THIRD EDITION

THE MIDDLE EAST AND CENTRAL ASIA

An Anthropological Approach

Dale F. Eickelman

Dartmouth College

PRENTICE HALL, UPPER SADDLE RIVER, NEW JERSEY 07458

Library of Congress Cataloging-in-Publication Data

Eickelman, Dale F.
The Middle East and Central Asia : An anthropological approach / Dale F. Eickelman. — 3rd ed.
p. cm.
Rev. ed. of: The Middle East, 2nd ed. c1988.
Includes bibliographical references and index.
ISBN 0-13-123019-0
1. Ethnology—Middle East. 2. Ethnology—Africa, North. 3. Ethnology—Asia, Central. 4. Middle East—Social life and customs. 5. Africa, North—Social life and customs. 6. Asia, Central—Social life and customs. I. Eickelman, Dale F. Middle East. II. Title.
GN635.N42E39 1997
306'.0956—dc21 97-14080
CIP

Editorial Director: Charlyce Jones Owen
Editor in Chief: Nancy Roberts
Associate Editor: Sharon Chambliss
Marketing Manager: Chris DeJohn
Editorial/production supervision
and interior design: Serena Hoffman
Buyer: Mary Ann Gloriande
Cover design: Bruce Kenselaar
Cover art: Reza/Imax

This book was set in 10/12 Palatino by D.M. Cradle Associates and was printed and bound by Courier Companies, Inc. The cover was printed by Phoenix Color Corp.

Printed in the United States of America

10 9 8 7 6 5 4 3 2 1

ISBN 0-13-123019-0

Prentice-Hall International (UK) Limited, *London*
Prentice-Hall of Australia Pty. Limited, *Sydney*
Prentice-Hall Canada Inc., *Toronto*
Prentice-Hall Hispanoamericana, S.A., *Mexico*
Prentice-Hall of India Private Limited, *New Delhi*
Prentice-Hall of Japan, Inc., *Tokyo*
Simon & Schuster Asia Pte. Ltd., *Singapore*
Editora Prentice-Hall do Brasil, Ltda., *Rio de Janeiro*

TO CHRISTINE EICKELMAN

CONTENTS

PREFACE

This book is intended as an anthropological introduction to the Middle East and Central Asia. A second, complementary goal is to point out the contribution that the study of the Middle East and Central Asia is making to the main currents of anthropology, especially those that relate to the analysis of complex societies.

As anthropological scholarship on the major civilizational areas of the world has reached a critical intensity, different dominant issues have emerged in each region that have then influenced ideas elsewhere. For example, in research on sub-Saharan Africa in the late 1940s and early 1950s, a predominant question was the nature of political order in "stateless" societies. Similarly, many anthropological studies of India focused on the cultural and social aspects of inequality, and this literature has profoundly influenced discussions of stratification and social class elsewhere.

Because of the Middle East's complexity and diversity, several interrelated themes prevail. One group of issues is suggested by the study of Islam, Judaism, and Christianity and how these world religions are understood, both as global movements and in their rich local manifestations in the Middle East. How do local understandings of Islam, for example, affect the wider currents of Muslim civilization? How does a world religion such as Islam shape, and become shaped by, the rapidly evolving economic and political contexts in which it is maintained and reproduced? What are the implications of mass higher education and mass communications for how people think about religion and politics?

Another set of issues concerns ideas that people hold about their cultural identity. In a region as complex as the Middle East, with its overlapping linguistic, ethnic, national, kin, gender, and class distinctions, the problems of how personal and collective identities are asserted and what they mean in differing historical and political contexts are especially crucial. With the rise of ethnonationalism and ethnoreligious nationalisms, such identities are sometimes more plastic or at others seemingly more fixed than many earlier assumptions concerning their cultural bases have allowed.

A third theme concerns the political contexts and consequences of economic activities—the production, allocation, and consumption of goods and services. Together with practitioners of other disciplines, anthropologists analyze the social and cultural impact of developments such as massive labor emigration from poorer countries, the accrual of oil and mineral wealth to others, urbanization, agricultural innovation, and competition over scarce resources such as water. Anthropologists, like their colleagues in other disciplines, are concerned with such issues as what happens to cultural values and social relationships in the context of rapid economic and political change, and the prospects for more "civil" societies in the Middle East and Central Asia.

A fourth theme concerns changing *interpretations* of Middle Eastern societies and cultures by Westerners and by Middle Easterners themselves. This issue, once considered an historiographic one related only indirectly to "real" anthropological inquiry, is now considered implicit in any problem in the human sciences. Ideas concerning what constitutes valid description and interpretation of a culture or society have changed dramatically over the last two centuries, especially as modern anthropological inquiry has ceased to be primarily a Western enterprise.

The first two editions of this book dealt only with the Middle East, a challenging task in itself. For all practical purposes, Central Asia (and Azerbaijan) were a world apart during the period of Soviet domination, sealed off from adjoining Middle Eastern countries. By the late 1980s, this situation had begun to change. Cross-border cultural and commercial ties between Middle Eastern and Central Asian countries were rapidly created or renewed, and Russian and Central Asian scholars intensified their cooperation with European and American colleagues, often working collaboratively with them.

Central Asia and the Muslim-majority regions of the Caucasus have decidedly different profiles from most countries in the Middle East, but many questions and issues applicable to the Middle East serve as useful points of departure for understanding Central Asia. We now know that Islam remains a basic (although not exclusive) element of identity for most people in the region, as did Judaism for a significant (although rapidly declining) minority, in spite of vigorous Soviet antireligious campaigns. The significant presence of Russian administrators and settlers throughout the region is not fully analogous to the situation of French settlers in colonial Algeria—many Russians and Slavs were deported to the region from elsewhere—but the privileged status of the Russian language, the "glass ceiling" for Central Asians in much of the Soviet bureaucracy, and an economic system weighted toward extracting resources from the region rather than developing it bears many similarities to the colonial situation that prevailed in the Middle East. Finally, exploring the interpretive framework by which Soviets and Russians sought to understand Central Asia and comparing developments in Central Asia with what Moscow-based scholars called the "foreign Muslim East" help us to understand better the strengths and weaknesses of our own interpretive frameworks.

It is not yet possible to deal with many essential anthropological topics in Central Asia with the same depth as is possible in many Middle Eastern contexts, although the quality of historical and ethnographic work now under way is rapidly changing this situation. In the interim, this third edition suggests points of departure for understanding Central Asia, especially the rising significance of ethnonational politics and the related "rewriting" of national and ethnic histories by some of the region's intellectuals.

This book is intended both as a textbook and as an interpretive essay. It introduces students, colleagues, and general readers to the Middle East and Central Asia and to the questions that have been and are being developed by scholars and writers concerned with the two regions. Although this book is necessarily a synthesis of major research, I seek to develop a particular style of anthropological inquiry and show its contribution to the study of these two complementary regions of complex and ancient civilizations. Many textbooks are derivative and unconvincing, in that they rarely convey the sense of discovery that leaps from the pages of the more extensive monographs that constitute the central substance of anthropological inquiry. I hope that this book contains the sense of discovery that I felt in creating it, and in re-creating it for the third edition, and that readers will be prompted to explore some of the monographs and articles mentioned in the text and footnotes. Most chapters conclude with an annotated list of further readings, to provide a general introduction to basic source and reference materials. The glossary, containing references to where terms are discussed in the text, provides an additional resource for comparison.

The manuscript for the first edition of this book was completed in the Sultanate of Oman in late 1979. In that politically turbulent year, an informal group of oasis dwellers in a small provincial capital, often including myself, met almost daily for afternoon coffee in the relatively cool date-palm tree gardens. There we compared notes on what we heard and understood of regional politics from shortwave broadcasts in various languages and from other sources. These afternoon "news" sessions, devoted to regional and international politics, were as integral a part of oasis life as concern over property and water rights. Topics at that time included the Soviet invasion of Afghanistan, revolutionary Iran, and the November 1979 siege of the Great Mosque in Mecca by militant Muslim radicals. Most of the older tribesmen had firsthand experience of war and rebellion and were fully aware of the fragile political environment in which they lived. It was no luxury to take fragments of information and "news," often recognized as imperfect or suspect, and to critically assess its basic and long-term implications in a manner not unfamiliar to good anthropological reporting and analysis. These "news" sessions, and similar ones conducted during return visits to Oman since then, underscored just how intertwined "local" political and economic events were with regional and international ones in the view of Middle Easterners from all walks of life.

Political and economic developments since that time have sustained and augmented interest in the Middle East, and interest in Central Asia has blossomed since the end of the Soviet era. Many of the anthropological studies that appeared in the 1980s reflect more directly than their predecessors how the "background" themes of religious understandings and institutions, kinship and family, loyalty and trust, gender relations, political authority, and the linkages between villages, regions, and states are linked to the "hard" political and economic events that are the stuff of newspaper headlines. For example, in

Afghanistan, Islam and ideas of tribal and regional loyalty ceased to be arcane topics by the early 1980s; instead, they now suggest the limits of state authority and external intervention.

My approach is not encyclopedic. For reasons of historical accident and rapidly shifting political climates for research, American, European, Russian, Iranian, Arab, Pakistani, Central Asian, and Turkish anthropologists and other scholars have been better able to conduct field studies in some areas than in others, just as the historical development of some countries has focused attention on specific issues. Thus many of the anthropological studies of Turkey by both indigenous and foreign researchers have concentrated on the themes of modernization and nation building, while those of North Africa have been concerned with the continuing impact of the colonial experience. Even if the various countries of the Middle East were known equally well through anthropological studies, there would be little point in attempting a single composite of these materials, any more than such an effort for Africa or Latin America would be intellectually rewarding.

In general, my procedure is to develop specific topics on the basis of the best available documentation for a particular country or region and then to sketch as far as possible how patterns of kinship, political comportment, and the like compare with similar patterns elsewhere in the Middle East. For example, Chapter 4 discusses nomadism, especially through an examination of the Basseri of southern Iran and the Rwāla bedouin of Saudi Arabia and Jordan. They are chosen not because they represent a "lowest common denominator" for nomads of the Middle East but because they have been the subject of anthropological studies sufficiently detailed to form a base for understanding pastoral activities elsewhere and for a discussion of the role of nomads and tribal societies in the premodern, preindustrial past.

This third edition has been extensively revised and rewritten, although the overall structure remains largely intact. Earlier editions, in addition to being used in courses in anthropology, have been adopted for courses in history, politics, religious studies, urban planning, international relations, and Middle Eastern civilizations in the United States, Australia, Canada, Great Britain, France, Germany, Italy (in translation), Japan (in translation), and the Middle East. In revising, I have sought to take the diversity of this audience into account.

Reviewers, colleagues, friends, and students at my own university and others have offered numerous helpful comments and suggestions, many of which have been incorporated into this edition. In particular, William Fierman, Mark Katz, Adeeb Khalid, Anatoly Khazanov, Theodore Levin, and Martha Brill Olcott have generously shared their knowledge of Central Asia and Russia, as have my Russian and Central Asian colleagues Vitaly Naumkin, Vyacheslav Ya. Belokrenitsky, Abdujabar Abduvakhitov, and Dimitri Makarov. Vanessa Maher and Bozkurt Güvenç made general suggestions that have contributed to this edition, as has Gene R. Garthwaite. In addition, the participants in the National Endowment for the Humanities 1995 Summer Seminar for College Teachers, "Re-Imagining Politics and Societies: The Middle East and Central Asia," gave me thoughtful advice and insight on our current state of knowledge about Central Asia and how to think about the two regions together.

Support from the Claire Garber Goodman Fund of the Department of Anthropology at Dartmouth College made possible the preparation of new maps for this edition. Nancy Fenton prepared the originals of all but two of the maps, and Chris Scott, the creative director of Nomad Communications, Norwich, Vermont, provided advice and facilities that made a significant difference in the quality of the final versions. Christine Eickelman and Deborah Hodges read the completed manuscript with a critical eye, and Matthew Silvia, as a work-study assistant and Presidential Scholar at Dartmouth College, also assisted in preparing this revision. Numerous colleagues and publishers have generously allowed the use of photographs and other materials, and they are acknowledged at appropriate places in the text.

The colleagues, friends, and reviewers who offered advice and support for the first two editions of this book are not listed here again, but my appreciation remains as strong as ever.

Dale F. Eickelman

NOTE ON TRANSLITERATION

One of the first books that I read on the Middle East was Carleton Coon's *Caravan.** As a beginning student of Arabic, I appreciated his careful transcription. It facilitated my identification of unfamiliar terms, and for languages that I did not speak it gave me a general idea of how words were spoken. In a time of publishing economies, the willingness of Prentice Hall to allow the full transcription of terms from Middle Eastern and Central Asian languages, particularly Arabic, reflects a concern for editorial quality that can no longer be taken for granted. I have in general followed the conventions of the *International Journal of Middle East Studies*, although in deciding on how to transliterate colloquial terms I have attempted to follow the pronunciation of the area being discussed. For Arabic, the stroke over a vowel indicates that it is lengthened: *ā* as in *ma*, *ī* as in bean, and *ū* as in noon; *ay* as in pay is a diphthong. The emphatic consonants (*ḍ, ṣ, ṭ, ẓ, ḥ*) are indicated by dots under them; *kh* is pronounced as in Bach; *gh* as the *r* of Parisian French. The *ᶜayn* is typeset with a small, raised ᶜ in the glossary and index and with an opening single quotation mark (‘) in the text, and the *hamza*, a glottal stop as in the Brooklynese "bottle," with a closing single quotation mark (’). Often in spoken language, even in educated speech, the *hamza* is dropped; but I have included it in transliteration in those instances where it seemed necessary to do so. Except where otherwise noted, only the singular form of Arabic words is indicated, with *-s* added for plurals. Adjectival forms of many Arabic place names and words are indicated with an *ī* at the end of the word, as in Arabic. Words and place names with common English forms appear as they do in English and are not fully transliterated. Thus Mecca, not Makka; Fez, not Fās; Quran, not Qur'ān; Allah, not Allāh; Islam, not Islām; and sultan, not sulṭān.

*Carleton S. Coon, *Caravan: The Story of the Middle East*, rev. ed. (New York: Holt, Rinehart and Winston, 1961 [1951]).

PART I
INTRODUCTION

1

ANTHROPOLOGY, THE MIDDLE EAST, AND CENTRAL ASIA

We need to think beyond the limits of existing political and geographic frontiers to grasp the subtle links among economic and political currents, religious movements, and the movement of people and ideas. An older notion of geography as physical frontiers still provides a significant point of departure for understanding the societies and politics of the Middle East and Central Asia, but traditional notions of "frontier" must be placed alongside complex transnational commercial, economic, religious, and intellectual links that contribute to creating national, religious, ethnic, and state identities. The increased pace of labor migration and the growing ease of travel and communication have played an important part in eroding the significance of physical frontiers. In particular, the collapse of the Soviet Union rapidly led to the dissolution of boundaries between the former Soviet republics of Central Asia and the Middle East, boundaries that had been almost impermeable for much of the twentieth century.

THE MIDDLE EAST AND CENTRAL ASIA: SHIFTING FRONTIERS

The terms "Middle East" and "Central Asia" appear clear when they are employed in general common-sense contexts. In contemporary usage the "Middle East" encompasses the region stretching from Rabat to Tehran, a distance of roughly 3400 miles (equal to the distance from New York City to Fairbanks, Alaska). To give another indication of its vastness, the Middle East includes territory on three continents—Africa, Asia, and Europe (the European section of Turkey). When certain features of the linguistic, religious, political, and historical complexities of the region are emphasized, the term is often extended to include Afghanistan and Pakistan.

The boundaries of Central Asia, across which the caravans of the Great Silk Route brought luxury goods from China to Europe in the Middle Ages, are similarly indistinct and have become more so since the dissolution of the Soviet Union and the growing diversity of Central Asia's commercial and political links with the outside world. For purposes of this book, "Central Asia" includes the former Soviet states of Uzbekistan, Turkmenistan, Tajikistan, Kyrgyzstan, and Kazakhstan (see Figure 1-1). Azerbaijan is not part of Central Asia, but because of its Muslim majority population and a partially shared administrative and political heritage, it is discussed in this book within the context of Central Asia.

If the limits of Central Asia appear indistinct today, they were more so before the expansion of the Russian Empire and the influx of Russian settlers in the latter half of the nineteenth century. Until then, the region was vaguely known as "Turkestan" or, as in a mid-nineteenth-century British map, "independent Tartary," a region of independent khanates, or principalities, stretching from the borders of present-day Iran in the south to northeast of the Caspian Sea.[1] Central Asian history has been neglected because the region exists in a "double periphery"—between the spheres of Inner Asian and Islamic civilizations, where Perso-Islamic and Turko-Mongolian traditions have converged since the Mongol invasions of the thirteenth century.[2]

Although Central Asia and the Middle East lack clearly defined natural frontiers, the sense of frontiers is intimately linked to the dynamics of history and political context. Robert Canfield argues that the traditional sense of "area studies" inadvertently perpetuated division of the world into spheres that made sense more for displaying artifacts in museums of an earlier era than for understanding changing political, social, and economic fields.[3] Assessing long-term historical developments in the Turkic- and Persian-speaking areas of the Middle East and Central Asia, he suggests that we replace the older term "culture area" with *ecumene* in order to emphasize the historically intertwined ebb and flow of political, economic, ethnic, and religious currents and practices that characterized Central Asia and the Iranian and Anatolian plateaus prior to the twentieth century and that characterize them again in the wake of recently unsealed and porous frontiers.

[1] Mark Katz, personal communication, July 15, 1996.

[2] Jo Ann Gross, "Introduction: Approaches to the Problem of Identity Formation," in *Muslims in Central Asia: Expressions of Identity and Change*, ed. Jo Ann Gross, Central Asia Book Series (Durham, NC, and London: Duke University Press, 1992), pp. 1, 16–17. The phrase "double periphery" originates with the Russian historian Yuri Bregel.

[3] Robert L. Canfield, "Preface," in *Turco-Persia in Historical Perspective*, ed. Robert L. Canfield (New York: Cambridge University Press, 1991), pp. xiii–xiv.

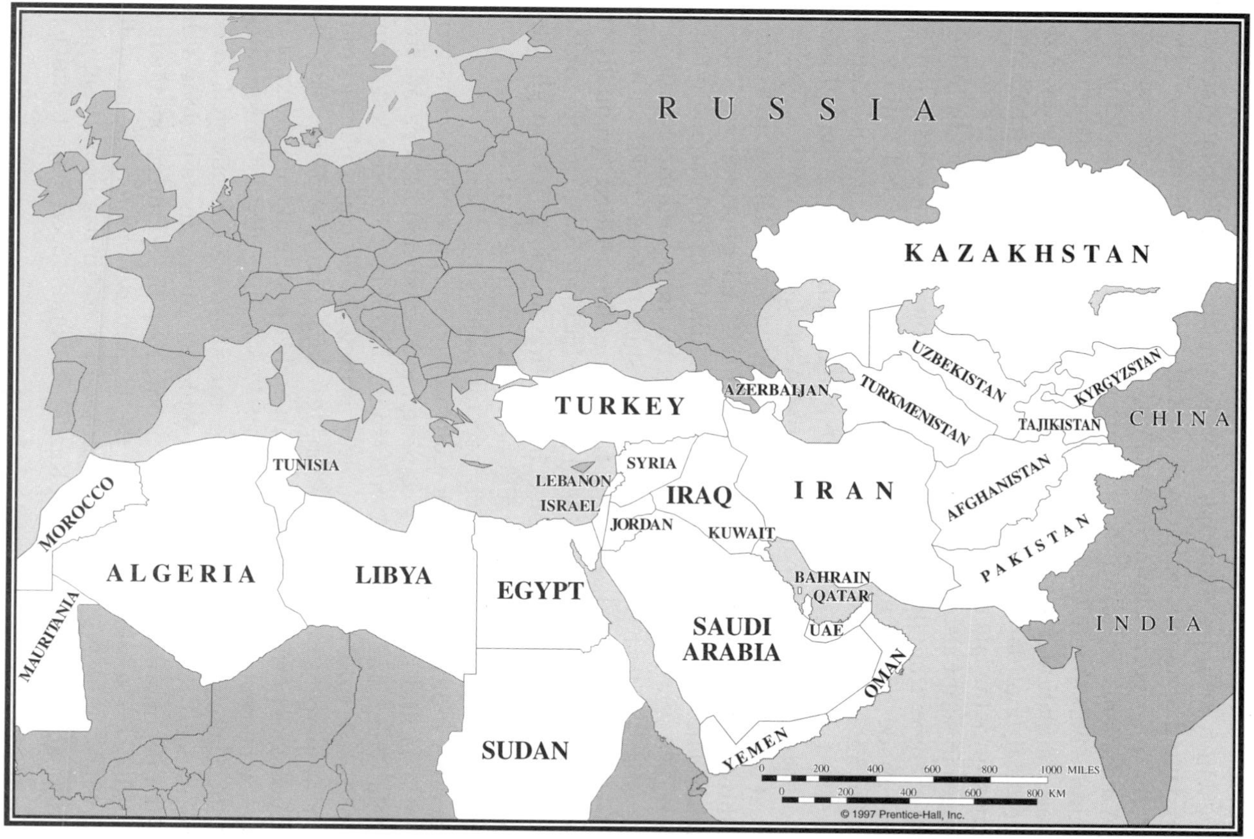

FIGURE 1–1. The Middle East and Central Asia: Political boundaries, 1990.

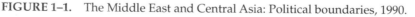

Azerbaijan, a country of 7.1 million people situated between Iran, Armenia, Turkey, the Caspian Sea, and Russia, provides an example of these fluctuating zones of influence. Geographically, oil-rich Azerbaijan is part of the Caucasus region, which includes Armenia, Georgia, and parts of Russia. Azeri is a Turkic language that significantly overlaps with Turkish. In terms of religion, native Azeris are overwhelmingly Muslim, unlike Christian Armenia and Georgia. Azerbaijanis share much in common with the peoples of northern Iran, a region where Azeri Turkish, not Persian, remains the first language of much of the population. Like several of its neighbors, including Turkey, Azerbaijan's political boundaries have been redrawn or significantly challenged several times since the late nineteenth century.[4]

Changes in script also suggest shifting political and social fields. In 1926, Azerbaijan changed from the Arabic to the Latin alphabet, two years before the change was made official in Turkey; but in 1940 Stalin ordered Latin script abandoned in favor of Cyrillic. In November 1992, Azerbaijan officially decreed a return to the Latin script, a move implicitly facilitating its ties with Turkey, which also uses the Latin alphabet, and the West. Of the twenty telephones arrayed next to the desk of Azerbaijan's president, Ayaz Mutalibov, in September 1991, three were direct connections to the Turkish telephone network. Business school teachers were already commuting regularly from Istanbul to Baku, and in 1991, 600 Azeri students were studying business and management in Turkey.[5] Azeris say that this latest alphabet shift restores links with their national past. In 1993, the other Central Asian republics decided "gradually" to implement the transition from the Cyrillic to the Latin alphabet, except for Persian-speaking Tajikistan, which opted instead for Arabic script.[6] In all these cases, however, Russian and the Cyrillic alphabet continue to play a major role as the dominant language and script of several generations.

As another indication of the ambiguity of frontiers, many observers write of "Central Asia and Kazakhstan," considering Kazakhstan as separate from Central Asia. There are significant differences. Kazakhs compose less than a majority of Kazakhstan's population, even if they are its major ethnic group, composing 42 percent of the population. Russians compose 37 percent, and Slavs, including deported populations from earlier eras, make up much of the remaining 21 percent of the population of 17.5 million (by 1993 estimates). Much of the Slavic population, including Russians, are concentrated in Kazakhstan's mineral-rich northern regions (oblasts), giving these regions a different economic, linguistic, and political profile than the southern ones, where ethnic Kazakhs predominate in all but the large urban centers. Some of the northern oblasts have Russian names, although Kazakh has been designated the state language since 1989. In 1996, Kazakhstan announced plans to move its

[4] See especially Tadeusz Swietochowski, *Russia and Azerbaijan: A Borderland in Transition* (New York: Columbia University Press, 1995).

[5] Interviews, Baku, September 18–20, 1991.

[6] Jacob M. Landau, *Pan-Turkism: From Irredentism to Cooperation* (Bloomington and Indianapolis: Indiana University Press, 1995), pp. 211–15.

capital from Almatay, in the southeast, to the north in order to be closer to the state's center of population and symbolically to underscore the country's unity.[7] When Kazakhstan adopted a new constitution in January 1993, it also changed the spelling of its capital city from Alma-Ata to Almaty, bringing it into conformity with "the rules of the Kazakh language."[8]

The flux in the names of cities, provinces, and countries applies to the names designating broader areas also; and these names are not politically neutral. The specialist's reluctance to speak of the "Middle East" or "Central Asia" without providing extensive glosses is due to the circumstances surrounding the terms' origins. Like older, more geographically limited labels such as "the Near East" and "the Levant" that remain in use, the term "Middle East" was not coined by inhabitants of the region. It originated with nineteenth-century European strategists and is unabashedly Eurocentered. In the geopolitics of the British military, for example, the "Middle East" meant the command responsible for the region from the Nile to the Oxus rivers; the lands to the east of the Oxus belonged to the Indian command.[9] In terms of civilizational boundaries, such a division made little sense because it cut the historically united (or at least interacting) Iranian plateau in two, but the term was not coined with scholars in mind.

The terms most commonly used to describe North Africa make sense against the backdrop of the pattern of nineteenth- and twentieth-century European colonial domination. Thus the term "North Africa" does not literally mean the entire northern part of that continent, but Morocco, Algeria, Tunisia, and Libya. For Arab-speakers, this region, excluding Egypt, is generally known as the "Maghrib," a term that means "the West" and, more poetically, "the land where the sun sets." This term reflects the geopolitics of an earlier epoch, when the first waves of Muslim invaders came from the Arabian peninsula in the seventh and eighth centuries. "Maghrib" is popularly used in French as well, largely because the region—less Libya (conquered by Italy), the Spanish Sahara, and a narrow mountainous zone in northern Morocco (ceded by the French to Spain in 1912)—was under French domination until the mid-twentieth century (see Figure 1-2). Even in this more compact region of French domination, the imposition of colonial boundaries created distinctions that remain significant today. Arab geographers considered the country now known as the Islamic Republic of Mauritania as part of the Maghrib. Yet, because Mauritania was attached to French West Africa and administered from Dakar during the era of colonial rule, it is often not considered part of the Middle East, despite the fact that the majority of its population is Muslim and Arabic-speaking and the country is a member of the Arab League and the Maghrib Arab Union. The

[7] See Anatoly M. Khazanov, *After the USSR: Ethnicity, Nationalism, and Politics in the Commonwealth of Independent States* (Madison: University of Wisconsin Press, 1995), p. 158; Philip S. Gillette, "Ethnic Balance and Imbalance in Kazakhstan's Regions," *Central Asian Monitor*, no. 3 (1993), pp. 17–23.

[8] Gillette, "Ethnic Balance," p. 18.

[9] Marshall G. S. Hodgson, *The Venture of Islam*, vol. 1 (Chicago: University of Chicago Press, 1974), pp. 60–61.

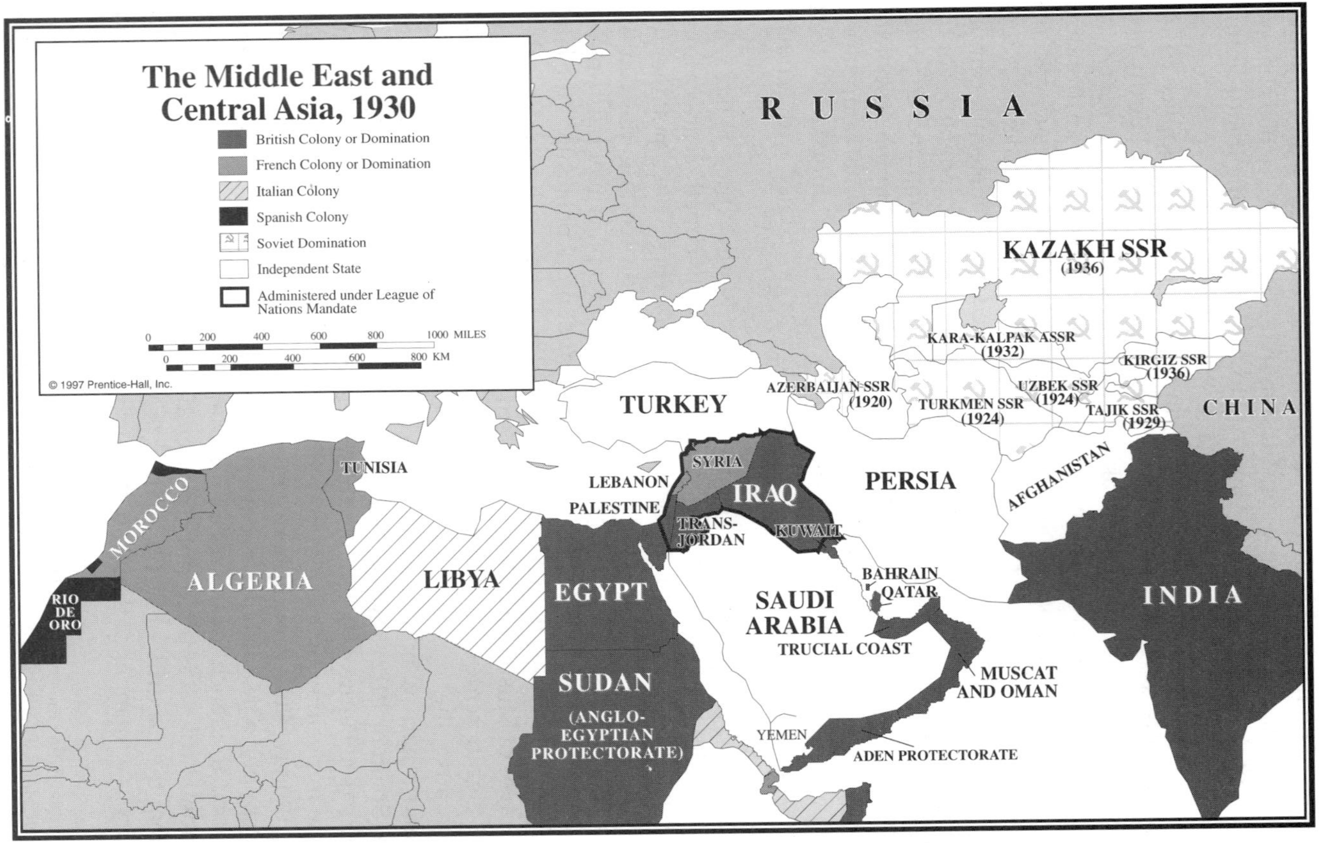
The Middle East and Central Asia, 1930
British Colony or Domination
French Colony or Domination
Italian Colony
Spanish Colony
Soviet Domination
Independent State
Administered under League of Nations Mandate
0 200 400 600 800 1000 MILES
0 200 400 600 800 KM
© 1997 Prentice-Hall, Inc.
RUSSIA
KAZAKH SSR (1936)
KARA-KALPAK ASSR (1932)
KIRGIZ SSR (1936)
AZERBAIJAN SSR (1920)
TURKMEN SSR (1924)
UZBEK SSR (1924)
TAJIK SSR (1929)
CHINA
TURKEY
SYRIA
LEBANON
PALESTINE
IRAQ
TRANS-JORDAN
KUWAIT
PERSIA
AFGHANISTAN
INDIA
BAHRAIN
QATAR
SAUDI ARABIA
TRUCIAL COAST
MUSCAT AND OMAN
YEMEN
ADEN PROTECTORATE
MOROCCO
RIO DE ORO
ALGERIA
TUNISIA
LIBYA
EGYPT
SUDAN
(ANGLO-EGYPTIAN PROTECTORATE)

FIGURE 1-2. The Middle East and Central Asia: Political boundaries, 1930.

Islamic Republic of the Sudan, despite its large non-Muslim, non-Arabic-speaking minority, has no such difficulty in being considered part of the Middle East, but, again, this is largely due to the accident of colonial rule—it fell under Egyptian rule about 1830, and from 1899 until 1955 was governed by what was formally an Anglo-Egyptian condominium.

The arbitrariness of colonial boundaries becomes especially apparent in Central Asia under Soviet rule. Figure 1-2 offers a "snapshot" of Middle Eastern and Central Asian frontiers as they appeared in 1930. Under Soviet rule, the political boundaries throughout the region were frequently altered, beginning with Russia's 1917 revolution and extending until the late 1930s. In the years immediately after the revolution, boundaries were often rearranged to reduce or remove the threat of seccession, and between 1924 and 1936, the region was "reconstructed" into autonomous republics in which a majority of the population shared the same nationality, but which also contained enclaves of peoples of other ethnic groups (*ethnies*) gathered into "homelands." As head of the People's Commissariat for Nationality Affairs (Russian, *Narkomnats*) after 1917, Joseph Stalin (1879–1953) played a major role in elaborating Soviet nationality policy.[10] Beginning in the 1920s, censuses were conducted in which people often were forced to choose a nationality, and these choices, once made, had significant political consequences. Thus an inhabitant of present-day Tajikistan might not have had a distinct consciousness at the time of the 1924 union-wide census of being an Uzbek or a Tājik but was forced to choose one category or the other.[11]

In sum, the terms "Middle East" and "Central Asia" have their drawbacks, but they remain useful, provided they are not taken to indicate a political, economic, or religious homogeneity. The shifting cultural and historical realities must be taken into account in any meaningful study of these regions. In any case, the term "Middle East" is now employed in a fairly neutral, descriptive sense by Middle Easterners themselves and is used in the same way in this book. In Arabic, it is also the title of a London-based daily newspaper, *al-Sharq al-Awsaṭ*. We employ Central Asia in a similar manner.

FIRST APPROXIMATIONS

Geography

As a whole, the Middle East is semiarid (although there are important local variations); since antiquity it has been a region of agriculture (since at least 8000 B.C.) and empire; and it lacks sharply defined natural boundaries. Although the region is partially cut off from sub-Saharan Africa and the Indo-Pakistani sub-

[10] For an excellent assessment of these policies, see Robert J. Kaiser, *The Geography of Nationalism in Russia and the USSR* (Princeton, NJ: Princeton University Press, 1994), esp. pp. 102–38.

[11] See the newspaper drawings reproduced in Edward Allworth, *The Uzbeks* (Stanford, CA: Hoover Institution Press, 1990), pp. 202–203.

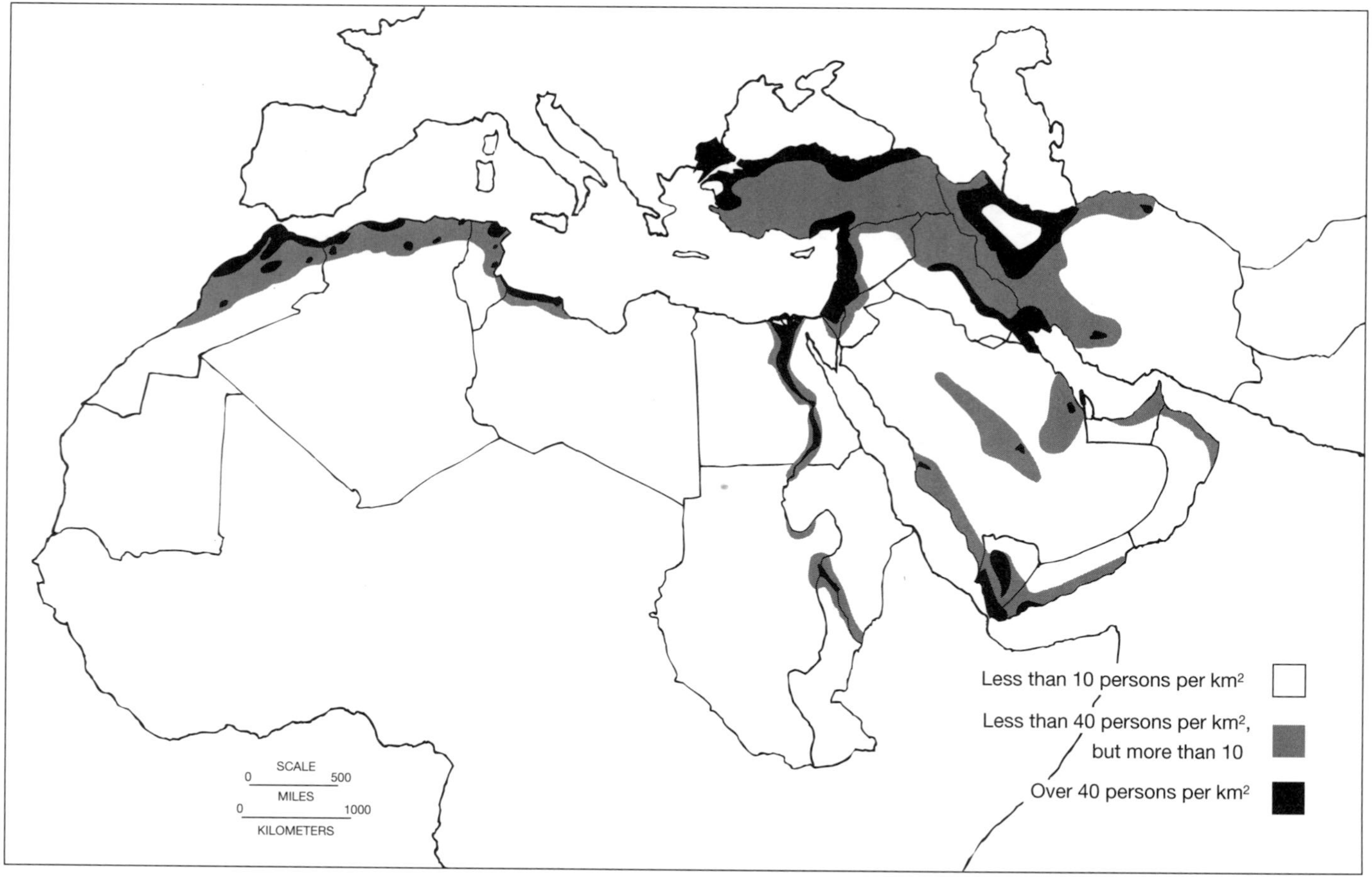

FIGURE 1-4. Population density of the Middle East.

to a few miles on either side of the Nile River, although the Nile Delta and the area between the Tigris and Euphrates Rivers in Iraq contain intricate webs of irrigation channels that support relatively dense populations.

Elsewhere in the Middle East there are other sorts of irrigation systems, both traditional and modern, adapted to local circumstances. Wells are often a source of water, although in Iran and in regions of Morocco such as Marrakesh, there are elaborate underground canals (called *ghaṭṭāra* in Morocco, *qanāt* in Iran, and *aflāj* in Oman) that carry water from underground streams in nearby mountain regions to the rich oases of the plains. Modern technology has greatly expanded the land that has been brought under cultivation, but where modern wells and pumps are introduced, they often remove water from fossil aquifers faster than it can be replaced and threaten to exhaust a nonrenewable resource. This calamity has happened in parts of Yemen; and the mismanagement of water resources in Central Asia poses a similar threat.

Because it is semiarid, large parts of the Middle East traditionally have been given over to a mode of livelihood that combines the extensive cultivation of crops such as wheat and barley with sheep and goat herding. Herds are usually moved in fixed patterns between adjacent ecological zones in the course of a year and graze on the stubble of cultivated fields after harvest. Such movement is called *transhumant pastoralism* or *seminomadism*, and it differs from the movement of nomadic groups who follow their herds (pastoral nomadism). Seminomadic pastoralists and pastoral nomads form a significant but declining minority in such countries as Saudi Arabia (probably less than 10 percent), Iran (5 percent), and Afghanistan (10 percent or more), and are less than 2 percent of the population in the countries of North Africa, with the exception of Libya and Mauritania. But pastoral nomadism as the sole or predominant activity of certain groups, to the full exclusion of cultivation, is today relatively rare. Only in Somalia have nomads (until recent droughts and political disturbances) constituted a majority of the population (about 75 percent in the early 1970s).[13] In Central Asia, where horse-riding pastoralists once dominated both the steppes and the mountain pastures (with mixed herds of sheep, goats, horses, cattle, and camels), Russian colonization beginning in the mid-nineteenth century and Stalin's forced collectivization of the 1930s had devastating effects on both live-

[13] These figures are derived from Donald Powell Cole, *Nomads of the Nomads* (Chicago: Aldine, 1975), p. 143; and Beaumont, Blake, and Wagstaff, *The Middle East*, p. 185. The tentative, and politically significant, nature of such overall estimates should always be kept in mind. To cite two extreme examples, population estimates for Afghanistan in 1968 ranged from 7 million to 17 million. No officials knew the real figures, but they all recognized that higher figures yielded the prospect of more international aid. A census in Saudi Arabia in 1962–1963 (the results of which were never officially recognized) revealed the population to be only 3.9 million as opposed to earlier estimates of 7 million and a 1972 estimate of 8 million. See Beaumont, Blake, and Wagstaff, *The Middle East*, pp. 176–77; and Robert J. Lapham, "Population Policies in the Middle East and North Africa," *Middle East Studies Association Bulletin* 11, no. 2 (May 1977), 16. In 1992, Saudi Arabia announced that it had completed a new census, its first since 1972, indicating a population of 16.9 million, of which Saudis made up 12.3 million and foreigners 4.6 million. It also concluded that Saudi Arabia had a growth rate of between 3.5 and 3.8 percent, one of the highest in the world. "Saudis' Census Counts 16.9 Million People," *New York Times*, December 16, 1992, p. A8.

stock and humans, although there are signs that post-Soviet officials in the national governments of Central Asia are taking a renewed interest in pastoral production.[14]

The significance of transhumant pastoralists and nomads has often been exaggerated as a factor in Middle Eastern history, although the great Mongol invasions of Central Asia and parts of Europe and the Middle East by Chingīz (Genghis) Khān (1155–ca. 1227) and his successors left a lasting impact on world history, including the sack of Baghdad and the destruction of the 'Abbāsid caliphate in 1258. Before the advent of modern technology, nomadic pastoral groups traditionally constituted a political and military threat to effective central government in many regions, including Morocco and Iran. Until 1922–1923, Iranian politics were constrained to some extent by tribally organized societies, not just pastoral ones, that limited the control of the central government. The same applies to Morocco. French and Spanish colonial rule began in Morocco in 1912, but it was not until the early 1930s that tribal resistance was overcome in all parts of the country.

Most Middle Eastern countries also possess mountainous regions—Kuwait and some of the Gulf states are the exceptions—and these regions have served as zones of refuge from central government control. Thus the Kurds of Iraq, Iran, and Turkey and the Berber-speaking tribal groups in Algeria's Kabylia Mountains and Morocco's Rif and Atlas mountain chains have managed to remain relatively autonomous until the recent past.

The interrelations among nomads, farmers, and city dwellers in the Middle East and Central Asia are important to understanding the region. The geographically limited area of the agricultural hinterlands of most cities and their vulnerability to adjacent pastoralists differentiate much of Middle Eastern and Central Asian history from that of Europe. This competition between city-based state apparatuses and outlying pastoralists, who could be raiders or "transportation specialists," over the farmlands between them continued until the 1940s.

The Middle East may have been a region of irrigation, agriculture, and pastoralism, but for many of the countries, significant mineral wealth, especially in oil, has in recent times created the potential for significant economic growth. Revenues from such resources dramatically increased in the 1960s and 1970s and have made possible substantial alterations in the social and material life of some of the region's inhabitants. Likewise, the discovery of new oil resources in Kazakhstan and the introduction of modern technology to renew the oil fields of Azerbaijan have the potential for significantly improving those countries' economic outlook. Oil prices have dropped significantly from their record highs in the early 1970s, but oil still constitutes the principal source of income for many states of the region.

[14] Thomas J. Barfield, *The Nomadic Alternative* (Englewood Cliffs, NJ: Prentice Hall, 1993), pp. 136–44, 176.

The Middle East is also a region of intense urban and commercial life, with ancient cities such as Damascus, Cairo, and Istanbul, as well as those of more recent origin such as Riyadh and Casablanca. Over 67 percent of the region's inhabitants were urban dwellers in 1990, as opposed to roughly 10 percent in 1900, and the proportion of urban dwellers to the overall population continues to rise.[15] Of course, the transformations occurring in these cities are not unique to the Middle East. Central Asia shows similar patterns of urban growth, and the same rapid rate of urbanization is occurring throughout the Third World. In the chapters of this book concerned with the nature of cities, these more general trends are considered, but equal emphasis is placed on the extent to which certain features of urban life continue to make these cities distinctly Turkish, Egyptian, Muslim, or Middle Eastern and how these culturally unique attributes influence and are affected by more general processes such as population growth and world economic currents.

The Middle East has often been characterized as a "mosaic," a metaphor that effectively evokes the area's linguistic, religious, political, and historical complexities and suggests its significant internal differentiation. Yet the juxtaposition of a range of cultural and noncultural features in the Middle East does not in itself make the region unique. Such a "mosaic" characterization can be applied equally to Central Asia, the Indian subcontinent, Southeast Asia, the Balkans, and Russia, among other locales.

Religion

In historical terms, the area designated by the broader, contemporary usage of the term "Middle East" coincides roughly with the first wave of Arab invasions and with the three largest Muslim empires at their greatest extent—the Ummayad (661–750), the early 'Abbāsid (750–ca. 800), and the Ottoman (from the sixteenth through the eighteenth centuries). Even if not always politically unified, the region shows significant social and cultural continuities. The first adherents of Islam and its initial carriers were from the Arabian peninsula, but thinking of the Arabian peninsula or even the wider Arab world as a "heartland" of Islam can lead to a distorted view of Islamic civilization. The epicenter of the total world Muslim population lies between Iran and Pakistan, on the eastern edge of the area with which this book is concerned. Muslims today are situated in a wide band that ranges from Indonesia and the Philippines through the Indo-Pakistani subcontinent, Central Asia, Iran, and Turkey to the Arabic-speaking regions of the Middle East and Black Africa (Figure 1-5).

Population figures for Muslims in Europe and North America are also substantial. By current estimates, Indonesia alone contains almost as many Muslims (140 million) as the Arab Middle East (162 million), and the Muslims of the Indian subcontinent (272 million) outnumber those of the Arab states,

[15] Alan Duben, *The Middle Eastern City: An Urban Management Perspective* (Istanbul: International Union of Local Authorities, 1992), p. 38; Lapham, "Population Policies," p. 4; and Beaumont, Blake, and Wagstaff, *The Middle East*, p. 185.

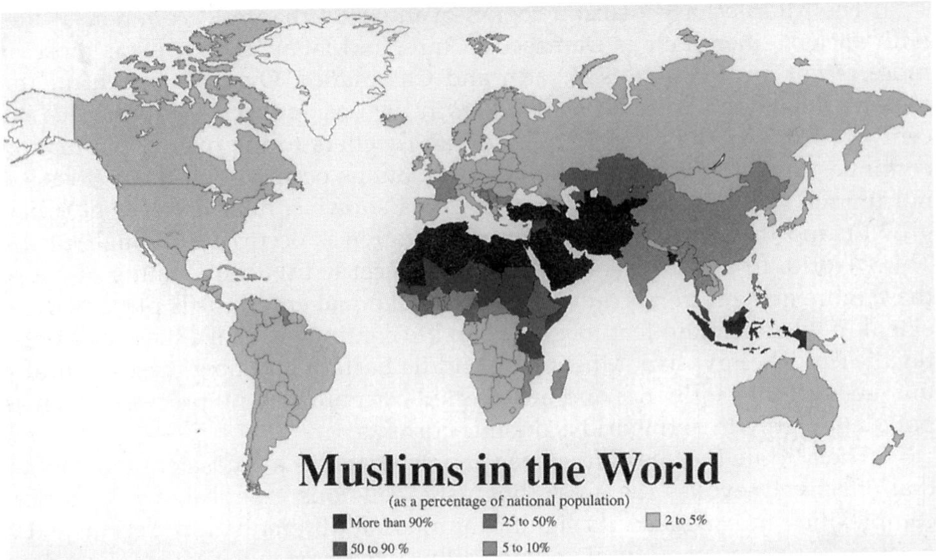

FIGURE 1-5. Although the Middle East is commonly considered as the "center" of the Muslim world, nearly half the world's Muslims live in Southeast Asia. Their political significance, like that of Muslims in Europe and North America, is growing rapidly. [From Dale F. Eickelman and James Piscatori, *Muslim Politics* (Princeton, N.J.: Princeton University Press, 1996). © Princeton University Press, 1996. All rights reserved.]

Iran, and Turkey combined (254 million). The 1989 census of the former Soviet Union, its last, which of course included the now-independent states of Central Asia and the Caucasus, indicated a Muslim population of 55 million, which gave the former Soviet Union the fifth largest Muslim population of any country in the world.[16] As of 1995, there were 5 million Muslims in France, making up some 5 percent of the population, and significant Muslim populations in Germany (2 million), Great Britain (1 million), Belgium, and the Netherlands. There were over 4 million Muslims in the United States in 1986; and if current trends in immigration, birth rate, and conversion continue, by the year 2000, there will be over 6 million, and Muslims will constitute the second largest religious group in the United States after Christianity.[17]

Most people in the Middle East are Muslim, but this has not always provided a basis for common sentiment and identity. Currently an irredentism

[16] Barbara A. Anderson and Brian D. Silver, "Growth and Diversity of the Population of the Soviet Union," *Annales of the American Academy of Political and Social Sciences*, no. 510 (July 1990), 155–77.

[17] Estimates of Muslim populations are derived from John L. Esposito, *Islamic Revivalism*, Occasional Paper No. 3 (Washington, DC: American Institute for Islamic Affairs, 1985), pp. 8–9; Carol L. Stone, "Estimate of Muslims Living in America," in *The Muslims of America*, ed. Yvonne Yazbeck Haddad (New York and Oxford: Oxford University Press, 1991), pp. 28–29; and Youssef M. Ibrahim, "Europe's Muslim Population: Frustrated, Poor and Divided," *New York Times*, May 5, 1995, pp. A1, A12. See also Gilles Kepel, *Les banlieues de l'Islam* (Paris: Éditions du Seuil, 1987), for a comprehensive survey of France's Muslim population.

based on common religion is on the upsurge in the Middle East, as elsewhere in the world, but this was not always the case. From the 1950s to the 1970s, an irredentism based on common Arab identity swept the Arab world, and millions of Arabs rejoiced at the creation of the United Arab Republic, joining Egypt and Syria (February 1958), which was soon complemented by a loose federation with Yemen (March 1958), the United Arab States, as a first step toward genuine Arab unity. Yet the federation with Yemen was never really implemented. No other states joined, and Syria seceded from the United Arab Republic in 1961, although Egypt retained the official title for many years. Although the idea of Arab unity remains a hope for many Arabs, later efforts at political union, such as that between Libya and Tunisia, have been equally short-lived.

Similarly, for over half a century the elite of Turkey have stressed their ties with Europe more than those with their Muslim neighbors. In the last years of the Ottoman Empire, European statesmen referred to it as the "sick man of Europe," implicitly accepting the Ottoman elite's claim to a European identity. Egyptian elites prior to the 1950s, and again in this decade in certain contexts, stressed their country's Mediterranean identity rather than its Arab or Middle Eastern identity. The same is true for the countries of North Africa. Notwithstanding questions of modern nationalist feeling, historians such as Fernand Braudel have persuasively argued the case for considering the countries on both sides of the Mediterranean as a single society for extended historical periods.[18] All Central Asian countries (except Kazakhstan) have overwhelmingly Muslim populations, but there are few signs that this shared identity is emerging as a significant political factor. At the same time, the seven decades of Communist rule failed to suppress the region's basic sense of "being Muslim."

Islam, of course, is the dominant religion of the Middle East. The state of Israel, where Jews constitute a majority of the population, is an obvious exception, but even in those countries where the majority of the population is Muslim, there are often significant Christian and Jewish minorities. In the Middle East as a whole, Muslims constitute 82 percent of the population, Christians 9 percent, Jews 7 percent, and other religions (primarily noncitizen workers in the Arabian peninsula states) 2 percent.[19] Roughly 8 percent of Egypt's population is Christian (mostly Coptic), as are 20 percent of Syria's and Iraq's and perhaps 40 percent of Lebanon's. Exact statistics on the size of these minorities are hard to obtain, especially in the case of Lebanon, where no census has been conducted since 1932 in an effort (which largely succeeded until 1975) to preserve a delicate political balance between various ethnic and religious groups—Maronite Christian, Armenian Greek Orthodox, Greek Catholic, Sunnī Muslim, Shī'ī Muslim, Palestinian Christians and Muslims, Druze, and other smaller groups. Elsewhere in the Middle East, there have been thriving Greek and

[18] Fernand Braudel, *The Mediterranean and the Mediterranean World in the Age of Philip II*, trans. Siân Reynolds (New York: Harper & Row, 1975 [French original, 1949]).

[19] Estimates taken from *The Atlas of Mankind*, ed. I. M. Lewis, Christophe von Fürer-Haimendorf, and Fred Eggan (Chicago: Rand McNally, 1982), p. 106.

Armenian Christian communities, especially in Egypt and Turkey, although since the beginning of this century their numbers have diminished considerably. The distribution of Jewish and Christian populations in the Middle East at the turn of the century was very different from the distribution of those populations today.[20]

Similarly, in Central Asia, Russian colonization and Soviet policies brought large numbers of Slavs to the region. In capital cities such as Tashkent (Uzbekistan), Almatay (Kazakhstan), Bishkek (Kyrgyzstan), and Dushanbe (Tajikistan), up to one-third of the population is Russian, although the non-indigenous population has dropped steadily since the dissolution of the Soviet Union in 1991. Similarly, in Kyrgyzstan, only 20 percent of the industrial workers are Kyrgyz (even less in management and engineering), and in Kazakhstan, only 18 percent of the industrial workers are Kazakh.[21] As was the case in the Middle East at the end of the colonial era, these numbers are likely to alter significantly in the coming decade. A significant problem posed in this book is to assess how precisely complex ethnic and religious identities are sustained and articulated in changing economic and political contexts.

Most of the countries of the Middle East have always had significant Jewish minorities, with the exception of Saudi Arabia and the states of the Persian/Arab Gulf (which, however, have Hindu minorities), and Jewish communities played a major role in the urban life of Central Asia. Jewish communities contracted in size after the creation of the state of Israel in 1948, the collapse of the colonial regimes of North Africa in the 1950s and 1960s, and, in the east, the Iraqi revolution of 1958. Sizable Jewish minorities remain, however, in Iran, Turkey, Tunisia, and Morocco, although today one is more likely to hear Central Asian Jewish music in Queens, New York, than in Bukhāra or Samarkānd. Another significant minority in many countries of North Africa was composed of colonial settlers, who were predominantly, although not exclusively, of French, Spanish, and Italian origin and Christian in religion.

Languages

Arabic is principally identified with Islam and the Middle East, yet this assumption engenders serious distortions, one of which is to diminish the role attributed to Persian culture in Islamic civilization. Although Arabic today is the principal language of the largest part of the Middle East, this was not always the case. For a considerable period after the Islamic conquests of the seventh century, Arabic had not become the principal language of either commoners or the indigenous elite of conquered regions such as Persia and North Africa. Likewise, at the peak of the Ottoman Empire's strength, from the fifteenth through the eighteenth centuries, Ottoman Turkish tended to be the

[20] See Youssef Courbage and Philippe Fargues, *Christians and Jews Under Islam* (London: I. B. Tauris, 1995 [French original 1991]).

[21] Khazanov, *After the USSR*, p. 117.

principal lingua franca of the elite in much of the region. Persian was also commonly employed in a similar role in regions beyond where it is spoken today.

The major language groups of the Middle East and Central Asia are indicated in Figure 1-6; note, though, that in many areas a number of languages and dialects of more limited scope also exist. In a small town of 12,000 inhabitants in northwestern Turkey, Susurluk, virtually the entire population spoke mutually intelligible dialects of Turkish in the late 1960s, but the older generation continued to speak Circassian and Georgian.[22] Kurdish is widely spoken elsewhere in Turkey, which also has an Arabic-speaking minority. In northern Iraq, there is a bewildering array of ethnolinguistic communities—Kurdish-speaking Gypsies, Kurds, Arabic-speaking pastoralists, and a range of groups with finely distinguished religious, ethnic, and linguistic identities. Similarly, in many border areas of the Middle East, such as that between Iraq and Iran, most of the population is bilingual (Arabic and Persian) in southerly portions of that particular border or trilingual (Arabic, Persian, and Kurdish) along its northernmost sections.

There are large Berber-speaking populations in North Africa, although most are becoming increasingly fluent in Arabic as well. In regions such as Egyptian and Sudanese Nubia, most of the male population is bilingual in Arabic and a Nubian dialect, although the advent of mass education in Egypt and the Sudan is increasingly limiting the use of the Nubian dialects to domestic contexts.[23]

European languages, especially those of the former colonial powers, continue to be important in large parts of the Middle East, just as Russian remains the common language of the educated elite of Central Asia, where the laws regarding the introduction of national languages to replace Russian remain more symbolic than actual.[24] Arabic is the national language in all the countries of France's former North African colonies, but the urban educated population is usually bilingual in French and Arabic. Algeria, Tunisia, and Morocco have adopted official policies of Arabization; yet two decades after independence in Morocco and Tunisia and a slightly lesser period for Algeria, many sections of the government bureaucracy continue to be run in French. Indeed, proportionately more Moroccans speak French today than was the case in the colonial era. The French language remains significant in the schools as well, although Arabization at the elementary and secondary levels is progressing. A network of French educational institutions formally intended for the children of the remaining French still exists, but children from elite North African families also

[22] Paul Magnarella, *Tradition and Change in a Turkish Town* (New York: Halsted Press, 1974), p. 33. For a general introduction to Middle Eastern languages, see Gernot L. Windfuhr, "Linguistics," in *The Study of the Middle East*, ed. Leonard Binder (New York: Wiley, 1976), pp. 347–97.

[23] Robert A. Fernea, "Ethnographic Essay," in *Nubians in Egypt: Peaceful People*, ed. Robert A. Fernea and Georg Gerster (Austin and London: University of Texas Press, 1973), pp. 15, 45–46.

[24] See William Fierman, "Independence and the Declining Priority of Language Law Implementation in Uzbekistan," in *Muslim Eurasia: Conflicting Legacies*, ed. Yaacov Ro'i, Cummings Center Series (London: Frank Cass, 1995), pp. 205–30.

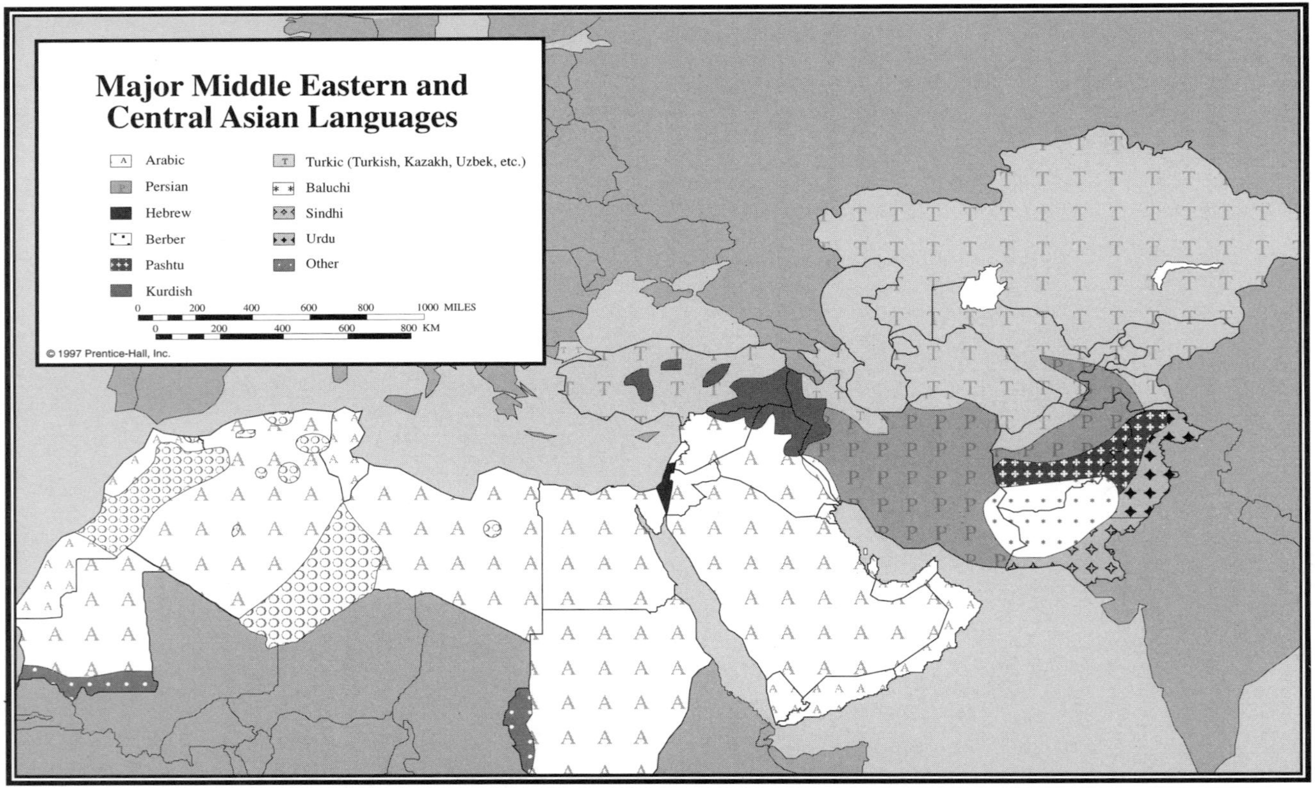

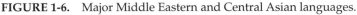

FIGURE 1-6. Major Middle Eastern and Central Asian languages.

attend these institutions. In the government-run schools in North Africa, French continues to be important as a secondary language.

ANTHROPOLOGY TODAY: PRACTICAL ASSUMPTIONS

The purpose of this book is not simply to convey information but also to convey a manner of thought. The language of social anthropology is not quite so laden with technical jargon as are the languages of other social sciences. This has the handicap in some circles of making anthropological inquiry appear initially as a codification of the obvious, but it is often the "obvious" assumptions about cultural conduct and social forms that appear so familiar that become almost impermeable to analysis. I seek to elucidate how an anthropological approach to the study of the Middle East has contributed to an understanding of the region and to the principal intellectual currents of the discipline. American anthropologists could only comment on Central Asian developments at a distance until the early 1990s, but the ethnographic and social historical studies of Russian and Central Asian scholars suggest interesting contrasts to their American and European counterparts.[25]

Anthropology as an academic discipline is notoriously difficult to define. In an earlier, theoretically less reflective era, social anthropology was commonly, although imprecisely, defined as that branch of sociology most concerned with the study of small-scale, technologically simple, nonliterate societies. Now that sociologists, political scientists, economists, and historians rub elbows with anthropologists in the study of both complex and "simple" societies, such a casual division of labor—always questionable—is fully inadequate. Hence two questions must be raised. The first concerns the nature of an *anthropological* study of a complex or simple society and the extent to which such a study can be differentiated from those of history and the other disciplines of the social sciences. A second issue, introduced here and implicitly answered by the structure of this book, is the means by which anthropological techniques, developed largely in the context of the study of small-scale societies and small groups, can contribute to the study of major civilizational areas. By specifying some of the central concerns of anthropological inquiry or, to be more precise, the style of anthropological inquiry developed in this book, I suggest a view of anthropology less heroic than a literal reading of our discipline's name—the science of man—implies, but a view that, at the same time, more accurately represents its unique contribution to the human sciences.

[25] See Sergei P. Poliakov, *Everyday Islam: Religion and Tradition in Rural Central Asia*, trans. Anthony Olcott (Armonk, NY: M. E. Sharpe, 1992), and the critical analysis of this popularizing Russian text in Asad AbuKhalil, "Islam and the Study of Central Asia: A Critique of the Western Scholarly Literature," *Arab Studies Journal* 4, no. 1 (Spring 1996), 115–29, who places Russian studies of Central Asia alongside other "Western" ones; and Dale F. Eickelman, "Introduction: The Other 'Orientalist' Crisis," in *Russia's Muslim Frontiers: New Directions in Cross-Cultural Analysis*, ed. Dale F. Eickelman (Bloomington: Indiana University Press, 1993), pp. 1–15.

The difficulty in defining anthropology reflects less a confusion on the part of its practitioners than the nature of anthropological inquiry itself: There is no clear agreement among its leading practitioners on a central paradigm for research or on the nature of the questions asked. Instead, anthropology is a field of inquiry in which competence is acquired by joining its central debates at any given moment.

In England and the United States, anthropology has existed as a formal academic discipline only since the turn of the century, but it has been a clearly demarcated field of inquiry since at least the 1880s. As with other scientific fields, its central concerns have shifted since then. In the late nineteenth century, anthropology was closely linked with Darwinian concepts of human evolution, so that the techniques and data of what are today separate subdisciplines—social and cultural anthropology (then less grandly known as *ethnography*), linguistics, archaeology, and physical anthropology—were all loosely united. New frames of reference and methodologies drew these subdisciplines apart for many purposes, although the departmental structure of most American universities still reflects the discipline's nineteenth-century organization.

The lack of a common central paradigm in anthropology makes it difficult to convey the concerns of the anthropologists, especially sociocultural anthropologists, to nonspecialists. In 1950, Edward Evans-Pritchard, a leading British anthropologist, described social anthropology to the British public in a series of radio lectures. He began by admitting that for most persons, anthropology still conjures up hazy connotations of apes and skulls, primitive rites, and curious superstitions.[26] But the subject he wished to introduce to his listeners, and which I introduce here, is in fact very different.

A cultural or social anthropologist studies contemporary societies or historical societies that are well enough documented for the purpose. One concern of anthropologists is with the shared symbols and interlocking patterns of meaning generated, maintained, modified, and reproduced by persons in a given society to make sense of the world about them and to act in it. An overlapping concern is with the study of regularities in observed social organization and the ideas held by a society about such organization—how the domestic and public activities of social groups are organized and the consequences of this organization for such concerns as social inequality, gender relations, and political authority. Many anthropologists, especially those concerned with the study of complex, historically known societies such as those of the Middle East, contrive to achieve a balance between concern with the organization and development of complex systems of meaning and practice and how these systems shape, and are shaped by, the contexts of political domination and economic

[26] E. E. Evans-Pritchard, *Social Anthropology and Other Essays* (New York: Free Press, 1964 [1950]), p. 1. For a more recent introduction to the discipline, see I. M. Lewis, *Social Anthropology in Perspective: The Relevance of Social Anthropology*, 2nd ed. (Cambridge and New York: Cambridge University Press, 1985) for a British perspective; and Robert R. Murphy, *Cultural and Social Anthropology: An Overture*, 2nd ed. (Englewood Cliffs, NJ: Prentice-Hall, 1986), for an American one.

relations among groups and societies of different levels of complexity and in different periods.

As an enthusiast of my discipline, I recognize that I am passing over several lively theoretical debates. I am doing this so as not to get bogged down in a technical discussion of the merits of Lévi-Straussian structuralism, the nearly cryptological study of symbols favored by others, deconstructionism, the reemergence of a somewhat musty evolutionary perspective to the study of society, postmodernism, or other concerns, although many will be raised in this book. Instead, I briefly sketch the nature of the discipline as it specifically relates to the study of the Middle East.

Anthropology, or at least a major tradition within it, is a human science, and as such, it shares many common features with history, the other major discipline through which the study of major civilizational areas is undertaken. Some anthropologists legitimize their enterprise by claiming that their goal is to develop universal "laws" of social organization or of cultural order that are somehow independent of specific societies or historical realities. Despite occasional programmatic essays proclaiming this goal, the enduring core of the discipline is contained in detailed, monographic studies of specific societies, cultures, and issues. Such details, and the means by which they are interconnected, are the essence of anthropological inquiry.

Comparative studies of societies and cultures are possible on the basis of such ethnographic studies, but the order thus discerned is not of the sort discerned by the natural scientist. In sciences such as physics, chemistry, and geology, the patterns of order that are described and analyzed are the products of communication among fellow specialists. There is no question of their speaking with the objects of their study. In anthropology and the other human sciences, the notion of objectivity acquires a special meaning, since the anthropologist must discern the meaning behind a social act in order to comprehend it. Briefly stated, humans are cultural animals. They communicate with others and comprehend the world through ordered, shared systems of symbols. Anthropologists are usually more concerned with making explicit the underlying logic of these shared patterns of meaning and codes of conduct than are historians, but studies such as Michael Chamberlain's analysis of the social and political role of knowledge in medieval Damascus underscore that both historians and anthropologists undertake this goal.[27] However, both anthropologists and historians tell stories. Some of these stories collar the reader with direct argument and interpretation, but others seek instead to provoke the imagination, allowing the reader to draw more than one moral. Most narratives in both disciplines combine both kinds of stories.

The problem of making explicit such shared meanings has been called the "translation of cultures," a phrase of Evans-Pritchard's. This problem is most vivid in working with the small scale, relatively isolated groups that have tra-

[27] Michael Chamberlain, *Knowledge and Social Practice in Medieval Damascus, 1190–1350*, Cambridge Studies in Islamic Civilization (Cambridge and New York: Cambridge University Press, 1994).

ditionally been the concern of anthropologists, for in such societies, basic concepts like *time, space,* and *person,* along with other aspects of the nature of the social order, are likely to be substantially removed from our own concepts. At the same time, such notions are often so taken for granted that they usually are not fully expressed by those who share a given cultural tradition. Yet they are public and demonstrable, and the explanation of such implicit concepts is central to making sense of other societies and cultures.[28] Such problems of translation are very real for anthropologists studying the rich, complex civilizations of the Middle East and Central Asia, although at first sight there is much more that is at least superficially known about shared patterns of meaning and social action in such societies. The same problem exists for a contemporary historian studying, for example, early nineteenth-century sectarian movements in upstate New York, when he or she seeks to determine the significance to audiences in that period of the frenzied descriptions of hell contained in surviving copies of sermons. In the New York case, the problem of translation initially appears less obvious, as the historian can "get by," although imperfectly, through a substitution of contemporary attitudes. Yet *some* set of hypotheses as to the underlying patterns of the social order must be made to render such evidence intelligible. Thus historians, just like anthropologists, principally (although not exclusively) concerned with contemporary societies, including their own, seek systematically to infer what is known or knowable about the beliefs and the social order of earlier periods.

Anthropologists and historians pursue styles of explanation that are complementary and interchangeable. Both disciplines entail abstractions from social reality and the shared social meanings that constitute such reality. Historians differ from anthropologists in the type of abstraction that is made from this reality, although this is more a difference of degree than of kind. A common-sense way of conceiving history is to consider it as a record of what happened in the past. Yet a moment's reflection (as Malinowski was fond of saying) makes it clear that any coherent narrative concerning the past requires abstractions from reality. The French philosopher Jean-Paul Sartre aphoristically defined history as "the deliberate resumption of the past by the present" and thus captures at least part of the enterprise involved.[29] Whether the historian is concerned with the Battle of Algiers or the 1933 World Series, no account would be duller or less meaningful than one that naively attempted to gather all relevant documents while imposing no order upon them. The historian must sift through what is known of events and abstract from them, discarding data that fail to contribute to a "story." The historian's primary goal is to elicit the cir-

[28] Clifford Geertz, "'From the Native's Point of View': On the Nature of Anthropological Understanding," in Clifford Geertz, *Local Knowledge: Further Essays in Interpretive Anthropology* (New York: Basic Books, 1983 [1975]), pp. 55–70.

[29] Jean-Paul Sartre, *Literary and Philosophic Essays* (New York: Collier, 1962), p. 206. The British historian and philosopher R. C. Collingwood made the same point as Sartre and developed its implications more thoroughly, if less epigrammatically. See Collingwood's *The Idea of History* (London: Oxford University Press, 1961 [1946]), pp. 282–302.

cumstances that are unique to a given event or to a sequence of events. The resulting explanations only partially entail the determination of fact. The more difficult issue, as the French sociologist Raymond Aron has emphasized, is in deciding the best way of arranging the facts to make them intelligible. Unlike scientific explanations, which can be tested and confirmed through success with replicable cases, historical explanations cannot be "tested." Instead, the best historical explanation is the one that is "most consistent, plausible, and in accordance with all the evidence."[30]

The historian may seek primarily to explain specific events but he must still rely on sociological (or anthropological) abstractions about the nature of religious beliefs, political relations, and the like in a given society to proceed with his narrative. The anthropologist is primarily interested in attempts to elicit and to confirm recurrent regularities in a society—such as the relation of certain systems of belief to social action, the nature of symbol systems, and the relation of types of political authority to various ideas of social inequality. Such explanations are closely intertwined with the understanding of specific historical events. Raymond Aron has gone so far as to say that the job of the sociologist—and sociology, as he uses the term, encompasses social and cultural anthropology as well—is "to render social or historical content more intelligible than it was in the experience of those who lived it."[31]

The relation between history and anthropology has often been obscured by theorists who presume that, because historical and anthropological (or sociological) explanations are separable as ideal types, the actual work of historians and sociologists is equally separable.[32] Even a casual comparison of key monographs in anthropology and in history indicates that the two forms of explanation are necessarily complementary.[33]

To prepare for fieldwork, in addition to immersion in anthropological monographs and social theory, an anthropologist characteristically, or at least ideally, spends several years learning the language and history of a region. Fieldwork itself generally lasts for a year or two and concentrates on a particular small-scale group or groups. The reason for this emphasis on small-scale,

[30] Raymond Aron, *Introduction to the Philosophy of History* (London: Weidenfeld & Nicolson, 1961), p. 124.

[31] Raymond Aron, *Main Currents in Sociological Thought*, vol. 2, trans. Richard Howard and Helen Weaver (New York: Doubleday/Anchor, 1970), p. 245. A similar argument, based in part on the arguments of classic anthropological monographs, can be found in W. G. Runciman, *Sociology in Its Place and Other Essays* (Cambridge: Cambridge University Press, 1970), pp. 1–44.

[32] An extreme formulation of this notion, which, for a time, blocked a more sophisticated consideration of the nature of anthropological thought, can be found in A. R. Radcliffe-Brown, *Structure and Function in Primitive Society* (London: Cohen and West, 1952), pp. 1–3.

[33] Compare, for example, Ernest Gellner, *Saints of the Atlas*, The Nature of Human Society Series (Chicago: University of Chicago Press, 1969), a study of political structure and organization in Morocco's High Atlas Mountains in the 1950s, with Roy P. Mottahedeh, *Loyalty and Leadership in an Early Islamic Society* (Princeton, NJ: Princeton University Press, 1980), a historical study of the implicit ideas of trust, loyalty, kinship, and patronage that governed political conduct during the Būyid dynasty of tenth- and eleventh-century Iraq and Iran, or with Richard Bulliet's *The Patricians of Nishapur*, Harvard Middle Eastern Studies, 16 (Cambridge, MA: Harvard University Press, 1972).

"primitive" societies was that in them most significant social relations were assumed to be face-to-face and geographically self-contained. Under these circumstances it was easier for the anthropologist to see the links among institutions—family and kinship relations, friendship and patron-client ties, land tenure, inheritance rules and practices, religious rituals, beliefs, politics—and, most important, the shared symbolic conceptions of the world that underlie these various forms of behavior.[34] On the basis of the intensive study of such societies (or, increasingly today, of small groups within larger societies, be they peasants or intellectual elites), the anthropologist then proceeds to the hardest job, that of creating out of the record of research a coherent representation of a society and the general principles of order within it. More self-consciously than most historians, the anthropologist relates this task to general theoretical issues.

Now that anthropologists are, or try to be, as much at home in cities, towns, villages, and regions encapsulated within modern and complex societies as in the rapidly disappearing isolated and small-scale societies, the question becomes more pressing of how the microsociological technique of fieldwork—the intensive, totalistic study of social forms—contributes to understanding larger units of society. How can the microsociological study of an anthropologist contribute to the understanding of larger entities such as nation-states? As Clifford Geertz asked with characteristic irony: "Are the petty squabbles of barnyard notables really what we mean by politics? Are mud huts and goat-skin tents really where the action is?"[35] Is there not the danger of getting lost in "mindless descriptivism" in the study of a pilgrimage center in Morocco or a tribe in the Yemen or at least of learning more about these entities than one really wants to know?

This book demonstrates that anthropologists, or most anthropologists anyway, study specific places, not for themselves or for the love of minute description of routine events in exotic places but to learn something beyond them. We do intensive analyses of political, economic, symbolic, and historical processes on a small scale. Like all other disciplines in the social sciences, we use data as a means of making hypotheses about larger wholes. As Geertz emphasizes, the question is not whether we generalize—any science generalizes—but *how* we generalize. In the human sciences, the microsociological technique of anthropology offers an alternative to the tendency to speak of tribe and peasants or rulers and ruled as if they were stock characters in a sociological morality play.[36] Given the significant linguistic, cultural, and political diver-

[34] The definition of *institution* varies significantly in the social sciences. By this term I mean customary, accepted ways of doing things in a given society. The emphasis in this definition is on the culturally shared patterns of meaning and mutual expectations that underlie such conventions.

[35] Clifford Geertz, "Comments," in *Rural Politics and Social Change in the Middle East*, ed. Richard Antoun and Iliya Harik (Bloomington and London: Indiana University Press, 1972), p. 460. This discussion owes much to Geertz's succinct presentation of the issues in pp. 460–67 of the Antoun and Harik volume.

[36] Ibid., p. 463.

Excavations of new areas at Harappa, an important archaeological site in Pakistan's Sindh province, reveal new information on the vast trading networks established during the heyday of the Indus valley cities (2600–1900 B.C., especially 2450–2200 B.C.). These trading networks cross-cut conventional understandings of frontiers between major world regions. In the photograph above (seated left), J. Mark Kenoyer (University of Wisconsin, Madison, codirector of the Harappa Archaeological Research Project with Harvard University's Richard H. Meadow), is excavating an important craft production area at the site. Assisted by Pakistani student archaeologists and local workers, he is mapping the newly exposed structures. The site area (Mound ET) is located just inside a major gateway and appears to have been a craft quarter or bazaar area. Traded materials included lapis lazuli and pottery from the highlands of Baluchistan and Central Asia; shells from Oman, Gujarat, and Pakistan's Makran coast; and copper from Rajastan, Baluchistan, and Oman. Each new season of excavation raises questions and significantly changes our understanding of the social and economic dynamics of the Indus Valley and its relation to other major regions. [Photograph by William Miller.]

sity of the Middle East, facile generalizations about common characteristics often prove misleading and deceptive.

Anthropologists are particularly concerned with eliciting the taken-for-granted, shared meanings that underlie conduct in given societies and are so familiar a part of routine that they are taken to be "natural." It is against such undramatic backgrounds that citizens participate in nation-states or have contact with the governments of such entities or even form a part of such governments. The petty squabbles of barnyard notables may not in themselves be of compelling interest, but they frequently offer a more advantageous means of determining the components of a political style than the more formal and generally less accessible deliberations of parliaments and cabinet meetings. The link between the unit of the anthropologist's study and the larger whole is not that of microcosm to macrocosm—as an earlier generation of community studies often naively assumed—but merely that of an arena of study that permits the elaboration of hypotheses about certain social and cultural processes.

Through the study of such mundane events as patterns of naming, seeking a husband or wife, the ways in which sickness is cured, settling a dispute, selling a sheep, local elections, and religious ceremonies, anthropologists seek to grasp what is distinctly Moroccan about Moroccan markets, Lebanese about Lebanese political factionalism, Alevi about Alevi conceptions of Islam, Omani about Omani notions of honor, or Egyptian about Egyptian styles of etiquette and deference. The microsociological perspective of the anthropologist can often provide valuable insights into just how participation in such larger entities is experienced. Through comparison of different societies and cultures and through careful attention to technique and theoretical assumptions, anthropologists seek an understanding of what is distinctive about general processes operating in specific historical and cultural settings. The following chapter indicates how notions of what constitutes an adequate description of Middle Eastern and Central Asian societies has changed over the past century and a half and suggests how "objective" assumptions of any society, including one's own, are linked to the social contexts in which, and for which, they are produced.

FURTHER READINGS

The Middle East and Central Asia are on the periphery of the declared scope of K. N. Chaudhuri, *Asia Before Europe: Economy and Civilization of the Indian Ocean from the Rise of Islam to 1750* (Cambridge and New York: Cambridge University Press, 1990), but in practice his scope and his "re-imagining" of conventional geographic frontiers directly contributes to understanding how the Middle Eastern and Central Asian civilizations have complemented one another throughout history, and suggests directions that future writings on Central Asia may take. See especially his discussion of "Animals and Their Masters: Nomads and Nomadism," pp. 263–96, which also pertains to Chapter 4 of this book. Ali Banuazizi and Myron Weiner, eds., *The New Geopolitics of Central Asia and Its Borderlands* (Bloomington and London: Indiana University Press, 1994), describe the contemporary situation.

2

INTELLECTUAL PREDECESSORS

East and West

The "West" rediscovered the Middle East in the early nineteenth century and Central Asia in the late nineteenth, although Central Asia almost disappeared from view again during the Soviet era (1917–1991). I specify "rediscovery" because, at least until the Christian conquest of Granada, Spain, in 1492 and the final expulsion of Muslims from Spain in 1609, for centuries Europeans had recognized the intellectual supremacy of the Muslim world in many fields. Indeed, many key aspects of Western heritage, including ancient Greek thought, were preserved and enhanced through their assimilation into early Islamic civilization.[1] Because of these many elements of shared heritage, Western—and Christian and Jewish—history has been so entangled with that of the Middle East and Islam that the area has never appeared to Westerners as safely different and exotic. Islam has always preoccupied the European imagination, although in an intensified and substantially altered manner since the end of the sixteenth century, when the notion of a distinct Muslim "orient" began to take hold. It reached full bloom in the seventeenth and eighteenth centuries.[2]

In some ways it is ironic to speak of the European rediscovery of the Middle East or Central Asia. Within the Muslim world there were sustained intellectual efforts to comprehend Muslim society as a totality. A salient, but by no means isolated, example is the medieval North African intellectual Ibn Khaldūn (d. 1406). One of his most important contributions was an effort to understand the nature of political authority. Recent scholars, including Ernest Gellner (1925–1995), who was concerned with understanding the nature of premodern political authority throughout the Muslim Middle East, and Richard Tapper,

[1] F. E. Peters, "Islam as a Western Civilization," *The Arabic World* 18, no. 3 (May–June 1972), 13–19, breaks with earlier conventions and looks at Islamic civilization as an integral part of the Western past. See also George Makdisi, *The Rise of Colleges: Institutions of Learning in Islam and the West* (Edinburgh: Edinburgh University Press, 1981).

[2] See Thierry Hentsch, *Imagining the Middle East*, trans. Fred A. Reed (Montreal: Black Rose Books, 1992), pp. 75, 81.

who has studied "tribe" and state in Afghanistan and Iran over the last two centuries, have used Ibn Khaldūn's theories of dynastic succession in empires with significant tribal populations as a point of departure.[3]

Like many of his contemporaries, Ibn Khaldūn acquired his education by traveling to centers of learning throughout North Africa and the Middle East. He served as counselor of state to a number of North African rulers and to Spanish rulers when Spain was still under Muslim domination. He makes for fascinating reading today, as he had to struggle to create a sociological vocabulary that could articulate the rise and decay of dynasties throughout the Muslim world.

Ibn Khaldūn must have been acutely sensitive to the problems of dynasties and political domination, for the Spanish Muslim principalities collapsed one after another during his lifetime. One clear threat was from Christian invaders; another was from sudden internal shifts in the political climate of the Muslim world. It has sometimes been argued that Ibn Khaldūn sought to provide a universal model for political developments. I believe that he was concerned primarily with medieval North Africa and southern Spain, from which he drew most of his examples. His observations on the nature of political domination make more sense in this context than if they are extended to encompass all forms of domination.

Ibn Khaldūn sees dynasties in terms of successive ideal stages. At its inception, a dynasty must possess "group feeling" (*'aṣabīya*), which can be roughly glossed by the idea of people acting as if compelling ties of obligation bind members of their group together. He argues that intense notions of group feeling are more likely to be found in rural or tribal contexts (the notion that group feeling is confined primarily to nomads or bedouin is based on a misinterpretation of Ibn Khaldūn's Arabic original). Group feeling need not depend on presumed "blood" relationships, but the bonds of solidarity must take precedence over all other bonds of association. Such ties imply that group members act together in a common interest over extended periods of time, and he provides examples from the North African dynasties at their origin. He also argues that a new dynasty is most likely to be established when it can claim a religious basis of legitimacy: prophecy, reform, or some other "religious coloring." Only with group feeling can a religious ideology be practically implemented; thus Ibn Khaldūn used the notion to link ideologies to their political contexts.

Like most political thinkers, Ibn Khaldūn chose a striking metaphor of the human life span—growth, maturity, and decay—to depict the nature of political change, with each stage of this cycle generating the conditions necessary for the next. With maturity, the dynasty becomes competent and bureaucratic, but overly confident. It begins to decay when it is taken over by luxury-loving successors who take their status for granted and lose the determination and sacrifice needed to maintain authority. In this sense his theory of dynastic change is pessimistic, because he saw the cyclical succession of stages as inevitable. Ibn

[3] See Ibn Khaldūn, *The Muqaddimah*, 2nd ed., vol. 1, trans. Franz Rosenthal, Bollingen Series 43 (Princeton, NJ: Princeton University Press, 1967), pp. 249–355.

Khaldūn's notion of history is also repetitive: Events in human history become disconnected incidents of an unchanging divine plan. Such a notion of fixed stages of human activity is not without parallels in more recent European social and political thought—some aspects of the thinking of Karl Marx and Arnold Toynbee come immediately to mind, although the contexts in which these later thinkers worked were quite different.

Central Asia also had its outstanding intellectuals and historians, such as Rashīd al-Dīn Ṭabīb (1247–1318), a near-contemporary of Chingiz Khān (?1167–1227), founder of the Mongol Empire whose Hordes (as its major confederations of tribes with elected leaders, or *khān*-s, were known) conquered Persia, parts of Syria and Mesopotamia, and Europe in the thirteenth century. Born in Persia and trained as a physician, he entered the service of the Mongol court in Persia, and around age 30 converted from Judaism, also his family's religion, to Islam. By this time, the Mongol rulers had themselves converted to Islam, and the *khān* whom Rashīd al-Dīn served was concerned that the Mongols were losing sight of their Mongol identity. With this in mind, Rashīd al-Dīn, who by 1298 also became a senior political figure (*wazīr*), was first commissioned to write a history of the Mongols in Persia, and later, on request, a world history (Ar. *Jāmi' al-tawārīkh*, lit. "Collection of Histories"), of the Mongols and all the peoples with whom the Mongols came into contact.[4] However, because Central Asia constituted a "double periphery" (as described in Chapter 1), it entered the Western imagination later than Persia, Turkey, and the Arab countries and regions.

Most areas of the Russian Empire with Muslim populations were annexed between the late eighteenth and nineteenth centuries. At the time of the first official census in Tsarist Russia in 1897, Muslims made up 11 percent of the population, or 13.6 million out of a total of 125.6 million. Partly in reaction to intensified efforts at Russification and Christianization beginning in the mid-nineteenth century, vigorous pan-Islamic and pan-Turkic movements developed in Russia, modeled in part on the pan-Hellenic, pan-Slavic, pan-Italian, and pan-German movements that had developed earlier in Europe.[5] Central Asia and Afghanistan became the focus of the "great game" of competition among imperial powers, and these concerns fueled scholarly interest in the West.[6]

This chapter describes the principal intellectual currents and geopolitical circumstances that have led to efforts to interpret Middle Eastern and Central Asian societies and cultures since the last century. The scholars and observers

[4] David Morgan, *The Mongols*, Peoples of Europe (Cambridge, MA, and Oxford: Blackwell, 1986), pp. 18–21, who also reviews the argument questioning the authorship of the "Collection of Histories."

[5] Jacob M. Landau, *The Politics of Pan-Islam: Ideology and Organization* (Oxford: Clarendon Press, 1990), pp. 143–46; and Jacob M. Landau, *Pan-Turkism: From Irredentism to Cooperation*, 2nd ed. (Bloomington and Indianapolis: Indiana University Press, 1995), p. 182.

[6] Jon W. Anderson, "Poetics and Politics in Ethnographic Texts: A View from the Colonial Ethnography of Afghanistan," in *Writing the Social Text: Poetics and Politics in Social Science Discourse*, ed. Richard Harvey Brown (New York: Aldine De Gruyter, 1992), pp. 91–115. See Morgan, *Mongols*, pp. 5–31; and Owen Lattimore's classic *Inner Asian Frontiers of China* (Boston: Beacon, 1962 [1940]).

whose works are discussed share, in varying degrees, three common features with modern social anthropologists: (1) they considered the study of the *contemporary* social order significant to their research, even when their primary goal was the comprehension of remote or "classical" historical periods; (2) they considered it important to describe and comprehend the ordinary activities and taken-for-granted conventions of daily life and sought to do so through direct and prolonged contact; and (3) they consciously made *systematic* observations (especially in the latter half of the century) and sought to make explicit the principles on which their inquiries were based.

There were three main reasons for the growing European interest in the Middle East (and, to a lesser extent, Central Asia) in the nineteenth century. First was a general curiosity about the customs of peoples elsewhere, but particularly those of the Muslim orient. The Muslim orient had been used since the late seventeenth century as a screen on which Europeans projected fantasies about the primitive or alien "other" and an often imaginary geography. This was reflected in part in the emerging field of "orientalism," which included everything from Muslim societies to the civilizations of India, China, and Japan. This interest was popularly reflected in a number of ways: Moors, Turks, and Persians characteristically appeared in operas of the period and painters such as Eugène Delacroix (1798–1863) romantically depicted what they considered the "private" life of Islam. Successful, if inaccurate, books such as Washington Irving's *Mahomet and His Successors* or more imposing artifacts of intellect such as Ernest Renan (1823–1892), "Islamism and Science," offered a general theory of the "decay" of Muslim civilization in contrast to Western vitality.[7] Inherent corruption and the decay of "oriental" government is a common theme in the Western "orientalist" literature of the period.

By the mid-nineteenth century, travel to the Middle East—at least to its major cities (but not Central Asia)—was no longer considered hazardous. Novelists such as Thackeray visited the region, and the reading public eagerly followed their accounts.[8] A succession of nineteenth-century world's fairs in Europe and North America "displayed" the orient in ways that, with the passage of time, reflected increasing colonial domination.[9] By the end of the century the fascination with the Muslim world merged, at least in Britain, with the

[7] Washington Irving (1783–1859), *Mahomet and His Successors* (New York: Putnam, 1868). Equally indicative of the kitsch literature concerning the Muslim orient is Washington Irving's *Legends of the Alhambra* (Philadelphia and London: Lippincott, 1909). Renan's essay can be found in his *Poetry of the Celtic Races and Other Studies*, trans. William G. Hutchinson (London: W. Scott, 1896). An essay on the life of Muḥammad can be found in Renan's *Essays in Religious History and Criticism*, trans. O. B. Frothingham (New York: Carleton, 1864), pp. 226–84. Renan's ideas struck a responsive chord among Middle Eastern intellectuals, including the important early Islamic reformer Sayyid Jamāl al-Dīn al-Afghānī (1838–1897). A standard study of al-Afghānī's writings, with extensive selections from them, is Nikki R. Keddie, *An Islamic Response to Imperialism*, 2nd ed. (Berkeley and Los Angeles: University of California Press, 1983 [orig. 1968]).

[8] William Makepeace Thackery (pseud. M. A. Titmarsh) (1811–1863), *Notes of a Journey from Cornhill to Grand Cairo* (New York: Wiley and Putnam, 1846).

[9] Zeynep Çelik, *Displaying the Orient: Architecture of Islam at Nineteenth Century World's Fairs* (Berkeley and Los Angeles: University of California Press, 1992).

romantic notion of the pure bedouin nomad as a primitive contemporary with the virtues of a Victorian gentleman. This strand of attraction to the Middle East might be called (anachronistically) the "T. E. Lawrence syndrome," after the now-legendary World War I British military intelligence officer (1888–1935) who encouraged Arab tribal leaders to revolt against Ottoman rule.

Such romantic assumptions about the Muslim orient were undeniably important in sustaining a scholarly and popular interest in the area, and some travel accounts, such as Charles Doughty's *Travels in Arabia Deserta* (1888), presented valuable and precise ethnographic data, although they were not intended as ethnographies even by the conventions of the time.[10] In the hands of later anthropologists, such accounts have been invaluable—for reconstructing the social organization of pastoral nomadic societies, for instance, prior to the effective imposition of modern state authority. Travel accounts of the Middle East and a rather diffuse concept of "oriental" society had a significant impact on some of the main theses developed by leading sociologists, including Karl Marx (1818–1883), Max Weber (1864–1920), and Émile Durkheim (1858–1917).

A second reason for interest in the Middle East in this period was heightened imperial activity in the region. It was a fertile ground for the enterprises of European financiers and was also considered ripe for direct political control. Napoleon Bonaparte's expedition (1798–1801) brought Egypt under French rule for a brief period, and completion of the Suez Canal in 1869 began a period of rapidly growing European economic interest in Egypt, which culminated with British occupation in 1882 and the annexation of the Sudan (technically, an Anglo-Egyptian condominium) shortly thereafter. Economic dependence, once established, often brought political intervention in its wake. In North Africa, Algeria was occupied by France in 1830 and soon thereafter was legally considered an integral part of the metropole; Tunisia was made a French protectorate in 1881, Morocco in 1912. If indirect forms of domination are included, such as the presence of British political advisers to the Trucial States of the Arab-Persian Gulf beginning in the early nineteenth century to protect imperial lines of communication to India (and subsequently oil supplies), then the magnitude of European political interest in the region is even more pronounced. In the years following World War I, direct European control (or control by mandate) over the countries of the Middle East expanded to encompass Libya (Italy), Syria and Lebanon (France), and Palestine and Iraq (Britain); in Central Asia, Russia intensified its economic and political hold in the last four decades of the nineteenth century.

Finally, interest in the Middle East converged with important trends in European scholarship, particularly the so-called "higher criticism" of the Bible. Bernard Lewis has written that one reason for this was a Jewish sympathy with

[10] Charles Doughty, *Travels in Arabia Deserta* (New York: Random House, n.d. [1888]). In literary style; Doughty's *Travels* is probably one of the greatest nineteenth-century travel accounts, although it had little success in the author's lifetime. For contemporary assessments of Doughty's significance, see Stephen Tabachnick, ed., *Explorations in Doughty's "Arabia Deserta"* (Athens and London: University of Georgia Press, 1987). See also Richard Bevis, "Spiritual Geology: C. M. Doughty and the Land of the Arabs," *Victorian Studies* 16, no. 2 (December 1972), 163–81.

Islam. As religious anti-Judaism gave way to racially expressed anti-Semitism in Europe, some Jewish scholars looked to other Semites for comfort. This affinity, Lewis says, was largely imaginary but accounted for part of the interest in Islam.[11] In addition, several prominent scholars trained in ancient and modern Semitic languages became explorers and ethnographers because they saw such research as necessary for understanding society in the time of the Old Testament patriarchs.

It is easy to think of the orientalist scholarship of this period as taking the same form in all European countries and over long periods of time, from the eighteenth through the twentieth centuries, but this would be misleading. Many studies of the Middle East in the nineteenth century do not conform to the passionately argued yet curiously ahistorical representation of scholarship on the Middle East from 1800 to 1950 contained in Edward Said's *Orientalism*.[12] Said describes how Western scholarly images of the Middle East have been constructed over the last two centuries. He is best when assessing the more imaginary and literary eighteenth-century accounts of Islam and the Arab East. For later periods, as some of his Arab critics have pointed out, he disregards the evidence of "orientalist" scholarship that runs contrary to his own broad assumptions, sustains the very assumptions about the "essential" features of "East" and "West" that he decries in Western literature on the Arab East, and places "orientalist" scholarship outside the main currents of history and politics by assuming that it was static throughout the period covered and had developed in an identical fashion in all Western countries. Western scholarship on the Arab world, Said's Arab critics argue, should be linked to the specific historical, cultural, and political contexts in which it was produced. Some Arab critics see *Orientalism* as contributing to an "orientalism in reverse," especially in the Arab world of the 1970s and the 1980s, in which "authentic" Islam and Arab character are asserted by some Arabs and Muslims to be essentially unchanged since the advent of Islam in seventh-century Arabia.[13] In Central Asia and the Caucasus, the "re-imagination" of the past creates a "minefield of subtle political nuances," in which the assimilation or shared heritage with neighboring peoples is omitted from the archaeological and historical record to justify contemporary nationalist claims.[14] Even musical traditions are not exempt from such direct political concerns.[15]

[11] Bernard Lewis, "The Study of Islam," *Encounter* 38, no. 1 (January 1972), 35–36.

[12] Edward W. Said, *Orientalism* (New York: Pantheon, 1978).

[13] See Emmanuel Sivan, "Edward Said and His Arab Reviewers," *Jerusalem Quarterly*, no. 35 (Spring 1985), 11–23.

[14] Philip L. Kohl and Gocha R. Tsetskhladze, "Nationalism and Archaeology in the Caucasus," in *Nationalism, Politics, and the Practice of Archaeology*, ed. Philip L. Kohl and Clare Fawcett (Cambridge: Cambridge University Press, 1995), p. 152. See also Daniel Brower and Edward J. Lazzerini, eds., *Russia's Orient: Imperial Borderlands and Peoples, 1700–1917* (Bloomington: Indiana University Press, 1997).

[15] See Theodore Levin, *A Hundred Thousand Fools of God: Musical Travels in Central Asia* (Bloomington: Indiana University Press, 1996).

BONAPARTE'S EXPEDITION TO EGYPT, 1798–1801

Bonaparte's expedition is often used by historians to symbolize the point at which the Muslim orient, forced to recognize growing Western hegemony, was compelled to acquire Western technology, especially military technology, and ultimately was to be profoundly shaken by contact with all aspects of European civilization. Bonaparte's expedition also marked the start of the European scholarly rediscovery of the Muslim East. Traveling with Bonaparte's fleet were 150 scientists and orientalists, whose task was to make a systematic inventory of Egypt—its geology, rivers, minerals, antiquities, and, of most concern in the present context, the "manners and customs" of its inhabitants. The motivation for the last was the hope that insight into contemporary society, especially that of the peasants, might provide clues to the social order of Pharaonic times. The implicit assumption was that peasant society was profoundly conservative and resistant to change. (Parenthetically, the notion that the study of some present societies is a valuable indication of the past of others dies hard. Indeed, it still dominates popular understanding of what anthropologists do.) In any case, the findings of the scholars accompanying Bonaparte were collected in the massive, meticulous, 24-volume *Description de l'Égypte* (1820).[16] Even if its ethnographic section was not always as accurate as the sections on geology and natural history, its authors aspired to the same high standards.

In the later French colonial conquests in North Africa, an initial by-product of conquest was the compilation of similar inventories of the new domains. The strength of the surveys of Algeria and Tunisia rests more on an inventory of the physical characteristics of the two territories than in an understanding of their populations. Nevertheless, they indicate in a perfunctory manner the nature of indigenous political activities and institutions. Interest in ethnographic inquiry during the colonial era in Algeria was linked directly to political conditions. For example, in periods of sustained local resistance to French rule, there was an increase in ethnographic investigation of political and religious topics. This interest waned when French rule was thought to be secure.[17]

In contrast, monographs written on Morocco just prior to the protectorate (1912–1956) and during its early years constitute one of the best collections of colonial ethnography to be found anywhere. One reason for the quality of this research, in contrast to most of that conducted in Algeria, was a conscious decision on the part of the French, at least in principle, to preserve and enhance indigenous institutions. Another clear impetus was the notion that rational, systematic ethnographic inquiry would facilitate the "scientific" implantation

[16] *Description de l'Égypte* (Paris: Éditions d'Art Albert Guillot, 1966).

[17] For a useful account of changing styles in the ethnography of Algeria, together with representative texts, see Philippe Lucas and Jean-Claude Vatin, *L'Algérie des anthropologues* [The Anthropologists' Algeria] (Paris: Maspéro, 1975); and for colonial Morocco, Edmund Burke III, "The Image of the State in French Ethnological Literature: A New Look at the Origins of Lyautey's Berber Policy," in *Arabs and Berbers: From Tribe to Nation in North Africa*, ed. Ernest Gellner and Charles Micaud (London: Duckworth, 1972), pp. 175–99.

of colonial rule. This tendency to regard the exercise of colonial rule as a science was already present at the time of Bonaparte's expedition to Egypt.

Another significant aspect of Bonaparte's invasion of Egypt was the attempt to legitimize the colonial enterprise in the eyes of the conquered population. On one of the expedition's ships was an Arabic printing press looted from the Vatican. This was used to print a proclamation, translated awkwardly into Arabic by an orientalist, announcing that Bonaparte had come in the name of Islam and would govern in a more Islamic fashion than the preceding corrupt Mamlūk regime. The invading troops were ordered to be scrupulously respectful of mosques. Bonaparte dressed as a Muslim and prayed in mosques, until the ridicule of his troops forced him to abandon the practice.[18] What is crucial about such actions is that they prefigure later, more systematic attempts by colonial regimes to legitimize their presence in the eyes of the ruled and, whenever possible, to win over key elements in the indigenous society. Ethnographic investigation was seen as an important contribution to this aspect of the colonial enterprise.

EXPLORERS: JOHN LEWIS BURCKHARDT (1784–1817) AND EDWARD LANE (1801–1876)

There is a special class of explorers whose works are particularly useful in tracing the rediscovery of the Middle East—those who could speak the languages of the region and who, through long residence in it, could describe its society with reasonable accuracy. For the purposes of ethnographic (or more precisely protoethnographic) description, the works of two nineteenth-century explorers and travelers suggest the enduring value of some accounts from this period.

Burckhardt was born into a well-to-do Swiss family and became attracted very early in his life to the "discovery" of the Middle East.[19] As a young man he traveled to England to study Arabic at Cambridge. During this time, he prepared himself for the anticipated rigors of life in the East by walking barefoot through the English countryside, living only on vegetables for long periods. In 1809, at the age of 25, he left for the Middle East and never returned, dying there of malaria eight years later.

Burckhardt's books reveal him to be an engaging, if compulsive, scholar who can be relied on for accuracy. He lived on a minute stipend provided by an English group, the Association for Promoting the Discovery of the Interior Parts of Africa. Throughout his stay in the Middle East, Burckhardt dressed in Turkish fashion, as did the urban elite of the period in much of the Middle East. He adopted the name of Shaykh Ibrāhīm, more out of convenience than an attempt to conceal his true identity. Burckhardt's Arabic was excellent—both

[18] Alan Moorehead, *The Blue Nile* (London: Four Square Editions, 1965), pp. 55–133, provides a well-written general account of the French occupation of Egypt.

[19] The biographical details presented here are derived from Katharine Sim, *Desert Traveler: The Life of Jean Louis Burckhardt* (London: Gollancz, 1969).

classical Arabic and several contemporary dialects—and while in Damascus he translated *Robinson Crusoe*. Although recognized as a Christian, he was accepted as an authority on Islamic law. Among his works are a collection of Arabic proverbs, an account of his travels in Nubia, and his detailed but elegant *Notes on the Bedouins and the Wahábys*, his most ambitious work.[20]

Notes on the Bedouins is evenly divided between an ethnographic description of bedouin society in Arabia and a detailed history of the Wahhābī movement, a form of Islamic puritanism that originated in the mid-eighteenth century in Arabia and reached its greatest territorial extent during Burckhardt's stay in the Middle East. He describes bedouin society in a coherent, organized fashion; there are sections on the layout of tents, the segregation of the sexes, dress, etiquette, domestic life and economy, religious practices, tribal organization, marriage, feuds, and warfare. No explicit sociological themes are explored, but an implicit concern with the nature of bedouin "independence" runs throughout the account. Burckhardt was fascinated by the bedouins' "uncorrupted manners" and their code of honor.

Admittedly, his point of departure is naturalistic description. He classifies the parts of the tent and the "parts" of tribal organization in the same way that a botanist would classify plants. One reason he appears to consider the bedouin as "uncorrupted" (in contrast to the "debauchery" of townsmen) is that he portrays them as timeless and unchanging. Even towns and the Ka'ba are described primarily by their physical form; many of the "ancient customs" he describes are part of the physical landscape. In general, Burckhardt makes it clear that the observer is the contemplator and that the bedouin, for all their initial charm, live a monotonous and unreflective life.[21] Still, his work is not as fully anchored in the "orientalist" assumptions of his period as other accounts, and it represents a genuine attempt to portray bedouin society.

After describing the rules of hospitality, blood revenge, and the autonomy of most bedouin tribes from the authority of central governments, Burckhardt asks: How is it possible to have an ordered society such as that of the bedouin, with a code of law and conventions of conduct but no written codes of law and no formal "legislation"? Burckhardt's question sounds awkward today, but it was one that interested many European political philosophers of the time.[22] Burckhardt's contribution to its discussion was to perceive the relevance of his direct experience with such a society. Segmentary lineage theory in social anthropology (see Chapter 6), which enjoyed considerable popularity from the publication of Evans-Pritchard's *The Nuer* (1940) until the mid-1960s, can in

[20] John Lewis Burckhardt, *Arabic Proverbs; or, the Manners and Customs of the Modern Egyptians* (Totowa, NJ: Rowman and Littlefield, 1972 [1830]); *Travels in Nubia* (London: John Murray, 1822); *Notes on the Bedouins and Wahábys* (London: Henry Colburn and Richard Bentley, 1831). All three books are available in reprint editions.

[21] These points are elaborated in Kenneth Sandbank, "Literary Representation and Social Legitimation: J. L. Burckhardt's Approach to 'The Orient,'" *International Journal of Middle East Studies* 13, no. 4 (November 1981), 497–511.

[22] Burckhardt, *Notes*, pp. 378–82.

many ways be considered a more systematic response to this question, as societies described as segmentary were said to exist without any formal leaders or governmental apparatus, all conflict within them being regulated by organized violence (feuds) among the groups involved.[23] On the basis of observations such as Burckhardt's, later social anthropologists have been able to construct more theoretically oriented arguments on the nature of political organization in pre-oil Arabia.[24]

The second section of the *Notes* concerns the Wahhābī movement. The ideological goal of this movement was the reform of Islam as it was then practiced. The "Unitarians" (*al-muwaḥḥidūn*), as the Wahhābiyya call themselves, were especially antagonistic toward the popular custom of venerating the shrines of Muslim saints. Their ideology remains strong in Saudi Arabia today. In their drive to reassert the Quranic doctrine of the equality of all men before God, the Wahhābiyya even destroyed the cupola built over the birthplace of the Prophet Muḥammad in Mecca. Because the Wahhābiyya politically united the tribes of Arabia, it was considered a threat to the Ottoman Empire, particularly to the Mamlūk regime of Egypt. After repeated attempts to crush the movement, an army of Muḥammad 'Alī, the ruler of Egypt, finally defeated it in 1818, shortly after Burckhardt wrote his account.

Burckhardt gathered reports of the Wahhābiyya and its doctrines from members of the movement and eyewitnesses. He carefully assessed the implications of the Wahhābī insistence on settling nomadic groups in order to better control them. He considered their leadership, the nature of their doctrines, and how they were viewed by Muslims outside the Arabian peninsula. Like many contemporary anthropological descriptions of religious movements, Burckhardt's account of the Wahhābī movement alternates between social history and background material on religious ideologies and social forms.

Edward Lane originally intended to enter the ministry, and in this context he acquired an enthusiasm for oriental studies. Later he became an engraver, but the work proved too taxing on his health. In 1825, at the age of 24, he set out for Cairo, where he lived more or less constantly until 1849. He adopted native clothes—the Turkish dress of Cairo's elite—but never concealed his identity as an Englishman and a Christian. He delicately reminded his Muslim friends that Christ was also seen as a prophet in the Quran. Lane mixed freely with Egyptians and was held in confidence by many of them. Fluency in Arabic such as he possessed may not be absolutely necessary for certain types of ethnographic inquiry (such as cultural ecology or certain forms of economic anthropology), but for any account of a society's beliefs, rituals, and social conventions it is essential.

[23] Burckhardt described in detail the institution of the feud as the Bedouin themselves conceived it. A segmentary diagram even appeared in his account (*Notes*, vol. 1, pp. 150–51).

[24] See, for instance, Madawi Al Rasheed, *Politics in an Arabian Oasis: The Rashidi Tribal Dynasty* (London and New York: I. B. Tauris, 1991).

FIGURE 2-1. Bridal procession in Cairo, 1835. [From Edward William Lane, *An Account of the Manners and Customs of the Modern Egyptians* (London: John Murray, 1860), p. 164.]

Lane's *An Account of the Manners and Customs of the Modern Egyptians* (1836)[25] provides a detailed account of urban Muslim society and thus complements Burckhardt's *Notes*. Lane does not appear to have considered *Manners and Customs* as his principal work, although it is considered so today. He intended it as a popular book to complement an account of the manners and customs of the ancient Egyptians (those of Pharaonic times) that was then in circulation. His other works included a translation of *A Thousand and One Nights* in a manner more accurate, if less sensational, than that provided by Burton and a massive Arabic-English lexicon that he never lived to complete.

Lane wrote that his intention in *Manners and Customs* was simply to make some of his countrymen "better acquainted with the domiciliated classes of one of the most interesting nations of the world, by drawing a detailed picture of the inhabitants of the largest Arab city." He regarded his book as an accessory to the reading of translations of Arabic literature that was then in vogue.[26] His descriptions of urban life are elegant in their economy and clarity. They include dress, child rearing, ceremonies associated with birth, marriage, and death, domestic life, the marketplace, government, Islam, and, above all, the nuances of etiquette and the taken-for-granted conventions of society. As with the writings of Burckhardt, there is no explicit theoretical orientation to Lane's writing, and there is a tendency to view Cairene society as an object to be contemplated and classified.

[25] Fifth edition (1860) reprinted (New York: Dover, 1973).

[26] Ibid., p. xxiii.

SCHOLARS: W. ROBERTSON SMITH (1846–1894)

The brilliant, tenaciously cosmopolitan W. Robertson Smith is the first of the scholars considered in this chapter to have a specific, conscious theoretical orientation toward the study of Arab society. As Thomas O. Beidelman has written in an appraisal of Smith's work, whatever Smith's shortcomings by today's perspectives, he "sought to define the essential nature of religious behavior and approached the analysis of social institutions through comparative and historical studies."[27] This explicit goal, and Smith's means of achieving it, remain one of the central concerns of contemporary social anthropology.

Smith acquired a dazzling reputation as a mathematician but quickly turned to biblical studies. In 1875, at the age of 29, he was given the extraordinary distinction of being named to a committee to produce an authorized English translation of the Bible. He also assumed editorship of the *Encyclopaedia Britannica*, where his wide-ranging interests and responsibilities "led him to a personal acquaintance with nearly every important intellectual in Britain and a large number on the Continent . . . men as different as Swinburne and Darwin, Huxley and Kelvin, Spencer and Burne-Jones."[28] He is said to have personally read every article submitted.

One of Smith's strongest personal interests was in "historical" criticism of the Bible. This approach to biblical study, already prevalent on the Continent, asserted that the texts of the Bible should be treated as any other historical document and analyzed for authorship and historical authenticity. Like other scholars of his time, Smith found this approach easier to apply to the Quran than to the Bible because of strong opposition from conservative Christians. By all accounts, however, he was strong-willed, independent, and had more than a touch of arrogance. His determination to express his views in an uncompromising manner eventually led to his dismissal for heresy from his professorship at Aberdeen by the General Assembly of the Free Church of Scotland.

Smith was fluent in Arabic and other Semitic languages, as well as the principal European languages. To improve his Arabic, he made several voyages to Egypt and North Africa between 1878 and 1890. He spent most of 1878–1879 in Cairo, making camelback tours of the Arabian peninsula, Palestine, and Syria.[29] As did many other travelers of the period, he wore native garb and adopted an oriental name, in this case the Arab one of 'Abdallāh Effendī. With his swarthy looks and dark beard, he often managed to pass as an Arab.

A true Victorian, Smith was profoundly pleased with his Britishness, and he sometimes shared the excesses and prejudices of his time in thinking about alien peoples.

[27] T. O. Beidelman, *W. Robertson Smith and the Sociological Study of Religion* (Chicago and London: University of Chicago Press, 1974), p. 29.

[28] Ibid., p. 13.

[29] Smith wrote extensively on his trip to western Arabia. See his "Journey in the Hejaz," in his *Lectures and Essays of William Robertson Smith*, ed. J. S. Black and G. Chrystal (London: A. & C. Black, 1912), pp. 484–597. This account was first published serially in *The Scotsman* (February–June 1880).

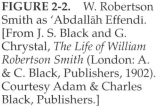

FIGURE 2-2. W. Robertson Smith as 'Abdallāh Effendī. [From J. S. Black and G. Chrystal, *The Life of William Robertson Smith* (London: A. & C. Black, Publishers, 1902). Courtesy Adam & Charles Black, Publishers.]

> It would be a mistake [he wrote] to suppose that genuine religious feeling is at the bottom of everything that justifies itself by taking a religious shape. The prejudices of the Arab have their roots in a conservatism which lies deeper than his belief in Islam. It is, indeed, a great fault of the religion of the Prophet that it lends itself so readily to the prejudices of the race among whom it was first promulgated, and that it has taken under its protection so many barbarous and obsolete ideas, which even Mohammed must have seen to have no religious worth, but which he carried over into his system in order to facilitate the propagation of his reformed doctrines.[30]

Despite these lapses into the stereotyped wisdom of his age, Smith considered the systematic study of contemporary Arab society—at least what he habitually referred to as that of the "pure" bedouin—as crucial in his attempt to comprehend how a people's experience in society relates to their religious and ethical conceptions. Smith's two principal books, *Lectures on the Religion of the Semites* (1889) and *Kinship and Marriage in Early Arabia* (1885), set out in a highly articulate fashion his principal assumptions concerning the origins and development of religion and society.[31]

First, like many of his contemporaries, Smith accepted the concept of the evolutionary progress of human society. As Beidelman stresses, this "evolutionary" perspective was encouraged by the basic Judeo-Christian belief in the ethical and intellectual development of a chosen people that, for Christians, culmi-

[30] Smith, *Lectures and Essays*, pp. 491–92.

[31] William Robertson Smith, *Kinship and Marriage in Early Arabia* (Boston: Beacon Press, 1967 [1885]); *Lectures on the Religion of the Semites* (New York: Schocken Books, 1972 [1889]). The account of Robertson Smith's ideas is largely derived from Beidelman, *W. Robertson Smith.*

nated in the message of Christ. Thus societies could be arranged on a sort of ladder, with Victorian England predictably on the highest rung. Smith considered his studies of Arab—which for him meant bedouin—kinship as key to understanding ancient Semitic society.

Second, Smith saw a close relationship between the stage of development of a social group and the nature of its intellectual, religious, and moral life. He assumed that our perception of nature and the universe is modeled on our experience in society. This idea is introduced in his *Lectures* but is even more sharply delineated in a separate study of prophecy in ancient Palestine.[32] Smith argued that each prophet could speak only for his own time and thus had to convey his message in terms that could be understood by members of his own society. The ideas of prophets could be ahead of those prevalent in their own society but not too far. Thus Smith conceived of the problems of the alienation of people from society and the means by which their ideas could affect social transformations. For example, for a scholar to grasp the message of Ezekiel, the social organization of that prophet's time had to be delineated, together with the cosmology and modes of thought and expression contemporary with it. If Ezekiel's prophetic message was then found to differ from that of Samuel, Smith argued, it is not because of any contradiction in the Bible but because Samuel addressed himself to different groups and situations.

Given Smith's assumption of stages of social development and their specific relationship to ideologies, his scholarly interest in the bedouin becomes more apparent. Smith saw bedouin society as relatively unchanged from the time of the Old Testament. Through studying the present-day bedouin and what was known of bedouin society just prior to and immediately after the time of the Prophet Muḥammad, he sought through analogy and comparison to "reconstruct" the state of society as it was in the time of the Patriarchs. Such an ahistorical assumption is no longer acceptable in contemporary social anthropology, but it is important to recognize that it led Smith to evaluate carefully the ideas about kinship and political organization of Arabs both at the time of Muḥammad (on which extensive information was available through traditional Islamic scholarship) and in the nineteenth century. It should also be noted that, contrary to the stereotypes still prevalent in some circles concerning "orientalists," Robertson Smith, like the Dutch scholar Snouck Hurgronje and other distinguished contemporaries, regarded Muslim scholars not only as sources or as objects of study but as colleagues to be respected.

Finally, Smith used ethnographic and historical data to support explicitly formulated theoretical assumptions about the nature of Arab social organization and its evolution. Part of his argument concerning the evolution of Arab society is simply wrong. In the second part of *Kinship and Marriage*, for example,

[32] W. Robertson Smith, *The Prophets of Israel and Their Place in History to the Close of the Eighth Century B.C.* (London: A. & C. Black, 1919 [1882]).

he presumes the existence of an earlier, matrilineal system of descent reckoning among the Arabs on the basis of what is today regarded as insufficient evidence. Yet the first section of the book is one of the enduring classics of anthropology, for it presents the first systematic account of the social structure of the feud and the basic principles of kinship and political organization among the Arab bedouin. Smith essentially sets forth the fundamental features of what later were to become known as segmentary societies. His argument was a direct inspiration for Evans-Pritchard's later (1940) study of segmentation among the Nuer of the southern Sudan.[33] Similarly, Smith's conviction that symbolic behavior was related to the nature of social groups was the basis on which Émile Durkheim derived inspiration for his own sociology of knowledge and of symbolic forms.[34]

Smith was one of the first Western writers to recognize that the genealogies used by the bedouin to describe their sociopolitical order were not descriptions of concrete, actual relations but ideological charters for the construction of social groups. He realized that ecological necessity and changing political conditions could result in shifts in the composition of groups. To gain political strength, for instance, ambitious chiefs would include as wide a group as possible of assumed kinsmen and clients in their following; and he was well aware of the means by which weaker groups and individuals could manipulate genealogies to establish claims to kinship with more powerful groups.[35]

In Chapter 6, Smith's influence on segmentation lineage theory and related concepts, especially in the work of E. E. Evans-Pritchard, Emrys Peters, and Ernest Gellner, is discussed more fully. The critical point to recognize for the present is that studies such as those of Robertson Smith reached a wide audience and provided considerable impetus to the understanding of the Middle East, the Arab world, and Islam. Even when Smith constructed theoretical arguments that are considered faulty in retrospect, he touched on many of the basic issues of anthropological inquiry, including the social base of symbolic behavior, the nature of the feud, and the ideological basis of kinship and "family" ties. Many of his insights remain fresh today. In particular, his theoretical arguments and documentation of them through ethnographic and historical sources were much more boldly conceived than many of the "functionalist" studies that were later to predominate in the study of the Middle East.

[33] See. T. O. Beidelman's review of the Beacon paperback edition of *Kinship and Marriage*, *Anthropos* 63–64 (1968–1969), 592–95. Beidelman, who studied under Evans-Pritchard at Oxford, provides the following clarification (personal communication, April 1977): "Evans-Pritchard told me that he got his insights on segmentation from Smith and also indicated that he read Smith either before or while at Cairo [where Evans-Pritchard held a teaching post prior to his fieldwork among the Nuer], so that would suggest that the notion was in his head before fieldwork. . . . He certainly had a complete and well-used set of Smith, some of which I now have."

[34] Beidelman, *W. Robertson Smith*, p. 65.

[35] Smith, *Kinship and Marriage*, pp. 5, 7, 42–43, 269.

SCHOLARLY INQUIRY AND IMPERIAL INTERESTS

Like the other human sciences, anthropology has become a critically reflexive discipline. By this I mean that its leading practitioners regard an awareness of their implicit theoretical assumptions and how these assumptions are indirectly, yet pervasively, influenced by the intellectual and political setting in which scholarly inquiry is carried out as an integral part of any research. In the late nineteenth and early twentieth centuries, such an explicit critical awareness was often absent from anthropological and related studies.[36] Nineteenth-century scholars were aware of many of the assumptions that pervaded their work, but even when directly concerned with the nature of non-Western political institutions, they remained remarkably silent on the exact consequences of imperial conquest and European colonial rule.[37] Scholarly investigations by Europeans of "oriental" societies were carried out in the context of impending imperial domination or, in some cases, of actual colonial rule, and this fact must be taken into account, as the direction of scholarly inquiry often merged with the interests of the colonial power.

It would be wrong, however, to interpret such a fusion of interests by contemporary standards and to regard all such research as politically sinister, as proponents of more simplistic versions of neo-Marxism often argue. Some anthropologists argue that ethnographic inquiry in this century and the last was carried out in the context of European bourgeois society expanding its political, economic, and intellectual domination. This is certainly true, but the *specific* consequences of such domination for patterns of inquiry still must be demonstrated. In any case, such an assumption in itself hardly invalidates anthropological inquiry. Many ethnographers who participated in colonial rule were quite aware of the context in which their work was carried out. A salient example is the French sociologist Jacques Berque (1910–1995), whose father was for many years director of Native Affairs for the French government in Algeria. Berque himself was raised in Algeria and had a distinguished career in the Moroccan colonial service. Even in the 1930s Berque's writings indicated a subtle awareness of the nature of the colonial situation that he experienced, a theme that in later years had become much more developed in his work. Of

[36] See Talal Asad, "Two European Images of Non-European Rule," in *Anthropology and the Colonial Encounter*, ed. Talal Asad (London: Ithaca Press, 1973), pp. 103–18. A thorough study has been made of the basic assumptions of leading "orientalist" scholars by J. D. G. Waardenburg, *L'Islam dans le miroir de l'Occident* [Islam in the Mirror of the West], 3rd ed. (Paris and The Hague: Mouton, 1969).

[37] One of the few exceptions I know of to this generalization is a small, neglected book by Arnold Van Gennep, better known for his *Rites of Passage* (Chicago: University of Chicago Press, 1960). Van Gennep's *En Algérie* (Paris: Mercure de France, 1914) devotes several chapters to the means by which French settlers appropriated land from native Algerians and the social consequences of these and similar acts of dispossession and political subjugation. Another exception, pointed out to me by Nicholas S. Hopkins, is Charles Le Coeur, *Le rite et l'outil* [Rituals and Tools], 2nd ed. (Paris: Presses Universitaires de France, 1969 [1939]), subtitled "An Essay on Social Rationalism and the Pluralism of Civilizations." Pages 59 to 131 concern the effect of French colonial administration on social categories and market activities in Azzemour, Morocco.

FIGURE 2-3. This is the earliest known photograph of the Ka'ba in Mecca, located in the courtyard of the Grand Mosque. The Ka'ba is covered by a cloth brought annually by pilgrims from Egypt. This photograph was taken by a Muslim Turkish doctor resident in Mecca and was published in Christian Snouck Hurgronje's *Bilder-Atlas zu Mekka* (The Hague: Martinus Nijhoff, 1888). Hurgronje (1857–1936), a leading Dutch orientalist who also played a major role in formulating Dutch colonial policy in Southeast Asia, resided in Mecca for six months in 1885 with permission from the local Ottoman authorities and notables. His *Mekka in the Later Part of the Nineteenth Century*, trans. J. H. Monahan (Leiden: E. J. Brill; London: Luzac & Co., 1931 [1889]), remains a valuable period account of Meccan life.

course, Berque, like other scholars, was profoundly affected by the milieu in which his research was conducted, but this fact hardly denies the possibility of competent anthropological inquiry.

More plausible than direct correlations between political context and scholarship is the argument that imperial domination and studies of the Islamic "orient" bear a subtle, abstract, and variable relation to each other. The activities of political domination and scholarship shared a general drive to impose "order" upon the non-European world. In one case this order was political and military; in the other it was the attempt to classify, arrange, and codify knowledge of an alien civilization.[38] The two sorts of order and control were often closely related, but they could also operate independently, as has been shown

[38] The linkage between political domination and ideas of medicine are skillfully portrayed in Nancy Elizabeth Gallagher, *Medicine and Power in Tunisia, 1780–1900* (Cambridge: Cambridge University Press, 1983).

by the radical transformations in the disciplines concerned with Middle Eastern and Islamic studies over the past century and a half.

The nature of traditional Muslim polities and the consequences of colonial rule are important issues and will be dealt with in detail in later chapters. In the present context it is sufficient to demonstrate that the situation of impending or actual colonial rule and economic domination did much to encourage scholarly investigations into the nature of Muslim and Middle Eastern society.

Ethnographic inquiry in the nineteenth and early twentieth centuries was often regarded in colonial contexts as an adjunct to political and military control, especially during periods of "native" unrest. This trend is especially prevalent in the ethnography of North Africa. In Algeria, as indicated earlier, the social institutions and beliefs of native Algerians were generally ignored during periods of unquestioned French domination, and were the subject of intensive analysis during periods of resistance to French rule. The movement against the French led by Amīr 'Abd al-Qādir in the 1830s and 1840s was one such occasion; the stiff resistance to the French in Berber-speaking Kabylia, the last region of Algeria to succumb to French domination in the 1850s, was another.[39] During and shortly after conquest of the region, studies of Kabylia were abundant. They created stereotypes about Berbers that were to persist for generations, but they also produced seminal studies of religion, state, and authority that had significance for the main currents of social thought. Alexis de Tocqueville (1805–1859), whose *Democracy in America* is a classic study in Western political analysis, also commented on Algeria and the French conquest.[40] A comparable level of ethnographic interest in Algeria was not rekindled until the 1950s, the final, violent years of colonial rule.

Organized ethnographic inquiry reached its fullest development in Morocco. The incorporation of Morocco as a protectorate within the *pax gallica* dates only from 1912, but from the late nineteenth century, French colonial interests began seriously to contemplate extending their "civilizing mission" to Morocco. The quality of the administrators and scholars first attracted to Morocco is in many ways comparable to the quality of scholars and officials attracted to India when it was a dominion of the British Empire. French Moroccanists were heavily influenced by the main sociological currents of their day, although admittedly, they were not unaffected by the romantic vision of France

[39] See Julia A. Clancy-Smith, *Rebel and Saint: Muslim Notables, Populist Protest, Colonial Encounters (Algeria and Tunisia, 1800–1904)*, Comparative Studies in Muslim Societies (Berkeley and Los Angeles: University of California Press, 1994).

[40] Émile Durkheim refers briefly to the ethnography of the Kabyle region in his classic *The Division of Labour in Society* (New York: Free Press, 1966 [1893]). The complex reasons for his not making more explicit reference to this body of ethnographic literature, most particularly to the work of Émile Masqueray (1843–1894), are discussed by Ernest Gellner, "The Roots of Cohesion," *Man* (N.S.) 20, no. 1 (March 1985), 142–55. See also the various contributions in *Connaissances du Maghreb: Sciences sociales et colonisation*, ed. Jean-Claude Vatin (Paris: Éditions du Centre National de la Recherche Scientifique, 1984). For selections from de Tocqueville's commentaries on Algeria, see Lucas and Vatin, *L'Algérie des anthropologues*, pp. 90–94. For an account of popular French perceptions of colonial nineteenth-century Algeria, see Malek Alloula, *The Colonial Harem*, trans. Myrna Godzich and Wlad Godzich, Theory and History of Literature 21 (Minneapolis: University of Minnesota Press, 1986).

as the first imperial power since the Romans to unite most of North Africa under one rule. By the late nineteenth and early twentieth centuries, several scholars, usually backed by colonial interests or the French government, had begun systematically to describe Morocco.

The collective investigation of Moroccan society began in 1904 with the founding in Tangier of the Mission Scientifique au Maroc.[41] This brought together a group of talented scholars and scholarly diplomats who spoke Arabic (and often Berber as well) and were well grounded in current sociology. This group produced extensive monographs on Moroccan history, the workings of the traditional Moroccan legal system and administrative apparatus, the organization of traditional crafts and commerce, Muslim education, religious beliefs and rituals, linguistic texts through which local dialects could be rapidly learned by administrators, tribal divisions, and translations of key legal, religious, and historical documents.[42] The studies undertaken were of a very utilitarian sort. This is not surprising, as the Mission Scientifique was formally attached to the protectorate administration shortly after the beginning of the protectorate. Later, in the 1920s, it became a part of the Institut des Hautes Études Marocaines (Institute for Higher Moroccan Studies), an organization whose principal task was to train colonial administrators.

One of the most distinguished members of the original team of scholars was Édouard Michaux-Bellaire, who became director of the Mission Scientifique in 1907. After the Mission Scientifique had been in existence for nearly two decades, Michaux-Bellaire described its initial purpose as the sociological "reconstitution" of Morocco's social life, not only through the study of books and manuscripts but through the collection of tribal traditions and the study of religious brotherhoods, economic life, and families.

> It was a question of creating . . . , so to speak, the catalogue of Morocco, its tribes, its towns, its religious orders, to rediscover through them origins, ramifications, struggles, and alliances, and to follow them in history through different dynasties, to study institutions and customs, in a word, to reconnoiter, so far as possible, the land in which we might be called to act one day, so as to permit us to act in full awareness of the consequences of our actions.[43]

[41] See Edmund Burke III, "La mission scientifique au Maroc," in *Actes de Durham: Recherches récentes sur le Maroc moderne* (Rabat: Publication du Bulletin Économique et Social du Maroc, 1979), pp. 37–56. See also his "The Sociology of Islam: The French Tradition," in *Islamic Studies: A Tradition and Its Problems*, ed. Malcolm H. Kerr (Malibu: Undena Publications, 1980), pp. 73–88; and "The First Crisis of Orientalism, 1890–1914," in Vatin, *Connaissances*, pp. 213–26. For the work of an influential later colonial sociologist, Robert Montagne, who first came to Morocco as a military intelligence officer, see David Seddon's introduction to Robert Montagne, *The Berbers: Their Social and Political Organisation*, trans. David Seddon (London: Frank Cass, 1973 [1931]), pp. xiii–xliv.

[42] Their investigations were published in two series of monographs, *Archives Marocaines* and *Villes et Tribus du Maroc*, as well as in several journals. The main journals were *Archives Berbères* (1915–1920), the *Revue du Monde Musulman* (founded in Tangier in 1906), and after 1921, *Hespéris*, which became *Hespéris-Tamuda* shortly after Morocco's independence.

[43] Cited in Abdelkabir Khatibi, *Bilan de la sociologie au Maroc* (Rabat: Association des Sciences de l'Homme, 1967), p. 10. My translation.

To sum up, a convergence of interests led to the ethnographic rediscovery of the Middle East in the nineteenth and early twentieth centuries. At the beginning of this period, the Islamic "orient" served as a screen on which European fantasies about the exotic and unknown could be projected, but this view was gradually replaced by more systematic observations under the impetus of growing colonial and imperial interests and the centrality that the ethnographic study of the region had to key intellectual topics of the period.

Earlier Western scholarship on the Middle East, including that of "orientalists," cannot be facilely summed up as projecting a foreign view onto the Middle East and gradually correcting it. A more subtle process of "understanding" was also at work. Western scholars often reproduced very exactly a "native" view of Muslim and Middle Eastern societies, especially the views of the learned Muslim elite, as articulated in their own writings. It can be argued that the attitude of the Muslim elite toward the "lower orders" could often be as disparaging and self-serving as the writings of any colonialist. Further, if prior orientalist views of the Middle East can be criticized as too text-oriented, this fault is shared with the representations of medieval (and contemporary) Muslim society held by the Muslim learned elite itself.

Good ethnographic work requires a delicate balance between an understanding of text and sociocultural context. Talal Asad makes this point nicely, emphasizing that a "desire to learn about the Other" is never disembodied from social practices and the ideas of disciplined knowledge associated with them: "Forms of interest in the production of knowledge are intrinsic to various structures of power, and they differ not according to the essential character of Islam or Christianity, but according to historically changing systems of discipline."[44] The Middle East does not lend itself to the sort of "hit and run" anthropology in which the learning of language and history is regarded as mere distraction from concern with social theory. Theoretical understandings are sharpened with an awareness of what were regarded as adequate prior ethnographic and historical accounts.

FUNCTIONALISM IN THE STUDY OF THE MIDDLE EAST

As expressed in its classical form in the 1930s by such anthropologists as A. R. Radcliffe-Brown and Bronislaw Malinowski, functionalism emphasizes the explanation of social phenomena on the basis of their interrelation with coexisting events or social forms, rather than in terms of how any of these came to be. The earlier use of functionalist orientations in the study of the Middle East clearly illustrates how theoretical preconceptions shape what a scholar "sees" in fieldwork or other research. Although functionalism as theory may now be moribund, it continues as a practical framework for organizing research. For

[44] Talal Asad, *The Idea of an Anthropology of Islam*, Occasional Papers Series (Washington, DC: Georgetown University Center for Contemporary Arab Studies, 1986), p. 5.

this reason, an analysis of its dominant conceptions is of interest for understanding both earlier and contemporary conceptions of the Middle East.

As a movement dominating social anthropology, functionalism can be traced from its origins in the second decade of the twentieth century through its apogee in the 1930s and its eventual decline (but not disappearance) as a theoretical doctrine in the late 1950s. Although it was a dominant trend in English and American anthropology, it never acquired the same firm hold upon German ethnology or in the work of French anthropologists and sociologists interested in the non-European world. Thus French human geographers continued to undertake a number of detailed studies of traditional ecological adaptations of villages and pastoralists throughout the region of France's Middle Eastern and North African colonial domains, and other French scholars produced valuable monographs on the social and economic life of the region's cities and towns. There were also pockets of anthropologists in the English-speaking world who ignored the functionalist movement, although for the most part such individuals were of a generation that followed earlier paradigms for scholarly investigation.[45] Generally speaking, however, the "official" history of anthropology omits reference to studies of the Middle East because, until recently, the discipline's priorities did not include the study of complex societies and civilizations.

A by-product of functionalism was the turning away of anthropological interest from the Middle East. Functionalism appeared to account much better for relatively simple, small-scale societies than for the larger scale, historically known societies that anthropologists typically encountered in the Middle East. Only by treating Middle Eastern villages and tribes as if they were small-scale, relatively isolated societies was it possible to make sense of them in terms of functionalist theory. Villages and tribes were treated as closed social worlds, even when large numbers of villagers and tribesmen regularly sought work in cities or overseas and depended on income from such temporary or permanent migration for their sustenance. Although the scale of labor migration has intensified in recent decades, it has long been a significant feature of Middle Eastern societies.

[45] One prominent example is the Finnish anthropologist Edward Westermarck (1862–1939), who taught at the University of London for most of his career (1904–1930). Beginning at the turn of the century, he lived intermittently in Tangier over a period of roughly two decades and produced monographs concerning various aspects of Moroccan rural society. Among his principal publications were *Ritual and Belief in Morocco* (New Hyde Park: University Books, 1968 [1926]); *Wit and Wisdom of Morocco* (New York: Horace Liveright, 1931), and *Marriage Ceremonies in Morocco* (London: Macmillan, 1914). Timothy Stroup, "Edward Westermarck: A Reappraisal," *Man* (N.S.) 19, no. 4 (December 1984), 575, argues that Westermarck, through cultural immersion and linguistic competence, established himself "as a pioneer of local anthropological fieldwork," preceding the influential Bronislaw Malinowski in intensive field research by more than a decade. Moroccan and international scholars recently collaborated in a reappraisal of Westermarck's work, *Westermarck et la société marocaine* [Westermarck and Moroccan Society], ed. Rahma Bourqia and Mokhtar al Harras, Publications of the Faculty of Letters and Human Sciences, Université Mohammad V, Rabat, Colloquia and Seminars 27 (Rabat: Faculté des Lettres et des Sciences Humaines, 1993). Many of the essays are in English and offer a model for rethinking earlier ethnographic work.

The most broad-gauged and influential attempt to apply functionalist theory to the Middle East was provided by the physical anthropologist Carleton Coon in *Caravan: The Story of the Middle East*, first published in 1951 and revised several times over the following decade. This book was the first general anthropological introduction to the area and enjoyed a sustained popularity. Yet *Caravan* also portrays the drawbacks of functionalism. The book's unity is sustained by the metaphor of the mosaic, a device that is useful for conveying some of the bare geographic and ethnographic facts concerning the Middle East and North Africa—modes of livelihood, physical characteristics of the population, religious and linguistic groupings, and political organization. Unfortunately, it is less adequate in explaining the interrelations among these elements or their known historical transformations. In fact, a principal negative virtue of *Caravan* is its clear exemplification of the weakness of functionalist theories in providing meaningful accounts of historically known societies. In his first chapter "The Picture and Its Pieces," Coon writes that the mosaic pattern of the region becomes clear if the "little pieces of plastic and broken glass" are removed. By plastic and broken glass he means essentially everything that is "modern" or in transition in the Middle East. Coon writes that "a culture in transition is hard to describe and harder to understand; we must find some period in history when the culture was, relatively speaking, at rest."[46]

This assertion means that Coon's method is, for instance, to describe Egyptian society as it presumably was prior to Bonaparte's invasion, Morocco as it existed in the late nineteenth and early twentieth centuries, and Turkey as it was in the nineteenth century, and then to assume that these descriptions essentially hold in all key respects for much longer periods of time. These are "base times" for Coon, and he assumes that for hundreds of years—from at least the fifteenth to the nineteenth century in most parts of the Middle East—societies were "frozen" in form. The notions of *base time* or *base line*, common among many American anthropologists during the functionalist era, are symptomatic of the cavalier treatment of the historical past. Recent historical research has underlined what was known before the publication of Coon's book: Ahistorical assumptions concerning Middle Eastern societies are profoundly inappropriate.

The extraordinary assumption of centuries of cultural "rest" creates a highly artificial and misleading way of looking at any society or civilization and is empirically inapplicable to the civilizational area he describes. Throughout the period of cultural "rest" that Coon assumes, highly significant transformations were occurring throughout the Middle East. To name only one, in the nineteenth century the Middle East was being increasingly drawn into the world capitalist economy. This was one of the principal factors leading to the instability of central governments in many regions, such as Morocco after the 1860s. The resulting instability provided a convenient excuse for European colonial intervention in some instances and the control

[46] Carleton S. Coon, *Caravan: The Story of the Middle East*, rev. ed. (New York: Holt, Rinehart and Winston, 1961), p. 8.

of vital governmental services such as customs revenues in others. Not all transformations of the society were related to external factors alone, of course. Much of the impetus for change came from developments internal to Middle Eastern societies themselves.

Elsewhere, Coon describes Islam as the "right" religion for the Middle East because it survived as the dominant religion in the area for such an extended period of time. Hence, he argues, Islam must be in "equilibrium" with the environment. A similar argument underlies his explanation of the prohibition on wine in the Islamic world. With so much of the area a desert and the Arabs so hospitable, it would be too cumbersome and expensive to carry goatskins of wine through the region.[47] Or consider his more general statement: "The keynote to the Islamic way of life is that it provided a maximum goodness of fit for a swarm of human beings, living in the environment of the Middle East, to a progressively deteriorating landscape."[48] Again, this statement constitutes a massive tautology. It could just as well be applied to Christianity in Europe or, in a functionalist account of the New World, to Aztec human sacrifice. All that needs to be argued is that such practices exist because they fulfill a function.

Coon's assertion of a "fit" between Islam and the Middle East ignores the fact that the center of gravity of the Muslim population in the world falls somewhere between Pakistan and Iran; in fact, the majority of the world's Muslims live on the Indian subcontinent and in Southeast Asia. Admittedly, Coon's argument also can be adapted to the environmental circumstances of these regions, although, again, the argument asserts no more than the fact that if things were not the way they are, then they would be different.

Coon was exceptional in writing about a civilizational area, for, as I have previously indicated, the professional work of anthropologists is primarily on a more minute scale. Whatever the shortcomings of functionalism as social theory, it has the decisive practical advantage of providing an organizing guide for anthropological fieldwork. It encourages anthropologists to conceive of societies in their totality—or, to be more modest about the scope of anthropology as actually practiced, it encourages fieldworkers to collect information on kinship, myths, politics, economics, and other aspects of social life and to seek out interrelations among these various activities, even when the linkages are not immediately apparent. As a consequence, a substantial number of ethnographies now exist that provide resource materials for purposes other than those for which they were originally intended. It can be argued that the notion of gathering documentation on the "total" social world of individuals, whether they be office workers in an industrial society or villagers who spend a large part of their lives in relation with others from the same immediate locale, constitutes a distinctively anthropological technique of viewing culture and society. As a theory, functionalism has limitations that are obvious once they are made explicit,

[47] Ibid., p. 347.

[48] Ibid., p. 346.

but its organizing concepts have proved to be an enduring ad hoc stratagem for effective field research.

Few anthropologists completely ignored the data of historical change in the heyday of functionalism, but such data fitted awkwardly into available theoretical frameworks. Because functionalist theory has the built-in bias of treating societies as if they were closed systems existing at one historical moment, there was a tendency to ignore the factors that led to the "transition" of a society from one state to another. Historical transformations were instead thought of in layer-cake images, with each slice of time superimposed. The limitation of this strategy is that it serves more to contrast the end points of certain processes than to focus on the nature of the changes taking place. This is because the "synchronic slices" approach encourages a conception of historical change in terms of discrete, episodic units, rather than as a continuous process. Emphasis was placed on the description of societies in periods when it was presumed there was little significant change rather than on periods of conflict, revolution, or major transition.[49] An alternate version of the same basic argument regarded social forms as cyclical, in which a tendency to social inequality, for instance, would begin to develop and then be replaced by a movement toward egalitarianism.[50]

The limitations of the concept of functionalism became particularly clear when the notion was applied to complex, historically known societies. By the 1950s, minor qualifications were being added to the basic arguments of functionalism, so that the "functional" description of a society was frequently complemented by historical description. Evans-Pritchard's *Sanusi of Cyrenaica* is a classic monograph by an anthropologist that embodies functionalism's limitations. One of these was the artificial bounding of units of social analysis by immediate locales, with the result that power relations existing in the wider society were often obscured. In the case of Libya, Evans-Pritchard's analysis downplays the bizarre situation of King Idrīs as a British protégé and the compromises at the United Nations that led to the creation of modern Libya.[51]

[49] Abner Cohen's *Arab Border Villages in Israel* (Manchester, UK: Manchester University Press, 1965) is a clear example of such an approach. For a detailed critique of Cohen's study, see Talal Asad, "Anthropological Texts and Ideological Problems: An Analysis of Cohen on Arab Villages in Israel," *Economy and Society* 4, no. 3 (August 1975), 251–82.

[50] This is one of the elements of the argument presented in Ernest Gellner's *Saints of the Atlas* (Chicago: University of Chicago Press, 1979). See also Paul Stirling, "Cause, Knowledge and Change: Turkish Village Revisited," in *Choice and Change: Essays in Honour of Lucy Mair*, ed. John Davis (New York: Humanities Press, 1974), pp. 191–229. Stirling's original fieldwork in Turkey was conducted at intervals between 1949 and 1952 and is presented in his monograph *Turkish Village* (New York: Wiley, 1965), now unfortunately out of print. In 1971, when it was still difficult for foreigners (or Turkish nationals) to conduct field research in Turkey, Stirling was allowed to return to the village he had studied 20 years earlier. His "Cause, Knowledge and Change," based on this visit, recognizes the problems of studying change within the compass of a functionalist framework.

[51] E. E. Evans-Pritchard, *The Sanusi of Cyrenaica* (Oxford: Clarendon Press, 1949). For an alternative view of the role of tribes in Libya's recent political history, see Lisa Anderson, *The State and Social Transformation in Tunisia and Libya, 1830–1980* (Princeton, NJ: Princeton University Press, 1986).

The goal of Evans-Pritchard's monograph is to describe how an Islamic religious order, the Sanūsīya, became in the nineteenth century the predominant religious order to which the transhumant bedouin tribes of Cyrenaica (Libya) were affiliated. He argues that the Sanūsīya was the only order to adapt effectively to the acephalous segmentary social organization of the tribes, in which each individual was presumably an equal of every other and no one occupied a position of full-time leadership. In the twentieth century, however, Italian conquest and colonization provided the sustained pressure necessary to transform the acephalous segmentary tribal society into a state organization under the leadership of the head of the Sanūsī religious order, who subsequently became Libya's first monarch. A closer examination of this study indicates that the section in which the social structure of bedouin tribes is described is abstract and totally separated from the much longer, straightforward historical account describing the growth of the Sanūsī religious brotherhood and the Italian conquest of Libya. Only in two crucial paragraphs (pp. 104–105) does Evans-Pritchard discuss how bedouin tribal society was presumably transformed from an acephalous segmentary society into a state organization. He speculates that prolonged external pressure forces "segmentary" societies into such transformations but, of course, provides no detailed description of this process. His historical account is fully intelligible without reference to the abstract description of the segmentary structure of bedouin society as it presumably was in the precolonial historical past (pp. 29–61). As social history, the book is adequate, but the ahistorical description of bedouin social organization is marginal to that success.

FURTHER READINGS

Ibn Khaldūn is a pivotal figure, not only for his own thought but also for the way his ideas have influenced contemporary scholarly thought. Muhsin Mahdi's *Ibn Khaldūn's Philosophy of History* (Chicago: University of Chicago Press, 1957) remains the standard study in English; Yves Lacoste, *Ibn Khaldun: The Birth of History and the Past of the Third World*, trans. David Macey (New York: Schocken Books, 1984 [1973]), provides a fresh reappraisal of Ibn Khaldūn's work. Ibn Khaldūn also forms the point of departure for an influential essay by Ernest Gellner, "Flux and Reflux in the Faith of Men," in his *Muslim Society*, Cambridge Studies in Social Anthropology 32 (Cambridge: Cambridge University Press, 1981), pp. 1–85. Richard Tapper provides a seminal discussion of Ibn Khaldūn in his "Introduction" to *The Conflict of Tribe and State in Afghanistan*, ed. Richard Tapper (London: Croom Helm; New York: St. Martin's Press, 1983), pp. 62–75. An especially useful recent essay showing how contemporary Arab anthropologists view him is al-Sayyid Aḥmad Ḥāmid, "Ibn Khaldūn's Influence in Social Anthropology: An Anthropological Reading of His *Muqaddimah*" (in Arabic), *Journal of the Social Sciences* (Kuwait) 15, no. 3 (Autumn 1987), 171–87.

For a brief evocation of an earlier Muslim polymath whose writings possess sufficient contemporary significance to claim him as a distinguished anthropological ancestor who "had exhaustively examined, and suggested a methodology for the study of caste and kinship in India . . . [a]lmost a thousand years before European Indianists," see Akbar S. Ahmed, "Al-Beruni: The First Anthropologist," *Royal Anthropological Institute*

News, no. 60 (February 1984), 9. Ahmed, evoking contemporary concerns, comments that al-Birūnī (973–1048) "is as impeccable an anthropologist as he is a Muslim."

Both medieval and contemporary accounts by Muslim pilgrims and travelers contain important accounts of how other peoples, Muslim and non-Muslim, were "imagined." See Dale F. Eickelman and James Piscatori, eds., *Muslim Travellers: Pilgrimage, Migration, and the Religious Imagination* (London: Routledge; Berkeley and Los Angeles: University of California Press, 1990).

For Central Asian views of medieval Europe, see Morgan, *Mongols*, pp. 167–95. Muḥammad aṣ-Ṣaffār, *Disorienting Encounters: Travels of a Moroccan Scholar in France in 1845–1846*, trans. and ed. by Susan Gilson Miller (Berkeley and Los Angeles: University of California Press, 1992), was entrusted by the Sultan of Morocco with describing French society. Susan Miller's introduction to the volume is essential reading for understanding Muslim accounts of the European "other."

The work of Europe's nineteenth-century "orientalist" scholars also facilitated the interest of Muslims in their own past. Only fragments of al-Ṭabarī's (839–923) *History of Prophets and Kings* were available until a scholarly edition was collected, edited, and published in Leiden between 1879 and 1901. Indeed, an enduring achievement of the nineteenth-century "orientalists" was to call attention to the texts of earlier Muslim thinkers and their contemporaries and to make them more accessible to Middle Eastern and European scholars than they had ever been previously. For an appraisal of the scope and value of al-Ṭabarī's *History*, now being made available in a 38-volume translation into English under the general editorship of Ehsan Yarshatar (Albany: State University of New York Press, 1985–), see Hugh Kennedy, "Invoking the Heroic Age of Islam," *The Times Literary Supplement* (London), March 14, 1986, pp. 263–64. Albert Hourani, *Islam in European Thought* (Cambridge: Cambridge University Press, 1991), offers more than the title suggests. This collection of essays deals not only with its stated subject matter, but the final three chapters deal with the interaction between Muslim and European intellectuals from the eighteenth century on.

The closest Russian counterpart for Central Asia to Carleton Coon's account of the Middle East is Sergei P. Poliakov, *Everyday Islam: Religion and Tradition in Rural Central Asia*, trans. Anthony Olcott (Armonk, NY, and London: M. E. Sharpe), originally intended as a popular account of Muslim societies for a Russian audience. In her introduction, Martha Brill Olcott (p. xix) notes that Poliakov's book also reflects how the ethnography of Muslim societies was taught to "talented undergraduate and graduate students at Moscow State University" prior to 1990. For an analysis of Poliakov's and other accounts of Central Asian societies by Muslim scholars, see Asad AbuKhalil, "Islam and the Study of Central Asia: A Critique of the Western Scholarly Literature," *Arab Studies Journal* 4, no. 1 (Spring 1996), 115–29. Prerevolutionary Russian understandings of Central Asia are assessed in Daniel Brower and Edward Lazzerini, eds., *The Russian Orient: Imperial Borderlands and Peoples, 1750–1917* (Bloomington and London: Indiana University Press, 1997), and I discuss the context of Russian studies of Central Asian and Middle Eastern societies in the 1980s and early 1990s in my "Introduction" to *Russia's Muslim Frontiers: New Directions in Cross-Cultural Analysis*, ed. Dale F. Eickelman, Indiana Series in Arab and Islamic Studies (Bloomington and London: Indiana University Press, 1993), pp. 1–15. See also Garay Menicucci, "Glasnost, the Coup, and Soviet Arabist Historians," *International Journal of Middle East Studies* 24, no. 4 (November 1992), 559–77.

PART II
LOCATIONS: REGION, ECONOMY, AND SOCIETY

3

VILLAGE AND COMMUNITY

In recent years as in the past, agricultural, pastoral, and trade activities throughout the Middle East and Central Asia combine in different ways. How people value activities depends on the shifting frameworks of political and economic domination in which they occur. These values and possibilities have frequently been subject to sudden shocks, such as the forced settlement and collectivization of Central Asian pastoralists under Stalin in the 1930s, the forced settlement of pastoral nomads in Iran during the reign of Reza Shah Pahlevi (1925–1941), the forced resettlement of the Kurds of northern Iraq under Ṣaddām Ḥusayn, the sudden influx of oil wealth in the Arab/Persian Gulf states, or the more incremental economic changes of North African states such as Morocco and Tunisia, in which the economy of entire regions today depends on remittances from extended family members working in distant cities or in Europe. Communities that might initially appear to be isolated are always linked to communities elsewhere, although the intensity and pace of such exchanges have increased dramatically with improvements in communication and transportation.

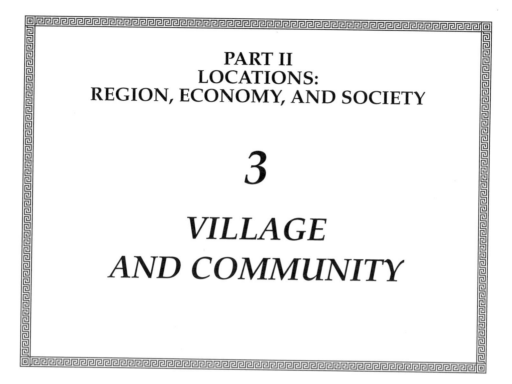

The frame of analysis chosen, whether a village or a herding group, a city quarter, a whole region, or the world market, makes a considerable difference as to how these ties are conceived and interpreted. The forms of interdependence are complex and changing, so that social groups do not fall readily into such seemingly distinct classificatory niches as villagers, pastoral nomads, or city dwellers. Ibn Khaldūn's observations on the overlapping nature and complementarity of the categories of tribespeople, peasants, and urban dwellers are as useful today as they were for the fourteenth century. Many gradations of these categories exist. A strong argument can be made, for example, for distinguishing between large, cosmopolitan cities and provincial towns, each with its distinct forms of intellectual and religious movements, and for the subtle linkages among highly dispersed people of common origin, whether they remain within their country of origin or, like Palestinians, are highly dispersed.

Most modern anthropological studies acknowledge these interrelations, although some modes of description and analysis—notably earlier functionalist studies—often muted their significance and reinforced the image of villages as closed social and economic worlds. We have already seen that a large proportion of Middle Easterners are farmers or peasants, and the proportion used to be larger. But a salient strand of indigenous Middle Eastern thinking conceives of social forms in the region, not so much in terms of socioeconomic categories or even of a continuum of ways of life, as in terms of a dichotomy between city and country.[1] In the Soviet era, the central government's creation of the Uzbek (oasis-dwelling cultivators) and Tājik (mountain-dwelling pastoralists) "nationalities" out of peoples who did not consider themselves as separate built on such an idealized dichotomy. The city/country dichotomy is sometimes conceived as one between civilization and its lack. In this view, the pinnacle of civilization is the great city with its mosques, markets, schools, seat of government. The opposite extreme, lacking all these things, is that of the presumed "fringe" of culture represented by the camel pastoralists. Many classical Middle Eastern scholars divided the region's inhabitants into the two ideal types of town dweller (Ar. *ḥaḍarī)* and "noble" pastoralist (Ar. *badawī*), or the equivalent of these terms in the other languages of the region, such as *shahrī* and *dashtī* in Persian. This popular dichotomy has been taken over by many writers on the region, even though it leaves the bulk of the population, the tribal and nontribal peasants (*fallaḥūn*), as an incomplete realization of one or another of the two ideal types.

The difficulty of understanding the relations between these different domains is increased by the image of tribalism. Both scholars and urban Middle Easterners often confound the notions of tribe, descent, and pastoralism, and the assumption is made that most tribal populations are pastoral. In Afghanistan, to take only one example, most tribespeople are settled cultivators. This is also true for Oman, the Yemens, Pakistan, and many other parts of the Middle East and Central Asia. The surplus of cultivator labor, collected in the form of rents from landlords and taxes from governments, has in some regions provided the traditional basis for the thriving states and civilizations of the Middle East. Both now and in the past, many tribes have had both nomadic and settled components, and political leadership and movements frequently have encompassed groups pursuing combinations of these forms of economic activity. The influx of oil wealth to some countries of the Middle East has prompted major internal and

[1] For an excellent discussion of these categories, see Gabriel Baer, *Fellah and Townsman in the Middle East* (London: Frank Cass, 1982), pp. 7–12, 18–22, 101–105.

regional economic transformations. These shifts and fluctuating opportunities for migratory work, both in the region and in Europe, have had important political, economic, social, and intellectual consequences.[2]

One of the more important recent changes has been in the military technology and communications commanded by the modern state, so that the balance between state and region has, for the most part, been significantly altered in favor of the state. Nonetheless, old views die hard. The Moroccan dichotomy between "lands of government" (*blād al-makhzan*—"makhzan" literally meaning "storehouse" but also referring to the sultan and his entourage) and "lands of dissidence" (*blād as-sība*) became a stock image in French colonial ethnographic literature. In the 1950s Carleton Coon gave the term further life by using it to characterize the entire Middle East as divided into lands controlled by states and those controlled by tribes. Many anthropologists have continued to use this dichotomy, at least to describe the "traditional" Middle East. Further, where villagers and farmers have also been tribesmen, they have been conceived as tribespeople and not as villagers. Curiously, what has been written about village life in Middle Eastern settings has been given relatively little emphasis by scholars interested in global characterizations of the region.

VILLAGE AND COMMUNITY STUDIES

For most of recorded history, the majority of the population of the Middle East has lived in agricultural settlements, and although large parts of Central Asia were given over to nomadic pastoralism prior to the influx of Russian settlers, oasis cultivation was also important throughout the region. The importance of agriculture was intensified with the forced collectivization schemes of the 1930s, which brought parts of the region, such as Uzbekistan, to the brink of ecological disaster.[3] Yet the social organization and economic significance of villages have often been neglected or taken for granted. Another contributing factor is that villagers often have low social status among Middle Easterners (and Central Asians) themselves. Nonetheless, both dry farming, the cultivation of seasonal crops that depend on rainfall, and irrigation farming, which depends on water from rivers and underground aquifers, have long been major economic activities of both the Middle East and Central Asia.

[2] See Ismail Serageldin, James Socknat, J. Stace Birks, and Clive Sinclair, "Some Issues Related to Labor Migration in the Middle East and North Africa," *Middle East Journal* 38, no. 4 (Autumn 1984), 615–42; and Roger Owen, *Migrant Workers in the Gulf*, Report No. 68 (London: Minority Rights Group, 1985). On migrant communities in Europe and Pakistan, see Pnina Werbner, *The Migration Process: Capital, Gifts and Offerings Among British Pakistanis*, Explorations in Anthropology (New York and Oxford: Berg, 1990); and Hastings Donnan and Pnina Werbner, eds., *Economy and Culture in Pakistan: Migrants and Cities in a Muslim Society* (Basingstroke and London: Macmillan, 1991).

[3] Martha Brill Olcott, *The Kazakhs*, Studies on Nationalities in the USSR (Stanford, CA: Hoover Institution Press, 1987), pp. 16–18, 49, 176–98; and Anatoly M. Khazanov, *After the USSR: Ethnicity, Nationalism, and Politics in the Commonwealth of Independent States* (Madison: University of Wisconsin Press, 1995), pp. 115–17, 121–23, 157–59.

Anthropologists have paid more attention to irrigation agriculture than dry farming in the Middle East. There were several converging reasons for the interest in irrigation agriculture in the 1950s. One was the impact of Karl Wittfogel's *Oriental Despotism*,[4] which argued that irrigation systems, or at least certain forms of them, necessitated the development of hierarchical forms of sociopolitical organization. The thesis attracted the attention of archaeologists and social anthropologists, offering what they considered a testable framework for understanding the interrelation between modes of production and social organization. Another reason was that studies of irrigation societies fit nicely with the conventions of functional explanation. After all, in a region such as the Middle East, irrigation systems and the scarce resource of water that they distribute are vital to agricultural production and social life. In such communities, ecological considerations sharply constrain local economic opportunities.

A clear example of functionalist assumptions skillfully applied to a community dependent on irrigation is the 1961 study of the Fadījī Nubians of Upper (southern) Egypt by the late Abdul Hamid el-Zein (1935–1979), at the time an ardent functionalist and later a leading proponent of the structural study of ritual and symbolism.[5] The people Zein studied were relocated in 1963 when the construction of the new Aswan dam resulted in the flooding of their old village sites, so that Zein's description is necessarily in the past tense. Prior to the flooding, settlements and fertile land were located in a narrow belt along the Nile, framed on both sides of the river by rocky, barren mountains. The region received only 1 inch of rainfall annually, so that agriculture was entirely dependent on irrigation. Even prior to relocation, there were land shortages induced by technological change. The first Aswan dam, built in 1902, raised the water level in the winter each year and thus reduced the land available for cultivation; the same effect followed heightenings of the dam in 1912 and 1933. In the low-water season of August and September, this land was briefly available

[4] Karl Wittfogel, *Oriental Despotism: A Comparative Study of Total Power* (New Haven, CT, and London: Yale University Press, 1957). Although now dated, Robert McC. Adams, *The Evolution of Urban Society: Early Mesopotamia and Prehispanic Mexico* (Chicago: Aldine, 1966), indicates how the ideas of Wittfogel and others have been used to interpret archaeological data. See also Adams's classic *Lands Behind Baghdad* (Chicago: University of Chicago Press, 1968).

[5] Abdul Hamid M. el-Zein, "Water and Wheel in a Nubian Village," M.A. thesis, American University in Cairo, 1966. A published summary of Zein's argument is his "Socioeconomic Implications of the Water Wheel in Adendan, Nubia," in *Contemporary Egyptian Nubia*, vol. 2, ed. Robert A. Fernea (New Haven, CT: Human Relations Area Files, Inc., 1966), pp. 298–322. Zein later turned away from functionalism and enthusiastically adopted structuralist theories to the study of Islamic societies in the Middle East and Africa. See Dale F. Eickelman, "A Search for the Anthropology of Islam: Abdul Hamid el-Zein," *International Journal of Middle East Studies* 13, no. 3 (August 1981), 361–65. For a general account of Nubian society accompanied by an outstanding photographic essay, see Robert A. Fernea and Georg Gerster, *Nubians in Egypt: Peaceful People* (Austin and London: University of Texas Press, 1973). Other useful studies include Bruce G. Trigger, *Nubia Under the Pharaohs* (Boulder, CO: Westview Press, 1976); John G. Kennedy, *Struggle for Change in a Nubian Community* (Palo Alto, CA: Mayfield, 1977); and Hussein M. Fahim, *Egyptian Nubians: Resettlement and Years of Coping* (Salt Lake City: University of Utah Press, 1983).

for cultivation. Wheat and beans were the principal crops, although many villagers also owned palm trees and harvested their dates.

Zein cites a Nubian proverb to reinforce his theme of the waterwheel as a central element in Fadījī society: "The water wheel is like a mosque, and those who serve it are like those who serve the mosque." He treats membership in the village, status in the local community, and central rituals as if they were all part of a closed system. Thus Zein emphasizes the land shortage and the ecological constraints that made it impossible for men to build up wealth in animals. He sees education, emigration, and market activities as partial solutions to the chronic land shortage, thus conceiving them as a sort of safety valve that enabled the system of the village to work.

Zein takes 300 pages to work out the implications of the waterwheel for the social life of the Fadīja. In the course of his argument, however, it becomes clear that the Fadīja never were agriculturally self-sufficient. In the nineteenth century their village was an important way station for the slave trade between Cairo and the Sudan; more recently it was important in the lucrative smuggling business between Egypt and the Sudan. In addition, Nubians have long emigrated to other parts of Egypt—a phenomenon that was already important in the nineteenth century. The remittances the emigrants sent home were necessary for the subsistence of their families. Significant in this respect, the principal crops of the Fadīja were insufficient for their subsistence, so that many villagers played active roles in the market as merchants and traders. But as Zein specifies, the Fadīja nonetheless claimed that their status in the community was linked principally to the ownership of land and water rights.

In describing the ownership and operation of the waterwheel, Zein emphasizes the functional justification of certain traditional arrangements. Thus the base of a waterwheel is hard to site—few locations are suitable for it—and difficult to repair. It must be owned by one man, writes Zein, because it is so crucial. The upper parts of the waterwheel, including the buckets, are individually owned or rented. In the case of a serious quarrel, certain upper parts (unlike the base) may be removed and replaced by those belonging to someone else without seriously disrupting the wheel's operation. Through case studies of disputes, Zein indicates how Fadījī social institutions prevent conflicts from interfering with their livelihood. Similarly, he indicates how patterns of marriage alliances are linked to the ownership of water rights. Co-owners of water rights seek intermarriage between their households to solidify their alliances and lessen problems of inheritance. The roles played in rituals are also closely associated with such rights. The waterwheel thus is a concrete artifact whose study reveals the components and functioning of the supposedly closed social system of the village.

Zein's densely packed monograph does not provide a "total" explanation of village life, as functionalist arguments often promise. Yet it provides an intricate description of a key institutional complex within Nubian life. Zein's description of the waterwheel, its maintenance and its relation to other aspects of village

FIGURE 3-1. Waterwheel, Egyptian Nubia. The wheel is partially covered by branches to retard evaporation. [Courtesy Abdul Hamid M. el-Zein.]

life, constitutes one of the best descriptive accounts for the 1960s of the social organization of irrigation practices available for the Middle East.[6] Less convincing is his conceptual framework, in which the components of society at a given moment are considered to be in a closed equilibrium with each other. In the classical functionalist tradition, Zein considers the waterwheel and ownership of water rights to be in direct relation to the cultural value of community ("moral" community in Durkheim's terms) maintained by the Fadīja and to the acquisition of social honor within the community. Yet Zein is such an able ethnographer that his own data suggest that the system of status that he described was more complex and less holistic than he claimed. For instance, villagers who could command cash from remittances or from trading activities fail to fit into the nicely

[6] Another early study of an irrigation society, based on fieldwork in Iraq (1956–1958) and directly inspired by Wittfogel's thesis, is Robert Fernea, *Shaykh and Effendi: Changing Patterns of Authority Among the El Shabana of Southern Iraq*, Harvard Middle Eastern Studies 14 (Cambridge, MA: Harvard University Press, 1970). Although Fernea's monograph adopts many conventions of functional analysis, it was innovative in clearly depicting the links between "outside" political forces and local authority structures. For an excellent postfunctional account linking irrigation practices with property rights and cultural definitions of wealth, see Abdellah Hammoudi, "Substance and Relation: Water Rights and Water Distribution in the Ḍrā Valley," in *Property, Social Structure, and Law in the Modern Middle East*, ed. Ann Elizabeth Mayer (Albany: State University of New York Press, 1985), pp. 27–57. For profiles of villages throughout the Middle East, see *The Middle Eastern Village: Changing Economic and Social Relations*, ed. Richard Lawless (London: Croom Helm, 1987).

established equilibrium of status tied to land and water rights that Zein asserts. When returning emigrants invested their money in land, Zein explained how it contributed to their role in the local status system. But when the funds were invested in education or new economic activities, his account is more ambiguous and treats such forms of status as if they were alien to the local community.

Zein explicitly states that although individuals entered and left the social system and that individual ownership of land and water rights was constantly shifting, the waterwheel and the system of allocating rights connected with it persisted. Yet he acknowledges that the "enduring" system of the allocation of rights he describes came into its present form only at the turn of the century. As a descriptive convention, Zein's assumption that the waterwheel and the social obligations connected with it were a central cohesive force works well so long as his account concerns only those activities directly related to the waterwheel. Leaks in the "closed" system show up as soon as other activities of the villagers are considered.

An incisive transitional account of the limitations of the functionalist approach was developed by the British anthropologist Emrys Peters (1916–1987). As a student of E. E. Evans-Pritchard, he worked with the bedouin of Cyrenaica, Libya, shortly after World War II. The principal results of that research have been a series of articles exploring the concept of segmentation and the feud (see Chapter 6). His most direct inquiry into the more general issue of functional theory is contained in two articles he wrote on a Shī'ī Muslim village in southern Lebanon, where he worked for a year in 1952 and again in 1956. The first analysis was published in 1963, although it had earlier been presented informally at scholarly conferences. A thorough "recantation" of his 1963 article then appeared in 1972.[7]

Peters's 1963 analysis details the social and economic organization of the village. He recognized that at least some individuals were highly mobile but assumed that the structure of the society—that is, the orderly arrangement of roles and statuses within it—remained the same. Rebellions against the social order did not bring about the collapse of the social order; rather, they provided opportunities for powerful persons or groups of persons to replace others whose power and influence had diminished.

Many characteristics of the village led Peters to believe that an equilibrium model of its social structure was appropriate in 1952 and for at least three generations prior to that time. In the first place, the village was territorially discrete, located on a high promontory with a cliff on one side and sharply delineated borders on the others, so that it was set off sharply from the other villages in the region. Its population of 1100 appeared prosperous and largely self-subsistent. There was abundant rainfall—50 to 60 inches—from November through March,

[7] Emrys L. Peters, "Aspects of Rank and Status Among Muslims in a Lebanese Village," in *Mediterranean Countrymen*, ed. Julian Pitt-Rivers (Paris and The Hague: Mouton, 1963), pp. 159–202. This has been reprinted in volume 2 of Louise E. Sweet, ed., *Peoples and Cultures of the Middle East* (Garden City, NY: Natural History Press, 1970), pp. 76–123. Peters's "recantation" (my term) is contained in his "Shifts in Power in a Lebanese Village," in *Rural Politics and Social Change in the Middle East*, ed. Richard Antoun and Iliya Harik (Bloomington and London: Indiana University Press, 1972), pp. 165–97.

though irrigation was needed the rest of the year. The luxurious array of crops included tomatoes, eggplant, peppers, beans, peas, carrots, cabbage, apples, oranges, quince, radishes, lettuce, cucumbers, plums, figs, pomegranates, sugar cane, olives, and grapes. Many villagers also had small herds of sheep and goats, although most of the meat consumed in the village was purchased elsewhere.

Another reason that Peters conceived the village to be self-contained was the emphasis the villagers placed on landownership as a criterion of social identity. Villagers asserted a special identity with their land and spoke of themselves as being its "sons."

In his 1963 article, Peters accepted the villagers' self-categorization into distinct groups as an adequate model of the social structure. Essentially, this division was composed of the "Learned Families," the commercial traders, and a peasant proletariat. The village was predominantly Shī'ī Muslim. Membership in the three Muslim categories could be primarily related to landownership and use and was reflected in patterns of dress, seating arrangements on social occasions, and other readily visible signs of comportment.

The first group, as seen by the villagers, the Learned Families, was composed in part of the descendants of 'Ali bin Abī Ṭālib, the Prophet Muḥammad's paternal cousin and son-in-law. They were called *sayyid*-s. The remainder of this group were known as *shaykh*-s. They claimed descent from an ancestor who fought alongside the Prophet's grandson at the Battle of Karbala in 680, an incident crucial to Shī'ī history. These families were called "Learned" not because they necessarily were educated but because they claimed a superior social and religious status based on descent. Some members of the Learned Families had been to traditional Shī'ī centers of learning in Iraq. This aristocracy constituted about 20 percent of the population of the village. They intermarried among themselves and with families of similar status in neighboring villages, and controlled local political offices. The Learned Families lived in better houses than did other villagers, performed no manual labor on their land (another indication of their status), and were said by the villagers to own the majority of the land.

Although the Learned Families claimed a common identity based on descent, it was possible for persons from other categories to assimilate with them through persistent effort and the expenditure of wealth in ways approved by the leaders of the Learned Families. Peters provides several specific examples of individuals in other categories who became wealthy and powerful and who, through proper deference and a willingness to become publicly known as clients of the Learned Families, could put forward a claim to Learned Family status themselves, at least in certain contexts. In his 1972 account, Peters acknowledges that he did not see such social mobility as a force in the realignment of sets of social relationships but only as a movement of persons within a fixed social system.[8]

[8] Peters, "Shifts in Power," p. 165.

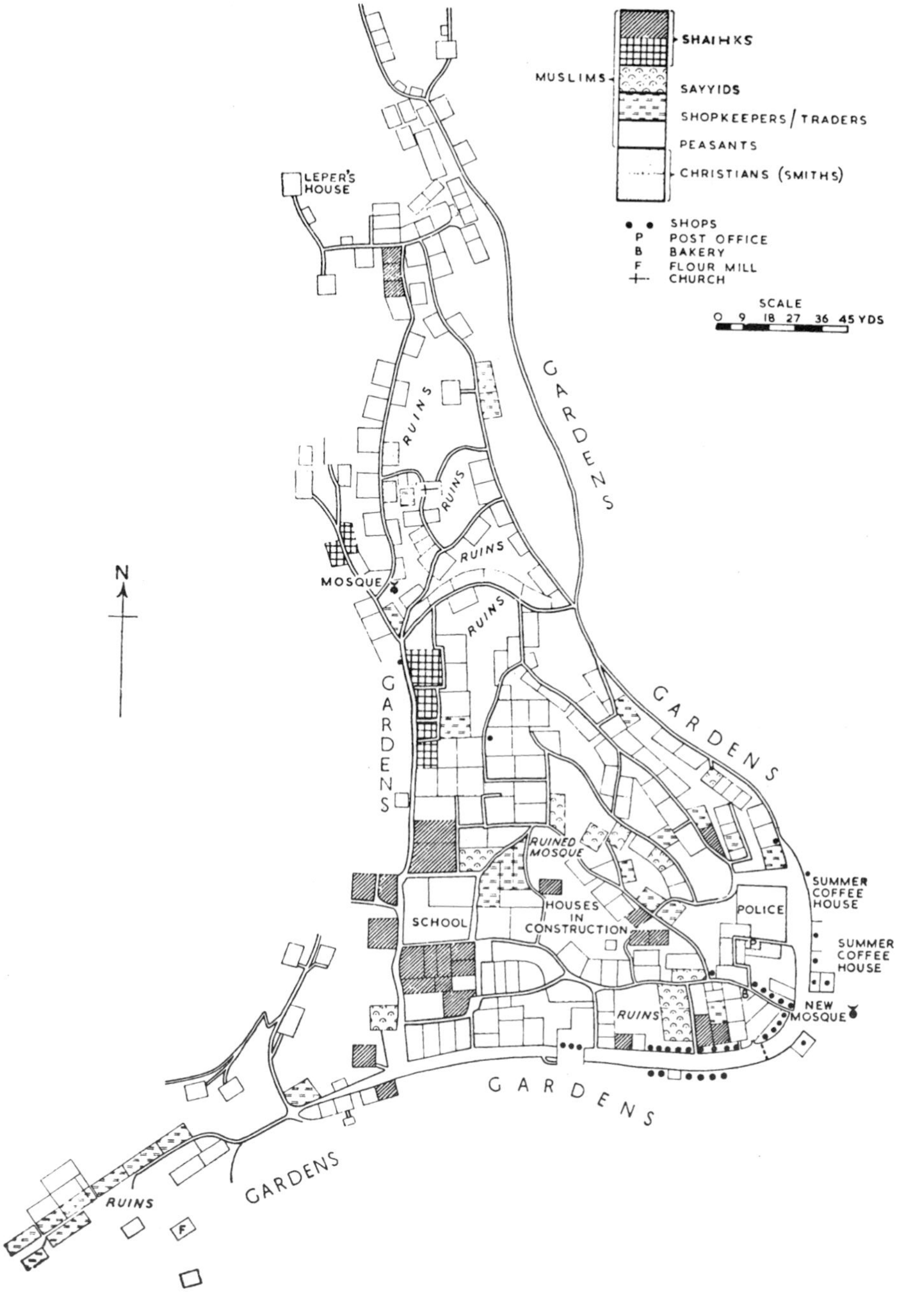

FIGURE 3-2. A village in southern Lebanon, 1950s. [From Emrys L. Peters, "Aspects of Rank and Status Among Muslims in a Lebanese Village," in *Mediterranean Countrymen*, ed. Julian Pitt-Rivers (Paris and The Hague: Mouton, 1963), p. 168. Courtesy Emrys L. Peters and Mouton & Co., Publishers.]

The second important group was the commercial traders. They were not so clearly defined as a category, although they cultivated small gardens, tended to wear European clothing, and belonged primarily to two patronymic groups. They constituted another 20 percent of the Muslim population.

The third, and largest, group was the peasant proletariat, the remainder of the population, with the exception of a few Christian households. Peasants worked their own land and served as laborers for the lands of the Learned Families. In his 1963 account of the village, in which he saw status as part of a single, overriding system related to the land, Peters regarded the high rate of migration among the peasant proletariat as an indication of pressure on the land. If persons of peasant origin migrated in large numbers to North and South America, Great Britain, and West Africa, it was because of the lack of locally available land. In his later study Peters acknowledged that earlier he had largely overlooked the effect of the improved access to schools of many of these emigrants, the substantial remittances they sent back to the village, and, especially in the case of those who remained in Lebanon, the active influence they maintained in village affairs. Because the villagers insisted to Peters that the Learned Families owned a lot of land and would not part with it, Peters inferred that ownership of land was the key to understanding stratification. He consequently directed his research strategies toward this topic and assumed that the social structure he so construed was stable over time.

Peters confirmed his earlier conception of a stable social structure through the analysis of two behavioral indices. One was the performance of the annual mourning (*ta'zīya*) plays commemorating the martyrdom of the slaying of Ḥusayn, the Prophet's grandson, by Sunnī Muslims in 680. Throughout the regions in which Shī'ī Islam predominates, such reenactments were, until recently, performed during the first ten days of the Muslim lunar month of Muharram, in some circumstances by professional actors and sometimes by the villagers. In the village studied by Peters, the roles of the Shī'a, supporters of 'Alī (the Prophet's son-in-law) and descendants of the Prophet, who lost the battle and suffered martyrdom, were performed by the Learned Families. The roles of the victorious but treacherous Sunnī Muslims were performed by the peasants, thus dramatically symbolizing what Peters took to be fixed elements of the status of and a symbolic warning to the peasants of the anarchy that would prevail if descendants of the Prophet were not allowed their rightful place in the social world.

Despite some signs of discontent, Peters noted that almost everyone in the village exhibited some form of deference to the Learned Families and in elections for various local offices, the candidates supported by the Learned Families invariably won through the manipulation of village factions.

Soon after his initial period of fieldwork, Peters saw the disintegration of what he had assumed to be a stable system of social structure. In 1953, there were municipal elections throughout Lebanon. One of the peculiarities of Lebanese elections of this period was that persons could choose to vote where they wished, although most enfranchised persons voted in their natal villages.

This fact alone renders suspect any account of local politics that considered only the presence of persons residing in the village itself, for no village in the country is more than half a day by bus from any other village, so that anyone with ties to a village could easily vote in it. In the 1953 elections the candidate supported by the Learned Families was soundly defeated and the Learned Families were unable to exert much political influence from that time on. The winner in the 1953 election was still in office 15 years later. He was instrumental in bringing a new school to the village, as well as a medical clinic, a paved road, and education for women, among other significant transformations.

The value of Peters's 1972 study is the meticulous account of why his earlier analysis and implicit theoretical assumptions were unsatisfactory. As Peters writes, his principal difficulty was that he accepted at face value the social categories used by the villagers. This directed his attention away from important economic and status transformations that were occurring. These transformations were not perceived by the villagers as patterned regularities, although Peters argues that an understanding of them was essential for an adequate account of village structure. The villagers asserted a central unitary value in the ownership of land, said that the Learned Families were the major landowners, and accused the Learned Families of coveting the land of the other groups. This obscured for Peters the fact that a large number of Learned Families were poor. Hard-pressed for funds, they found themselves selling their land to an emerging group of commoners whom Peters called the "Professionals" in his 1972 article.[9] They were the children of commoners who had attended American missionary schools in the region and who were thus enabled to acquire further technical and university training. Because of their status, the Learned Families were compelled to send their children only to Shī'ī religious schools, a restriction that commoners could ignore. Thus a number of commoner children became prominent doctors, lawyers, merchants, bureaucrats, and managers in Lebanon and abroad.

Similarly, the commercial skills acquired by peasant emigrants familiarized them with modern administrative techniques. They had considerable money for investment and put at least part of it in village lands. Whereas the Learned Families maintained their land in nonmarket crops, the Professional and trader classes were more aware of the possibilities for export crops and invested in such things as apples. By the time the Learned Families became aware of the income to be derived from such crops, the market value had diminished so that much of the initial advantage of investing in them was lost.

[9] Subsequent studies of Lebanon suggest some of the mechanisms that led to major transformations in Lebanese social structure and the instability of power and authority within it. See Michael Gilsenan, *Lords of the Lebanese Marches: Violence and Narrative in an Arab Society* (Berkeley and Los Angeles: University of California Press, 1996); Gilsenan's earlier "Against Patron-Client Relations," in *Patron and Clients in Mediterranean Societies*, ed. Ernest Gellner and John Waterbury (London: Duckworth, 1977), pp. 167–83; and Samir Khalaf, "Changing Forms of Political Patronage in Lebanon," also in *Patrons and Clients*, ed. Gellner and Waterbury, pp. 185–205. Factionalism in the 1975–1985 Lebanese "civil" war is discussed in Chapter 8 of this book.

Also, the Professionals chose to make the heavy investment necessary to acquire merit in the eyes of the Learned Families.

In many ways, Peters wrote in his 1972 reanalysis, there was a disadvantage to the high rank of the Learned Families. Only a few of them were actually large landowners. Poor *sayyid*-s and shaykhs had to live on loans because it was beneath their dignity to work their own lands. Similarly, the high degree of literacy exhibited by the Learned Families as an aggregate was acquired almost exclusively through the traditional religious education necessary to maintain their status. This education limited their ability to perceive modern economic and political opportunities and to take advantage of them.

The social networks and ties of patronage and clientship of the Learned Families also showed sharp contrasts to those of the other two groups. The Learned Families tended to marry only among themselves or with persons of similar rank in neighboring villages. The peasant Professionals had weblike connections through marriage and patronage with people of many different walks of life in Beirut and elsewhere—bankers, politicians, doctors, educators, emigrants, and entrepreneurs—and used these ties to advantage in the acquisition of political influence. The Learned Families were caught up in a narrow web of relations and were pursuing what had become a defunct economic policy of investing their wealth in land, although the locus of significant economic activities had shifted elsewhere. The Professionals had acquired the training, the connections, and the resources to replace the Learned Families as the dominant social group. They were capable of enhancing the welfare of the community as a whole through the effective manipulation of these ties.

Peters saw the error of his first analysis as the attempt to fit all the facts of village life into a single pattern. In his reanalysis, he concluded that the "system" the anthropologist looks for is necessarily open-ended and must be explained, at least in part, by looking for historical transformations. The key components of status present in any situation must be looked at comparatively in order to be comprehended, both in different social settings and at different historical periods. The components of the system thus described become apparent by the historical analysis of shifts in power. Patterned regularities exist in such open-ended systems, but not the elusive and misleading single system presumed by the functionalists. Rank, as perceived by the villagers, operated differentially—that is, to the detriment of some members of the Learned Families and to the advantage of some people in the other categories. Ownership of land was not of equal significance to all villagers.

In fairness to Peters, few anthropologists in the 1950s and 1960s realized the full importance of the cultural and social impact of emigration, education, exposure to the West, and the feedback of these factors on the political and cultural fate of the region. Even earlier in the century, to take only the countries of North Africa as an example, the presence of large numbers of North African laborers in France led to the development of organized labor movements in the colonies and the coalescence of a nationalist movement. The same was true for the large number of North Africans who fought in France's armies and a smaller but influential number of North African students who studied in France. More recently, in the 1950s and 1960s, some key political issues in countries such as Brazil, France, and West Germany can be traced directly to Middle Eastern immigrant populations.

When workers return to their country of origin, they bring changed notions of housing, marriage, family, and society. Their changed tastes in clothing, housing, and other commodities have contributed to the precipitate decline of many traditional crafts such as weaving and rug making. Whether their experience with the West is one of bitterness and disillusionment or one of partial liberation from some of the constraints of their own society, their lives are profoundly altered. Emigration in countries such as Morocco, Algeria, Tunisia, Lebanon, Egypt, Yemen, and Syria profoundly affects the lives of virtually every town and village. Immigration into oil-rich countries such as Libya, Saudi Arabia, and the Gulf states (where immigrants sometimes outnumber local residents) has had a similarly profound impact. Additionally, it has only been in the last two decades that substantial numbers of school-age women have had access to higher education in many Middle Eastern countries. The consequences of such change are often delayed, which may be one of the reasons that Peters underestimated its importance in his earlier study. But, as he realized in his reanalysis, the cumulative and long-term impact of such changes can often be substantial.[10]

ECONOMY AND VILLAGE SOCIETY

Although often mundane, the details of village economic and social life can be of vital importance to understanding Middle Eastern polities. Since the 1970s, anthropologists and social historians have shown a renewed interest in understanding Middle Eastern villages, peasant (and proletariat) ideas of self and society, work and wealth, community, and responsibility in specific economic and political contexts. The examples presented here of village and settled community research conducted since the late 1950s suggest how available theoretical approaches shape anthropological description and how ethnographic research in turn contributes to the reformulation of social theory. They also suggest how ethnographic analysis often transcends the constraints of the theories and assumptions according to which the research was initially formulated.

An interesting ethnographic study to consider in these terms is Shelagh Weir's splendidly illustrated *Qat in Yemen*,[11] based on library research and fieldwork in 1977 and 1979–1980 in Razīḥ, a northern province in the Yemen Arab Republic. Her monograph indicates how the earlier genre of community study

[10] Peters, "Shifts in Power," pp. 174–85.

[11] Shelagh Weir, *Qat in Yemen: Consumption and Social Change* (London: British Museum Publications Limited, 1985). In 1990, the People's Democratic Republic of Yemen, also known as South Yemen (and under British rule until a Marxist takeover in 1967), was united with the Yemen Arab Republic.

has been transformed. The monograph, solidly based on field research in a specific locale, depicts wider economic, political, and social developments.

The basic question posed by Weir's study is deceptively recondite: Why has *qāt* (*Catha edulis*) cultivation and consumption flourished and increased when it could have disappeared, like so many other "traditional" practices? Since at least the 1600s, the *qāt* tree has been cultivated in the highlands of southwestern Arabia. Its leaves are chewed as a mild stimulant, and its consumption is a major feature of Yemeni social life. It is "chewed communally at social gatherings which take place every afternoon throughout the country, and the consumption and production of *qāt* involve the expenditure and circulation of huge sums of money." By 1979–1980, Weir estimates that Yemeni consumers were spending between a quarter to a third of their earned incomes on *qāt*.[12] Its use is also widespread in Kenya, Somalia, Djibouti, and northern Ethiopia. By the mid-1980s, regular air shipments made the highly perishable leaf regularly available even to Brooklyn's Yemeni community.

Weir notes that prior to the 1970s, "regular *qāt* consumption was mainly confined to a small, rich, mainly urban elite." During the 1970s its regular use spread to nearly three-fourths of the entire Yemeni population of all social categories, an expansion made possible by large-scale labor migration and the consequent influx of remittances. The unprecedented prosperity of the Yemenis facilitated increased consumption but does not in itself explain why this particular "traditional" practice, unlike others, spread to all Yemeni social classes and generations and to both sexes. Weir notes that some observers dismiss the issue by saying that *qāt* consumption is addictive. She disputes the evidence for this claim and looks for the causes of its popularity in social explanations: "The significance of *qāt* parties in Yemen can no more be understood in terms of the physical effects of *qāt* than the importance of coffee houses in seventeenth-century London can be explained by the effects of caffeine."[13]

Weir then links the shifting consumption patterns of *qāt* with the issue of social stratification. Expanded *qāt* consumption came about with the post-1970 increase in and wider distribution of wealth between social strata and generations and "changes in male and female working patterns and conditions." The importance of wealth relative to other factors, such as birth and occupation, as determinants of social prestige has increased significantly in the economic conditions of the post-1970 era.[14] As in many other countries, agricultural production has fallen off precipitously in the Yemeni highlands, so that Yemen, once self-sufficient in terms of food, now is a net food importer as wage labor abroad

[12] Ibid., p. 8.

[13] Ibid., p. 9. See also John G. Kennedy, *The Flower of Paradise: The Institutionalized Use of the Drug Qat in North Yemen Culture, Illness and Healing* (Boston: Kluwer Academic Publishers, 1987); and Daniel Martin Varisco, "On the Meaning of Chewing: The Significance of *Qāt (Catha edulis)* in the Yemen Arab Republic," *International Journal of Middle East Studies* 18, no. 1 (February 1986), pp. 1–13.

[14] Weir, *Qat*, pp. 25, 89, and, in general, on the economics of *qāt* production, pp. 83–108; and her "Economic Aspects of the Qat Industry in North-West Yemen," in *Economy, Society and Culture in Contemporary Yemen*, ed. B. R. Pridham (London: Croom Helm, 1985), pp. 64–82.

FIGURE 3-3. Farmers taking a midmorning coffee break among their *qāt* bushes in Razīḥ, Yemen Arab Republic, 1980. [From Shelagh Weir, *Qat in Yemen: Consumption and Social Change* (London: British Museum Publications Limited, 1985), p. 33. Courtesy of the author.]

becomes a more attractive alternative to agricultural work and high labor costs make grain production less viable.[15] It can be argued that *qāt* production, which, because of the perishability and fragility of the plant, favors small farmers over major producers, especially in the conditions of hillside agriculture of northern Yemen, has the short-term advantage of keeping cultivated land in production that would otherwise be abandoned.

After reviewing the social history of northern Yemen, past and present Western and Yemeni views toward *qāt*, and the social history of *qāt* consumption itself, Weir argues that, despite the 1962 Yemeni revolution (in which rule by a hereditary imam, or religious leader, was replaced by a republican regime), an eight-year civil war between Saudi- and Western-backed royalists and republicans, and increased prosperity, the social separateness of the earlier social categories remains. These categories are the *sayyid*-s, claimed descendants of the Prophet Muḥammad; the *qāḍī*-s, hereditary legal specialists; the *qabīlī*-s, or people of tribal descent; and the *nuqqāṣ*, a term that literally means "deficient" and refers to persons of "despised" birth and occupations, such as butchers, street sweepers, tanners, and barbers. The 1962 revolution in the

[15] Varisco, "On the Meaning of Chewing," pp. 6–7. See also Richard Tutwiler and Sheila Carapico, *Yemeni Agriculture and Economic Change*, Yemen Development Series 1 (Sana'a: American Institute for Yemeni Studies, 1981).

Yemen Arab Republic notwithstanding, endogamous marriages among the *nuqqāṣ* and marriage prohibitions among the *sayyid*-s, who can marry *qabīlī* women but will not offer women from their own social category in return, contribute to the persistence of existing status hierarchies.[16] Although the traditional social hierarchy still exists, Weir argues that its importance may well be declining and attitudes toward it changing, although not necessarily in the direction of egalitarianism.

A major contributing factor is the changing distribution of wealth. In earlier periods, wealth in land and social prestige were highly correlated, but as households developed other sources of income, they were no longer forced to sell land to survive. Land, especially close to settlements, became increasingly valuable as a capital investment because remittance money was used to build new houses. *Qāt* is also sufficiently lucrative to finance expensive terrace maintenance and has the advantage of being less labor-intensive than grain.

In the region of Yemen that Weir discusses, seating patterns at the afternoon *qāt* sessions and other social gatherings, like regular participation in them, provide a more finely tuned indicator of a person's economic status than the possession and display of imported consumer durables. As with fashions in the West, scarcity and availability add to the prestige value of *qāt* as a commodity. Because *qāt* is not food, everyone brings his own, with no obligation to share. "In a manner of speaking a man is only as good as his last lunch party or his last bunch of *qāt*."[17] The order of seating, forms of discourse, and the manner of manipulating the *qāt* leaves are among the indicators of status.

Some ethnographers have concluded that the "flux" in seating patterns indicates a trend toward more egalitarianism.[18] For Weir, the flux merely indicates that "a new social order is emerging in those areas in which different (and possibly conflicting) hierarchical principles are becoming predominant."[19] The

[16] Weir, *Qat*, pp. 22–26.

[17] Ibid., p. 162.

[18] See ibid., pp. 130–36; and Varisco, "On the Meaning of Chewing," p. 9, who downplays the importance of seating arrangements.

[19] Weir, *Qat*, p. 136. Paul Dresch (personal communication, June 22, 1987), an ethnographer who has conducted field research in the plateau areas to the east of where Weir worked, notes that there are significant regional differences in the importance of seating patterns in Yemen. In some regions, such as Razīḥ, they are highly significant; elsewhere, "apart from where the host goes, there is very little fixed pattern." Daniel Martin Varisco and Najwa Adra, "Affluence and the Concept of the Tribe in the Central Highlands of the Yemen Arab Republic," in *Affluence and Cultural Survival*, ed. R. F. Salisbury and E. Tooker, *Proceedings of the American Ethnological Society* (Washington, DC: American Ethnological Society, 1985), p. 138, also note significant regional variation. In making anthropological abstractions, geographic specificity can often be very important. These regional differences contribute in part to conflicting interpretations of whether ideas of stratification are changing in Yemen. On the underlying theoretical issue, Dresch continues: "It's interesting that Shelagh [Weir] sees flux as a transition from one hierarchy to another, not the advent of egalitarianism. The joke, analytically, is that where one has no historical evidence one now assumes transition, such as [Emrys] Peters in the same position naturally assumed fixity. [Weir is] probably right . . . but the shift in unsecured assumptions since Peters's time seems to reflect something about fashions in anthropology."

issue is an important one because it indicates the relationship between massive and rapid economic change, intricately linked with wider economic and political currents, the durability of specifically Yemeni notions of hierarchy and social order, and how these notions shape participation in and understanding of economic and political choices. From a Western perspective and that of many non-Yemeni Arabs, an intensive study of *qāt* consumption initially appears to be an issue of strictly local importance. Its discussion, however, raises many of the same basic issues of political economy and ideas of wealth, community, and status that apply everywhere.

Weir's monograph is one of many new approaches to the study of villages. If an older genre of village ethnography was intended primarily to indicate the presumed stable and enduring elements of village organization,[20] contemporary studies experiment with the most effective ways of representing how villagers and peasants, in the past as in the present, find that their livelihoods and conceptions of work and society significantly shift over time. Such studies take many forms. They include a sustained Marxist approach to analyzing the "changing local class structure and ideology within the broader political economy of the Moroccan state,"[21] a major contribution to social theory using elements of an ethnography of Algerian peasants as a point of departure,[22] a social historical account of changing patterns of property, landownership, production, and social organization in Tunisia,[23] accounts of the lives of contemporary villagers that are at the same time experiments in

[20] For example, Hani Fakhouri, *Kafr el-Elow: An Egyptian Village in Transition*, 2nd ed. (Prospect Heights, IL: Waveland Press, 1987 [1972]). A classic, and still useful, example of such an earlier approach is Winifred S. Blackman, *The Fellāhīn of Upper Egypt* (London: Frank Cass, 1968 [1927]), especially concerned with "survivals" from Pharaonic times. For a more controlled effort to link contemporary ethnography with past practices, see Patty Jo Watson, *Archaeological Ethnography in Western Iran*, Viking Fund Publications in Anthropology 57 (Tucson: University of Arizona Press for the Wenner-Gren Foundation for Anthropological Research, 1979).

[21] David Seddon, *Moroccan Peasants: A Century of Change in the Eastern Rif, 1870–1970* (Folkestone, Kent, UK: Dawson Press, 1981), p. xv. See also Paul Pascon, *Capitalism and Agriculture in the Haouz of Marrakesh*, trans. C. Edwin Vaughan and Veronique Ingman (New York: Methuen, 1986 [1977]); and James A. Miller, *Imlil: A Moroccan Mountain Community in Change* (Boulder, CO, and London: Westview Press, 1984). An excellent study in political economy in the macropolitical sense of the term is John Waterbury, *Hydropolitics of the Nile Valley* (Syracuse, NY: Syracuse University Press, 1979).

[22] Pierre Bourdieu, *Outline of a Theory of Practice*, trans. Richard Nice, Cambridge Studies in Social Anthropology 16 (New York and London: Cambridge University Press, 1977), which can be usefully compared with his earlier ethnographic writings, including three classic essays that originally appeared in French between 1963 and 1972 and are reprinted in *Algeria 1960: The Disenchantment of the World, The Sense of Honour, The Kabyle House of the World Reversed*, trans. Richard Nice, Series in Modern Capitalism (Cambridge: Cambridge University Press, and Paris: Éditions de la Maison des Sciences de l'Homme, 1979), and his *The Algerians*, trans. Alan C. M. Ross (Boston: Beacon Press, 1962 [1958]), published at the height of the Algerian struggle for independence.

[23] Lucette Valensi, *Tunisian Peasants in the Eighteenth and Nineteenth Centuries*, trans. Beth Archer, Studies in Modern Capitalism (Cambridge: Cambridge University Press; Paris: Éditions de la Maison des Sciences de l'Homme, 1985 [1977]).

ethnography,[24] a long-term, multivolume study of livelihood, community, politics, and religious ideas and practice in Jordan,[25] a Polish study of an Iraqi Kurdish community after its "resettlement" in the late 1970s,[26] a study of settled communities and changing social identities in Afghanistan,[27] and others describing the effects of the last Shah's "White Revolution" on village political and economic life.[28] This incomplete enumeration suggests how far contemporary ethnographers have moved from an earlier era of describing villages as self-contained and slow to react to wider economic and political currents. As the following chapter indicates, the same problem has pervaded studies of pastoral societies.

FURTHER READINGS

In addition to Ibn Khaldūn's classic statement on the relationship among cities, peasants, and tribally organized people (including, but not limited to, nomads) contained in *The Muqaddamah* [The Prologue to History], 2nd ed., vol. 1, trans. Franz Rosenthal, Bollingen Series 43 (Princeton, NJ: Princeton University Press, 1967), pp. 249–355, there are numerous excellent modern studies. In recent anthropological writing, the work of Richard Tapper, especially "Anthropologists, Historians, and Tribespeople on Tribe and State

[24] Jean Duvignaud, *Change at Shebeika: Report from a North African Village*, trans. Frances Frenaye (Austin: University of Texas Press, 1977 [1968]). Henry Habib Ayrout, *The Egyptian Peasant*, trans. John Alden Williams (Boston: Beacon Press, 1963 [1938]), can be usefully compared with journalist Richard Critchfield's later *Shahhat: An Egyptian* (Syracuse, NY: Syracuse University Press, 1978). Timothy Mitchell, "The Invention and Reinvention of the Egyptian Peasant," *International Journal of Middle East Studies* 22, no. 2 (May 1990), 129–50, raises major ethical questions concerning Critchfield's work, which purports to depict the life and thoughts of a young peasant in the 1970s, but in which major passages are remarkably parallel in structure and content to Father Ayrout's book from the 1930s. See also Richard Critchfield, "A Response to 'The Invention and Reinvention of the Egyptian Peasant,'" *International Journal of Middle East Studies* 23, no. 2 (May 1991), pp. 277–79, and Mitchell's reply, pp. 279–80.

[25] Richard T. Antoun, *Arab Village: A Social Structural Study of a Transjordanian Peasant Community* (Bloomington: Indiana University Press, 1972), his *Low-Key Politics: Local-Level Leadership and Change in the Middle East* (Albany: State University of New York Press, 1979), and *Muslim Preacher in the Modern World: A Jordanian Case Study in Comparative Perspective* (Princeton, NJ: Princeton University Press, 1989), which deals with religious life in the same village.

[26] Leszek Dziegiel, *Rural Community of Contemporary Iraqi Kurdistan Facing Modernization*, Studia i materialy 7 (Kraków: Agricultural Academy in Kraków, 1981). "Resettlement," as Dziegiel explained in a later publication, became a euphemism for an Iraqi project (of which the Poles were not informed) to deport Kurds to "development" centers, destroying former villages and water wells in the process. See Dziegiel's "Kurdistan as a Subject of Research," in *In Search of a Paradigm*, ed. Anna Zambrzycka-Kunachowicz, trans. Krzysztof Kwasniewicz (Kraków: Platan, 1992), pp. 235–53, which also contains an account of the study of Kurds and Kurdish villages in different national ethnographic traditions.

[27] Robert L. Canfield, *Faction and Conversion: Religious Alignments in the Hindu Kush*, Anthropological Papers 50 (Ann Arbor: University of Michigan, Museum of Anthropology, 1973), and his "Ethnic, Regional, and Sectarian Alignments in Afghanistan," in *The State, Religion, and Ethnic Politics: Afghanistan, Iran, and Pakistan*, ed. Ali Banuazizi and Myron Weiner (Syracuse, NY: Syracuse University Press, 1986), pp. 75–103.

[28] Grace E. Goodell, *The Elementary Structures of Political Life: Rural Development in Pahlevi Iran* (New York: Oxford University Press, 1986); and Eric Hooglund, *Land and Revolution in Iran, 1960–1980* (Austin and London: University of Texas Press, 1982).

Formation in the Middle East," in *Tribe and State Formation in the Middle East*, ed. Philip S. Khoury and Joseph Kostiner (Berkeley and Los Angeles: University of California Press, 1990), pp. 48–73, and his earlier "Introduction," in *The Conflict of Tribe and State in Afghanistan*, ed. Richard Tapper (London: Croom Helm; New York: St. Martin's Press, 1983), pp. 1–82, has been important in articulating in nuanced historical detail the multiple and complex relations between tribe and state and among villagers, pastoralists, townspeople, and city dwellers. See also Ira M. Lapidus, "Tribes and State Formation in Islamic History," in *Tribe and State Formation*, ed. Khoury and Kostiner, pp. 25–47, which includes a discussion of Central ("Inner") Asia. Michael Edward Bonine, *Yazd and Its Hinterland: A Central Place System of Dominance in the Central Iranian Plateau*, Marburger Geographische Schriften 83 (Marburg: Geographischen Institutes der Universität Marburg, 1980), discusses regional economic integration within the context of central place theory. In contrast to many British and American anthropologists, French ethnographers and human geographers have consistently focused on regions. See *Le Maghreb: Hommes et espaces*, 2nd ed., ed. Jean-François Troin (Paris: Armand Colin, 1987), with a thorough bibliography of studies in French. For the Arab Gulf and an introduction to contemporary German scholarship on pastoral societies, see Fred Scholz, ed., *Beduinen im Zeichen des Erdöls: Studien zur Entwicklung im beduinischen Lebensraum Südost-Arabiens*, Beihafte zum Tübinger Atlas der Vorderen Orients, Series B, vol. 45 (Weisbaden: Reichart Verlag, 1981), with an English summary and excellent maps.

The abundant ethnographic accounts of Yemeni society offer especially rich accounts of village life. These include Tomas Gerholm, *Market, Mosque and Mafraj: Social Inequality in a Yemeni Town*, Stockholm Studies in Social Anthropology 5 (Stockholm: University of Stockholm, Department of Social Anthropology, 1977); Thomas B. Stevenson, *Social Change in a Yemeni Highlands Town* (Salt Lake City: University of Utah Press, 1985); and Susan Dorsky, *Women of 'Amran: A Middle Eastern Ethnographic Study* (Salt Lake City: University of Utah Press, 1986). For urban women, see Anne Meneley, *Tournaments of Value: Sociability and Hierarchy in a Yemeni Town* (Toronto and Buffalo: University of Toronto Press, 1996). For South Yemen, officially the People's Democratic Republic of Yemen from 1970 until 1990, Abdallah S. Bujra, *The Politics of Stratification: A Study of Political Change in a Southern Arabian Town* (Oxford: Clarendon Press, 1971), remains the classic account of stratification prior to the 1967 Marxist takeover. For indications that earlier social hierarchies, especially concerning marriage, strongly persisted and pervaded the comportment even of dedicated party cadres, see Helen Lackner, *P.D.R. Yemen: Outpost of Socialist Development in Arabia* (London: Ithaca Press, 1985), pp. 106–22, esp. p. 108; and Norman Cigar, "State and Society in South Yemen," *Problems of Communism* 34, no. 3 (May–June 1985), 41–58. For an example of Russian ethnography in English, see Vitaly Naumkin, *Island of the Phoenix: An Ethnographic Study of the People of Socotra*, Middle East Cultures 16 (London: Ithaca Press, 1993). Paul Dresch, *Tribes, Government, and History in Yemen* (Oxford: Clarendon Press, 1989), offers an excellent social and political history of northern Yemen as well as an incisive account of village life.

4

PASTORAL NOMADISM

Nomadic pastoralism seems always to have been part of a larger system that includes peasants and urban trading centers. Some accounts give the impression that herding societies were once self-contained, and only recent political and economic transformations have reduced their scope and autonomy. But links with other ways of life have always been indispensable. Pastoral nomadic groups in the Middle East and Central Asia maintain regular access to settlements for a variety of agricultural products and other goods that must be obtained through trade or, on occasion in the past, by force.

Pastoralism is the herding and management of animals, which in the Middle East usually means camels, sheep, and goats. In Central Asia, the herds "consist, as the Mongols say, of the *five animals*: sheep, goats, horses, cattle, and camels. Of these, sheep and horses are the most important, but the ideal is to have all the animals necessary for both subsistence and transportation so that a family or tribe can approach self-sufficiency in pastoral production."[1] As Thomas Barfield indicates, which of the five animals predominates in any given herd depends on local ecological conditions—more cattle in wetter areas and more camels at the edge of deserts.[2] Most *pastoral societies* also cultivate some crops. The apparent exception is the deep-desert camel herders of the Arabian peninsula. But even these herders have a symbiotic relation with settlements.

Nomadism describes groups that move from place to place in a purposeful, but not always predictable, manner. Nomadism is a very broad category, including groups that may move a few miles up and down the Zagros or the southern edges of Morocco's High Atlas Mountains or groups that travel over a thousand miles each season in the Arabian peninsula.

Tribe signifies a group of people often conceptualized in terms of genealogy. In fact, even the language of genealogy is applied to a wide range of organ-

[1] Thomas J. Barfield, *The Nomadic Alternative* (Englewood Cliffs, NJ: Prentice-Hall, 1993), p. 137.

[2] Ibid.

izational systems, including pastoral nomads, settled farmers, or even urban dwellers. Tribes are often, although not always, politically unified.

The bedouin (Ar. *badawī*, pl. *badū*) are Middle Eastern peoples who live in a symbiotic relationship with settled peoples, or in some instances claim ancestors who have done so, and adhere to ideologies of autonomy and equality. Both Westerners and urban Arabs think of the *badū* as camel herders. They do not fit neatly into any single category based on economic activities, such as agriculture or pastoralism. Their identity is more complicated.

Badāwa, or being bedouin (I do not capitalize the term to indicate that it does not refer to a specific ethnic group or people) is the opposite of *ḥaḍāra*, who, as we noted in Chapter 3, are those whose claimed "roots" are in towns and cities. Yet some of the "bedouin" mentioned by Ibn Khaldūn cultivated silkworms, and many of their modern counterparts are settled cultivators, as is the case in southern Arabia. Most often these bedouin are organized into tribes, so that one almost automatically thinks of them as "tribespeople" in English, with all that the term suggests, accurately or not, of autonomy, ferocity, and other "bedouin" virtues. Some pastoralists are neither tribal nor bedouin, and some of the tribes of the northern Oman interior (such as the Ḥaṭātla) are tribal pastoralists, but neither nomadic nor bedouin. Many tribes in western Morocco, Iran, Iraq, and elsewhere herd sheep and goats and live in tents for part of the year but combine these activities with agriculture and the use of permanent settlements for other seasons.

Most bedouin are Arabic speakers and claim Arab descent. The exceptions are several small tribes in the southern part of the Arabian peninsula, such as the Ḥarāsīs of the Sultanate of Oman, who speak a South Arabian Semitic dialect. So are the Kabābish Arabs of the northern Sudan, who have mixed herds of camels, sheep, and goats. The camel-herding "noble" tribes of the Arabian peninsula that displace themselves in regular patterns throughout the year in search of water and pasture are bedouin, nomads, and pastoralists, but not all tribespeople are nomadic. Thus only some of the Rwāla bedouin are nomadic, but all members of this large tribe of Syria, Jordan, Saudi Arabia, and Iraq call themselves bedouin, are proud of the fact, and are considered bedouin by other Arabs. However, calling someone *badawī* to his face in northern Oman is a grave insult because the term implies ignorance and primitiveness.

The important point about all these terms is that they are primarily social categories, not empirical ones. Even the word *nomad*, a term favored by geographers, is difficult to apply in a culturally neutral way. Arabs often use the term *badū raḥḥāl*, for instance, which means "traveling, or nomadic, bedouin," indicating that not all bedouin are nomadic pastoralists. Perhaps the best question to ask is not "What is a bedouin?" but "Who says of which group that they are bedouin, and why?"[3]

[3] The distinctions between these concepts owe much to discussions with William and Fidelity Lancaster and with Paul Dresch.

Nomadism is a geographic term; pastoralism is one of several (not necessarily exclusive) economic options; "tribe" is a form of social organization and an ideology; and bedouin is a form of cultural identity. This chapter is concerned with tribespeople who are nomadic and pastoral, and later in this chapter we concentrate on a group that is nomadic and pastoral and call themselves bedouin. In Chapter 6 we discuss the more general notion of "tribe."

As of 1970, pastoral nomads constituted only slightly more than 1 percent of the population of the Middle East, yet until the late 1960s such nomadic societies were more extensively studied by anthropologists than villages, towns, or cities. There are major anthropological studies in English of pastoral nomads in Iran, Turkey, Somalia, Afghanistan, Israel, Saudi Arabia, the Sudan, Algeria, and Libya, as well as an extensive literature in the professional journals. In contrast, the Middle East has been the only world region for which no equivalent range of studies has been available until the 1970s for its major populations, the peasants or settled "tribal" communities.[4]

A partial explanation for the disproportionate emphasis on pastoral nomadism continues to be the romantic attraction to some anthropologists of nomadic life and virtues, but there are also more important theoretical and practical reasons. First, pastoral nomadism offers the appropriate conditions for social groups that conceive their identity primarily in terms of segmentary organization, a subject that raises basic questions about the nature of political order and the comparative study of society in the Middle East and Central Asia.[5] A second reason is an anthropological concern with human ecology. Studies of pastoral societies contribute to an understanding of human adaptation to difficult environments and to the constraints that ecological and economic conditions place on social organization. A third reason is a practical one: Many Middle Eastern governments, for a mixture of political, economic, and humanitarian motives, have been anxious to settle their pastoral populations and consequently have often encouraged the work of both foreign and indigenous anthropologists with pastoral groups. In cases where tribal populations, settled and nomadic, have been deemed contemporary political threats, academic access to them was allowed only after their economic and political base had been effectively undermined to the point where they were deemed to be "harmless relics of a previous age." This was how the central government viewed tribes in Pahlavi Iran by the early 1970s, although tribal political identity (not itself limited to pastoralists or nomads)

[4] Clifford Geertz, "Studies in Peasant Life: Community and Society," in *Biennial Review of Anthropology, 1961,* ed. Bernard J. Siegal (Stanford, CA: Stanford University Press, 1962), p. 17.

[5] On the significance of studying lineage organization in the context of pastoral societies as opposed to those of towns or villages, see Emrys Peters, "Aspects of Affinity in a Lebanese Maronite Village," in *Mediterranean Family Structures,* ed. J. G. Peristiany, Cambridge Studies in Social Anthropology 13 (London: Cambridge University Press, 1976), pp. 30–32, which, in spite of the narrowly focused title, ranges far and wide in the Mediterranean. One of the most thoughtful comparisons between Central Asian and Middle Eastern patterns of kinship structure and political authority is in Charles Lindholm, *Frontier Perspectives: Essays in Comparative Anthropology* (Karachi and New York: Oxford University Press, 1996 [1988]), pp. 147–71.

in some regions of revolutionary Iran and in Afghanistan under Soviet domination (1978–1989) and the subsequent collapse of central authority has undergone a partial resurgence.[6]

PASTORAL NOMADISM: CHANGING POLITICAL CONTEXTS

The reasons for the seemingly irreversible decline in the numbers of pastoral nomads beginning in the eighteenth century are multiple and vary considerably with region, but among them are the steady expansion of cultivated land, to the detriment of lands available for grazing, the declining attractiveness of herds to merchants and other nonpastoralists as a capital investment, the disappearance of significant caravan traffic as alternative investments have become available, and the increasing ineffectiveness of nomads as a military force. Census figures for Iraq indicate the scope of this decline. In 1867, pastoral nomads constituted about 35 percent of the population, as compared with only 2.8 percent (about 300,000 people) of the population in 1970.[7] The decline of nomadism began at different times in various countries, but in almost all cases the rate of decline brought about by large-scale economic and political shifts has been rapid.

The major factors involved in the decline of pastoralism are suggested by the case of Egypt, which, in the early nineteenth century, became the first country in the Middle East to experience a rapid expansion of agricultural production due to increasing involvement in the world capitalist economy and a consolidation of its central government under Muḥammad 'Alī (r. 1804–1848).[8] To increase agricultural production and tax revenues, Muḥammad 'Alī sought to settle the bedouin tribes, and to this end he used a combination of tactics. One was to give land grants to bedouin tribal leaders (*shaykh-s*) and to tax this land at a low rate. The drawback to this policy was that many shaykhs preferred to lease their land to peasants rather than induce their followers to settle. Another technique was to appoint bedouin leaders to government offices, keeping members of their families as hostages in Cairo to ensure their loyalty. In order to carry out their tasks and to enjoy the wealth usually associated with such offices, many of these leaders settled in towns and often built palaces for themselves as an indication of their new status. At the same time, they maintained a firm hold upon fellow tribespeople as their formal representative with the gov-

[6] Richard Tapper, "Introduction," in *The Conflict of Tribe and State in Iran and Afghanistan,* ed. Richard Tapper (London: Croom Helm; New York: St. Martin's Press, 1983), pp. 52–53; Lois Beck, "Revolutionary Iran and Its Tribal Peoples," *Merip Reports,* no. 87 (May 1980), 14–20. See also Beck's *The Qashqa'i of Iran* (New Haven, CT, and London: Yale University Press, 1986), pp. 296–347.

[7] Peter Beaumont, Gerald H. Blake, and J. Malcolm Wagstaff, *The Middle East: A Geographical Study* (New York: Wiley, 1976), p. 187. Cf. p. 124, where the figure is given as 1.1 percent for 1947.

[8] The following account is based on Gabriel Baer, *Studies in the Social History of Modern Egypt* (Chicago: University of Chicago Press, 1969), pp. 3–16.

ernment and persuaded many of them to settle, exacting from them tax revenues and other obligations.

An associated tactic to encourage settlement was to allow bedouin shaykhs to register uncultivated land in their own names, leaving them to induce their fellow tribespeople by whatever means available to settle and cultivate this land. The process of land registration was confusing enough to illiterate tribespeople (who often thought it to be a prelude to military conscription), so that even when tracts of land were intended for tribes as a whole, tribal leaders found it easy to acquire personal title to such land and progressively to convert fellow tribespeople into peasants and sharecroppers. A similar process occurred elsewhere in the Middle East, including the former Ottoman provinces of Iraq, Syria, and Palestine.[9]

The decline in pastoral nomadism has accelerated with the economic and political transformations that have occurred since the end of World War II and the influx of oil wealth into several Middle Eastern countries. For example, roughly 40 percent of Saudi Arabia's population was nomadic in the 1950s, as compared with 11 percent in 1970 and less than 5 percent today. These figures do not reveal the even more significant shift of many nomadic groups from camel herding to the raising of sheep and goats and a motorized nomadism in which trucks are used to facilitate seasonal migrations.[10] In Libya, 25 percent of the population was nomadic in 1962, as compared with 3.5 percent in 1970.[11] In some regions, notably those adjoining the Sahara and the Horn of Africa, this trend has been hastened by the drought and famine that occurred in the early 1970s. Prior to the drought, 75 percent of Somalia's population was nomadic; subsequently, most pastoralists had to be relocated to refugee camps as conditions worsened. The Somali government, like many other governments in the affected zones, responded to the crisis by taking steps to settle the pastoralists permanently and to seek to replace their clan and tribal identities with wider notions of ethnicity and nation.

[9] The appropriation of lands intended for collectivities by personal title was not confined to attempts to induce nomads to settle. In Syria and Palestine it was common for cultivated lands to be collectively held by villages under a system of land tenure known as *mashā'a*. In 1858, the Ottoman administration enacted a major reform involving land registration intended to eliminate the earlier system of tax farming and its accompanying abuses by making cultivators directly responsible for the tax on their lands. Like many reforms, this one had unintended consequences. It provided an opportunity for unscrupulous village headmen to acquire personal title to the lands of entire villages. See Talal Asad, "Anthropological Texts and Ideological Problems: An Analysis of Cohen on Arab Border Villages in Israel," *Economy and Society* 4, no. 3 (August 1975), 261; and Scott Atran, "*Ḥamula* Organization and *Mashā'a* Tenure in Palestine," *Man* (N.S.) 21, no. 2 (June 1986), 271–95. See also Philip Khoury, "The Tribal Shaykh, French Tribal Policy and the Nationalist Movement in Syria Between Two World Wars," *Middle Eastern Studies* 18, no. 2 (April 1982), 180–93; and Philip Carl Salzman, ed., *When Nomads Settle* (New York: Praeger, 1980).

[10] Beaumont, Blake, and Wagstaff, *The Middle East*, pp. 187, 321; and Dawn Chatty, "Leaders, Land, and Limousines: Emir versus Sheikh," *Ethnology* 16, no. 4 (October 1977), 385–97.

[11] Beaumont, Blake, and Wagstaff, *The Middle East*, p. 187; also Abdalla Said Bujra, "The Social Implications of Development Policies: A Case Study from Egypt," in *The Desert and the Sown: Nomads in Wider Society*, ed. Cynthia Nelson, Research Series 21 (Berkeley: University of California, Institute of International Studies, 1973), p. 156.

FIGURE 4-1. Ja'da camel driver, Ḥaḍramawt, southern Arabia. Roads and trucks have profoundly transformed the life of nomadic pastoralists. [From Freya Stark, *Seen in the Hadhramaut* (London: John Murray, Publishers, Ltd., 1939), p. 3. Courtesy of the author and publisher.]

Anthropological studies of contemporary pastoralists indicate that the process of settlement has a variety of consequences for social organization. The Yörük of southeastern Turkey, who began large-scale settlement only after World War II, regard sedentarization as one of a number of economic strategies. As the economic rewards of pastoralism became increasingly marginal, households and groups shifted to settled life whenever possible, basing the decision to settle primarily on economic considerations. This shift implied significant changes in the distribution of wealth (fixed inequalities of wealth are generally not as pronounced among fully nomadic groups), but it did not result in any "massive change in formal institutions or social rules."[12] A similar conclusion was reached by a study of the impact of a government project initiated in the early 1960s to settle the bedouin of Egypt's western desert, one aspect of which was to encourage participation in an agricultural cooperative movement in order to weaken tribal and lineage loyalties. The socialist cooperatives quickly became popular, but not for the reasons envisaged by government planners. Nomads regarded the cooperatives as offering an economically advantageous

[12] Bates, *Nomads and Farmers*, p. 222.

alternative to traditional herding practices, which also permitted the *strengthening* of traditional group loyalties and leadership.[13]

In other cases, settlement is resisted even when there are economic advantages to abandoning traditional pastoral activities. This is reported to be the case for some of the camel-herding "noble" tribes of Saudi Arabia, who have opposed settlement because it often involved their mixture with nontribal groups they considered inferior in the system of social stratification that was prevalent in the region until recently. Likewise, there was an initial reluctance to shift to the herding of sheep and goats because herding was an activity traditionally carried out only by "weaker" (that is, inferior) tribal groups. Because the economic advantages gained from such a shift have enabled some weaker groups to raise their status significantly, the reluctance of "noble" tribes to adapt themselves to the commercial raising of sheep and goats is rapidly diminishing, only to be replaced by the major ecological problems of lack of water and overgrazing of available pastures.[14]

Although many anthropologists have concentrated on recent economic and political pressures that have reduced the numbers and strength of pastoral nomads, others have explored their historical role in the Middle East and Central Asia in the formation of state organizations, or as Anatoly Khazanov specifies, "dynasties which are nomadic by origin," and the organizational and leadership problems that result as they expand and incorporate existing states or peasant populations.[15]

One notable study for the Middle East is that of Madawi Al Rasheed (Āl Rashīd), *Politics in an Arabian Oasis: The Rashidi Tribal Dynasty*.[16] At one level, an ethnohistory of political centralization among the Shammār tribe and the rise and fall of the Rashīdī dynasty of central Arabia before the consolidation of Āl Sa'ūd rule and the formation of "Saudi" Arabia, her book also concerns the politics of memory. Her account draws on British, French, and Egyptian archives and nineteenth-century travelers' accounts; anthropological writings concerning Middle Eastern politics; and the narratives and poems of Rashīdis in exile. For her relatives, "the interviews became the means to socialize me and enrich my knowledge of my own history."[17]

[13] Another reason for the strengthening of traditional leadership and loyalties appears to be the large-scale involvement of the bedouin in smuggling activities. Livestock is smuggled into Libya, where prices are much higher than in Egypt. Such practices had to be concealed from government officials, at least at a formal level. See Bujra, "Social Implications," p. 150; and Lila Abu-Lughod, "Change and Egyptian Bedouins," *Cultural Survival Quarterly* 8, no. 1 (Spring 1984), 6–10.

[14] Cole, *Nomads*, pp. 144–63; see also his "The Enmeshment of Nomads in Saudi Arabian Society: The Case of Āl Murrah," in *Desert and Sown*, ed. Nelson, pp. 113–28, and "Tribal and Non-Tribal Structures Among the Bedouin of Saudi Arabia," *Al-Abhath* (Beirut) 30 (1982), 77–93.

[15] Anatoly M. Khazanov, *Nomads and the Outside World*, 2nd ed., trans. Julia Crookendon (Madison: University of Wisconsin Press, 1994), especially pp. 228–302, which offers a magisterial overview of "nomadic" state formation in Central/Inner Asia and the Middle East.

[16] (London: I. B. Tauris, 1991.)

[17] Ibid., p. 6.

Al Rasheed juxtaposes three types of argument: anthropological discussions of tribes, segmentation, leadership and succession to high office, and marriage strategies; a written historical narrative of the Rashīdī dynasty and central Arabia, tied principally to European (and Ottoman) accounts but supplemented by sources in Arabic; and the oral narratives (*salfa*) of the Rashīdis themselves. These narratives, in which members of her extended family told about "events that they themselves neither witnessed nor took part in" and that "cannot be found in textbooks," are known to all Shammār and are often interspersed with oral poetry (*qaṣīda-s*) attributed to the participants in the events of the last century.[18] The authenticity of these accounts depends on the status of the narrator, his age and reputation for reliable memory, and his (and sometimes her) relationship to predecessors. The narratives highlight political struggle, but Al Rasheed argues that they incorporate emotions and "human experiences" to a greater extent than acknowledged by anthropologists who posit a sharp dichotomy between them and "political" poetry.[19]

Al Rasheed compares Shammār tribal organization and Rashīdī dynastic rule with similar developments elsewhere, including the Qashqā'i and Bakhtiyari of Iran and various Arab tribes, invoking anthropological notions of segmentation in the process. The result is a fascinating narrative of how successive tribal leaders converted shaykhly influence into princely authority by promoting commerce and protecting Shī'ī merchants, developing a non-tribal militia, acting with a combination of generosity and firmness to maintain authority over their tribe, and managing internal and external threats to their rule.

Al Rasheed is especially good at sociologically enhancing earlier accounts. If prior scholars call attention to the *khuwwa*, or "brotherhood" tax, among the Shammār (in which a dominant group would exact tribute from a weaker one in exchange for protecting them against external raids, including from the dominant "brothers") as an economic transaction established to protect the weaker party in a relationship, Al Rasheed explores its nuances more thoroughly, suggesting how such an arrangement is subtly modified as the power relations shift between the contracting parties.[20] European accounts of the Barzān palace of the Hā'il oasis are enriched when Al Rasheed relates the spatial organization of the oasis and its symbolic significance in exercising political authority.[21] Likewise, her detailed narrative of internal disputes within the dominant Rashīdī lineage—no fewer than six of the twelve Rashīdī *amīr*-s, or princes, who governed the tribe's principal oasis of Hā'il between 1836 and 1921 acquired leadership by assassinating close male relatives,

[18] Ibid., pp. 159–60.

[19] Ibid., pp. 168–69, 181.

[20] Henry Rosenfeld, "The Social Composition of the Military in the Process of State Formation in the Arabian Desert," *Journal of the Royal Anthropological Institute* 95 (1965), 75–86, 174–94. Rosenfeld depicts the military and political role of pastoral nomads in northern Arabia in the nineteenth century and prior to World War I.

[21] Al Rasheed, *Politics*, pp. 49–53.

including infants—offers fascinating insight into how "internal" Rashīdī rivalries and uncertain succession related to the wider framework of changing economic opportunities from pilgrim caravans and commerce, Sa'ūdī and Wahhābī expansion into the Najd, and increasing Ottoman and European involvement in Arabian affairs. The explanation of marriage strategies indicates how key Rashīdī families used marriage as a means to consolidate their authority, then were obliged, when their power waned, to offer women to the Sa'ūdī *amīr*.[22] A final chapter on the Rashīdī *amīr*-s in exile in Riyadh offers rare insight into the politics of Ibn Sa'ūd's wife-taking, a mini-essay on patronage and authority in contemporary Saudi Arabia, and how the rise and fall of tribal dynasties is linked to the creation and maintenance of state authority, the conflicting principles of family and kinship loyalties, and the exigencies of state authority.

The basic tension that Al Rasheed describes between authority in tribal societies and that exercised by the ruler of a state and his entourage continues to prevail in several states of the Arab/Persian Gulf. A common pattern prior to the 1950s was for coastal rulers to have economic and political interests closely tied to maritime commerce and only nominal control over the tribal leaders of both nomadic and settled groups in the interior. The tacitly contractual loyalties of these leaders were maintained through subsidies, political intermarriages, and associated strategies. These tactics continue to be significant in the region, and tribal loyalties are far from being remnants of the past.[23] The case is the same in Somalia, where nationalist politics prior to independence in 1960 and political activities since then under both democratic and military governments are significantly associated with lineage and clan loyalties, albeit in modified forms.[24]

[22] The theme of marriage as a political strategy in tribal societies for consolidating domestic (household) status and managing political and economic conflict and competition is richly explored in Nancy Tapper, *Bartered Brides: Politics, Gender and Marriage in an Afghan Tribal Society*, Cambridge Studies in Social and Cultural Anthropology 74 (Cambridge and New York: Cambridge University Press, 1991).

[23] For useful discussions of the Arab/Persian Gulf states, see J. B. Kelly, "A Prevalence of Furies: Tribes, Politics, and Religion in Oman and Trucial Oman," in *The Arabian Peninsula: Society and Politics*, ed. Derek Hopwood (London: Allen and Unwin, 1972); Fuad I. Khuri, *Tribe and State in Bahrain*, Publications of the Center for Middle Eastern Studies 14 (Chicago: University of Chicago Press, 1980); and Peter Lienhardt, "The Authority of Shaykhs in the Gulf," *Arabian Studies* 2 (1975), 61–75. For further east, the essays contained in *Tribe and State in Iran and Afghanistan*, ed. Tapper, are pertinent, especially Tapper's own contribution, "Nomads and Commissars in the Mughan Steppe: The Shahsevan Tribes in the Great Game," pp. 401–35, based in part on the analysis of contemporary nineteenth-century documents on tribal history and politics. Other studies making extensive use of combined anthropological and historical sources are Gene R. Garthwaite, *Khans and Shahs: A Documentary Analysis of the Bakhtiyari in Iran* (Cambridge and New York: Cambridge University Press, 1983); and Beck, *The Qashqa'i*.

[24] Lewis, *Pastoral Democracy*, pp. 266–95; see also his "The Politics of the 1969 Somali Coup," *Journal of Modern African Studies* 10, no. 3 (October 1972), 383–408, and "Kim Il-Sung in Somalia: The End of Tribalism?" in *Politics in Leadership*, ed. William A. Shack and Percy S. Cohen (Oxford: Clarendon Press, 1979), pp. 13–44.

ARABIAN PENINSULA PASTORAL NOMADS: THE RWĀLA BEDOUIN

So far this chapter has provided a general view of the historical, economic, and political contexts of pastoral nomadism in the Middle East and Central Asia. The remainder of this chapter involves the more detailed ethnographic analysis of the Rwāla bedouin of the northern Arabian Desert, among whom William Lancaster conducted over three and one-half years of field research together with his wife, Fidelity, and their children, in visits beginning in 1972. As Lancaster states, the fact of their living in the encampment of a tribal leader (*shaykh*) of the Sha'lān family led to many Rwāla assuming that he was a half-brother to the shaykh, who had grown up in England. Moreover, their presence as a family among the Rwāla facilitated an understanding of all aspects of Rwāla life, including access to both the male and female sides of tents. As relations with the Lancasters grew progressively more cordial, "the sheikhly family found it easier to acquiesce than to try to explain to the tribesmen" exactly what they were doing. The Lancasters' prolonged residence among the Rwāla led to their increasing acceptance into the ordinary social fabric. It also provided them an almost unique perspective to observe firsthand the changes taking place in bedouin society throughout the decade.[25]

Lancaster's *The Rwala Bedouin Today* is especially valuable for its thorough account of the role and status of women in bedouin society, as perceived both by the women themselves and by the men. Likewise, the monograph offers a nuanced account of how the bedouin perceive shifting economic and political opportunities while sustaining kinship and tribal loyalties.

In the mid-1970s there were between a quarter and a half million Rwāla, although the Rwāla themselves sometimes assert that their population numbers up to 1.5 million. The ambiguity of such estimates indicates one problem facing development planners in the Middle East. Most Rwāla today are found in Saudi Arabia, although they are spread out in a vast territory of about half a million square kilometers that extends into Jordan, Syria, and Iraq. This vast area was not exclusive to them. Other tribes used the same territory at different times of the year. Until 1958 virtually all of the five major sections of the Rwāla herded camels. Since the 1920s one section herded sheep as well, an activity that has become more common in recent years, as the Rwāla are increasingly drawn into the cash economy.[26]

The nomadic cycle for the camel-herding Rwāla was to move south to the edge of the Nafūd desert of Saudi Arabia in late winter and early spring, then to move northward in late spring and summer, crossing international boundaries

[25] Lancaster, *Rwala*, pp. 4–6. A sensitive parallel account of field research in a bedouin society is contained in Lila Abu-Lughod, "Fieldwork of a Dutiful Daughter," in *Studying Your Own Society: Arab Women in the Field*, ed. Soraya Altorki and Camillia Fawzi El-Solh, Modern Arab Studies (Syracuse, NY: Syracuse University Press, 1988), pp. 139–61.

[26] Lancaster, *Rwala*, pp. 8–10. See also Carl R. Raswan, "Tribal Areas and Migration Lines of the North Arabian Bedouins," *Geographical Review* 20, no. 3 (July 1930), 494–502.

in the process. Exact migratory routes depended not only on highly uneven patterns of rainfall but also on the preferences of subgroups and international political conditions. Rainfall for the entire area was less than 10 inches (25 centimeters) annually and highly erratic. Permanent sources of water were in short supply. Temperatures dropped as low as freezing in the north (Syria) during winter, but could rise to 113°F (45°C) in the summer, with a range of up to 77°F (25°C) between daytime and nighttime temperatures throughout the year.

Given their large numbers, the Rwāla rarely migrated as a tribe. (The past tense is used because about half the Rwāla were still herding in the mid-1970s.) The substitution of motor transport for camel caravans after World War I, the disappearance of traditional raiding by the 1930s, the formation of modern state systems and borders, a severe drought in the late 1950s that further curtailed nomadic pastoralism, plus opportunities for wage labor through enlistment with the Saudi National Guard, work for oil companies, and smuggling—all incrementally encouraged many Rwāla to develop new skills and entrepreneurial activities. The particular mix of available economic activities has frequently shifted. As Lancaster points out, bedouin society has never been static in the known 4000-year history of camel nomadism. The Rwāla have never lived in a self-sufficient environment; their "assets and options" have always involved a consideration of the economic opportunities available outside of pastoral society. In the present century, however, the pace of adaptation has accelerated.[27]

The Rwāla live in both temporary herding camps and in permanent structures. In both cases, the basic spatial organization of the tents or buildings is by claimed genealogy. These settlements are known as *gawm* (classical Ar. *qawm*). The term *gawm* "is not geographical nor genealogical but indicates a conglomeration of people with an identity of interest." Even when settlement structures are permanent, Lancaster cautions against assuming a stable population. Of the approximately 500 family units present at ar-Rishā, the settlement he joined in 1972, "only about 8 remained in 1979; the other 200 were newcomers."[28]

Each camping cluster worked as an economic unit. A subgroup within one of the *gawm*-s to which Lancaster belonged consisted of some 35 households of relations, clients, and dependents, including servants and "slaves." Lancaster specifies that "slave" is presently a social and not a legal category, although slavery was not abolished in Saudi Arabia until 1962. Slaves could own property, were protected by the laws of blood feud, and in some cases rose to positions of great influence. A slave, however, "only reflected the honour of his owner" in a society in which major importance is attached to personal and household reputation, and he was unable to marry a "free" *badū* woman. Nor do bedouin males marry women of slave origin or take them as concubines.

[27] Lancaster, *Rwala*, pp. 8–9, 99–100, 119. See also Fredrik Barth, "The Land Use Pattern of Migratory Tribes of South Persia," *Norsk Geografisk Tidsskrift* 17 (1959) [Bobbs-Merrill Reprint A-11], 1–11. For the implications of camel pastoralism for long-term social change in the premodern era, see Richard W. Bulliet, *The Camel and the Wheel* (Cambridge, MA: Harvard University Press, 1975).

[28] Lancaster, *Rwala*, p. 10.

The Rwāla utilize complex multiple interrelationships among cooperating group members—patrilineal descent, matrilateral descent (traced through the patriline of one's mother), and ties created through marriage—to justify particular instances of coresidence or economic activity. The individual or group taking such action knows exactly which ties are being invoked, but observers, including other Rwāla, can never be entirely certain. This ambiguity facilitates a constructive flexibility in interpreting specific social relationships and responsibilities. Much political and economic cooperation takes place among members of the same named patrilineal group, "but relationships through women cut across patrilines and markedly extend economic or political options." The "patrilineal genealogy" is generally used to justify loyalties and choices to outsiders, but in practice other relationships are also significant. Thus, many relationships are referred to as *ibn 'amm* (father's brother's son) relationships, to imply very close ties of loyalty based on genealogy. In practice, "so widely is the term used that it could be applied to any Rweli, any Bedu or even any human being."[29]

The Rwāla bedouin are what anthropologists call a *segmentary* society. Thus, any "segment" of society—from individuals to small, cooperating groups of close patrilineal relations, tribal sections, and tribes—in ascending order of inclusion, "sees itself as an independent unit in relation to another segment of the same section, but sees both segments as a unity in relation to another section."[30] Groups are defined not in isolation or by some shared essence, but relationally. Moreover, elements at the same "level" are formally equal and defined by "balanced opposition." In the cases at hand, this definition of groups by mutual contradistinction is apparent in notions of shared honor (Ar. *sharaf* or *'irḍ*), not to arbitrary patterns of cooperation and support. "Balanced opposition" implies a moral equilibrium, not one of opposed "social masses" of tribal groups of equal strength.[31] In situations of

[29] Ibid., pp. 11–13, 21–23. Daniel Bradburd, *Ambiguous Relations: Kin, Class, and Conflict Among Komachi Pastoralists,* Smithsonian Series in Ethnographic Inquiry (Washington, DC, and London: Smithsonian Institution Press, 1990), pp. 114–15, similarly stresses that the criteria which the Komachi in Iran use to calculate kin are "not a beautifully articulated web but a collection of jury-rigged lashings" which were neither "categorical nor given."

[30] E. E. Evans-Pritchard, *The Nuer: A Description of the Modes of Livelihood and Political Institutions of a Nilotic People* (Oxford: Clarendon Press, 1940), p. 147. For an excellent discussion of segmentation, arguing that political authority in segmentary systems is based on persuasion and shared cultural notions of the social order, see Steven C. Caton, "Power, Persuasion, and Language: A Critique of the Segmentary Model in the Middle East," *International Journal of Middle East Studies* 19, no. 1 (February 1987), 77–102. For the idea of honor in pre-Islamic Arabia, a neglected classic is Bichr Farès, *L'honneur chez les Arabes avant l'Islam* (Paris: Librairie d'Amérique et d'Orient, 1932), a study very much in the tradition of Durkheimian sociology but curiously ignored by anthropologists.

[31] Chapter 6 contains a further discussion of segmentary societies and their importance in the study of the Middle East. The moral basis of segmentary societies is emphasized in a comparative study of several Middle Eastern contexts by Michael Meeker, "Meaning and Society in the Near East: Examples from the Black Sea Turks and the Levantine Arabs," *International Journal of Middle East Studies* 7, no. 2 (April 1976), 243–70, and no. 3 (July 1976), 383–422. The distinction between the moral basis of segmentary societies and theories assuming the "social masses" view is forcibly advanced by Paul Dresch, "The Significance of the Course Events Take in Segmentary Systems," *American Ethnologist* 13, no. 2 (May 1986), 309–24. Dresch also provides an insightful review of recent understandings of segmentary theory and its contribution to the anthropological study of the Middle East.

conflict, it is difficult to determine in advance which names or "levels" of segmentation will be invoked. The principle of segmentation remains fixed but can be applied in a variety of accepted ways.

Lancaster writes that the Rwāla view all humanity as "ultimately descended in the male line from a common ancestor." Hence they are all *Banī Ādam,* "the sons of Adam."[32] Their principal concern, however, is with Arabs, whom they divide into the bedouin, seen as genealogically "close" to them, and nonbedouin, who are not. The Rwāla have five tribal "sections" (Ar. *fakhdh*; pl. *fukhūdh,* literally "thigh"), or major divisions: the Mur'adh, the Dughmān, the Ga'ādza'a, the Frajja, and the Kwātzba. The first three of these named groups make up the larger named group of Abyāth. The Frajja claim descent from Asmar. These parts of the tribal genealogy are fixed, in that any effort to manipulate this part of the genealogy is a major political act. Such is the case for the Kwātzba, who originally broke off from another tribe to join the Rwāla. They did not initially fit into the larger genealogical framework provided by patronyms such as Murādh and Abyāth, and some groups objected to their assimilation. They were eventually accepted, however, and no one presently is actively concerned with their incongruous lack of fit into the overall patronymic system. No Rwāla asserts that the patronym Murādh or Abyāth, for example, signifies actual persons.

Below the "level" of the tribal section, however, genealogies are more malleable and are "exclusively concerned with actual living groups on the ground." Lancaster argues that this "gap" in the genealogy, which no one tries to fill, is significant for the concept of "jural equality" which it engenders. A named group within a tribal section remains just that, and no one group can claim supremacy over others. Each named group below the level of the tribal section is responsible for the conduct of its members. These groups, which Rwāla call the *ibn 'amm,* or minimal section group, are reputedly descended from a male line five generations distant. No one can "remember" the precise link to the inclusive tribal section (e.g., Murādh), so feuds between two minimal sections never involve the entire tribal section. Descent groups below the level of section are slowly manipulated over time to accommodate shifting economic and political realities.

The "formal" upper levels of the segmentary genealogy remain fixed, but at lower levels there is considerable autonomy in the formation of responsible groups. Frequent intermarriage offers multiple pathways through which individuals can claim ties. The fact that women's roles are not public and women do not appear in the formal genealogies provides the necessary latitude for flexibility of these cooperating groups. Lancaster provides an instance of a man who could show 11 different genealogical paths through which he was related to his wife.[33]

[32] Lancaster, *Rwala,* pp. 24–25.

[33] Ibid., pp. 39–41, 49.

To an outsider, the segmentary system of the Rwāla appears confused because it is in a constant state of flux. Even the terms for the various inclusive "levels" of tribal organization—"tribe" (*qabīla* and *'ashīra*), "section" (*fakhdh*), and "minimal section" (*ibn 'amm*) must be used with caution because in various contexts they can refer to various "levels" as well. *Ibn 'amm,* which literally means "father's brother's son," can be used in a number of ways, of which patrilineal descent is only one. The term *ibn 'amm* can also refer to three-generation groups which have no name but whose members intermarry extensively. They are "really economic units whose members co-operate very closely with each other." He explicitly avoids calling these groups lineages, because patrilineal ties cannot be traced with precision. Acting as if one is an *ibn 'amm* "proves" the relationship, and the thicket of intermarriages and other ties makes assertions of realignment possible. Such realignments are more difficult among the shaykhly Sha'lān, whose formal genealogy is known for some 15 generations; but even in this case the "must be" argument legitimizing actual practice within the segmentary system is possible. "As political and economic motives change with time, so the genealogy must change to accommodate changing assets and new options." Lancaster goes so far as to say that it "is not *the* genealogy leading to *a* relationship, but rather *the* relationship leading to *a* genealogy."[34]

The role of women is complex. Lancaster emphasizes how the choice of marriage partner maintains and extends long-term relationships. The political and economic arenas are recognized as short-term and rapidly changing. For the long term, what is important is the reputation of the spouse-to-be. Men are expected to demonstrate such virtues as honor, bravery, generosity, political acumen, and mediatory abilities. Lancaster carefully documents how these virtues are inculcated from an early age for both men and women. An excess of these virtues has its own built-in limits. An excess of generosity, for instance, leads to an inability to fulfill obligations. From the age of two onward, a male child is in the public gaze. The children of fathers with a good reputation, especially tribal leaders, have a decided advantage because they have more opportunity to observe how delicate political situations are mediated.[35] Women's reputations are known primarily within the group but are equally important for enhancing the group's reputation. "In structural terms, if not in theoretical ones, women are equal partners." The confinement of women to the private sector among the Rwāla is not a relegation to a second-class status but "a measure of their extreme importance to society as a whole: they are simply too valuable and important to be allowed to embroil themselves publicly in the maelstrom of politics and feud."[36]

[34] Ibid., pp. 35, 151. Compare Lancaster's account of the *ibn 'amm* relationship with the earlier one of Alois Musil, *The Manners and Customs of the Rwala Bedouin* (New York: AMS Press, 1978 [1928]), pp. 46–47.

[35] Ibid., pp. 43–44.

[36] Ibid., p. 58.

Some Rwāla, especially the tribal prince (*amīr*) of the Sha'lān and the leading shaykhs, are economically and politically influential beyond the confines of bedouin society. They live in towns and have greater access to governmental authorities than ordinary tribespeople. Nonetheless, Rwāla shaykhs have no formal coercive powers over the tribe. They maintain their leadership through skill at achieving consensus and representing the tribe to state authorities, access to information, and success at maintaining a reputation for managing influence and control over persons and resources in the best interests of the collectivity. Thus although leading Rwāla are considerably more wealthy than average tribespeople, they must be prepared to use this wealth in the interests of fellow tribespeople. Lancaster's description of a lavish formal entertainment for a visiting official suggests how the Rwāla engage in political role-playing to impress outsiders with the prestige and authority of their shaykhs:

> All these services were performed by slaves and servants at a sign from the sheikh and every action was carried out promptly. . . . As soon as the visitors had left, it became apparent that the whole scene was a charade designed solely to impress. The slaves lolled in the recently vacated seats, the sheikhs poured their own tea, the servants ate up the titbits or simply left. Later on, when it became obvious that I wasn't worth impressing, I heard the same slaves, those paragons of domestic service, telling the sheikh that it was too hot to do what he had asked, he'd have to do it himself.[37]

Among nomadic pastoralists, reputation is based on the display of bedouin virtues, not on wealth or control over resources in themselves. As Lila Abu-Lughod writes of the Awlād 'Alī bedouin of Egypt's Western Desert, authority is thought to derive "neither from the use of force nor from ascribed position, but from moral worthiness." Among both the Rwāla and the Awlād 'Alī there are major status differentials, but these are conceived as "relations not of domination and subordination but of protection and dependency."[38] The ideology of honor and respect for personal autonomy is interpreted among both the Rwāla and the Awlād 'Alī so that recognition of a leader's authority is seen as a voluntary act by reasonable, autonomous persons. This shared ideology effectively channels personal ambition. In the past, the Rwāla conducted raids on other bedouin groups and settlements, which served as a de facto means of allocating and redistributing resources in uncertain desert environmental conditions. The bedouin virtues of personal autonomy and mutual support honed many of the same skills needed by the Rwāla today to succeed as entrepreneurs and to take advantage of rapidly fluctuating economic and political opportunities. Some bedouin have become highly proficient at raiding the modern capitalist economy as entrepreneurs. To succeed in this sphere, bedouin see tribal values and mutual support as more stable and enduring than the frailty of state authority and institutions.

[37] Ibid., p. 83. But this "role playing" could be backed with the ability to coerce followers. See Musil, *Manners and Customs*, pp. 58–59.

[38] Lila Abu-Lughod, *Veiled Sentiments: Honor and Poetry in a Bedouin Society* (Berkeley and Los Angeles: University of California Press, 1986), p. 85; see also Lancaster, *Rwala*, pp. 119–23.

FIGURE 4-2. Shaykh Nūrī Sha'lān of the Rwāla (slightly right of center) with official guests, 1974. [From William Lancaster, *The Rwala Bedouin Today* (New York and London: Cambridge University Press, 1981), p. 90. Courtesy of the author.]

Lancaster describes the division of labor between the *amīr* of the Rwāla and his brothers, as they are variously engaged in overseeing small agricultural holdings, commercial and entrepreneurial activities, smuggling (very effective for keeping in touch with the tribe), and diplomacy in several neighboring countries. They act as a unit, exchanging information and providing mutual support. Although the scale and complexity of shaykhly entrepreneurial activities are wider than those of other tribespeople, these opportunities are seen as open to all, with shaykhs facilitating the activities of their tribespeople whenever possible. Again, bedouin ideology emphasizes the equality and personal autonomy of tribespeople and perceives the sustained success of some over successive generations as due to personal honor and skill. In a practical political sense, the ability of Rwāla tribal leaders to maintain ties with several contiguous countries and to adapt to changing notions of territory has enabled them to preserve more autonomy and political influence than is the case for nomadic pastoral groups more closely tied to single states.[39]

[39] Ibid., pp. 89–90, 93, 116, 130, 146. See also William and Fidelity Lancaster, "The Concept of Territoriality Among the Rwala Bedouin," *Nomadic Peoples* no. 20 (March 1986), 41–48.

FIGURE 4-3. Xinjiang, China, 1987. In the Altai mountains of Central Asia, the Kazakh nomads of Kazakhstan and the Kazakh Autonomous Region of China live in cylindrical *yurts*, in some ways the functional equivalent of the cloth tents of Middle Eastern pastoralists. The sturdy lattice framework of the *yurt* and its heavy felt panels withstand the region's cold winters and high winds. [Courtesy Thomas Barfield.]

THE IDEOLOGY OF EQUALITY: FURTHER CONSIDERATIONS

It is clearly important to distinguish between Arab bedouin values, especially those of political autonomy and egalitarianism, and the process by which these become reformulated and take on new meaning in changed economic and political contexts. Such transformations have frequently been accelerated in recent times but are not unique to the modern era. The preceding section stressed the egalitarian aspects of Rwāla life, but the egalitarian chiefs of Lancaster's account appear as tyrants in the analyses of other scholars dealing with earlier historical periods, and the political implications of bedouin society as a whole depend very much on the degree to which they are involved with outside power and resources. The point is that the "same" cultural system in different circumstances can produce very different political formations, that authority often requires constant assertion, and that the society of the Rwāla, like most others, contains strong elements of inequality of resources and control over them, notwithstanding the ideology of equality. It is important to keep in mind that the Rwāla political system is not "essentially" egalitarian, and the Lūr-s (described below) are probably not "essentially" inegalitarian.

Nomadic pastoralists in Iran provide salient examples of the ethic of egalitarianism existing in circumstances of substantial economic and political inequality. Like the Rwāla bedouin, many other pastoral and nonpastoral tribal groups throughout the Middle East consider themselves equals within their own community. Consider the sheep- and goat-herding Lūr-s in western Iran.[40] They assert that success as a herder is determined by personal qualities and luck. Yet, as their ethnographer, Jacob Black, indicates, the probabilities are high that the wealthiest 10 percent of the population will be able to maintain or increase their wealth, and the remaining 90 percent will have difficulty in maintaining economic viability. In the sense that the Lūr-s possess "no acknowledged leaders, no officers, and no named ranks," they are equal.[41] However, the majority of the population requires economic patrons from the upper stratum of society, which controls larger herds, requires shepherds, and can provide work and salaries for those of the lower strata. Lower strata members have fewer animals, work for others to make up for their lack of capital in animals, and are usually obliged to offer the labor of their sons to larger herd owners, so that control over their sons is weakened.[42] Animal mortality figures provide an index to the consistent and marked difference in control of economic and political resources between the upper and lower strata of Lūr society. The mortality rate for animals owned by the lower 90 percent of the population is 50 percent higher than that for the upper 10 percent.[43]

Lūr-s claim that as equals they are free to opt out of dependent contractual relationships, as Black points out, but doing so essentially means that they must find another patron, which is not always easy. The situation of inequality described by Black may be more extreme than elsewhere in the Middle East, but it calls into question the adequacy of accounts of tribal society that presume that the locally maintained ideologies of equality can be accepted without recourse to an analysis of how they affect, and are affected by, the changing economic and political contexts in which they are maintained and reproduced. Among the Lūr, a few dominant individuals or lineages have effectively controlled political and economic resources over long periods of time, including access to the government over important matters, the allocation of jobs, and other eco-

[40] Jacob Black, "Tyranny as a Strategy for Survival in an 'Egalitarian' Society: Luri Facts versus an Anthropological Mystique," *Man* (N.S.) 7, no. 4 (December 1972), 614–34. A fuller account, unfortunately a posthumous one, is provided by the same author, under the name Jacob Black-Michaud, *Sheep and Land: The Economics of Power in a Tribal Society* (London: Cambridge University Press; Paris: Éditions de la Maison des Sciences de l'Homme, 1986). For a study of another Iranian tribe emphasizing similar themes, see Daniel A. Bradburd, "Never Give a Shepherd an Even Break: Class and Labor Among the Komachi," *American Ethnologist* 7, no. 4 (November 1980), 603–20, and his *Ambiguous Relations.* See also Lois Beck, "Herd Owners and Hired Shepherds: The Qashqa'i of Iran," *Ethnology* 19, no. 3 (July 1980), 327–51.

[41] Black, "Tyranny," p. 623.

[42] Ibid., p. 627. See Bradburd, *Ambiguous Relations,* pp. 106–110, for an illustration of the complexity and bitter awareness of "market forces" with which such negotiations are carried out.

[43] Ibid., p. 631. For an alternative account of the effects of economic processes on social differentiation and settlement as a consequence both of wealth at one end of the economic spectrum and poverty at the other, see Barth, *Nomads,* pp. 101–11.

nomic opportunities. Other Lūr tribespeople have consistently lacked such resources. In these circumstances, the inadequacies of accepting local ideological assertions as adequate "explanations" of political and economic perceptions and practices become increasingly evident. In any case, pastoral nomadic societies are not "closed" societies. Pastoral nomads necessarily sustain economic, political, and social ties with settled communities, both in historical and present-day contexts. Ecological conditions place significant constraints upon pastoral nomadic groups and their social and political options, but the wider political and social contexts in which pastoral nomadic societies exist are of equal, if not greater, significance.

This chapter has indicated some of the reasons why there has been a pronounced concentration by anthropologists on pastoral nomads in their study of the Middle East. I have emphasized shortcomings in the consideration of bedouin society as essentially "closed" and have stressed the need to recognize and study the sustained and necessary ties between pastoralists and nonpastoralists, both in historical and present-day contexts. Ecological conditions place significant constraints upon pastoral nomadic groups and their social and political affairs, but I have indicated reasons why the wider political and social contexts in which pastoral groups exist are also significant.

By providing an extended example of the social organization of a single pastoral group, I have shown that ethnographic description necessarily implies a set of theoretical assumptions and have indicated the problems associated with certain types of anthropological explanation. The next chapter examines these issues in more detail and relates them to the more general topic of the cultural nature of social identity.

FURTHER READINGS

Two books that offer a comprehensive survey of nomads and pastoralists are Anatoly M. Khazanov, *Nomads and the Outside World,* 2nd ed., trans. Julia Crookenden (Madison: University of Wisconsin Press, 1994 [1983]); and Thomas J. Barfield, *The Nomadic Alternative* (Englewood Cliffs, NJ: Prentice Hall, 1993). Khazanov includes a comprehensive assessment of work in Russian on Central and "Inner" Asia and an extensive introduction to the second edition that discusses recent developments in policies toward pastoral peoples and studies of them. The most comprehensive and accessible bibliography of books, maps, and articles on nomads and pastoralists is Fred Scholz, *Nomadismus: Bibliographie* (Berlin: Das Arabische Buch, 1992). Brian Spooner, *The Cultural Ecology of Pastoral Nomads,* Addison-Wesley Module in Anthropology 45 (Reading, MA: Addison-Wesley, 1973), provides a useful review essay of earlier studies, which should be supplemented by the conference proceedings of the Équipe Écologie et Anthropologie des Sociétés Pastorales, *Pastoral Production and Society* (London: Cambridge University Press; Paris: Éditions de la Maison des Sciences de l'Homme, 1979).

Important studies include Fredrik Barth, *Nomads of South Persia* (Prospect Heights, IL: Waveland Press, 1986 [1965]), which is discussed extensively, but unevenly, in Emrys L. Peters, "The Paucity of Ritual Among Middle Eastern Pastoralists," in *Islam in Tribal Societies,* ed. Akbar S. Ahmed and David M. Hart (London and Boston: Routledge &

Kegan Paul, 1984), pp. 187–219; Daniel G. Bates, *Nomads and Farmers: A Study of the Yörük of Southeastern Turkey,* Anthropological Papers 52 (Ann Arbor: University of Michigan, Museum of Anthropology, 1973), showing how nomadic groups decide to settle; I. M. Lewis, *A Pastoral Democracy: A Study of Pastoralism and Politics Among the Northern Somali of the Horn of Africa* (New York: Holmes & Meier, 1982 [1961]); Emanuel Marx, *Bedouin of the Negev* (Manchester, UK: Manchester University Press, 1967); Talal Asad, *The Kababish Arabs: Power, Authority and Consent in a Nomadic Tribe* (London: C. Hurst, 1970); Abbas Ahmed Mohamed, *White Nile Arabs: Political Leadership and Economic Change,* L.S.E. Monographs on Social Anthropology 53 (London: Athlone Press, 1980); Abd al-Ghaffar Muhammad Ahmad, *Shaykhs and Followers: Political Struggle in the Rufa'a al-Hoi Nazirate in the Sudan* (Khartoum: Khartoum University Press, 1974); Abdel Ghaffar M. Ahmed, ed., *Some Aspects of Pastoral Nomadism in the Sudan* (Khartoum: Sudan National Population Committee, 1974); Jeremy M. Keenan, *The Tuareg People of Ahaggar* (New York: St. Martin's Press, 1977), a study of the matrilineal Tuareg; Thomas J. Barfield, *The Central Asian Arabs of Afghanistan* (Austin and London: University of Texas Press, 1981); Richard Tapper, *Pasture and Politics: Economics, Conflict and Ritual Among the Shahsevan Nomads of Northwestern Iran* (New York and London: Academic Press, 1979); Lois Beck, *Nomad: A Year in the Life of a Qashqa'i Tribesman* (Berkeley and Los Angeles: University of California Press, 1991), a fascinating, almost day-to-day account of the personal and collective decisions that nomadic pastoralists must face almost daily; Roy Behnke, Jr., *The Herders of Cyrenaica: Ecology, Economy, and Kinship Among the Bedouin of Eastern Libya,* Illinois Studies in Anthropology 12 (Urbana and London: University of Illinois Press, 1980); and Emanual Marx and Avshalom Shmueli, eds., *The Changing Bedouin* (New Brunswick and London: Transaction Books, 1984). Dawn Chatty, *From Camel to Truck: The Bedouin in the Modern World* (New York: Vantage Press, 1986), provides a readable introduction to the bedouin in Syria; and her *Mobile Pastoralists: Development Planning and Social Change in Oman* (New York: Columbia University Press, 1996), offers equal insight into Oman's present-day pastoralists and the sociology of development bureaucracies. Other monographs dealing with Arabian peninsula bedouin include Donald Powell Cole, *Nomads of the Nomads: The Al Murrah Bedouin of the Empty Quarter* (Prospect Heights, IL: Waveland Press, 1984 [1975]); and William Lancaster, *The Rwala Bedouin Today* (New York and London: Cambridge University Press, 1981). There is an equally impressive literature in French and German. A representative study in French is Jean-Pierre Digard, *Techniques des nomades baxtyâri d'Iran* (Cambridge: Cambridge University Press; Paris: Éditions de la Maison des Sciences de l'Homme, 1981). Representative of German work is Jörg Janzen, *Nomads in the Sultanate of Oman: Tradition and Development in Dhofar,* trans. Alexander Lieven (Boulder, CO, and London: Westview Press, 1986 [1980]), who provides an excellent account of the changing economic and social conditions of settled and pastoral tribal groups in southern Oman and the consequences for them of a major insurgency, officially ended in 1975, and the oil boom. German scholarship is especially well represented in studies of the "Northern Tier" states of the Middle East: Turkey, Iran, and Afghanistan, as well as the Arabian peninsula in recent years.

Another important work is Michael E. Meeker, *Literature and Violence in North Arabia,* Cambridge Studies in Cultural Systems 3 (New York and London: Cambridge University Press, 1979), whose point of departure is the ethnography of the Rwāla bedouin.

5

CITIES IN THEIR PLACE

"Cities aren't isolates, but wide-ranging flows of people, authority systems, cultural symbols, capital innovations."[1] The complexities of urban life pose particular challenges for analysis. Anthropologists, social historians, sociologists, and area specialists have written substantially on cities in the Middle East—less to date on the great cities of Central Asia—but until recently, these discussions have been hampered by several factors. One has been a lack of communication across disciplinary boundaries. Social scientists, on the one hand, knew social theory but were less familiar with materials dealing specifically with the Middle East. For their part, area specialists tended to be so wrapped up in their immediate data that their descriptions rarely posed broad sociological questions. A second factor is that scholars concerned with the nature of the Islamic city as an ideal type by and large did not seek to integrate their analyses with those of scholars concerned with contemporary Middle Eastern cities, who considered the consequences of major economic changes, migration, and rapid population growth.

A final factor—political isolation—has affected work on Central Asia. Until 1970, Russian scholars were obliged to describe urban developments within the strictures of Marxism-Leninism and had only restricted access to Western sources. An additional problem was that historical sources for Central Asian cities are still more limited than those available for the Middle East. Moreover, as many of my Russian and Central Asian colleagues have pointed out, scholars working on the "foreign Muslim East" in the 1970s and late 1980s were subject to less ideological supervision than colleagues working in Soviet Central Asia, so that many preferred not to work intensively within the Soviet Union itself. Moreover, scholars outside of Moscow had only restricted access to Western sources. As a consequence, full-scale studies of Central Asian urban

[1] Robert McC. Adams, "World Picture, Anthropological Frame," *American Anthropologist* 79, no. 2 (June 1977), 268.

history after the Mongol invasions of the thirteenth century began only in 1970. Some of this work took the form of archaeological excavations. Historical work concerned the rapid development of cities such as Tashkent after the eighteenth century (but prior to 1917), development "due to an active commercial relationship between the Russians and the Kazakh nomads."[2] Many of these archaeological and historical studies were directed to supporting theories of the "ethnogenesis" of the various nationalities of Central Asia, a trend that has continued with the post-1989 "new nationalist" ideologies.[3] Notwithstanding these limitations, some excellent work has appeared, such as O. A. Sukhareva's ethnohistory of Bukhara, which includes a history of its 220 urban quarters from the eighth century through the early twentieth century. Notably understudied until the last years of Soviet rule, however, was the role of religious figures in Bukhara's urban history.[4]

Within the last two decades, scholars have joined historical to contemporary concerns in studying Middle Eastern and Central Asian cities. Urban planners who once disregarded or downgraded local traditions in architecture and urban planning now have a renewed interest in it, as do their elite sponsors in the Middle East. As a result, the insights of "area" scholarship are rejoined with broader disciplinary trends in sociology and social history.[5]

In considering cities past and present and their implications for culture and society in general, the magnitude of the growth of the urban population of the Middle East and Central Asia in recent years is an important consideration. In 1900, less than 10 percent of the inhabitants of the Middle East were urban; by midcentury, 28 percent were. By 1980, 47 percent lived in towns and cities, and projections for the year 2000 are for 60 percent. In 1960, only 11 cities in the Middle East had more than 1 million inhabitants. By the late 1980s there were 38 such cities, and another 250 with populations between 100,000 and 500,000.[6]

[2] Hisao Komatsu, "Central Asia," in *Islamic Urban Studies: Historical Review and Perspectives*, ed. Masahi Haneda and Toru Miura (London and New York: Kegan Paul International, 1994), p. 293.

[3] Ibid., and E. N. Chernykh, "Postscript: Russian Archaeology After the Collapse of the USSR—Infrastructural Crisis and the Resurgence of Old and New Nationalisms," in *Nationalism, Politics, and the Practice of Archaeology*, ed. Philip L. Kohl and Clare Fawcett (Cambridge: Cambridge University Press, 1995), pp. 139–48; and Philip L. Kohl and Gocha R. Tsetskhladze, "Nationalism, Politics, and the Practice of Archaeology in the Caucasus," in ibid., pp. 149–74.

[4] Adeeb Khalid, "The Residential Quarter in Bukhara Before the Revolution (The Work of O. A. Sukhareva)," *Middle East Studies Association Bulletin* 25, no. 1 (January 1991), 15–24; and Komatsu, "Central Asia," pp. 295–318.

[5] The best introduction to these trends is presented in the publications of the Aga Khan Award for Architecture (Cambridge: Aga Khan Award for Architecture), based on a series of international seminars: *Toward an Architecture in the Spirit of Islam* (2nd ed., 1980), *Conservation as Cultural Survival* (1980), *Housing Process and Physical Form* (1980), *Architecture as Symbol and Self-Identity* (1980), and *Places of Public Gathering in Islam* (1980). These Aga Khan Award Program volumes convey a lively, multidisciplinary exchange. Several collections of essays serve as guides to major research.

[6] Peter Beaumont, Gerald H. Blake, and J. Malcolm Wagstaff, *The Middle East: A Geographical Study* (London and New York: Wiley, 1976), p. 206; and Abdulaziz Y. Saqqaf, "Introduction," in *The Middle East City: Ancient Traditions Confront a Modern World*, ed. Abdulaziz Y. Saqqaf (New York: Paragon House Publishers, 1987), p. xviii.

Anatoly Khazanov notes that the rural population of Central Asia and Kazakhstan "is usually characterized by low mobility even within their own republics"—only 9 out of 1000 people moved from rural areas to cities in Uzbekistan in 1989, in contrast to 33 out of 1000 in the Soviet Union in general—the figures for urban growth are nonetheless significant, and squatter districts have mushroomed on the outskirts of many Central Asian cities.[7] Thus 23.8 percent of Uzbekistan's population was urban in 1926 (but only 18.3 percent of all Uzbeks lived within their "national" territory), 36.7 percent in 1970 (23 percent of all Uzbeks), and 40.7 percent in 1989 (30.5 percent of all Uzbeks). For Kyrgyzia, 12.0 percent of the population was urban in 1926 (0.8 percent of all Kyrghyz), 37.4 percent in 1970 (14.5 percent of all Kyrghyz), and 38.2 percent in 1989 (21.7 percent of all Kyrghyz).[8] These figures point to a significant non-national population living in the cities and in that sense is analogous to the colonial era in North Africa until midcentury. The seemingly slow growth of the urban population is also explained by a high rural birth rate. Post-1989 figures suggest an increasing out-migration of Russians.

As elsewhere in the world, urban growth in the Middle East and Central Asia tends to be overconcentrated in a few centers. Thus, in Morocco, which, despite accelerated urbanization, remains 55 percent rural, much of the urban population is concentrated on a narrow strip of land extending 150 kilometers north from Casablanca and 50 kilometers inland.[9] Statistics for Casablanca and Cairo dramatize the rapidity of this growth. At the turn of the century, Casablanca had a population of 20,000. By 1936, it had grown to 260,000, one-third of which was European. By 1963, it had over 1 million inhabitants, despite the fact that the European population had dropped to less than 10 percent of the total (and it continues to decline). By 1980, Casablanca's population exceeded 2 million.[10]

Cairo, in 1800, had a population of about 250,000, 600,000 by the turn of the century, 3.7 million by 1960, and 5.7 million by 1970. With the absorption of refugees from the Suez Canal zone after the June 1967 war and a continuing influx of immigrants from other areas, its population reached 8.7 million by 1980. In mid-1986, Egyptian officials reported that the country's population had reached 50 million, having grown by 1 million in the preceding 250 days alone, with about three babies born every minute. Egypt's population has grown tenfold in the last century and a half (and is expected to reach 100 million by the year 2025), but in the same period Cairo's population increased thirtyfold.[11]

[7] Anatoly M. Khazanov, *After the USSR: Ethnicity, Nationalism, and Politics in the Commonwealth of Independent States* (Madison: University of Wisconsin Press, 1995), p. 119.

[8] Figures cited in ibid., p. 261.

[9] Robert Escallier, *Citadins et espace urbain au Maroc*, Research Series 7–8 (Poitiers: Centre Interuniversitaire d'Études Méditerranéenes, 1981), vol. 1, pp. 7–46.

[10] J. Martin, H. Jouver, J. Le Coz, G. Maurer, and D. Noin, *Géographie du Maroc* (Casablanca: Librairie Nationale, 1967), p. 175; and Jean-François Troin, *Le Maghreb: Hommes et espaces*, 2nd ed. (Paris: Armand Colin, 1987), p. 160.

[11] Saad Eddin Ibrahim, "A Sociological Profile," in *The Middle East City*, ed. Saqqaf, p. 216; *The Times* (London), July 24, 1984, p. 14.

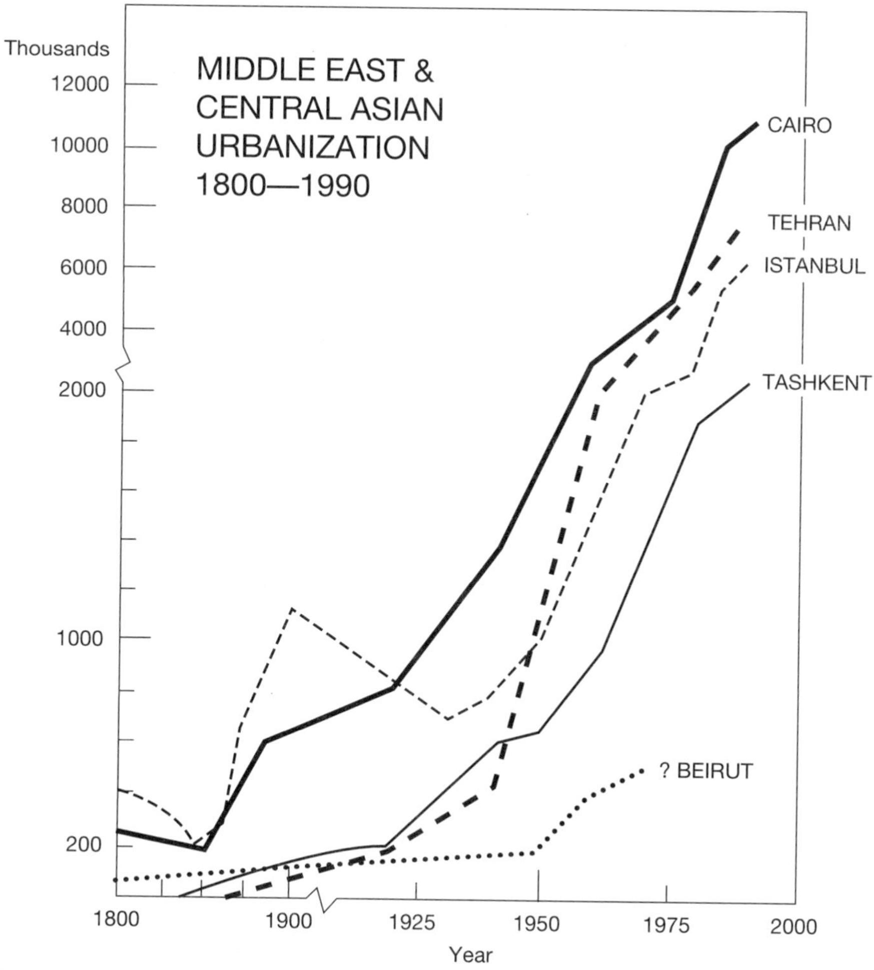

FIGURE 5-1. Urbanization of the Middle East, 1800–1980 (figures are in thousands). [L. Carl Brown, ed., *From Madina to Metropolis* (Princeton, NJ: Darwin Press, 1973), p. 107; and Alan Duben, *The Middle Eastern City: An Urban Management Perspective* (Istanbul: International Union of Local Authorities, 1992).]

Whatever the strains placed on Egyptian society at large, and these were very considerable, they have been intensified and multiplied in the capital city, with an infrastructure created for a much smaller population.

Urban growth in other countries is equally pronounced, with over half of Lebanon's population concentrated in the capital area and less than one-fourth in villages; Tunis contains over half of the country's population, and the Tel Aviv district over half of Israel's. Similar overconcentration occurs elsewhere and shows no sign of reversal.[12]

[12] Beaumont, Blake, and Wagstaff, *The Middle East*, p. 207.

The current pace of urban growth is particularly critical. Historians consider the period 1800–1850 one of rapid urban growth in Europe because the urban population nearly doubled during that time. Yet between 1950 and 1965 alone, the overall population of the Middle East nearly doubled, and the urban population increased at an even faster rate. The population base on which this doubling occurred is, of course, larger than that for early nineteenth-century Europe. But the urban "leaps" in Western Europe and the United States took place in the context of rapid economic development and industrialization. This has not been the case for much of the Middle East, and the resource base is unlikely to increase substantially over what it is today.

The implications of such rapid and massive population growth for the economy, society, and politics of the region cannot be predicted from statistical trends alone, although one scholar, reflecting on the "rapid" population growth in the 1950s and 1960s, suggested that its consequences included a "segmental" modernization, with some elements of the population benefiting from economic growth disproportionately; a greater tendency for the politics of the street, with urban crowding and the flow of political and economic refugees into the centers of power threatening political stability; and the greater challenge faced by all states, regardless of their capacities or inclinations, to improve the welfare of their subjects.[13] This prediction has proven generally accurate.[14]

THE "ISLAMIC" CITY IN THE MIDDLE EAST

Any assessment of the social and political implications of contemporary urban growth in the Middle East and Central Asia necessitates an understanding of the social history of urban development in the two regions. The discussion here primarily concerns the Middle East, although the issues posed for Central Asia, on the basis of available studies in English, appear largely comparable to those of the Middle East. Until recently, scholars tended to deal with earlier urban forms in terms of the "Islamic" city. Taken literally, the notion implies that Islam prescribes or encourages particular urban forms; but most scholars have applied the term only to cities where Muslims have been predominant, and it is in this sense that the term is being reintroduced.

Earlier approaches were handicapped by the question posed by the German sociologist Max Weber. Why, Weber asked, did a distinct form of urban organization, the commune, arise only in medieval Europe and not elsewhere? Weber discerned a distinctly urban, corporate form of social organization in European towns that distinguished them from the larger society of which they

[13] J. C. Hurewitz, "The Politics of Rapid Population Growth in the Middle East," *Journal of International Affairs* 19, no. 1 (1965), 26–38.

[14] See Guilain Denoeux, *Urban Unrest in the Middle East: A Comparative Study of Informal Networks in Egypt, Iran, and Lebanon*, SUNY Series in the Social and Economic History of the Middle East (Albany: State University of New York Press, 1993).

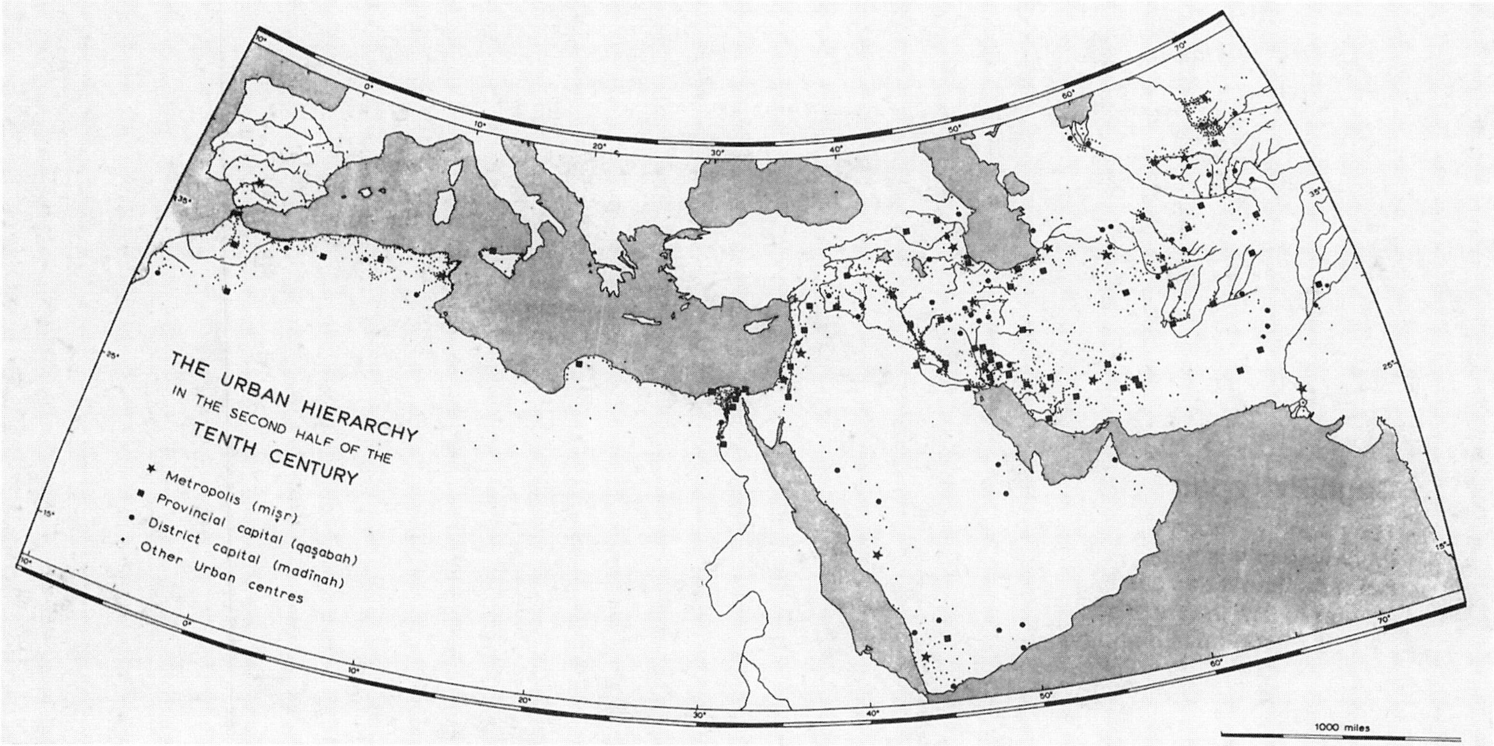

FIGURE 5-2. Urban hierarchy of the Islamic Middle East in the tenth century. [From Paul Wheatley, "Levels of Space Awareness in the Traditional Islamic City," *Ekistics* 42, no. 253 (December 1976), 360. Courtesy of the author and publisher.]

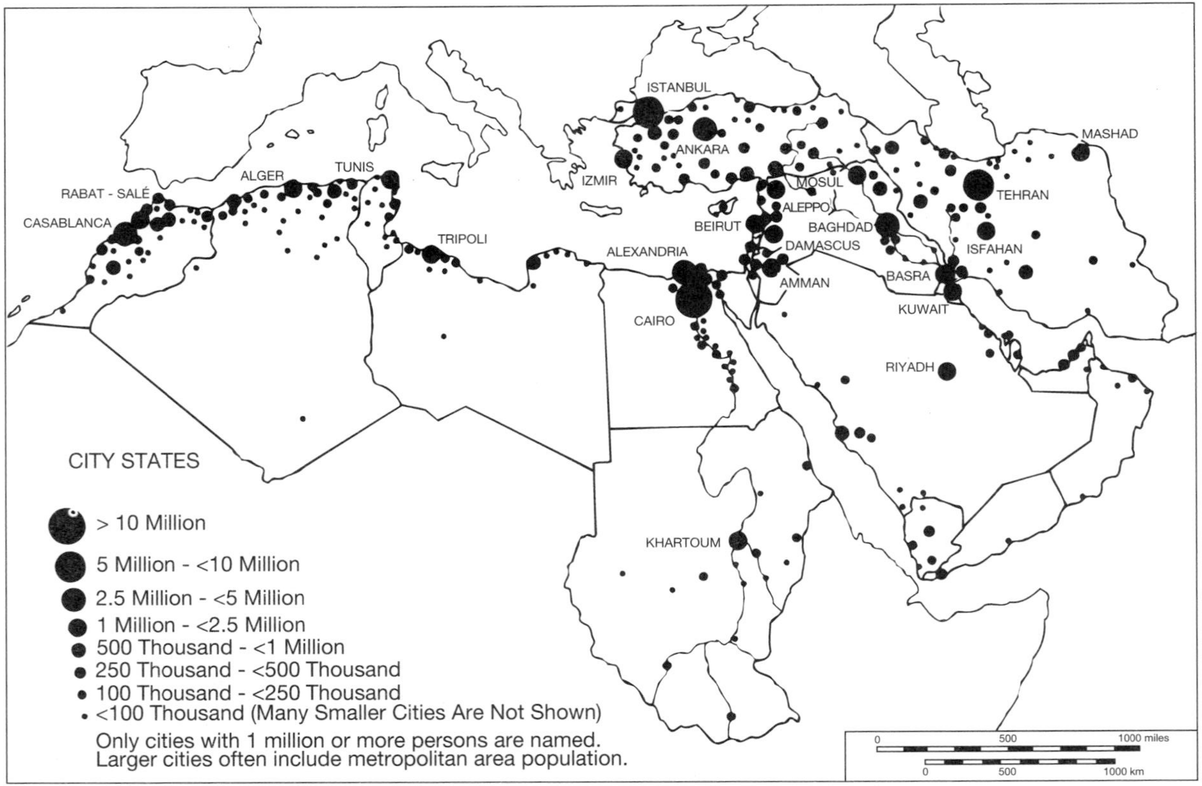

FIGURE 5-3. The distribution of cities today suggests that population is overconcentrated in a few major cities. (Not all smaller cities are shown on this map.) [Compiled and designed by Michael E. Bonine. Data from *The Middle East and North Africa*, 34th ed. (London: Europa Publications Ltd., 1987); G. Blake, J. Dewdney, and J. Mitchell, *The Cambridge Atlas of the Middle East and North Africa* (New York: Cambridge University Press, 1987); publications of URBAMA (Tours); and other written sources and maps.]

formed a part, but he found no equivalent in the orient.[15] His discussion of cities elsewhere merely served as a backdrop for what he regarded as the uniqueness of cities in the West. Despite the fact that many traditional cities in the Muslim world were often set apart from their surroundings by towering walls (as were many cities in medieval Europe), in general they possessed little autonomy from the state and no distinctive *formal* organization.

Led by Weber's formulation of comparative urbanism and similar notions posed by other scholars, some orientalists unsuccessfully sought the equivalent to European communes in the Muslim world. For example, the French orientalist Louis Massignon (1883–1962) argued that the "guilds" of merchants and craftsmen in the Muslim Middle East served much the same purpose as the communes, but he never produced evidence to support his assertion. As one critic commented, despite Massignon's stature as a scholar, his work on urban forms abused evidence and constituted no more than a "tissue of fallacies."[16] Other scholars got bogged down in descriptivism, enumerating the features that appeared to characterize particular Islamic cities or "the" Islamic city as an ideal type. Features such as the presence of mosques, marketplaces, and public baths were suggested as essential characteristics of Islamic cities, but exceptions can be found to each of these enumerations. For example, virtually every rural local community in Morocco has a mosque, although not, of course, as impressive as those of the great urban centers, and many markets in Morocco occurred independently of cities. An enumeration of such features cannot in itself distinguish towns from villages. Other scholars have represented the characteristics of towns as enumerated by Muslim theologians.[17]

As the morphology and functioning of cities throughout the Islamic world became better known, the inadequacies of stereotypic notions of Islamic cities became increasingly apparent. For instance, Bonine argued that the grid-like form of medieval Iranian cities is derived primarily from the exigencies of irrigation systems and is not an outgrowth of specifically Islamic influences. Lapidus reminded scholars that Muslim conquerors often took over cities from earlier rulers and did not build them anew, and the balance between urban and nonurban populations was not significantly changed by the Islamic conquests,

[15] Max Weber, *Economy and Society*, ed. Guenther Roth and Claus Wittich (New York: Bedminster Press, 1968), pp. 1212–36, esp. pp. 1226 and 1233. For the relevant literature concerning the Middle East, see A. H. Hourani, "The Islamic City in the Light of Recent Research," in *The Islamic City*, ed. A. H. Hourani and S. M. Stern (Philadelphia: University of Pennsylvania Press, 1970), pp. 9–24; Dale F. Eickelman, "Is There an Islamic City? The Making of a Quarter in a Moroccan Town," *International Journal of Middle East Studies* 5, no. 3 (June 1974), 274–78; Bryan S. Turner, *Weber and Islam: A Critical Study* (London and Boston: Routledge & Kegan Paul, 1974), pp. 93–106; and Janet Abu-Lughod, "The Islamic City—Historic Myth, Islamic Essence, and Contemporary Relevance," *International Journal of Middle East Studies* 19, no. 2 (May 1987), 155–76.

[16] S. M. Stern, "The Constitution of the Islamic City," in *The Islamic City*, ed. Hourani and Stern, pp. 37–42.

[17] For example, Gustave E. von Grunebaum, "The Sacred Character of Islamic Cities," in *Mélanges Ṭaha Ḥuṣain*, ed. A. Badawī (Cairo: Dār al-Ma'ārif 1962), pp. 25–37.

FIGURE 5-4. Traditional southern Arabian architecture. For defensive purposes, there are no windows on lower stories. [From Freya Stark, *Seen in the Hadhramaut* (London: John Murray, Publishers, Ltd., 1939), p. 19. Courtesy of the author and publisher.]

despite the fact that many orientalists have characterized Islam (misleadingly) as an "urban" religion.[18]

Many meticulously detailed descriptive monographs concerning "representative" Islamic cities have emerged over the last half century. Thus Le Tourneau built his massive study of Fez on the assumption that the city's spatial layout and its economic, political, and social institutions until just prior to French conquest in 1912 had remained essentially the same for half a millennium.[19] This presumed stasis of urban forms encouraged some scholars to think of Islamic cities as living counterparts to medieval European cities. The atemporal assumptions and misplaced analogies of the French tradition concerning the nature of Islamic cities did not prevent the resulting descriptive ethnographies and historical studies from becoming irreplaceable primary documentation.

One of the first breakthroughs in the scholarly impasse of how Islamic cities were studied was the appearance in 1967 of Ira Lapidus's *Muslim Cities*.[20]

[18] Michael E. Bonine, "The Morphogenesis of Iranian Cities," *Annals of the Association of American Geographers* 69, no. 2 (June 1979), 208–24; Ira M. Lapidus, "The Evolution of Muslim Urban Society," *Comparative Studies in Society and History* 15, no. 1 (January 1973), 21–50.

[19] Roger Le Tourneau, *Fès avant le Protectorat*, Institut des Hautes Études marocaines, Publications 45 (New York: AMS Press, 1978 [1949]). For contemporary Fez, see Anton Escher and Eugen Wirth, *Die Medina von Fes*, Erlanger Geographische Arbeiten 53 (Erlangen: Fränkische Geographische Gesellschaft, 1992), with outstanding maps.

[20] Ira M. Lapidus, *Muslim Cities in the Later Middle Ages*, 2nd ed. (Cambridge and New York: Cambridge University Press, 1984 [1967]). This study should be supplemented with Michael Chamberlain, *Knowledge and Social Practice in Medieval Damascus, 1190–1350*, Cambridge Studies in Islamic Civilization (Cambridge: Cambridge University Press, 1994).

Essentially, Lapidus changed the sociological questions asked. Rather than search for social forms that were unique to cities, as suggested by the approach of Weber, Lapidus instead sought to delineate the social forms that were *in* cities and allowed for the orderly conduct of social life. His emphasis was on such fundamental social institutions as families and quarters, religious organization, and how the administrative machinery of the state effectively worked. For Lapidus, "Muslim cities are cities by virtue of social processes which are not peculiar to any given culture, but they are Muslim by virtue of the predominance of subcommunities which embodied Muslim beliefs and a Muslim way of life." It is the interaction of the various subcommunities and of the various elites that created the urban community and achieved a "sufficiently good order."[21] There were informal, but crucial, cross-cutting patterns of kinship, religion, politics, and economics. He focuses on the nature and the comparison of social structures rather than cities themselves, firmly breaking with Weber's approach to discussing urban forms.

Lapidus's analysis is in general congruent with the recurrent argument of this book that many of the most significant patterns of constancy and order in Middle Eastern cultures are to be found in what scholars earlier dismissed as "informal" social groupings. There are shared cultural perceptions of how people relate to each other that do not necessarily manifest themselves in the form of organized groups or classes.

One of the ways in which these underlying cultural notions of the social order are manifested is in their influence on spatial perceptions and use.[22] This relationship has been a long-standing concern in Middle Eastern studies, but the way the issue is discussed has shifted substantially in recent years. An earlier generation of colonial ethnographers considered the confusing—from a European perspective—maze of narrow, winding streets and blind alleys of traditional North African cities (*madīna*-s) a direct spatial projection of the "alogical" disorder of the "indigenous mentality," a notion that unfortunately has not entirely disappeared from the scholarly corpus.[23] There is no generalizing principle that allows a person to get from one place to another on the basis of abstract spatial criteria. In essence, one learns how to get from one point to another by having gone there before. Even in smaller towns in North Africa, it is not uncommon for people from one part of town to get lost in unfamiliar sec-

[21] Lapidus, "Evolution," 47–48. See also Richard W. Bulliet, *The Patricians of Nishapur*, Harvard Middle Eastern Studies 16 (Cambridge, MA: Harvard University Press, 1972). Roy P. Mottahedeh, *Loyalty and Leadership in an Early Islamic Society* (Princeton, NJ: Princeton University Press, 1980), has most thoroughly developed the notion of implicit "informal" assumptions concerning self, community, and loyalty in an argument confined neither to an urban elite nor to "early" Muslim societies.

[22] See Wheatley, "Levels."

[23] *Madīna* in Arabic means "town" or "city." In North Africa it has taken on the narrower connotation of the older "native" component of contemporary cities. The quotations are from Louis Brunot, in Georges Hardy, *L'âme marocaine d'après la littérature française* (Paris: Librairie Émile Larose, 1926), p. 20; and Xavier de Planhol, *The World of Islam* (Ithaca, NY: Cornell University Press, 1959), pp. 14–15 [original French 1957].

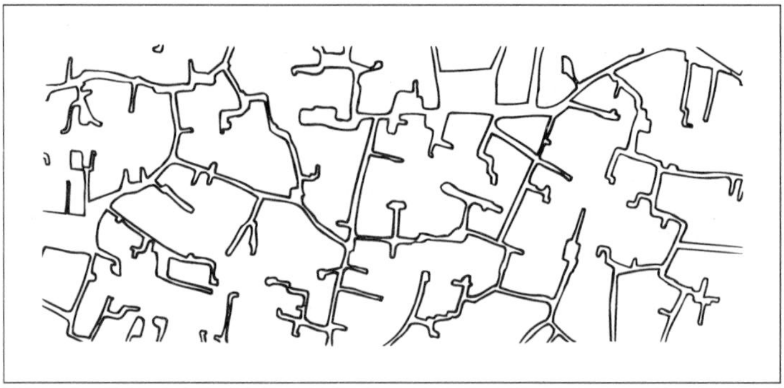

FIGURE 5-5. The winding streets and blind alleys of traditional North African cities constituted a puzzle for colonial ethnographers. [Courtesy of the author.]

tions, and residents routinely ask "strangers" from elsewhere in the town what they are doing there. Residential quarters and houses within them have never been clearly distinguishable in any exterior way, by wealth or other criteria, although in southwest Asian cities such as Antioch, Beirut, Damascus, and Baghdad, sectarian groups generally cluster in separate urban quarters.[24] With the exception of the former Jewish quarters (*mallāḥ*-s) in many towns, such separation is generally lacking in North Africa.

Four discernible patterns of spatial order can be found in most precolonial Middle Eastern cities: the relation of towns to the state, the market (*sūq*) or economic complex, the relation of religious institutions to the town, and the organization of residential and domestic space.[25] These various principles of order overlap. The presence of the central power is often represented by a separate, fortified quarter either within the larger cities or alongside them. In North Africa such a compound is called a *qaṣba*, or fortress. Soldiers or government representatives were settled in this compound and usually were distinguishable from other townsfolk. The traditional patterns of the complex of economic

[24] Jacques Weulersse, "Antioche: Essai de géographie urbaine," *Bulletin d'Études Orientales* 4 (1934), 27–80; John Gulick, "Baghdad: Portrait of a City in Physical and Cultural Change," *AIP Journal* 33 (July 1967), 246–55.

[25] F. Stambouli and A. Zghal, "Urban Life in Precolonial North Africa," *British Journal of Sociology* 27, no. 1 (March 1976), 1–20. In spite of their regional specificity, the principles of order applied specifically to North Africa serve as useful guides, especially their interesting summary of the "informal" status of elite authority and the general lack of importance of organized groups and classes. See the text and accompanying photographs in James Kirkman, ed., *City of Ṣan'ā'* (London: World of Islam Festival Publishing Co., 1976); and the encyclopedic *Ṣan'ā': An Arabian Islamic City*, ed. R. B. Serjeant and Ronald Lewcock (London: World of Islam Festival Trust, 1983). A note on terminology is useful here. *Sūq* is an Arabic term. Its equivalents in the Northern Tier are *bāzār* in Persian, perhaps the term most familiar to Anglophones, and *çarşi* in Turkish. The equivalent term for towns or cities is *shahr* (*şehir* in Turkish). Sometimes reversals in meaning occur as terms migrate from language to language. Thus the Arabic *qaṣba* ("fortress") becomes *qasaba* in Persian and means "small town" or "village," and the Turkish *kasaba* likewise means "town." I am grateful to Richard Tapper for pointing out these usages.

FIGURE 5-6. Covered *sūq*, Tetouan, Morocco. Major commercial streets are often partially separated from residential ones. [Courtesy of the author.]

activity have been analyzed by Clifford Geertz.[26] There is a tendency for commercial and craft activities to be separated from places of residence, so that, with the exception of small shops within residential quarters, most mercantile activities and the circulation of people, carts, and animals associated with them are removed from the semiprivate space of residential quarters. There is also a tendency for commercial and artisanal activities to be hierarchically ordered, with the more prestigious closest to the principal mosque and others located on the main arteries.

The religious institutions cross-cut many of the other notions of order. In larger urban centers such as Tunis and Fez, the principal mosque is the place for the Friday sermon and the rituals associated with major feast days. In the past, it also served as a place of learning, and frequently it was the focal point for public protest in times of civil unrest. This symbolic centrality of the mosque was often replicated by its spatial centrality. In Tunis, the mosque is accessible by major arteries leading to the principal gates of the *madīna*, facilitating access from all residential quarters. Finally, there are the maraboutic, or saint's,

[26] Clifford Geertz, "Suq: The Bazaar Economy in Sefrou," in Clifford Geertz, Hildred Geertz, and Lawrence Rosen, *Meaning and Order in Moroccan Society: Three Essays in Cultural Analysis* (New York: Cambridge University Press, 1979), pp. 123–313. There are numerous excellent studies in French for the entire Middle East and in French and German for Afghanistan and Iran. For example, on the social and ritual organization of guilds in Tashqurghan in northern Afghanistan, see Pierre Centlivre, *Un bazar d'Asie centrale* (Wiesbaden: Reichert, 1972).

shrines associated with each city or town, which even today serve occasionally as focal points of communal activities.

A final principle of order is the division of traditional *madīna*-s into residential quarters, with the households of each quarter claiming multiple personal ties and common interests based on varying combinations of kinship, common origin, ethnicity, patronage and clientship, participation in factional alliances, and spatial propinquity itself. In a small Moroccan town in which I conducted research between 1968 and 1970, residents divided the town into anything from 30 to 43 quarters. The fact that there is such a discrepancy in how townspeople evaluate space even in such a small setting indicates that space is not conceived entirely in a fixed way. How quarters were evaluated depended on what people knew of the social history of the town, which varied with generation and social position, and formative experiences shared with other people in the community. The demarcation of quarters cannot always be discerned by physical signs. Many are clustered around impasses, but this is not always the case. For one thing, the social boundaries of many quarters are subject to modification; for another, not all houses are necessarily thought to be part of quarters. Only those clusters of households sustaining a particular quality of life are known as quarters.

In Morocco, that quality of life is defined by the extension in contiguous physical space of the notion of "closeness" (*qarāba*); component households in a quarter assume that they share a certain moral unity, so in some respects social space in the quarter can be regarded as an extension of the households within it. This closeness is symbolized in a number of ways: the exchange of visits on feast days; assistance and participation in the activities connected with births, circumcisions, weddings, and funerals of component households; and the like. The heads of a quarter's households share certain minimal collective responsibilities. They often construct and maintain a mosque and hire a Quranic teacher for it. Because of the multiple ties that link the residents of a quarter, respectable women who never venture to the main market can circulate discreetly within the quarter, because the residents all assume a closeness to each other. As long as a quarter had notables or prominent persons capable of acting as their leaders, some sort of claim of common descent or origin, and the ability at least in some contexts to act collectively, it constituted a feature in people's shared conceptual image of the town.

As the distribution of power, authority, and prestige shifts, so does the conception of space. Thus, despite the apparent "disarray" of such spatial conceptions to outsiders, they follow an articulate cultural logic. Similar conceptions of space appear to prevail elsewhere in the Middle East. To use Kevin Lynch's term, the *imageability* of residential space in the Middle East is not principally in terms of physical landmarks but in shared conceptions of the social order. The cultural bases of these conceptions can be abstractly delineated, but a particular knowledge is needed for orientation in the social space of each town. John Gulick's study of Tripoli, Lebanon, suggests that the notion of imageability is more useful when it encompasses not only visual form (Lynch's emphasis) but also those that are socioculturally significant in both "modern" and traditional settings. A study of Amman, Jordan, indicates significant continuities between the social and spatial orders discerned for both "Islamic cities and contemporary urban forms, especially in neighborhood mosque constructions, government-sponsored architectural innovations, and the use of space by men and women.[27] For Central Asia, the network of urban quarters (*mehelle*-s) remains one of the few features not destroyed by decades of Soviet rule. At a Tājik wedding in Samarkand in October 1992, for example, quarter residents informally gathered together to frustrate the efforts of security officials who would not allow foreign guests to speak privately with "unrecognized" Tājik community leaders.[28]

COLONIAL CITIES AND THEIR LEGACY

Colonial principles of spatial order are particular instances of the projection of dominant cultural values or, to be more precise, the values of the dominating political power. The colonial cities of French North Africa, especially in Morocco, provide particularly clear examples of the basic principles of colonial urban planning. If India was the colony on which Great Britain lavished the most elaborate attention, then Morocco was its equivalent for France. Colonial cities were not just the juxtaposition of the urban forms of the dominating power and the dominated. They were new creations with specific and lasting social consequences.[29] In cities such as Casablanca, commercial and economic interests were so powerful and growth so rapid that colonial authorities were unable to plan effectively for rational growth and development. Elsewhere, however, the French developed almost Cartesian plans to articulate the legitimizing ideology of colonial domination. One of the myths of legitimacy used by the French in Tunisia and Morocco was that they were not a colonial power. "Native" regimes were maintained intact in both countries, and these regimes were "aided" by the authorities of the protectorate, who acted in the name of the Muslim rulers. Technically, the French role was one of preserving native institutions.

The consequence for urban planning—and, in the case of Morocco, every town had a developmental plan by the 1930s—was a basic dualism in urban

[27] Kevin Lynch, *The Image of the City* (Cambridge, MA: MIT Press, 1960); John Gulick, "Images of an Arab City," *Journal of the American Institute of Planners* 29, no. 3 (August 1963), 196–97. For Marrakesh, Morocco, see Mohamed Boughali, *La représentation de l'espace chez le marocain illettré* [The Representation of Space Among Illiterate Moroccans] (Paris: Éditions Anthropos, 1974). On Amman, see Eugene Lawrence Rogan, "Physical Islamization in Amman," *Muslim World* 76, no. 1 (January 1986), 24–42.

[28] Dale F. Eickelman, field notes, October 1992. The same incident is described by Mark Katz, "On the Silk Road," *National Interest* (Winter 1992/93), 84–86.

[29] See Anthony D. King, *Colonial Urban Development: Culture, Social Power and Environment* (London: Routledge & Kegan Paul, 1976); also Janet L. Abu-Lughod, *Rabat: Urban Apartheid in Morocco* (Princeton, NJ: Princeton University Press, 1980).

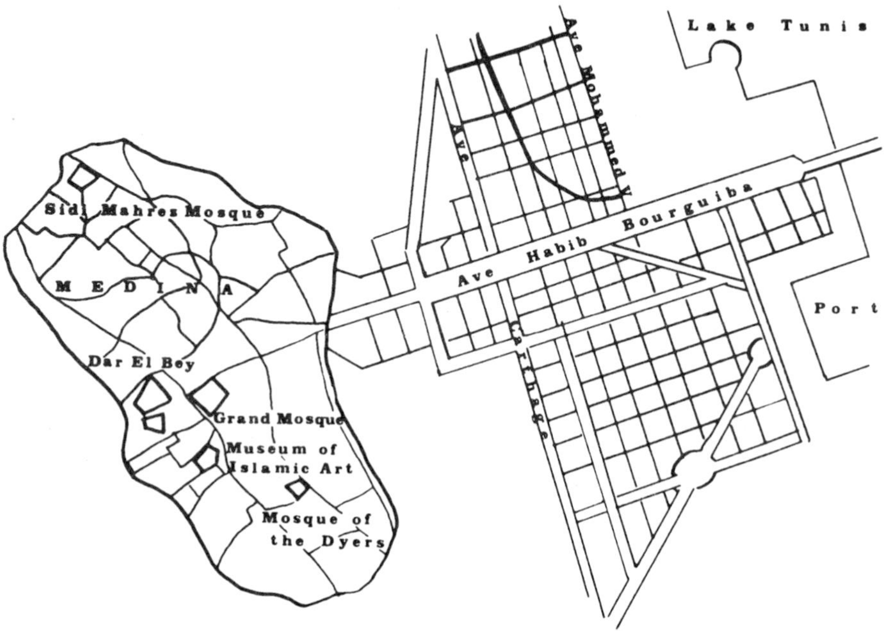

FIGURE 5-7. "Tunis showing juxtaposition of old and new city, and Bourguiba Avenue as battering ram against old city." [From L. Carl Brown, ed., *From Madina to Metropolis* (Princeton, NJ: Darwin Press, 1973), p. 29. Courtesy L. Carl Brown and Darwin Press, Inc.]

growth. In nearly every case, the "traditional" *madīna* was preserved more or less intact, while a "new" town, meant primarily but not exclusively for Europeans, grew up alongside it. In some cases, two "new" towns were created: one for "evolved" natives, another for Europeans. The overall shape of the town of Tunis (see Figure 5-7) suggests how this philosophy was spatially projected. As some Tunisians comment, the overall street plan takes the form of a cross being rammed into the *madīna*, making the colonial imagery even more suggestive. One plan for Tunis, elaborated during the Vichy regime but never carried out, took colonial planning one step farther. The "modern" part of Tunis was divided along one main axis between Christians and Muslims (with a few "neutral" places in between) and along the other axis between bourgeoisie and workers, thus using the principles of religion and class for the spatial ordering of society. In the name of security and hygiene, colonial urban planning, like its postcolonial successors, often provides a physical projection of state authority, controlling and disciplining in the ways so skillfully described by Michel Foucault for ideas of disease and punishment in the West.[30]

[30] I am grateful to Ellen C. Micaud (personal communication) for describing Vichy plans for Tunis. For Michel Foucault, see his *Birth of the Clinic: An Archaeology of Medical Perception*, trans. A. M. Sheridan Smith (New York: Vintage Books, 1975), and *Discipline and Punish: The Birth of the Prison*, trans. Alan Sheridan (New York: Vintage Books, 1979).

The initial colonial planning for Morocco, from the inception of the protectorate in 1912 until the 1930s, was highly coherent and based on three principles.[31] The first was that *madīna*-s were to be separated from European quarters. This division corresponded to what the French saw as the fundamentally "different" mentalities of Muslims and Europeans. Thus it was argued that most "traditional" Moroccans preferred to be insulated from the outside world so that the vitality of traditional life could be preserved. Although an effort was made to provide the *madīna*-s with improved sewers, water systems, and electricity, the seeds were planted for many *madīna*-s to deteriorate into historic slums, dying a slow death of benign neglect. There were exceptions for cities such as Salé and Tetouan, where many of the traditional bourgeoisie maintained houses for reasons of prestige, but the overall trend, especially after the economic dislocations of World War II, was to abandon such housing to impoverished rural immigrants.

A second principle was for town planning to protect the cultural heritage. Colonial planners enforced strict regulations designed to protect the town as an overall monument, a notion that began to be applied internationally in most countries only by the 1960s. As Jean Dethier suggests, whatever the intentions of the planners, Moroccans often interpreted the decision to retain walls around the *madīna* as a security measure. In fact, some of the older "native" housing developments, one in the phosphate mining center of Khouribga and the other in Casablanca, had walls with guards posted at the gates for just such a purpose, although the security was ostensibly for the inhabitants of the developments and not against them.

The final notion was that of constructing the "new" cities according to the most up-to-date principles of planning. The result for many Moroccan towns was the provision of parks and green spaces (often serving as a buffer between European and Moroccan quarters) and zoning regulations that, except for Casablanca, adequately managed to control the direction of growth. The state also purchased tracts of land that were then sold under strict controls to prevent speculation. Public buildings were designed and situated to contribute to the overall symmetry of towns, and town planners took special care to use distinctive features of local topography. With the exception of the provision of "evolved" native quarters, until the late 1940s, such planning was primarily for the benefit of Europeans, as if the political and economic transformations of the colonial regime could leave the indigenous population undisturbed. And in the "evolved" settlements, the proviso that construction had to begin immediately and according to strict (and expensive) specifications ensured that only wealthier Moroccans could take advantage of them.

Despite the efforts of colonial authorities, "clandestine" housing emerged, especially in the form of the shantytowns, or *bidonvilles*, whose inhabitants were primarily emigrants from rural areas. Such "temporary" housing has

[31] Jean Dethier, "Evolution of Concepts of Housing, Urbanism, and Country Planning in a Developing Country: Morocco, 1900–1972," in *From Madina to Metropolis*, ed. L. Carl Brown (Princeton: Darwin Press, 1973), pp. 197–243; and Abu-Lughod, *Rabat*, pp. 131–274.

FIGURE 5-8. Bidonville, Bni Msīk, Casablanca, 1968. Such "temporary" housing as this has become a permanent feature of many Middle Eastern cities. [Photograph by D. Papini. Daniel Noin, *La population rurale du Maroc* (Paris: Presses Universitaires de France, 1970), plate 48. Used by permission of the publisher.]

become a permanent feature of most large Middle Eastern cities, with local variations such as Cairo's "City of the Dead," where families have taken above-ground tombs for housing. Studies that have been conducted on the value of land in shantytowns indicate that unscrupulous realtors can realize a larger profit from collecting rents from such lands than in building more expensive housing. When the land is needed for other purposes, the shacks on it technically can be cleared, although actual exercise of such rights involves political risks. Planners often have thought of shantytowns as a passing phenomenon, but attempts after World War II by the protectorate government and by Morocco's independent government have never effectively managed to stem their growth. Analogous developments occurred throughout the Middle East; in Turkey fully 13 percent of the urban population live in shantytowns (*gecekondu*-s), and in many towns of the Middle East, the figure may be significantly higher.[32]

The planning policies of independent regimes throughout the Middle East unsurprisingly reflect the ideology of dominant groups which often incorporate the legacy of colonial assumptions concerning urban life. Ellen Micaud has produced what amounts to an ethnography of successive urban plans for postindependence Tunis. Immediately after independence in 1956, the Tunisian elite viewed the *madīna* as an obstacle to be surmounted so that the country could have "a capital worthy of the active modernizing image being fashioned on all fronts."[33] After independence, the exodus of all who could afford to leave

[32] Alan Duben, "Review of Kemal Karpat, *The Gecekondu: Rural Migration and Urbanization*," *Middle East Studies Association Bulletin* 12, no. 3 (December 1978), 50.

[33] Ellen C. Micaud, "Urbanization, Urbanism, and the Medina of Tunis," *International Journal of Middle East Studies* 9, no. 4 (November 1978), 433.

the *madīna* for other housing accelerated rapidly, leaving the *madīna* to rural immigrants and others who had no active say in its future; and the nationalization of pious endowments in 1957 radically changed its economic and legal structure.

Some visionary urban planners called for the neglect of the *madīna*, considering it an obsolete relic of a colonial past (after all, colonial authorities considered the old quarters as historic monuments) to be overcome. This stage of postindependence planning can in some ways be considered an implicit acceptance of the colonial devaluation of the *madīna*, in the sense that it was associated with an inferior status and an unvalued past. In the late 1960s, with the burgeoning of the tourist industry, there was a tendency to regard the *madīna* as part of the cultural heritage, and various plans, some the subject of international competitions, were evolved in an effort to regard it as part of the national tourist business.

A final, more realistic phase was begun in 1973 with more modest projects but ones designed to encourage the maintenance of housing within the *madīna* (through legislation to facilitate owner-occupied dwellings) and to provide subsidies for various craft and artisanal activities. Planners began to realize that it was not possible to allow any further deterioration of the *madīna*, given the housing crisis throughout the capital region. Only after two decades of independence has it been possible to regard the *madīna* as an integral and enduring part of Tunisia's heritage and living present.

The Soviet/Russian legacy in Central Asia also reflects a colonial heritage. Tashkent is today a city of over 2 million people. Although the Russian population is rapidly diminishing, it remains important, as do the large number of Uzbeks who are, as Ted Levin writes, "not only bi-ethnic, but in their daily lives, actively bi-cultural."[34] In the 1880s, Uzbeks and other Asians lived in the old quarters on one side of the Ankhor River, while the Russians built a new town on the other side. Levin describes Tashkent today as four cities in one. First, there is the old city of "crooked streets, walled-off houses set in courtyards, . . . and small neighborhood shops and bazaars." Much of this part of the city disappeared with the earthquake that destroyed part of Tashkent in 1966. For instance, "the rambling central bazaar has been superseded by a circular concrete domed market surrounded by a large parking lot." The second city is what remains of Russian Tashkent of the colonial era, with broad avenues radiating from a central square, and smaller streets leading to "thick-walled one-story bungalows and villas set in large gardens." The third city, "creeping out like a fungus" into both colonial Tashkent and the old city, is Soviet Tashkent, built with little regard for local sensibilities and dominated by massive public buildings and rectangular apartment blocks.[35] Finally, on the outskirts of Soviet

[34] Theodore Levin, *The Hundred Thousand Fools of God: Musical Travels in Central Asia* (Bloomington: Indiana University Press, 1996), p. 7.

[35] Ibid., p. 9, where Levin narrates a fascinating interview with the architect who designed much of Soviet Tashkent, explaining the lack of fit between his personal interest in the "harmony" of Islamic architecture with what he created in Tashkent.

Tashkent is the "new Uzbek Tashkent," a "reimagination" of traditional life "in newly built neighborhoods of individual houses, each with its own walled courtyard," in which the newly rich "try to outdo one another in the grandeur of their houses, especially in the room for entertaining guests."[36]

CITIES NOW

The study of cities necessarily involves interdisciplinary approaches. Fuad I. Khuri, who studied urbanization in the greater Beirut region prior to the 1975 Lebanese civil war, sees Middle Eastern urban studies as falling into three categories that remain valid today.[37] First is what he calls the survey approach: the compilation of demographic data that indicate something about the age distribution of urban residents as opposed to those of the country, levels of consumption, size and density of urban areas, and other such indices. In the main, he states, such compilations of statistics are part of international efforts to assess the extent of urbanization and the administrative problems associated with it.[38]

A second major approach is the study of particular issues—religious beliefs and practices, child rearing, social classes, and educational practices—in terms of urban-rural contrasts, sectarian differences, and socioeconomic backgrounds. According to Khuri, the difficulty with most such studies is that they accept uncritically the validity of the categories used, such as rural and urban. They often do not provide a comprehensive theory of the nature of urban life with which the various characteristics attributed to urban and rural communities or to various socioeconomic classes can be systematically linked. He suggests that many studies (with the exception of Janet Abu-Lughod's meticulous analysis of the demography, socioeconomic characteristics, and social history of every major district of Cairo) have ignored the impressive changes that have modified the "social character" of Middle Eastern cities since the 1930s, and are written, instead, as if villages or cities were constants.[39] Khuri's community study of two contrasting Beirut suburbs did not assume such constancy. His approach to their analysis was to deal "with a wide range of structures, organizations, institutions, customs, socioeconomic differentiation, and political action." In contrast to the Western pattern of specialized suburban communities, many of which serve as dormitories for nearby business and industrial districts, Khuri indicated that there was a tendency for Lebanese suburban communities to be economically independent and self-contained. He concluded that in the communities studied, "class is the least

[36] Ibid., p. 9.

[37] Fuad I. Khuri, *From Village to Suburb: Order and Change in Greater Beirut* (Chicago and London: University of Chicago Press, 1975), pp. 1–15.

[38] Ibid., p. 2.

[39] Janet L. Abu-Lughod, *Cairo: 1001 Years of the City Victorious*, Princeton Studies on the Near East (Princeton, NJ: Princeton University Press, 1971).

important instrument of organization. Neither neighborhoods, quarters, or suburbs, nor voluntary associations, societies, clubs, or political constellations are based on class affinities."[40]

Reflecting on Beirut more than a decade after the 1975 civil war, Khuri described its semi-independent urban nuclei as separate "tents," opportunistically combining and opposing one another for short-term advantage. (It is interesting to note that Khuri employs a "bedouin" imagery to evoke for readers a state of near-anarchy.) In 1980, together with his students, he counted 42 militias, parapolitical and paramilitary "associations" that divided up the city "perhaps consciously, and more likely unconsciously, into mutually exclusive spheres or zones of influence, or what they call 'operation grounds' "; the presence of one excludes the others. In this situation, the twisted streets mirror "social agglomerations interwoven by kinship and traditional ties of neighborliness," one in which "the urban society is fitted into a social map, not a spatial one."[41] In his view, these various "endogamous solidarities" are grafted onto the wider polity without being assimilated by it. His description in many ways echoes Roy Mottahedeh's account of trust and loyalty in the time of the Būyid dynasty of tenth- and eleventh-century Iraq and Iran, a time in which political authority was weak or unreliable, but commercial and social life carried on in a reasonably orderly fashion.

Khuri's argument concerning sectarian identity and residential area deserves careful attention because elsewhere in the Middle East spatial differentiation based on wealth, migrant status, and other key variables has become more and more common and suggests the increasing importance of class, occupation, and wealth as organizing factors of the social order. The analysis of settlement patterns in many Middle Eastern cities suggests the continued importance of residence groupings heavily influenced by sectarian identity, region, and tribe.[42] Nonetheless, Abu-Lughod's overall characterization of post–World War II urban trends in Morocco applies equally, with appropriate differences in timing, to many other countries of the region: a growing economic involution, coupled with rising unemployment, rapid population growth, an exacerbation of housing shortages, and a continued trend toward separation of the population by economic level.

[40] Khuri, *Village to Suburb*, p. 217. For prewar contrasting views of the importance of class in Lebanon, see Suad Joseph, "Muslim-Christian Conflict in Lebanon: A Perspective on the Evolution of Sectarianism," in *Muslim-Christian Conflicts: Economic, Political and Social Origins*, ed. Suad Joseph and Barbara L. K. Pillsbury (Boulder, CO: Westview Press, 1978), pp. 63–97; and Michael Gilsenan, "Against Patron-Client Relations," in *Patrons and Clients in Mediterranean Societies*, ed. Ernest Gellner and John Waterbury (London: Duckworth, 1977), pp. 167–83.

[41] Fuad I. Khuri, "Ideological Constants and Urban Living," in *The Middle East City*, ed. Saqqaf, pp. 72–73.

[42] Abu-Lughod, *Rabat*, p. 258. An excellent interdisciplinary assessment of current urban trends in the Arab world is provided in URBAMA, *Petites villes et villes moyennes dans le monde arabe* (Tours: Institut de Géographie, 1986). For an Israeli "development town," see Harvey E. Goldberg, *Greentown's Youth* (Assen, The Netherlands: Van Gorcum, 1984).

In many of the oil-wealthy Gulf states, which have experienced massive building growth since the 1960s, it has been common to construct large blocks of housing for particular occupational categories, with regions of villas reserved for engineers, merchants, and other people of high status, and three-storied walk-up apartment buildings for those of more limited income groups. Such a pattern is also common in older cities. Baghdad has large sectors marked off for particular types of housing—for military officers, civil service employees, and those of particular industries such as oil, railroads, utilities, and banks.[43]

Another sort of spatial order is provided by the settlement of migrants in cities, a phenomenon that accelerated at the end of World War II and has continued unabated ever since. Abu-Lughod has presented a portrait of a "typical" migrant to Cairo in the late 1950s. He was a young male who spent his first days in the city with a relative or friend from his village of origin. When he found more permanent lodging, it usually was in a neighborhood or subsection of the town occupied by other migrants from the same region. A similar pattern prevails today, although assistance might be provided by a group with a shared religious orientation. Such migrants often formed benevolent associations to look after their common interests. To help them to adjust to city life, migrants have a network of primary personal associations "far beyond" what is deemed possible in the West, enmeshing "not hundreds but thousands of individuals."[44]

Likewise, Evelyn Early describes the delicate balance of lower-middle-class migrant women to maintain appearances and make ends meet. "Country" (*baladī*) are many, but to appear too *baladī* is to appear rustic, while acting like a higher-status urban person (*afrangī*, from "Frank" or "French") leaves one open to accusations of putting on airs.[45] A similar pattern of settlement and the use of personal networks to adapt to new situations, including migration for oil wealth and refugee status due to wars and civil conflict, prevails elsewhere in the Middle East and erodes hard and fast distinctions among city, village, and town.[46]

Not all recent settlements of migrants consist of shantytowns; individuals move out of them when their financial circumstances allow. For modest civil

[43] On Kuwait, see Saba George Shiber, "Kuwait: A Case Study," in *From Madina to Metropolis*, ed. Brown, pp. 168–93. On Baghdad, see Gulick, "Baghdad."

[44] Janet Abu-Lughod, "Migrant Adjustment to City Life: The Egyptian Case," in *Arab Society in Transition*, ed. Saad Eddin Ibrahim and Nicholas S. Hopkins (Cairo: American University in Cairo Press, 1977 [1961]), pp. 395, 402. For a later, more disruptive pattern of migration, see her "Recent Migrations in the Arab World," in *Arab Society: Social Science Perspectives*, ed. Nicholas S. Hopkins and Saad Eddin Ibrahim (Cairo: American University in Cairo Press, 1985 [1978]), pp. 177–95.

[45] Evelyn A. Early, *Baladi Women of Cairo: Playing with an Egg and a Stone* (Boulder, CO, and London: Lynne Rienner, 1993).

[46] See Khuri, *Village to Suburb*; Colette Petonnet, "Espace, distance et dimension dans une société musulmane: à propos du bidonville marocain de Douar Doum à Rabat," *L'Homme* 12 (1972), 47–84; Alan Dubetsky (Duben), "Class and Community in Urban Turkey," in *Commoners, Climbers and Notables*, ed. C. A. O. Van Nieuwenhuijze (Leiden: E. J. Brill, 1977), pp. 360–71; John Waterbury, *North for the Trade: The Life and Times of a Berber Merchant* (Berkeley and Los Angeles: University of California Press, 1972), pp. 37–88.

FIGURE 5-9. Modern construction in Oman dates almost entirely from the post-1970 era. [Courtesy of the author.]

servants, employees of factories, bus conductors, and persons of similar occupation, this means renting or buying a house in a neighborhood such as Casablanca's ʻAyn Shuq (Aïn Chok). This is a neighborhood about half an hour to the east from the center of town by municipal bus, named after one of the first post–World War II housing developments constructed for Moroccans by the French. It is close to what in 1979 was still the periphery of a rapidly expanding Casablanca; by 1986, the neighborhood had been totally engulfed by the expanding city. The original development consists of carefully laid out rectangular streets; only the principal streets can be used by automobiles. Shops, a bath, and a mosque are located along these main internal streets; impasses lead off them, and the whole complex is accessible from the outside by only a few streets, so that the overall spatial principles of a traditional *madīna* are replicated, overlaid by a rectangular grid of European inspiration. Most of the inhabitants of the original houses in the quarter are older retired people or elderly soldiers, including many initially granted rights to housing in the development. Because rents for government developments are lower than commercial ones, such rights are jealously protected.

The original project is now dwarfed by adjoining privately constructed housing. Principal shops are located along a major highway and boulevard which determine the limits of the quarter. These are almost the only streets lined with trees. The remaining sides of the quarter are bounded by empty lands. Large primary and secondary schools and an orphanage adjoin the quarter. Every morning thousands of schoolchildren cross paths through the garbage-strewn empty spaces to various schools, some for boys and girls together, others with separate education. Most of these schools are of recent construction, a desperate effort to keep up with a demographic crisis in which over half the population is under the age of 15.

Because schools can be a symbol of progress and improvement, it is important to indicate how they are experienced by the children of the quarter. The under-18 population spends a great deal of time in school or in school-related activities, and despite the increasingly difficult odds in a poor economy and the large number of unemployed school-leavers, look upon educational success as a means of securing their future. This audience is particularly receptive to the message of "fundamentalist" Islam.[47] After the January 1984 riots in many of Morocco's major cities, the government began to forbid student demonstrators to continue their education. Students told me at the time that this measure, even more than the threat of prison sentences, had a chilling effect upon even the most politically committed.

The quarter's secondary school (*lycée*) is modestly but adequately designed, with a high wall cutting it off from the outside, adequate lighting, and small internal courtyards. Until 1984 there were periodic student demonstrations against the growing inadequacies of an educational system unable, despite valiant efforts, to cope with rapid expansion. Fewer than 10 percent of the entering school students eventually obtain diplomas, and even they cannot be assured of gainful employment. School furniture is broken or defective; blackboards and books are few. Students show a marked enthusiasm for the teachers who take an interest in them. For the other teachers, especially when official visitors are present to evaluate teaching performance, students deliberately show inattention or indifference. In the mid-1980s, some 30 years after Morocco's independence, many teachers in the secondary cycle were still foreigners, some from France and other European countries, including Eastern Europe, and a few from the Arab East. Almost none of the European teachers made any effort to learn Arabic, to converse with their Moroccan colleagues outside of formal meetings, or to meet with their students outside of classroom situations. The moment school was over, they left for other parts of Casablanca, much like many teachers in America's inner cities. By 1990, the last of these foreign teachers had left Morocco's public secondary schools. Only the younger Moroccan teachers live in the quarter itself, unless they have family or relatives elsewhere in Casablanca.

Few of the quarter's streets are paved, but it possesses the bare essentials of an adequate urban infrastructure. Houses are provided with sewers, electricity, and water. Until 1981, few other amenities were provided. After serious riots in Casablanca in 1981, municipality administrative reforms and a speech by the king suggesting that the city needed more green space and better archi-

[47] On the audience for fundamentalism in North Africa, including Morocco, see François Burgat and William Dowell, *The Islamic Movement in North Africa*, Middle East Monograph Series (Austin: University of Texas Press, 1993); and Dale F. Eickelman, "Re-Imagining Religion and Politics: Moroccan Elections in the 1990s," in *Islamism and Secularism in North Africa*, ed. John Reudy (New York: St. Martin's Press, 1994), pp. 253–73.

FIGURE 5-10. A secondary school in 'Ayn Shuq, Casablanca. Fewer than 10 percent of entering secondary school students eventually obtain diplomas. [Courtesy of the author.]

tecture led to the provision of small, vest-pocket parks and investments by private landlords in at least the facades of their properties.

Only a few of the larger stores on the periphery of the quarter are well stocked. Most stores sell in small quantities, carry only basic commodities, and sell at higher prices to their clients in exchange for extended credit. Several garages have been converted into mosques without minarets. Houses are mostly two-storied, but the houses of the entire quarter, with their gaudy facades of pink, light blue, green, yellow, and orange, indicate that many inhabitants gradually constructed their own properties. The interiors of many houses show that originally they were single-storied with open courtyards. As owners acquire the funds, they add a room or a story at a time. Many owners rent part of their houses to other families or to single civil servants such as teachers to pay for additional construction. Casablanca has rent control laws, as do many other cities in the Middle East, but in practice they work effectively only for long-term tenants.

There are virtually no factories near the quarter, and many inhabitants are underemployed or support people not in the labor force. Outside of school hours, the streets are crowded with children playing; radios blare throughout the daytime, and in the early evening they are joined by the noise of television sets. There are some cars parked on the streets and a much larger number of scooters, but many residents depend on public buses. Bus rides in the city are long and often uncomfortable, but the lower rent and cost of housing in peripheral, popular quarters outweigh such inconvenience.

Most of the quarter's residents come from elsewhere in Morocco, but there are no evident patterns of settlement by region. Neighbors are civil and cooperate with each other but at a fairly minimum level. The structure of ownership and the feeling of many residents that they belong to the quarter only until they find more substantial housing militate against more permanent bonds. Teenagers and young adults—both men and women in the case of Casablanca—are attracted by the bright lights and amusements of promenading in Casablanca's center or sitting in its cafés, where they are freer than in their own quarter to meet friends and to project what Susan Ossman calls *le look*, a carefully cultivated image of self through hairstyles and dress that leaves behind the exigencies of life at the economic edge, a post-modern combination of imagined European and Moroccan chic that also seeks to convey a personal presence and authority.[48] In 'Ayn Shuq itself, there are few cafés and no cinemas or recreational facilities beyond the streets. There is less room for *le look*. In spite of the outward appearances of a minimal neighborhood solidarity, the quarter's frayed look and genteel poverty are not incompatible with strong, enduring bonds of kindness, generosity, and cooperation.

Several anthropological monographs deal with cities today, but not all seek to combine anthropological approaches with social history to understand the long-term implications of transformations. One such effort is Kenneth L. Brown's *People of Salé*, a substantial social historical attempt to relate the impact of long-term shifts in world economic currents to the social order of a North African city. Brown makes the important point, confirmed by other studies, that status and social relations were not determined by any fixed characteristics. Attributes such as Arab or Berber identity, religious learning, patrilineal descent, and membership in occupational groups and religious brotherhoods constituted "cultural categories, not concrete, isolated social aggregations or classes." Social relations were instead "characterized by a pattern of shifting coalitions, of networks of patrons and clients" based on common interests that were "sometimes strengthened (but not determined) by descent, marriage, or friendship." His description of the city's elite is likewise congruent with descriptions of other Middle Eastern contexts. They were persons "who dominated crosscutting social networks" and who were less leaders of "powerful extended families" than "men who controlled clientele groups held together by mutual interests, not ties of consanguinity."

The long-range consequences of capitalist and colonial penetration, Brown argues, were to create a situation in which a few entrepreneurs amassed

[48] Susan Ossman, *Picturing Casablanca: Portraits of Power in a Modern City* (Berkeley and Los Angeles: University of California Press, 1994).

considerable wealth, while the majority of small merchants, artisans, and peasants became increasingly impoverished and social mobility became more difficult. Stated in the abstract, this theme of the growth of class relationships instead of vertical ones of patron-client and other ties recurs in contemporary anthropological and social historical literature. Brown analyzes in detail and over long historical periods the consequences for particular crafts and mercantile activities of these economic and political changes; other studies often merely juxtapose before-and-after contexts without assessing the interplay between market forces and social relations. Brown argues that the "local patterns of relationships," which he meticulously describes, remain largely intact and to date have not led to a "class-based social structure."[49] Thus, even with the growing differentiation of people along lines of wealth, individuals perceived their "interests" in a multiplicity of settings and manipulated an intricate range of identities and loyalties.

If the growing importance of economic differentiation was apparent in the critical period dealt with by Brown through the 1930s, it has become much more so in the accelerated social change of the post–World War II era. For this more recent period, Alan Duben's (Dubetsky's) 1970–1971 research in a *mahalle* (neighborhood) of 30,000, which he calls Aktepe, located on the outskirts of Istanbul, remains valuable for understanding notions of trust and loyalty that pervade both rural and urban settings. Aktepe's population is heterogeneous in origin, ranging from the "religiously conservative" Black Sea Sunnī Muslims to Alevi Muslims from east and east-central Anatolia. Duben is concerned with understanding the interplay between older notions of consociation, which he glosses as "the moral community which is Islam," and "the organization of individuals according to social class."[50]

Aktepe is divided into two principal quarters. One is occupied by people of Black Sea origin ("Laz" territory, after the principal ethnic characterization of the Black Sea region). The other consists predominantly of people of eastern Anatolian origin. It is known as "Kurdish" territory, although not all residents of this region are Kurds. A few people from other regions are interspersed in the two quarters. This regional/ethnic distinction is also taken as a religious one. The Kurds (Alevi-s) live in the lower part of the neighborhood. There are no mosques there, and during Ramāḍan many residents do not keep the fast. In contrast, the upper Sunnī (Laz) part of the neighborhood has two mosques. Although administratively united, Duben characterizes the upper and lower quarters of Aktepe as "two rather different moral communities," or self-conscious separate social units, in terms of the "objective facts" of regional ties, marriage patterns, and "different religious belief systems."[51]

[49] Kenneth L. Brown, *People of Salé: Tradition and Change in a Moroccan City, 1850–1950* (Cambridge, MA: Harvard University Press, 1976), pp. 6, 56, 60, 224. See also Suad Joseph, "Family as Security and Bondage: A Political Strategy of the Lebanese Working Class," in *Arab Society*, ed. Hopkins and Ibrahim, pp. 241–56.

[50] Dubetsky, "Class and Community," p. 360.

[51] Ibid., p. 362.

The pattern of migrants settling in Aktepe is much the same as that described by Abu-Lughod for Cairo. People from the same village or general region settle together. In the case of Aktepe, a common pattern is for incomers to construct single-story makeshift homes and later to move into four- and five-floor modern apartment buildings nearby. There is an evident differentiation of wealth and occupation, as a few laborers have formed their own small workshops or as others become successful entrepreneurs in real estate or commerce. Most residents of the quarter remain laborers, either in the small workshops and factories within Aktepe or in the large industrial zone that adjoins it.

Duben views classes "as conflict groups determined by their relation to the means of production." He argues that it is more useful to consider classes as one type of conflict group, along with others such as "status groups, sects, or regional groupings."[52] There is an unequal distribution of wealth and power among Aktepe's residents, as elsewhere in Turkey, but for Duben the nature of significant groupings within this inegalitarian framework remains to be classified empirically; he does not regard the formation of social classes as a self-evident phenomenon or the existence of other forms of conflict groups as a "false" consciousness. All such groupings that are significant to the members of a particular society and that serve as a guide to social action must be taken into consideration. For Duben, any use of terms such as *class* must take into account both the social and historical institutions of the society being studied and the economic and social forms outside the area.[53]

In fact, he reviews recent work on the consequences of industrialization in non-Western contexts that suggests that increasing social differentiation, including the separation of kinship ties from those of work, is not a necessary concomitant of industrial development. He points out that in many of the small factories and workshops of Aktepe, workers are hired according to the patron's assessment of a worker's reliability and trustworthiness (*dürüstlük*). Such relationships of trust are particularly developed among people with a common religious identity. Patrons and workers are linked by a complex of social obligations that extends beyond the workplace. Some of the larger workplaces even provide mosques on their premises. These complex bonds of social obligations ensure the workers' loyalty. The principle of recruiting workers with such common bonds is also followed by larger industries such as textile factories. Only when a high level of skill is necessary are technical factors given predominance. Duben's argument is that these "traditional" social alignments structure the workplace and contribute to its effective functioning. In short, the more important grouping for patrons and workers is community instead of class, and bonds of class solidarity are not inevitably a consequence of increasing economic differentiation. Neighborhood improvement associations among both the Alevi Kurds and the Sunnī Laz populations pay for the support of various community facilities, including primary schools, dispensaries, and (for the

[52] Ibid., p. 364.

[53] Ibid., pp. 364–65.

Sunnī population) a mosque, and the wealthier members of the two communities are the leaders in these associations.[54]

Duben acknowledges the development of a "politically conscious" labor movement and the growth of class consciousness among some Turks. He concludes that such consciousness has become increasingly important, particularly in Turkey's larger industries and among workers returning from Europe, but in Aktepe, where most individuals work in smaller factories and workshops, a sense of distinct class has developed most clearly only among the patrons. Their wealth and mobility enable them to meet others in similar positions elsewhere in the city, and many are becoming distinguished by a distinctive style of dress and manners. Class differentiation is becoming more significant, but a comprehension of *how* it shapes Turkish notions of society and identity necessitates understanding other forms of social cohesion as well. Class consciousness alone will not shape the future.[55] Work, including the necessity in urban settings for women to enter the job market, contributes significantly to changed notions of society and political community. For Istanbul, Jenny B. White offers the women's equivalent for what Duben has described for the local association of male labor and the implications of these emerging forms of association for political life in Turkey.[56]

Both anthropology and social history offer a balance between sociological abstraction—charts and numbers showing urban growth, population trends, educational levels, and economic indices—and narratives indicating how these transformations are perceived and acted upon. An unusually effective collective enterprise representing the multiple voices in a contemporary Middle Eastern society is *Téhéran au dessous du volcan* [Tehran Under the Volcano], a joint work by French and Iranian scholars.[57] This study uses a combination of narrative, maps, photographs, and the personal testimony of intellectuals, women, students, *mullah*-s, Revolutionary Guards, former prisoners, wealthy businessmen, minorities, the "disinherited" poor, rural immigrants, and others to portray the changes in postrevolutionary Iran. The more analytically oriented contributions deal with such topics as Tehran's stunning demographic growth since the revolution, its division into residential and class areas, and the shifting political and economic importance of the various sectors of the city. The mix of first-person narratives (or narratives told as if they were in the first person) and "conventional" ethnographic, geographic, and social historical narrative lends strength to the presentation.

[54] Ibid., p. 367. See also Dubetsky's "Kinship, Primordial Ties, and Factory Organization in Turkey: An Anthropological View," *International Journal of Middle East Studies* 7, no. 3 (July 1976), 433–51. For accounts of the effective forms of solidarity among Muslim immigrants in France, see the special issue of *Esprit*, "Français/immigrés," no. 102 (June 1985), 173–236.

[55] Dubetsky, "Class and Community," pp. 368–69.

[56] Jenny B. White, *Money Makes Us Relatives: Women's Labor in Urban Turkey* (Austin: University of Texas Press, 1994), which, for politics, should be complemented with her "Islam and Democracy: The Turkish Experience," *Current History* 94, no. 1 (January 1995), 7–12.

[57] Bernard Hourcade and Yann Richard, eds., *Téhéran au dessous du volcan, Autrement,* Hors série 27 (Paris: Autrement Revue, 1987).

Similarly, Cairo has had an abundance of excellent studies of social class, politics, and community that suggest the importance of understanding the linkages between "domestic" and extended family, decisions regarding marriage, employment, housing, and the use of resources and politics and religious expression and practice in a more conventional sense.[58]

This chapter has assessed how the main contours of urban life, past and present, have been interpreted by anthropologists and scholars in related disciplines. It also suggests some of the main social and cultural consequences of the rapid transformation of the urban landscape over the last four decades. If there has been a "great divide" until now between scholars interested in "premodern" Middle Eastern cities and contemporary cities, this is in part because of the lack of adequate social theory to deal with processes and change in values and institutions. Even if such theory is not yet fully developed, anthropologists and sociologists are fully aware of the necessity of describing the direction of change and of making full use of social historical materials.

In discussing the emergence of class relationships and other large-scale social processes, the importance of distinguishing between anthropology *in* cities and the anthropology *of* cities becomes paramount. The emergence of class relationships is a process that affects entire economies and regions and cannot be confined to a discussion of urban milieus. The social organization of work in cities and the intensity with which urban residents are exposed to a wide spectrum of economic and political currents are such that processes of class formation are often more visible in cities. Certain transformations may appear more pronounced in urban contexts but cannot be explained within those contexts alone. Many studies that are categorized as urban anthropology make significant contributions to anthropological topics in urban milieus but do not concern the characteristics of cities in themselves. Such studies have been referred to throughout this book and are reintroduced here only briefly, sometimes by reference to discussions in earlier chapters. The anthropology of cities, of urban forms, is more distinctive in scope. This chapter has been particularly concerned with the anthropology of cities and the consequences of massive and rapid population growth for urban forms.

Of course, the two approaches to the study of cities, anthropology *in* cities and *of* cities, are not entirely separable. The importance of studying regions and the interconnectedness of city and town dwellers, agriculturists, and pastoralists was stressed in Chapter 3. In a parallel manner, although peasants and farmers are discussed at length under various headings throughout this book, no single, separate chapter is devoted to them. The reason for not doing so is to focus attention on common elements in seemingly small-scale yet pervasive concerns with personal and group identity cross-cutting urban, agricultural, or

[58] See, in particular, Diane Singerman, *Avenues of Participation: Family, Politics, and Networks in Urban Quarters of Cairo*, Muslim Politics (Princeton, NJ: Princeton University Press, 1994); Arlene Elowe MacLeod, *Accommodating Protest: Working Women, the New Veiling, and Change in Cairo* (New York: Columbia University Press, 1991); and Early, *Baladi Women*.

pastoral settings and how these are linked with the great themes of "civilization" (*ḥaḍāra*) and "barbarism" (*badāwa*), of economic activity and governance, and attitudes toward just rule, which shape important elements of Middle Eastern and, as they become better known, Central Asian conceptions of self and society.

FURTHER READINGS

Understanding cities and urban environments in the historical and contemporary Middle East has been greatly facilitated by Masashi Haneda and Toru Miura, eds., *Islamic Urban Studies: Historical Review and Perspectives* (London and New York: Kegan Paul International, 1994), a critical bibliography that is organized by major regions—the Maghrib, the Mashriq, Turkey, Iran, and Central Asia. It deals with relevant work in all major scholarly languages, including Russian and the various languages of the Middle East. As a guide to the literature, Michael E. Bonine, Eckart Ehlers, Thomas Krafft, and Georg Stöber, eds., *The Middle Eastern City and Islamic Urbanism: An Annotated Bibliography of Western Literature*, Bonner Geographische Abhandlungen 91 (Bonn: Ferd. Dümmlers Verlag, 1994), is a comprehensive work of 7500 entries, including journal articles, books, and chapters of books. The editors point out (p. 9) that works in Middle Eastern languages and Russian are not included.

There are several key surveys of urban issues and problems. A. H. Hourani and S. M. Stern, eds., *The Islamic City*, Papers in Islamic History 1 (Oxford: Bruno Cassirer; Philadelphia: University of Pennsylvania Press, 1970), concentrates on research concerning the premodern period. L. Carl Brown, ed., *From Madina to Metropolis*, Princeton Studies on the Near East (Princeton, NJ: Darwin Press, 1973), is an excellent collection of amply illustrated essays; and Kenneth Brown, Michèle Jolé, Peter Sluglett, and Sami Zubeida, eds., *Middle Eastern Cities in Comparative Perspective* (London: Ithaca Press, 1986), is especially good at distinguishing various scholarly traditions—including British, French, Arab, and American. Useful review essays include Michael E. Bonine, "From Uruk to Casablanca: Perspectives on the Urban Experience of the Middle East," *Journal of Urban History* 3, no. 2 (February 1977), 141–80; Paul Wheatley, "Levels of Space Awareness in the Traditional Islamic City," *Ekistics* 42, no. 253 (December 1976), 354–66; Janet Abu-Lughod, "The Islamic City: Historic Myth, Islamic Essence, and Contemporary Relevance," *International Journal of Middle East Studies* 19, no. 2 (May 1987), 155–76, more concerned with contemporary urban forms than her title suggests; and T. Yukawa, ed., *Urbanism in Islam: Proceedings of the Second International Conference on Urbanism in Islam (1990)* (Tokyo: Middle Eastern Culture Center in Japan, 1994), which includes recent work on Central Asia. Finally, Abdulaziz Y. Saqqaf, ed., *The Middle East City: Ancient Traditions Confront a Modern World* (New York: Paragon House, 1987), is especially good in depicting urban issues since the 1967 Arab-Israeli war and the oil boom of the 1970s.

In addition to the social historical studies previously cited, two others stand out: Abraham Marcus, *The Middle East on the Eve of Modernity: Aleppo in the Eighteenth Century* (New York: Columbia University Press, 1989); and Alan Duben and Cem Behar, *Istanbul Households: Marriage, Family, and Fertility, 1880–1940*, Cambridge Studies in Population, Economy, and Society in Past Time (Cambridge and New York: Cambridge University Press, 1991). Using nineteenth-century Ottoman urban census data and archival and sociological research, Duben and Behar describe life in a prosperous quarter (*mahalle*) and the succession of residential, family, and marriage choices in one of the first large-scale Muslim cities to experience "Westernization." Westernization is a topic usually treated in terms of political institutions, education, and town planning. Duben and

Behar trace Westernization through the more "intimate" domestic choices that people make concerning marriage, dress, wedding celebrations, furnishings, and residence patterns. Their book is nicely complemented by Zeynep Çelik, *The Remaking of Istanbul: Portrait of an Ottoman City in the Nineteenth Century* (Berkeley and Los Angeles: University of California Press, 1993 [1986]). There are two complementary studies of Ceuta (Arabic, Sibta), one of Spain's last toeholds on the coast of northern Morocco, which also merit attention: Manuel Gordillo Osuna, *Geografía urbana de Ceuta* (Madrid: Instituto de Estudios Africanos, 1972); and Eva Evers Rosander, *Women in a Borderland: Managing Muslim Identity Where Morocco Meets Spain*, Stockholm Studies in Social Anthropology 26 (Stockholm: University of Stockholm, 1991). Taken together, the two studies explore the meaning of "frontier" from different perspectives.

Syria and Turkey are also the subject of lavishly illustrated geographic studies that lend themselves to anthropological inquiry. In particular, there is an ongoing series, *Geographical Views in the Middle Eastern Studies: I, Turkey*, ed. Akinobu Terasaka (Ibaraki, Japan: Ryutsu Keizai University, 1989), *II: Syria*, ed. Akinobu Terasaka and Masanori Naito (Ibaraki, Japan: Ryutsu Keizai University, 1990), and *III: Ankara*, ed. Akinobu Terasaka and Itsuki Nakabayashi (Ibaraki, Japan: Ryutsu Keizai University, 1992), all of which are in English.

Jerusalem has a special significance for Muslims, Christians, and Jews, and is a source of both reverence and competition between these three world religions and sectarian groups within them. Michael Romann and Alex Weingrod, *Living Together Separately: Arabs and Jews in Contemporary Jerusalem* (Princeton, NJ: Princeton University Press, 1991), is a good point of departure for considerations of urban space. Gerald Caplan, *Arab and Jew in Jerusalem: Explorations in Community Mental Health* (Cambridge, MA, and London: Harvard University Press, 1980), has less to do with mental health than with the challenge of negotiating government and public spaces in a divided city. Finally, two works of historical geography offer an excellent basis for thinking anthropologically about Jerusalem: Yehoshua Ben-Arieh, *Jerusalem in the Nineteenth Century: The Old City* (New York: St. Martin's Press, 1984); and Ruth Kark, *Jerusalem Neighborhoods: Planning and By-Laws (1855–1930)* (Jerusalem: Magnes Press, 1991).

PART III
CONSTRUCTED MEANINGS

6

WHAT IS A TRIBE?

KHANTARĪSH [loud]: What kind of question is that, "What is a tribe?" Can I ask you, "What is the state of Israel?" Why do you think that the first question is easier? Is it because "a tribe" is something you didn't grow up with?[1]

"Tribal" identities at first appear more exotic to Westerners than those based on kinship, religion, or city quarters and therefore serve as an apt introduction to how shared ideas about loyalties and the nature of society relate to the social order. In part, tribal identities have appeared exotic because of their initial unfamiliarity and because of the way in which some anthropologists have chosen to depict such social forms. That is why it is useful to discuss ideas of the "tribe" in the Middle East and Central Asia before considering other bases of social identity. Terms such as "tribe" or, for Central Asia, "horde" (Mongol *juz*), a "relatively stable territorial-political formation" of confederated tribes under an elected leader (*khān*),[2] are also clouded by early Western understandings of evolutionary "stages" of social and cultural growth and, in some contexts, their perjorative connotations. Of course, "tribal" identities do not occur in all Middle Eastern contexts, although there are significant nomadic and settled populations that are tribally organized throughout the entire region, from Morocco to the eastern frontiers of Central Asia.

[1] Smadar Lavie, *The Poetics of Military Occupation: Mzeina Allegories of Bedouin Identity under Israeli and Egyptian Rule* (Berkeley and Los Angeles: University of California Press, 1990), p. 168.

[2] Anatoly M. Khazanov, *Nomads and the Outside World*, 2nd ed., trans. Julia Crookenden (Madison: University of Wisconsin Press, 1983).

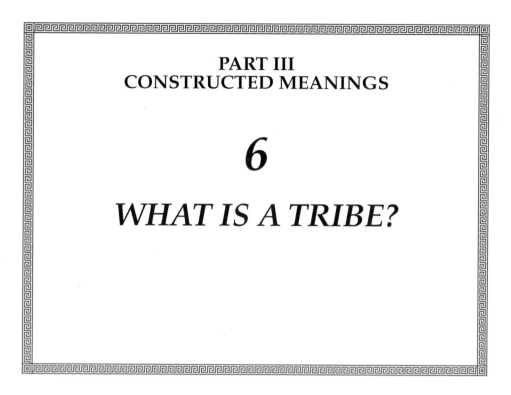

Because the single word *tribe* is used to describe a range of ideas about society and social forms throughout the world does not mean that these ideas are all intrinsically related. Understanding ideas of tribe in the Middle East and Central Asia is not advanced by adding together all the various meanings of tribe or in writing about tribes in general. Take, for example, the notion of tribe still prevalent in many archaeological discussions, where "tribe" is an organizational level between "bands" and "states." In this formulation, not only are tribes assumed to be something independent of states, but they are thought to be the evolutionary predecessors of states. The problem is further compounded by the views of some Middle Eastern urban intellectuals—and, with the demise of Soviet rule, Central Asian intellectuals "re-imagining" their pre-Soviet identities—who have adopted nineteenth-century evolutionary views of society with a vengeance and assume that tribes exist only at the fringes of states or that they are the residue of pre-state formations. Both now and in the past, many states work through tribes, rather than against them.[3] Tribes can be thought of as "family resemblances," to use Wittgenstein's phrase, possessing partial similarities that can be compared and contrasted rather than exact identities asserted by less accurate theoretical assumptions. In the sense of family resemblances, tribes in the Middle East (and Central Asia at least before forced collectivization in the 1930s) have many characteristics in common and a shared cultural logic.

The first thing to emphasize is that tribal identity, like other bases of social identity, including kinship relations, citizenship, and national identity, is something that natives (and sometimes ethnographers) create. These forms do not exist as objects that can be torn from social and cultural contexts by anthropologists for recording and classification into typologies.[4] Such patterns of meaning change with historical situations. It makes a great deal of difference whether they occur in the context of strong or weak state organizations or a colonial society.

There are four principal forms in which people create tribal identity in the Middle East: (1) the elaboration and use of explicit "native" ethnopolitical ideologies by the people themselves to explain their sociopolitical organization; (2) concepts used by state authorities for administrative purposes; (3) implicit, practical notions held by people that are not elaborated into formal

[3] This is the case even for self-declared "revolutionary societies." See John Davis, *Libyan Politics: Tribe and Revolution*, Society and Culture in the Modern Middle East (London: I. B. Tauris, 1987), pp. 95–106, for a discussion of how Libya's revolutionary government works through tribal structures, which, as Davis points out, "never were the sole generators of political action" (p. 95).

[4] Pierre Bourdieu, *Outline of a Theory of Practice*, trans. Richard Nice, Cambridge Studies in Social Anthropology 16 (Cambridge and New York: Cambridge University Press, 1977), pp. 35–36. See also Daniel Bradburd, *Ambiguous Relations: Kin, Class, and Conflict Among Komachi Pastoralists*, Smithsonian Series in Ethnographic Inquiry (Washington, DC: Smithsonian Institution Press, 1990), pp. 172–85.

ideologies; and (4) anthropological concepts.[5] All but the last are actor's notions, in the sense that they are implicitly or explicitly held by participants in a society and used as a practical guide to some form of social action. The anthropologist's notion of tribe is for analytical rather than practical purposes, although the sociological observer, whether native or foreign, also participates in the "observed" society in a special sense and is engaged in the practice of theoretical discourse. It should be emphasized that, although these various notions of tribe are separable for analytical purposes, in practice they are by no means mutually exclusive and frequently overlap.

Native, or locally held, ethnopolitical ideologies of tribal identity vary throughout the Middle East, but they are generally based on a concept of political identity formed through common patrilineal descent. A major exception is the Tuareg of the Sahara, where tribal identity is based on matrilineal descent—that is, descent traced through the mother. Political action in such tribes—the patterns in which groups of people will combine or dispute in a predictable manner—has generally been explained by anthropologists in terms of segmentary theory. People in such tribes also sometimes hold that the principles of segmentary ideology explain the "essence" of their political activities, although, as Emanuel Marx points out, this is simply not the case.[6] Other grounds for political action may coexist with segmentary ones, and if the notion of family resemblances among notions of personal and collective loyalties is accepted, then alternatives to a search to reducing political action to a sole "essential" principle can be explored, as they are in this chapter. Moroccan tribespeople, for example, when discussing their notion of *qbīla* ("tribe"), elaborate it in different ways, depending on their generation and social status. Individuals who are socially and politically dominant often elaborate such ideologies in complex ways and use them to fix political alliances with members of other tribal groups and to enhance their own position vis-à-vis state authorities. Ethnographers working in tribal societies have frequently based their accounts of kinship relations and tribal organization on information provided by such socially and politically dominant individuals, although the notions of tribal identity main-

[5] The following discussion builds on Bourdieu, *Outline*; Talal Asad, "Political Inequality in the Kababish Tribe," in *Essays in Sudan Ethnography*, ed. Ian Cunnison and Wendy James (London: C. Hurst, 1972), pp. 126–48; and Dale F. Eickelman, *Moroccan Islam: Tradition and Society in a Pilgrimage Center*, Modern Middle East Series 1 (Austin and London: University of Texas Press, 1976), pp. 105–21. As Linda L. Layne, *Home and Homeland: The Dialogics of Tribal and National Identities in Jordan* (Princeton, NJ: Princeton University Press, 1994), pp. 96–107, points out, these various usages, including the scholarly ones, "inform" one another and often have immediate political implications.

[6] Emanuel Marx, "The Tribe as a Unit of Subsistence: Nomadic Pastoralism in the Middle East," *American Anthropologist* 79, no. 2 (June 1977), 356; Philip Carl Salzman, "Tribal Organization and Subsistence: A Response to Emanuel Marx"; and Emanuel Marx, "Back to the Problem of Tribe," *American Anthropologist* 81, no. 1 (March 1979), 121–25. Note, however, that the Rwāla, as defined by Marx ("Tribe," pp. 348, 358), do not correspond with the Rwāla as they define themselves, a problem noted in Chapter 4 and raised at greater length below.

tained by ordinary tribesmen, not to mention tribeswomen, often differ significantly from such formal ideologies of the dominant.

The second notion of tribe is based on its use as an administrative device in contexts as varied as the Ottoman Empire, Morocco, Central Asia under Russian domination, other countries prior to and during the period of colonial rule, and a number of independent Middle Eastern countries, including Iran. Administrative assumptions concerning the nature of tribes are generally based, to some degree, on locally maintained conceptions modified for political purposes. Thus administrative concepts of tribe frequently assume a corporate identity and fixed territorial boundaries that many "tribes" do not possess and give privileges and authority to tribal leaders that are dependent on the existence of a state organization and not derived from concepts of leadership as understood by tribespeople themselves.[7] In cases such as Morocco and the Sudan, the colonial powers formally promoted "tribal" identities and developed tribal administration to a fine art in an attempt to retard nationalistic movements. In reaction, the postindependence governments of these and other countries signaled an ideological break with the colonial past by formally abolishing tribes as an administrative device, although such identities continue to be highly significant at the level of practical local administration.

Practical notions of tribe, the third analytical category considered here, are those implicitly held by tribespeople as a guide to everyday conduct in relations between larger social groups. The term *practical* emphasizes that these concepts of identity emerge primarily through social action and not through abstract reflection upon the social order. Such notions are often difficult for anthropologists to elicit, for they are not always formally articulated by tribespeople in ordinary situations, and because social alignments based on these notions frequently shift. Practical notions of tribe and related concepts of social identity implicitly govern crucial areas of activity, including factional alignments over land rights, pastures, and other political claims, marriage strategies (themselves a form of political activity), and many aspects of patronage.[8]

Finally, there are the analytical conceptions of tribe held by anthropologists. A preliminary caution regarding these notions—I emphasize the plural—is in order. In both popular and anthropological usage, the concept of tribe figures in a variety of sociological, evolutionary, and ecological typologies. In some contexts "tribe" is even partially synonymous with "primitive," a usage

[7] A good example of this is the leadership of the Qashqa'i of Iran. See Lois Beck, *The Qashqa'i of Iran* (New Haven, CT, and London: Yale University Press, 1986).

[8] These issues become even more complicated when some tribal leaders claim to rule on the basis of consent but behave almost despotically in some contexts with the support of state authorities, who in turn have their own view of what constitutes a tribe. See Norman N. Lewis, *Nomads and Settlers in Syria and Jordan, 1800–1980*, Cambridge Middle East Library (Cambridge: Cambridge University Press, 1986). See Nancy Tapper, *Bartered Brides: Politics, Gender and Marriage in an Afghan Tribal Society*, Cambridge Studies in Social and Cultural Anthropology 65 (Cambridge and New York: Cambridge University Press, 1991), pp. 91–100, for an especially clear discussion of the strategies and political implications of marriage in a tribal society.

decidedly out of place in most of the Middle East and Central Asia.[9] In black Africa the term is generally regarded as pejorative among the elite, yet a minister of foreign affairs from an Arabian peninsula state, discussing political issues with me in a suite at the remarkably untribal Waldorf Towers in late 1985, casually remarked with pride that the success of his country in facing modern political challenges was derived in part from its tribal identity. Far from being a relic of the past or a "primitive" vestige of social organization, as seen by many urban Arabs from outside the Arabian peninsula, "tribe" in some modern contexts can be a constructive element in sustaining modern national identity. To compound the ironies in usage of "tribe" in black Africa and the Middle East, the political forms glossed as "tribe" in the two areas often have little in common. Tribes have often been kingdoms in sub-Saharan Africa, absorbing or dominating other tribes. Middle Eastern tribes either coexisted with royal or state authority or served as antikingdoms, and where tribal leadership formed royal dynasties in the Middle East in the past, it has not continued to rule in tribal terms.

Anthropological conceptions are intended primarily to make sociological sense of "tribal" social relations. Like the "native" conceptions outlined above—and "natives," of course, can also be anthropologists—anthropological notions exist for a purpose, usually that of acquiring a theoretical understanding of the cultural bases of social identity, but they parallel the uses of native ideologies and can be used to "order" understandings of society. Anthropological notions of tribe are not more real than "native" conceptions or superior to them; instead, they are a more explicit form of knowledge of social relations, or at least they are intended as "authoritative" explanations of such social relations.

There is a drawback to providing a general, abstract definition that ignores these various overlapping notions of tribe. What an ethnographer "sees" of social forms in any given cultural contexts depends on such factors as whether the ethnographer is regarded as friendly or dangerous or as possessing a greater or lesser degree of understanding of society and authority over decisions that may affect that society. Ethnographers, whether "native" or not, are almost inevitably perceived as "learned," so their questions nearly always elicit the most "learned" representations of society from informants, in accordance with the informant's conceptions of learning and of conscious literary tradition. In tribal societies, such learned representations generally entail the elaborate use of written or oral traditional (memorized) genealogies. Such ideological representations are important in themselves, but they do not take into account the implicit, practical cultural understandings of society that are so basic that (to paraphrase Bourdieu) they find expression only in silence.[10] The anthropologist's problem is to balance out these various conceptions of tribe

[9] For a review of these usages, see Marx, "Tribe," pp. 343–44.

[10] Bourdieu, *Outline*, p. 18. For a comprehensive review of how anthropologists have discussed the notion of tribe in Afghanistan and Iran, see Richard Tapper, "Introduction," in *The Conflict of Tribe and State in Afghanistan*, ed. Richard Tapper (London: Croom Helm; New York: St. Martin's Press, 1983), esp. pp. 1–12, 42–75; and Beck, *Qashqa'i*, pp. 11–21.

and to arrive at one that is "real." The anthropologist's objective is to achieve as adequate an understanding as possible of how people in a given society conceive of social forms, use this knowledge as a basis for social action, and modify these conceptions in practice and over time.

THE PRINCIPLE OF SEGMENTATION

The principle of *segmentation* raises a basic question of European social philosophy: What are the minimal, or essential, conditions needed for individuals to cooperate in society in an orderly fashion? The seventeenth-century English philosopher Thomas Hobbes posed the question in the following manner: How could the wills, passions, and desires of individuals be coordinated so that there would not be anarchy, a war of all against all? Given his particular image of man and society, Hobbes answered that, while all men sought to satisfy their desires to the full, no one could do so in a state of total anarchy. Hence humans possess a "spark of reason" that enables them to agree to at least a minimal "sovereign" control over themselves in order to pursue their self-interest. In segmentary societies, no permanent "governmental" authority exists, so there is a minimum of such control. The "native" concept of the social order and analytical "model" of political structure were thought to coincide. In segmentary societies, political order was (in principle) exclusively through the segmentary principle, often expressed in terms of the metaphor of common descent. Violence, self-help, or appeal to the shared moral conventions of the social group allow for the maintenance of order.

Segmentation theory has had the added attraction of providing a key notion by which a wide range of political forms in certain types of societies could be explained. Interest in the concept of segmentation, although not exactly labeled as such, is evident in such influential sociological studies as *The Division of Labor in Society* (1893), in which Émile Durkheim writes of "mechanical" or "segmental" societies where individuals and groups tend to resemble each other to the point that he compares their forms to the rings of an earthworm.[11] Even if cut up, each part is capable of existing on its own. One of his examples of such a society was the Kabyle of Algeria.[12] The notion of segmentation was especially developed in ethnographies on black Africa published in

[11] Émile Durkheim, *The Division of Labor in Society*, trans. George Simpson (New York: Free Press, 1933 [1893]), p. 175.

[12] Ibid., pp. 174–81. Although Durkheim mentioned Kabyle ethnography only in passing, he appears to have been heavily influenced by the work of Emile Masqueray and others. The best discussion in English of Masqueray's work and its relation to subsequent French sociology is Ernest Gellner, "The Roots of Cohesion," *Man* (N.S.) 20, no. 1 (March 1985), 142–55. One virtue of Gellner's *Saints of the Atlas*, The Nature of Human Societies Series (London: Weidenfeld & Nicolson, 1969), is that he firmly links the discussion of segmentation theory to the main currents of European political philosophy. On the negative aspects of Gellner's approach, see Talal Asad, "The Concept of Cultural Translation in British Social Anthropology," in *Writing Culture: The Poetics and Politics of Ethnography*, ed. James Clifford and George E. Marcus (Berkeley and Los Angeles: University of California Press, 1986), pp. 141–64.

the 1940s and 1950s, where it appeared to provide a framework within which anthropologists could undertake comparative research.[13]

The most thorough ethnographic application of segmentary theory was E. E. Evans-Pritchard's *The Nuer*, which first appeared in 1940.[14] This book made almost no explicit reference to its sociological predecessors, but in earlier writings and conversations with students and colleagues, Evans-Pritchard acknowledged the profound effect of Robertson Smith's writing on Arab kinship on his work.[15] Figure 6-1 shows the essentials of the idea of segmentation. The bottom "level" refers to discrete camping clusters, as among the Rwāla, or to rural local communities, as among Morocco's Bnī Batāw (discussed later in this chapter). Such groups may share a common territory or herd together, but they expect other group members to support their interests. Many households claim common kinship ties. As indicated in the earlier discussion on the Rwāla, these ties often can be traced in multiple ways and can, over time, be assimilated to ties of kinship if people act "as if" they were related to one another.

Conflict with other groups, including a feud (Ar. *th'ar*) resulting from a homicide or the theft of animals, can be defined as an attack upon collective honor (Ar. *sharaf*). In such a situation, members of the segmentary group are expected to support one another. The support group is situationally defined. For example, if someone from group C (level 1) attacks the honor of someone in group A, then members of groups A and E are expected to support A. Members of C and F are expected to support C. Likewise, a challenge by B to A involves a higher, more inclusive level of participation (at level 3 in Figure 6-1). The terms in the system have meaning only in opposition to the others, and all "higher" loyalties are activated only in case of perceived need.

An integral element of segmentation is the high value placed on the autonomy and honor of individuals, and a "balanced opposition" of honor-bearing people and groups. Not all people and groups involved in a feud may respond to an appeal for mutual assistance, for some potential participants may not define a specific situation in the same way. Groups may refrain from supporting their "brothers" and still occupy the same status in the segmentary system. But if they support another group, as illustrated by the competitive displays of horsemanship among Morocco's Bnī Batāw, their position within the segmentary system is irrevocably altered. Again, the principle of segmentation does not require that people and groups adhere to fixed lines of conduct and responsibility.

[13] See, for instance, M. G. Smith's early review of the use of the concept in "Segmentary Lineage Systems," *Journal of the Royal Anthropological Institute* 86, no. 2 (July–December 1956), 78.

[14] E. E. Evans-Pritchard, *The Nuer: A Description of the Modes of Livelihood and Political Institutions of a Nilotic People* (Oxford: Clarendon Press, 1940).

[15] E. E. Evans-Pritchard, "The Nuer: Tribe and Clan (part 3)," *Sudan Notes and Records* 18, no. 1 (1935), 37–87, and his review of G. W. Murray's *Sons of Ishmael*, in *Africa* 11, no. 1 (January 1938), 123. I am grateful to Paul Dresch for these references. Dresch's "Segmentation: Its Roots in Arabia and Its Flowering Elsewhere," *Cultural Anthropology* 3, part 1 (1988), 50–67, should be consulted for a thoughtful social history of segmentation theory in anthropological thought.

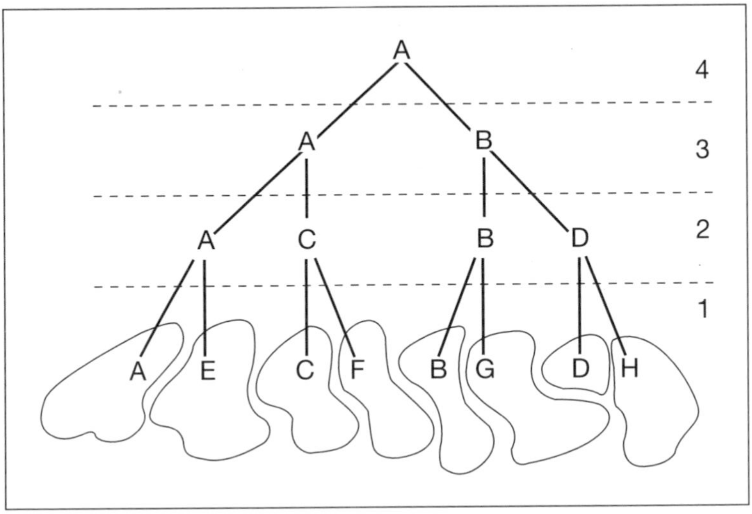

FIGURE 6-1. The concept of segmentation. [From Dale F. Eickelman, *Moroccan Islam*, p. 207. Copyright © 1976 by University of Texas Press. All rights reserved.]

As Paul Dresch explains, the actor in such a system "is not just a point, with position but no cultural extent, around which meaning coalesces. Far from being given, the actor is constituted in accord with the same structural principle as the categories with which he works and the forms of action available to him. People may alter their place in the set of categories, but they cannot be without a place."[16] In other words, the cultural notions of honor, person, and loyalty are inherently bound up with the "principle" of segmentation. These notions are cultural principles, not directly observable accounts of "actual" social action.

The principle of segmentation and associated notions of person, responsibility, and honor serve as "native" models of the social order in many tribal societies throughout the Middle East. A question remains about the extent to which the segmentary principle has been described and developed as an adequate analytical mode of the social order in societies so characterized. A major difficulty has been the confusion between segmentation and what anthropologists call *segmentary lineage theory*. Segmentation, as Dresch writes, characterizes "the types of events possible." It involves cultural principles that shape and inform possible conduct. Segmentary lineage *theory* concerns "sequences

[16] Paul Dresch, "The Significance of the Course Events Take in Segmentary Systems," *American Ethnologist* 13, no. 2 (May 1986), 319. See also his "The Position of Shaykhs Among the Northern Tribes of Yemen," *Man* (N.S.) 19, no. 1 (March 1984), 31–49. Dresch's two articles, together with Steven Caton, "Power, Persuasion, and Language: A Critique of the Segmentary Model in the Middle East," *International Journal of Middle East Studies* 19, no. 1 (February 1987), 77–102, provide good points of departure for understanding the issue of segmentation in the Middle East. For a review of earlier approaches in North Africa, see Dale F. Eickelman, "New Directions in Interpreting North African Society," in *Contemporary North Africa: Issues of Development and Integration*, ed. Halim Barakat (Washington, DC: Georgetown University, Center for Contemporary Arab Studies, 1985), pp. 164–77.

of events at the level of observation."[17] It also implies that political relationships are conceived primarily or exclusively in terms of lineal descent (either patrilineal or matrilineal), with groups at each "level" of society balanced by others of roughly equal strength. Segmentation requires a "moral" balancing of concepts of honor; segmentary lineage theory purports to ignore cultural principles and to involve, instead, the political balancing of actual groups.[18]

One of the earliest and most important clarifications of the concept of segmentation was made by Emrys L. Peters, a student of Evans-Pritchard at Oxford who carried out fieldwork among the tribes of Cyrenaica between 1948 and 1950, when they were still camel-herding pastoralists.[19] In the first part of his article, Peters explains that the bedouin see the basic unit of their social organization as the camp—that is, groups that herd together. Over 80 percent of the males in these camps, each with a population of 200 to 700 (in 1960 he gave the figure as 150 to 200), were agnatically related. Acceptance into such a group implies full political responsibility. Such "tertiary" groups (as they are designated by Peters) are corporate for most purposes. Moreover, each camp has its own wells, ploughland (the bedouin of Cyrenaica also cultivate), and pasture. In Figure 6-1 such groups are represented as level 1, where the irregularly drawn spheres associated with them are meant to indicate the territory possessed by each descent group. The ultimate test of membership in such a tertiary group is conduct during feuds and the payment of blood money. If someone does not participate as expected in such matters, he risks splitting from the group. Bedouin say that homicide within a tertiary group is unthinkable, as the group is supposed to respond to the injury of any of its number as "one body." Such homicides occur nonetheless, but Peters points out that the bedouin do not think of them in terms of murders requiring revenge. The most common result is the voluntary exile of a slayer or his expulsion from the group.

For homicide between tertiary sections, such as A and E in Figure 6-1, Peters argues that there is compelling pressure to settle such feuds quickly. Although each group possesses its own wells and territory, social relations between them are fairly intense, and a prolonged feud would seriously disrupt them. In most cases, settlement is arranged through an agreement to pay "blood money" (*diya*). The amount agreed upon is rarely paid in full, for, debt, like the feud itself, is a form of social relationship. So long as the debt is not

[17] Dresch, "The Significance," 309.

[18] Evans-Pritchard's *The Nuer* can be read either way, as Caton, "Power, Persuasion, and Language," 79, indicates. Evans-Pritchard's subsequent *The Sanusi of Cyrenaica* (Oxford: Clarendon Press, 1949) deals with segmentary lineage theory principally in terms of opposing social forces, as is the case with Gellner's *Saints*. See Hildred Geertz's review of *Saints* in the *American Journal of Sociology* 76, no. 4 (January 1971), 763–66. For a detailed discussion of the difficulties with Gellner's ethnographic argument by a Moroccan ethnographer, see Abdellah Hammoudi, "Segmentarity, Social Stratification, Political Power and Sainthood: Reflections on Gellner's Thesis," *Economy and Society* 9, no. 3 (August 1980), 279–303.

[19] Emrys L. Peters, "Some Structural Aspects of the Feud Among the Camel-Herding Bedouin of Cyrenaica," *Africa* 37, no. 3 (July 1967), 261–81. See also his earlier (orig. 1960) "The Proliferation of Segments in the Lineage of the Bedouin of Cyrenaica," in *Peoples and Cultures of the Middle East*, vol. 1 (Garden City, NY: Natural History Press, 1970), pp. 363–98.

fully paid, the social relationship endures. At the next level of segmentary integration (level 2 in Figure 6-1), groups usually occupy different ecological regions, so there is no urgent necessity to reach a settlement, although, even here, there are limitations to hostilities. They do not occur, for instance, at tribal markets. Quite often, hostile groups arrange to be present at different times to avoid meeting one another.[20] At higher levels, feuding can be even more prolonged. It should be kept in mind, however, that Peters's "tertiary" groups can, at one and the same time, be adjacent "secondary" or "primary" groups; hence his tidy argument about ecological pressures limiting the possibility of conflict is not as convincing as an explanation based on bedouin ideas of community and responsibility—in short, shared ideas of moral community. Outside the tribe itself, to continue Peters's argument, there were, at least in principle, no conventional restraints upon hostilities.

Peters's account provides specific examples of how segmentary lineage ideology is applied by its adherents to specific, historically known situations. Yet his goal is essentially the negative one of showing that, as a sociological model of "actual" social relations, segmentary lineage theory is inadequate. Thus his article demonstrates that segmentary groups among the Cyrenaican bedouin were not in a "balanced opposition" to one another in terms of numbers or resources in lands and herds. Nor did groups combine as dictated by segmentary lineage theory. "Power" was unevenly distributed among groups; the genealogical "equality" of groups claiming descent from a common ancestor could mask a considerable disparity of political strength, and tribal leadership did not always occur along the lines indicated by segmentation theory. Finally, significant political and economic links were created through marriage ties and other ties through women, a point already made in the earlier discussion of the Rwāla.[21]

Peters's analysis of the feud is excellent for showing how the Cyrenaican bedouin account for discrepancies between their political and economic alliances and their asserted adherence to segmentary principles. Yet, as was seen earlier with the Rwāla, the various "shortcomings" and sociological "contradictions" enumerated by Peters do not directly detract from the importance of segmentation as a culturally maintained principle informing social action in many Middle Eastern tribal contexts.

As Steven Caton argues, the indigenous models, of which Peters describes one,

[20] David Montgomery Hart, *The Aith Waryaghar of the Moroccan Rif: An Ethnography and History*, Viking Fund Publications in Anthropology 55 (Tucson: University of Arizona Press for the Wenner-Gren Foundation, 1976), pp. 38, 87, describes a situation in the Moroccan Rīf prior to colonial rule in which feuds were so endemic that each house had next to it a mud-and-stone masonry pillbox, where a man could have a commanding view of the terrain and take refuge if necessary. Hart does not accept the argument advanced by earlier ethnographers (whom he cites) that because women were not subject to attack, the existence of separate women's markets in the Rīf developed so that essential supplies could be obtained even during prolonged hostilities.

[21] Bourdieu, *Outline*, pp. 30–71, is one of the earlier social anthropologists to recognize the importance of such ties in Middle Eastern tribal societies.

> should be given far more emphasis in explaining social action. . . . When one examines the ethnographic record to determine what it is that Middle Eastern tribesmen are doing in political acts, one finds that they are talking to each other probably more than they are fighting, . . . with the consequent or attendant belief that the basis of power is persuasion rather than the exercise of force.[22]

Cultural notions of persuasion, together with mediation, honor, and negotiation, are basic to the shared moral community of tribespeople, not the use of sheer force. As Caton acknowledges, power as force certainly exists in some situations, but power as persuasion is equally real. By learning how to be persuasive, one becomes a man of honor in tribal societies, and persuasion is more central to the workings of tribal society than the use of force. In spite of the importance of persuasion and oratory—for instance, in the Berber societies of North Africa—Caton points out that there is no study of their oratory, of how people persuade others to adopt particular strategies or courses of action.

The confusion between segmentation as a cultural principle and as a means of shaping social action and segmentary lineage theory has, until recently, blocked the development of more satisfactory ways of understanding tribal societies in the Middle East and, by extension, Central Asia, where ethnographers have often adapted ideas from colleagues working in Middle Eastern contexts.[23] Thus some anthropologists, notably Ernest Gellner, have presented elaborate theories accounting for how presumably acephalous and egalitarian tribes organized by segmentary lineages coexisted with the inegalitarian and stratified social order of the cities and states of the region, at least in the "traditional" past. He asserted that the High Atlas region of Morocco possessed "traditional [segmentary lineage] institutions" that, until the 1930s, "had survived untouched . . . in a kind of sociological ice-box" until the mid-1950s, when he conducted his field research.[24] Yet significantly, Gellner provided no specific examples of political action by High Atlas Berbers for the earlier periods, and the evidence that he provided for later periods is irrelevant or contradictory to his understanding of segmentary lineage theory, although perceptive in posing questions of general political and sociological importance.[25]

As for the principle of segmentation, it has been extended by other scholars to apply to virtually any situation of conflict in the Middle East. Thus a political scientist has used the notion loosely to account for political factions

[22] Caton, "Power, Persuasion, and Language," p. 89.

[23] See, for example, Khazanov, *Nomads*, esp. pp. 169–97, who notes the many "exceptions" to the principle of segmentation.

[24] Ernest Gellner, "Political and Religious Organization of the Berbers of the Central High Atlas," in *Arabs and Berbers: From Tribe to Nation in North Africa*, ed. Ernest Gellner and Charles Micaud (London: Duckworth, 1972), pp. 25–58.

[25] Gellner's insistence that segmentation is the only political principle at work in tribal society (*Saints*, p. 42) limits his argument. On the nineteenth-century co-presence of tribal and state authority in the High Atlas region on which Gellner's ethnography is based, see Hammoudi, "Segmentarity," and Aḥmad al-Tawfiq, *Moroccan Society in the Nineteenth Century: Īnūltān, 1850–1912* [in Arabic], 2nd ed. (Rabat: Publications of the Faculty of Arts and Human Sciences, Université Mohamed V, 1983).

among the Moroccan elite, when all that is meant is that political rulers have sought to "divide and rule" in order to maintain their own hegemony.[26]

A MOROCCAN EXAMPLE: THE BNĪ BATĀW

The Bnī Batāw is a semitranshumant, Arabic-speaking group of roughly 18,000 (as of 1980) located on the plains of western Morocco near the foothills of the Middle Atlas Mountains.[27] Their livelihood derives from a combination of pastoralism and seasonal agriculture. Each fall they sow fields of wheat and barley on the plains; then they take their herds of sheep and goats to the forested foothills of the mountains, where there is sufficient forage for the winter. Especially in years of drought, there are running disputes with the government's forest guards over the use of these lands. In the past, the Bnī Batāw often moved their herds far into the Berber-speaking highlands, but French colonial restrictions, and since 1956 the restrictions of the Moroccan government, substantially limited the timing and extent of these annual moves. During March or April, depending on ecological conditions, the Bnī Batāw return with their herds to the plains. Today most of the Bnī Batāw live in dwellings of stone and dried mud on the plains and use their tents only in the winter transhumant months. After their fields are harvested in June, the herds are allowed to graze on the stubble in the fields. Water and forage become scarcer as the summer progresses. Eventually, people are compelled to move with their herds toward their winter pastures.

How do Bnī Batāw tribespeople conceive of their identity? *Bnī* is an Arabic word literally meaning "sons of." *Batāw* is a Berber word meaning "fragment." Bnī Batāw leaders and the government consider the tribe to be part of a larger tribal "confederation," but the larger grouping exists primarily as administrative entity and as an ideological framework in which wider political alliances were concluded in the past. There is no historical evidence to indicate that these wider entities acted as a collectivity. Within the Bnī Batāw itself, tribesmen speak of their identity in terms of *agnation*, or shared patrilineal descent. (I specify tribesmen because women, although they know the general outline of tribal structure, are vague about detail and usually trace their social ties through personal connections and *female* descent ties, although their accounts are not as comprehensive as those offered by "authoritative" male notables.) As for tribesmen, the problem remains of how they can be "sons of a fragment" or the "sons of" the place names that are used to designate certain

[26] On the application of segmentary theory to the Moroccan political elite, see John Waterbury, *The Commander of the Faithful: The Moroccan Political Elite* (New York: Columbia University Press, 1970), pp. 61–80. The notion of segmentation is quickly abandoned in this exemplary political ethnography of a Third World political elite. Gellner himself, *Muslim Society*, Cambridge Studies in Social Anthropology 32 (Cambridge: Cambridge University Press, 1981), p. 72, takes exception to such extensions of his notion of segmentation.

[27] Eickelman, *Moroccan Islam*, pp. 105–21; see also Eickelman, "Time in a Complex Society: A Moroccan Example," *Ethnology* 16, no. 1 (January 1977), 39–55.

subgroupings of the Bnī Batāw. The nature of social identity becomes clear if we pursue the way in which this language of social identity is used in practice.

Tribesmen explain their relation to each other and to outsiders such as anthropologists in terms of metaphors. Sometimes the metaphor is based on the parts of a tree—twigs, branches, and trunk; at other times, parts of the human body such as veins and arteries are used. Ordinarily, these metaphors are applied only in a general sense to the three "levels" of the Bnī Batāw. These are known abstractly as the rural local community (*dawwār*), the section (*fakhda*), and the tribe (*qbīla*). Members of such groups claim common descent or, more specifically, "closeness" to each other. Briefly described, the smallest unit of these levels is the *dawwār*. Literally, the word means "circle." Until the 1930s, tribespeople lived in tents throughout the year. Especially when the Bnī Batāw moved their herds into the highlands controlled by Berber-speaking groups, they pitched their tents in a circle, herding their animals into the center at night for security. Few groups camp like this any more, because the French managed to limit most intertribal hostilities and raiding. Today, the remaining tents (for the tribe is becoming increasingly settled and is abandoning herds for irrigation agriculture due to persistent water shortages) are more widely spaced during the winter months, just as the permanent dwellings of the Bnī Batāw are located on their agricultural lands, which are individually owned. These dwellings are not clustered into villages. Each local community is composed of 50 to 100 "tents" (*khayma*-s), also frequently called "households" (*dār*-s).

The next level is the section, which is usually composed of three or four local communities. The Bnī Batāw use a number of terms to designate sections,

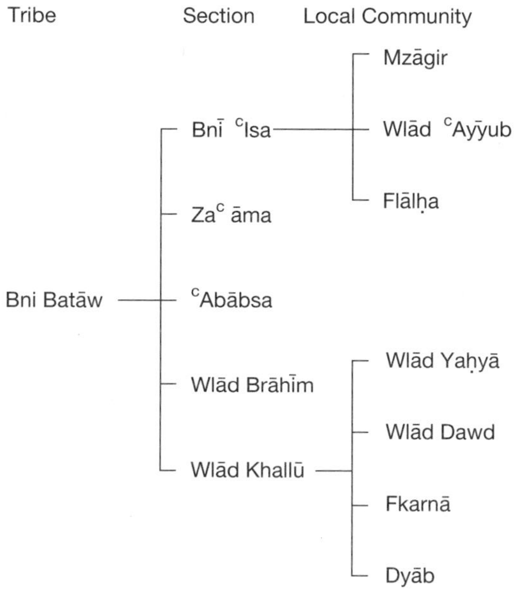

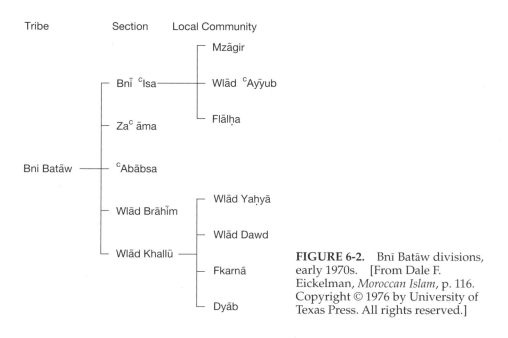

FIGURE 6-2. Bnī Batāw divisions, early 1970s. [From Dale F. Eickelman, *Moroccan Islam*, p. 116.]

one of which is thigh (*fakhda*), a term also used by the Rwāla. The Bnī Batāw are presently divided into five such sections.

To understand how tribespeople comprehend their society, the first important thing to notice is that they do not emphasize their relations with each other through patrilineal descent, although this notion is associated with the metaphors of social organization provided by the imagery of blood and the parts of a tree. As one tribesman put it, "We are like the branches of a tree, but each branch is on its own," emphasizing that the claim of common descent does not necessarily determine the lines of faction and political alliance. Actually, in explaining how the metaphors of the parts of trees and the human body relate to their social structure, tribespeople in western Morocco rely heavily on the concept of "closeness" (*qarāba*). *Qarāba* does not necessarily imply real or assumed kinship, even for tribespeople. Closeness flows along a number of lines. It can develop through cooperation with nearby households, mutual herding arrangements, kinship and patronage relations, and other bonds of mutual interest. The notion of "closeness" is an important one and is discussed at length in the following two chapters. On a practical level, moreover, the enumerations of groups and their divisions at any moment never exactly tally. Although tribespeople conceive of the relations between individuals and groups within the same framework (that is, the metaphor of the tree or of "blood"), there are variations in how these organizing concepts are applied to actual groups.

These variations are particularly clear at the "level" of the rural local community, the most important "level" in terms of everyday activities. Every tent belongs to such a local community. They are not set apart from each other by formal boundaries, only by shifting understandings of the identity of groups and their composition.

Tribespeople in a rural local community claim patrilineal relation to each other (among other ties), but no one can specifically demonstrate how all members of a group are mutually related. When pressed to indicate exact ties, tribespeople generally say that "older" persons know or that such ties derive from "early" (*bakrī*) times, an unspecified ahistorical past that is used to legitimize present-day social alignments.[28] Tribespeople do not ask each other for exact demonstrations of such ties. What counts is who acts together in a sustained way on ritual and political occasions. This flexibility is seen in the council (*jmā'a*) found in each local community. This is not a formal body but is constituted of adult male heads of tents who informally consult on such issues of mutual concern as transhumant movements, quarrels over water and pasture rights, the hiring and payment of a Quranic teacher to reside with them and teach their children the rudiments of the Quran, maintenance of the white-

[28] Eickelman, "Time," 50–52; and *Moroccan Islam*, pp. 115–21. Michael A. Marcus, in "History on the Moroccan Periphery: Moral Imagination, Poetry, and Islam," *Anthropological Quarterly* 58, no. 4 (October 1985), 152–60, and in "'The Saint Has Been Stolen': Sanctity and Social Change in a Tribe of Eastern Morocco," *American Ethnologist* 12, no. 3 (August 1985), 455–67, discusses how tribal poetry and ties with marabouts can be used to maintain a sense of local history distinct from that imposed by the state elite and townspeople, who relegate tribal and rural groups to the periphery.

washed building that serves as a tomb for their marabout, or saint (every local community is identified with one), and similar collective obligations.

Individual tents and groups of tents dissatisfied with belonging to a particular rural local community may break away to join another rural local community or to form their own whenever circumstances permit. This reshuffling also occurs among the Rwāla and among Libyan tribes, and it in no way challenges the ideology of shared identity and of exclusivity and opposition maintained in the tribal environment. Again, they compose a moral community, not a "natural" community.[29] Marriage ties, land inherited by a wife, or even the purchase of land from an individual from another rural local community can serve as the basis for such a realignment. Realignments frequently entail no physical relocation of households, as, for practical purposes, only nearby rural local communities are involved. Because of these shifts of identity, "official" administrative designations of rural local communities are almost always inaccurate and are considered by tribespeople as a category of identity used only in formal contact with local officials.

Because rural local communities are constantly re-forming, one way of determining links is to see the camping arrangements at the annual festival (*mūsim*) of the major marabout of the region, Sīdī Mḥammad Sharqī. His shrine and living descendants are located in the town of Boujad. This festival occurs each fall, just before the move to winter pastures. Groups are distinguished both by the placement of tents on these occasions and by the competitive displays of horsemanship and shooting (*taḥrīk*-s), sometimes called powder-plays (*la'b al-barūd*), in which they engage. The idea of these competitions is for groups to ride in a gallop in a straight line and to fire their guns simultaneously. Heavy betting accompanies these occasions. Participation in the competitions reflects new social alignments, and some realignments are due to disputes over the competitions themselves. Because the marabout's festival is also the one time in the year that tribespeople gather from a large area, such powder-plays, in effect, constitute public announcements of new social arrangements. As the conception of patrilineal descent is a relative one that changes with actual social arrangements, the groups involved legitimize their new relations by shifting the way in which they represent their ancestors and links with particular marabouts.

The identity of sections among the Bnī Batāw is somewhat more stable over time. Unlike the Rwāla, however, Bnī Batāw sections are subject to gradual shifts, not only in composition but also in formal identity. They acquire and lose people all the time, although there is greater stability in the structure of the names of groups and the locally shared conceptual framework in which they are situated.[30] One reason for their greater stability over lower tribal levels is

[29] For Libya, see Davis, *Libyan Politics*, pp. 63, 269–70.

[30] Khazanov's account of Kazakh tribal structure prior to the 1920s is broadly analogous to the account described here, with the Kazakh herding group (*aul*) taking the place of the Moroccan rural local community (*dawwār*), and the *yurt*, the Central Asian pastoralist's circular portable dwelling erected on wooden poles and covered with skins, taking the place of the Middle Eastern tent. See Khazanov, pp. 172–79.

FIGURE 6-3. Competitive riding at a *mūsim*, Morocco, 1968. [Courtesy Maurice Grosser.]

that they are recognized as administrative entities. The precolonial, colonial, and independent governments have invested the rights to collective pastures in sections and still allocate many taxes through the administrative apparatus associated with them. Prior to the colonial period, sections also performed significant functions. Each section, for instance, constructed fortified compounds of mud and stone that were used for defense in times of intertribal raiding. Sections also made collective arrangements for grazing rights to pastures controlled by neighboring groups, but there were many other "levels" at which such arrangements could also be made. Individuals from different tribal groups, for instance, could make arrangements among themselves if they had confidence in each other.

More formal arrangements between relatively stable groups were also frequent. A common sort were "ritual alliances" (*ṭāṭā*) made between rural local communities and sections of the same or different tribes. In such alliances, groups agreed to refrain from fighting and raiding each other and, at least in principle, to aid each other in the event of threats from third parties. Such alliances generally involved the exchange of herding rights as well. The patterns of such alliances occasionally coincided with "closeness," as reckoned by the formal ideology of patrilineal descent, but such ideology was not the primary factor in their formation.

These ties worked in the following way. The Flālḥa (see Figure 6-2) local community of the Bnī 'Īsa section of the Bnī Batāw concluded an alliance with the 'Abābsa section of the tribe; the fact that the two groups were at different "levels" of organization was not considered significant by the Bnī Batāw. They met at the shrine of one of the marabouts in Boujad and swore an alliance.

Each collectivity had multiple alliances of this sort. The Wlād Khallū section had three such alliances with other sections just before the colonial era.

One section was part of an Arabic-speaking tribe with adjacent agricultural lands; another involved an Arabic-speaking tribe at some distance from their own; a third alliance was with a neighboring Berber-speaking group, the Ait Bū Ḥaddū.

These alliances were concluded by different ritual means. In one case the groups involved had a communal meal, at the end of which all the men removed one of their slippers and placed them in a pile, one pile for each of the two groups. Slippers from the two piles were then matched at random. The men whose slippers were paired became companions with a special relation to each other. Whenever one needed permission for pasture rights or other matters, he approached his companion in the other group. In another case, the lactating women of the two contracting groups nursed the children of the opposite group after the men's communal meal. In a third case, the councils of the two groups had a communal meal in which the milk from lactating women of the two groups had been mixed in one of the plates, thus creating an enduring tie of milk brotherhood. Once such an alliance was concluded, any violation invited supernatural (as well as human) retribution.

The implication of these formal alliances carries the corresponding one that there is no *natural* tie of obligation between men and groups, but that these must be maintained. If someone says, "You're a member of A, so you must join us in opposing B," the reply can be, "Yes, I am a member of A, but I won't come to your assistance." The obligations that derive from identity are not necessarily binding in and of themselves. This is one of the reasons that identities can be so flexible in practice, even as the structure in which they are ordered remains relatively stable.[31]

Little mention has been made so far of the level of tribe. From the historically known precolonial period, it appears to have existed more as a set of ordered names that provided a range of potential identities for various groups at different times than as a base for sustained collective action, although coalitions of various sections and rural local communities within the "tribes" frequently occurred. When these coalitions did occur, it was not necessarily along lines of lineal descent. This is demonstrated by the patterns of resistance in which people from various sections and tribes aligned themselves against the French. Precolonial accounts of disputes in western Morocco also suggest that alliances followed much more flexible lines than those predicted by formal classifications.

An interesting aspect of the French colonial understanding of tribal structure is that it depended more on the ideology of agnatic relationships than did that of Moroccan tribespeople themselves. The French were in a dominant position, so their interpretation and codification of Moroccan ideas of tribe became the "official" form of social knowledge, which then permeated Moroccan understandings of tribal society. Segmentary ideology was administratively

[31] For more discussion of this issue, see Paul Dresch, "Placing the Blame: A Means of Enforcing Obligations in Upper Yemen," *Anthropos* 82, part 4–6 (1987), 427–43.

convenient as an "official" representation of local social structure. How were these administrative understandings translated into practice? Each winter, as indicated earlier, the Bnī Batāw moved with their herds to the Berber highlands. Yet, for the French, the Berber highlands were under military rule, and the lowland plains were under the civil native affairs administration. In the precolonial period, pasture rights could be arranged between individuals or several tents of different tribal groups when peaceful conditions prevailed. In some circumstances, the host person or group charged a price for such rights; in other cases, reciprocity at a later date was expected. Of course, disputes occurred frequently, but these only served to emphasize the wide range that such pastoral arrangements could take. The French found this flexibility confusing for administrative purposes, especially when tribesmen crossed administrative boundaries.

Colonial archives for the 1930s indicate that some administrators went so far as to propose a ban on pastoral movements that crossed administrative boundaries, unaware that such radical restrictions would drastically reduce the size of herds and make the survival of the Bnī Batāw precarious. In the end, a compromise was adopted in which movements of herds were authorized, but only on a reduced scale and only involving entire sections. The French argued (in line with popular sociological assumptions of the period) that only collective arrangements were "traditional."

French administrative divisions, however, worked more along the lines of a quasi-genealogical framework than the Moroccan tribes. For example, if a pastoral dispute broke out between the Bnī Batāw and a group of Berber tribesmen while the Bnī Batāw were with their herds in the Middle Atlas Mountains, the French civil official in Boujad who was responsible for the Bnī Batāw was not allowed to communicate directly with his military counterpart 20 miles away who was responsible for the Berber group. Instead, he was obliged to communicate with his immediate superior in a neighboring town, who communicated with his civilian superior. This administrator in turn contacted the ranking military officer responsible for the Middle Atlas region, who communicated with his subordinates. These rigid administrative hierarchies had no counterpart in Moroccan tribal organization, although the genealogical grid used by the French to indicate relations among various groups naturally had important consequences, as pasture rights and taxes were determined by them, and local strongmen had their privileges reinforced by the support they received from the French by appointment as unsalaried officials with the power to offer "authoritative" advice to administrators. The French were concerned with the vertical axis described in Figure 6-1, which suggests lines of control, whereas tribespeople themselves were primarily interested in the horizontal axis, which corresponds more to autonomy.

Now what is important about these complex patterns of association and identity? To say that some rural Moroccans are "tribal" suggests to other Moroccans a style of comportment and of managing social relations about which there can be a range of perceptions and misperceptions. Lines of political cleavage depend on the interpretation of complex factors of residence, kinship, herding, and land arrangements, among other considerations. Those interests that are most salient are often legitimized through the notion of segmentation. "Tribal" people do not respond in a semiautomatic way to challenges to the various social collectivities to which they belong. In the Moroccan case, the notion of "closeness," outlined earlier, and informed for some Moroccans by the principle of segmentation, allows considerable latitude in the course events take and how political choices can be legitimized. Despite many regional variations, however, there is a common "family resemblance" among Middle Eastern and Central Asian notions of tribe. Tribespeople think of themselves, at least in part, as being opposed to other morally equivalent tribal units, although they also contend with nontribal peoples.

Of course, the social organization of a Moroccan tribe cannot in itself be taken as representative of all Middle Eastern tribes or Central Asian ones, although Anatoly Khazanov pursues Middle Eastern and Central Asian family resemblances in detail.[32] But the *type* of analysis offered here can serve as a guide to understanding tribes in other contexts. Such analysis involves an account of how people in a given society explicitly and implicitly conceive of the social order and act on these assumptions. It also involves seeing how these assumptions become transformed in different historical contexts. Although Middle Eastern countries and regions within them share numerous economic, social, and cultural similarities, they differ in just as many ways. Comparisons of "tribal" societies in these countries, based solely on a single point of resemblance, such as the ways in which ideologies of patrilineal descent are used and manipulated, can be highly misleading because such ideologies are inadequate for describing the political organization and ideas of a moral community of Middle Eastern tribal groups.

The appropriate use of the notion of segmentation, like an understanding of the notion of tribe, is not confined to the Middle East's (or Central Asia's) past or to an archaic form of political order. The principle of segmentation applies to cultural ideas of political and social order, not to the "course events take." Nor are tribal identities becoming irrevocably eroded in favor of identification with state and nation, in spite of the often brutal efforts of colonial and national governments to eliminate all actual or potential alternatives to state authority. As Richard Tapper points out, the state opposes the idea of tribe not only as an "external force" but also as an ideal of political authority. Tribes have rarely been entirely free from state influence and control. Tapper suggests analyzing both historical sequences of greater and lesser state authority and control and the ideas of state and tribe as "frontiers of the mind," or opposing cultural values.[33] Although tribes and tribal authority were systematically and ruthlessly undermined in twentieth-century prerevolutionary Iran, for exam-

[32] Khazanov, *Nomads*, 119–97.

[33] Tapper, "Introduction," *Tribe and State*, pp. 70–71.

ple, they appear to have enjoyed at least a temporary resurgence since the Iranian revolution.[34]

Nor is it appropriate to accept at face value the claim of modern states that they best represent the notions of modernization and progress. As Tapper writes, tribal societies "have been less savage than historical states and empires, less 'clannish' than many ruling elites; neither the evils that the twentieth century has ameliorated (such as ignorance and disease), nor the evils that it has brought (such as overpopulation, alienation, ecological disaster, and mass destruction) can be attributed to tribalism. . . . Tribalism has its faults and limitations, but its provision of social security and its long-term survival value should recommend it as no anachronism in the last decades of the twentieth century."[35]

It is unnecessary to view acceptance of the idea of tribe or of the principle of segmentation as an either/or proposition or to assume that one description of a segmentary system can somehow account for all social organizations or tribes in the Middle East. Studies of tribe and comparisons among them are best advanced through looking for "family resemblances" that can be compared and contrasted rather than exact identities asserted by simpler but less accurate theoretical assumptions. This notion of "family resemblances" applies equally to the study of personal and family relationships in the Middle East, the subject of the next chapter.

IDEOLOGIES

We have noted that "tribe" is an ideological term denoting a particular form of social identity. Before we turn to other such notions in the next chapter, it is useful to clarify what we mean by "ideology." In current popular usage, *ideology* often acquires the connotation of a system of illusory "unreal" beliefs concerning the nature of the social (or economic or political) world. The notion that ideologies are illusory is unfortunate and contrary to how the term is used by most sociologists and social anthropologists, who regard them as significant and irreducible components of any cultural order. Ideologies inform social practice and provide it with meaning. The problem is to specify more precisely what is meant by ideology and its relation to society. The authors of such a classical discussion as *The German Ideology* insisted that ideologies shape and are shaped by the particular social, economic, and historical formations in which they occur.[36]

[34] See Gene R. Garthwaite, "Reimagined Internal Frontiers: Tribes and Nationalism—Bakhtiyari and Kurds," in *Russia's Muslim Frontiers: New Directions in Cross-Cultural Analysis*, Indiana Series in Arab and Islamic Studies (Bloomington: Indiana University Press, 1993), pp. 130–45.

[35] Tapper, "Introduction," *Tribe and State*, pp. 74–75.

[36] Karl Marx and Frederick Engels, *The German Ideology*, ed. C. J. Arthur (New York: International Publishers, 1970 [1846]), esp. pp. 46–47. This general principle holds not only for what might be termed social knowledge but also for the underlying assumptions of scientific thought, despite the popular notion that "science" is somehow immune from social vicissitudes. See Barry Barnes, *Interests and the Growth of Knowledge* (London and Boston: Routledge & Kegan Paul, 1977).

The central problem posed by Karl Marx of the relationship between ideology and society continues to inform contemporary social thought. The primary theoretical issue is *how* the relation between ideologies and social forms should be described and elaborated.

In the past, many sociologists have been concerned principally with those ideologies or beliefs that are consciously elaborated and maintained. Such ideologies, especially in the political domain, are undeniably important and merit intensive analysis as explicit, categorical accounts of how the world is supposed to work. There are also implicit, shared notions of the social order, which are so taken for granted that they are not usually codified or presented in an explicit manner. These implicit and explicit notions often collide with one another. American law concerning the family and family responsibilities may strike some as either idealized or utopian, but anyone caught up in the mechanisms of family court soon recognizes that these notions of "family values" are authoritative and can profoundly affect the course of events. These explicit and implicit shared notions of the social order also exist in specific times and spaces. They structure social activity and its interpretation and in turn are shaped by configurations of political domination and economic relations. Shared cultural understandings are elaborated by social categories, groups, and classes in divergent ways and often change in significance when taken up by new carriers or adapted to novel contexts.[37]

The term *ideology*, as I use it above, encompasses a wider set of notions than formal ideologies alone. Anthropologists and other social theorists are additionally concerned with what might be called *practical ideologies*, sets of beliefs constituted by implicit, shared assumptions concerning such basic aspects of the social order as notions of tribe, kinship, family, person, sexuality, nation, religion, and worldview. Most of these notions overlap in various ways, and some are more encompassing than others. *Worldview*, for instance, is one of the broader concepts and is used by anthropologists to designate shared cultural assumptions concerning the overall nature of the social order. Many of the practical ideologies remain incompletely systematized by those who maintain them, although forms of conduct—patterns of naming, marriage, residence, and ritual—can be used to document them.

The fact that many of these ideologies are so "natural" and taken for granted means that in ordinary circumstances they are not consciously or fully articulated. Thus Americans, in looking at their own beliefs and social forms, are not ordinarily prepared to elaborate their shared assumptions concerning family, sexuality, and the like. Or more precisely, to make the anthropologist's task more intriguing, when some "natives" express formal beliefs concerning family, religion, and economic conduct, these beliefs may only obliquely account for the actual, implicit principles that form the basis of their practical ideology. The same is, of course, true of Middle Eastern and Central Asian soci-

[37] See Dale F. Eickelman, "The Political Economy of Meaning," *American Ethnologist* 6, no. 2 (May 1979), 386–93, which discusses the work of Pierre Bourdieu; and Anthony Giddens, *The Constitution of Society* (Berkeley and Los Angeles: University of California Press, 1984), pp. 1–40.

eties. In dramatic instances, such as the former Marxist Somali Democratic Republic, now a lapsed state for all practical purposes, tribalism and lineage loyalties were declared illegal and officially ceased to exist, yet through mundane but critical indices such as patterns of livestock investment and the lineage composition of governments since the 1969 "revolution," it can readily be demonstrated that lineage loyalties continued to thrive, although it was illegal to say so publicly.[38] How formal and practical ideologies overlap and influence each other is one of the principal themes raised in the discussion of "tribe."

There are genuinely puzzling problems of analytical strategy and substance that concern the relation of ideologies to society. Notions of tribe, kinship, ethnicity, sexuality, and religion all constitute shared cultural meanings, ways of making sense of the social world and of informing action within it. All patterns of cultural meaning are generated, maintained, and often transformed through social use, but these forms of social use are not reducible to individual choice alone, and some social forms are immensely resilient and long-lived. The distinction between *ḥaḍāra* and *badāwa* is a case in point. If patterns of meaning are reproduced through social action, why do so many of them (such as notions of family) appear to remain relatively stable over long periods of time, despite the massive economic, political, and social transformations of many parts of the Middle East (or elsewhere, for that matter)? Or is it just that some patterns of meaning appear more stable—for instance, those practical ideologies so taken for granted that they are not fully articulated and thus not subject to conscious manipulation?

A related issue concerns the limits of ambiguity and multiple interpretations of symbolic statements and how such ambiguity often facilitates the accommodation of major social and cultural changes. In the last half century in countries such as Morocco, Iraq, and the Sudan, and in the last decade or two, in countries such as the Yemen Arab Republic and Oman, and currently in all the states of Central Asia, there have been massive changes in how people make a living, where they live, how they are educated, and what they expect from each other and from the state. The theme of change is pursued in historical as well as contemporary contexts because the scope of some changes in the past has often posed similar problems of the relation of cultural meanings to social forms. Such issues are not only of major interest to social theorists; they also provide people who live in rapidly changing societies with a means of reflecting upon their own lived experience.

FURTHER READINGS

For Emrys Peters's more general views on the use and misuse of segmentary lineage theory in Middle Eastern contexts, see his "Aspects of Affinity in a Maronite Lebanese Village," in *Mediterranean Family Structures*, ed. J. G. Peristiany, Cambridge Studies in

[38] I. M. Lewis, "Kim Il-Sung in Somalia: The End of Tribalism?" in *Politics in Leadership: A Comparative Perspective*, ed. William A. Shack and Percy S. Cohen (Oxford: Clarendon Press, 1979), pp. 13–44.

Social Anthropology 13 (London: Cambridge University Press, 1976), p. 32. See also his "The Tied and the Free: An Account of a Type of Patron-Client Relationship Among the Bedouin Pastoralists of Cyrenaica," in *Contributions to Mediterranean Sociology*, ed. J. G. Peristiany (Paris and The Hague: Mouton, 1968), pp. 167–88. Peters's "Cultural and Social Diversity in Libya," in *Libya Since Independence*, ed. J. A. Allan (London: Croom Helm, 1982), pp. 103–20, brings his account forward by three decades. The best comparative discussion of the feud in Mediterranean "tribal" societies is Jacob Black-Michaud, *Cohesive Force: Feud in the Mediterranean and the Middle East* (New York: St. Martin's Press, 1975). See also the interesting case studies in Joseph Ginat, *Blood Disputes Among Bedouin Rural Arabs in Israel: Revenge, Mediation, Outcasting, and Family Honor* (Pittsburgh: University of Pittsburgh Press, 1987).

The blurred distinction between segmentation as a cultural principle and segmentary lineage theory became particularly apparent in ethnographies on Morocco published in the 1960s and 1970s. Ernest Gellner's *Saints*, published in 1969 but available in summary form since at least 1963, makes no such distinction. Subsequent studies of Moroccan society labeled as "interpretive" anthropology, in spite of significant differences in the points of view of individual authors, including Clifford and Hildred Geertz, Lawrence Rosen, Paul Rabinow, and Dale Eickelman, emphasized cultural notions of self and person and sought to explain how social action was perceived within the cultural framework of the Moroccan social order.

Some scholars, including Eickelman, in "Ideology and Regional Cults: Maraboutism and Ties of 'Closeness' in Western Morocco," in *Regional Cults*, ed. Richard P. Werbner, ASA Monograph 16 (New York and London: Academic Press, 1977), pp. 3–24, and Ernest Gellner, *Muslim Society*, Cambridge Studies in Social Anthropology 32 (New York and Cambridge: Cambridge University Press, 1981), pp. 214–20, have directly cited the views of opposing scholars. More often, however, the opposing arguments are not cited, making the scholarly debate opaque. For example, Raymond Jamous, *Honneur et baraka: Les structures sociales traditionelles dans le Rif* (Cambridge: Cambridge University Press; Paris: Éditions de la Maison des Sciences de l'Homme, 1981), makes virtually no reference to the work of other contemporary scholars on Morocco. This lack of scholarly contextualization makes Jamous's thorough but idealized account and analysis of Rifian notions of honor and segmentation particularly hard to relate to alternative views or, for that matter, to the region's social and economic history.

A major contribution of later studies has been to break down the earlier presumption of a sharp distinction between tribal and urban society in Morocco and between tribes in the "traditional" past and in historically known periods. See, for example, Michael A. Marcus, " 'Horsemen Are the Fence of the Land': Honor and History Among the Ghiyata of Eastern Morocco," in *Honor and Shame and the Unity of the Mediterranean*, ed. David D. Gilmore, American Anthropological Association Special Publication 22 (Washington, DC: American Anthropological Association, 1986), pp. 49–60. Elaine Combs-Schilling, "Family and Friend in a Moroccan Boom Town: The Segmentary Debate Reconsidered," *American Ethnologist* 12, no. 4 (November 1985), 659–75, argues that segmentation "coexists" with other "organizational idioms" (p. 660) and, as an organizational principle with long-term strategic significance, need not be placed into operation for day-to-day affairs (p. 671). Her account is best in analyzing how claims to kinship obligation are articulated in Morocco's small urban centers, but it is less convincing in equating such ties and obligations with segmentation.

Charles Lindholm, "Kinship Structure and Political Authority: The Middle East and Central Asia," reprinted in his *Frontier Perspectives: Essays in Comparative Anthropology* (Karachi and New York: Oxford University Press, 1996 [1986]), pp. 147–71, leaps too quickly from a discussion of kinship structures, which he categorized as "segmentary," to macrohistorical political ones, but he suggests interesting, if not always convincing, comparisons between the two major civilizational/cultural/geographic regions. See also his "The Segmentary Lineage System: Its Applicability to Pakistan's Political Structure" (originally written in 1977), pp. 121–44, in the same volume.

The next step in the discussion of segmentation is the emergence of Moroccan interpretations of Moroccan society, an example of which is Aḥmad al-Tawfīq, *Moroccan Society in the Nineteenth Century: Inūltān, 1850–1912* [in Arabic], 2nd ed. (Rabat: Publications of the Faculty of Arts and Human Sciences, 1983), who deals, as a social historian, with roughly the same region discussed in Gellner's *Saints*, but he comes to different conclusions regarding the nature of political authority and economic ties with the "outside" world.

Discussions concerning the applicability of Gellner's version of segmentation theory were most intense in the 1970s and early 1980s, but the issue was revisited in one of the last notes that Gellner wrote before his death in 1995. See Henry Munson, Jr., "Rethinking Gellner's Segmentary Analysis of Morocco's Ait 'Atta," *Man* (N.S.) 28, no. 2 (June 1993), pp. 267–80, who argues that Gellner's depiction of the Ait 'Atta is "fundamentally flawed." Gellner responded with a long comment, "Segmentation: Reality or Myth?" *Journal of the Royal Anthropological Institute* 1, no. 4 (December 1995), pp. 821–29, to which Munson replied on pp. 829–32 of the same issue. Gellner stressed that segmentation is an "absolutely indispensable" tool for understanding "Agrarian" societies, an important "brick" in his conceptual apparatus for understanding human social and political development. This exchange, like others cited in this book, offers useful insight into how such debates shape ideas in the social sciences.

Andrew Shryock, *Nationalism and the Genealogical Imagination: Oral History and Textual Authority in Tribal Jordan*, Comparative Studies in Muslim Societies 23 (Berkeley and Los Angeles: University of California Press, 1997), discusses how the "genealogical" representation of political relationships prevalent in tribal settings becomes transformed when tribes become incorporated into the modern state or, as in Jordan, become a significant component of state identity, and how authoritative genealogical representations become transformed when conveyed in writing rather than orally.

7

PERSONAL AND FAMILY RELATIONSHIPS

WHY STUDY KINSHIP?

People create kinship ties, and with them they establish social relationships and mark distinctions among themselves. Meticulous descriptions of how these cultural identities are established, elaborated, reproduced, and modified when applied to new contexts, instead of treating them as fixed ethnographic artifacts, however, are only now becoming common. But kinship, family relationships, and other associated cultural ideas must be studied in the context of complementary, locally held notions of patronage, neighborliness, friendship, and the economic and political contexts in which these are maintained and reproduced. The overlapping of kinship with other forms of identity, including those of residential proximity, is found throughout the Middle East and Central Asia.

Understanding kinship and family ties cross-culturally involves several related issues. Anthropologists must elicit the shared cultural notions of family and relationship prevalent in any given society rather than presuming their content (for example, shared genetic substance—the concept of "blood" ties in American culture) in advance. Whatever the actual groupings of people who feel obliged to one another through "family" relationships, these groupings act in cultural terms that have a genetic reference. Nonetheless, how people behave toward one another as "kin" and "family" cannot be accounted for entirely in terms of obligations defined in genetic terms.[1]

In the past, many American and European anthropologists have implicitly and inappropriately imported their own cultural stress on genetic ties when interviewing people in the Middle East and analyzing their notions of kinship

[1] David M. Schneider, *American Kinship: A Cultural Account*, 2nd ed. (Chicago: University of Chicago Press, 1980 [1968]. See also Rodney Needham, "Polythetic Classification: Convergence and Consequences," *Man* (N.S.) 10, no. 3 (September 1975), 349–69; and Marilyn Strathern, "Kinship and Economy: Constitutive Orders of a Provisional Kind," *American Ethnologist* 12, no. 2 (May 1985), 191–209.

The principal kinship terms for family of origin in formal Arabic are *ab* (father), *umm* (mother), *'amm* (father's brother), *'amma* (father's sister), *khāl* (mother's brother), *khāla* (mother's sister), *akh* (brother), *ukht* (sister), *ibn* (son), and *bint* (daughter). The principal terms indicating ties through marriage, called *affinal* links by anthropologists, include *zawj* (husband), *zawja* (wife), and *nasīb* (father-in-law); *ansibā'*, the plural of *nasīb*, designates in-laws in general. There are other terms, such as *hafīḍ* and *hafīḍa* (grandson and granddaughter) and *jadd* and *jadda* (grandfather and grandmother). Anthropologists call kinship terminology such as that used by Arabs *denotative* because the terms designate specific relatives rather than classes of them. Relatives other than those specified above are generally designated by combinations of these terms. For instance, *ibn 'amm* is a father's brother's son, and *abū zawja* is a wife's father. There are other combinations of terms to designate half-siblings, co-wives, and other types of relationships. Colloquial usage tends to follow this general pattern described, with many local variations.

and family. In Central Asia, Russian ethnographers were almost the only "outsiders" to have had regular access to rural regions until the 1990s, and they were discouraged from studying kinship and family ties. For ideological reasons, ideas about kinship and family were often taken for granted or regarded as devoid of interest. As a result, Russian-language studies on the subject are only now beginning to appear.[2] Scholars from outside the region were even more strictly controlled, and prior to 1991, it was unusual for Westerners to gain access to homes or rural areas. One could sense the significance of family and kinship ties in conducting "approved" research, such as Theodore Levin's ethnomusicological studies of the region, but researchers were discouraged from studying the topic.[3] This situation is changing rapidly. The result has been an overemphasis on

[2] I am grateful to Anatoly Khazanov (personal communication, August 3, 1996) for discussing Russian-language ethnographic studies related to kinship and family. His suggestions are included in the Further Readings section of this chapter. See, however, Sergei P. Poliakov, *Everyday Islam: Religion and Tradition in Rural Central Asia*, trans. Anthony Olcott (Armonk, NY, and London: M. E. Sharpe, 1992), pp. 53–58, for brief, general comments; and Elizabeth E. Bacon, *Central Asians Under Russian Rule: A Study in Culture Change* (Ithaca, NY, and London: Cornell University Press, 1980 [1966]). Although specific anthropological studies of kinship and family remain sparse, demographic data yield considerable information on recent trends. See, for example, Mark Tolts, "Modernization of Demographic Behaviour in the Muslim Republics of the Former USSR," in *Muslim Eurasia: Conflicting Legacies*, ed. Yaacov Ro'i, Cummings Center Series (London: Frank Cass, 1995), pp. 231–53.

[3] See Theodore Levin, *The Hundred Thousand Fools of God: Musical Travels in Central Asia* (Bloomington and London: Indiana University Press, 1996). He discusses at length the kinship and family relations of singers and musicians and the way that ties of family, neighborhood, and friendship provide an important framework for getting things done. However, as William Fierman (personal communication, August 3, 1996) indicates, until 1991, the movements of Western scholars and the people they could see were strictly controlled, and foreigners were not allowed to speak to people without official supervision. Under such circumstances, the silence about kinship and domestic life is easy to understand.

genealogical kinship ideologies, which have their main and clearest form for Muslims in the Quranic inheritance code and for all Middle Easterners in kinship terminology, both terms of address—that is, the terms used when speaking to a person—and terms of reference, those used to a person.[4]

Because there are certain similarities between, for example, Arabic formulations and American ones, some anthropologists have, wittingly or unwittingly, extrapolated their own cultural notions into Middle Eastern data. This has been particularly the case in limiting family ties to "blood" ties and in assuming that the notions of "clan" and "tribe" have more significance in the ordering of behavior and the determining of choices in moral situations than relationships with neighbors (or members of the same herding group, in the case of nomadic pastoralists) and friends.[5] Such assumptions have contributed to the popularity of notions such as segmentary lineage theory, discussed in Chapter 6. Two related issues are involved here: one concerns how coercive kinship norms are in themselves; the other concerns the independence of kinship norms from other kinds of social obligation.

Anyone interested in understanding Middle Eastern and Central Asian life should follow "native" constructs and logic as thoroughly as possible. Knowledge of the full context in which ideas of family and personal relationships are held is especially important for understanding Middle Eastern societies and will become equally important as studies of Central Asian kinship and family become more readily available. This is because kinship forms and the personalization of social relationships permeate even bureaucratic and industrial settings, often in an effort to make such relationships more reliable. It is not unusual to find the key offices of governments in the Middle East com-

[4] For Morocco, see Hildred Geertz, "The Meanings of Family Ties," in Clifford Geertz, Hildred Geertz, and Lawrence Rosen, *Meaning and Order in Moroccan Society*, Cambridge Studies in Cultural Systems (New York: Cambridge University Press, 1979), pp. 356–63; for Egypt, see Hani Fakhouri, *Kafr el-Elow: An Egyptian Village in Transition*, 2nd ed. (Prospect Heights, IL: Waveland Press, 1987 [1972], pp. 57–61; for South Yemen, see R. B. Serjeant, "Kinship Terms in Wadi Ḥaḍramaut," *Der Orient in der Forschung* (Wiesbaden: Franz Steiner, 1967), pp. 626–33. Kinship terms in Persian and Turkish tend to be more classificatory than denotative. For Turkish, see Paul Stirling, *Turkish Village*, The Nature of Human Society (New York: Wiley, 1965), pp. 151–55; and Brian Spooner, "Kinship and Marriage in Eastern Persia," *Sociologus* 15, no. 1 (1965), 22–31. The partial exceptions are linked to the other language groups in the area. For example, David Montgomery Hart, *The Aith Waryaghar of the Moroccan Rif: An Ethnography and History*, Viking Fund Publications in Anthropology 55 (Tucson: University of Arizona Press for the Wenner-Gren Foundation, 1976), pp. 203–13, notes the term *ayyām*, used by some of Morocco's Berber-speaking groups to refer equally to father's sister's child, sister's child, daughter's child, and (asymmetrically) son's child. Among the Pukhtun of Pakistan's North-West Frontier Province and Afghanistan, both father's sister and mother's sister are called *tror*. See David M. Hart, *Guardians of the Khaibar Pass* (Lahore: Vanguard Books, 1985), pp. 25–26, 176.

[5] For an elaboration of this argument in an Algerian context, see Pierre Bourdieu, *Outline of a Theory of Practice*, trans. Richard Nice, Cambridge Studies in Social Anthropology 16 (New York: Cambridge University Press, 1977), pp. 30–71; for a Moroccan example that indicates in detail how people can have genealogical models "suggested" to them by anthropologists, see H. Geertz, "Family Ties," pp. 349–56. Emrys Peters, "Aspects of Affinity in a Lebanese Maronite Village," in *Mediterranean Family Structures*, ed. J. G. Peristiany, Cambridge Studies in Social Anthropology 13 (New York: Cambridge University Press, 1976), pp. 27–28, discusses the perils of drawing unwarranted inferences from kinship terminology alone, citing examples from contemporary anthropological literature.

posed of close relations, presumably because kinship ties are assumed to be a guarantee of loyalty. This is the case, not only in the monarchies of the region, such as Saudi Arabia, Oman, and Morocco, but in other regimes as different as Iran (and the significant roles of Ayatollah Khomeini's son and son-in-law), Egypt, Syria, Turkey, and Lebanon. Nor are such actions necessarily regarded as an abuse of political authority. Many businesses are organized along the same lines.

The study of kinship in the Middle East, like the study of tribes, has often been regarded primarily as an anthropological preserve, although this has not prevented scholars in other fields from making assumptions about the nature of family and group identity. Such assumptions can become highly politicized. In the 1970s, for instance, Edward Said took a distinguished sociologist to task for writing that "co-operation in the Near East is still largely a family affair and little of it is found outside the blood group [*sic*] or village," on the grounds that it suggests a diminished capacity of Middle Easterners to organize "institutionally, politically [and] culturally."[6] Yet, because a large number of Middle Eastern personal relationships are cast in the language of family relationships, and because such ties pervade government offices, understanding kinship relations and how ties of trust are forged among people is also crucial to understanding how formal institutions work. The term *family* can be put to many different uses in Middle Eastern societies, and, as we learn more about the region, in Central Asia as well. Many of Ṣaddām Ḥusayn's closest associates are from his immediate family, and his presidential body guards (*al-ḥimāya*) are "almost to a man from the president's tribal and geographical zone."[7]

As with concepts of "tribe" in the Middle East and Central Asia, there are no single notions of kinship and family in the two regions, nor can variations between the kinship systems be used to classify them taxonomically. Cultural notions of personal and kin relationships vary considerably from Rabat to Kabul and Almaty, from rural to urban settings, and among different educational and socioeconomic categories of society.

PRACTICAL KINSHIP

The term *kinship*, as used by anthropologists, can be considered an *experience-distant* concept—formulated for analytically inclined participants in a society

[6] Edward W. Said, *Orientalism* (New York: Pantheon, 1978), p. 312. Said's quote is from Morroe Berger, *The Arab World Today* (Garden City, NY: Doubleday/Anchor, 1964), p. 151. Value judgments such as Berger's are not restricted to the Middle East. "It is worth observing that each of the nations of Europe believes the others to be guilty of nepotism to a far greater degree than themselves," writes Julian Pitt-Rivers, *The Fate of Shechem or the Politics of Sex*, Cambridge Studies in Social Anthropology 19 (Cambridge and New York: Cambridge University Press, 1977), p. 107. I am grateful to Paul Dresch for pointing out this reference.

[7] Amatzia Baram, "Re-Inventing Nationalism in Ba'thi Iraq, 1968–1994: Supra-Territorial and Territorial Identities and What Lies Below," *Princeton Papers*, no. 5 (Fall–Winter 1996).

or its observers to comprehend or compare social phenomena, either typologically or through "family resemblances." *Experience-near* concepts are those that individuals use "naturally and effortlessly" to define what they see, feel, think, and imagine and that they "readily understand when similarly applied by others."[8]

Used comparatively as a first-order, experience-distant approximation, "kinship" serves as a useful framework for comparing experience-near concepts from different parts of the Middle East and Central Asia that can be glossed as "kin": the notion of *qawm* (Afghanistan), *ḥamūla* (Arabs in Israel), and *qarāba* (Morocco). In Afghanistan, *qawm* refers to a socially united and territorially contiguous group of people who speak of themselves as if they were also linked by agnatic kinship, although such a group actually includes affines, neighbors, and others. The term does *not* apply to persons or households who do not cooperate with other members of the *qawm*, in spite of close agnatic or affinal ties. A *qawm* is ideally "a territorially and socially integrated group, joined together through ties of kinship, political action, and religious belief and ritual."[9] Although *qawm* can also refer to people sharing common agnatic descent, it would be incorrect to regard such a usage as primary and its reference to "a territorially and socially integrated group" as derivative. The central feature of the Afghan concept of *qawm* is the active maintenance by its members of a shared notion of relationship. It is this ideological form that is primary, not a "native" recognition of "blood" ties, even if such assumptions are metaphorically important.

The same general point holds for some of the shared notions of identity among Arab villagers in Israel. In a study conducted in 1958–1959, Abner Cohen found that most (but not all) households were identified with a number of patronymic associations called *ḥamūla*-s. The shared identity of the *ḥamūla* was expressed in the idiom of patriliny, although villagers themselves were aware that not all the claimed patrilineal links were historically valid.[10] To emphasize the fact that he was not writing of lineal descent, Cohen used the term *patronymic group* to stress that the shared element of *ḥamūla* identity was the name of a claimed agnatic ancestor. Cohen was one of the first ethnographers to break with the more conventional assumptions of lineage theory in a Middle Eastern context. In a later publication he referred to the *ḥamūla* by the more appropriate term *patronymic association* rather than *group* better to emphasize the flexibility inherent in the cultural

[8] This distinction is elaborated in Clifford Geertz, *Local Knowledge* (New York: Basic Books, 1983 [1975]), p. 57.

[9] Robert Leroy Canfield, *Faction and Conversion in a Plural Society: Religious Alignments in the Hindu Kush*, Anthropological Papers 50 (Ann Arbor: University of Michigan, Museum of Anthropology, 1973), pp. 34–35. For a clear distinction between *qawm* and related terms as categories rather than empirical groupings, see also Nancy and Richard Tapper, "Marriage Preferences and Ethnic Relations Among Durrani Pashtuns of Afghan Turkestan," *Folk* 24 (1982), 162–63.

[10] Abner Cohen, *Arab Border Villages in Israel* (Manchester, UK: Manchester University Press, 1965), pp. 2–3, 105–29.

principle of *ḥamūla* and its frequent lack of sharp principles of exclusion in social practice.[11]

For certain specific purposes such as inheritance, a calculation of agnatic relations and affines was made in principle in terms of the tenets of the Quran. However, everyday domestic arrangements and the political alignments of the *ḥamūla* were governed by principles of social identity that were not based solely on ties created through "blood" and marriage, as Cohen's case studies meticulously demonstrate. In practice, *ḥamūla* identity was based on a complex web of patrilineal, affinal, and matrilateral ties, neighborliness (most *ḥamūla* households were located in the same section of the village), and sustained cooperation in political, economic, and ceremonial activities. As political alignments and interests altered, some households shifted their *ḥamūla* identity, although such realignments generally occurred only among households not clearly identified with the *ḥamūla*'s core. Nonetheless, when asked to define a *ḥamūla*, villagers did so in terms of common descent, although they privately stated to the ethnographer that such claims could not always be demonstrated. As with other forms of social identity, *ḥamūla* affiliation in itself did not determine the lines of cooperation and political action, despite the fact of such identity being couched in the idiom of patrilineal descent. Cohen provides numerous examples of cross-*ḥamūla* ties of friendship, patronage, and common economic and political interests that served equally as bases for unity and cooperation. Ties created through marriage were similarly used. He points out that intra-*ḥamūla* marriages were relatively common, but that marriages outside the *ḥamūla* could also serve as the base for close economic and political cooperation.[12]

A third example, from the "far West" of the Middle East, is the Moroccan concept of "closeness" (*qarāba*), briefly introduced in its rural/tribal context in Chapter 6.[13] As used by urban and rural Moroccans, "closeness" carries contextual meanings that range imperceptibly from asserted and recognized ties of kinship to participation in factional alliances, ties of patronage and clientship,

[11] Abner Cohen, "The Politics of Marriage in Changing Middle Eastern Stratification Systems," in *Essays in Comparative Social Stratification*, ed. Leonard Plotnicov and Arthur Tuden (Pittsburgh: University of Pittsburgh Press, 1970), pp. 195–209. Scott Atran, "*Ḥamūla* Organization and *Masha'a* Tenure in Palestine," *Man* (N.S.) 21, no. 2 (June 1986), 281, refers to *ḥamūla*-s as "corporate patronymic groups that were not genealogically integrated. Nevertheless, membership in the corporation was expressed in a patrilineal idiom."

[12] See Cohen, *Arab Border Villages*, pp. 71–93, for his best example of historical changes in the politics of marriage alliances and the elasticity with which normative claims of marriage "rules" are interpreted. In his study of a provincial urban center in Turkey, Peter Benedict, also reacting against prevailing assumptions of lineage theory and the solidarity of extended families, found that even when there was a compact arrangement of the houses of married sons within a natal courtyard, "many of the households so arranged . . . had virtually nothing to do with their close agnatic neighbors." See Peter Benedict, "Aspects of the Domestic Cycle in a Turkish Provincial Town," in *Mediterranean Family Structures*, ed. Peristiany, p. 239.

[13] See Dale F. Eickelman, *Moroccan Islam: Tradition and Society in a Pilgrimage Center*, Modern Middle East Series 1 (Austin and London: University of Texas Press, 1976), pp. 95–105, 183–210. Lila Abu-Lughod, *Veiled Sentiments: Honor and Poetry in a Bedouin Society* (Berkeley and Los Angeles: University of California Press, 1986), pp. 51–59, discusses a similar use of the term among the Awlād 'Alī of Egypt's western desert.

and common bonds developed through neighborliness. Closeness is constituted by compelling ties of obligations. Often closeness is expressed as a "blood" tie, even when no demonstrable lineal ties exist, because however such ties are valued in practice, they are considered permanent and cannot be broken. Yet, in contexts other than those governed by inheritance law, closeness based on family ties is generally not sharply differentiated from closeness based on other grounds. Most frequently, people try to make the various bases for closeness overlap.

The concept of "closeness" as used in present-day Morocco, the Palestinian *ḥamūla*, the Afghan *qawm*, the *ibn 'amm* groups of the Rwāla, and other notions such as the Omani "family cluster" (*ḥayyān*) have their counterparts elsewhere in the Middle East and are not just accommodations to recent developments. The idea that descent can be a means of invoking or expressing solidarity but is not anything "natural" that guarantees solidarity comes across very clearly in Ibn Khaldūn's notion of "group feeling" (*'aṣabiya*) (described in Chapter 2).[14] He stresses how artificial "blood" relationship is and indicates the multiple bases on which group feeling can be asserted among both townspeople and tribes. He ultimately claims that the "naturalness" of "blood" ties makes them superior to all other modalities as a basis for group feeling. Nonetheless, Ibn Khaldūn is clear that the underlying cultural construct of *'aṣabiya* is not based primarily on "blood" ties.

How kinship, also glossed as "closeness" in Morocco, serves as a guide to practical social relationships is illustrated by a prominent maraboutic (saintly) patronymic association in the town of Boujad, which had a population of approximately 20,000 in 1973 (35,000 by 1992). Boujad is a local pilgrimage center located on Morocco's western plains, next to the foothills of the Middle Atlas Mountains. Roughly a third of Boujad's population claim descent from the marabout Sīdī Mḥammad Sharqī (d. 1601). Collectively, these descendants are known as the Sharqāwa—*Sharqāwa* being the plural for Sharqī in Arabic. The town has 26 maraboutic shrines of varying importance; 23 of them are Sharqāwī shrines. Despite the decline in recent years of popular belief in the efficacy of marabouts as intercessors with the supernatural, the town remains an important regional pilgrimage center and is also the administrative and market center for its rural hinterland.

Because of the advantages of wealth, prestige, and education that derived from the reputation as marabouts of some Sharqāwa in the past, many have managed to maintain prominence in Morocco today as merchants, entrepreneurs, officials, and politicians. Although today Sharqāwī prominence is justified principally on grounds other than maraboutic descent, some Sharqāwa still

[14] Ibn Khaldūn, *The Muqaddimah*, trans. Franz Rosenthal, 2nd ed., vol. 1, Bollingen Series 43 (Princeton, NJ: Princeton University Press, 1967), pp. 249–310, esp. p. 264. For the concepts of *ḥasab* (honor acquired through the deeds of one's self or ancestors) and *nasab* (descent) as used in tenth- and eleventh-century Iraq and Iran, see Roy P. Mottahedeh, *Loyalty and Leadership in an Early Islamic Society* (Princeton, NJ: Princeton University Press, 1980), pp. 98–100. For Oman, see Christine Eickelman, *Women and Community in Oman* (New York and London: New York University Press, 1984), pp. 80–111.

derive considerable material and status benefits from the gifts they receive from their largely rural clientele.

What exactly does the claim to Sharqāwī descent mean in Boujad today? The Sharqāwa do not act collectively as a group and never did so consistently in the past. Descent was one of a number of identities that they shared. In Boujad itself there are currently eight Sharqāwī patronymic associations. All claim descent from sons of Sīdī Mḥammad Sharqī, although none can trace exact genealogical links to him. Nonetheless, this information is said to repose in books and records. Of the eight Sharqāwī patronymic associations in Boujad, the members of two of them additionally claim descent from prominent nineteenth-century Sharqāwī marabouts. In addition, there are people who claim Sharqāwī descent elsewhere in Morocco.

Each patronymic association is associated with a residential quarter in Boujad. One of the two most prominent Sharqāwī associations in Boujad is that of the 'Arbāwa. Although identification with a patronymic association does not imply an obligation to act in common with other individuals who belong to it, as recent experiences in local electoral politics and disputes over various local issues amply demonstrate, 'Arbāwī quarter is one of the most tightly knit in Boujad. Approximately 86 percent of its 300 or so residents (as of 1970) were born in the town itself, as opposed to an average of 54 percent for the town as a whole. A majority of the households in the quarter claim bonds of kinship with each other. In fact, many of them have shared inheritance rights from agricultural estates and other holdings. More important, among the descendants of the leading Sharqāwī marabout of the nineteenth century, after whom this quarter is named, are prominent administrators, merchants, politicians, a brother-in-law of Morocco's king, and even a leading sociologist. There are advantages of prestige in claiming identification with this particular patronymic association.

Ideally, the households of a quarter are bound together by multiple personal ties and by common interests. In fact, a "traditional" residential quarter in Morocco can be defined as the extension of "closeness" (*qarāba*) in physical space. For closeness to exist in a patronymic association, as in a residential quarter in a traditional urban setting such as Boujad, the limits of the patronymic association and the quarter must overlap; the quarter must be capable of collective social action in at least some significant contexts. This usually means that there are men of standing (*kubbār*) in the patronymic association or quarter who can act as spokesmen on critical occasions and can mobilize the heads of the quarter's households. Ideally, the notions of patronymic association and residential quarter converge. When this overlapping occurs, as in the case of the 'Arbāwī patronymic association/residential quarter, mobilization of the collectivity forms a regular part of the fabric of social life.

In many "traditional" spatial settings, neighbors who cooperate with each other claim to outsiders that they have common descent as a means of enhancing their prestige. Thus the inhabitants of another residential quarter in Boujad claim common origin from a nearby tribal group and assert kinship with one another. Although certain households of the quarter are related by ties of kinship and marriage, others are linked solely by occupation, neighborliness, and other common attributes not related to the attribute of descent. Again, the one feature common to all the quarter's households was their ability to act successfully as a collectivity.

The quarter in question, Qṣayra ("The Little Fortress"), is so named because it adjoins a fortified, high-walled Sharqāwī quarter and, in fact, looks like a scaled-down version of it. How closeness is demonstrated by residents of the quarter serves to indicate how notions of "family" and "kinship" are understood in their Moroccan context. Most residents of the quarter claim that they or their ancestors came from Ait Ṣāliḥ, a tribal grouping west of Boujad. Without denying their Ait Ṣāliḥ origin, others prefer to stress their relations with Ḥājj Bū Bakr, reputedly of Ait Ṣāliḥ, who founded the quarter at the turn of the century and whose household serves as the core with which other households claim affinity.

Bū Bakr was a tannery owner and grain merchant when the French arrived in 1913. He made a fortune through his commercial activities and soon converted his fortune into social honor, first by making the pilgrimage to Mecca and thereby acquiring the title of Ḥājj ("Pilgrim"), then by constructing an imposing house for himself and by marrying a second wife. As his sons matured and married, he built adjacent houses for them, in the manner of other men of prestige. He also constructed a small mosque for the quarter and made a major contribution toward hiring a Quranic teacher (*fqīh*) to teach in it. He died shortly after World War II; his sons and widows continue to reside in the quarter.

The means vary by which residents of Qṣayra quarter claim "closeness" with Ḥājj Bū Bakr. Most claim closeness by descent and marriage, although in most cases no exact genealogical links can be demonstrated. There are some 30 dwellings in the quarter, but when I asked residents to enumerate them for me, several were invariably excluded. These turned out to be living units that somehow did not qualify as households—men sleeping in shops, the dwellings of several poor and often childless couples, and all those people excluded from the circle of closeness for some assumed moral defect. These nonhouseholds did not share the visiting patterns of the counted households of the quarter or engage in their reciprocal exchanges.

It is useful to examine the asserted ties of one resident in detail because they illustrate virtually the entire range of means by which closeness can be claimed. Ma'ṭī (1),[15] a local shopkeeper, at first claimed that Bū Bakr was of his "blood" (*min dammī*). This he elaborated by claiming that the relation was through his "father's brother" (3), who had married a woman of Ḥājj Bū Bakr's household. This notion is interesting, for such a tie would not be considered "blood" by American concepts of kinship. I had earlier asked Ma'ṭī to enumerate his kinsmen. I was preparing a "formal" kinship chart, as do many anthropologists, diagramming in an abstract manner his claimed relatives. When I reminded Ma'ṭī that he had previously said his father had no brothers, he replied that, since he was "close" (*qrīb*) to Ḥājj Bū Bakr, it must be through a

[15] The identifying numbers are keyed to Figure 7-1.

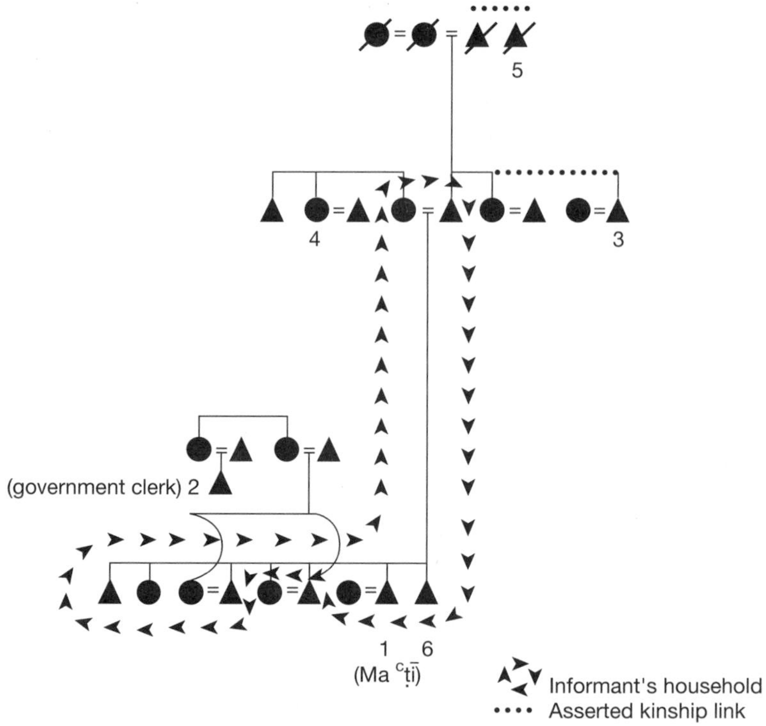

FIGURE 7-1. Kinship ties of Ma'ṭī, Qṣayra quarter. [From Dale F. Eickelman, *Moroccan Islam: Tradition and Society in a Pilgrimage Center* (Austin: University of Texas Press, 1976), p. 101. Copyright © 1976 by University of Texas Press. All rights reserved.]

half-brother of his grandfather (5). In other words, the knowledge of closeness came first, then its justification. He added that there "probably" was a second link through the marriage of his mother's sister (4), who lived in the same quarter. Again, this tie could not be demonstrated.

Finally, Ma'ṭī said that Bū Bakr's people act *as if* (*b-ḥāl*) they are related (*qrīb*), so they must be, and he recited at length the informal visiting patterns that prevailed between their households. No one can remember such genealogical ties clearly, he said; and although—in perfectly comprehensible Catch-22 reasoning—no one can verify them in any exact way, they must exist. He went on to link himself in a similar manner with a minor, but locally significant government official (2), also of the quarter founded by Bū Bakr and related to Ma'ṭī through the marriage ties of his brother and sister. The tracing of significant kinship ties through affines and the bilateral reckoning of kin in practical social contexts are very common features of Moroccan notions of kinship, the formal emphasis on the ideology of patrilineal descent notwithstanding.[16]

[16] Peters, "Aspects of Affinity," p. 32, also emphasizes this point.

In the "Little Fortress" quarter, as in the 'Arbāwī quarter, both "kinship" and involvement in local exchange networks are invoked to justify assertions of closeness. Given the role of the maraboutic Sharqāwa in Boujad's past, one way the residents of Qṣayra sought to enhance their prestige was to build a tomb for a claimed ancestor next to some of the Sharqāwī tombs on the outskirts of town. The effort ultimately met stiff opposition from the Sharqāwī and failed, but its near success managed to raise the prestige of the quarter's inhabitants in the eyes of most Boujadis because they acted together as a collectivity.[17] Significantly, this process of merging social ties based upon asserted kinship and residential proximity is also characteristic of older residential quarters elsewhere in North Africa and in the shantytowns that have grown up around many of the region's towns and cities.[18]

I have presented this Moroccan example in detail because it shows the complex idea of "relationship," involving kinship, neighborliness, reciprocity, responsibility, and space and the ways they are asserted and expressed. The details in the account are particular to Morocco, but the implicit principles can be used to discern relationships in many other contexts elsewhere, such as the relationships among lineages and households within the pastoral Maduzai tribe in Afghanistan,[19] the framework for doing business in Central Asia, and the interplay of family and professional ties among Arabs and Saudis during the 1990–1991 Gulf War against Iraq.[20]

ANALYTICAL CONSIDERATIONS

I have emphasized the flexibility with which notions of family and interpersonal relationships are conceived and utilized. Because of the many variations in cultural concepts of social identity that occur throughout the Middle East, it is especially important to understand how anthropologists explain and document them. For this purpose, Hildred Geertz's "The Meanings of Family Ties," based on extensive field research in Sefrou, Morocco, in the 1960s, remains an

[17] For details of the incident, see Dale F. Eickelman, "Is There an Islamic City? The Making of a Quarter in a Moroccan Town," *International Journal of Middle East Studies* 5, no. 3 (July 1974), 289–93.

[18] See Colette Petonnet, "Espace, distance et dimension dans une société musulmane: À propos du bidonville marocain de Douar Doum à Rabat," *L'Homme* 12, no. 2 (April–June 1972), 47–84. Barbara K. Larson, "Tunisian Kin Ties Reconsidered," *American Ethnologist* 10, no. 3 (August 1983), 551–70, provides a similar discussion of the importance of bilateral kinship, residential proximity, and patrilocal residence, but not patrilineal descent. Also see Kazuo Ohtsuka, "A Note on Kin Group Endogamy and Social Categories in Lower Egypt," *Bulletin of the National Museum of Ethnology* (Osaka) 8, no. 3 (September 1983), 563–86.

[19] Nancy Tapper, *Bartered Brides: Politics, Gender and Marriage in an Afghan Tribal Society*, Cambridge Studies in Social and Cultural Anthropology 74 (Cambridge and New York: Cambridge University Press, 1991), pp. 67–100.

[20] See the fascinating book by Khaled bin Sultan (with Patrick Seale), *Desert Warrior: A Personal View of the Gulf War by the Joint Forces Commander* (New York: HarperCollins, 1995). Prince Khaled's highly readable account concerns relations within the Saudi royal family, of which he is a member, and how "things get done" within a modern military organization.

important point of departure because she spells out step by step what anthropologists do to make these notions explicit.[21] She describes: (1) prior anthropological approaches to studying Middle Eastern kinship; (2) living arrangements—the use of space and the "webs" of relationship in which cultural notions of kinship are used to inform and to interpret social action; (3) cultural understandings or "constructs" concerning family; and (4) how marital choices are made and their significance. In the two decades since her study appeared, many subsequent studies of other regions of the Middle East (but, again, not yet Central Asia) have complemented or modified several of her observations. Nonetheless, the comprehensiveness of her presentation continues to make her study a ready point of departure for comparison with kinship and domestic organization elsewhere in the Middle East.

After reviewing prior studies of Middle Eastern kinship, with their emphasis on lineage theory and the so-called "preference rule" for father's brother's daughter (*bint 'amm*) marriage, Geertz situates the study of kinship concepts and ties in the wider context of the complementary notions of friendship and patronage because the lines between these various forms of relationships are not sharply drawn in the Moroccan context. To document the practical contexts in which notions of personal and family relationships are elaborated, Geertz describes in detail the kinship ties and living arrangements of a wealthy and conservative high-status extended family in Sefrou. This family is, admittedly, not "typical," but, as Geertz argues, the fact that it is tightly organized and possesses other unique characteristics makes it easier to discern "the underlying patterns which inform familial relationships."

At the time of Geertz's field research, the houses of the 'Adlūn extended family were still clustered in a neighborhood or quarter (*darb*) that bears their name. Since then, in line with trends throughout Morocco, the family has moved to new residences elsewhere. The strong family ties remain, but they no longer are clearly represented in neighborhood space. Geertz details how space was used in 'Adlūn quarter and more particularly in one of the oldest, largest, and most distinguished of the 'Adlūn houses, Dār Bū 'Alī ("the house of Bū 'Alī"). Even in the late 1960s, many of the larger houses in the older sections of North African cities were subdivided and tenanted by unrelated poorer families, but in the case of Dār Bū 'Alī, 11 related adults, including several married couples (and in the past, their servants), shared the same house. Twenty-five adults living elsewhere were also associated with the household.

As Geertz emphasizes, the notion of "house" deserves particular attention. The house is known by the name of the dominant adult male (or ancestor) associated with it. He was known as the "owner" or "master" of the house (*mūl ad-dār*). Bū 'Alī was the paternal grandfather of the older residents of the house. The inhabitants of the house, including its women, are collectively known as the "masters" of the house (*mwālīn ad-dār*), but there is no sharp dividing line between members of the household and other relations. Bū 'Alī's claimed

[21] H. Geertz, "Family Ties," pp. 315–91.

descendants are sometimes referred to as "Bū 'Alī's people" (*nās Bū 'Alī*); 'Adlūn refers to the entire extended family, but there is no sharp division made between *nās 'Adlūn* and *nās Bū 'Alī*. The connotations of both these terms and of family (*'ā'ila*) are multiple and refer to a number of overlapping categories of kinsmen. Bū 'Alī's people (*nās*) are not just a neatly delineated subdivision of the 'Adlūn people. The categories cannot be accommodated by lineage theory.

In the past, a number of material circumstances encouraged the daily interaction of quarter residents, especially for the women. To a more limited extent, this remains the case today. In the past, when there was no piped water—many poorer households still lack it—the women of the household had to use a public fountain. The shared fountain, a public bath in the quarter constructed by the 'Adlūn family, inheritance laws that tend to subdivide the ownership of houses among relatives who thus share common economic interests, and the use of space such as rooftops (from which women from different houses can talk with each other as they do their chores) facilitate interaction among neighbors and kinsmen and blur the distinction between neighbors and relatives.

Geertz's discussion of the web of actual social relationships has a special interest for the anthropological study of kinship because she poses a series of related questions that form comprehensive guides to the study of practical kinship that transcend her focus on a single, high-status urban extended family.

The first issue concerns the size and shape of the daily interacting group of relatives and neighbors, especially women. In the residential quarter, the clustering of houses, the shared water resources, the communal expenses (such as the maintenance of a small mosque), and the large number of kinsmen living together mean that many relatives have intense daily contact. Of course "relations" means not only patrilineally related people but also those related matrilaterally and through marriage. Through generations of marriage, kinship ties often become so dense that people are related to one another in all three ways. Muslims can marry first cousins, and when such marriages occur, the result strengthens the multiple ties among relatives. As Geertz explains, "One's cousin is also one's brother-in-law, one's ex-husband has married a woman next door, one's uncle is one's father-in-law, one's husband is a former playmate, and one's child seemingly is shared by everyone."[22] Additionally, the feelings and activities of neighbors and relatives in such close physical proximity mean that their behavior is "entirely a matter of open argument and explicit social pressure."[23] This constant pressure of "publicity," to use Geertz's term, is an integral part of Moroccan family life and makes privacy difficult to obtain.

The pressures of public scrutiny are equally important for the "family clusters" (*ḥayyān*) of the northern Oman interior. *Ḥayyān* "specifies a fairly well defined cluster of persons living in several households that are often adjacent to one another and commonly within walking distance." Births, deaths, marriages, Quran recitals, and the practical matters of daily life bring members of

[22] Ibid., p. 333.

[23] Ibid., p. 334.

the family cluster together. Women visit members of their family cluster and form their most intimate friendships with other women in it. Indeed, most marriages are contracted between members of the extended family cluster, and collectively they seek "to hide all internal dissent and to present as smooth a front as possible to the rest of the community."[24]

Such pressures were even more intense in the large households of an earlier generation of the wealthy throughout the Middle East, reminding observers to be sensitive not only to differences in class and social category but to change over generations in ideas of family and household and how these ideas should be realized in practice. An historian of Egyptian origin, Afaf Lutfi al-Sayyid Marsot, drawing on the recollections of her family and friends, writes: "I was given multiple examples of houses where three generations lived together and who with their servants and retainers came to well over sixty inmates—the women could not exactly remember the names of all the retainers so only accounted for the major ones."[25]

Geertz's second point draws attention to the boundary between informal ("private") and formal ("public") spheres of social action. In the "conservative" setting that she describes, the higher the status of women, the less they are seen in public, although there is considerable variation between generations and according to whether women are young or old and unmarried or married. Age, social status, education, and many other complex factors enter into how and when a veil and other covering garments are worn, and how they are worn symbolizes the division between the public and the private spheres.

In rural settings in North Africa, for instance, women often go unveiled, although they conceal themselves and act with socially appropriate modesty when outsiders are present. In urban settings, women are commonly unveiled before marriage and assume the veil afterwards. The use of the veil can often serve as an indicator of higher social status, although, once again, there is considerable flexibility as to when and where it is used. Young, educated women, for instance, often do not veil and find other means of indicating propriety and status. Comparing Geertz's account on the complex meanings of veiling with later accounts of its situational religious, political, class, and moral significance is also a comment on the changing nature of family and public life in the Middle East. In Casablanca and Fez, for example, teenage daughters of some middle-class families seem to wear headscarves or even to veil less for religious reasons than to assert independence from their parents, who are often more relaxed about such matters.

In Turkey, as elsewhere, the use of headscarves can be as powerful a political and religious symbol as the veil. The Turkish Republic outlawed the fez, the traditional men's hat, in the 1920s but made no provision for women's dress. With the Islamic resurgence in Turkey in the 1970s, many women, including

[24] C. Eickelman, *Women and Community*, pp. 81, 91.

[25] Afaf Lutfi al-Sayyid Marsot, "The Revolutionary Gentlewomen in Egypt," in *Women in the Muslim World*, ed. Lois Beck and Nikki Keddie (Cambridge and London: Harvard University Press, 1978), p. 275.

FIGURE 7-2. Women returning from market in rural Morocco. Lack of veiling can have complex implications of origin, social status, and relationships with others present, including in this case the photographer, at the time a resident of the village and known to those photographed. [Courtesy Paul J. Sanfaçon.]

those with "modern" education, adopted what they considered to be "traditional" Islamic dress. A major public controversy erupted in 1984 when a school administrator refused to allow a class valedictorian to address an assembly because she wore traditional dress.[26] The issue becomes more complex as both village and urban women compare their experiences with those of relatives living and working in Europe.[27]

The third issue in the analysis of practical kinship is the prevalent pattern of hospitality and visiting. In the Moroccan context, there is continuous visiting among relatives and neighbors. When relatives are neighbors, these patterns of activity are particularly intense. There is also considerable visiting among relatives and close friends at greater distances. As Geertz indicates, men are considerably more mobile than women, but even their travel patterns are "to a striking degree determined by the location of family connections."[28] These patterns vary according to whether members of the family are urban or rural, wealthy or poor, concentrated in one particular locality or widely dispersed. Even with the impact of the modern economy and its pressures, at least for the educated middle class, who occupy modern housing where it is difficult for relatives to be immediate neighbors (as was traditionally the case), Geertz finds a

[26] See Emelie A. Olson, "Muslim Identity and Secularism in Turkey: 'The Headscarf Dispute,'" *Anthropological Quarterly* 58, no. 4 (October 1985), 161–69.

[27] Ruth Mandel, "Turkish Headscarves and the 'Foreigner Problem': Constructing Difference Through Emblems of Identity," *New German Critique*, no. 46 (Winter 1989), 27–46; and Angeles Ramírez, "Las inmigrantes marroquíes en España, emigración y emancipación" [Moroccan Female Immigrants in Spain, Emigration and Emancipation], in *Mujeres, democracia y desarrollo en el Maghreb*, ed. Gema Martín Muñoz (Madrid: Editorial Pablo Iglesias, 1995), pp. 143–55.

[28] H. Geertz, "Family Ties," p. 934.

FIGURE 7-3. Girls in Dhaḥyān, a town in Yemen's northern province of Sa'da, returning from school in 1985. One girl is balancing a schoolbag on her head, and all are wearing the *shila*, the black outer garment characteristic of this region of northern Yemen. Whether indoors or outdoors, women cover their bodies completely when in the presence of unrelated males. Thus "public" can be inside or outside the house, as Gabriele vom Bruck explains in "A House Turned Inside Out: Inhabiting Space in a Yemeni City," *Journal of Material Culture* 1, no. 1 (March 1997). These girls are the first generation to attend state schools; their mothers received a religious education from their male relatives and husbands. [Photograph courtesy Gabriele vom Bruck.]

persistence of strong familial ties expressed in patterns of visiting, a trend largely confirmed by studies conducted elsewhere in the Middle East.[29]

A fourth issue in the analysis of practical kinship is the relative importance of the conjugal family in Middle Eastern settings. In the residential quarter described by Geertz, the conjugal bond is one of many cross-cutting ties of kinship and affinity, so that household units are not built primarily around the conjugal bond. In an older pattern of polygamous marriages (by Islamic law men are permitted up to four legal wives, provided they can be "equally" maintained), affinal links through women were used by wealthier individuals

[29] Women's visiting patterns is a subject central to many contemporary studies. See, among others, C. Eickelman, *Women and Community*, pp. 150–79; Soraya Altorki, *Women in Saudi Arabia: Ideology and Behavior Among the Elite* (New York: Columbia University Press, 1986), pp. 99–105; and Nancy Tapper, "Gender and Religion in a Turkish Town: A Comparison of Two Types of Formal Women's Gatherings," in *Women's Religious Experience*, ed. P. Holden (London: Croom Helm, 1983), pp. 71–88.

to secure complex political and economic alliances. In modern Egypt, for example, only 0.05 percent of contemporary marriages are polygamous.[30]

The overall trend throughout the Middle East is toward separate housing for each nuclear family and the strengthening of the conjugal bond, with consequent shifts in the tenor of relationships among members of the family. Mübeccel Kiray argues that a wife's status rises when she lives alone with her husband and children rather than under the same roof as her husband's relatives, although the woman also becomes more dependent on her husband. She shares more in the decision making of the household and in many of her husband's activities. Extended families remain very important, even when relatives do not live in the same house or immediate neighborhood. Kiray argues that the changes that have occurred with large-scale labor emigration to Europe—a trend now diminishing in importance—and other economic and political shifts have brought about fundamental reinterpretations of family and kinship roles. At the same time, she sees a continued importance of the extended family and the bonds of obligation and trust that unite family members, facilitate their movement from one region of the country to another, and secure employment.[31] Many variations in household composition, however, are not directly related to issues of tradition or modernity but to changes in the domestic cycle, as people marry, raise children, grow older, and establish, when economically feasible, a degree of autonomy by setting up independent households.[32]

A final consideration is the linkage between kinship and patterns of social status, influence, and authority. Geertz suggests that economic and political achievement in Morocco is "almost entirely an individual matter. An ambitious man may use the help of kinsmen in his climb, and in return may help them, but these exchanges are personally arranged and by no means obligatory."[33] Significant ranges of wealth can be found within a single extended family, and Geertz provides numerous case studies indicating this variation. At the same time, the presence of powerful and influential individuals within a single extended family substantially increases the likelihood of the next generation's possessing a competitive advantage in retaining their social status. Studies of rural leadership in Morocco suggest that, despite the changes from the precolonial regime to colonial domination and later to independence, economic and political advantage has often remained within the same extended families.[34]

[30] Marsot, "Revolutionary Gentlewomen," p. 263.

[31] Mübeccel Kiray, "The New Role of Mothers: Changing Intra-familial Relationships in a Small Town in Turkey," in *Mediterranean Family Structures*, ed. Peristiany, pp. 261–71. See also Jenny B. White, *Money Makes Us Relatives: Women's Labor in Urban Turkey* (Austin: University of Texas Press, 1994).

[32] An outstanding account of urban-rural, class, and generational differences is Andrea B. Rugh, *Family in Contemporary Egypt* (Syracuse, NY: Syracuse University Press, 1984).

[33] H. Geertz, "Family Ties," pp. 339–40.

[34] Rémy Leveau, "The Rural Elite as an Element in the Social Stratification of Morocco," in *Commoners, Climbers and Notables*, ed. C. A. O. van Nieuwenhuijze (Leiden: E. J. Brill, 1977), pp. 268–78; D. Eickelman, *Moroccan Islam*, pp. 211–37.

FIGURE 7-4. Bukhāran Jewish entertainer Tohfakhān Pinkhasova with guests at a Muslim wedding in Bukhāra, Uzbekistan, 1991. Male and female guests at Bukhāran weddings celebrated separately in the past. In recent years, however, mixed celebrations have become increasingly common. [Courtesy Theodore Levin.]

How family ties are articulated depends substantially on the economic situation of the families involved. Vanessa Maher, in her study of a small town in Morocco's Middle Atlas region, suggests that marriages are much more stable among the urban middle classes than among the less affluent in rural areas. When the main inheritance is land, men and women are likely to retain important shared property rights and service obligations with their own kin, and such ties tend to be incompatible with a primary allegiance to the spouse. Marriages in such circumstances are arranged, less with a view to conjugal happiness than to serve the long-term interests of those who arrange them, the parents of the spouses and the intermediaries.[35] Maher estimates that for 70 percent of the population of the town she studied, marriages served to maintain the economic and social status quo of the couple. For another 20 percent it meant cultural assimilation to the Arabized and politically dominant group (she studied in a Berber-speaking region); for the remaining 10 percent, the urban elite, women possessed movable capital as opposed to land rights. Marriage to such women was regarded principally as an alliance, with long-term economic and integrative significance between extended families, and hence marriages tended to be more stable. For groups lacking such capital, divorce entailed no

[35] Vanessa Maher, *Women and Property in Morocco*, Cambridge Studies in Social Anthropology 10 (Cambridge: Cambridge University Press, 1974), p. 157.

significant loss, as there was no capital to lose. This was decidedly not the case for the urban elite.[36] Clearly, any study of kinship that neglects the practical domain of economic relationships, as many studies have tended to do in the past, must be treated with some caution.

MARRIAGE

> Arranging marriages is a highly serious matter, like waging war or making big business deals.[37]

As this statement suggests, marriage in most Middle Eastern contexts involves not only the personal wishes of the man and woman concerned but the responsibility of their relatives. In the past, at least among wealthier families, marriages could be said to have been almost entirely the responsibility of the father or guardian of a boy and girl, although under contemporary circumstances this is no longer the case. Actual marriage practices vary significantly throughout the region, so that studies of particular locales must be consulted for appropriate ethnographic detail. When a girl is married at the average age of 12 or 13, despite the legal requirement that she be 16, as reported by Hamed Ammar for an Egyptian village at midcentury, or, on the average, between the ages of 13 and 15, as the Gulicks reported for Isfahan, Iran, in the 1960s, she had a minimal say in her fate.[38] However, such statistics are snapshots of a certain earlier period. Throughout the region, for reasons explained below, the age of marriage is becoming significantly later. In general, however, marriage choices usually are made by a group of people from the extended families of the conjugal pair, whether the marriage is among Muslims, Christians, or Jews, and views about marriage, like those about family, can serve as another indicator of shared assumptions concerning the nature of the social order.[39]

In Morocco, as in the other countries of the Middle East, much depends on the reputation, social status, and educational background of the prospective couple. Half a century ago in upper-class families, the couple had little say in the choices imposed upon them; today, of course, this is less so. In the case of a young man with a living father, the father is expected to take a significant role in the negotiations, and the same is true for a young woman. If questioned, men aver that marriage negotiations are their concern alone, since they claim to have an understanding of the social obligations involved superior to that of women.

[36] Ibid., pp. 191–220.

[37] A Moroccan discussing marriage practices with Hildred Geertz, cited in "Family Ties," p. 363.

[38] Hamed Ammar, *Growing Up in an Egyptian Village* (London: Routledge & Kegan Paul, 1954), p. 183; and John Gulick and Margaret E. Gulick, "The Domestic Social Environment of Women and Girls in Isfahan, Iran," in *Women*, ed. Beck and Keddie, p. 504.

[39] For an elaboration of the similarities of Muslim and Jewish practices in many domains, see S. D. Goitein, *A Mediterranean Society: The Jewish Communities of the Arab World as Portrayed in the Documents of the Cairo Geniza. Volume III: The Family* (Berkeley and Los Angeles: University of California Press, 1978). Although Goitein is principally concerned with the tenth through the thirteenth centuries, he frequently introduces comparative material from contemporary periods.

Women take a different view of the process and in fact take quite an active role in suggesting marriage partners and in preliminary negotiations.[40]

Informal go-betweens are often used in the first stages of such discussions. They are chosen from among kinspeople and friends trusted by both parties. For example, a young man might ask a classmate to sound out the other family or enlist the assistance of his sister or mother. The person selected to explore such possibilities depends on the social ties between the parties and cannot be predicted from abstract considerations of kinship roles alone. Women's baths and women's social gatherings are one place where exploratory talks can take place. After all, as one woman explained to me, since Moroccan men presume that women tend to have less "reason" (*'qāl*) than men, with *reason* being defined as the ability to act effectively in a wide range of social situations,[41] women are especially useful in exploratory discussions. Anything said by a woman can be denied by men as not accurately representing their views. Although the initiative is supposed to come from the groom's family, the bride's family often begins negotiations, especially if there have been previous marriages between the two extended families or if the marriage is within the extended family itself, as is the case for a father's brother's daughter, or "parallel cousin" marriages, which are permitted in Islamic law.

If the suggestion of a marriage is accepted, discussions follow concerning the date of the wedding and the conditions to be included in the marriage contract (a woman can, for instance, specify that her husband may not take a second wife without granting her a divorce). The subject of the most protracted negotiations is the size of the bridewealth (*ṣdāq*), or the sum which the groom's family must pay to the bride's family, part of which goes for the provision of certain furnishings that remain the personal property of the wife. Bridewealth is not usually paid in full but is used as a device to discourage a husband's seeking divorce, as in such an event the wife or her family can demand the balance.

The amounts involved in bridewealth payments continue to escalate, and bridewealth constitutes only a part of the cost involved in a wedding. Because the ceremonies involved in marriage indicate to the wider public the social standing of the couple, the expenses for gifts and entertainment are often excessive. A 1975 study conducted in Fez estimated that the cost of marriage for a junior civil servant, including all gifts and the multiple entertainments of guests, came to approximately $14,000. Of this, the groom's family contributed

[40] On changes in Saudi elite marriages and marriage negotiations, see Altorki, *Women in Saudi Arabia*, pp. 124–47. William Lancaster, *The Rwala Bedouin Today*, Changing Cultures (New York and Cambridge: Cambridge University Press, 1981), p. 54, notes that although the Rwāla likewise claim the strict segregation of the sexes, the vehicles of young men "just happen" to break down in front of the tent of women in whom they are interested, at the same time as the veil of a young woman "accidentally" falls out of place. To use the language of Washington, D.C., "deniability" is maintained, and no reputation suffers. Similarly, for well-to-do households in Oman, the telephone has become an instrument tolerated, if not approved, for premarital communication.

[41] Note the self-fulfilling cultural definition of *reason*. Because women traditionally have been restricted from participating fully in a wide range of public activities, such as law courts, it follows that when they do participate, they often do so less effectively than men. See D. Eickelman, *Moroccan Islam*, pp. 130–38.

$5000 and the bride's family the rest. The cost equalled the income of the married couple for a period of four years. For the more modest wedding of an ordinary worker, costs were estimated at $1900, with $1314 paid by the groom's family and the rest by the bride's. The expense equalled the man's estimated income for the first 22 months of his marriage. With the cost of marriage so high, many couples prolong their engagement for several years in order to acquire the necessary resources.[42]

There are other reasons for the later age at which marriages are contracted throughout the region. These include deteriorating economic conditions, housing shortages, enforcement of higher age requirements, more years in school, and, above all, changing attitudes toward marriage.[43] Only since midcentury has mass education spread throughout the Middle East. Mass education, combined with rapidly changing economic conditions, contributes to a significantly revised sense of self, gender, and person.

In the oil-wealthy Gulf states, costs are much more extravagant and have become a major social problem. In some cases, however, the inflation in bridewealth is deceptive.[44] Among the Rwāla, it is principally a means of making a public statement on the value a family places upon a woman. In most cases, it is never entirely paid, and it discourages "outside" suitors.[45]

Once the financial negotiations are satisfactorily concluded, the fathers of the bride and groom or the relatives acting as their guardians sign a formal agreement before a notary, although there still are marriages in rural areas where an older tradition prevails, at least among families with very modest resources, of concluding agreements in front of reliable witnesses so that the matter, if contested, can later be brought before a court. Either procedure is regarded as legally binding and occurs near the time of the *khaṭba*, the formal public request for the woman's hand during a ceremonial dinner at her home.

The *khaṭba* is usually preceded by a large gift of sugar, publicly delivered, to the woman's household. If the families involved are well off, it will be accompanied by musicians and women from neighboring households. In general, the more socially prominent the families involved, the more public the delivery of the gift. If the gift is not declined, the engagement feast takes place the following day.

The wedding may be delayed considerably after the formal legal agreement. Not only are financial considerations involved, but in many Middle Eastern cities there is an acute housing shortage, so that many couples postpone marriage until suitable accommodations can be found and until they can afford to live together.

[42] Abdelhaq Cohen, "Le coût du mariage à Fes," *Lamalif* (Casablanca), no. 69 (March 1975), 14–16.

[43] See Mounia Bennani-Chraïbi, *Soumis et rebelles: Les jeunes au Maroc* [Subjects and Rebels: The Youth of Morocco] (Paris: CNRS Éditions, 1994); and Susan Ossman, *Picturing Casablanca: Portraits of Power in a Moroccan City* (Berkeley and Los Angeles: University of California Press, 1994).

[44] Among the Yorük of southeastern Turkey, one means of coping with the escalation of bridewealth is by kidnapping, usually done by prearrangement with the couple involved and their trusted relatives. See Daniel G. Bates, *Nomads and Farmers: A Study of the Yorük of Southeastern Turkey*, Anthropological Papers 52 (Ann Arbor: University of Michigan, Museum of Anthropology, 1973), pp. 59–86.

[45] Lancaster, *Rwala*, p. 51. See also N. Tapper, *Bartered Brides*, pp. 141–56.

Shortly before the wedding, the bride's family delivers to the groom's house the various goods purchased with the bridewealth—mattresses, blankets, trays and silverware, cups, clothing, cooking utensils, and so on. For the weddings of wealthy families, goods are carried on flatbed trucks and are circulated throughout the town, accompanied by musicians drumming and playing woodwind instruments and clapping and dancing by some of the women of the households involved and their neighbors. These occasions involve considerable status competition, for they publicly announce the social standing of the couple and the prestige of their extended families.[46]

On the day of the wedding, a farewell celebration is held at the bride's house. At the groom's house, in the meantime, there is a long evening of feasting and talking. Later, some of the groom's relatives, but not the groom himself, set out to collect the bride. There is much weeping and crying as the bride is taken from her family. On arrival at the groom's house, the bride is ceremonially dressed in heavy layers of fine brocades and jewels, often rented. The groom finally leaves his guests, lifts his bride's veil, drinks milk with her, and offers her dates. Depending on the region of the country, close relatives and kinsmen may visit the new couple briefly at this stage. Wedding gifts are presented at this time, with each gift publicly announced and displayed. The wedding party continues throughout the night, culminating, so to speak, when proof is brought to the guests of the bride's virginity. In country weddings, this is done by having a hired female dancer place a tray of fruit on her head, over which is placed a handkerchief spotted with the bride's virginal blood. As more Moroccans become exposed to Western and urban sensibilities, the practice of insisting on such direct confirmation of virginity is gradually disappearing. Several days of feasting often follow, during which the bride is expected to feign exhaustion and remain immobile, visited only by close female friends. Perhaps in part to accustom the bride to her new surroundings (when the bride and groom are not previously related) and to accustom her to new patterns of domestic authority, the bride will not see her father, brothers, and other male relatives for at least three months.

Moroccans, as well as other Middle Easterners, stress the multiple forces involved in marriage arrangements, of which the feeling of the man and woman for each other is only one factor. The social networks of the two are more or less directly involved and enter into calculations of a good marriage. Statistics on marriage and divorce are hard to come by because most experts acknowledge that divorces which do not involve property settlements go largely unreported in most Middle Eastern countries. In one village in Morocco studied by Vanessa Maher, 49 percent of all marriages ended in divorce, and

[46] Again, there are significant variations in this pattern throughout the Middle East. In the Omani interior, weddings confined to the family cluster are so private that outsiders become aware of the event only after it has taken place. They involve no music or public display. The birth of a child, on the other hand, is the occasion for much intracommunity visiting. Such contrasting patterns depend, of course, on significantly different notions of person and community. See C. Eickelman, *Women and Community*, pp. 106–109. For an extended discussion of the semiotics of marriage and wedding rituals among Berbers in the Moroccan Rif, see Roger Joseph and Terri Brint Joseph, *The Rose and the Thorn: Semiotic Structures in Morocco* (Tucson: University of Arizona Press, 1987).

this figure appeared to be relatively constant for those born between 1895 and 1915. Maher's study brought out significant contrasts between marriage stability in the rural setting and in the neighboring town that served as a regional administrative center. Divorce rates were highest in the village—52 percent—as against an average of 38 percent in the town.[47] Maher states that the crucial factor in determining the rate of divorce was the economic and social situation of women. If inheritance was in land instead of liquid assets, if minimal bridewealth was paid, if the bride was young (80 percent of marriages of women under the age of 14 ended in divorce), and if marriage partners retained stronger links with their natal family than that of their spouse—all factors more prevalent in the village than the town—divorce was more likely.

Another factor is whether a couple has children. Until a woman has children, her primary source of moral—and sometimes financial—support often remains her own kin. She can always go back to them if the need arises, and this option remains open even after the couple has children.

THE IMPORTANCE OF KIN AND FAMILY

Marriage strategies and patterns of kinship obligations reveal underlying notions of personal identity and conceptions of the social self. There has been a tendency in earlier writing on the Middle East to treat kinship rights, practices, and obligations as self-contained objects that can be reduced to fixed rules or normative structures that generate the various practices analyzed by anthropologists.

An earlier concern with father's brother's daughter (*bint 'amm*) marriages, to the exclusion of other topics, derives from a wider anthropological interest in forms of exchange in social relationships and at least normative claims in the Middle East that such forms of marriage are "preferred." Such marriages are permissible in Islam, and at least in some social contexts Middle Easterners assert that if a woman and her family choose not to marry a father's brother's son, his consent and that of his family must be obtained.[48] Proverbs are sometimes cited as evidence for this preference, but proverbs stating contrary opin-

[47] Maher, *Women and Property*, pp. 17, 196–98. Maher's comparison of her findings with those of other scholars on pp. 196–97 is particularly useful. For an excellent empirical account, including a discussion of polygamous households, see Gillian Lewando-Hunt, "Conflicts Among Bedouin Women," *Royal Anthropological Institute Newsletter*, no. 19 (April 1977), 4–7.

[48] For example, Antoun, *Arab Village*, p. 74. Donald Powell Cole, *Nomads of the Nomads: The Āl Murrah Bedouin of the Empty Quarter* (Prospect Heights, IL: Waveland Press, 1984 [1975]), pp. 71–72, states that the Āl Murra "prefer" *bint 'amm* marriages, but he explicitly states that the meaning of this "preference" in practice is that marriage within lineages or among people of equal status is preferred. An account of the whole issue, which includes a historiographic discussion of why anthropologists got interested in this issue to the exclusion of other issues, is contained in Bourdieu, *Outline*, pp. 30–71. The most comprehensive and thoughtful recent essay on the topic is Ladislav Holy, *Kinship, Honour and Solidarity: Cousin Marriage in the Middle East*, Themes in Social Anthropology (Manchester and New York: Manchester University Press, 1989). Holy comprehensively reviews the many discussions of the topic, indicating its significance as a symbolic expression of what gender relations, agnatic solidarity, and marriage ought to be but also as an important element in marriage strategies (pp. 104–27).

ions are equally prevalent. Thus the Moroccan proverb in favor of *bint 'amm* marriage, "He who marries the daughter of his father's brother is like him who celebrates his feast with a sheep from his own flock" (that is, one who shows wealth and prestige by having sufficient resources within the family on which to draw) has its contrary in "Keep away from your blood before it defiles you" (in quarrels between the relatives of the spouses).[49]

Some anthropologists have sought to document the statistical rate of "actual" occurrence of such marriages or of claims of its normative preference. Yet among the Rwāla, as in many other Middle Eastern societies, there is considerable flexibility in who counts as a *bint 'amm*, or a father's brother's son (*ibn 'amm*); "so widely is the term used that it could be applied to any Rweli, any Bedu or even [with possible hyperbole on the part of the author] any human being."[50] Estimates of the "actual" incidence of such marriages vary from 43 percent in tribal Kurdistan to 2 percent in Lebanon, with a region-wide estimate of 10 to 15 percent. Such estimates are often made from incompatible assumptions, confound "practice" with normative statements and cultural categories, and should therefore be treated with considerable caution.[51]

As Pierre Bourdieu illustrates through detailed examples drawn from the Kabyle of Algeria, genealogically identical marriages may have different, even opposite, meanings and may be the outcomes of very different strategies involving a wide range of symbolic and material interests such as fertility, filiation, residence, inheritance, marriage, and the values of honor and prestige.[52] Nancy Tapper, whose work on the Durrānī Pashtuns of north-central Afghanistan, has done much to return the study of kinship and marriage in the Middle East to the center of anthropological thought, similarly argues that the contextual interpretations of any specific marriage relates ultimately to what is exchanged: "men, women, productive resources and valuables, and intangibles such as prestige and political support." The rates of exchange between these spheres may change over time and thus have different implications for status and (in the case of the Durrānī) ethnic identity. Indeed, any given marriage or strategy is capable of multiple interpretations by the Durrānī themselves and does not demonstrate any fixed set of rules or "preferences." Seen synchronically, patterns of exchange involving both honor and control over resources show the interplay of contradictory values. Seen over time, the emphasis is on the "alternative structures" of hierarchy and equality implicit in Durrānī ideology. This ideology encompasses notions of religious and tribal equality, seen in terms of honor, and competition over the control of resources, in which "the

[49] Cited in Edward Westermarck, *Wit and Wisdom of Morocco* (New York: AMS Press, 1980 [1931]), p. 72.

[50] Lancaster, *Rwala*, p. 22. For Oman, see C. Eickelman, *Women and Community*, p. 94, who notes the tendency to describe all marriages within the family cluster as *bint 'amm* marriages, regardless of the precise relationship of the spouses.

[51] Richard T. Antoun, "Anthropology," in *The Study of the Middle East*, ed. Leonard Binder (New York: Wiley, 1976), pp. 166–68.

[52] Bourdieu, *Outline*, pp. 43–52.

weak lose control of resources of all kinds, lose honour and become weaker still, while the strong gain control of resources, gain honour and become stronger." Tapper writes that, at the very least, "the symbolic and material implications of Middle Eastern marriage systems will only be disentangled by treating them as part of a wider exchange system."[53]

As for genealogies and claims of the importance of lineal descent, many anthropologists have taken their importance for granted and have analyzed them as static ethnographic artifacts, ignoring how they are used and how their meaning can change with context and over time. In my own ethnographic experience in Oman and Morocco, people's use of complex genealogies reaching back over many generations tends to be correlated closely to wealth and social class. Individuals and groups who have something to gain by imposing their interpretation of genealogies upon the social order will strive to do so. It would be considered inappropriate and dangerous to one's reputation, in both tribal and nontribal settings, for people without claims to high social status to make elaborate claims of descent.

Bourdieu argues that anthropologists have tended to neglect the role of genealogies and the significance of the occasions when a genealogical representation of relationships (as opposed to other representations) is invoked. He argues that anthropologists easily forget that genealogies are the product of multiple strategies and thus treat the meaning of kinship relations genealogically defined as a resolved question.[54] Instead, anthropologists should seek to specify the types of situations in which the use of genealogies and relationships defined by them are particularly dominant. Although emphasis is placed on patrilineal relationships, matrilateral relations have equal importance in many social situations, although they have tended to be neglected, as they are not "official" genealogical representations of the social order.

Richard Antoun has written that any scholarly approach that concentrates almost exclusively on one type of kinship tie or social relationship and the "problems" derived from it constitutes a "museum" approach, which creates artifacts of kinship exotica.[55] Although it can be argued that his comment unjustly characterizes current trends in museology, I concur with the intention of his comment. Kinship studies have often been considered an arcane anthropological preserve, except when more general writers choose to make sweeping generalizations concerning the importance of family ties in the Middle East. This chapter has suggested a less arcane way of looking at Middle Eastern and, when similar studies of the region become accessible, Central Asian notions of social identity.

[53] Nancy Tapper, "Direct Exchange and Brideprice: Alternative Forms in a Complex Marriage System," *Man* (N.S.) 16, no. 3 (September 1981), 400–405.

[54] Bourdieu, *Outline*, p. 35. Emrys L. Peters, "Aspects of Rank and Status Among Muslims in a Lebanese Village," in *Mediterranean Countrymen*, ed. Julian Pitt-Rivers (Paris and The Hague: Mouton, 1963), pp. 159–202, presents a sprawling genealogy and indicates how it was manipulated by an elite keeper of the culture.

[55] Antoun, "Anthropology," pp. 166–68.

FURTHER READINGS

Examples of marriage negotiations and ceremonies elsewhere in the Middle East and Central Asia are included in Hamed Ammar, *Growing Up in an Egyptian Village* (London: Routledge & Kegan Paul, 1954), pp. 192–201; Paul J. Magnarella, *Tradition and Change in a Turkish Town* (New York: Halsted Press, 1974), pp. 107–30; Richard T. Antoun, *Arab Village: A Social Structural Study of a Transjordanian Peasant Community* (Bloomington: Indiana University Press, 1972), pp. 114–59; and C. Eickelman, *Women and Community in Oman* (New York: New York University Press, 1984), pp. 93–110. For Central Asia, see Audrey C. Shalinsky, *Long Years of Exile: Central Asian Refugees in Afghanistan and Pakistan* (Lanham, MD: University Press of America, 1994), pp. 68–75; and Veronica Doubleday, *Three Women of Herat* (Austin, TX: University of Texas Press, 1990). Elizabeth E. Bacon, *Central Asians Under Russian Rule: A Study in Culture Change* (Ithaca, NY, and London: Cornell University Press, 1980 [1966]), contains short discussions best pursued through the index references. For older Middle Eastern accounts of nineteenth- and early twentieth-century marriage practices, see Edward Westermarck, *Marriage Ceremonies in Morocco* (London: Curzon Press; Totowa, NJ: Bowman & Littlefield, 1972 [1914]); C. Snouck Hurgronje, *Mekka in the Latter Part of the Nineteenth Century*, trans. J. H. Monahan (Leiden: E. L. Brill; London: Luzac & Co., 1931), pp. 83–144, which provides a fascinating account of women's "freedom" among elite families in a pre-Westernized cash economy; and Edward William Lane, *An Account of the Manners and Customs of the Modern Egyptians* (New York: Dover, 1973 [1836]), pp. 155–85. Photographs of marriage practices in a small village near Bethlehem taken by the Finnish ethnographer Hilma Granqvist and a summary of her ethnographic work related to marriage appear in Karen Seger, ed., *Portrait of a Palestinian Village: The Photographs of Hilma Granqvist* (London: Third World Centre for Research and Publishing, 1981), pp. 74–101. A useful account dispelling the notion that pastoral nomads have no coherent rituals, especially those related to marriage, is Daniel A. Bradburd, "Ritual and Southwest Asian Pastoralists: Implications of the Komachi Case," *Journal of Anthropological Research* 40, no. 3 (Fall 1984), 380–93. On polygamy, see Irwan Altman and Joseph Ginat, *Polygamous Families in Contemporary Society* (Cambridge and New York: Cambridge University Press, 1996), a study that also discusses polygamy in non-Muslim societies. On family and extended groupings in time of crisis, see Joseph Ginat, *Blood Revenge: Family Honor, Mediation, and Outcastings*, 2nd ed. (Sussex: Sussex Academic Press, 1996 [1987]).

Despite significant legal reforms throughout the Middle East (and Central Asia), there are limits in many regions even today to how actively women participate in marriage choices. In Turkey, a country with a tradition since the 1920s of legal reform favoring the equality of women and men, women in small urban centers continue to be "severely segregated" from the age of 11 onward. One Turkish scholar, Fatma Mansur Coşar, "Women in Turkish Society," in *Women in the Muslim World*, ed. Lois Beck and Nikki Keddie (Cambridge and London: Harvard University Press, 1978), p. 138, reports (somewhat implausibly, unless in response to self-reporting?) that "63 percent of the girls who live in small towns see their husband for the first time on their wedding day, while the proportion for the three large cities and the villages are 16 and 19 percent respectively." June Starr, *Law as Metaphor: From Islamic Courts to the Palace of Justice* (Albany: State University of New York Press, 1992), assesses the increasing sophistication and success of rural women in using the court system to claim their civil rights. Ann Elizabeth Mayer, *Islam and Human Rights: Tradition and Politics*, 2nd ed. (Boulder, CO: Westview Press, 1995 [1991]), pp. 93–142, provides an authoritative survey of women's legal status in Islamic law and the legal codes of various Middle Eastern states.

For the complementary images that men and women hold of one another in Morocco, see Lawrence Rosen, *Bargaining for Reality: The Construction of Social Relations in a Muslim Community* (Chicago: University of Chicago Press, 1984), pp. 32–33, 38–42, 45–47; and

Daisy Hilse Dwyer, *Images and Self-Images: Male and Female in Morocco* (New York: Columbia University Press, 1978). An excellent account of variations in women's self-perceptions in Afghanistan, with implications for understanding other societies, is Nancy Tapper, "Matrons and Mistresses: Women and Boundaries in Two Middle Eastern Tribal Societies," *European Journal of Sociology*, no. 1 (May 1980), pp. 59–78. The work of medical anthropologists also makes important contributions to women's (and men's) conceptions of self. See Marcia C. Inhorn, *Quest for Conception: Gender, Infertility, and Egyptian Medical Traditions* (Philadelphia: University of Pennsylvania Press, 1994), and her *Infertility and Patriarchy: The Cultural Politics of Gender and Family Life in Egypt* (Philadelphia: University of Pennsylvania Press, 1996).

For a comprehensive view of households in Turkey in the late nineteenth and early twentieth centuries, see Alan Duben and Cem Behar, *Istanbul Households: Marriage, Family and Fertility, 1880–1940*, Cambridge Studies in Population, Economy and Society in Past Time 15 (Cambridge and New York: Cambridge University Press, 1991).

See Arlene Elowe MacLeod, *Accommodating Protest: Working Women, the New Veiling, and Change in Cairo* (New York: Columbia University Press, 1991), pp. 97–124, for an excellent account of contemporary practices among lower-working-class women in Cairo; and Valerie J. Hoffman-Ladd, "Polemics on the Modesty and Segregation of Women in Contemporary Egypt," *International Journal of Middle East Studies* 19, no. 1 (February 1987), 23–50. For Oman, see C. Eickelman, *Women and Community*, p. 126; and Unni Wikan, *Behind the Veil in Arabia* (Baltimore and London: Johns Hopkins University Press, 1982), pp. 94–99. Two outstanding accounts, unfortunately available only in French, are Hinde Taâriji, *Les Voilées de l'Islam* [Islam's Veiled Ones], 2nd ed. (Casablanca: Éditions Eddif), the account of conversations of a secular woman journalist who traveled throughout the Arab world and Turkey asking women to explain their decision to wear the headscarf. Farida Abdelkhah, *La révolution sous le voile: Femmes islamiques d'Iran* [Revolution Beneath the Veil: Islamic Women in Iran] (Paris: Karthala, 1991), is a wide-ranging study by an anthropologist of Iranian origin. For Central Asia, see M. A. Tolmacheva, "The Muslim Woman in Soviet Central Asia," *Central Asian Survey* 12, no. 4 (1993), 531–48. On the political significance of veiling and the headscarf, see, for Saudi Arabia, Eleanor A. Doumato, "Gender, Monarchy, and National Identity in Saudi Arabia," *British Journal of Middle Eastern Studies* 19, no. 1 (1992), 31–48; and, for Muslims in France and the Middle East, Dale F. Eickelman and James Piscatori, *Muslim Politics* (Princeton, NJ: Princeton University Press, 1996), pp. 1–2, 90–91.

8

CHANGE IN PRACTICAL IDEOLOGIES

Self, Gender, and Ethnicity

Cultural concepts of kinship, family, person, community, and sect do not occur in isolation, but rather are interconnected in complex ways. Thus change in any one domain is often irregularly accelerated or impeded by the others. Taken together, these concepts form matrices of symbolic representations that mediate the conditions of existence. These representations are "generative schemes" that produce recurring practices and perceptions of reality. In ordinary circumstances, however, these representations are not consciously apprehended. In analogy with ideas of structure in language, these symbolic representations (Pierre Bourdieu uses the Latin term *habitus*, which carries the meaning of a settled practice or disposition to act in a certain way) produce a large variety of "surface" expressions, which vary with such factors as person, class, social category, generation, and gender.[1] Massive and rapid economic and political change affects basic symbolic representations, but the influence of such "objective" conditions is often uneven and not fully predictable because people's perceptions of these objective conditions are mediated by the symbolic representations themselves. Periods of crisis or rapid transformation often provide the conjuncture of circumstances suitable for constructing or reformulating new practical, or implicit, ideologies—of lineage, tribe, kinship, sect, religion, loyalty, and nation. However, as dramatic as some changes may appear in legislative act, they unevenly affect practice and popular understandings. Thus Morocco abolished tribes as political units in the early 1960s and replaced them with "communes," although many communes were designed on the basis of established tribal boundaries. Other countries have legislated changes in the personal status of men and women that often contrast dramatically with popularly understood rights and expectations.

[1] Pierre Bourdieu, *Outline of a Theory of Practice*, trans. Richard Nice, Cambridge Studies in Social Anthropology 16 (Cambridge and New York: Cambridge University Press, 1977), pp. 82–88.

Early studies of self, kinship, gender, and ethnicity often treated such notions as if they were relatively fixed and enduring, but there is now more awareness of how such representations are affected by the historical contexts in which they were generated and reproduced and the social location (or status, roles, and influence) of their carriers within a given society. Ideologies and practices concerning person, gender, sect, and *ethnos* are fundamentally dependent on the social institutions through which they are communicated and reproduced. Some meanings are shared, others are challenged or denied, and most are consciously or implicitly altered in the process of transmission. Class, social category, generation, gender, and status all provide different conjunctions from which ideas and practices are learned, valued, transmitted, and reproduced.

Take the notion of *person*. Anthropologists often distinguish between notions of individual and person. *Individuals* are mortal human beings, the objects of observation and self-reflection. *Person* refers to the cultural concepts that lend the individual social significance. Personhood, which varies according to culture, provides individuals with socially recognized criteria through which their actions achieve social significance. Thus ideas of person, or self, are not just individually held, nor are they shared in an undifferentiated manner throughout a society. Indeed, this internal differentiation provides the sense of "other" and of "otherness" necessary to maintain a distinctive sense of honorable self. Steven Caton, for instance, illustrates how notions of personal and collective honor in tribal society emerge in the course of men's poetic competitions (*bālah*) in North Yemen. *Bālah* are intertribal competitions that entail the concept of an "Other *against* whom a glorious deed," a poetic composition, is performed. This other must be considered worthy of competition, from whom subsequent challenges can be expected. The result of such challenges and responses is an ongoing construction and reconstruction of self.[2]

This chapter looks at three of the most sensitive contexts of cultural projections of person and self: naming, a practice that, because usually not consciously systematized, is a good index of implicit notions of person and change; gender and sexuality, which, in part, are also regarded as private, immutable, and implicit; and ethnic identities, which, like sectarian identities, have posed special challenges in both enhancing and threatening the existence of contemporary nation-states. As shall become clear, coverage for Central Asia reflects the strictures of pre-1990 research. Studies concerning ethnicity and nationalism are relatively abundant, but those concerning gender issues, women's consciousness of their roles in society, religious beliefs, and similar topics remain fewer than for the Middle East, or they conform suspiciously to pre-1990 Soviet

[2] Steven C. Caton, "The Poetic Construction of Self," *Anthropological Quarterly*, Special Issue on "Self and Society in the Middle East," ed. Jon W. Anderson and Dale F. Eickelman, 58, no. 4 (October 1985), 142. The articles in this issue provide a useful introduction to notions of person and self in the contemporary Middle East. For intertribal poetry contests in the Sudan, see Ahmed al-Shahi, "Pride and Vilification—Two Tribal Viewpoints," *Journal of the Anthropological Society of Oxford* 12, no. 2 (Trinity 1981), 87–102.

ideals. When women are discussed, it is largely in terms of educational statistics and participation in the labor force.[3]

NAMING

Patterns of naming provide privileged insight into the assumptions concerning cultural ideas of the person, as S. D. Goitein indicates in his analysis of female names in the Geniza documents. These documents depict the social life of the Jewish (and Muslim) communities of the southern Mediterranean, especially Cairo, in the tenth through thirteenth centuries. Goitein's analysis has produced a description of the social life and values of the period that is more thorough than that provided by many contemporary ethnographies. In the Geniza documents, women rarely speak for themselves; many were illiterate, and those who were not were frequently constrained to speak through male guardians. From inheritance papers, correspondence, and other fragmentary evidence, Goitein elicited the implications of naming patterns and what they reveal of attitudes toward self.

Names were "living words," the meanings of which were well known to those who bestowed them. Women were primarily responsible for the names given to daughters, so that the meaning of a name and the frequency of its occurrence are good indicators of what a woman wished for her daughter and, by implication, for herself.[4] The wide variety of names given to women had a number of common characteristics. In contrast to the names of men, which often contained references to God or to religious concepts, women's names consistently emphasized secular themes. The exceptions were principally confined to upper-class families. Goitein takes the sexual dichotomy in naming patterns to imply a "chasm" between the worldwide Hebrew book culture of the men and the local popular subculture of the women.

Additionally, many female names—over 70 percent, and an equivalent proportion among Muslim names—suggest ideas of "ruling, overcoming, and victory," such as Sitt al-Kull ("She Who Rules over Everyone"), Sitt al-Nās ("Mistress over Mankind"), Sitt al-Fakhr ("Mistress of Glory"), and Labwa ("Lioness"). As Goitein argues, such names suggest a self-image of women diametrically opposed to the traditional view of women as frail, domestic, or dependent on men. Indeed, names implying chastity or fertility, attributes regarded by men as praiseworthy, were almost entirely absent, perhaps because such attributes were so taken for granted. Other names implied noble

[3] M. A. Tolmacheva, "The Muslim Woman in Soviet Central Asia," *Central Asian Survey* 12, no. 4 (1993), 531–48; and Michael Paul Sacks, "Roots of Diversity and Conflict: Ethnic and Gender Differences in the Work Force of the Former Republics of Soviet Central Asia," in *Muslim Eurasia: Conflicting Legacies*, ed. Yaacov Ro'i, Cummings Center Series (London: Frank Cass, 1995), pp. 269–87, based on a careful assessment of demographic trends.

[4] S. D. Goitein, *A Mediterranean Society: The Jewish Communities of the Arab World as Portrayed in the Documents of the Cairo Geniza. Vol. III: The Family* (Berkeley and Los Angeles: University of California Press, 1978), p. 314.

lineage or a mere welcoming of the newborn, such as Mūna ("Wishes Fulfilled"), Ghunya ("Gain"), Yumn ("Good Luck"), Sa'āda ("Long Life"), and Bāqa ("Substitute"—for a child who died). Because such names were fairly common, Goitein suspects that they were a protest against the male preference for boys.

Changing fashions in naming can also be used as documentary indices of shifting religious and national consciousness, another crucial dimension of ideas of self.[5] One such study is Richard Bulliet's discussion of trends in Turkish naming patterns from the early nineteenth century to the 1950s.[6] For instance, the Turkish names of Mehmet, Ahmet, and Ali are all derived from Arabic and have religious connotations. These names were highly popular prior to the secularizing Ottoman reforms (called the Tanzimat) that were enacted from the 1840s onward. There was a sharp plunge in their popularity, and they reached a low in 1885–1889, when the reforming spirit was most intense. Afterward, religious names slowly recovered in popularity, only to reach a new low in 1905–1909, when the Young Turk movement was strong. Later there was a gradual but steady recovery of the incidence of religious names through 1920–1924, after which they maintained a fairly stable level.

Concurrently, the political circumstances from the rise of the Young Turks in the final years of the Ottoman Empire through the declaration of the Turkish Republic in 1923 were correlated with the replacement of names of Arabic origin by those that were Turkish and secular, reflecting a distinctly Turkish national identity. Such names were only 8 percent of the total of the sample in 1910–1914, rose to 65 percent from 1930 to 1941, and have declined only slightly in subsequent years. Yet, as Bulliet emphasizes, the new trend in the popularity of Turkish secularized names did not radically diminish the use of names with a religious base. This suggests that, despite the militantly secularist ideology of the Turkish state promulgated by Atatürk and his successors, a significant component of the population retained its distinctly religious identity. Increasing literacy among villagers in Turkey is linked in part to a revitalized use of older Persian and Arabic terms, which a secular-minded Turkish elite has sought to purge since the 1920s. A resurgent Islamic influence has brought names with religious connotations back into vogue, as well as words from the Ottoman era that were falling into disuse among the elite.[7]

By analogy with Turkey, naming patterns in Central Asia and Azerbaijan are already showing significant changes over those that prevailed in the Soviet era, when many people, especially the elite, Russified their names. The trend now is to follow more distinctly "national" naming conventions. Thus ethnomusicologist Theodore Levin's faculty adviser at the Academy of Music in the 1970s was Faizullah Muzaffarovich Karamatov. "Faizullah," his personal name,

[5] Ibid., pp. 315–19.

[6] Richard W. Bulliet, "First Names and Political Change in Modern Turkey," *International Journal of Middle East Studies* 9, no. 4 (November 1978), 489–95.

[7] See "A Kokteyl Culture," *The Economist*, April 11, 1987, p. 92.

was the same then as today. His patronymic, in Russian style and with a Russian suffix, is "Muzaffarovitch," or "son of Muzaffar." "Karamatov" is his family name, again with a Russian suffix. Since independence, in 1991, his name has become more Uzbek, and he has dropped the Russian style and suffixes. He calls himself "Faizullah Karamatli"—his personal and family names. Some traditionalists refer to him as "Faizullah Muzaffar oglu" (*oglu* is Uzbek for "son of"). Just as frequently, he is addressed by his first name alone, Faizullah, to which an honorific for teachers is added, *Domullah*.[8] What in proper English usage would be "Honored Professor Levin" becomes "Honored Professor Ted" in proper Uzbek usage, with no family or clan names added.

Another important aspect of naming as a key to the idea of the person in the Middle East and Central Asia is a greater flexibility as to how a person can be referred to and addressed in comparison with Western societies. In the early years of French rule in Morocco, for instance, when letters of safe conduct and a system of land registration that required the precise legal identity of people was being put into effect, it was not uncommon for the French to issue papers that referred to individuals by numerous alternative (and equally appropriate) names.[9] For example, a man called Aḥmad could also be known as:

Aḥmad wuld Drīss al-Baqqāl	Aḥmad, son of Drīss, the Grocer
Aḥmad wuld Drīss wuld Muṣṭafā	Aḥmad, son of Drīss, son of Muṣṭafā
Aḥmad "wuld 'Msh"	Aḥmad, "son of the man with poor eyesight" (a nickname)
Aḥmad al-Tādilī	Aḥmad from Tādla
al-Tādilī	the one from Tādla
Wuld Drīss	son of Drīss
Aḥmad wuld Drīss ash-Sharqāwī	Aḥmad, son of Drīss, of the Sharqāwī (patronymic association)

As in the West, only with the spread of the legal registry of births and the necessity, principally for administrative reasons, of identifying people unambiguously by a single name, has the variety of naming choices been lessened. Indeed, the need of state authorities to control populations and identify individuals unambiguously for the purposes of taxation, military service, health, and education is one of the hallmarks of modern states, be they revolutionary or conservative. Nonetheless, flexible patterns of naming persist in many parts of the Middle East. Moroccan naming patterns suggest how flexible are the ways in which people can identify themselves, although there are variations in how these different components are emphasized. Moroccan names can be composed of the following elements: (1) personal names, such as Muḥammad, Aḥmad, and Būzkrī; (2) nicknames (*laqab*-s), generally relating to some predominant personal identifying feature, such as "the one-eyed," "the colorful," or

[8] Personal communication, Theodore Levin, August 8, 1996.

[9] Hildred Geertz, "The Meanings of Family Ties," in *Meaning and Order in Moroccan Society*, ed. Clifford Geertz, Hildred Geertz, and Lawrence Rosen (New York and London: Cambridge University Press, 1979), pp. 341–56.

"the fast one"; (3) names derived from occupation and origin (*nisba*); (4) patrifiliative names; and (5) "family" names (*kunya*-s), made obligatory by the government in the 1950s but earlier maintained by wealthy government officials, merchants, marabouts, and descendants of the Prophet (pl. *shurfā*).[10]

Personal, or "first" names, can be drawn from a range of religious and secular sources. These names are not always distinctive. In one set of census material, Hildred Geertz found that out of 982 male names, 156 were called Muḥammad.[11] Quite a few names reflect little more than the time of year a child was born. An infant born near the feast day of the Prophet ('Īd al-Mīlūd) often is given the name Mīludī. Similarly, one born near the Feast of Abraham ('Īd al-Kabīr) will often be known as al-Kabīr. If an earlier child has died, the later child may be given the same name or a name indicating that he or she is a replacement. A child may also be named after an immediate relative who has recently died. In Morocco, naming a child after a living person is considered an ill omen for the child and is therefore not done.

There are fashions in naming, and names often acquire a political significance. In earlier generations almost all male names were religiously based (in a pattern reminiscent of that described by Goitein, many female names were not). A name once given is not ordinarily changed, although in some regions, such as the Sultanate of Oman, a man or woman may change his or her personal name at marriage if the name is thought to be incompatible with that of the proposed spouse. In such contexts, each letter of the alphabet is thought to be correlated with certain values (such as fire and water), some of which are incompatible with others. If the names of a couple intending marriage lack the proper correspondence, then the name of one is changed.[12]

Nicknames can be acquired for a number of reasons. Usually they refer to a distinctive personal characteristic or an outstanding incident in a person's life. A Moroccan in one small town was named Bin Shaqrūn, after a prominent Casablanca merchant of the 1890s, because he used to sell things as a child to other children in his quarter. In a Jordanian village, one man is called al-Hamshārī, a Turkish word meaning "countryman," because his father served in the Ottoman army in World War I. Upon returning to his village the father greeted the first man he saw with: "How are you, *hamshārī*?" using the Turkish

[10] Part of the following discussion on naming is adapted from Dale F. Eickelman, "Time in a Complex Society: A Moroccan Example," *Ethnology* 16, no. 1 (January 1977), 48–50. A thorough discussion of names, one of the best for a Middle Eastern context, which relates them to the notions of kinship and patronymic association, is found in Geertz, "Family Ties," pp. 341–56. For naming ceremonies in Egypt and the effect of government-imposed civil registries on patterns of naming, see Hamed Ammar, *Growing Up in an Egyptian Village* (London: Routledge & Kegan Paul, 1954), pp. 91–93, 97.

[11] Geertz, "Family Ties," p. 342.

[12] Abdul Hamid M. el-Zein, Temple University, personal communication (June 1979). Ammar, *Growing Up*, pp. 92–93, points out that in Middle Eastern contexts where formal naming ceremonies for children do not exist (such as Palestine in the 1930s), the names of children are sometimes changed in later years. This is almost never the case where formal naming ceremonies exist, as occurs seven days after the birth of the child in Egypt and Morocco, among other Middle Eastern countries.

term. Another man known for his piety was called al-Shihādī ("Testifier" of faith in God) because a male child was born to him at the end of his life.[13]

Nicknames fall into two categories. Those of people and groups that convey either neutral or positive images tend to be public. Names conveying less desirable, invidious personal characteristics, such as *daggār* ("busybody"), can be used as effective means of social control in the contexts of everyday use.[14] Many such terms have an inherent ambiguity that permits them to be used either pejoratively or simply as signs of intimacy. One Moroccan secondary student is called Al-Muqayhir ("the down-and-out") because, unlike his classmates, he ostentatiously dresses in his oldest clothing. The same nickname might be applied of course to a student who really was in desperate financial circumstances.

Names derived from occupation, origin, and affiliation (for instance with a religious brotherhood) are called *nisba*-s, "a combination of a morphological, grammatical, and semantic process which consists of transforming a noun into what we would call a relative adjective, but what for Arabs becomes just another sort of noun."[15] Thus the location with which people are identified can become part of their name: al-Marrākshī for a man and al-Marrākshīya for a woman who comes from Marrakesh. Depending on context, the same people can be referred to by the name of a quarter in Marrakesh, or by the name of a tribe in the region or subgroup of it, or by the name of a larger geographic or social entity. For example, in Cairo, Ḥasan al-Marrākshī might be known as Ḥasan the Maghribi ("the Moroccan"); in Morocco itself such a *nisba* would hardly be distinctive, nor would be al-Marrākshī in Marrakesh. *Nisba*-s can also be derived from occupations, such as al-Khayyāṭī ("the tailor") and al-Baqqālī ("the grocer"); from affiliation with a religious brotherhood, for example, an-Nāṣirī for a member of the Nāṣirīya brotherhood; and from the name of a maraboutic descent group such as ash-Sharqāwī (of the Sharqāwī patronymic association), or 'Alāwī from the son-in-law of the Prophet (thus indicating prophetic descent). The characterization of a person by *nisba* is highly flexible: "Calling a man a Sefroui is like calling him a San Franciscan; it classifies him but it doesn't type him; it places him without portraying him."[16] Combined with other types of naming and situating people in social contexts, a *nisba* provides one more means by which notions of self can be specified and expressed.

Teknonyms, in which people are known after the names of their children, are also common: Abū Nāṣir (Nāṣir's father), Abū 'Umār, and Umm Muḥammad (Muḥammad's mother) are examples. There are variations within and between

[13] Richard T. Antoun, "On the Significance of Names in an Arab Village," *Ethnology* 7, no. 2 (April 1968), 159. Richard Tapper informs me that *hamshārī* originally derives from the Persian *ham* ("same") and *shahr* ("city").

[14] Ibid., 164–69.

[15] Clifford Geertz, *Local Knowledge* (New York: Basic Books, 1983), p. 65. For a more extended discussion by Geertz of the significance of *nisba*-s in relation to economic roles, see his "Suq: The Bazaar Economy," in *Meaning and Order*, ed. Geertz, Geertz, and Rosen, pp. 140–50.

[16] C. Geertz, *Local Knowledge*, p. 68.

regions in the use of such names, with their use more prevalent in the Levant and the Arabian peninsula, for example, than in North Africa. Among some nomadic tribes in Oman a man can be given a teknonym based on his daughter's name, although among the settled population of the coast and in the Jabal Akhḍar region, a teknonym is based inevitably on the name of a son.

Patrifiliative names, such as Abū Bakr bin Fu'ād (Abū Bakr, son of Fu'ād), situates people in the social context of their paternal predecessors and elder contemporaries. In ordinary usage, the name of only one ascending generation is indicated, although for clarity or to emphasize particular features of one's genealogy, a string of claimed predecessors may be added, as in Abū Bakr bin Fu'ād bin Drīss, in which the grandfather's name is also added. Occasionally, a mother's name is added as a sort of nickname, especially in the case of plural marriages. Occasionally a matrifiliative link is also indicated, as in Fāṭima bint Ẓahra (Fāṭima, daughter of Ẓahra). Children and young adults are commonly referred to only as someone's child, as in Bint Ḥasan (Ḥasan's daughter), until with maturity their own social identity becomes distinct.

One of the principal features of patrifiliative name chains is that, although ideally they can be extended infinitely into the past, in reality they rarely extend back farther than two generations. The assertion that a name chain can be traced back over many generations usually implies a claim to high social status, "noble" antecedents, or descent from the Prophet Muḥammad. As Ibn Khaldūn (see Chapter 2) pointed out many centuries ago, there is nothing "natural" in invoking common descent as a basis for community; in the end, those who align together seek or claim common descent to legitimate sustained cooperation. Indeed, the most assiduously elaborated genealogical claims are usually associated with political, religious, and social leadership.[17]

Until fairly recent times, the use of family names, or *kunya*-s, was largely confined to members of the elite in many Middle Eastern countries. In Morocco such names became obligatory only in the 1950s and are still known in rural areas and small towns as "government" names. Sometimes family names were chosen for individuals from printed lists of available names, if the person did not suggest one. Some illiterates in fact have to ask other people to read their "government" names for them, so little are these names a part of ordinary social contexts. Often names that can be thought of as *nisba*-s, such as Sharqāwī, are adopted as family names, and names connoting place of origin and of occupation imperceptibly merge with those of family.

As a basis of social identity, names primarily signify the actual person carrying the name, not abstract groups or genealogical "lines" with an extended

[17] See, for instance, C. C. Stewart, *Islam and the Social Order in Mauritania* (Oxford: Clarendon Press, 1973), pp. 62, 134–35; and Abd-al-Ghaffar Muhammad Ahmad, *Shaykhs and Followers: Political Struggle in the Rufu'a al-Hoi Nazirate in the Sudan* (Khartoum: Khartoum University Press, 1974), pp. 84–92. On Ibn Khaldūn's notions of descent and collective identity, see his *The Muqaddimah*, 2nd ed., vol. 1, trans. Franz Rosenthal, Bollingen Series 43 (Princeton, NJ: Princeton University Press, 1967), pp. 249–355. Daniel Martin Varisco, "Metaphors and Sacred History: The Genealogy of Muhammad and the Arab 'Tribe,'" *Anthropological Quarterly* 68, no. 3 (July 1995), 139–56, indicates how female as well as male ancestors can be invoked in making claims to inherited status.

temporal reality. The structure of possible ways of naming a person ensures that the temporal depth is markedly attenuated, as is the notion of the person having a fixed social location. Naming patterns and how they are used thus indicate that there is considerable flexibility in how people are identified and how they can choose to identify themselves. In American and European contexts, such flexibility is not entirely lacking. The terms of address, such as the use of the first name without titles or honorifics, can suggest intimacy or disrespect, according to context and the speaker. Media personalities may simplify or change their names to further their careers, and one may go to court to change one's name. The same is true of course in Middle Eastern situations, but the variety of means by which a person can be identified is considerably greater.

WOMEN, MEN, AND SEXUALITY

Until the 1970s, women tended to be portrayed unidimensionally in studies of the Middle East, so that analyses of marriage and domestic life concentrated on formal roles and procedures. A brief quotation from Sergei Poliakov's late Soviet-era study of rural Central Asia may suggest the quality of work there until very recently:

> An important factor in a girl's willingness to marry even a boy whom she does not know is the opportunity marriage gives her to wear a new dress, to adorn herself, to try on all the clothes she gets as her dowry. It makes no difference here whether the young woman is able to go outside of her new home, which is very rare, or whether she stays at home; she gets equal satisfaction from both.
>
> Most women also like their position in the family, which might be described as "unthinking."[18]

On the next page, Poliakov notes a "high" rate of female suicide, with "self-immolation" and "poisoning—most commonly by drinking vinegar essence" as the "usual" methods. He offers no statistics, claiming that suicides are rarely noted in official records, and asserts that the only community response is to "quash any attempts to blame such tragedies on traditionalism," and he goes on to state that even education cannot raise Central Asians from their "usual orbit."[19]

In community studies of the Middle East, women were often described as "a world apart" or as inhabitants of a "private" sphere of "limited" significance.[20] The publication in the 1970s of two major collections of scholarly essays

[18] Sergei P. Poliakov, *Everyday Islam: Religion and Tradition in Rural Central Asia*, trans. Anthony Olcott (Armonk, NY: M. E. Sharpe, 1992), p. 85.

[19] Ibid., pp. 85–86.

[20] Roxann A. Van Dusen, "The Study of Women in the Middle East: Some Thoughts," *Middle East Studies Association Bulletin* 10, no. 2 (May 1976), 2.

and primary sources on women in the Middle East brought the study of women and gender to the center of social thought.[21] Beginning in the 1980s, full-scale monographs reporting on major field or social historical research analyzing women's roles in society became relatively abundant, and many studies now explore intraregional comparisons, differences of age and generation, residence patterns (urban and rural), classes and social strata, education, and participation in the work force. By the 1980s, studies were more likely to depict how women's cultural and social roles are internally differentiated within contemporary societies and how women's images and self-images have been transformed over time. These changes in how historians and ethnographers have portrayed women in society are due not just to "progress" but also to greater attention to the "informal" roles of women, who sometimes, working in partnership with men of an extended family, engage in politics as fully as men but in a "deniable" way not amenable to official control or public scrutiny.[22]

The themes discussed here include gender and sex roles; the implications for women's status of changing political, legal, and economic conditions; and how the seemingly more durable cultural understandings of gender roles relate to basic understandings of self and society, as social constructions, change over time.

Gender Roles and Sexuality

Anthropological knowledge has a way of calling into question the most fundamental assumptions concerning "human nature." Throughout the Middle East, the public discussion of women and gender roles can be highly politicized, and it is necessary to get beyond the public statements of normative roles. These formal statements often are at considerable variance with both practice and accepted conventions. Shahla Haeri writes of sexuality and gender relations, "It is evident that such control and segregation may appear to

[21] Elizabeth Warnock Fernea and Basima Qattam Bezirgan, eds., *Middle Eastern Muslim Women Speak* (Austin and London: University of Texas Press, 1977), is an anthology of writings by and about Middle Eastern women. It has been updated by a new anthology, *Women and the Family in the Middle East: New Voices of Change*, ed. Elizabeth Warnock Fernea (Austin: University of Texas Press, 1985). Another major collection from the 1970s, *Women in the Muslim World*, ed. Lois Beck and Nikki Keddie (Cambridge, MA, and London: Harvard University Press, 1978), contains more analytical essays. Cynthia Nelson, "Public and Private Politics: Women in the Middle Eastern World," *American Ethnologist* 1, no. 3 (August 1974), 551–63, remains valuable for its discussion of how women have been treated in earlier ethnographic accounts. For a survey of evidence—historical and contemporary—concerning the "informal" political leadership of women, especially among the elite, see James A. Bill and Robert Springborg, *Politics in the Middle East*, 3rd ed. (Glenview, IL, and London: Scott, Foresman/Little, Brown, 1990), pp. 107–17. See also Suad Joseph, "The Study of Middle Eastern Women: Investments, Passions, and Problems," *International Journal of Middle East Studies* 18, no. 4 (November 1986), 501–509; and Lila Abu-Lughod, "Zones of Theory in the Anthropology of the Arab World," *Annual Review of Anthropology* 18 (1989), 267–306.

[22] Christine Eickelman, *Women and Community in Oman* (New York: New York University Press, 1984), pp. 80–111; Diane Singerman, *Avenues of Participation: Family, Politics, and Networks in Urban Quarters of Cairo*, Princeton Studies in Muslim Politics (Princeton, NJ: Princeton University Press, 1995).

an outside observer to be more immutable, uniform, and static than they really are."[23]

Tunisian sociologist Abdelwahab Bouhdiba suggests what a comprehensive study of sexuality should be and the available documentary sources. His *Sexuality in Islam* analyzes attitudes toward sexuality in the medieval Islamic world and in the contemporary period both through texts and (by reference to a few relevant colonial and contemporary studies of Tunisia) sociological accounts. He insists that although the Islamic community considers itself rightly as a unity, Islam and Muslim society is fundamentally "plastic" in its essence, so that none of the ambiguities of existence are sacrificed, including the serious and playful, collective and individual components of sexuality. For Bouhdiba, one can speak of a Malay Islam, an Arab Islam, an Iranian Islam, a Tunisian Islam, and other manifestations of Muslim civilization, each suggesting attitudes that cannot be reduced to "folklore"or to a composite essence.[24] His text suggests how the sexual dimension of identity has been elaborated in the context of various expressions of Islamic belief and practice and in a multiplicity of settings.

However, it is not just setting that contributes to variations in gender differences. It is also the changing practices and intents of women and men. In Iran, for example, Azam Torab points out that there are continual debates among Shīʿī religious scholars over what it is to be male and female. She also provides examples of the increase in female religious leaders, called "speakers" (*guyandeh*), who animate women's study groups and religious gatherings and sometimes challenge conventional assumptions of "gendered" authority. Gendering, she insists, is not a fixed and unchanging disposition: "Gendering is about how women and men make their femininities and masculinities known to themselves and to each other, through saying and doing things in specific instances."[25] It is fluid and changeable between individuals. Women may accept dominant cultural notions of gender, but, as with the growing strength of women's religious study groups, they can also speak and behave in ways that contest these dominant notions.

Most studies concerning gender and sex roles point to the markedly different patterns of socialization of the two sexes. As indicated earlier in this chapter, the different types of names given to boys and girls strongly suggest the different attitudes toward the two sexes and their respective roles in society. Hamed Ammar's discussion of childhood socialization in an Egyptian village, now nearly half a century old, remains a significant point of departure and an

[23] Shahla Haeri, *Law of Desire: Temporary Marriage in Shiʿi Iran* (Syracuse, NY: Syracuse University Press, 1989), pp. 207–208. See also Jon Anderson, "Social Structure and the Veil: Comportment and the Composition of Interaction in Afghanistan," *Anthropos* 77 (1982), 397–420, who indicates how stylized communications between unrelated women and men can occur without exceeding the bounds of propriety.

[24] Abdelwahab Bouhdiba, *Sexuality in Islam*, trans. Alan Sheridan (London and Boston: Routledge & Kegan Paul, 1985 [1975]), pp. 127–28.

[25] Azam Torab, "Piety as Gendered Agency: A Study of *Jalaseh* Ritual Discourse in an Urban Neighbourhood in Iran," *Journal of the Royal Anthropological Institute* (N.S.) 2, no. 2 (June 1996), 238.

indication of earlier practices. Boys, he writes, tend to be regarded as a capital investment in peasant settings and are thought to contribute more to a family's social prestige. A man with numerous sons speaks with more authority as they mature. Consequently, midwives are given more substantial presents on the birth of a boy than for a girl. Ammar indicates that, although a girl's birth is greeted with less enthusiasm, normatively it is reprehensible (*makrūh*) to show dissatisfaction. Villagers are frequently reminded of the pre-Islamic custom of burying female infants alive and of Islam's superiority in this regard, as the Quran forbade the practice. Nonetheless, villagers say they regard girls as burdensome and a potential source of shame to the family, so that girls must be carefully protected until their marriage.[26] Ammar lists what villagers consider the positive attributes of women, such as possessing greater compassion than men, yet his account clearly indicates the greater reserve that accompanies the birth of girls.

In Ammar's village, girls are shown comparative indulgence in infancy but are expected to reach "sociological adulthood" more rapidly than boys. They soon form separate play groups and are differentially treated throughout their young adulthood. Perhaps the most striking experience that the two sexes undergo is circumcision, which is practiced on *both* sexes in the Aswan region of Egypt. For boys, this occurs between the ages of three and six and is accompanied by a public communal celebration involving both adult male relatives and friends and a separate meal for women. Girls are circumcised (that is, the internal labia are cut off) at the age of seven or eight, ostensibly "to prevent any suspicion on the bridegroom's part that the bride is not a virgin." Whereas the occasion of male circumcision is regarded as a religious occasion, that of female circumcision is confined to women, and men are not even supposed to evince an interest in it.[27] On reading Ammar, it is easy to concur with Paul Vieille's statement concerning the status of women in Iran that their "progressive deval-

[26] Ammar, *Growing Up*, pp. 94–96. Other, more recent accounts of socialization in village and small town settings include Susan Schaefer Davis and Douglas A. Davis, *Adolescence in a Moroccan Town* (New Brunswick, NJ, and London: Rutgers University Press, 1989); and C. Eickelman, *Women and Community*, pp. 180–215.

[27] Ammar, *Growing Up*, pp. 116–18. Despite legislation enacted in 1959 prohibiting female circumcision in Egypt, the practice continues in rural areas. An even more radical practice—infibulation—occurs, despite legislation forbidding it, in the Sudan and certain other Middle Eastern countries. Infibulation involves the deliberate mutilation of the female genitalia so as to close off the vaginal opening almost completely. It is an excruciatingly painful operation and sometimes results in death. See Rose Oldfield Hayes, "Female Genital Mutilation, Fertility Control, Women's Roles, and the Patrilineage in Modern Sudan: A Functional Analysis," *American Ethnologist* 2, no. 4 (November 1975), 617–33; Janice Boddy, "Womb as Oasis: The Symbolic Context of Pharaonic Circumcision in Rural Northern Sudan," *American Ethnologist* 9, no. 4 (November 1982), 682–89; Virginia Lee Barnes, *Aman: The Story of a Somali Girl*, as told to Virginia Lee Barnes and Janice Boddy (New York: Vintage Books, 1994) (which contains a first-person account of a clitoridectomy, pp. 52–60); and Scilla McLean and Stella Efua Graham, eds., *Female Circumcision, Excision, and Infibulation: Facts and Proposals for Change*, Report No. 47 (2nd rev. ed.) (London: Minority Rights Group, 1985). The latter report indicates that it is difficult for women to find a marriage partner without undergoing the practice. Predictably, the topic is a sensitive one that Sudanese, especially educated ones, approach with caution in public discussion because of the disapproval such practices arouse in the West and

uation" is apparent, despite the value placed on their importance as counters of exchange in "good" marriages.[28]

Woman and Status

"Status" can mean the formal rights and obligations of a person, as citizen or subject as enacted by law. It can also mean religious or normative prescriptions that, although they may not have the force of law, are difficult to transgress in public or conventional and accepted ways of comportment. The status of women is closely tied to gender roles, but it is also linked, as in Kuwait and Saudi Arabia, to issues of national identity, family law, Islamic and "international" views on human rights, employment opportunities, and education. The result is to make all public discussions volatile and politicized.[29] As a Syrian colleague recalled, "In the first Friday sermon in my Damascus mosque after the June 1967 Arab-Israeli war, the preacher blamed our defeat on the corruption of our women."[30]

Emrys Peters, whose work we encountered in earlier chapters, undertook a comparative study of the gendered division of labor in four Middle Eastern settings—the bedouin of Cyrenaica, Libya (where he worked in the late 1940s), a settled Libyan bedouin community, a Shīʿī peasant village in south Lebanon (see Chapter 3), and a Maronite Christian community in Lebanon. Peters observed that the status of the two genders is strongly correlated with the division of labor: domestic versus "man's" work.[31] This observation is echoed in

in Muslim countries such as those of the Maghrib, where equivalent rites are unknown. It should be noted that such physically painful rites are not entirely confined to women. Although male circumcision occurs in most parts of the Middle East at an early age, in some parts of Yemen, circumcision occurs only between the ages of 12 and 15. Surrounded by a crowd of men and women, the child recites the Muslim creed, "There is no God but God and Muḥammad is his Prophet," three times. The foreskin is cut and thrown into the crowd and then picked up by the youth, who proudly displays it. He is placed on his mother's shoulders, where he continues to show it off and then, brandishing a dagger, he leads a procession of dancers. A boy is humiliated for life if he shows any signs of pain or distress. The practice is outlawed, but see the photographs taken of one such ceremony in 1972 in Claudie Fayein, *Yemen* (Paris: Éditions du Seuil, 1975), pp. 34–35. In general, such brutally direct rituals of "sculpting" the body to achieve social identity are beginning to disappear, in part through government action and in part through the homogenizing effect of mass education and exposure to "standard" Islamic practices.

[28] Paul Vieille, "Iranian Women in Family Alliance and Sexual Politics," in *Women*, ed. Beck and Keddie, p. 452.

[29] See Eleanor A. Doumato, "Gender, Monarchy, and National Identity in Saudi Arabia," *British Journal of Middle East Studies* 19, no. 1 (1992), 31–47; and Anh Nga Longva, "Kuwaiti Women at a Crossroads: Privileged Development and the Constraints of Ethnic Stratification," *International Journal of Middle East Studies* 25, no. 3 (August 1993), 443–56. She argues that constraints on women's public dress, rather than being "timeless," are imposed by ethnic stratification. Kuwaiti women are obliged to wear national dress—the *ʿabāya*, a black, head-to-foot outer garment which symbolizes power and prestige—in public places. Between the mid-1950s and 1970s, women increasingly abandoned this outer garment in favor of Western-style clothes, but by the mid-1980s, with the influx of foreign workers to the region, they reverted to the *ʿabāya* as a form of protection (p. 449).

[30] Interview, Damascus, March 11, 1996.

[31] Emrys L. Peters, "The Status of Women in Four Middle East Communities," in *Women*, ed. Beck and Keddie, pp. 311–50.

many subsequent studies on the implications of sex roles in the Middle East. As Nadia Hijab and others point out, changing economic fortunes have a significant impact on how ideologies of gender are expressed. When large numbers of Jordanian men emigrated to the Arab Gulf for high-paying jobs, significant numbers of women entered the Jordanian work force. When the men were forced to return to Jordan because of a downturn in the economy, women were removed from many of these jobs to make way for the returning men. The justifications men invoked for this policy shift were often religious.[32]

Many studies have concentrated on the impact of greater educational opportunities for women, legislative reforms, generational change, and the effect of changing economic and political conditions on women's roles and the image of women in society. In countries such as Egypt and Turkey, some women of the middle and upper classes participate in organized movements for the explicit purpose of enhancing the status of women, and such associations today have a significant impact on policies in most of the countries of the Middle East.[33]

Legal reforms that have benefited women have been enacted in most Middle Eastern settings, with substantial improvements in the status of women in countries such as Tunisia, Iran, and Turkey.[34] There are notable omissions in such reforms. Only Turkey, Israel, Tunisia, and the countries of Central Asia (still following Soviet legal codes) have, for instance, prohibited polygamy, although in other countries, including Iraq and Pakistan, legal permission must be obtained for marrying more than one wife. In Morocco and Lebanon,

[32] Nadia Hijab, *Womanpower: The Arab Debate on Women at Work*, Cambridge Middle East Library (Cambridge: Cambridge University Press, 1988), pp. 105–15. For Egypt, see Arlene Elowe Macleod, *Accommodating Protest: Working Women, the New Veiling, and Change in Cairo* (New York: Columbia University Press, 1991), pp. 42–43. See also the thoughtful essay by Deniz Kandiyoti, "The Paradoxes of Masculinity: Some Thoughts on Segregated Societies," in *Dislocating Masculinity: Comparative Ethnographies*, ed. Andrea Cornwall and Nancy Lindesfarne (London and New York: Routledge, 1994), pp. 196–213; and two special issues of *Middle East Report*: 24, no. 5 (September–October 1994), 1–22, "Gender, Population, Environment: The Middle East Beyond the Cairo Conference," and 26, no. 1 (January–March 1996), 4–39, "Gender and Citizenship in the Middle East." For an excellent overview of sociological studies of women in Middle Eastern societies, see Deniz Kandiyoti, "Introduction," in *Women, Islam and the State*, ed. Deniz Kandiyoti, Women in the Political Economy (Philadelphia: Temple University Press, 1991), pp. 1–21, and, in the same volume, her "End of Empire: Islam, Nationalism and Women in Turkey," pp. 22–47.

[33] For earlier historical periods, see Afaf Lutfi al-Sayyid Marsot, "The Revolutionary Gentlewoman in Egypt," in *Women*, ed. Beck and Keddie, pp. 261–76; Fatma Mansur Coşar, "Women in Turkish Society," ibid., pp. 124–40; Mangol Bayat-Philipp, "Women and Revolution in Iran, 1905–1911," ibid., pp. 295–308; Mark A. Tessler, "Women's Emancipation in Tunisia," ibid., pp. 141–58; Andrea B. Rugh, "Women and Work: Strategies and Choices in a Lower-Class Quarter of Cairo," in *Women and Family*, ed. Fernea, pp. 273–88; and Henry Rosenfeld, "Men and Women in Arab Peasant to Proletariat Transformation," in *Theory and Practice: Essays Presented to Gene Weltfish*, ed. Stanley Diamond (Paris and The Hague: Mouton, 1980), pp. 195–219.

[34] The best survey of the legal situation is Ann Elizabeth Mayer, *Islam and Human Rights: Tradition and Politics*, 2nd ed. (Boulder, CO, and London: Westview Press, 1995). See also her "Reform of Personal Status Laws in North Africa: A Problem of Islamic or Mediterranean Laws?" *Middle East Journal* 49, no. 3 (Summer 1995), 432–46, which argues that the reform of family and marriage laws in the countries of Muslim North Africa has many parallels with recent efforts to reform personal status codes in the countries of southern Europe. See also Elizabeth H. White, "Legal Reform as an Indicator of Women's Status in Muslim Nations," in *Women*, ed. Beck and Keddie, pp. 52–68.

FIGURE 8-1. Postage stamps in revolutionary Iran depict the official ideology toward women. "Woman's Day" is celebrated on the birthday of the Prophet's daughter, Fāṭima Zahra, and the mother of Ḥusayn, one of the principal Shīʿī martyrs. The stamp above left shows a militant woman urging her companions forward. The stamp to the right depicts a woman holding a child wearing a headband already designating him as a future martyr. The extent to which women share this official representation of their role is uncertain. [From Peter Chelkowski, "Stamps of Blood," *The American Philatelist* 101, no. 6 (June 1987), 560. Used with permission of the author and the American Philatelic Society.]

women can insert restrictions into marriage contracts against husbands taking second wives.[35] Minimum ages for marriage are in effect in most Middle Eastern countries, and reforms limiting a husband's unrestricted ability to divorce have been enacted in most countries. Laws related to inheritance, on the other hand, have met with greater resistance because of specific Quranic prescriptions. Of course, legal reforms do not necessarily change social practice, although they reflect the changing values of legislators or rulers. In Turkey, which introduced secular civil and criminal codes in 1926, marriages in rural areas were, until recent decades, never officially validated by civil courts, and inheritance disputes were often settled outside the formal judicial system, often to the disadvantage of women. In recent years, that situation has altered dramatically, as education has become more pervasive, and women have become more aware of their rights and able to use the courts.[36]

[35] For recent developments in Morocco, see Ann Elizabeth Mayer, "Moroccans—Citizens or Subjects? A People at the Crossroads," *New York University International Journal of Law and Politics* 26, no. 1 (Fall 1993), 63–105.

[36] June Starr, *Law as Metaphor: From Islamic Courts to the Palace of Justice* (Albany: State University of New York Press, 1992). On the impact of legal reform in the Sudan, see the relevant sections of Carolyn Fluehr-Lobban, *Islamic Law and Society in the Sudan* (London: Frank Cass, 1987). Also see her *Islamic Society in Practice* (Gainesville: University Press of Florida, 1994), pp. 115–41.

FIGURE 8-2. Student in Beirut. Education is a major force in changing women's status. [Courtesy *Aramco World Magazine*, March–April 1971.]

The status of women in revolutionary situations is more difficult to ascertain. Women in the regions of large Muslim populations in Central Asia have enjoyed equal legal rights and educational opportunities since the 1920s, although in practice, their access to schooling, especially in rural areas, and to social services is less than that available to men.[37] Revolutionary countries such as the former People's Democratic Republic of Yemen (1970–1990) and liberation movements throughout the Arab world have often proclaimed the full equality of women, but actual practice often falls far short of declared intent.[38] During Algeria's struggle for independence in the 1950s, some women participated fully in the revolutionary movement. Because the French rarely searched them, women were often used for carrying bombs and as couriers. Since independence, however, women have had less de facto access to education and

[37] See, for example, Kathleen Kuehnast, *Women and Economic Changes in Kyrgyzstan: Coping Mechanisms and Attitudes Towards Social Policies* (Washington, DC: World Bank, 1993).

[38] On the former PDRY, see Helen Lackner, *P.D.R. Yemen: Outpost of Socialist Development in Arabia* (London: Ithaca Press, 1985), pp. 106, 108, 117; and Norman Cigar, "State and Society in South Yemen," *Problems of Communism* 34, no. 3 (May–June 1985), 47–49. On Beirut during its civil war, see Maroun Baghdadi and Nayla de Frieze, "The Kalashnikov Generation," in *Women and Family*, ed. Fernea, pp. 169–82, and, in the same volume, Rosemary Sayigh, "Encounters with Palestinian Women Under Occupation," pp. 191–208.

have been discouraged by public policy from competing with men in the labor market.[39] Islamic resurgence has had a mixed impact, in some instances leading to a greater voice for women, as in Turkey, and in others relegating them to supportive roles for men.[40]

No clear pattern has emerged from the 1978–1979 Iranian revolution, except that the initiatives under the rule of the late Shah toward women's suffrage and legal enfranchisement, ready access to higher education, and access to public employment appear to have been stalled, or in some cases reversed, since the revolution. On the other hand, many women adopted the veil for the first time in 1978–1979 in a display of support for the revolution. Since then, women's religious gatherings have proliferated, and the state, recognizing the political importance of women "speakers" at these gatherings, is making efforts to bring them under official control.[41] Prior to the Iranian revolution, many observers had assumed that the conservative ideology that allocates women a subordinate status to men was most strongly supported by "small-scale peasant and merchant communities."[42]

As the economic and political base of these communities was eroded by modernization, especially in the 1960s and 1970s, it was assumed that the support for the older ideologies concerning male and female roles would also wane. If anything, the "old ideology" has become more pervasive. Like most conservative ideologies, however, traditional Shī'ī attitudes concerning women have been flexible, and these are reflected to some extent in the enactment and adjudication of laws pertaining to marriage and the family.[43]

Women have actively participated in Iranian political protest since at least the mid-nineteenth century.[44] Shī'ī institutions such as *mut'a* marriage, a form of temporary marriage not requiring the consent of a woman's family, indicate the flexibility with which doctrines can be interpreted and adapted to individual situations. This form of marriage, once primarily an urban phenomenon and

[39] See the eloquent and scathing account of the status of Algerian women by the Algerian journalist Fadèla M'rabet, excerpted from her *Les Algériennes* and translated in *Women Speak*, ed. Fernea and Bezirgan, pp. 319–58. For the situation since 1991, when the military took over the government to halt an electoral process that seemed likely to bring Islamists to power, see Boutheina Cherlet, "Gender, Civil Society and Citizenship in Algeria," *Middle East Report* 26, no. 1 (January–March 1996), 22–26.

[40] For a thoughtful analysis of Arab women's participation in revolutionary movements throughout this century, including "resurgent" Islam, with ample quotations and references, see the important article by Yvonne Y. Haddad, "Islam, Women and Revolution in Twentieth Century Arab Thought," *The Muslim World* 74, nos. 3–4 (July–October 1984), 137–60. Also see Valerie J. Hoffman, "An Islamic Activist: Zaynab al-Ghazali," in *Women and Family*, ed. Fernea, pp. 223–54. (Al-Ghazali was a senior female activist in Egypt's Muslim Brotherhood.)

[41] Torab, "Piety," pp. 235, 248.

[42] Michael M. J. Fischer, "On Changing the Concept and Position of Persian Women," in *Women*, ed. Beck and Keddie, pp. 189–215.

[43] Ziba Mir-Hosseini, *Marriage on Trial: A Study of Islamic Family Law*, Society and Culture in the Modern Middle East (London and New York: I. B. Tauris, 1993), esp. pp. 54–83.

[44] See Nahid Yeganeh and Nikki R. Keddie, "Sexuality and Shi'i Social Protest in Iran," in *Shi'ism and Social Protest*, ed. Juan R. L. Cole and Nikki R. Keddie (New Haven, CT, and London: Yale University Press, 1986), pp. 108–196.

linked to pilgrimage centers and long-distance travel, has, according to one Iranian anthropologist, undergone a "conceptual metamorphosis" since the revolution, so that it now has "an almost completely new meaning, and is addressed to a completely different audience," even including the sanctioning of "trial marriage for the period of engagement."[45] Although *mut'a* marriage may not be widely practiced, its reinterpretation to meet changed political and social contexts in recent years points to the viability of "conservative" ideologies and institutions and their ability to adapt to new circumstances.

Access to education is in many ways a prerequisite for change in women's status throughout the region. In the Middle East as a whole during the 1960s, the proportion of adult women (age 15 and over) who were literate was only 13 percent—ranging from a low of 4 percent for Algeria, Libya, and Morocco to a high of 30 percent for Turkey.[46] Of course, the higher proportion of women in school in more recent years indicates the capability and commitment of most countries of the region to provide for women's education.

The comparison of female enrollment rates for school-age children between 1960 and 1992 reveals dramatic progress. In Tunisia in 1960, 43 percent of primary school-aged females were enrolled, and 112 percent in 1986 (the figure exceeds 100 percent because enrollments for adult literacy courses are included in the available statistics). For Morocco the respective figures are 27 percent and 57 percent; 36 percent and 91 percent for Iraq (in 1981—no figures are available for 1992); 27 percent and 104 percent for Iran; 58 percent and 107 percent for Turkey; 59 percent and 105 percent for Jordan; and 22 percent and 75 percent for oil-rich Saudi Arabia. The statistics for less affluent countries show similar improvement: 14 percent and 41 percent (in 1981) for the Sudan, and 7 percent in 1970 (no figures are available for 1960) for the Yemen Arab Republic to 37 percent of the school-aged female population in 1986.[47] Statistics for secondary school and university education show corresponding rates of increase for women.

Many studies suggest that the higher the direct involvement of women in nondomestic economic activities, the more open the social roles they can perform. At the same time, recent intensive studies of the economic role of women have documented a greater traditional and nontraditional range of roles that women can occupy than has often been reported previously. Susan Davis reports a total of 22 different income-earning activities engaged in by rural Moroccan women.[48]

[45] Shahla Haeri, "The Institution of Mut'a Marriage in Iran: A Formal and Historical Perspective," in *Women and Revolution in Iran*, ed. Guity Nashat (Boulder, CO: Westview Press, 1982), pp. 231–51.

[46] Nadia H. Youssef, "The Status and Fertility Patterns of Muslim Women," in *Women*, ed. Beck and Keddie, p. 88.

[47] World Bank, *World Development Report 1984* (New York: Oxford University Press for the World Bank, 1984), Table 25, pp. 266–67; World Bank, *World Development Report 1995* (New York: Oxford University Press for the World Bank, 1995), Table 29, pp. 220–21. Comparable figures are not available for Central Asia.

[48] Susan Schaefer Davis, *Patience and Power: Women's Lives in a Moroccan Village* (Cambridge: Schenkman, 1983), pp. 71–83. See also Hijab, *Womanpower*.

In a study of both rural and urban women, Vanessa Maher presents a complex picture of how recent economic transformations have affected the status of women in rural areas and small towns. These include women of "high bourgeois" origin who have been able to use their status and access to higher education to win a considerable measure of political and social autonomy; "new women," educated women of the "petty bourgeoisie," who have assumed professional roles as teachers, nurses, and secretaries; dependent wives of upwardly mobile petty administrators and teachers, for whom a rise in social status usually means a strict seclusion from men and the organization of activities in time and space so that the social worlds of men and women rarely coincide; "free" women—professional dancers, some divorced women, some wives of migrant workers, and prostitutes—often of rural origin, who trade off their ambiguous status for autonomy from male tutelage;[49] and women who, because of their precarious economic situation—widowed, divorced, kinless, or with unemployed husbands—are forced into factory work or work considered socially marginal.[50] Fatima Mernissi's interviews with women working in craft industries such as weaving textiles and rugs indicate how dependent women are on men as intermediaries, a situation that only increases their precarious economic position.[51] Maher writes that the progressive impoverishment of the Moroccan countryside with recent economic transformations has had "particularly devastating" consequences for women and children.[52]

Rapid economic transformations, mass communication, and mass education have brought conventional ideologies concerning male-female relations into question throughout the Middle East and increasingly so in Central Asia, sometimes reinforcing traditional attitudes by adapting them to new situations and at other times facilitating a greater internal diversity within particular societies. Even when changes in the status of women appear to move at a glacial pace, women in rural areas are increasingly aware of the opportunities available to them and are beginning to question the roles assigned to them by prevailing ideological assumptions. This is clear as states confront practical issues. Iran, for example, has developed population policies that encourage women to play a major role in decisions of family size, and this has resulted in an "accom-

[49] For what such "free" women think of men and marriage, see the poems translated by Elizabeth Fernea in "Seven Women's Songs from the Berber Mountains of Morocco," in *Women Speak*, ed. Fernea and Bezirgan, pp. 127–34. For a fascinating study of recent attitudes and the consequences of education and a changing economy, see Deborah Kapchan, *Gender on the Market: Moroccan Women and the Revoicing of Tradition* (Philadelphia: University of Pennsylvania Press, 1996).

[50] Vanessa Maher, "Women and Social Change in Morocco," in *Women*, ed. Beck and Keddie, pp. 100–23.

[51] Fatima Mernissi, "The Degrading Effects of Capitalism on Female Labour," *Peuples méditerranéens/Mediterranean People*, no. 6 (January–March 1978), 41–57, and her *Doing Daily Battle: Interviews with Moroccan Women*, trans. Mary Jo Lakeland (London: Woman's Press, 1988). See also Brinkley Messick, "Subordinate Discourse: Women, Weaving, and Gender Relations in North Africa," *American Ethnologist* 14, no. 2 (May 1987), 210–25.

[52] Maher, "Women," p. 113.

modating" attitude toward women's public roles.[53] The lack of participation of Muslim women in public life in the past means that when women assume modern professional roles, they often experience fewer obstacles in their careers than has been the case for women in the United States.[54]

Cultural Understandings of Gender

The ideological conventions concerning women and gender vary considerably throughout Middle Eastern and Central Asian societies. There is no single Islamic view, any more than there is a single Jewish or Christian one, although there is no shortage of authorities, often self-appointed, who assert that they know *the* Islamic view. Because of major differences of time, place, and social condition, assuming a pervasive "Islamic attitude" concerning sex roles leads to serious distortion.[55] In the West, use of a term such as "the Christian woman" would immediately signal a partisan conception not clearly related to specific historical or social contexts. Yet precisely this sort of transhistorical abstraction is commonly used in writing about women and sex roles in the Middle East, both by outsiders and by those living within the region.

One cause for the continuing popularity of such ahistorical abstractions comes from the way that both those advocating maintenance of the status quo and those advocating a rethinking of sex roles, like other significant aspects of social identity and social policy, seek legitimacy for their views. Revolutionaries, modernists, and traditionalists all assert that their positions are identified with the "authentic" message of the Quran and of Islam. Thus those who wish to emphasize the constraints that Islam places on women in society emphasize Quranic verses such as the following:

> Your women are your field, so act
> upon your field as you wish.
> (Sura 2, "The Cow," verse 223)

[53] Homa Hoodfar, "Devices and Desires: Population Policy and Gender Roles in the Islamic Republic," *Middle East Report* 24, no. 5 (September–October 1994), 11–17.

[54] Elizabeth Fernea, personal communication, 1978. See also Fernea and Bezirgan's translation of "Excerpts from The Umm Kulthum Nobody Knows, as Told by Umm Kulthum," in *Women Speak*, ed. Fernea and Bezirgan, pp. 135–66, a poignant account of the famous singer's transformation from a village girl into an international celebrity managing her own career.

[55] This is a difficulty with Fatima Mernissi's *Beyond the Veil: Male-Female Dynamics in a Modern Muslim Society*, rev. ed. (Bloomington: Indiana University Press, 1987 [1975]), which summarizes Robertson Smith's speculations concerning a matriarchal society in pre-Islamic Arabia, the Prophet Muḥammad's treatment of women in the seventh century (taking them at face value), a superficial analysis (based only on the translated English text) of the writings of the twelfth-century mystic and scholar al-Ghazzālī, interviews with 14 Moroccan women, and an analysis of letters written to a Moroccan radio program to construct an Islamic "ideal type" of male-female relations not clearly related to historical or regional context. Despite these shortcomings, Mernissi's book is passionately argued and represents one point in the spectrum of polemic that permeates contemporary Middle Eastern societies. Yeganeh and Keddie, "Sexuality and Shi'i Social Protest," presents a strong case against assuming a uniform "Islamic" attitude toward sexuality. See also Mervat Hatem, "Class and Patriarchy as Competing Paradigms for the Study of Middle Eastern Women," *Comparative Studies in Society and History* 29, no. 4 (October 1987), 811–18.

> Men watch over women because God
> has preferred some of you over others and because
> (men) support them from their means. . . .
> And if they challenge you, (first) caution them, (then) confine them to their (sleeping) couches,
> and (finally) beat them (if necessary).
> But do not treat them unjustly.
> (Sura 4, "Women," verse 34)[56]

Taken in a literal sense, as some conservative Muslims do, such verses can legitimize the relegation of women to an inferior status in public life and to subordinate them to men. After all, God's directive is addressed to men ("*Your* women"), not to women. However, it is possible to read such verses in a more liberal sense by emphasizing the contexts in which they occur: legal prescriptions that specified the rights of women and frequently improved upon existing customs in seventh-century Arabia. A verse following Sura 4, verse 38, for instance, recommends that if a husband and a wife quarrel, arbiters should be appointed from the kin of each to seek a resolution of the conflict. And the Prophet's example, where he sometimes heeded the advice of his wives, can be cited. Moreover, through various judicial and customary interpretations of Islamic doctrine, considerable modifications of doctrine and practice can occur, despite the fact that the authors of such changes legitimate them by claiming that no change is involved, only a "return" to pure Islamic principles. Many Muslim thinkers, both women and men, have put forward radically different interpretations of the Quran, which argue that its proper interpretation suggests an equality of women and men, and that the conditions specific to seventh-century Arabia do not constitute binding precedents for all time.[57] Unfortunately, the ideological claim that no change occurs has blocked some analysts from perceiving often dramatic variations and innovations.

One approach to the study of gender roles in Islamic society was to note the disparity between the "Great Tradition"—a distillation of what was considered Islamic law and Quranic ethics—and locally elaborated practices and traditions. When the study of gender roles and ethics was conceived in terms of transcultural norms and local comportment, observers saw various village practices as "accommodations" of the assumed normative Islamic

[56] My translation.

[57] See Amina Wadud-Muhsin, *Qur'an and Women* (Kuala Lumpur: Penerbit Fajar Bakti Sdn. Bhd., 1992); and Dale F. Eickelman, "Islamic Liberalism Strikes Back," *Middle East Studies Association Bulletin* 27, no. 2 (December), 163–68, for an assessment in English of the argument of Muhammad Shahrour, *al-Kitāb wa-l-Qur'ān: Qirā'a Mu'āṣira* [The Book and the Quran: A Contemporary Reading] (Beirut: Sharikat al-Maṭbū'āt li-l-Tawzī' wa-l-Nashr, 1992), which has become a best-seller throughout the Middle East.

tradition to the exigencies of village and urban life.[58] The principal drawback to this approach is the artificial normative tradition against which local practices are assessed. Muslim intellectuals ranging from Saudi conservatives to liberal modernists construe a particular Islamic tradition and measure contemporary practices and expectations against it. By asserting that there is an identifiable Islamic normative tradition independent of particular situations and carriers, anthropologists who study the "problem" of accommodation ignore the continuing and pervasive internal debates within Muslim societies—the plural is deliberately used—as to what is normative. As a Moroccan colleague has written, a proper understanding of Islam and Islamic law enjoins dialogue, a willingness to understand the opinions of others, and a disposition to good relations (*ḥusnā*) with them. This dialogue entails adaptation and the continual renewal of understandings about Islam within a framework of civility.[59]

Another cluster of related approaches to the cultural study of women can be called *structuralist*. Many of them deal with the themes of honor and shame. As Carol Delaney notes, these notions are not uniform throughout the Mediterranean area and the Muslim Middle East. The English glosses of "honor" and "shame," in fact, "cover a variety of terms, meanings and practices" that are best thought of not in terms of something like a dress code but as "a kind of genetic code—a structure of relations—generative of possibilities."[60] Structuralists seek to elicit these relationships and their underlying elements, and few analysts who pursue this approach confine their analysis to issues of sexuality or gender alone. Pierre Bourdieu, writing on the Kabyle Berbers of Algeria, situates his discussion of women in the broader context of issues of honor and a wide range of social relations. Honor "is the basis of the moral code of an individual who sees himself always through the eyes of others, who has need of others for his existence, because the image he has of himself is indistinguish-

[58] See, for instance, Richard T. Antoun, "On the Modesty of Women in Arab Muslim Villages: A Study in the Accommodation of Traditions," *American Anthropologist* 70, no. 4 (August 1968), 671–97; see also Nadia M. Abu-Zahra, "'On the Modesty of Women in Arab Villages': A Reply," *American Anthropologist* 72, no. 5 (October 1970), 1079–88; and Antoun's reply 1088–92. For a discussion of tradition that captures the nuances of local (or "Little Tradition") debates and their two-way influence with the carriers of the "Great Tradition," see Richard T. Antoun, *Muslim Preacher in the Modern World: A Jordanian Case Study in Comparative Perspective* (Princeton, NJ: Princeton University Press, 1989), pp. 17–29.

[59] Sa'īd Bensa'īd, "al-ḥiwār wa-l-fahm lā al-qaṭ'iyya wa-l-jahl" [Dialogue and Understanding, Not Alienation and Ignorance], *al-Sharq al-Awsaṭ* (London), 7 July 1993, p. 10.

[60] Carol Delaney, "Seeds of Honor, Fields of Shame," in *Honor and Shame and Unity of the Mediterranean*, ed. David Gilmore, Special Publication 22 (Washington, DC: American Anthropological Association, 1987), p. 35, and her *Seed and the Soil: Gender and Cosmology in Turkish Village Society*, Comparative Studies on Muslim Societies (Berkeley and Los Angeles: University of California Press, 1991). See also Julian Pitt-Rivers, *The Fate of Schechem, or the Politics of Sex: Essays in the Anthropology of the Mediterranean* (Cambridge: Cambridge University Press, 1977); and Unni Wikan, "Shame and Honour: A Contestable Pair," *Man* (N.S.) 19, no. 4 (December 1984), 635–52.

able from that presented to him by other people."[61] Hence the dynamics of honor necessarily involve those of social exchange in general. When speaking of dishonor in Kabyle society, the formulas employed generally refer to how certain problems appear before others. Social honor in general, Bourdieu argues, is maintained through a series of challenges and ripostes.

Kabyles distinguish between two complementary forms of honor: *nīf* (a term that literally means "nose") and *ḥurma* ("all that is prohibited under the penalty of committing sin, or is sacred").[62] Bourdieu translates *ḥurma* as "honor" and *nīf* as "point of honor." *Ḥurma* implies both that which is sacred and that which is respectable (it is also a word used for "woman" in some parts of the Middle East, at least among an older generation). The integrity of honor requires a "punctilious and active vigilance" of the point of honor (*nīf*). At times, points of honor can be manipulated as in a game of two parties seeking to outbid the other, but any challenge to honor deals with the "most fundamental divisions" of Kabyle culture, "those which control the whole mythico-ritual system."[63] Bourdieu identifies *ḥurma* with all that concerns femininity, the "sacred of the left hand"—sexuality, food, magic, and privacy—and *nīf* with the sacred of the right hand—masculinity, all which concerns social and political exchanges, religion, and public life.[64] The propriety of women and the privacy of the family are thus, for Bourdieu, crucial components of the broader discussion of the role of women and sex roles.

In a complementary essay, Bourdieu links the architecture of the traditional Kabyle house, the practical functions associated with each of its sections, and its cultural connotations with dualistic categories (male/female, house/fields and market, day/night, upper/lower, right/left) that make the house a microcosm of "the same oppositions which govern all the universe."[65] Women and sex roles, in this view, are components of a more comprehensive set of cultural assumptions concerning the world that are shared by people in a given society.

An alternative but equally comprehensive approach to the study of sexuality and gender roles is to study them as part of a larger goal of eliciting ordered systems of categories "in terms of which the experience of another is perceived and articulated."[66] People in a given society may share common cultural assumptions yet interpret reality in systematically different ways. One set

[61] Pierre Bourdieu, "The Sentiment of Honour in Kabyle Society," in *Honor and Shame: The Values of Mediterranean Society*, ed. J. G. Peristiany, The Nature of Human Society Series (Chicago: University of Chicago Press, 1966), p. 211.

[62] Ibid., p. 216.

[63] Ibid., pp. 216–17.

[64] See chart, ibid., p. 222.

[65] Pierre Bourdieu, "The Berber House or the World Reversed," in his *Algeria 1960*, trans. Richard Nice (New York: Cambridge University Press, 1979 [1970]), pp. 133–53.

[66] Lawrence Rosen, *Bargaining for Reality: The Construction of Social Relations in a Muslim Community* (Chicago: University of Chicago Press, 1984), p. 148. Parts of his argument had appeared earlier as a series of articles beginning in 1968.

of assumptions concerns the nature of sexuality and gender roles. As Lawrence Rosen argues, the possession of such common understandings does not necessarily imply that both sexes will elaborate shared assumptions in quite the same way.

Drawing upon explanations provided to him by Moroccan townspeople and villagers, Rosen depicts some of the assumptions that Moroccans make concerning how men and women differ as persons. Although his argument is specific to Morocco, it has strong parallels elsewhere in the Muslim world.[67] The essential contrast that Lawrence Rosen draws is between the complementary concepts of *nafs* ("passion, appetite") and *'qāl* ("reason").[68] *Nafs* is possessed by all living creatures—angels, men, animals, and *jnūn* (sing. *jinn*-s). It is composed of all the passions and lusts; unchecked, it can lead men to bad and shameful conduct. *'Qāl*, explained a Moroccan to Rosen, is "reason," the ability to use our heads in order to keep our passions from getting hold of us and controlling us."[69] Through following God's word, as it is known from the Quran and the teachings of Islam, man can avoid being a slave to his passions, can distinguish right from wrong, and can live as God intended him to live. Through discipline and learning, a child gradually learns to control his passions. Women also possess reason but cannot develop it as fully as men. "It's just in their nature. Women have very great sexual desires and that's why a man is always necessary to control them, to keep them from creating all sorts of disorder. . . . It's like the saying goes: 'A woman by herself is like a Turkish bath without water,' because she is always hot and without a man she has no way to slake the fire."[70]

The notion that women are subordinate to men is an ideological assumption shared by both genders, but in practice it is elaborated in different ways by men and women. Men tend to emphasize the supposedly natural differences between the two sexes when they seek to understand their ties with women. Women, for their part, tend to emphasize the social relations between the two sexes and the "ways in which men can be ignored, outflanked, or outwitted by the arrangement of various social pressures within the household or family."[71] In short, women's actions suggest that they regard their subordination as social rather than natural. Rosen then documents how the definition of "reality" is negotiated in such matters as arranging marriages, just as it is in other aspects of social identity, including ethnicity, class, and perceived social origins.

The analytical approach exemplified by Rosen avoids assuming that the "nature" of social reality is fixed and derived from rules. Both the cultural assumptions concerning reality and their articulation in practical social circumstances are subject to redefinition or "negotiation." Although the underlying

[67] See, for example, Torab, "Piety," 241–44.

[68] Rosen, *Bargaining*, pp. 31–34.

[69] Ibid., p. 31.

[70] Ibid., pp. 32–33.

[71] Ibid., pp. 38–39. See also Daisy Hilse Dwyer, *Images and Self-Images: Male and Female in Morocco* (New York: Columbia University Press, 1978); and M. Elaine Combs-Schilling, *Sacred Performances: Islam, Sexuality, and Sacrifice* (New York: Columbia University Press, 1989).

cultural theme shared by men and women is that women are subordinate to men, women can exercise considerable influence and independence.

In theoretical terms, a structuralist interpretation (in the generic way the term is used here) of categories such as gender roles goes beyond the explicit perceptions of "natives," just as Rosen's discussion of gender beliefs points to underlying cultural views of human nature that inform and pervade social relations in Morocco. A parallel structural argument can be made without projecting the particulars of Moroccan conceptions of gender onto the entire Muslim world. Nancy and Richard Tapper, for instance, argue that, although men in Turkey are most closely identified with "orthodox" religious activities, recitals by and for women of the *mevlûd*, a panegyric poem praising Muḥammad, his life and his miracles, are an intrinsic component of Islamic thought and practice in Turkey. These performances occur regularly and frequently, particularly in commemoration of family and neighborhood deaths. The Tappers describe these activities as humanizing the Prophet's person and allowing individuals to identify with him, something not done in the formal religious activities of men and in the centrality attached to the word of the Quran. Participation in *mevlûd*-s provides women with opportunities for leadership and self-expression outside the domestic sphere. Women's *mevlûd*-s are disparaged by men, who "nonetheless tolerate and even encourage the participation of women of their own households." As the secular Turkish state has imposed controls upon men's religious activities, "the women seem to have become the repositories of spiritual values to which both women and men subscribe but which, paradoxically, only women can experience with performative immediacy because of their inferior status." The religious establishment regards women as subordinate in religious matters and regards women's activities as relatively autonomous. But, as the Tappers argue, understanding the Islamic tradition in Turkey and in comparable societies elsewhere in the Muslim world depends on examining the complementary beliefs and practices of *both* men and women.[72]

An ethnographic caveat is essential. The notion of the "subordination" of women is subject to considerable contextual variation. Shahla Haeri, for instance, reports that *muṭ'a* marriage in Iran has in the past been used by elite women to legitimize sexual liaisons in terms of religious law.[73] Likewise, Christine Eickelman, discussing the political roles of women in the Arabian peninsula, suggests that the effective political units in the tribe are family clusters (*ḥayyān*) in which the related activities of their component men and women are needed to maintain alliances and assert an effective political voice.[74] Once

[72] Nancy Tapper and Richard Tapper, "The Birth of the Prophet: Ritual and Gender in Turkish Islam," *Man* (N.S.) 22, no. 1 (March 1987), 69–92, esp. 86–87, a study that will be discussed in another context in Chapter 10.

[73] Haeri, "Institution."

[74] Christine Eickelman, "Women and Politics in an Arabian Oasis," in *A Way Prepared: Essays on Islamic Culture in Honor of Richard Bayly Winder*, ed. Farhad Kazemi and R. D. McChesney (New York and London: New York University Press, 1988), pp. 199–215; and Mary Elaine Hegland, "Shi'a Women of Northwest Pakistan and Agency Through Practice: Ritual, Resistance, Resilience," *Polar: Political Anthropology Review* 18, no. 2 (November 1995), 65–79.

again, an effective understanding of gender roles requires more than a recitation of normative claims.[75] In Chapter 9 we return to the discussion of how notions of gender are best understood within more all-encompassing notions of person and society.

ETHNICITY AND CULTURAL IDENTITY

Notions of ethnicity are cultural constructions, although in popular usage, especially in the form of ethnogenesis in Central Asia, it is sometimes assumed to be almost a biological given and the basis for national identity. In Russia and Central Asia, ethnogenesis is understood as "a lengthy and continuous process of development of the main characteristics of an ethnic community, including the physical characteristics of its members, language, and other cultural features," and it is used to create national ideologies and "lay claim to scarce resources, whether they be political, social, economic, or demographic."[76] Thus even the past can be claimed to support contemporary boundary disputes or the favoring of one people over another.

Ethnicity in modern Western usage refers to "the way individuals and groups characterize themselves on the basis of their language, race, place of origin, shared culture, values, and history. . . . Central to the notion of ethnicity is a conception of a common descent, often of a mythic character."[77] Ethnicity is often considered a matter of birth, but the exceptions are as frequent as the rule, especially as the social and political significance of ethnic and religious identities alters according to specific historical contexts. The experience of large-scale migration in search of wage labor—Pakistanis to Saudi Arabia, North Africans to France and Belgium, and Turks to West Germany—has had a major impact on how ethnic identity is conceived. At the very best, "ethnicity" is an "experi-

[75] See Lila Abu-Lughod, *Veiled Sentiments: Honor and Poetry in a Bedouin Society* (Berkeley and Los Angeles: University of California Press, 1986).

[76] Victor A. Shnirelman, *Who Gets the Past? Competition for Ancestors Among Non-Russian Intellectuals in Russia* (Baltimore and London: Johns Hopkins University Press for the Woodrow Wilson Center, 1996), pp. 1–2. Shnirelman offers an excellent analysis of the "re-imagination" of identities following the Soviet collapse and an account of the rise and fall of Soviet theories and practice concerning ethnicity and nationalism. For scathing, even patronizing, comments on Central Asian intelligentsia efforts to "construct" national identities independent of approved Soviet ones, see Poliakov, *Everyday Islam*, pp. 130–35, for which (as an indication of his own ideological stance) he acknowledges the "feebleness of our own counterpropaganda" (p. 136).

[77] Ali Banuazizi and Myron Weiner, "Introduction," in *The State, Religion, and Ethnic Politics: Afghanistan, Iran, and Pakistan*, ed. Ali Banuazizi and Myron Weiner (Syracuse, NY: Syracuse University Press, 1986), pp. 2–3. In addition to the Banuazizi and Weiner volume, which offers an excellent overview of recent work on politics, sectarianism, and ethnicity in the countries specified, see *Revolutions and Rebellions in Afghanistan: Anthropological Perspectives*, ed. M. Nazif Shahrani and Robert L. Canfield, Research Series 57 (Berkeley: University of California, Institute of International Studies, 1984). On the ambiguity of the term *ethnicity*, see also Jon W. Anderson, "Ethnic Dilemmas in Pakistan, Iran and Afghanistan as Security Problems," in *Soviet-American Relations with Pakistan, Iran, and Afghanistan*, ed. Hafeez Malik (London: Macmillan, 1987), pp. 70–89.

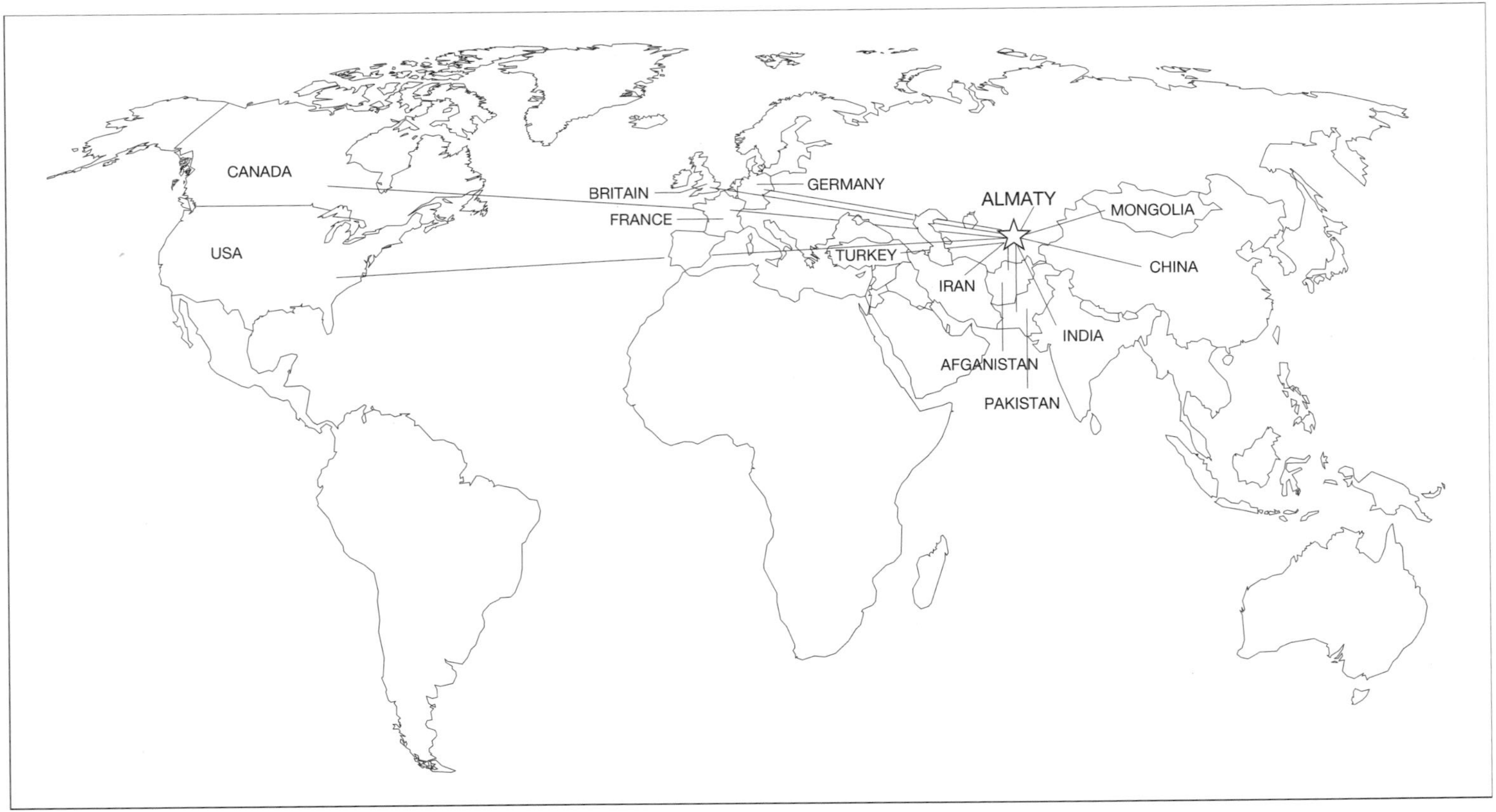

FIGURE 8-3. This map, published in Almaty on the occasion of the October 1992 world assembly (*kurultay*) of Kazakhs, represents Kazakhs throughout the world. Such maps are part of the politics of ethnonationalism. Note that although Kazakhs are represented in Germany, the United States, and Canada, none are indicated for Russia. [From *Asia* newspaper (Almaty), no. 15 (1992). All rights reserved.]

ence-distant" term, much like "kinship" (see Chapter 7) but perhaps even more problematic because of its varying contemporary political significance and the sheer diversity of the forms of identity characterized (primarily by outsiders to the region) as "ethnic" throughout the Middle East. Indeed, it is difficult to find a specific counterpart in Middle Eastern languages for the English "ethnicity." Take the term *qawm* ("people") in Afghanistan (see Chapter 7). Depending on context, it can mean a tribe or a subdivision of one, a people sharing a common origin or region of residence, or more generally, a shared identity of religion and language.[78]

For Benedict Anderson, the notion of political "imagined community" implies the conscious or inadvertent social and historical construction implicit in notions of ethnicity and nationalism, even as their advocates assert that they are "natural" and fixed for all time.[79] Our Russian and Central Asian colleagues have difficulty with this term, for they are acutely aware of the deliberate and forceful creation and manipulation of ethnic and national identities from the 1920s to the present and the eruption of virulent, "Bosnia-like" ethnonationalisms following the collapse of Soviet rule.[80] The creation of nations was thorough in the Soviet era and included both script changes and what one scholar has called the "Europeanization" of Persian and Central Asian languages. Unsurprisingly, since the early 1990s, these processes are being reversed, although the "national" languages created during the Soviet era remain intact.[81]

Assertion of an "ethnic" identity is often a political claim and has very different implications, depending on context. In Afghanistan, opposition to the state during the period of Soviet military intervention (1979–1989) came largely from tribally organized (and foreign-backed) ethnic groups, for whom attachment to Islam served as a common denominator. In Pakistan, especially after the secession of Bangladesh in 1971, the country's ruling Punjabi elite viewed with suspicion the country's other ethnic groups, which include Sindhis, Pashtuns, Muhajirs (Muslim refugees who migrated after 1947 from what is now India), and Baluch. The Pakistani state emphasizes its Islamic identity because this crosscuts the ethnic identities for a majority of the population (Pakistan has, however, a significant non-Muslim population). In addition to Bangladesh, ethnic ties formed the basis of a Baluch insurgency, which fought for regional autonomy from 1973 to 1977. It was

[78] An excellent survey of the specific "ethnic" and "people" terms used in Iran and Afghanistan is presented in Richard L. Tapper, "Ethnicity, Order and Meaning in the Anthropology of Iran and Afghanistan," in *Le fait ethnique en Iran et en Afghanistan*, ed. Jean-Pierre Digard (Paris: Centre National de la Recherche Scientifique, 1988), pp. 21–34.

[79] Benedict Anderson, *Imagined Communities: Reflections on the Origins and Spread of Nationalism* (New York: Verso, 1991 [1983]).

[80] See Shnirelman, *Who Gets the Past?*

[81] Jan W. Weryho, "Tajiki Persian as a Europeanised Oriental Language," *Islamic Studies* 33, nos. 2–3 (Summer-Autumn 1994), 341–73; and William Fierman, "Independence and the Declining Priority of Language Law Implementation in Uzbekistan," in *Muslim Eurasia*, ed. Ro'i, pp. 205–30.

unsuccessful but contributed to a heightened Baluch national consciousness that cut across tribal divisions.[82]

Understanding "ethnicity" requires an analytic framework that presents the principles of ethnic stereotyping (notions concerning the motivations and attributes of the members of "other" ethnic groups and what can be expected of them, as well as those of one's own ethnic group) and how these notions are maintained in changing historical contexts. Ethnic identities, like linguistic, sectarian, national, family, and other forms of social definition, can be comprehended only in the context of more general cultural assumptions in a given society concerning the nature of the social world and social relationships. Such identities must be analyzed in terms of the specific historical contexts in which they are maintained, transformed, and reproduced and not as blocklike units of an ahistorical mosaic of objective "culture traits" amenable to mapping.

In a seminal essay written in the late 1960s, Fredrik Barth reviewed the drawbacks to defining ethnicity as a fixed and unchanging, almost biologically given, element of personal identity or set of prescriptive cultural "traits" or rules. He sought instead to focus on the "*socially* effective" ways in which notions of ethnic group identities and boundaries were produced and maintained, as opposed to what he called the identification of "cultural stuff," which he considered merely the content, not amenable to sociological analysis, used to fill in social forms.[83] Barth's approach has been termed an *instrumentalist* one in that it maintains that subjective claims to ethnic identity are sustained by the manipulation of culture to support the collective political and economic interests of particular groups. Barth focuses on the organizational forms of social groups whose principle of unity is presumed to be that of ethnicity, rather than alternate or complementary attributes that could form the base of organizational cohesiveness. For example, the essay in his volume concerning Fūr cultivators and Baggāra pastoralists in the Sudan avoids consideration of the historical process of personal shifts of ethnic identity between the two neighboring groups. It assumes that when people change the means by which they utilize resources, their ethnic identities change as well. Even were this to be the case, little attention is paid to precisely what ethnicity means in the setting of the Fūr and the Baggāra, and only Fūr views of social identity are provided in detail.[84]

[82] Selig S. Harrison, "Ethnicity and the Political Stalemate in Pakistan," in *State, Religion, and Ethnic Politics*, ed. Banuazizi and Weiner, pp. 267–98, esp. pp. 274–75. See also Zelig Harrison, *In Afghanistan's Shadow: Baluch Nationalism and Soviet Temptations* (New York: Carnegie Endowment for International Peace, 1981); and Brian Spooner, "Who Are the Baluch? A Preliminary Investigation into the Dynamics of an Ethnic Identity from Qajar Iran," in *Qajar Iran: Political, Social and Cultural Change, 1800–1925*, ed. Edmund Bosworth and Carole Hillenbrand (Edinburgh: Edinburgh University Press, 1984), pp. 66–78.

[83] Fredrik Barth, "Introduction," in *Ethnic Groups and Boundaries: The Social Organization of Cultural Difference*, ed. Fredrik Barth (Boston: Little, Brown, 1969), pp. 10–15. For an analysis of the continued use of the "mosaic" model of ethnicity, see Bryan S. Turner, *Marx and the End of Orientalism*, Controversies in Sociology 7 (London and Boston: Allen & Unwin, 1978), pp. 39–52.

[84] Gunnar Haaland, "Economic Determinants in Ethnic Processes," in *Ethnic Groups*, ed. Barth, p. 71.

In his own case study in the volume, Barth elaborates the economic and productive contexts in which it is useful for Pathans to stress their identities as Pathans and those in which it is not. By confining his discussion to "traditional" Pathans and to social groups distinguished by their exploitation of particular ecological "niches," he disregards some of the most significant tests of ethnicity in contemporary and complex urban and transnational settings.[85]

Barth developed his argument in a later study of Ṣuḥār, an ethnically, religiously, and linguistically complex coastal town in the Arabian Gulf.[86] Each group in this complex society is seen as a carrier of distinctive cultural "traits," organized like threads in a piece of Baluch needlework into "cultural syndromes," which Barth seeks to sort into their component parts.[87] In spite of the interesting description of social organization in a complex setting, the notion of culture he advances does not really move past an earlier notion of culture as material and ideational "stuff."

Most modern notions of culture have little to do with the notion of mappable cultural "traits" of an earlier generation. Instead, they emphasize how cultural meanings are socially employed, produced, and transformed through social action and interaction. The social production of cultural meaning is an important component of such an approach. Barth's approach to ethnicity is logically elegant, but it lacks an adequate notion of how social processes relate to the production of the cultural conceptions with which people distinguish themselves from "other" ethnic categories and with which they account for, evaluate, and weigh the importance of these distinctions. Cultural notions of identity are constantly adjusted to changing requirements and are not reducible to implicit aggregate notions of "interest."[88]

The Kurds are a case in point. How Kurds construct their ethnic and religious identity in changing economic and political contexts, or have the label "Kurd" applied to them by others, indicates the difficulties involved in treating ethnic identities either as primordial givens or as locally held "apparent" ideologies of identity that serve aggregations of collective interests.

Kurdistan is a region that crosses several international boundaries. The majority of Kurds are located in Turkey (10–12 million, perhaps 20 percent of the country's population), Iran (5–6 million, perhaps 10 percent of the population), and Iraq (4 million, about 23 percent of the population), with smaller numbers in the USSR (600,000–1 million) and Syria (500,000–600,000), and per-

[85] Fredrik Barth, "Pathan Identity and Its Maintenance," in *Ethnic Groups*, ed. Barth, p. 117.

[86] Fredrik Barth, *Sohar: Culture and Society in an Omani Town* (Baltimore and London: The Johns Hopkins University Press, 1983).

[87] Ibid., p. 86.

[88] See G. Carter Bentley, "Ethnicity and Practice," *Comparative Studies in Society and History* 29, no. 1 (January 1987), 24–55.

haps 1 million elsewhere, including West Germany.[89] The number of Kurds is a significant issue, with Kurdish spokesmen offering the higher figures. Those wishing to diminish their political importance offer lower estimates.

Kurds in Turkey are officially designated as "mountain Turks" who possess an incomplete command of Turkish. Although other minorities in Turkey, including Greeks, Armenians, Sephardic Jews (who speak Ladino), and Arabs, are allowed to speak their non-Turkish languages and have their mother tongue recorded in official censuses, Kurdish is not officially recognized as a language. The media are permitted to broadcast only non-Turkish foreign languages "which have contributed to human civilization,"[90] a phrasing that Turkish political scientist Binnaz Toprak explains is designed to exclude Kurdish, which until recently has not been a written language. However, the Turkish state, like states elsewhere, tolerates an interesting compromise with Kurdish ethnonationalists, perhaps in an attempt to dampen support for the Kurdish insurgents and to strengthen Turkey's case for joining the European Community. Several local television stations broadcast in Kurmanci and Zaza, which are Kurdish dialects (see Chapter 10). There are also several magazines in Zaza, and the popular singer Ibrahim Tatlises has several cassettes in the dialects. The last Turkish census lists Kurmanci- and Zaza-speakers, avoiding use of "Kurdish." Although some ethnonationalists have pressed for elementary education in Kurdish (which is offered to migrants in Germany by the German state), it is still not allowed as a medium of education.[91]

Many Kurds in Turkey are also Alevi Muslims, a sectarian group looked upon with disdain by most Sunni Turks. Thus they differ from other Turks in terms of both language and religion.[92] To compound the Alevi sense of difference, many were also suspected of membership in the Bektashi religious brotherhood, a once-powerful order associated with the elite of the Ottoman Empire

[89] Figures derived from Amir Hassanpour, "The Kurdish Experience," *Middle East Report* 24, no. 4 (July–August 1994), 3; and supplemented by Patricia J. Higgins, "Minority-State Relations in Contemporary Iran," in *State, Religion, and Ethnic Politics*, ed. Banuazizi and Weiner, p. 178. Population figures for all minority groups are politically sensitive and subject to considerable variation. Thus Stephen C. Pelletiere, *The Kurds: An Unstable Element in the Gulf* (Boulder, CO: Westview Press, 1984), p. 16, numbers the Kurds in Turkey at only 3 million, with a total in all neighboring countries of 7–7.5 million. Similar political interests plague the substantial disparity between the population claims of Egyptian Coptic spokesmen (7 million) and official estimates (2.6 million as of 1976). See Makram Samaan and Soheir Sukkary, "The Copts and Muslims of Egypt," in *Muslim-Christian Conflicts: Economic, Political, and Social Origins*, ed. Suad Joseph and Barbara L. K. Pillsbury (Boulder, CO: Westview Press, 1978), p. 130.

[90] A legal regulation cited in Binnaz Toprak, "Civil Society in Turkey," in *Civil Society in the Middle East*, ed. Augustus Richard Norton, vol. 2 (Leiden: E. J. Brill, 1996), p. 114.

[91] Personal communication with a Turkish colleague, August 13, 1996.

[92] The situation is highly complex. Ruth Mandel, "Ethnicity, Heterodoxy, and Historical Paradigms: A Turkish Muslim Community's Experience in the Diaspora," unpublished paper, February 1987, used with the author's permission, pp. 5–6, distinguishes between the "Kurdish Alevis" of eastern Anatolia who speak Zaza, an Iranian language, as well as Kurmanci (the principal Kurdish language spoken in Turkey), Arabic-speaking Alevis near the Syrian border, and recently sedentarized Alevi Turkomen (but Turkish-speakers) in southwest and western Anatolia, who identify with their Alevi co-religionists of the east "only on the most abstract of levels." This discussion of Alevi identity has benefited significantly from discussions with Mandel.

but banned in republican Turkey since 1925, along with other religious orders. The Alevis in the region of Dersim in eastern Anatolia held out against republican rule until 1938, when successful military "pacification" resulted in a victim toll estimated by some at 80,000. Renewed anti-Alevi violence in the late 1970s left hundreds dead.[93]

Kurdish identity sometimes emphasizes secular elements, as in Iraq, until the Kurdish movement was temporarily crushed in 1975, when the Shah cooperated with the Iraqi regime by denying sanctuary to nationalist supporters. In contrast, the Islamic Republic of Iran, which has treated its own Kurdish minority ruthlessly, supports Iraqi Kurdish separatists with funds, arms, and sanctuary.[94]

Although Kurds in each country seek autonomy, there is no clear support for a unified Kurdistan composed of Kurdish regions in Turkey, Iran, and Iraq. In Turkey, explicit claims to Kurdish and Alevi identity are fraught with political risk. Kurds in Turkey have been subject to repressive assimilationist policies. It has been said that Kurdish children are often beaten when they enter Turkish schools without knowing Turkish. Alevi religious gatherings, because they constitute religious orders, all of which are banned, are similarly forbidden. The repressive treatment of Kurdish-speaking Alevis, combined with the poverty of eastern Anatolia, has led to their disproportionately high representation in the Turkish migrant community in West Germany, estimated to be as large as 2 million.[95]

Ruth Mandel argues that Alevi identity, like all Muslim identities in Turkey, is continually negotiated. From an early age, Alevi children are socialized into seeing themselves as a subordinated people whose religious identity is suppressed by a Sunni majority. Alevis share a "mytho-historical charter" expressed in communal rituals. Alevi ideas of the past and their martyrdom at the hands of the Sunni majority become reworked as they "reimagine" themselves in different spatial and historical contexts. Subordinated to a Sunni majority in Turkey and regarded as "backward," Kurdish-speaking Alevis in West Germany find themselves free to express themselves as Kurds and as Alevis. They are also more receptive than their better-educated Sunni (and often urban) counterparts to "European" codes of conduct, including European-style clothes for women and girls.[96] Kurdish-speaking Alevis are also more likely to be regarded as "progressive" and antiauthoritarian by their German hosts. Ironically, because Turks form such a large number of migrant workers, Ger-

[93] Estimates reported in Ruth Mandel, "Sectarian Splits: Interpretations of Turkish Muslim Identities and History," unpublished paper, 1986, pp. 4–5.

[94] "A Kurdish Litany," *The Economist*, June 13, 1987, p. 42.

[95] Ruth Mandel, "From Economic Miracle to Ethnic Conundrum: A Quarter Century of Turks in the Federal Republic of Germany," unpublished manuscript, p. 5.

[96] Ruth Mandel, "Shifting Centres and Emergent Identities: Turkey and Germany in the Lives of Turkish *Gastarbeiter*," in *Muslim Travellers: Pilgrimage, Migration, and the Religious Imagination*, ed. Dale F. Eickelman and James Piscatori (Berkeley and Los Angeles: University of California Press, 1990), pp. 162–67.

mans tend to confuse Turks with Greeks, prompting a critical rethinking of identities by workers carrying both national labels. In a similar manner, Sunni and Alevi Turks critically rethink their differences as they interact with one another more intensely than in Turkey. The same is true of second-generation migrants in Germany.

Conscious identity as Kurds or as Alevi is not a given, but a socially constructed phenomenon. As mentioned, all Alevis do not share a common collective identity. The same is true for speakers of the various dialects of Kurdish. A Turkish political scientist, Şerif Mardin, has argued that Alevis began to identify themselves as a collectivity only in the 1970s, and Mandel points out that the various Alevi political and religious movements in the German diaspora owe much to the earlier, secular Kurdish separatist movements, appropriating "the folk categories of ethnicity and nationalism common to political discourse in the west."[97] Ethnicity, in Mandel's view, can best be considered "a malleable label employed by groups of intentioned actors in diverse contexts, rather than as a universally applicable cross-cultural comparative" term or as an "objective," fixed component of identity. It is used by actors "seeking to establish and justify social boundaries," either for themselves or for others, as is the case with dominant groups imposing themselves upon subordinates.[98] In both cases such identities are subject to reinterpretation as they are used in changing historical realities.[99] A sociological comprehension of ethnicity necessitates a historical understanding of how ethnic identities articulate and are manipulated.

Lebanon is at least as complex as Syria, Iran, Iraq, Afghanistan, Turkey, or Central Asia in ethnic and sectarian identities, but Europeans and Americans are more aware of Lebanese realities. Prior to 1975, Lebanon was often portrayed as "an almost miraculous balance between different communities and interests,"[100] a beacon of democracy and comparative neutrality in the complex intercommu-

[97] Şerif Mardin, "Centre-Periphery as a Concept for the Study of the Social Transformation of Turkey," in *'Nation' and 'State' in Europe: Anthropological Perspectives*, ed. R. D. Grillo (London: Academic Press, 1980), pp. 173–89, and Mandel, "Ethnicity, Heterodoxy," p. 12.

[98] Mandel, "Economic Miracle," p. 17.

[99] For a fascinating case study of the Shabak, a Shī'ī Kurdish group near Mosul in northern Iraq, who maintain a separate identity in the immediate vicinity of a variety of ethnolinguistic communities—Shī'ī Turkomen tribes in villages along the Tigris, Sunnī Muslim Arabs in Mosul, Christian villagers (Monophysites, Assyrians, and Nestorians, many supported by European Christian groups in the nineteenth and early twentieth centuries), Sunnī, Arabic-speaking bedouin, Kurdish-speaking Gypsies, and (until 1958) Jews both in Mosul and in settled agricultural communities—see Amal (Rassam) Vinogradov, "Ethnicity, Cultural Discontinuity and Power Brokers in Northern Iraq: The Case of the Shabak," *American Ethnologist* 1, no. 1 (February 1974), 207–18; and Amal Rassam (Vinogradov), "Al-Taba'iyya: Power, Patronage and Marginal Groups in Northern Iraq," in *Patrons and Clients in Mediterranean Societies*, ed. Ernest Gellner and John Waterbury (London: Duckworth, 1977), pp. 157–66. (To avoid bibliographic confusion, note that studies by Amal Rassam prior to 1976 appeared under the name of Amal Vinogradov.)

[100] For an excellent short introduction to Lebanon, see Albert Hourani, "Political Society in Lebanon: A Historical Introduction," Emile Bustani Middle East Seminar (Cambridge, MA: Massachusetts Institute of Technology, Center for International Studies, 1986), complemented by Helena Cobban, "Thinking About Lebanon," *Arab-American Affairs*, no. 12 (Spring 1985), 59–71.

nal and regional politics of the eastern Mediterranean, and a liberal example for other countries in the region, although the country was on the verge of civil war several times in the 1950s and 1960s, prior to the tragic conflagration that began in 1975. Often the fighting has been reported in the foreign press as between "rightists" and "leftists" (these terms were on the wane by the early 1980s) or between Christians and Muslims. The situation is considerably more complex and involves ephemeral, shifting alliances between sects and factions in often cross-sectarian boundaries.

As of 1975, Lebanon, a country roughly the size of Connecticut but only 35 miles wide, had an estimated population of 3 million, with 17 recognized religious sects. As Helena Cobban says, the sectarian divisions (as opposed to geographic ones) among these groups "have not changed in any substantial way since the Druze stopped proselytizing in 1043 A.D."[101] Because Lebanese electoral politics were linked to the strength of the various sects as recorded in an official 1932 census, which gave a slight majority (51.2 percent) to the Christian population, there has been no official census since then. Nonetheless, there has been a major shift of population over time in favor of Shī'ī Muslims. Population estimates for 1975 (with the figures from the 1932 official census in parentheses) indicate that the Maronite Christian population was 23 percent (29 percent in 1932), 7 (10) percent Greek Orthodox, 5 (6) percent Greek Catholic, and 5 (7) percent other Christians, including Armenian Catholics, Armenian Orthodox (many of whom arrived as refugees from Turkey in the early part of this century), Protestants, Jacobites, Syrian Catholics, Syrian Orthodox, Nestorians, and Latin Rite Catholics. Sunnī Muslims constituted 26 percent of the population (22 percent in 1932), with 27 (20) percent Shī'ī Muslims and 7 (7) percent Druze. Lebanese demographers in 1983 estimated a further population shift since the start of the civil war, with the total Christian population dropping from 40 percent of the total in 1975 to 33 percent in 1983, and the Muslim total increasing from 60 percent to 66 percent, with the Shī'ī accounting for the bulk of this increase.[102] Lebanon's small Jewish community (about 4000 in the 1960s) has virtually disappeared.

A further complexity concerns citizenship. An estimated one-third of Lebanon's inhabitants were noncitizens in 1975. These included 500,000 Syrians (both Christian and Muslim) and an estimated 300,000 Palestinians (again, both Christian and Muslim). Although earlier immigrants to Lebanon, including Armenian Christians and many of the Palestinian refugees who arrived in 1948, were accorded Lebanese citizenship, most of the later arrivals were not. These population pressures contributed to a major shift in Lebanon's political makeup.

Lebanon's system of intersectarian rule had been in existence since the early sixteenth century. In 1516 the entire region of "greater Syria," including

[101] Cobban, "Thinking About Lebanon," 62.

[102] Ibid. Her figures for 1975 are based on an estimate by Youssef Courbage. Figures for 1932 have been rounded to the nearest percentage point.

Lebanon, came under Ottoman rule. Because the Druze had supported the Ottoman conquests, they were given responsibility for administering part of the area, including its Maronite Christian community, which was granted a degree of autonomy to keep them loyal. In the early eighteenth century, "there came into existence, more fully than before, something which can be called, without too much distortion of the term, a Lebanese feudal system, a hierarchy of families having formal relations with each other, controlling cultivation and demanding personal services from the peasants." Albert Hourani explains that the symbiotic relations "between three families, the Sunni Shihabs, and Druze Jumblats, and the Maronite Khazins, explain much of the history of the period. There were fights between factions or parties, but not between religious communities as such."[103]

By the late eighteenth century, the Maronite community gained strength. In an event that Hourani terms "perhaps unique" in Ottoman history, part of the Shihab family was converted from Sunnī Islam to Maronite Christianity, and the Maronites reached a formal agreement with the Papacy in 1736. By the early nineteenth century, European interests began to be strongly felt in Lebanon, with the French establishing direct links with the Maronite community, the British with the Druze, and the Russians with the Orthodox Christian community.[104] Part of the reason for this heightened interest in Lebanon was economic, and part was an extension of European rivalries, which became increasingly intertwined with local conflicts and had unanticipated consequences for all levels.[105] Hourani's appraisal of the nineteenth century could easily be transposed and applied to Lebanon of the 1970s and 1980s: "The local forces might believe that the great powers would support them more fully than in fact they did; the great powers might believe that they had more control over the actions of their local clients than in fact they had."[106]

Dissolution of the Ottoman Empire after World War I led to political disturbances, major population movements, and the creation of "Greater Lebanon" as a separate state in 1920, with boundaries larger than those of the former Ottoman province. As a result, the Maronites were no longer a majority, although they still constituted the largest sectarian community. Indeed, the

[103] Hourani, "Political Society," p. 8. See also Cobban, "Thinking About Lebanon," 63.

[104] Hourani, "Political Society," p. 8.

[105] See Leila Tarazi Fawaz, *An Occasion for War: Civil Conflict in Lebanon and Damascus in 1860* (Berkeley and Los Angeles: University of California Press, 1994).

[106] Ibid., p. 10. Compare Hourani's observation on Lebanon in the nineteenth century with journalist Jonathan Randal, *Going All the Way: Christian Warlords, Israeli Adventurers, and the War in Lebanon* (New York: Vintage Books, 1984), p. 241, on the July 1982 Israeli invasion of Lebanon: "[The Israelis] found it a lot easier to know in whose garage the Palestinians had stashed a tank than to figure out what was going on in a Maronite leader's head." Elsewhere (p. 261) Randal refers to Israeli lack of concern for Lebanon's "twisted sociology" as a major factor contributing to its failure to achieve its goals in invading Lebanon. The same could be said of other outside powers, including Arab ones. For one of the best Israeli accounts, see Itamar Rabinovich, *The War for Lebanon, 1970–1985*, rev. ed. (Ithaca, NY, and London: Cornell University Press, 1985), esp. pp. 174–99, and the appendix, pp. 201–36, which reprints a 1976 speech by Syrian President Ḥāfiẓ al-Asad assessing the Lebanese situation.

slight (1 percent) majority of Christians recorded in the 1932 census remained unchallenged largely in order to make the overall political system work in spite of its growing dissonance with demographic realities—in particular, the growing numbers and political strength of the Shīʿī community.[107]

At the same time, the economic base of the country had altered. Even after absorbing refugees from Palestine after the 1948 Arab-Israeli war, most of Beirut's population, for example, still lived in clearly defined neighborhoods, within which ethnic and religious affiliations were relatively homogeneous. Beirut's rapid growth since the early 1950s was the result not only of an increasing rural exodus but also of the need to assimilate waves of Palestinian refugees after 1948 and, since the 1970s, refugees from Lebanon's war-torn south. Lebanon also became a major financial and intellectual center, absorbing large amounts of capital from Arabs in wealthier but seemingly less secure states. The Lebanese sociologist Samir Khalaf estimates that by 1975, greater Beirut "was probably absorbing 75 percent of Lebanon's urban population and close to 45 percent of the inhabitants of the country."[108] In spite of the growing sectarian heterogeneity of many communities, religious and sectarian ties remained strong. Writing prior to the 1975 civil war, the Lebanese anthropologist Fuad Khuri noted that, although most neighborhoods were not distinguished by class, settlement by sectarian identity was marked. Nonetheless, the geographic and social boundaries between Muslim and Christian communities (and various divisions within these religious groups) were not always sharp. In general, areas of concentration for one sect serve as a magnet for fellow sectarians elsewhere. Khuri's description of interaction between sectarian groups prior to 1975 indicated the restraint that allowed ordinary life to go on without violence: "Interaction between confessional groups is, by and large, limited to business transactions and to formal occasions: festivals, weddings, and funerals. To interact openly and freely with other confessions requires both knowledge and hypocrisy: knowledge of the etiquette, manners, and cultural sensitivities of the other group; hypocrisy in pretending to appreciate the ways of others while manipulating them."[109]

Suad Joseph also conducted field research in pre-1975 Beirut. She emphasizes that the boundary markers among various sects, even after 1975, have shifted with changing historical realities and opportunities. Her study of Burj Ḥammūd, an independent municipality about 5 kilometers from downtown

[107] Hourani, "Political Society," p. 12. For the dynamics of sectarian politics and shifting regional political alliances in Lebanon, see Augustus Richard Norton, *Amal and the Shiʿa: Struggle for the Soul of Lebanon*, Modern Middle East Series 13 (Austin and London: University of Texas Press, 1987). For the leading Sunnī families, see Michael Johnson, *Class and Client in Beirut: The Sunni Muslim Community and the Lebanese State, 1840–1985* (London: Ithaca Press, 1986).

[108] Samir Khalaf, *Lebanon's Predicament* (New York: Columbia University Press, 1987), pp. 219–20.

[109] Fuad I. Khuri, *From Village to Suburb: Order and Change in Greater Beirut* (Chicago and London: University of Chicago Press, 1975), p. 57. This point is also developed in Michael Gilsenan, *Lords of the Lebanese Marches: Violence and Narrative in an Arab Society* (Berkeley and Los Angeles: University of California Press, 1996).

Beirut, depicts the practical implications of sectarian identity.[110] Population movements in and out of Burj Ḥammūd reflect the political and economic currents affecting the entire country. In 1920, the municipality had a population of 2000, which increased to 20,000 in 1942 and to about 200,000 in 1973, with a high population turnover. Every one of Lebanon's 17 major sectarian groups was represented in its population,[111] although, since the civil war, there has been a tendency for sectarian communities to cluster together more intensively. Less than 1 percent of the municipality's pre-1975 population was composed of its original settlers.

Joseph stresses the sociological importance of the various waves of migrants who settled in the community, a factor also noted by others. The first major wave of migrants was the Armenians, who arrived following the massacres in Turkey in 1920. Through the assistance of various Armenian organizations, they bought land in the region and encouraged other migrants to join them. Through the end of World War II, the Armenians predominated in the region, set up small industries, and built schools, clinics, clubs, and churches. They also gained control of the municipal board, which they still dominate. Palestinians began arriving after 1948, with wealthier ones settling directly in the community and impoverished ones living in a nearby camp. In the 1960s, a large number of Syrians, mostly Sunnī Muslims but also from other Muslim and Christian sectarian groups, arrived following the political upheavals in Syria. Later refugees in the 1970s were largely Shīʿa from Lebanon's south. As a consequence, Joseph estimates that the pre-1975 population distribution was roughly 40 percent Armenian Christians, 40 percent Shīʿa, and 20 percent Palestinian. Some of the municipality's neighborhoods were mixed in sectarian orientation, but in most cases a single group predominated.

Several sorts of bonds emerge from daily interaction. Almost every street constituted a neighborhood, with households of various sectarian groups mixed together. Neighbors tended to share their goods and to participate in each other's feast days and other special occasions. Women formed intersectarian friendship and visiting networks. These networks maintained some semblance of security, social control, and unity in the street, even in the face of deteriorating political conditions. On the other hand, the sectarian identities and the armed militias maintained by the strongmen of various groups increasingly became part of the fabric of social life. Here the international repercussions of Lebanese "internal" politics become apparent. In Burj Ḥammūd, as elsewhere in the country, each sectarian group can call upon its compatriots elsewhere. In fact, many of the Lebanese residents of Burj Ḥammūd did not vote there when elections were held (one of the reasons that the Armenians maintained their

[110] Suad Joseph, "Muslim-Christian Conflict in Lebanon: A Perspective on the Evolution of Sectarianism," in *Muslim-Christian Conflicts*, ed. Joseph and Pillsbury, pp. 64, 85, and her "Working Class Women's Networks in a Sectarian State: A Political Paradox," *American Ethnologist* 10, no. 1 (February 1983), 1–22.

[111] Suad Joseph, "Women and the Neighborhood Street in Borj Hammoud, Lebanon," in *Women*, ed. Beck and Keddie, pp. 544, 548–53.

local political strength) but in their villages of origin, where they were indebted to particular strongmen (*za'īm*-s).

Similarly, sectarian groups that were strong locally but weak nationally coalesced with others and shifted these coalitions opportunistically. Thus the Katā'ib party, whose principal base is the Maronite Christian community, was supported by the Armenians at the time of Joseph's study, although at other times the Armenians have allied themselves with various Palestinian factions. Although some groups are more powerful than others—because of their limited numbers, for example, the Armenians have been unable to play a major role—no one group can completely dominate the others, so the various militias must constantly ally with other groups. Yesterday's targets not infrequently become today's allies, and both outside powers and insiders seek to manipulate one another to advantage. Yet, despite the appearance, for outsiders, of nearly total anarchy, little transpires in the tightly knit neighborhoods that is not known, providing a semblance of local order.[112]

Khuri was one of the first to argue convincingly that Lebanese political parties, curiously called "right wing" and "left wing" in the American press of the late 1970s, as if the classical template of European politics could be transplanted to Lebanon, are based primarily on personal relationships and sectarian alignments and not on ideologies. He goes so far as to say that ideological political parties, such as the Ba'thists and the Communists, appeal primarily to the young and unmarried, many of whom desert these parties once they have family responsibilities and material interests to protect. Alliances often cross sectarian lines, but only with the agreement of major leaders.[113]

Because ethnic and religious identities are rarely the sole attributes shared by persons and groups in the Middle East, it is crucial to consider how such social distinctions figure in the overall context of social and personal identity and not to stop at a mosaiclike enumeration of distinctions such as ethnic group, sect, family origin, and occupation. Lawrence Rosen provides a useful

[112] A Lebanese colleague described his kidnapping in 1984 by militiamen at one of Beirut's many roadblocks. As a precaution, he always informed his wife of the exact routes he intended to take when driving. When he did not reach home at the agreed time, she began telephoning the family's contacts with the different militias along the route. She finally reached the militia holding her husband, and its leader arranged for his release. Not all Lebanese are so fortunate as to have high-level contacts in a wide range of factional groups or the ability to keep their "cognitive maps" of the shifting checkpoints up to date. And not all militia leaders can systematically exercise control over their component units. On shifting Armenian alignments in Beirut (and, in particular, Burj Ḥammūd) in the 1980s, see Xavier Raufer, *La nébuleuse: Le terrorisme du Moyen-Orient* (Paris: Fayard, 1987), pp. 87–109.

[113] Khuri, *Village to Suburb*, pp. 200–201. For dated but still valuable explorations of organized violence and political leadership in Lebanon, see Michael Gilsenan, "Lying, Honor, and Contradiction," in *Transaction and Meaning: Directions in the Anthropology of Exchange and Symbolic Behavior*, ed. Bruce Kapferer, ASA Studies in Social Anthropology 1 (Philadelphia: Institute for the Study of Human Issues, 1976), pp. 191–219; and, for Gilsenan's argument that class conflict was at the root of current Lebanese political unrest and not locally held ideologies of sectarian and factional divisions, see his "Against Patron-Client Relations," in *Patrons and Clients*, ed. Gellner and Waterbury, pp. 167–84. See also his "Reflections on a Village in a Time of War," *Middle East Reports* 15, no. 5 (June 1985), 25–29.

FIGURE 8-4. Berber men and women, High Atlas region, Morocco. [Courtesy Robert A. Fernea.]

assessment of the significance of such concepts in Morocco, where part of his work concerned the significance of politically volatile cultural notions of self and community as applied to the "ethnic" distinction between Arabs and Berbers and between Moroccan Muslims and Jews.[114] The essential background is as follows.

French colonial administrators, first in nineteenth-century Algeria and subsequently in twentieth-century Morocco, sought to nurture the notion that "Berber" identity was distinct from that of Arab and Muslim. In Morocco, the French considered it politically useful to emphasize real and imagined differences of Berbers, largely residing in mountainous regions and in Morocco's south in the earlier part of the century, from the "Arab" society of the towns and the agricultural plains. French policy turned out to be a major political miscalculation. In 1930 the French issued their famous "Berber proclamation" in Morocco, legally excluding regions designated as Berber from the jurisdiction of Islamic law courts. The proclamation set off protests throughout Morocco and the Muslim world. (Nonetheless, the French continued to treat "Berbers" and "Arabs" as antagonistic to the end of colonial rule in 1956.) The 1930 decree was supplemented by policies affecting military recruitment, local administration, education ("Berbers" were forbidden to learn Arabic in schools, although most students found the means to do so anyway), which

[114] Rosen, *Bargaining*, pp. 133–64. Rosen's argument incorporates material that originally appeared in a pair of articles published in 1972. For commentary on Rosen's argument, see Norman A. Stillman, "The Moroccan Jewish Experience: A Revisionist View," *Jerusalem Quarterly*, no. 9 (Fall 1978), 111–23, and his *Jews of Arab Lands—A History and Source Book* (Philadelphia: Jewish Publication Society of America, 1979). See also Mark A. Tessler, "The Identity of Religious Minorities in Non-Secular States: Jews in Tunisia and Morocco and Arabs in Israel," *Comparative Studies in Society and History* 20, no. 3 (July 1978), 359–73. For an excellent collection of readings and an annotated bibliography, see *Jewish Societies in the Middle East*, ed. Shlomo Deshen and Walter P. Zenner (Washington, DC: University Press of America, 1982).

were designed to cultivate a distinctly "Berber" elite. The issue continues in many ways to be a delicate one for the independent Moroccan government, many of whose senior French-educated administrators from the urban milieu, even if skeptical of the ideological justifications of French colonial policy, assimilated its basic assumptions concerning the structural divisions of Moroccan society.[115]

Another major identifying axis in Moroccan society, as with several other Middle Eastern societies, is that of Muslim and Jew. The Jewish community in Morocco remains one of the largest in the Middle East outside Israel itself, although significant Jewish minorities remain in other Middle Eastern countries.[116] Several recent studies suggest major cultural similarities between Moroccan Muslims and Jews.[117] As Rosen writes, the status of Jews in the Middle East has historically differed significantly from the status of Jews in Europe and has in some respects been superior. Through the advent of French colonial rule in Morocco, Jews were scattered throughout the country. Many were in larger towns, where they often, but not always, lived in separate quarters called *mallāḥs*; in many of the smaller centers, regions of Jewish residence were not so sharply set off from their Muslim neighbors.[118] Jews practiced a range of occupations; they were butchers, sellers of charcoal, shoemakers, artisans in gold and silver, money changers, grain traders, cloth merchants, and itinerant

[115] See Edmund Burke III, "The Image of the Moroccan State in French Ethnological Literature: A New Look at the Origin of Lyautey's Berber Policy," in *Arabs and Berbers: From Tribe to Nation in North Africa*, ed. Ernest Gellner and Charles Micaud (London: Duckworth, 1972), pp. 175–99; Kenneth Brown's "The Impact of the Dahir Berbère in Salé," in the same volume, pp. 201–15; and Charles F. Gallagher, "Language and Identity," in *State and Society in Independent North Africa*, ed. Leon Carl Brown (Washington, DC: Middle East Institute, 1966), pp. 73–96.

[116] Estimates of the Jewish population as of 1982 in various Arab countries, together with the estimates (in parentheses) of the 1948 populations, when known, are as follows: Morocco: 17,000 (225,000 in 1948, and still 162,420 in 1960, according to census figures; 7000 as of 1995), Tunisia: 3700 (100,000), Lebanon: 250, Syria: 4000 (30,000), Iraq: 200 (130,000), Algeria: 300 (140,000), Egypt: 250 (80,000), Yemen Arab Republic: 1200 (70,000), and Libya: nil (35,000). These figures are derived from U. O. Schmelz and Sergio DellaPergola, "World Jewish Population, 1982," *American Jewish Yearbook, 1985* (Philadelphia: Jewish Publication Society of America, 1985), p. 328. The 1982 estimate for Iran was 30,000, down from 85,000 in the early 1970s. See Laurence D. Loeb, *Outcaste: Jewish Life in Southern Iran*, Library of Anthropology (New York: Gordon and Breach, 1977), p. 4.

[117] See especially Shlomo Deshen, *The Mellah Society: Jewish Community Life in Sherifian Morocco* (Chicago: University of Chicago Press, 1989).

[118] See Dale F. Eickelman, *Moroccan Islam: Tradition and Society in a Pilgrimage Center*, Modern Middle East Series 1 (Austin and London: University of Texas Press, 1976), pp. 45–48, 78. Important monographs dealing with North African Jewish communities include Abraham L. Udovitch and Lucette Valensi, *The Last Arab Jews: The Communities of Jerba, Tunisia*, Social Orders 1 (New York: Harwood Academic Publishers, 1984); Elizabeth Friedman, *Colonialism and After: An Algerian Jewish Community*, Critical Studies in Work and Community (South Hadley, MA: Bergin & Garvey, 1987); Daniel J. Schroeter, *Merchants of Essaouria: Urban Society and Imperialism in Southwestern Morocco, 1844–1886*, Middle East Library (Cambridge and New York: Cambridge University Press, 1987); Mordechai Ha-Cohen, *The Book of Mordechai: A Study of the Jews of Libya*, ed. and trans. by Harvey E. Goldberg (Philadelphia: Institute for the Study of Human Issues, 1980); and *Communautés juives des marges sahariennes du Maghreb*, ed. Michel Abitbol (Jerusalem: Ben-Zvi Institute and the Hebrew University of Jerusalem, 1982). For an evaluation of earlier anthropological monographs, see Lawrence Rosen, "North African Jewish Studies," *Judaism* 17, no. 4 (Fall 1968), 422–29.

traders in rural regions.[119] Various European Jewish organizations made contact with Middle Eastern Jewish communities in the 1880s and eventually helped establish Jewish schools and community services modeled on European ones.

As a consequence of these early efforts of European Jewish organizations in Morocco and the provision of separate schools for Jews after the establishment of colonial rule in 1912, Jews had a competitive edge in commerce, often serving as local representatives for European commercial interests and as minor functionaries in the protectorate administration. By the 1930s, European-style primary education had become almost universally available to the Jewish community, while in the same period, fewer than 2 percent of Morocco's Muslims had access to such education. After 1948 large numbers of Jews began to emigrate, especially from the smaller communities of the interior. The largest wave of emigration, however, began with Morocco's independence in 1956, with wealthier, educated Jews tending to emigrate to North America (especially to French-speaking Quebec) and to France, and those with fewer skills or connections to Israel.

Even during periods of serious crisis, such as during World War II, when the Vichy regime sought to deport Morocco's Jewish population and that of Tunisia, North African Jews were protected. Morocco's Sultan reminded the French that "protected" Morocco was nonetheless formally a sovereign nation and that Moroccan Jews were his subjects, enjoying full protection. The consequence was that Jews holding French citizenship were subject to Vichy laws and deportation, but not Moroccan nationals. In addition, many Muslims offered protection to their Jewish neighbors. As late as the 1967 and 1973 Arab-Israeli wars, many Moroccan Muslims took steps to ensure the safety of Jewish households with which they had ties.[120]

What does the tenor of the Muslim-Jewish distinction in Morocco have in common with that of Arabs and Berbers? Rosen's answer is to indicate ways by which people in Moroccan society tend to categorize others. He stresses the Moroccan tendency to render social relationships stable and more or less predictable through the creation of multiple bonds of interpersonal obligation. Rosen argues that in Moroccan society in general (for "Berbers" as well as "Arabs" and for "Jews" as well as "Muslims"), personal obligations are not prescribed by kinship roles or by any other generalized, collective obligations. There is a wide latitude in how social bonds, even those of kinship, are expressed and considerable flexibility in how an individual can choose to elaborate particular kinds of relationships. Ties of kinship, like those of occupation

[119] See Clifford Geertz, "Suq: The Bazaar Economy," in Geertz, Geertz, and Rosen, *Meaning and Order*, pp. 164–72; and Dale F. Eickelman, "Religion and Trade in Western Morocco," *Research in Economic Anthropology* 5 (1983), 335–48, which deals with parallels between the economic organization of itinerant Jewish traders and their Muslim counterparts.

[120] Norman A. Stillman, "Muslims and Jews in Morocco: Perceptions, Images, Stereotypes," in *Proceedings of the Seminar on Muslim Jewish Relations in North Africa* (New York: World Jewish Congress, 1975), pp. 13–39, especially the comments by Paul Raccah and Moise Ohana, pp. 28–29. See also Lawrence Rosen, "A Moroccan Jewish Community During the Middle Eastern Crisis," *American Scholar* 37, no. 3 (Summer 1968), 435–51; and Harvey E. Goldberg, "The Mellahs of Southern Morocco: Report of a Survey," *Maghreb Review* 8, nos. 3–4 (May–August 1983), 61–69.

FIGURE 8-5. Moroccan Jews who have emigrated to Israel have been accompanied by their sacred geography. This woman in Beit She'an, an Israeli "new town," established a shrine for Rabbi Avraham Uriwār in her own home. His original shrine is located on the outskirts of Settat, Morocco. For an account of the founding of Rabbi Avram's shrine in Israel, see Yoram Bilu and Galit Hasan-Rokem, "Cinderella and the Saint: The Life Story of a Jewish Moroccan Female Healer in Israel," *The Psychoanalytic Study of Society* 14 (1989): 227–260. [Photograph courtesy Yoram Bilu.]

and "ethnicity," provide minimal, baseline information about the social location of individuals but do not preclude considerable variation in the social constructions of interpersonal obligations based on a wide variety of attributes.[121]

Within this general framework of cultural conceptualizations of social bonds and obligations, the meaning of Berber identity becomes more apparent. Berbers are chiefly distinguished from other Moroccans by the fact that they speak a Berber language, usually in addition to Arabic, but even this characteristic says little of personal identity. Rosen considers patterns of occupation, residence, marriage, urban and rural origin, and other factors to show that distinctions in these domains do not coincide with languages spoken or with political and economic conduct. He concludes that Berber ethnicity in the region of Morocco he studied "is a factor that varies with situational contexts and the additional affiliations by which each of the participants [in social exchanges] are characterized. Identity as a Berber or an Arab is not, however, in almost any context an all-pervasive typification in terms of which one views and relates to another person."[122]

[121] Rosen, *Bargaining*, pp. 141–48, esp. p. 144.

[122] Ibid., p. 147.

Muslim and Jewish relations in Morocco can be considered in terms of the same overall framework with which Moroccans culturally typify other interpersonal ties. As is the case in the distinction between Berbers and Arabs, it is not possible to differentiate Jews and Muslims in terms of the economic roles they play. The major distinctions are instead between urban merchants and Jews, on the one hand, with the distinctive social roles they play, and people of rural and Berber-speaking origin on the other, although even this distinction is not a sharp one. There is, however, one important element of differentiation. Rosen argues that Muslims as a group share a "sociological pool" of prestige resources in that there is an intense and open competition among people that ranges from economic transactions to political and marital ties. Jews in Morocco are placed outside this sociological pool, in the sense that few marital ties are possible, and Jewish participation in politics is indirect and restrained. Relations of Jews with the Muslim community, both Arab and Berber, were principally economic, without the open-ended competitive ramifications engendered by the more complex and diffuse relations among Muslims. As with most other social ties in Moroccan society, those between Muslims and Jews were highly personal; in addition, however, they were noncompetitive in all but the economic sense. Thus a traditional role of Jews was to act as economic intermediaries between townsmen and the rural, tribalized population in central Morocco. Rosen writes that Muslims did not risk their social independence in elaborating ties with Jews. Often the ties were those of friendship. Even with the transformation of Muslim-Jewish relationships that occurred with the increasing identification of part of the Jewish community with European ways and economic interests in the colonial period, Jews continued to be treated as "face-to-face consociates" rather than as distant and undifferentiated members of a different ethnic or religious group.[123]

The fundamental and general conceptualizations of personal and collective identity that prevail in Morocco allow for considerable flexibility in how ethnic and sectarian identities are elaborated. Yet, as elsewhere in the Middle East, ethnicity and other forms of identity make sense when considered in the context of other social identities and in terms of specific historical contexts. The social and cultural context of "oriental" Jews in Israel illustrates the importance of considering ethnic identities in terms of time and social location.

Briefly, here are some essential features of Israeli society as related to the situation of "oriental" Jews, decidedly an "outsider's" term used by some Israelis of European origin to designate Jews of North African or Middle Eastern origin who emigrated to Israel or whose parents did so.[124] Roughly half of Israel's Jewish population (about 15 percent of the country's population, excluding the occupied territories, is Christian and Muslim) consisted of oriental Jews in the mid-1980s. Because the majority of immigrants in the 1950s and 1960s had little formal education and possessed only traditional skills that were of minimal

[123] Ibid., pp. 151–53.

[124] See Moshe Shokeid, "A Case of Ethnic Myth-Making," in *Cross-Currents in Israeli Culture and Politics*, ed. Myron J. Aronoff, Political Anthropology 4 (New Brunswick, NJ, and London: Transaction Books, 1984), pp. 39–49.

use in Israel, they were usually obliged to become manual laborers and agricultural workers. Their reduced status and the strong secularizing influence of Israeli society put severe strains on them. As an aggregate through the early 1970s, Middle Eastern immigrants and their children had considerably less success than their counterparts of European origin; unemployment among them was significantly higher, and they were proportionately less represented in the cabinet and in the Knesset (parliament) than their counterparts of European origin. The same held true for Jews of Middle Eastern origin in the upper ranks of the military and in the civil service through the early 1970s. These disparities were not the result of deliberate discrimination. Yet the changing perceptions of intercommunal relations among Israeli Jews from the 1960s to the early 1970s indicated a growing problem. In a public opinion poll taken just after the 1967 Six-Day War, 84 percent of Israeli Jews thought that intercommunal relations were good; this figure had dropped to 48 percent by 1971.[125]

What do these statistics mean for the perception of ethnic identity among Israeli Jews, especially those of Middle Eastern origin? As one Israeli anthropologist, Shlomo Deshen, reports, Israel's official immigration policies were founded on the notion of assimilating refugee immigrants and encouraging them to think of themselves principally as Jews, without regard to their cultures of origin. A common pattern has been for North African Jewish immigrants first to shed traditional practices that mark them off from other Jews. As they face the realities of adjustment in Israel, they gradually resume important aspects of their particular identities, such as the publication of folktales and scholastic writings peculiar to their own communities, the support of immigrant associations based on country of origin, the production of unleavened bread (*matzot*) in forms distinctive to each community of origin, political support for candidates concerned principally with the problems of immigrants of North African origin, and the maintenance or even proliferation in intensified forms of "local" religious practices such as visits to Jewish saints, in a manner somewhat similar to the visits to maraboutic shrines by some of North Africa's Muslim population.

The identities that Middle Eastern Jewish immigrants to Israel seek to project are not simply reconstitutions of identities possessed prior to their arrival in Israel. Writing in 1976, Deshen argued that Moroccan, Yemeni, Iraqi, and Tunisian Jews now in Israel "are making a stand for certain elements of their culture which they have retained and want to nurture. They seek to identify themselves also in autonomous subethnic terms, but they want that identification to be within the bonds of their overarching identity as Israelis."[126] Ethnic identities forged in other, earlier contexts in Tunisia, Morocco, and Iran are the base from which subsequent transformations of these systems of meaning occur: "The derivation is there, even if continuity is most tenuous and subtle;

[125] Amnon Rubenstein, "Jewish Panthers and Other Problems," *Encounter* 38, no. 6 (June 1972), 80–85.

[126] Shlomo Deshen, "Ethnic Boundaries and Cultural Paradigms: The Case of Southern Tunisian Immigrants in Israel," *Ethos* 4 (1976), 292.

and often it is quite overt."[127] Because of the size and early presence of the Moroccan Jewish community in Israel, they were the first to achieve wide political and "ethnic" visibility in Israeli society. Their *mimūna*, an outdoor festival involving visits to saints' shrines following Passover, came to the fore in the 1960s and, by the 1970s, was associated with the growing political strength of Moroccan Jews as a voting bloc and claims for legitimacy for specifically Moroccan Jewish practices. A specifically "Iranian" Jewish identity followed by the late 1970s. As Judith Goldstein reports: "The category 'Iranian' is itself specific to Israel and not to Iran as Iranians follow the pattern of 'In Iran I was Jewish; in Israel I'm Iranian.'"[128] Only with the greater influx of Iranian Jews to Israel in the late 1970s did a specifically Iranian identity emerge, and the cultural performances that marked this identity were modeled in part on the prior successful examples of Ashkenazim (for the most part of European origin) and Moroccan Jews. Goldstein's argument that Iranian Jews in Israel, by participating in "Iranian" cultural performances, are creating a "mutually agreed upon and a mutually shared common past" that thus creates a "heritage" of core historical symbols,[129] parallels in many respects Mandel's argument, presented earlier in this chapter, concerning recent transformations in identity of Kurdish-speaking Alevi-s in Germany.

Several conclusions can be drawn from the studies of ethnic and sectarian identities discussed so far. Sex and gender roles, ethnicity, kinship, and the like are all simultaneous components of social identity and cannot be analyzed independently of more general underlying assumptions. In practice, they often go together. Second, such identities must be analyzed in the specific historical contexts in which they are maintained, transformed, and reproduced, and not as parts of an ahistorical mosaic. The theoretical points of departure of contemporary studies of ethnicity vary widely: from an emphasis primarily on ethnicity as embedded in a system of social meanings to ethnicity and sectarianism as principally a product of global economic and political circumstances, or analyses combining aspects of these two approaches. The majority of current studies recognize that research into notions of identity entails attention both to cultural meanings and to the practical contexts in which they are produced and transformed. Anthropologists, like other scholars concerned with social theory, are not in a position to produce universal schema indicating the precise interrelationships between economic and political transformations and their associated ideologies of identity. But they recognize that both these dimensions must be carefully analyzed and that systems of meaning cannot be treated as if they were unchanging, as they have been treated in the past.

[127] Ibid., p. 293.

[128] Judith L. Goldstein, "Iranian Ethnicity in Israel: The Performance of Identity," in *Studies in Israeli Ethnicity*, ed. Weingrod, pp. 237–57.

[129] Ibid., p. 244.

A corollary to this is that ethnic distinctions, like those of region, sect, sex, language, and even tribe, are not being erased, as an earlier generation of analysts once facilely assumed, but provide the base from which newer social distinctions are forged. Even when there is a popular consensus or a desire among intellectual and political leaders to facilitate the reshaping of identities and responsibilities, either to mute the importance of divisive ethnic or sectarian identities or in transforming the roles of women and men in society, the point of departure from which such transformations are made must be considered in assessing their direction and tenor. Some governments and political leaders seek to ease tensions that arise from making such group definitions by denying their existence, but it would appear more reasonable to recognize them for what they are and to seek to harness them constructively. Shared notions of community by ethnic group or region can often provide the basis of trust and solidarity necessary for the effective functioning of and participation in modern society.

FURTHER READINGS

On the politicization of women, family, and gender roles, see Dale F. Eickelman and James Piscatori, *Muslim Politics*, Princeton Studies on Muslim Politics (Princeton, NJ: Princeton University Press, 1996), pp. 80–99.

In interviewing on "sensitive" subjects such as gender roles and sexuality in the Middle East (and in Central Asia), scholars have used various approaches to get beyond formulaic responses. One approach is suggested by Paul Pascon and Mekki Bentahar, "Ce que disent 296 jeunes ruraux," in *Études sociologiques sur le Maroc*, ed. A. Khatibi (Rabat: Bulletin Économique et Social du Maroc, 1971), pp. 147–48, 211–21. The authors found that collective interviewing and group discussions, instead of the individual interviews more common in American and European contexts, allayed much of the initial suspicion of the interviewers, who were sociology students at Mohammad V University in Rabat. Long-term studies can also establish high degrees of trust between interviewers and interviewees, as is evident in the transcripts of taped interviews concerning changing gender relations and sex roles presented in an excellent study of adolescent socialization by Susan Schaefer Davis and Douglas A. Davis, *Adolescence in a Moroccan Town: Making Social Sense*, Adolescents in a Changing World (New Brunswick, NJ: Rutgers University Press, 1988). See Mounīa Bennani-Chraïbi, *Soumis et rebelles: les jeunes au Maroc* (Paris: CNRS Éditions, 1994), pp. 21–23. Her book won a Moroccan literary prize in 1996, the Prix Atlas, indicating a growing internal market for books critical on social issues.

On women in Middle Eastern history, two works stand out. Leslie P. Peirce, *The Imperial Harem: Women and Sovereignty in the Ottoman Empire* (New York and Oxford: Oxford University Press, 1993), deals with the Ottoman imperial harem in the sixteenth and seventeenth centuries, a period popularly known as "the sultanate of women" because of the ability of women to manipulate political factions, act as agents for their sons, and endow monuments, charities, mosques, hospitals, markets, and commercial centers. Other works on the historical past include Afaf Lutfi al-Sayyid Marsot, *Women and Men in Late Eighteenth Century Egypt* (Austin: University of Texas Press, 1995); and Nikki R. Keddie and Beth Baron, eds., *Women in Middle Eastern History: Shifting Boundaries in Sex and Gender* (New Haven, CT, and London: Yale University Press, 1991). Bridging the historical and modern periods is Fedwa Malti-Douglas, *Woman's Body, Woman's Word: Gender and Discourse in Arabo-Islamic Writing* (Princeton, NJ: Princeton University Press, 1991). For a good sociological account of the significance of women's formal associations, see Şirin Tekeli, "Women in the Changing Political Associations of the 1980s," in *Turkish State, Turkish Society*, ed. Andrew Finkel and Nükhet Sirman (London and New York: Routledge, 1990), pp. 259–87. See also Chris Hann, "Culture and Anti-Culture: The Spectre of Orientalism in New Anthropological Writing on Turkey," *Journal of the Anthropological Society of Oxford* 24, no. 3 (1993), 223–43. Elizabeth Warnock Fernea, *Children in the Muslim Middle East*, Modern Middle East Series 18 (Austin: University of Texas Press, 1995), is a useful introduction to the topic of contemporary child socialization. See also Donna Lee Bowen and Evelyn A. Early, eds., *Everyday Life in the Muslim Middle East*, Indiana Series in Arab and Islamic Studies (Bloomington and Indianapolis: Indiana University Press, 1993). On women in Oman, in addition to Christine Eickelman, *Women and Community in Oman* (New York: New York University Press, 1984), see Unni Wikan, *Behind the Veil in Arabia: Women in Oman* (Baltimore and London: Johns Hopkins University Press, 1982). For Yemen, see Anne Meneley, *Tournaments of Value: Sociability and Hierarchy in a Yemeni Town* (Toronto: University of Toronto Press, 1996). For Iran, see also Erika Friedl, *Women of Deh Koh: Lives in an Iranian Village* (Washington, DC, and London: Smithsonian Institution Press, 1989). For Afghanistan, see Audrey C. Shalinsky, "Women's Roles in the Afghanistan Jihad," *International Journal of Middle East Studies* 25, no. 4 (November 1993), 661–75.

On Soviet and post-Soviet studies of ethnicity and ethnonationalism, in addition to citations in the text, see Anatoly Khazanov, *After the USSR: Ethnicity, Nationalism, and Politics in the Commonwealth of Independent States* (Madison: University of Wisconsin Press, 1995); and Philip L. Kohl and Gocha R. Tsetskhladze, "Nationalism, Politics, and the Practice of Archaeology in the Caucasus," in *Nationalism, Politics, and the Practice of Archaeology*, ed. Philip L. Kohl and Clare Fawcett (Cambridge: Cambridge University Press, 1995), pp. 149–74. Robert J. Kaiser, *The Geography of Nationalism in Russia and the USSR* (Princeton, NJ: Princeton University Press, 1994), offers the most comprehensive overview of state-initiated inventions of national groups and nationalism; and Tone Bringa, *Being Muslim the Bosnian Way: Identity and Community in a Central Bosnian Village*, Princeton Series in Muslim Politics (Princeton, NJ: Princeton University Press, 1995), pp. 197–231, offers a gripping account of the collapse of civil society and the transformation of neighbors into bitter ethnonational rivals. Also see the essays in Jo-Ann Gross, ed., *Muslims in Central Asia: Expressions of Identity and Change* (Durham, NC: Duke University Press, 1992).

For Afghanistan, additional sources include Robert Leroy Canfield, *Faction and Conversion in a Plural Society: Religious Alignments in the Hindu Kush*, Anthropological Papers 50 (Ann Arbor: University of Michigan, Museum of Anthropology, 1973), and his "Islamic Coalitions in Bamyan: A Problem in Translating Afghan Political Culture," in *Revolutions and Rebellions in Afghanistan: An Anthropological Perspective*, ed. M. Nazif Shahrani and Robert L. Canfield (Berkeley: University of California Institute of International Studies, 1984), pp. 211–29.

The Kurds are poorly represented in specifically anthropological studies, as most ethnographers have spent only brief periods (several weeks to two months) in Kurdistan and were not familiar with Kurdish or the other languages of the region. The principal studies are E. R. Leach, *Social and Economic Organization of the Rowanduz Kurds*, London School of Economics, Monographs on Social Anthropology 3 (London: Percy Lund, Humphries and Co., 1940); Fredrik Barth, *Principles of Social Organization in Southern Kurdistan, Universitetets Etnografiske Museum Bulletin* 7 (Oslo: Brødrene Jørgensen A/S, 1953); and Henny Harald Hansen, *The Kurdish Woman's Life: Field Research in a Muslim Society*, Hal, Nationalmuseets Skrifter, Etnografisk Raekke 7 (Copenhagen: National Museum, 1961). The best modern study is Martin van Bruinessen's *Agha, Shaikh and State: The Social and Political Structures of Kurdistan* (London: Zed Books, 1992). See also his "The Kurds Between Iran and Iraq," *Middle East Report* 16, no. 4 (July–August 1986), 14–27; and Hakan Yavuz, "Turkey's 'Imagined Enemies': Kurds and Islamists," *The*

World Today 52, no. 4 (April 1996), 98–102, and the special issue of *Middle East Report* 24, no. 4 (July–August 1994), 1–23, "The Kurdish Experience." Leszek Dzięgiel, *Rural Community of Contemporary Iraqi Kurdistan Facing Modernization*, Studia i Materialy 7 (Krakow: Agricultural Academy, 1981), is a Polish anthropologist's account of an Iraqi project to resettle villagers in "development" centers. T. F. Aristova, *Material 'naia kul'tura kurdov XIX-pervoi poloviny XXV.: problema traditisionno-kul'turnoi obshchnosti* (Moscow: "Nauka," 1990), provides a comprehensive discussion of "traditional" Kurdish economy and material culture, as well as an example of Soviet ethnography on the Middle East. I am grateful to Leszek Dzięgiel of the University of Kraków, Poland, for bringing this reference to my attention, and in general for sharing his knowledge of Kurdish studies.

On Jewish ethnicity in the Middle East, see Shlomo Deshen and Moshe Shokeid, *The Predicament of Homecoming: Cultural and Social Life of North African Immigrants in Israel*, Symbol, Myth, and Ritual (Ithaca, NY, and London: Cornell University Press, 1974); Moshe Shokeid and Shlomo Deshen, *Distant Relations: Ethnicity and Politics Among Arabs and North African Jews in Israel* (New York: Praeger, 1982); and Moshe Shokeid, "Cultural Ethnicity in Israel: The Case of Middle Eastern Jews' Religiosity," *AJS Review* 9, no. 2 (Fall 1984), 247–71. See also Harvey E. Goldberg, "The Mimuna and the Minority Status of Moroccan Jews," *Ethnology* 17, no. 1 (January 1978), 75–87; Shlomo Deshen, "Israeli Judaism: Introduction to the Major Patterns," *International Journal of Middle East Studies* 9, no. 2 (May 1978), 141–69; *Studies in Israeli Ethnicity: After the Ingathering*, ed. Alex Weingrod (New York: Gordon and Breach, 1985); and Kevin Avruch, "The Emergence of Ethnicity in Israel," *American Ethnologist* 14, no. 2 (May 1987), 327–39. See also Kenneth Brown and Jean Mohr, "Journey Through the Labyrinth: A Photographic Essay on Israel/Palestine," *Studies in Visual Communication* 8, no. 2 (Spring 1982), 2–81. The best recent collective work, with a comprehensive introduction, is Harvey E. Goldberg, ed., *Sephardi and Middle Eastern Jewries: History and Culture in the Modern Era* (Bloomington: Indiana University Press, 1996).

9

THE CULTURAL ORDER OF COMPLEX SOCIETIES

WORLDVIEW

Kinship, community, tribe, responsibility, and trust are subjectively held ideas about social relations shared by members of a society and embodied in rules, customs, symbolic actions such as ritual, and the conduct of everyday affairs. Such patterns of meaning have been analyzed by some anthropologists as parts of formal systems of classification and symbol systems and not as part of social practice. A complementary approach, emphasized throughout this book, focuses on how patterns of symbolic representations are generated in the everyday world of social experience, how they shape social practice, and how they are in turn modified by it. This emphasis on the production of meaning through practice (*praxis*, in the vocabulary of some writers) sets apart most contemporary analyses of *worldview* (shared symbolic representations concerning the nature of the social world) from earlier studies, which were primarily concerned with a "logical fit" among the key symbols of a cultural tradition. The notion of the production of symbolic representations of the world can be traced back at least to the writings of prominent nineteenth-century social theorists, including Marx and Engels.[1] What is new in recent writings, at least on the Middle East—comparable studies are not yet available for Central Asia—is the effort to explore the production of such representations in specific ethnographic and social historical contexts.

Notions of worldview overlap and build upon more specific conceptions such as family, community, ethnicity, and sexuality but differ in that they are more integrative and comprehensive. The idea that symbolic representations of social practice, as well as practices themselves, form part of the same generative framework has been introduced in the last few chapters through the discussion

[1] See, for example, the writings of Pierre Bourdieu, cited in earlier chapters; and Anthony Giddens, *The Constitution of Society: Outline of the Theory of Structuration* (Berkeley and Los Angeles: University of California Press, 1984).

of tribe, kinship, the use of genealogies, naming practices, gender roles, and ethnicity. I have stressed that these topics can be comprehended analytically only through the matrix of social representations of reality through which everyday life and actions become meaningful to Middle Easterners and Central Asians themselves. The elaboration of concepts of worldview in the Middle East and Central Asia is a challenging task, because the societies of the two regions are complex and historically known, unlike many of the "primitive" societies about which many social anthropologists originally elaborated the notion of worldview (or *cosmologies*, as many British anthropologists use the term).

As with any sociological study, earlier approaches to the understanding of worldview—or as it has sometimes been called, "national character"—must be taken into account. In the past, the national character of a people was sometimes considered unchanging. The attitudes and practices of Egyptian peasants of the twentieth century were thought to be very similar to those of peasants of Pharaonic times.[2] Such portraits of changelessness were used to justify colonial domination. French colonial ethnographers, for example, drew upon those elements of European social thought which emphasized the fixed "primitive mentalities" of certain populations as one means of legitimizing the colonial enterprise. Handbooks prepared for European teachers of Moroccan children emphasized the fixed values and traditions of Moroccans, disregarding the impact of European domination and economic penetration. Such guides advised that "respect" for religious and social beliefs and practices required European teachers to limit what they conveyed to their students, so that education could not be used as a means of transforming the "traditional" social hierarchy, the status of women, or other sensitive topics.[3] France's "civilizing mission" (*mission civilisatrice*), to use the phrase of the epoch, had its limits. Comparable accounts of "oriental" character were prepared for areas under English colonial domination. As Edward Said and others rightly insist, the "mosaic" representations of Middle Eastern societies that avoid discussion of the impact of political and economic changes lend themselves readily to such assumptions, as do vague assertions concerning the "Arab mind" or "Islamic thought."

Contemporary anthropological discussions of worldview are at once more ambitious and more limited in scope. They are more limited in that they do not assume that such representations are shared by all members of a given society, let alone from one end of the Arab and Middle Eastern world to the other. They do not purport to represent all implicit shared understandings, only

[2] Winifred S. Blackman, *The Fellahin of Upper Egypt* (London: Frank Cass, 1968 [1927]); Henry Habib Ayrout, *The Egyptian Peasant* (Boston: Beacon Press, 1968), which must be read in conjunction with Timothy Mitchell, "The Invention and Reinvention of the Egyptian Peasant," *International Journal of Middle East Studies* 22, no. 2 (May 1990), 129–50. For a review of earlier studies, see Fouad M. Moughrabi, "The Arabic Basic Personality: A Critical Survey of the Literature," *International Journal of Middle East Studies* 9, no. 1 (February 1978), 99–112.

[3] An example of such a guide is Louis Brunot, *Premiers conseils* [First Advice] (Rabat: École du Livre, 1934). Brunot was director of Muslim education in Morocco in the early 1930s.

those most related to the comprehension of particular patterns of social action—status, kinship, participation in maraboutic ("saintly") cults, friendship, and sincerity, to mention only the examples that will be elaborated in this and later chapters.

The more ambitious aspect of contemporary analyses of worldview is that they seek to articulate those taken-for-granted attitudes and values that make everyday social action possible, shared understandings that are so deeply rooted that they flow almost automatically. Yet these shared understandings do not exist independently of the situations in which they are used. Individuals control how symbolic representations are interpreted, and in so doing, they shape the symbolic representations.

Lloyd Fallers (1925–1974) writes that an anthropologist concerned with analyzing such basic symbolic representations must learn to cultivate

> especially the receptive side of communication—the ability to spend most of one's time listening instead of speaking, watching instead of acting; he learns to remember and to record in great detail what he sees and hears. These are difficult disciplines requiring rigorous training for academic intellectuals, who usually would rather talk than listen and who find boring or repulsive what they see as the "trivia" of ordinary life, particularly in their own societies.[4]

Taken together, such "trivia" documents a set of "natural" assumptions concerning the social world. These assumptions, which are considered "natural" and not "conventional," are constructed and transformed through social practice and made up of everyday, incompletely systematized, common-sense understandings of how the world "really" is.[5] Under ordinary conditions these basic assumptions form the implicit background against which social action is planned and carried out, even though they are not fully articulated by members of a society. Special frames of reference, such as formal religious ideologies, specialized knowledge of commerce and crafts, medicine, political strategies, and the interpretation of dreams, are elaborated against the background of such understandings.

Anthropologists have had different, albeit largely complementary, concerns in the elaboration of systems of worldview. Some scholars have been particularly concerned with the logico-meaningful relations among the cultural assumptions that make up particular worldviews. Others, while not neglecting this task, have paid particular attention to analyzing how such basic assumptions toward the social world are related to changing economic and political conditions. Because such implicit understandings are not fully systematized, they cannot be represented as neatly organized "cognitive maps"; there *is* a

[4] Lloyd A. Fallers, *The Social Anthropology of the Nation-State* (Chicago: Aldine, 1974), p. 8. For an example of equivalent "listening" by a social historian, see Abraham Marcus, "Privacy in Eighteenth-Century Aleppo: The Limits of Cultural Ideals," *International Journal of Middle East Studies* 18, no. 2 (May 1987), 165–83.

[5] The notion of the "natural" attitude toward the social world is developed in Alfred Schutz, *Collected Papers, I: The Problem of Social Reality* (The Hague: Martinus Nijhoff, 1967); and in Clifford Geertz, *The Interpretation of Cultures* (New York: Basic Books, 1973).

meaningful fit among the assumptions that make up particular worldviews, but the fit is best represented as jagged and uneven. In any case, what we hypothesize about any particular worldview is documented by the fragmentary and often inconsistent outward actions and statements of people in a given society. The ultimate test of an adequate description of worldview, therefore, consists of its ability to render intelligible wide varieties of behavior in a given society. Many recent studies have sought to depict such matrices of cultural meaning and to place them in the context of historical and sociopolitical change. An assessment of the basic approaches used in the study of worldview serves to tie together the discussion of the preceding three chapters and forms an essential backdrop to the discussion in later chapters of religion, politics, and the economy.

LANGUAGE AND ETIQUETTE

The best means of eliciting the background conventions and assumptions that make possible the routines of daily life is through concrete examples. Turns of phrase, bodily movements, dress styles, and patterns of etiquette are all valuable indicators of what these underlying assumptions are.

Within countries as complex as Lebanon, Iran, many of the Arab Gulf states, and Turkey, there is a recognizable diversity of personal and collective interests and beliefs, the commingling of which requires exercise of civility, a collective self-restraint, and willingness to coexist with other people and groups, even if they do not share all basic assumptions about the conduct of daily affairs. Moreover, such basic assumptions are not fixed, and stereotyped metaphors such as "the Arab mind" and "the French mentality" are beginning to disappear from educated usage.

Still, it remains true that there are styles of social conduct indicating background assumptions specific to particular cultural groups. Anyone who has conducted international negotiations realizes that one of their most difficult components is not what is formally said but the informal nuances of what is *not* said that figure significantly in the development or lack of common trust necessary for satisfactory agreement. Gestures and complexes of beliefs form coherent rhetorical patterns. To take several obvious examples, for Americans (except New Yorkers?), normal conversational distance is 3 to 4 feet apart, with closer distances corresponding to greater degrees of intimacy and greater distances suggesting more formality. Deans, business executives, ambassadors, and other high-status people often have large desks not out of practical necessity but to distance themselves from visitors and to suggest an authority of office. Such functionaries usually also have couches and less formal seating arrangements (and hidden liquor cabinets), which can set a tone of lesser formality upon occasion and convey this informality by distance and setting.

Among most Middle Easterners, by contrast, normal conversational distance is 2 to 3 feet, a proximity at which many Americans begin to feel uncom-

FIGURE 9-1. Men of the "lower classes" (Lane's designation). Older ethnographic accounts such as Lane's remain valuable for understanding changing patterns of greetings and ideas of rank. [From Edward William Lane, *An Account of the Manners and Customs of the Modern Egyptians* (London: John Murray, Publishers, Ltd., 1860), p. 33.]

fortable. Male friends or even relative strangers on good terms in the Middle East and Mediterranean will frequently hold hands or touch during conversation, without conveying the sexual intimacy that such gestures are often thought to convey in American contexts. Similarly, notions of time and how long a person can be kept waiting have cultural registers capable of subtle reading and orderly interpretation. Successful negotiators in international contexts develop a flair for comprehending such background understandings; they may not possess the ability to articulate such assumptions, as is necessary for the anthropological analysis of them, but they nonetheless acquire a practical mastery and understanding of the delightfully complex problem of how to intermingle these contrasting codes in transnational settings.[6]

A study in the late 1950s of the marsh dwellers of southern Iraq by Shākir Muṣṭafa Salīm, a distinguished Iraqi anthropologist, suggests how manners and etiquette are closely related to social ranking and the concept of person.[7] Although a few wealthy men have guest houses, most are collective ones maintained by lineages (see Figure 9-2). Most male social life centers on these guest

[6] These attitudes toward the practical use of time and space are discussed by Edward T. Hall, *The Silent Language* (New York: Doubleday, 1959).

[7] S. M. Salim, *Marsh Dwellers of the Euphrates Delta*, L.S.E. Monographs on Social Anthropology 23 (London: Athlone Press, 1962), pp. 72–80.

FIGURE 9-2. Tribal guest house (*muḍīf*), southern Iraq. [From S. M. Salim, *Marsh Dwellers of the Euphrates Delta* (London: Athlone Press, 1962), plate 5A. Used by permission of the London School of Economics.]

houses. Participants in guest house activity are expected to be formally dressed, with their head rope and outer cloak. One defers to people of higher status, and jokes and unnecessary laughter must be avoided in their presence. Even in the case of anger and major quarrels, those present are expected to speak clearly and calmly. Salīm recounts that one day the agitated father of two quarreling sons ran into the headman of his lineage in the guest house and asked him to intervene. The father had entered with such haste that he forgot his head rope and was unable to speak clearly. The headman listened, then criticized the father for speaking in a confused way, adding insultingly, "I thought one of your old wives had run away with a lover." The underlying assumption is that in almost all social situations a respectable man is expected to show reason and self-control.[8]

It is unlikely that many guest houses (*muḍīf*-s) remain among the remaining marsh dwellers in southern Iraq (see Figure 9-2). For "security" reasons, Saḍḍām Husayn's government has been draining the marshes and dispersing the largely Shī'ī population. However, this pattern of etiquette in Iraq, as elsewhere in the Gulf, also clearly reveals relative social ranking.[9]

[8] Ibid., p. 77.

[9] Similar patterns prevail among women. See Anthony Shay, "*Bazi-ha-ye Nameyeshi*: Iranian Women's Theatrical Plays," *Dance Research Journal* 27 no. 2 (Fall 1995), 16–24. For elsewhere, see Christine Eickelman, *Women and Community in Oman* (New York: New York University Press, 1984); and Anne Meneley, *Tournaments of Value: Sociability and Hierarchy in a Yemeni Town* (Toronto: University of Toronto Press, 1996).

FIGURE 9-3. A reception following the opening of a Quranic school near Nizwā, Sultanate of Oman, 1978. Guest house etiquette offers a key index of notions of person and value. [Courtesy of the author.]

Each person sits in the place corresponding to his social rank. High-status people, such as descendants of the Prophet Muḥammad, sit in places set off by carpets and pillows. The senior elder or owner of a guest house shows his respect to an esteemed visitor or stranger by leading him to his proper place or ordering the preparation of tea as well as the usual coffee. When a man of higher status enters a guest house, those assembled show respect by rising to their feet. For those of lesser status, they merely make the gesture of rising. Each man greets the newcomer, who responds separately to each greeting, rising or making as if to rise as each case merits. Overestimating a person's social status makes a newcomer look ridiculous; underestimating it is insulting. The whole procedure can be quite complicated, and adult Iraqi males are expected to have mastered these complexities. The search for "information" is hence an essential prerequisite for effective social comportment. Questions of rank are not explicitly discussed, but their accurate perception forms a necessary component of social life. If, because of long absence, a man is uncertain as to his relative rank, he will sit at a lower-ranking place and wait for someone to correct him.

IRAN

Iranian linguistic conventions and social forms suggest the "basic schemas," as one linguistic anthropologist has called them, with which Iranians interpret and engage in social action. The "architecture" of Iranian verbal interaction indicates a pervasive distinction between the "external" (*zaher*), public aspects of social action and speech and an "inner" (*baten*) core of integrity and piety revealed only to one's family and trusted intimates. In the "external" social world, characterized by insecurity and uncertainty, the cultural ideal is the clever dissimulator (*zerangī*), the shrewd and cynical manipulator capable of maintaining a "proper public face" and holding "true" feelings in check to protect the "inner" self. This inner self is revealed only to a narrow circle of trusted family and intimates, and ideally is pure, constant, and spiritual.[10] This basic distinction shows up in domestic architecture and in the use of domestic space, where a separate room or part of a room is set aside for public receptions and visiting, while another part of the house is reserved for family intimacy.

In collective action, William Beeman provides an example of a village in which there was ambiguity, at least for outsiders, as to who was the village headman. One person was recognized by outside administrators, but another was recognized by the villagers themselves. "Far from reflecting manifest uncertainty, the eventual state of affairs demonstrated the flexibility with which villagers were able to deal with the demands of different situations and value systems. Only an outside observer would try to fix on any one statement about the [headman] as the actual state of affairs."[11]

A promising approach to the study of worldview in complex societies is to analyze the relation between conventions of social and linguistic etiquette and social structure. This approach is particularly appropriate for Iran, where the conventions of etiquette (*ta'āruf*) permeate the representation of self. In English, *etiquette* connotes prescribed routine, an unwritten code of honor, and a set of conventions to maintain the dignity of people or professions. In Iran, the notion

[10] The most thorough account of this distinction is William O. Beeman, *Language, Status, and Power in Iran* (Bloomington and London: Indiana University Press, 1986), pp. 10–21. Beeman's book also marks a shift in anthropological linguistics away from a narrow concern with narrow technical issues to the broader goal of understanding "how language works in affecting the course of human events for individuals and larger groupings in human society" (p. 19). For the distinction applied to the psychiatric domain, see Byron J. Good, Mary-Jo DelVecchio Good, and Robert Moradi, "The Interpretation of Iranian Depressive Illness and Dysphoric Affect," in *Culture and Depression: Studies in the Anthropology and Cross-Cultural Psychiatry of Affect and Disorder*, ed. Arthur Kleinman and Byron Good (Berkeley and Los Angeles: University of California Press, 1985), pp. 369–428; and Karen L. Pliskin, *Silent Boundaries: Cultural Constraints on Sickness and Diagnosis of Iranians in Israel* (New Haven, CT: Yale University Press, 1987). For a review of earlier studies of Iranian "national character," see Ali Banuazizi, "Iranian 'National Character': A Critique of Some Western Perspectives," in *Psychological Dimensions of Near Eastern Studies*, ed. L. Carl Brown and Norman Itzkowitz (Princeton, NJ: Darwin Press, 1977), pp. 210–39.

[11] Beeman, *Language*, pp. 11, 24.

entails a discipline of the inner self in the service of the public self. Indeed, notions of self and status are relative to individuals and situations. Beeman observes, "Every time tea is offered to a group, every time several persons wish to proceed through one door, every time friends meet on the street . . . the constant unceasing ritualization of the assessment of climate of relative superiority and inferiority occurs and recurs. . . . Rights and obligations shift constantly with changes in one's social environment, mak[ing] these constant social gestures important tools in everyday social relations."[12] Only in the most superficial manner can etiquette be interpreted as insincerity or as the use of empty forms. Knowing how to employ *ta'āruf* (and when to disregard it) is linked to the possession of those human refinements, such as reason, that separate humans from nonhumans. Those unable to apply this code of conduct properly are thought to be "childlike," regardless of age and not in possession of their senses. Rudeness, as Beeman argues, conveys not only social inappropriateness but a lack of honor and human features.[13] Although Iranian civility possesses forms different from those of other Middle Eastern countries, the elaborate codes of hospitality found throughout the Arabian peninsula, North Africa, and elsewhere can be interpreted similarly.[14] Etiquette and hospitality can serve to establish, through implicit negotiations, relative rank and the rights and obligations associated with it.

For Beeman, the manipulation of style in language and etiquette is the means by which individuals seek to define ambiguous cultural contexts to their own advantage. In almost every case it involves the concealment of true (or "inner") feelings or opinions. Such control is regarded as a highly positive public virtue. Beeman further argues that a careful analysis of the use of *ta'āruf* indicates the shared notion of Iranians that the social order is inegalitarian and without reference to fixed rank or stratification. The control and formal reserve of *ta'āruf* enable people to avoid committing themselves to one course of action or set of assumptions concerning social ranking that might prove difficult to maintain should the relative position of people subsequently shift.

[12] Ibid., p. 58.

[13] Ibid., p. 85.

[14] A particularly complex example of linguistic conventions is provided by "straight" (*dugri*) speech among native-born Israelis of European descent, or *sabra*-s. The term comes from the Arabic *dughrī* but carries different contextual implications. Tamar Katriel, *Talking Straight: Dugri Speech in Israeli Sabra Culture*, Studies in the Social and Cultural Foundations of Language (Cambridge: Cambridge University Press, 1986), pp. 11–12, writes: "In Hebrew, *dugri* speech is contrasted to lack of sincerity, hypocrisy, talking behind one's back, or at times diplomacy. In Arabic, speaking the *dugri* stands opposed to concealment in an attempt to mislead or in the service of [smoothness in interpersonal relations]. . . . What stands in the way of truth speaking in the Hebrew *dugri* mode is sensitivity to face concerns [in the sense of "saving face"], interpreted as a lack of courage and integrity. What stands in the way of truth speaking in the Arabic *dugri* mode is the high value placed on smoothness in interpersonal encounters." Of course, these differences derive in part from contrasting notions of self among speakers of Arabic and Hebrew, their close proximity to one another in Israel and Palestine notwithstanding. For an argument concerning how sustained interaction (in this case in a sports team) can lead to imputing rationality to "other" groups across cultural divides, see Dan Rabinowitz, "Trust and the Attribution of Rationality: Inverted Roles Amongst Palestinian Arabs and Jews in Israel," *Man* (N.S.) 27, no. 3 (September 1992), 517–37.

James Bill has described how such conventions are related to political forms.[15] Writing prior to the Shah's abdication in 1979, he argues that in spite of the existence of formal political organization in Iran, notably the state apparatus, the exercise of political power is played out primarily within networks of informal factions, cliques, coteries, and ad hoc collectivities. These networks of interlocking personal coteries are called *dawra*-s. Each *dawra*—the word literally means "circle"—is an informal group of individuals who meet periodically, usually rotating the place of meeting among its members. These circles may be formed around any of a number of ties: professional, familial, religious, intellectual, political, or economic. This form of consociation has deep historical roots. Sufi mystics and darvishes, for instance, formed *dawra*-s with their disciples, and many of the groups regularly meet in coffeehouses. Bill says there are perhaps 2000 of them in Tehran alone. Among merchants and craftsmen in the bazaar, membership in *dawra*-s often partially overlaps with that of guild.

One reason for the pervasiveness of such informal organizations is the suppression of formal ones by the prerevolutionary Iranian state and, to all appearances, the postrevolutionary one as well. Even when formal political parties exist, most Iranians assume that real access to authority is through informal channels. The existence of personal ties is considered more important than ideological preferences. *Dawra*-s fragment and re-form as the interests of their members change, and most individuals belong to a number of these circles.

From the intimate circles around the Shah in the past and the informal coteries that surround Iran's present leaders to the level of informal village politics, the style of the *dawra* permeates Iranian political life. If a governor visits a village, villagers presume, with reason, that a request to his driver, secretary, guard, or even his guests constitutes an effective intervention. Iranians expend a great deal of energy in determining how best to approach people for a given request. Similarly, in the last days of the Shah, members of the foreign press corps were surprised to find announcements of the Shah's intentions made by persons with no formal capacity but who, in retrospect, were the most reliable sources as to what was going on. Successive postrevolutionary governments have shown a similar lack of clear lines of organization.

The *dawra* makes sense in a setting where the cultural assumption is that "real" power does not flow from institution to institution, as suggested by the formal apparatus of government, but from person to person and from groups of which effectively manage to impose their authority. The common force that unites the membership of *dawra*-s is a personal one; relationships that are not face-to-face and created out of multiple obligations are not as trusted. Because each person belongs to a multitude of *dawra*-s, information is rapidly passed among them.

[15] James A. Bill, "The Plasticity of Informal Politics: The Case of Iran," *Middle East Journal* 27, no. 2 (Spring 1973), 131–51.

The underlying conception of asymmetrical interpersonal relationship means that Iranians tend to assume that their survival and success depend on their ability to cultivate the right personal contacts and to use those contacts to achieve their goals. That attitude in itself does not sharply distinguish Iranians from Americans. Informal "circles," "crowds," and "cliques" exist in every society and are always deeply involved in political ties and administrative functioning. The real difference rests in the degree to which such perceptions and social forms in societies such as Iran are taken to be normative and just. "Circles" are culturally recognized or even stressed in Iranian social situations and also given sense and legitimacy through connection to, and meaningful association with, fundamental ideas about "natural" social relationships. To draw a parallel between two Middle Eastern contexts, the Iranian term *nazdīk*, which means "nearness" and implies reliable close acquaintances, kin, or friends, has much the same contextual meaning as the North African notion of *closeness*, introduced earlier in this book.

Another point made by Bill is that the Iranian assumption of the instability of social hierarchies is easily borne out in practice. In Iran's recent past, gardeners, water carriers, stableboys, the children of drivers, and military conscripts have all had excellent opportunities for advancement, provided they performed their services close to men of power. But there are just as many opportunities for decline, and the scramble for personal power takes these shifts into account. Bill recounts an anecdote of the prominent Iranian who clipped obituaries (which contain lists of who attended funerals) from all the daily newspapers to fill in, and change when necessary, a large chart he used to figure out the intricate links between the living. He used the chart to figure out the appropriate people to contact among the vast chains of linked interpersonal obligations in order to get things done.[16] Important families and people at all levels of Iranian society try to spread their members over a number of key positions because of the assumption that all formal offices and ranks are unstable.

In such a social order, the seeming pleasantries of *ta'āruf* acquire more significance. *Ta'āruf* is a means of avoiding direct, decisive encounters in a political and social world perceived as inherently unstable. Pleasantries, courtesies, politeness, and flattery abound at every level of social encounter, just as do uncertainty and doubt. Western-style organizational practices and seemingly unambiguous management messages may appear to operate by fundamentally similar rules in the Iranian context, but in practice they add another level of ambiguity to an already complex message system.[17] This applies to the military as well. A recent study of the Iranian military notes that "the strength and practical day-to-day influence of many high-ranking intelligence officials assigned to the professional military do not seem to derive from their positions. Instead, their power appears to correspond directly to the degree of access they have—

[16] Ibid., 138. See also Beeman, *Language*, pp. 36–48.

[17] Ibid., pp. 34–35.

through kinship or other ties—to leading clerics."[18] Similar extraorganizational connections were important in the military under the Shah (although in that era ties with the clergy were far from beneficial). *Ta'āruf* buffers opposing views, loosens lines of tension, and enables individuals to keep their options open to protect themselves against sudden shifts in political currents.

MOROCCO: GOD'S WILL, REASON, AND OBLIGATION

In the 1960s and early 1970s, several anthropologists used their ethnographic studies of Morocco as a basis for exploring complementary aspects of worldview and culture. Most of the resulting publications also address wider issues, so they form a useful point of departure for discussing the theoretical significance of ideas of worldview and their importance to the study of the Middle East.

A brief analysis of the relevant sections of *Moroccan Islam* suggests some of the decisions facing an anthropologist in any discussion of worldview. In that study, I sought to indicate the implicit set of cultural assumptions through which Moroccans make sense of the local interpretations of Islam and of transformations in these interpretations, especially over the last century. I worked with the initial assumption, shared in part with the participants in the study of Sefrou and its region—Clifford Geertz, Hildred Geertz, Lawrence Rosen, and Paul Rabinow—that Morocco's social structure was best conceived with *persons* as its fundamental unit, rather than their attributes or status as members of groups.[19] Moreover, persons are not arranged in layerlike strata or classes but are linked in dyadic bonds of subordination and domination that characteristically are dissolved and re-formed. The relatively stable element in this type of social structure is not the patterns that actual social relations form but the culturally accepted *means* by which people contract and maintain bonds and obligations with one another.

[18] Nicola B. Schahgaldian, *The Iranian Military under the Islamic Republic*, Report R-3473-USDP (Santa Monica, CA: Rand, 1987), p. 34.

[19] Monographs or book-length essays elaborating such notions or reacting to them include Clifford Geertz, *Islam Observed* (New Haven, CT, and London: Yale University Press, 1968); Clifford Geertz, Hildred Geertz, and Lawrence Rosen, *Meaning and Order in Moroccan Society: Three Essays in Cultural Analysis* (New York: Cambridge University Press, 1979); Dale F. Eickelman, *Moroccan Islam: Tradition and Society in a Pilgrimage Center*, Modern Middle East Series 1 (Austin and London: University of Texas Press, 1976); Paul Rabinow, *Symbolic Domination: Cultural Form and Historical Change in Morocco* (Chicago and London: University of Chicago Press, 1975), and *Reflections on Fieldwork in Morocco* (Berkeley and Los Angeles: University of California Press, 1977); John Waterbury, *North for the Trade: The Life and Times of a Berber Merchant* (Berkeley and Los Angeles: University of California Press, 1972); Kenneth L. Brown, *People of Salé: Tradition and Change in a Moroccan City, 1830–1930* (Cambridge, MA: Harvard University Press, 1976); Vincent Crapanzano, *Tuhami: Portrait of a Moroccan* (Chicago and London: University of Chicago Press, 1980); Kevin Dwyer, *Moroccan Dialogues: Anthropology in Question* (Prospect Heights, IL: Waveland Press, 1987 [1982]); Lawrence Rosen, *Bargaining for Reality: The Construction of Social Relations in a Muslim Community* (Chicago and London: University of Chicago Press, 1984); and Henry Munson, Jr., *The House of Si Abd Allah* (New Haven, CT, and London: Yale University Press, 1984).

How are such implicit notions of the social order made to appear natural and taken for granted? In a chapter entitled "Impermanence and Inequality: The Common-Sense Understanding of the Social Order," I sought to delineate five of the key concepts through which Moroccans comprehend social experience. These five concepts are God's will (*qudrat Allāh*), reason (*'qāl*), propriety (*ḥshūmīya*), obligation (*ḥaqq*), and compulsion (*'ār*).[20] The emphasis given to these five concepts is, admittedly, arbitrary in the sense that any description of worldview is largely shaped by the range of social action that it attempts to render meaningful. Had my study concerned notions of sexuality rather than religious ideologies, for example, emphasis would have been placed on Moroccan concepts that in my account were treated only in a subordinate fashion.

There is a problem of boundaries to these concepts, in two senses. In the first sense, I deliberately used the term *Moroccan* rather than the name of the particular locale in which I worked, for my experience in research elsewhere in Morocco (and in trying out my formulations on interested Moroccans) suggested that with regional nuances, the same ideas applied elsewhere and in all likelihood did not stop abruptly at the country's frontiers. Indeed, many of the basic Moroccan assumptions concerning the social world are expressed in the form of Islamic ideas that are hardly unique to Morocco or to North Africa.

In the second sense of boundary, the concepts that make up a worldview are not in fixed relation to one another. They are maintained insofar as they are actualized by individuals and meaningfully explain and render coherent action in the social world. When they cease to do so, they shift in emphasis. This flexibility accounts for their ability to accommodate and accounts for major shifts in the loci of economic and political power. Notions such as "God's will" and "reason," for instance, have rich historical layers of meaning and are used elsewhere in the Muslim world. Both terms occur in the Quran and have been the subject of an interesting study of the worldview of seventh-century Arabs, as well as an account of changing perceptions of the world in northern Sumatra.[21] The occurrence of these terms in Morocco is not unique, but they appear in a different semantic field, although in ordinary contexts most Moroccans never consider the possibility that these notions could be understood in any way but their own. The fact that these implicit notions are tacitly construed by Moroccans as Islamic as well as human universals makes the resulting vision of the world all the more reasonable and compelling to them.

Let me briefly sketch how these key notions articulate with each other. *God's will* is a basic notion for Moroccans. Any expression of future actions or events is almost inevitably prefaced by saying "if God wills" (*in shā' Allāh*),

[20] The discussion of these notions is adapted from Eickelman, *Moroccan Islam*, pp. 123–54. Copyright © 1976 by the University of Texas Press. All rights reserved.

[21] Toshihiko Izutsu, *God and Man in the Koran* (Tokyo: Keio Institute of Cultural and Linguistic Studies, 1964); and James Siegal, *The Rope of God* (Berkeley and Los Angeles: University of California Press, 1969). On the notion of "reason" among Iranian women, see Azam Torab, "Piety as Gendered Agency: A Study of *Jaleseh* Ritual Discourse in an Urban Neighbourhood in Iran," *Journal of the Royal Anthropological Institute* 2, no. 2 (June 1996), 241–44.

which is also tied to the notion of "that which is written" (*maktūb*). French colonial ethnography glossed this notion as "Islamic fatalism," suggesting a Moroccan passivity and resignation toward the events of this world. This interpretation was congruent with the colonizing power's image of Moroccans but is almost exactly opposite the way in which Moroccans use the term. Let us consider the notions of social structure described earlier.

For Moroccans, the inequality of men in this world is so matter of fact as not to be a matter of speculation. The actual state of affairs in this world at any moment is a manifestation of God's will; being inevitable, it cannot be questioned. An understanding of one's present social situation in terms of God's will legitimizes the momentary—and ephemeral—distribution of social honor as the God-given state of affairs. Men are free to take the world as it is and to determine action on the basis of their empirical observations. God's will attenuates speculation on why particular projects succeed or fail and blocks metaphysical speculation on the fate of the individual in this world. The wide-awake, common-sense person is much more concerned with adjusting to circumstances as they arise than with considering how things might have been or should be. Provisionality, the acceptance of God's will, thus focuses attention on assessing exact differentials of wealth, success, power, and social honor among particular men as a prelude to effective, specific social action, not upon speculation over the general order of the world.

A corollary to this notion is that the responsibility of people for one another is limited. There are abstract, normative obligations incumbent upon each Muslim, but how the obligations that arise from particular ties are valued varies significantly. Here is how one educated Moroccan explained the limits of one person's responsibility toward another:

> God created differences among people. . . . Let people do as they want. God distinguishes between them. A Muslim's duty is just to show people the path to those who wish to be with God, and that is that. Either they take it or they leave it. The Prophets allow them the choice. There is paradise and there is hell, and God will select who goes to each.[22]

Linked to the notion of God's will is that of *reason*, a notion introduced in the discussion of sexuality in Chapter 8. In Morocco and elsewhere in the Muslim world, the concept of reason is more explicitly tied to social context than most Western uses of the term. Reason in the Moroccan context is primarily the capacity to discern the meanings of the actions of other people and, on the basis of such perceptions, to engage in effective social action. Reason signifies adroitness or cleverness (without the pejorative English connotations of these terms) more than a capacity for dealing with abstract rational phenomena. Its possession assumes a capacity to perceive the empirical ties between people and to adapt them to one's own interests, within the shared code of conduct of society. Reason enables a person to perceive what will pass as acceptable and approved

[22] Cited in Eickelman, *Moroccan Islam*, p. 128.

conduct in the management of social obligations to kinsmen, neighbors, merchants, clients, people with influence, and people without.

The word for reason, *'qāl*, comes from an Arabic root that also means "confinement" or "control." It implies an ability of people to dominate their passions and to act as Muslims. Children are said not to possess reason because they do not yet know the Islamic law and code of conduct. Although Moroccans are highly affectionate toward their children, they say that at birth children are like animals, because they only gradually acquire the code of conduct and the ability to abide by it that distinguishes them from animals. As children begin to participate in the fast of Ramaḍān and to assume adult patterns of comportment, they are considered to have acquired reason.

Similarly, as was pointed out in Chapter 8, reason is popularly considered to be more fully developed in men than in women. This is not considered to be due entirely to any innate masculine capacity but to the fact that women's activities are confined primarily to the household and its immediate milieu. Hence a woman's ability to engage in a wide range of social relations and to have full control over expression of her passions is considered less than that of a man.[23] Some women are attributed a full capacity for reason, usually when high social class, education, or other circumstances enable them to participate effectively in the wider social world. One Moroccan explained the general difference between the sexes as follows:

> A man will think. He sees a quarrel leading to [court]; he knows that the other man has more "pull" with the [court] than he does. He knows how to deal with people bigger and weaker than he is. A woman is light-headed. She doesn't know how to do these things. If she goes to the [government offices], who pays attention to her? Better that she stay at home, where she can teach her daughters to cook and sew. They don't know Islam like men do; they even have tricks to avoid fasting.[24]

In the same way that women are considered deficient in reason, townsmen often claim that tribesmen are deficient because of their relative lack of skill in dealing with the government and merchants.

The notion of reason is clearly linked to the Islamic code of conduct in the complex symbolism associated with Ramaḍān, the month of fasting. The ability of Muslims to follow the arbitrary pattern of the fast and to refrain (among other restrictions on appetites) from food and drink from dawn to dusk for one month each year is taken as a key metaphor by which men can discipline their desires in accordance with the arbitrary code of conduct laid down by God. People's capacity to follow the divine model reaffirms that they are not bound by their passions to live in a totally anarchic world. The five ritual daily prayers also symbolize the divine template for conduct, but Ramaḍān is recognized as a more intensive, sustained discipline of human nature and as an opportunity for the collective exercise of self-control that signals the possession of reason.

[23] See also Torab, "Piety," 244.

[24] Ibid., p. 133.

FIGURE 9-4. Market street, Muṭraḥ, Sultanate of Oman. "The flow of words and the flow of values are not two things; they are two aspects of the same thing."—Clifford Geertz, "Suq: The Bazaar Economy in Sefrou," in Clifford Geertz, Hildred Geertz, and Lawrence Rosen, *Meaning and Order in Moroccan Society* (New York: Cambridge University Press, 1979), p. 199. [Photograph courtesy of the author.]

Obligation (*ḥaqq*) fits into the same pattern of comprehension of the social world. Men cannot control God's allocation of success and prestige, but they can render the actions of others more predictable by contracting and maintaining bonds of obligation. In the Moroccan context, all exchanges, invitations to meals, services as intermediaries, and even offers of rides in a car are seen as obligations that must be reciprocated. Some obligations are prescribed by Islamic law and "the way things are done," such as certain obligations toward kinsmen and communal religious ties. These obligations can be fulfilled within a wide latitude of acceptable conduct. Even exchanges of greetings, with their complex code of gestures and manners, impose obligations, because they publicly assert what one person would like the other, and observers, to think regarding their relations.

If a person repeatedly asks for a service to be rendered but is incapable of reciprocating, then he falls into a client relationship with the other. The dominant partner in the relationship is said to hold an "obligation" (*ḥaqq 'lā*) or "word" (*kalma*) over the other. The complex web of personally contracted bonds of obligation is always asymmetrical, just as all relationships impose obligations of calculable intensity. Exchanges of obligations can be finely tuned. There is a carefully nuanced vocabulary for the discussion of gradations in them that depends on a wide range of factors, such as education, wealth, kinship ties, and networks of obligations held or thought to be held over others.

In general, the reasonable individual strives for flexibility in relations in which he is under obligation to others, while at the same time fixing as firmly as possible relations in which he holds obligations "over" others. Because by God's will, the social world is viewed as in constant flux, an individual strives to be as free as possible to change the weight of obligations within his personal network, yet to remain within the bounds of propriety (*ḥshūmīya*) or acceptable social conduct.

Compulsion (*'ār*), the fifth of the concepts that I sketched in *Moroccan Islam*, is a special sort of impossible obligation that provides culturally accepted means of mending serious breaks in the web of obligations that bind people together. Essentially, it involves such a profound public effacement of the person or group seeking to oblige another to act in a certain way or to restore ordinary social relations that refusal risks divine punishment and severe social disapproval.

Taken as a group, all five concepts are logically articulated with one another and form a major part of the backdrop against which social relationships are elaborated. There is nothing fixed about these assumptions; some people question them some of the time, but usually they are accepted as an adequate and necessary base for daily social conduct and the assessment of the actions of others. These interrelated notions cannot be extended to cover other societies in the Middle East, although, as previously mentioned, some of the concepts figure elsewhere in modified form and in different cultural contexts. Likewise, the content of these terms, and equivalent ones elsewhere in the Middle East, is far from unchanging. By clinging to earlier understandings of some of these key terms, people can sometimes paint themselves into corners, as was the case with the "Learned Families" of southern Lebanon described by Peters (see Chapter 3).

NORTH AFRICANS IN ISRAEL: CONTINUITY AND CHANGE

The reanalysis of a monograph on North African Jewish immigrants in Israel, Moshe Shokeid's *The Dual Heritage*,[25] suggests some of the means by which basic shared assumptions concerning the social world become modified and how at other times they persist, even in substantially altered political and economic circumstances. As discussed in Chapter 8, Israeli immigration policy in

[25] Moshe Shokeid, *The Dual Heritage: Immigrants from the Atlas Mountains in an Israeli Village*, augmented edition (New Brunswick, NJ, and Oxford: Transaction Books, 1985 [1971]). "Augmentation" in this instance means a helpful introductory essay that reviews scholarly responses to the monograph's initial publication as well as later developments. The monograph is complemented by Shokeid's contributions to Shlomo Deshen and Moshe Shokeid, *The Predicament of Homecoming: Cultural and Social Life of North African Immigrants in Israel*, Symbol, Myth, and Ritual (Ithaca, NY, and London: Cornell University Press, 1974). See also Shokeid's *Children of Circumstances: Israeli Emigrants in New York* (Ithaca, NY, and London: Cornell University Press, 1988); and Harvey E. Goldberg, *Cave Dwellers and Citrus Growers: A Jewish Community in Libya and Israel* (Cambridge: Cambridge University Press, 1972).

many cases sought to "transplant" entire communities of North African Jews during the 1950s and 1960s, so that villages in North Africa were reconstituted in Israel and had to undergo major social and economic disruption.

Shokeid's later work concerned changing religious values, but *The Dual Heritage* is concerned explicitly with social change. Hence some background discussion is necessary to adapt his study to the discussion of worldview. Shokeid uses the sociological notion of *reference situation*, a complex of values appropriate to a past (or different) situation applied to a novel context. The reference situation for the residents of the Israeli immigrant community he studied was their former village of some 350 persons located in Morocco's High Atlas Mountains to the east of Marrakesh. To specify the nature of the reference situation, Shokeid tried to reconstruct the social organization of the community as it once existed.[26]

The reanalysis of Shokeid's monograph is especially interesting for the similarities it reveals in shared notions of society between North African Muslim and Jewish communities. The Jewish community studied by Shokeid had a myth of how they came to be settled in the High Atlas. He speculates that a quarrel may have led to the splitting apart in the nineteenth century of an earlier village, an event recalled by the villagers in mythical form: A leading rabbi warned the villagers' ancestors not to emigrate to the new location until a fountain was discovered under a tree near the site where they later constructed their synagogue. A similar type of settlement myth is told by Muslims in various parts of Morocco to account for the location of their villages.[27]

This particular North African Jewish village was surrounded by villages of Berber-speaking Muslims, and the social structure of the Jewish community appears to have significantly resembled that of its Muslim neighbors. Shokeid acknowledges that the memories of the past of the villagers now in Israel are idealized, so that their recollection of "permanent insecurity" is a generalized perception without necessary historical accuracy. However, the region was unquestionably insecure for both Muslims and Jews at the time of French entry into the area, and later, at the announcement in late 1955 of Morocco's imminent independence, there was a threat of renewed disorder that contributed to the departure of most of the community for Israel in 1956.[28]

[26] A useful ethnographic account exists in French for a nearby Jewish community in the early 1950s, prior to massive emigration. See Pierre Flamand, *Un méllah en pays berbère: Demnate*, Institut des Hautes-Études Marocaines, Notes et Documents 10 (Paris: Librairie Générale de Droit et de Jurisprudence, 1952). A more contemporary social history of a Jewish community in an urban setting is Shlomo Deshen, *The Mellah Society: Jewish Community Life in Sherifian Morocco* (Chicago: University of Chicago Press, 1989). See Mohamed Kenbib, *Juifs et musulmans au Maroc, 1859–1948: Contribution à l'histoire des relations inter-communautaires en terre d'Islam* [Jews and Muslims in Morocco, 1859–1948: Contribution to the Study of Intercommunal Relations in an Islamic Land], Publications of the Faculty of Arts and Sciences, Rabat (Rabat: Mohammed V University, 1994), for a comprehensive social history of Moroccan Jewish society.

[27] Shokeid, *Dual Heritage*, p. 17; for a parallel Muslim settlement myth, see Eickelman, *Moroccan Islam*, pp. 163–68.

[28] Shokeid, *Dual Heritage*, p. 22.

Shokeid's account of the internal differentiation of the community indicates that both in the High Atlas Mountains and later in Israel it was divided into patronymic groupings or agnatic clusters, each claiming descent from a common male ancestor, a pattern also common to rural and urban Muslims in Morocco.[29] In Morocco these groupings were stratified, with the one possessing the most influential political and economic contacts on the top, skilled itinerant craftsmen next, and the unskilled workers at the bottom.

On arriving in Israel, the settlers were assigned to a settlement called Yashuv, organized by one of Israel's leading socialist parties. The first settlement did not succeed. Representatives of several of Israel's religious parties told the Moroccan settlers that their sponsors were antireligious, would compel their daughters to serve in the army, where they would lose their virtue, and would not allow their sons to study the Torah. There were also scandals concerning the allocation of wage labor that resulted in demonstrations and some violence. In 1957 many of the settlers moved to Romema, another settlement in the Negev, the principal locus of Shokeid's field study.[30]

According to Shokeid, the villagers from the three principal patronymic groupings saw themselves as a single cooperating entity upon their arrival in the Negev, but their cooperation collapsed when they began to dispute over the allocation of leadership positions. He argues that the new situation of the Negev was more conducive to egalitarian relations. By 1958–1959, Israeli settlement officials thought of writing off Romema as a failure and moving some of the villagers, but by then it was difficult to shift immigrants to new locations.

In reading Shokeid's intricate description of the political maneuvers for land allocations and political office in Romema, I was struck by the similarity of his account to others describing contemporary local politics in Morocco.[31] There the principal alliances were not necessarily along the lines of patronymic groups but along the lines of any available kinship or other form of relationship that could be used as the basis for concerted action.[32] Shokeid acknowledges that kinship relationships in themselves did not necessarily induce cooperation. Only when there were other social links or economic factors or common economic interests did cooperation actually occur.

Perhaps the best indication of the villagers' notion of community is their conception of the committee that was organized to run their agricultural colony (*moshav*). The immigrants' use of Hebrew was, admittedly, imperfect, but the errors appear to have accurately reflected their conceptions. Shokeid explains that the proper way in Hebrew to refer to a member of the *moshav* governing committee was to call him *havier va'ad*, "a member of the committee." The com-

[29] Ibid., pp. 23–28. His use of *patronymic grouping* is essentially equivalent to the term *patronymic association* used in Chapter 7 of this book.

[30] Ibid., pp. 34–47.

[31] Ibid., pp. 62–83; Rosen, *Bargaining*, pp. 99–111; Dale F. Eickelman, "Royal Authority and Religious Legitimacy: Morocco's Elections, 1960–1984," in *The Frailty of Authority*, ed. Myron J. Aronoff, Political Anthropology 5 (New Brunswick, NJ, and Oxford: Transaction Books, 1986), pp. 181–205.

[32] Shokeid, *Dual Heritage*, p. 71.

mittee itself was *va'ad*. But the villagers consistently referred to this committee as *va'adim*, "committees," and to each committee member as *va'ad*, "a committee." The implication of this linguistic fact and of other documentation introduced by Shokeid was that each committee member in himself represented a committee. Shokeid's conclusion is that each committee member, instead of drawing his status from the fact that he belonged to the committee, contributed *his* status to the committee. He documents this interpretation through a detailed analysis of how the committee handled the allocation of water during a shortage.[33] The situation in Romema is congruent with the Moroccan notion of social structure, where the basic components of social structure are persons rather than groups and where the stable cultural element is the means by which people secure bonds with each other.[34]

Let me suggest a reinterpretation of Shokeid's analytic framework, made possible by the quality of his ethnographic documentation. Shokeid concentrates on idealized patterns of social interaction and tends in *The Dual Heritage* not to analyze underlying cultural values. Although he occasionally refers to past conflict and strife, he gives no elaborate examples of them. By juxtaposing an idealized past to a present in which the lines of conflict do not follow normative statements concerning the unity of patronymic groups, he concludes that the immigrants suffered a "breakdown" of their prior community.[35] I would argue that Shokeid's account demonstrates a marked continuity of values and assumptions concerning interpersonal obligations, an interpretation supported by his passing remark in the conclusion that most Romemites were "fairly modern" in their economic comportment (and adaptation to political life in Israel), despite the fact that "on the whole, their value system hardly changed" and that the "new" forms of behavior were legitimized "within the traditional set of norms."[36]

VEILED SENTIMENTS: MULTIPLE IDEOLOGIES

Lila Abu-Lughod's study of honor and sentiment among a small group of settled bedouin pastoralists, the Awlād 'Alī in Egypt's western desert, offers insight into complementary forms of discourse prevailing within a given

[33] Ibid., pp. 118–29, 143–47.

[34] See also Emanuel Marx, *The Social Context of Violent Behaviour: A Social Anthropological Study in an Israeli Immigrant Town* (London and Boston: Routledge & Kegan Paul, 1976), pp. 63–74. What Marx calls "appealing violence" shares significant parallels with the Moroccan notion of *compulsion*. Also see Alex Weingrod, *The Saint of Beersheba*, SUNY Series in Israeli Studies (Albany: State University of New York Press, 1990).

[35] Shokeid, *Dual Heritage*, p. 62. For a reinterpretation, see Shokeid's "The Impact of Migration on the Moroccan Jewish Family in Israel," in *The Jewish Family: Myths and Reality*, ed. Steven M. Cohen and Paula E. Hyman (New York and London: Holmes & Meier, 1986), pp. 82–96. Other "reconstructions" with which Shokeid's can be compared include Shlomo Deshen, "Women in the Jewish Family in Pre-Colonial Morocco," *Anthropological Quarterly* 56, no. 3 (July 1983), 134–44, and Harvey E. Goldberg, "Jewish Life in Muslim Tripoli in the Late Qaramanli Period," *Urban Anthropology* 13 (1984), 65–90.

[36] Shokeid, *Dual Heritage*, p. 230.

society.[37] In discussing the work of the Tappers (see Chapter 8), we have already seen how an understanding of the complementary beliefs and practices of men and women are necessary for understanding the Islamic tradition in Turkey. Abu-Lughod's monograph extends the argument to understanding basic notions of person and self, and in so doing it touches upon key issues in current anthropological thought.

Between October 1978 and May 1980, Abu-Lughod lived in one of the 15 households in a small community of related bedouin families. The "core" families had large sheep herds, small herds of camels kept for prestige, olive and almond trees, and some agricultural lands. The head of the most prestigious household had additional investments in urban real estate. When relations with Libya were better, many of the bedouin of this region, like their counterparts elsewhere (such as the Rwāla), engaged in smuggling, but such opportunities have become more scarce in recent years.[38]

The monograph strikes a delicate balance between making the encounter between anthropologists and their hosts "the sole object of inquiry," as some current anthropological discussions have done, and presents an "authoritative" account in which the anthropologist and the anthropological encounter are all but invisible. She describes her "proper" subject, to which other issues are subordinate, as "the relationship between Awlad 'Alī sentiments and experiences and the two contradictory discourses that express and inform them: a genre of oral lyric poetry of love and vulnerability on the one hand, and the ideology of honor in ordinary conversation and everyday behavior on the other."[39]

Possessing an Arab surname is not in itself a guarantee of fluency in Arabic, and Abu-Lughod describes how little she at first understood of what people said. Her father had introduced her to the Awlād 'Alī, thus firmly identifying her as an Arab and a Muslim, which obliged her to conform to accepted local standards of propriety. She initially "sought to move back and forth between the men's and women's worlds," but increasingly found that she had to "declare [her] loyalties firmly in order to be accepted in either," and she chose the women's world.[40]

Abu-Lughod had no particular interest in poetry when she began her study, although she noticed how often people "sang or punctuated their conversations with short poems," especially *ghinnāwa*-s, "lyric poems, like Japanese haiku in form but more like the American blues in content and emotional tone. They usually described a sentiment and were perceived by others as personal statements about interpersonal situations."[41]

[37] Lila Abu-Lughod, *Veiled Sentiments: Honor and Poetry in a Bedouin Society* (Berkeley and Los Angeles: University of California Press, 1986). See also her beautifully illustrated "Bedouin Blues," *Natural History* 96, no. 7 (July 1987), 24–33.

[38] Abu-Lughod, *Veiled Sentiments*, p. 8.

[39] Ibid., p. 10.

[40] Ibid., pp. 11–16. Quote from p. 16.

[41] Ibid., pp. 25, 27.

The first part of Abu-Lughod's monograph concerns familiar components of Middle Eastern societies (see Chapters 5 and 6). The Awlād 'Alī bedouin value autonomy but respect the hierarchical relationships that adhere in family identity and the ideology of honor, for which the complementary virtue for women and other dependents is modesty (*ḥasham*), "voluntary deference to those in the system who more closely embody its ideals."[42]

The ideology of honor she describes depends in part on nobility of descent (*aṣl*). Agnates—people united by claims to common patrilineal descent—are thought to share an identifying substance of "blood and flesh" (*dam wlḥam*). The bedouin term for kinship is "closeness" (*garāba*), a concept much like that found in Morocco, where the same term (pronounced *qarāba*) is used, as we have seen in Chapter 7. The bedouin ideology of kinship is "dominated" by the "ideology of natural, positive, and unbreakable bonds of blood" but, as elsewhere, is not limited to it.[43] There are inequalities of control over people and resources within lineage groups, as well as between them, but in an analogy with the notion of the extended family, the Awlād 'Alī assert that these are not ties of "domination and subordination" but of "protection and dependency" based on the greater abilities of some and what the bedouin consider the "natural" dependency of those who are less able. As Abu-Lughod points out, this construct "masks the arbitrary control over resources that allows one group to be autonomous" and creates "a differentiation that the Bedouins then use to validate their various social statuses." The tension between "ideals of equality and independence, on the one hand, and the reality of status differentials, on the other," is mediated through the idea that hierarchy depends on the possession of moral attributes and not force or ascribed status.[44] Men use "reason" (*'agl*, the equivalent in Awlād 'Alī Arabic to the Moroccan *'qāl*, discussed earlier) to control themselves so that they can act effectively in this system of moral authority.[45]

If the ideal qualities of men in this system are to be honorable, assertive, proud, generous, and fearless; women are modest, shy, deferential, and self-restrained. They are socialized into a modesty code that emphasizes "self-restraint and effacement." Women can also be assertive, honorable, proud, and generous, but not in interactions with men. They are expected to defer to those in authority, and this deference, or modesty, is the honor of the weak.[46] Honor for women necessarily entails being the wards and dependents of men.

[42] Ibid., p. 34. For the presentation and analysis of a similar code of honor elsewhere in the Middle East, see Charles Lindholm, *Generosity and Jealousy: The Swat Pukhtun of Northern Pakistan* (New York: Columbia University Press, 1982), esp. pp. 209–38. On honor in both Western and Middle Eastern contexts, with an extensive bibliography, see Frank Henderson Stewart, *Honor* (Chicago and London: University of Chicago Press, 1994).

[43] Abu-Lughod, *Veiled Sentiments*, pp. 41, 49, 51.

[44] Ibid., p. 85.

[45] Ibid., p. 91.

[46] Ibid., p. 152.

FIGURE 9-5. A Durrānī headman and his daughter, Afghanistan, 1972. Codes of honor and modesty are complemented by values of sentiment and attachment. [Courtesy Nancy Lindisfarne-Tapper.]

There is no "false consciousness" involved in participating in this moral system. The ideology of honor, with its complementary emphasis on modesty, contributes to a particular form of hierarchy both between lineages and family groups and between genders. Men and women do what they want, but their actions, motivated by a desire for moral understanding, justify and reproduce structures of inequality.

An especially useful element in Abu-Lughod's presentation is the steady stream of references to related studies. As mentioned earlier, good ethnographic writing strikes a balance between describing ethnographic encounters, in this instance with the Awlād 'Alī, and describing indigenous sentiments, understandings, and experiences. The other balance is between the ethnographer's fieldwork encounter and a continuing dialogue with anthropological predecessors and contemporaries engaged in analyzing related situations and issues. Abu-Lughod makes this dialogue explicit, providing a valuable introduction to the genre of contemporary ethnographic writing and the principal influences shaping it. In this respect, the first part of her ethnography provides an elegantly argued narrative of sometimes familiar material, and is a highly original account of how sexuality and veiling fit into the ideology of honor and modesty.

The second part of the monograph, "Discourses on Sentiment," consists of a close analysis of personal poetry, which is usually recited only in the presence of intimates. Contrary to the display of honor and modesty that prevails in ordinary discourse, the sentiments expressed in the poetry of both men and women (although never in mixed company) generally suggest a self that is vulnerable and weak. The poems concern loss, love, vulnerability, and other intimate feelings about situations and human relationships, all at odds with the discourse on honor and modesty.

Abu-Lughod uses the term *sentiment* rather than *emotion* to describe these values to emphasize that the discourse of the poetry is culturally as important as the better known discourse of honor and modesty. Poetry expresses sentiments that go against the code of honor not as individual rebellions against it but as part of a great cultural tradition. Poetry is "a modest way of communicating immodest sentiments of attachment and an honorable way of communicating the sentiments of dependency." The culturally structured sentiments expressed in poetry, mostly by those disadvantaged in the social system, also have meaning. That is why they are celebrated. "Poetry as a discourse of defiance of the system symbolizes freedom—the ultimate value of the system and the essential entailment of the honor code."[47] The sentiments expressed in poetry are just as much a part of Awlād 'Alī culture as the experiences sanctioned by the ideology of honor and modesty.

Abu-Lughod argues that the ideology inherent in discourse about honor and modesty and that provided by poetry represent coexisting ideologies, each of which provides "models of and for different types of experience," languages that people can use to express themselves. The discourse of poetry provides a "corrective to an obsession with morality and an overzealous adherence to the ideology of honor. . . . And maybe the vision is cherished because people sense that the costs of this system [of honor ideology], in the limits it places on human experience, are just too high."[48]

Throughout this book I have emphasized the necessity of considering the patterns of cultural values and social practice as they are found in each Middle Eastern and Central Asian setting. Nonetheless, the analysis of ideology and social practice in contexts as diverse as Morocco, Iraq, Iran, and Israel discussed in this chapter suggests important points of "family" resemblance. It also suggests the importance of patterns of social order that earlier would have been labeled "informal" or even "nonstructured." Each of the studies analyzed in this chapter makes sense of such flexible and pragmatic patterns of social action. They seek to discern cultural assumptions concerning the nature of the social world that inform these actions and serve as guides to them. An exami-

[47] Ibid., pp. 34, 240, 250–51.

[48] Ibid., pp. 258–59.

FIGURE 9-6. Codes of honor and ideas of justice mix in complex ways. A student from the Egyptian countryside suspected one of her four roommates at al-Azhar University, Cairo, of stealing 300 Egyptian pounds (about $90). To clear themselves of suspicion, the four students agreed to *bish'a*, a customary law ordeal in which those wishing to prove their innocence lick a white-hot ladle. If the tongue is not burned, innocence is confirmed. In this 1992 photograph, one of the students prepares to lick the ladle, while the other three await their turn. Only one of the students was burned, and she confessed to the theft. [Photograph courtesy Joseph Ginat. All rights reserved.]

nation of contemporary accounts of worldview and of social identity points to a renewed anthropological interest in how the relation between meaning and social practice changes historically. This attention to historical transformations is essential in making sense of events in the Middle East today. Finally, the insight that a given society may contain competing ideologies rather than a single "dominant" ideology in which all values are subsumed is especially useful for making sense of world religious systems as they are elaborated and experienced in the Middle East, the subject of the next chapter.

FURTHER READINGS

Other discussions of poetry and speech acts, as they relate to social practice and cultural values, include Michael Meeker, *Literature and Violence in North Arabia*, Cambridge Studies in Cultural Systems 3 (New York: Cambridge University Press, 1979), which analyzes the political poetry of the Rwāla and its relationship to authority; and Steven C. Caton, *"Peaks of Yemen I Summon": Poetry as Cultural Practice in a North Yemeni Tribe* (Berkeley and Los Angeles: University of California Press, 1990). Other studies of poetry in its social context include Said S. Samatar, *Oral Poetry and Somali Nationalism: The Case of Sayyid Mahammad 'Abdille Hasan* (Cambridge: Cambridge University Press, 1982); Saad Abdullah Sowayan, *Nabaṭi Poetry: The Oral Poetry of Arabia* (Berkeley and Los Angeles: University of California Press, 1985); and Michael A. Marcus, "History on the Moroccan Periphery: Moral Imagination, Poetry, and Islam," *Anthropological Quarterly* 58, no. 4 (October 1985), 152–60.

Another important study is Benedicte Grima, *The Performance of Emotion Among Paxtun Women: "The Misfortunes Which Have Befallen Me,"* Modern Middle East Series 17 (Austin: University of Texas Press, 1992). She discusses the telling of women's life stories among the Paxtun of Afghanistan and Pakistan, which, as is the case for Awlād 'Alī women, are related "in specific contexts of intimacy and privacy" (p. 120). Margaret A. Mills, *Rhetorics and Politics in Afghan Traditional Storytelling*, Publications of the American Folklore Society (Philadelphia: University of Pennsylvania Press, 1991), explores how storytelling offers a means of discussing ethics and religious and political authority and contributes to establishing personal identity. For North Africa, see Deborah Kapchan, *Gender on the Market: Moroccan Women and the Revoicing of Tradition*, Publications of the American Folklore Society (Philadelphia: University of Pennsylvania Press, 1996); and Sabra J. Webber, *Romancing the Real: Folklore and Ethnographic Representation in North Africa*, Publications of the American Folklore Society (Philadelphia: University of Pennsylvania Press, 1991). Food and cooking, often neglected expressions of cultural expression, are the focus of Sami Zubeida and Richard Tapper, eds., *Culinary Cultures of the Middle East* (London and New York: I. B. Tauris, 1994).

On contemporary Israeli Judaism, see the anthology *Israeli Judaism*, ed. Shlomo Deshen, Charles S. Liebman, and Moshe Shokeid, Studies of Israeli Society 7 (New Brunswick, NJ, and London: Transaction, 1995), including Shlomo Deshen's introduction, "The Study of Religion in Israeli Social Science" (pp. 1–17), and Moshe Shokeid, "The Religiosity of Middle Eastern Jews" (pp. 213–37), a paper originally published in 1982, which is almost prescient in highlighting the political significance of Jewish (and many other) communities in "reimagining" their history and "tradition" and the political significance of these activities.

PART IV
RELIGION AND EXPERIENCE

10

ISLAM AND THE "RELIGIONS OF THE BOOK"

WORLD RELIGIONS IN THE MIDDLE EAST AND CENTRAL ASIA

The key traditions of major world religions remain vital and meaningful through the actions of their carriers, who maintain and shape them over long historical periods and in highly diverse contexts. Thus religious traditions are inextricably linked to the changing relations of authority and domination in which they are shaped and transformed. By definition, world religions are not confined to any one society or cultural tradition. They transcend specific cultures, including their culture of origin. Adherents of world religions are aware, at least in principle, of a diversity of practice and interpretation that ranges well beyond the confines of localized, face-to-face communities. Some carriers of world religions often claim as doctrine that their tradition possesses a core of formative ideals and immutable religious truths, and most share common rituals. Yet these ideals, truths, and rituals must be sufficiently open to reformulation and reinterpretation by their carriers over successive generations and in novel contexts, even if the carriers of these traditions may be unaware that they have been reshaped.

Three world religious traditions have their origins in the Middle East—Judaism, Christianity, and Islam—but there are also a number of more highly localized traditions, such as Zoroastrianism (primarily in Iran), as well as the Druze of Lebanon, Syria, and Israel, and the Kurdish-speaking Yazīdī-s of northern Iraq, each with their own traditions of religious identity and practice. The past and present of these religious traditions intricately intertwine, even if some of their carriers are disinclined in some circumstances or unaware in others of how close these interrelationships are. Jerusalem provides perhaps the most poignant symbol of all that Judaism, Christianity, and Islam share and contest in the Middle Eastern context and beyond and how the significance given to religious symbols, space, and places ranges well beyond the local carriers of the three religious traditions.[1] The attitudes of the carriers of these three world religions toward gender provides an example at a more implicit level of a domain in which they share much in common.[2] At the same time, the Mongol invasions of the thirteenth century of many areas of Muslim rule, quickly followed by the conversion of the Mongol conquerors to Islam, suggests the surprising reversals of directions that world religions can take. In a similar fashion, Europe and North America are emerging in the late twentieth century as major centers of creativity in reformulating and "reimagining" the Islamic tradition.

This chapter primarily concerns the Muslim tradition, although the discussion shows that many of the themes often apply equally to Middle Eastern Christians and Jews. From a Western perspective, the Islamic tradition is frequently construed as the least familiar of the three major religious traditions of the area. Yet the Christian and Jewish traditions in their Middle Eastern contexts also contain many unfamiliar elements. Middle Eastern adherents to all three religions have been subject, of course, to the same nexus of political and social developments. For example, the "cultural" distance in Israel between Falasha Jews from Ethiopia or Yemeni Jews, on the one hand, and Jews of European origin, on the other, can be greater than the relations of these groups with their non-Jewish neighbors in their countries of origin.

Thus the Islamic reform or "renewal" movement that got under way in the Middle East in the late nineteenth century had its parallels among the carriers of the region's other religious traditions, including Egypt's Coptic Christian community and, until the 1960s, Libya's relatively isolated Jewish community. These developments were in part generated by political and economic develop-

[1] See Jonathan Webber, "Religions in the Holy Land: Conflicts of Interpretation," *Anthropology Today* 1, no. 2 (April 1985), 3–9, and Glenn Bowman, "Unholy Struggle on Holy Ground: Conflict and Interpretation in Jerusalem," *Anthropology Today* 2, no. 3 (June 1986), 14–17, for short anthropological accounts of "interpreting" Jerusalem. See also F. E. Peters, *Jerusalem: The Holy City in the Eyes of Chroniclers, Visitors, Pilgrims, and Prophets from the Days of Abraham to the Beginnings of Modern Times* (Princeton, NJ: Princeton University Press, 1985), and on the three world religions in the Middle East, his *Children of Abraham* (Princeton, NJ, and London: Princeton University Press, 1983). See also "Jerusalem: Vox Populi, Civitas Dei," *The Economist* (London), November 7, 1987, pp. 23–26.

[2] Carol Delaney, "The Meaning of Paternity and the Virgin Birth Debate," *Man* (N.S.) 21, no. 3 (September 1986), 494–513; and "Seeds of Honor, Fields of Shame," in *Honor and Shame and Unity of the Mediterranean*, ed. David Gilmore, Special Publication 22 (Washington, DC: American Anthropological Association, 1987), pp. 45–46. The carriers of each of these religions, however, possess multiple gender ideologies, making unitary comparisons between each tradition misleading unless comparisons within each tradition and their ongoing debates are also taken into account. For women in the Jewish ultra-Orthodox tradition, for example, see Tamar El-Or, *Educated and Ignorant: Ultraorthodox Jewish Women and Their World* (Boulder, CO, and London: Lynne Rienner, 1994).

ments within the Middle East itself, by intellectual and social developments elsewhere in the Muslim world, and, especially in the case of the Christian and Jewish communities, by an intensified contact with their European coreligionists. In all cases there were subtle and sometimes intense links between these various religious communities. In the Arab East, Christians played a significant role in the formulation of modern Arab political and national identity and, in the Arab West, even some members of the Jewish elite participated in the twentieth-century Moroccan nationalist movement.[3]

As with other great religious traditions, Islam is rich and varied in its creativity and expression, so it is a challenge for Muslim believers and scholars, both Muslim and non-Muslim, to account for the variations of Islam as it has been expressed over 1400 years and in the context of diverse cultural traditions. As a response to this complexity, some scholars dismiss local practices they consider not in accord with "central" Islamic truths as non-Islamic or as incorrect understandings of Islam, even though people who hold such beliefs consider themselves fully Muslim. Thus one leading Muslim intellectual, who has produced a rich and sensitive account of the Islamic tradition and is himself a leading reformist, dismisses all "mystical" and popular understandings of Islam, especially those that came to dominate many parts of the Middle East after the twelfth and thirteenth centuries, as being perpetrated by charlatans and "spiritual delinquents" and accepted only by the ignorant. Others argue that the major shift in popular religious expression, which took place in much of the Muslim world and which placed emphasis on the veneration of saints and participation in religious brotherhoods, was as important as the major shift in early Latin Christianity in the third through sixth centuries, when the veneration of saints came to the fore as part of a major reconfiguration of popular religious thought.[4]

[3] See E. J. Chitham, *The Coptic Community in Egypt: Spatial and Social Change,* Occasional Papers Series 32 (Durham, England: University of Durham, Centre for Middle Eastern and Islamic Studies, 1986), p. 108. On the situation of Copts, see Luc Barbulesco, "Babylone ou qahira," *Autrement,* no. 12 (February 1985), 192–97. For the Libyan Jewish community, see Mordechai Ha-Cohen, *The Book of Mordechai: A Study of the Jews of Libya,* ed. and trans. Harvey E. Goldberg (Philadelphia: Institute for the Study of Human Issues, 1980); and for Jews in Middle Eastern societies in general and their relationships with the Muslim and Christian communities, Bernard Lewis, *The Jews of Islam* (Princeton, NJ: Princeton University Press, 1984). On the development of an Arab national identity from the nineteenth century through the present, see Dale F. Eickelman, "Arab Society: Tradition and the Present," in *The Middle East: A Handbook,* ed. Michael Adams (New York: Facts-on-File, 1988), pp. 765–81. One of the best anthropological essays on how world religious traditions influence one another in changing temporal and political contexts is Robert W. Hefner, "The Political Economy of Islamic Conversion in Modern East Java," in *Islam and the Political Economy of Meaning,* ed. William R. Roff, Comparative Studies on Muslim Societies 1 (London: Croom Helm; Berkeley and Los Angeles: University of California Press, 1987), pp. 53–78.

[4] Fazlur Rahman, *Islam,* 2nd ed. (Chicago: University of Chicago Press, 1979). For an example of his original and influential interpretation of the Quran, see *Major Themes of the Quran* (Minneapolis and Chicago: Biblioteca Islamica, 1980), and *Islam and Modernity* (Chicago: University of Chicago Press, 1982). For early Latin Christianity, see Peter Brown, *The Cult of the Saints: Its Rise and Function in Latin Christianity* (Chicago and London: University of Chicago Press, 1981). I owe the comparison with the shift in popular Muslim religious sensibilities to Richard Bulliet (personal communication, September 18, 1987).

To account for these diversities, anthropologists in the 1940s introduced the notion of "Great" and "Little" traditions. When first applied, the Great Tradition/Little Tradition contrast rekindled an interest in how popular understandings of religion—the "little," localized, traditions—were related to more elite, literary ones. It also encouraged attention to the "carriers" of particular religious interpretations and practices—people influential in their own society or marginal to it—so that links among religion, authority, and influence could be explored.

Nonetheless, in many anthropological monographs the concept meant little beyond juxtaposing statements of "essential" Islamic principles, as elaborated in standard scholarly texts and by educated Muslims, with inventories of local religious practices. For example, the study of "trance" and "possession" states, often indicative of the affective side of religious traditions, has suffered from being relegated to the Little Tradition side of the divide. Only in recent years has the study of such rites become more clearly related to comprehensive studies of the person and to religious understandings of the world.[5]

Critical discussion of what is meant by Islam and the Islamic tradition is needed for both analytic and practical reasons. Especially in recent years, a number of studies of Islam have appeared that combine attention to textual analysis, a venerable tradition in the study of Islam, with analysis of the ethnographic and social historical contexts in which notions of Islam are developed, transmitted, and reproduced. Many earlier studies, based primarily on the study of key religious texts or of certain types of religious experience (formal rituals or mysticism, for example), tended to concentrate on the search for an Islamic "essence." This earlier analytic tradition, which is still vigorous, coincided in part with the ideological premise held by many Muslims that Islamic beliefs and practices are unaffected by historical change.

Recent ethnographic and social historical studies suggest a more complex notion of Islamic tradition than can be extracted by reliance on religious or legal texts. As a consequence, the notion of an Islamic "essence" has been difficult to sustain. The idea of "tradition," after all, need not necessarily imply a fixed or unitary set of principles existing independently of specific political and social conditions. The idea of what is "traditional" changes with generations and between social groups and classes and usually does not involve a unitary set of assumptions. It involves ongoing discussion, debate, and practice. In most contexts, people who have competing notions of religion or tradition coexist.

[5] Compare, for example, Vincent Crapanzano, *The Ḥamadsha: A Study in Moroccan Ethnopsychiatry* (Berkeley and Los Angeles: University of California Press, 1973), with Nancy Tapper and Richard Tapper, "The Birth of the Prophet: Ritual and Gender in Turkish Islam," *Man* (N.S.) 22, no. 1 (March 1987), 69–92, a study that relates "local" practices and beliefs to the more universal and "standardized" facets of a world religious tradition. Their study also raises basic questions for exploring the role of gender in religious traditions. Janice Boddy, *Wombs and Alien Spirits: Women, Men, and the Zar Cult in Northern Sudan* (Madison: University of Wisconsin Press, 1989), discusses spirit possession (*zār* cults), indicating that the practice is not confined to women, and she shows (much as Peter Brown does for saint cults in early Latin Christianity) how the practice offers a way of imagining and expressing alternative social realities.

Sometimes they are in opposition, but sometimes the choice between alternatives is not explicit.

Depending on context, carriers of a religious tradition adhere to practices and beliefs that are seen as incompatible by religious authorities or intellectuals (or scholarly observers) and that, therefore, cannot be reduced to a single, cohesive set of principles. In one dimension, these opposing (or complementary) conceptions of Islam are particularistic and significantly intertwined with the local social order. Other conceptions are universalistic, more amenable to generalization and application in a wide number of contexts. These opposing conceptions are co-present and in dynamic tension with one another. Some ideologies, such as those characteristic of "reformist" Islam and the beliefs of many educated Muslims, tend to be *universalistic*. Others, including North African "saint" cults (although "saint," for reasons to be explained, can be a misleading gloss), are *particularistic*.

The co-presence of these alternative ideologies and practices, some of which are not formally elaborated, means that the strength of one or another ideological form cannot be attributed *solely* to its relation to a specific social context. Such notions need not be perfectly integrated (and usually are not), nor can the universalistic and particularistic elements be neatly arrayed in terms of center and periphery. Within the Muslim world, there exist multiple linkages among the various ethnic, kinship-based, regional, political, and religious communities that do not arrange themselves into agreed-on hierarchies. Some pious Muslims claim Mecca as the spiritual center of the Muslim world, which it certainly is from some perspectives. But from other perspectives, the most profound religious innovations do not emanate from the centers, nor are they explicitly planned. In France, for example, labor migration and immigration have brought about more profound religious changes than innovations from traditional religious leaders. New forms of Muslim religious expression in France have had, in turn, a profound impact upon Islam, as it is practiced in North Africa and black Africa, the regions of origin for most immigrant Muslims in France. Far from being marginal to the Muslim world, Muslims in Europe are becoming increasingly central, in terms of the role they play not only in the Muslim world but also in the European states where they reside.[6]

In what is perhaps an extreme reaction to the earlier analytic tradition, which largely accepted the ideological premise held by many Muslims of the immutability of "true" Islamic belief and practice, an Egyptian Muslim anthropologist, Abdul Hamid M. el-Zein, has suggested replacing the term *Islam* by *islams*, better to emphasize the multiplicity of Islamic expression and to show that the "islams" of elite and nonelite, literate and illiterate, theologians and

[6] Gilles Kepel, *Les banlieues de l'Islam: Naissance d'une religion en France* [Suburbs of Islam: Birth of a Religion in France] (Paris: Éditions du Seuil, 1987). See also Pnina Werbner, "The Making of Muslim Dissent: Hybridized Discourses, Lay Preachers, and Radical Rhetoric Among British Pakistanis," *American Ethnologist* 23, no. 1 (February 1996), 102–22.

artisans, tribesmen and peasants are equally valid expressions of a fundamental, unconscious (in the structuralist sense) set of principles.[7]

The islams approach was a reaction against both the orientalist search for an ahistorical Islamic "essence" and the somewhat parallel venture of some Muslim fundamentalists who declare their own beliefs and practices "Islamic," in opposition to the practices of Muslims who do not agree with them. Ironically, by considering all expressions of Islam as transformations based on a single set of principles, the conceptual end product of the islams approach likewise reduces Islamic tradition to an essentialist, ahistorical core. Ideas and practices take on radically different meanings, depending on who introduces, advocates, and supports them. Some understandings of Islam are more valued than others because of their identification with certain carriers and groups. The islams approach, although intellectually productive when originally introduced because it focused attention on nonelite expressions of Islamic belief and practice, neglects the important dimensions of authority and domination in the transmission and reproduction of ideas and organizations. It neglects the historical conditions that favor the emergence of particular institutional arrangements or beliefs over alternative, coexisting ones.

This chapter discusses Islam and the other "religions of the book" as they appear in today's Middle East and Central Asia, with an emphasis on the richness and variety of these traditions. A complementary goal is to provide the critical perspective necessary for placing studies of these traditions in their appropriate contexts.

PRODUCING ORTHODOXY FOR ISLAM: THE "FIVE PILLARS"

Zein used the concept of *islams* to account for the lack of a common core of accepted dogma. Wilfred Cantwell Smith has suggested that in the Islamic case it is preferable to talk of *orthopraxy*, a commonality of practice and ritual, rather than of *orthodoxy*, the commonality of belief, on the grounds that Muslims share common rituals, even if they interpret them differently.[8]

Yet the notion that Muslims share a common orthopraxy also has its limitations. Even if there is a growing consensus among educated Muslims of some elements of practice, if not of belief, the notion still implies an authoritative formula that is "taught" to be correct, whether by "untutored parents" (Talal Asad's term), peers, self-appointed mosque preachers, or leading religious

[7] Abdul Hamid el-Zein, "Beyond Ideology and Theology: The Search for the Anthropology of Islam," *Annual Review of Anthropology* 6 (1977), 227–54. Michael Gilsenan, *Recognizing Islam*, adopts a similar stance. As Asad, "Idea," p. 2, reminds us, "there are Muslims everywhere who say that what other people take to be Islam is not really Islam at all," and that beliefs about the practices of others are their own beliefs as well. Such beliefs "animate and are sustained" by social relations with others and cannot be considered independently of hierarchies of authority and domination.

[8] Wilfred Cantwell Smith, *Islam in Modern History* (Princeton, NJ: Princeton University Press, 1957), p. 28.

scholars. As Asad writes, a "practice is Islamic because it is authorized by the discursive traditions of Islam, and is so taught to Muslims," a notion that has an advantage over the islams approach or the claim of common, "essential" practices or beliefs because it emphasizes the relationship between belief and authority.[9]

In any consideration of what constitutes Islamic practice, it is important to consider three elements: *time,* or the historical contexts in which given practices are introduced and interpreted; *scale,* or the extent to which given practices or traditions are universalistic or particularistic, deriving their strength from highly localized factors; and *internal debate* over "correct" traditions, a dimension that focuses attention on existing power relations within and impinging on particular societies.

Nonetheless, delineating the basic themes and the five "pillars" of faith from the many competing voices serves as a useful point of departure for considering how Islam is locally received and understood. The "five pillars" do not constitute a lowest common denominator of Islam, but they suggest some of the elements of belief and practice over which Muslims argue.

Islam is the only world religion to have had a built-in name from the outset. *Islam* (Ar. *islām)* means "submission," submission to the will of God. Whoever submits is called a *Muslim.* These terms occur repeatedly in the Quran. The word *qur'ān* itself means both "reading" and "recital."[10] It is the word of God revealed to the Prophet Muḥammad (570/80–632), beginning in 610 by the Angel Gabriel. Something is known of how these revelations first came to Muḥammad from verses in the Quran itself. On the first occasion, Muḥammad saw a glorious being standing high in the sky toward the horizon; then this being approached closer and closer to him. Muḥammad's first thought was that the being was God, but later he recognized it as Gabriel. No one is certain which part of the Quran was first revealed to Muḥammad, but many Muslims think it is this verse:

> O thou wrapped up (in a mantle),
> Arise and warn!
> Praise thy Lord
> Cleanse thy garments
> Shun defilement!
> Do not grant blessings
> (Expecting) a greater return
> For thy Lord, show fortitude.
>
> (Sura 74:1–7, "The Shrouded One"[11])

[9] Asad, "Idea," p. 15.

[10] The content and context of Quranic recitation are important themes explored in Richard C. Martin, "Understanding the Qur'an in Text and Context," *History of Religions* 21, no. 4 (May 1982), 361–84; and Kristina Nelson, *The Art of Reciting the Qur'an,* Modern Middle East Studies 11 (Austin and London: University of Texas Press, 1986). The latter deals with how modern Egyptian Quranic reciters use their voice to convey the perfection of the words and at the same time communicate moods and sentiments appropriate to various passages.

[11] Translation by Dale F. Eickelman.

Most Muslims hold every word of the Quran to be the word of God. The Quran states that God had earlier communicated His word through other prophets, those recognized by both Jews and Christians, but that over time their messages had become distorted. So Muḥammad was made the "Seal of the Prophets," to warn humankind one last time of their wrong ways and to provide them again with God's word, this time "in clear Arabic."

Any translation from one civilizational tradition to another is treacherous, but a comparison with Christianity is useful here. The Quran should not be seen as the exact equivalent of the Bible. Most Christians see the Bible as a record of the prophets and of Christ, but not directly as God's word, as Muslims see the Quran. This is why many Muslims, even those who do not speak Arabic, regard translations of the Quran as guides to its meaning rather than substitutes for the original. For most Christians it is the person of Christ, the Son of God, that personifies God because Christ is God. In contrast, the Quran insists that Muḥammad is merely the messenger of God. Some Muslims, especially certain mystics, have considered the person of Muḥammad a saintlike figure, but most Muslims consider Muḥammad the most perfect of men.

Clearly, belief in the Quran and the eternal nature of its message are important components of the Islamic tradition, but the word of God as embodied in the Quran is made meaningful to Muslims in different ways according to time and place. Problems of revelation and the legitimation of political authority, to consider only two major issues, are interpreted in various ways throughout the Muslim world.

A Moroccan *qāḍī*, or religious judge, had this to say concerning how the Quran should be interpreted:

> How can ordinary men, no matter how much they study, understand by themselves the words of the Quran? Those are high words, the words of God. Instead, you must look at what the Prophet did, the sayings of the Prophet, and the conduct and decisions of the Muslim community in the past. These tell you what is the *sharī'a* [the law of Islam or the "straight path"].

He then drew two parallel lines on a sheet of paper and explained that conduct within the two lines was permitted by Islam and all else was not. The fact that *he* was drawing the lines underscored (literally) his role as an authoritative interpreter—indeed, definer, although the *qāḍī* would deny this explicit, activist role—of "orthodox" tradition. Since the Quran, in the view of the Moroccan *qāḍī*, cannot be a direct guide to conduct, one must discern what Muslims at any given time regard as authoritative tradition.

The belief that the Quran cannot be a direct guide to conduct is not prevalent everywhere in the Muslim world but is an example of one of the ways in which the ideological notion of the immutability of Islamic belief can be maintained yet adjusted to accommodate local traditions. Much "Islamic" practice depends on *consensus* (*ijmā'a*) of Muslims, especially those considered religious scholars, in any part of the Muslim world. The notion of consensus has precise

FIGURE 10-1. "How can ordinary men, no matter how much they study . . . understand by themselves the words of the Quran?"—Moroccan *qāḍī*, 1969. [Courtesy of the author.]

legal connotations in Islam, but here I am primarily concerned with indicating popular conceptions of religious tradition.

Every Muslim participates in the *umma,* the community of living Muslims everywhere who are committed to what Marshall Hodgson has called the "venture of Islam." The *sharī'a,* the straight path of the ritual observances required of Muslims, is the most visible component of that venture. Muslims differ as to who legitimately succeeded Muḥammad in the leadership of the Muslim world. Sunnī Muslims, who constitute about 90 percent of Muslims worldwide, accept the notion that any Muslim could be Muḥammad's successor in all matters except prophecy, whereas the Shī'a, who constitute the remaining 10 percent and are principally located in Iran, East Africa, India, southern Iraq, Lebanon, and parts of the Arabian peninsula, feel that succession rightly belongs to the descendants of Muḥammad through his daughter Fāṭima and his son-in-law 'Alī. There are many elaborations and intermediary positions of these principal themes. Despite these differences, Islam is thought of by Muslims as imparting a tone and style to all aspects of their lives—familial customs, sociability, learning, even styles of personal grooming. *Sharī'a* can be translated as "law," but it is much more than the concept of law in English usage. Religiously speaking, the *sharī'a* governs all aspects of one's conduct as a Muslim.

There are "five pillars" (pl. *arkān)* of Islamic faith incumbent upon most Muslims; I say *most* because many Muslims modify or deny the normative nature of even these pillars because of their own interpretations of Islam. These

Some contemporary Middle Eastern states regard the *sharī'a* as a main source of laws, while others regard it as *the* main source. For most Muslims, however, the *sharī'a* refers more broadly to divinely ordained norms and ideals of just conduct that bind rulers and ruled alike—whether or not these principles are embodied in a formal legal code. A case recently brought before an English court helped clarify these complementary spheres of the *sharī'a*.

In the summer of 1996, the State of Qatar initiated litigation in Europe and elsewhere against its former ruler, Shaykh Khalīfa bin Ḥamad Āl Thānī, seeking to recover assets estimated between $3 to $7 billion that had been transferred from the Qatar state treasury to his personal accounts. In an English court, Shaykh Khalīfa argued that as a ruler, there were no restraints on his use of state funds. He argued that the *sharī'a* bound him only to the extent that it was explicitly incorporated into the constitution and laws of Qatar. In a letter to *The Economist*,* Qatar's Minister of Justice, Najeeb bin Mohamed al-Nauimi, argued otherwise and offered one of the clearest recent statements of the relation of *sharī'a* and legal obligation in a modern Muslim society:

> In describing the litigation between the state of Qatar and its former emir, Sheikh Khalifah Bin Hamad Al-Thani,** you fail to mention Islamic law.
>
> When Sheikh Khalifah recently transferred vast sums from the public treasury to his personal bank accounts in Switzerland, England, and elsewhere, he violated state budget laws enacted during his own term as emir. More fundamentally, he violated *sharia*, the Islamic law that governs all Qatari heads of state and the people they serve.
>
> Contrary to the suggestion made in your article, a legal distinction between the state's purse and that of its ruler is not "radical," and certainly not new. The *sharia* makes it clear that state funds are not the personal property of the *imam* or, in this case, the emir. Indeed, it is his duty to ensure that the public treasury is devoted to public purposes. He may receive enough to provide for the reasonable needs of himself and his family, but if he takes more he is guilty of *ghulul* (theft).
>
> Sheikh Khalifah himself took decisive steps to honour and institutionalise these rules when he deposed his predecessor in 1972. One of his first official acts as emir was to issue a decree halting the practice by which Sheikh Ahmed received payments directly from oil companies operating in Qatar. Sheikh Khalifah ordered that this money be restored to the public treasury for the general budget of the state.

On October 18, 1996, Qatar and its former ruler reached an out-of-court settlement that halted litigation.† Nonetheless, the case publicly reaffirmed the strength and pervasiveness of *sharī'a*, both as enacted in legislation and as generally upheld in contemporary Muslim political and social life.

*Najeeb bin Mohamed al-Nauimi, "Qatar's Purse Strings," *The Economist*, October 5, 1996, p. 8.

**"Qatar: Whose Cash Is It?" *The Economist*, August 31, 1996, p. 39.

†John Mason and Robin Allen, "Qatar Settles Billion-Dollar Suit," *Financial Times* (London), October 21, 1996, p. 3.

five pillars are the declaration of faith, the five daily ritual prayers, almsgiving, fasting, and the pilgrimage to Mecca.[12]

The declaration of faith (*shahāda*) is quite simply that there is no god but God and Muḥammad is His messenger (*rasūl*). This simple declaration of faith is so elemental that all Muslims can agree on it, whatever other differences they may have had for thirteen and a half centuries.

The second pillar is the *ṣalāt*, or five daily ritual prayers. All Muslims are supposed to cleanse themselves ritually, face Mecca, and pray at dawn, noon, midafternoon, sunset, and dusk. In towns, prayer callers climb to the top of minarets, even when loudspeakers are prevalent, and announce each prayer. Muslims may pray where they want. The use of mosques is not obligatory, although many believers congregate in mosques at least on Fridays for the midday prayers. The obligatory prayers are fixed in form and content, although personal invocations to God may be added to them upon their completion. Many Muslims say that the uniformity of these prayers symbolizes humankind's equality before God as well as their submission to His will.

Almsgiving (*zakāt*) is the third pillar. In some countries at certain periods the *zakāt* has been an obligatory tax on all Muslims who can afford to pay it. The Quran enjoins the wealthier to set aside part of their wealth for the destitute of the Muslim community. Most almsgiving throughout the Middle East remains personal; the donor often has a direct contact with his clients, unlike the anonymous pattern of giving that prevails in many Western societies.

The fourth pillar of Islam is fasting (*ṣawm*), which occurs each lunar year during the month of Ramaḍān. Adult Muslims in good health are expected to fast, and despite the fact that many people privately may choose not to do so, public fasting is observed almost everywhere. During Ramaḍān, Islam is consciously brought into daily activities; religious lessons are given nightly on the radio and television and in mosques. Ramaḍān is the month of repentance and purification. Some Muslims rationalize the fast by praising its supposed medical virtues in cleansing the vital organs of the body. Yet, as indicated in Chapter 9, its more important meaning is the ability of Muslims to follow the code of conduct fixed by Islam and thus to demonstrate their self-discipline and control over self. The fast carries a variety of elaborate interpretations, as Lloyd and Margaret Fallers indicate in their account of the fast in Turkey and Richard Antoun in his account for rural Jordan, but the public manifestation of the community's ability to observe the fast is a key and universal aspect of belief and practice.[13] Eating, drinking, smoking, and sexual intercourse are

[12] Codifications of orthopraxy into "five pillars" or their equivalent are an internal development of the Muslim community, not just an "Orientalist" convention. See, for example, an "authoritative" handbook written for English-speaking Muslims, *Introduction to Islam*, enl. edition, ed. Muhammad Hamidullah, Publications of the Centre Culturel Islamique (Paris), 1 (Hyderabad, India: Habib & Co., 1959). The following account of the formal steps in the pilgrimage, the fifth pillar, is based primarily on Gustave E. von Grunebaum, *Muhammadan Festivals* (New York: Henry Schuman, 1951), pp. 15–49; and *Aramco World Magazine* 26, no. 6 (November–December 1974).

[13] L. A. Fallers, assisted by M. C. Fallers, "Notes on an Advent Ramadan," *Journal of the American Academy of Religion* 42, no. 1 (March 1974), 35–52; and Richard T. Antoun, "The Social Significance of Ramaḍān in an Arab Village," *Muslim World* 58 (1968), 36–42, 95–104.

FIGURE 10-2. Tunisia, 1973. Pilgrims often visit local shrines before departing for Mecca. [Courtesy Nicholas S. Hopkins.]

prohibited between dawn and sunset, and, more significantly, Muslims are expected to engage in spiritual self-renewal. At night, in contrast, sociability is in many ways increased; visiting among friends and relatives is intensified, and the practical meaning of what it is to be a Muslim is enhanced for the entire community.

The fifth pillar is the pilgrimage (*ḥajj*) to Mecca, obligatory once in a lifetime for every Muslim economically and physically able to do so. Even more than the month of fasting, the pilgrimage is an obligation that removes Muslims from the constraints of ordinary, particular obligations. From the moment pilgrims set out on the journey, they are removed from ordinary society and become "liminal" in the sense of the term made popular by Victor Turner.[14] Pilgrims agree to dedicate their lives to Islam and must be in a state of ritual consecration to make a valid pilgrimage. They may not uproot plants or shed blood; if they do so, they must atone for it by ritual means. Sexual intercourse is also forbidden. If pilgrims die while on pilgrimage, they are thought to enter paradise immediately.

During the pilgrimage, ordinary social relationships with kinsmen, neighbors, and others assume diminished importance. One's identity as a Muslim and brotherhood in Islam are of paramount significance. Every step of the way becomes highly symbolic of the pilgrim's wider identification with Islam; the

[14] Victor Turner, "The Center Out There: Pilgrim's Goal," *History of Religions* 12, no. 3 (February 1973), 191–230.

web of particularistic social relationships is supposed to be transcended. Ritually speaking, some Muslims regard the Ka'ba as the symbolic center of the world, however peripheral it might be in terms of the ordinary social and political systems in which pilgrims are otherwise enmeshed.

In recent years, more than a million pilgrims annually have made the voyage. Its timing changes each year, for as with other key Islamic rituals, the time of the pilgrimage is set by the lunar calendar. In the past, as with equivalent rituals in Europe, the pilgrimage was a long and arduous journey from which many never returned. Every step of the way was fraught with danger, but this enhanced its spiritual richness. A voyage of a year or longer was not uncommon for pilgrims coming from North Africa, so that before they left on the *ḥajj,* they set their affairs in order in case they failed to return. Even in the mid-nineteenth century, when modern sea transport and relative peace and security made the pilgrimage easier, it still had its uncertainties. For many, it was a voyage of intellectual, and even commercial, discovery. Religious scholars at Mecca and along the way had contact with major intellectual currents elsewhere. Merchants could use the pilgrimage as an occasion to establish bonds that were of use in the conduct of international trade.

There are many descriptions of both the transformation that the pilgrimage effects upon Muslims and its ritual significance. In most parts of the Muslim world, it is a pious act for pilgrims to write an account of their journey for the guidance of others, although it is the unusual pilgrims whose accounts best reveal the intense meaning that the pilgrimage carries for the community of the faithful. Indeed, changes over time in how these accounts are written provide important indicators of altered social conceptions of person and self.[15]

Malcolm X was one such unusual pilgrim. Given the bitterness of his experience with race issues in America, his remarks are especially poignant. He remarked on the fact that the tens of thousands of pilgrims "were of all colours, from blue-eyed blondes to black-skinned Africans. But we were all participating in the same ritual, displaying a spirit of unity and brotherhood that my experiences in America had led me to believe could never exist."[16] He observed color patterns in the crowds in which like stayed with like but concluded that "true brotherhood" existed when these patterns implied no hierarchies of superiority and inferiority.

The claim of some Muslims that Mecca is the spiritual center of the Muslim world is subject to political interpretations, a point to which we shall return. For the moment, it suffices to note that Muslims possess identities in addition to that of Muslim. These coexisting identities were implicit in the attitude of Gamal Abdel Nasser (1918–1970), Egypt's leader in the heyday of the Arab

[15] See Barbara D. Metcalf, "The Pilgrimage Remembered: South Asian Accounts of the Hajj," *Muslim Travelers: Pilgrimage, Migration and the Religious Imagination,* ed. Dale F. Eickelman and James Piscatori, Comparative Studies in Muslim Societies 9 (Berkeley and Los Angeles: University of California Press, 1990), pp. 85–107.

[16] Malcolm X, with the assistance of Alex Haley, *The Autobiography of Malcolm X* (New York: Grove Press, 1966), pp. 338–39.

nationalist movement in the 1950s and 1960s. In his speeches and political acts, Nasser encouraged participation in the *ḥajj* as a demonstration of the power of the nonaligned nations in world politics and, in particular, of the strength of Arab nationalism. Nasser's endorsement of the pilgrimage also displayed to the leaders of conservative Arab states such as Saudi Arabia his view that most Arab pilgrims were not only committed Muslims but also Arab nationalists, both Sunnī and Shī'a, sympathetic to his political message. It would be difficult to ascribe primacy to any one of these identities at a given time or to separate "religious" from political and other sensibilities, much less to assign a hierarchy of motivation to all Muslims or to the adherents of other religions in the fulfillment of their religious obligations.

There are nine ritual steps to the pilgrimage itself.[17] Here my intent is not to present a structuralist explanation of the significance of these events but to outline them and to suggest some aspects of their symbolic richness. (1) First is the donning of the *iḥrām*, a white seamless garment that for many Muslims symbolizes the pilgrims' search for purity and their separation from the ordinary world. The *iḥrām* may be donned anywhere along the route up to the fixed points marking the confines of Mecca. No jewelry or other personal adornment may be worn, nor are pilgrims supposed to engage in disputes. Providing that the pilgrims have declared their intention (*nīya*) of making the pilgrimage, they are ready to enter the *ḥaram*, the sacred enclosure of Mecca itself, thought to have been established by Abraham and confirmed by Muḥammad. Non-Muslims are not allowed within its confines. Then (2), on the eighth day of the lunar month of Dhū l-Ḥijja, the month of the pilgrimage, pilgrims proceed to Mina, a small uninhabited village five miles east of Mecca. They spend the night there meditating and praying.

The next morning, the pilgrims move as a group to the plain of 'Arafa for the central rite of the pilgrimage, the (3) "standing" before Mount 'Arafa, the Mount of Mercy. They face Mecca, meditate, and pray. Many stand from noon to sunset. Some climb almost to the summit of the 200-foot mountain, at the foot of which the Prophet was supposed to have delivered his last sermon.

Just before sunset, a cannon sounds and the pilgrims proceed to (4) Muẓdālifa, a few miles back toward Mina. There they worship and sleep under the stars, after gathering a number of pebbles for use on the following day. The next morning, before daybreak, they return to Mina, where they throw the pebbles at three white-washed masonry pillars, especially the one thought to represent Satan, who three times tried to persuade Abraham not to obey God's command to sacrifice his son. Throwing the pebbles symbolizes the repudiation of evil.

[17] See, in particular, the sensitive, beautifully illustrated account by the Turkish scholar Emel Esin, *Mecca the Blessed, Madinah the Radiant* (London: Elek Books, 1963), which cites copiously from literature concerning Mecca and the pilgrimage. See also Muhammad Abdul-Rauf, "Pilgrimage to Mecca," *National Geographic* 154, no. 5 (November 1978), 581–607; and David Long, *The Hajj Today: A Survey of the Contemporary Makkah Pilgrimage* (Washington, DC: Middle East Institute, 1979). Numbers in the following discussion, identifying the stages in the pilgrimage, are keyed to Figure 10–3.

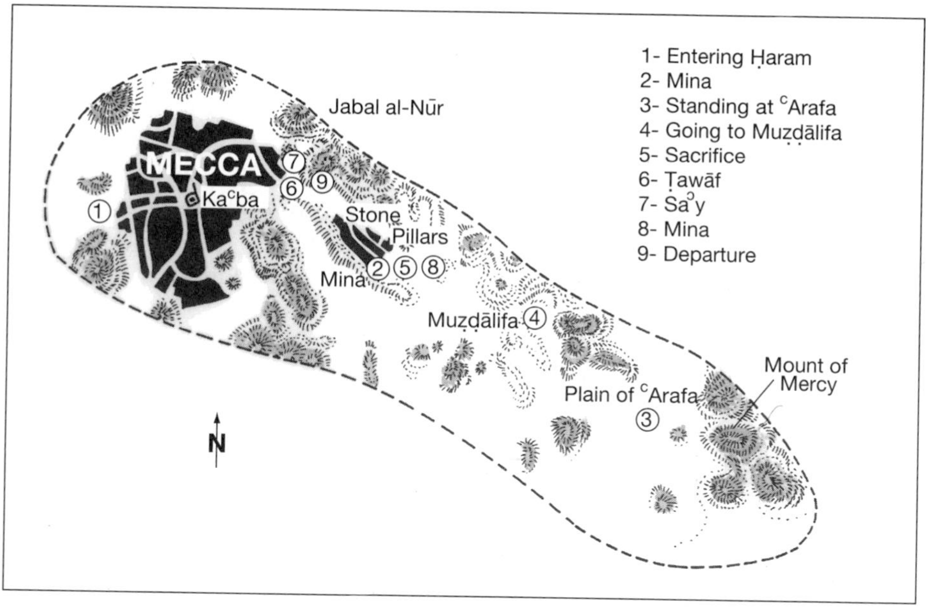

FIGURE 10-3. Principal steps of the *ḥajj*. [Based on an illustration in *Aramco World Magazine*, November–December 1974.]

(5) For the Feast of the Sacrifice (*'Īd al-Kabīr*), all pilgrims who can afford to do so buy a sheep or other animal for sacrifice and give away part of it to the poor, although given the quantity of meat sacrificed, most of it is not consumed (the Saudi government arranges for its shipment to needy Muslims throughout the world). This sacrifice has a range of meanings. It commemorates Abraham's willingness to sacrifice his son; it symbolizes the readiness to give up what is dearest to the pilgrim if commanded by God; it offers thanksgiving to God for having communicated with humans; and it reminds pilgrims to share their blessings with the less fortunate. Muslims throughout the world vicariously share in the elation of the pilgrims by performing their own sacrifices on the same day.

Once pilgrims have offered their sacrifices, they have completed a major part of the pilgrimage. Men shave their heads and women cut off a lock of their hair to symbolize their deconsecration. Pilgrims are now free to bathe and remove the *iḥrām,* although the prohibition on sexual intercourse remains.

The pilgrims next proceed directly to Mecca and perform (6) the *ṭawāf,* the circling. They circumambulate the Ka'ba seven times on foot, reciting a prayer on each circuit. This circling is said by some to symbolize the unity of God with man and of heaven with earth and reminds believers of the importance attached to the Ka'ba by the Patriarch Abraham, his son Ishmael, and Muḥammad. During the circling, many pilgrims try to touch the black stone that is embedded in one corner of the Ka'ba.

The key ceremonies of the pilgrimage are now completed, and pilgrims have the right to call themselves *ḥājji*-s. Most pilgrims, however, proceed to the "Place of Abraham," where Abraham is supposed to have offered his devotions to God. Then pilgrims reenact (7) the "running" (*sa'y*), the search for water by Hagar, the wife of Abraham (and Sarah's rival in the Bible). Hagar ran back and forth desperately searching for water for herself and her child until the Angel Gabriel appeared, stamped the ground with his heel, and brought forth water from the well of Zamzam for them. Pilgrims drink from this well before starting the running; many return home with bottles of water from it.

Pilgrims then customarily return for a third and last time (8) to Mina, where they cast their remaining pebbles at each of the three pillars—seven stones at each pillar for each day of the pilgrimage. This is also a time to visit with other pilgrims and to bid farewell to friends. Their final visit is to Mecca again, where pilgrims again circumambulate the Ka'ba (9) before returning home.

There is a rich tradition of myths associated with each step of the pilgrimage, and these myths have been variously interpreted throughout the Muslim world. If the pilgrimage is intended to convey the unity of the Muslim world, it also underscores its diversity. The *ḥajj* may hold the same significance for all Muslims, but the visit (Ar. *ziyāra*) to neighboring Medina carries a special significance for Shī'ī Muslims, whose beliefs are discussed in detail in the next section, because the al-Bāqī cemetery near the city is supposed to contain the grave of Fāṭima, the Prophet's daughter, and four of the twelve Shī'ī imams. In 1924 the Saudis banned access to the cemetery, but as a major concession to Iranian pilgrims, they reopened it in 1986 for visitation and prayer.

Over the past few centuries there have been repeated conflicts over Shī'ī access to these tombs. Since the Iranian revolution, conflict has intensified. In part, the Iranian Shī'a have been denied access to other revered Shī'ī shrines in southern Iraq since the outbreak of the Iran-Iraq war in 1980, and there were incidents throughout the 1980s in Mecca involving Iranian pilgrims (some 18 percent of the annual total), culminating with a violent confrontation on July 31,1987, in which 402 people died, including 275 Iranian pilgrims.[18] One reason for the violence is the political undercurrent challenging the legitimacy of Saudi custody of the holy shrines and conservative Saudi claims to leadership of the Muslim world. The fact that the Saudi monarch officially changed his title from "His Majesty" to "Servant of the Two Sacred Shrines" (*khādim al-ḥaramayn al-sharīfayn*) in 1986 suggests the importance the Saudi leadership attaches to its Islamic identity.

[18] For an account of this confrontation and prior ones, see Martin Kramer, "Behind the Riot in Mecca," *Policy Focus*, Research Memorandum 5 (Washington, DC: Washington Institute for Near East Policy, 1987).

THE SHI'A

The Iranian revolution of 1979 dramatically demonstrated the continued vitality of the Shī'ī tradition and its political influence in the modern world. Shī'ī belief and practice constitute a *source of motivation* to social action, not just a convenient vehicle for expressing social and economic discontent.[19] Said Amir Arjomand asserts that Shī'ism constitutes a world religion in its own right in a *sociological* sense. He is fully aware that most Shī'a, like other Muslims, assert the unity of Islam and the integrity of the Muslim community; nonetheless, the Shī'a know that their beliefs and practices set them apart from Sunnī Muslims in how they interpret Islam and express their belief.

The word *Shī'a* means "party" or "sect." This label reflects the origin of Shī'ism as a political movement in seventh-century Arabia. 'Alī (r. 656–661), the son-in-law of the Prophet Muḥammad, was the fourth of Muḥammad's caliphs (*khalīfa*-s), or successors.[20] 'Alī was assassinated by his opponents, as was Ḥusayn, the Prophet's grandson, in 680. The Shī'a consider both men martyrs. After 'Alī's assassination, the party of 'Alī in Kufa, in southern Iraq, demanded that succession be vested in 'Alī's descendants alone. This legitimist claim continues to be a principal Shī'ī belief. One contributing factor to Shī'ism, at least in its formative years, was the tension between newly conquered non-Arabs and their Arab rulers. In doctrinal terms, the Shī'a hold that the only legitimate successors to Muḥammad were his descendants through his son-in-law 'Alī and his daughter Fāṭima. Yet adherents of Shī'a Islam are no more homogeneous than those of Sunnī Islam. At the beginning of the Islamic era, most politically active Shī'a engaged in movements of protest and awaited the return of a *mahdī*, or "rightly guided one," to redress injustices and return the Muslim community to its proper course.[21]

With the exception of the Zaidī Shī'a of North Yemen, one component of Shī'ī doctrine is *taqīya*, or "concealment." In the face of persecution, the Shī'a are allowed to dissimulate their real beliefs if their expression would result in grave physical danger or a threat to the community. Thus 'Alī, whose caliphate was contested throughout his lifetime, "concealed" his belief in the right of his descendants to be Muḥammad's successors because of such a threat. This doctrine has allowed the Shī'a to adjust to diverse situations. This is the case for the Alevi (Ar. *'Alawī*) Muslims of Turkey, Iran, and Syria (where

[19] Said Amir Arjomand, *The Shadow of God and the Hidden Imam: Religion, Political Order, and Societal Change in Shi'ite Iran from the Beginning to 1890* (Chicago and London: University of Chicago Press, 1984), p. 3.

[20] See Marshall G. S. Hodgson, "How Did the Early Shī'a Become Sectarian?" *Journal of the American Oriental Society* 75, no. 1 (January–March 1955), 1–13, for an account of how the "basic principles" of Shī'ī thought and practice came into being.

[21] The notion of a *mahdī* is not unique to the Shī'a. The takeover of the Great Mosque at Mecca in November 1979 by a band of armed militants, mostly Sunnī, who proclaimed that one of their number was the *mahdī*, indicates the continuing political potential of such a belief and its challenge to traditional religious authorities. See Joseph A. Kechechian, "The Role of the Ulama in the Politics of an Islamic State: The Case of Saudi Arabia," *International Journal of Middle East Studies* 18, no. 1 (February 1986), 53–71, esp. 58–63.

the current president is an 'Alawī whose rituals and formal beliefs are such that some of their Sunnī and other Shī'ī neighbors have not accepted them as Muslims).

Religious leadership in the Shī'ī community relates closely to the level of popular support. Strictly speaking, there are no formal, appointative patterns of institutional leadership among the Shī'a, but pervasive informal ones enable Shī'ī men of learning to mobilize their followers. Because the patterns of leadership are informal and not centrally directed, they have been difficult for hostile governments to penetrate and suppress. *Mullah*-s, or village preachers, are associated with each mosque, as are a number of lesser religious figures. At the higher level are the *mujtahid*-s, scholars and leaders who by study and personal piety are recognized by their followers and peers as capable of making independent judgments and interpreting Islamic tradition. In contemporary Iran, *mujtahid*-s acquire recognition by publishing books outlining their methods and views for public comment. At a level above *mujtahid*-s are scholars called *Āyatullāh*-s, a term that literally means "sign of God." At the very apex of the hierarchy of deference is a scholar called the "Supreme" Āyatullāh, the *Āyatullāh al-'Uẓma,* considered the most learned scholar of his age and one whose piety is beyond question. Recognition at this highest level has been in the hands of a group of 30 or 40 religious scholars residing at Qum, one of Iran's holy cities, many of whom are related by ties of intermarriage and common studies or are descendants of leading religious scholars of the past. Leadership still depends in the end on a contemporary reputation for religious learning.[22]

Although some posts have revenues built into them, most of the higher members of the clergy depend on voluntary contributions from supporters, who have usually been large landowners and major merchants. Individual Shī'a often have considerable latitude in selecting the *mujtahid* from whom they will seek guidance and counsel, which creates room for independent entrepreneurs. Moreover, followers often can vote with their feet, so to speak, and shift allegiance from one *mujtahid* to another. Religious hierarchy among the Shī'a is based on deference, not institutionalized authority. This means that the Shī'a in Iran, as in Lebanon and the Arab Gulf states such as Kuwait, Bahrain, Saudi Arabia, and Oman, have independent leadership, although transnational lines of influence are not uncommon, given the shared training of Shī'ī men of learning and shared shrines—a pattern disrupted, however, by hostilities between Iran and Iraq.

[22] Arjomand, "Revolution," pp. 238–39, 246. Arjomand notes an inflation in the number of clerics claiming religious titles and competing for religious prestige in the nineteenth century. See also Leonard Binder, "The Proofs of Islam: Religion and Politics in Iran," in *Arabic and Islamic Studies in Honor of Hamilton A. R. Gibb,* ed. George Makdisi (Leiden: E. J. Brill, 1965), pp. 118–40. On the complex social and familial ties among leading Shī'ī scholars, see Michael M. J. Fischer, *Iran: From Religious Dispute to Revolution* (Cambridge, MA: Harvard University Press, 1980), and Fischer's "Becoming Mollah: Reflections on Iranian Clerics in a Revolutionary Age," *Iranian Studies* 13 (1980), 83–117, on the wide range of ideological positions taken by Iranian clerics and their varied audiences. Even in Iran of the late 1980s, there were Āyatollahs other than Khomeini, and some people considered them superior to Khomeini in religious authority. See A. V. Khan, "Ayatollah Attacks Khomeini Regime as Worse Than Shah's," *The Independent* (London), November 11, 1987, p. 10.

A key ritual and symbolic focus is the annual mourning (*ta'zīya*) in commemoration of the death of Ḥusayn, the Prophet's grandson and one of the Shī'ī *Imām*-s, at Karbala, Iraq, in the lunar month of Muḥarram in A.D. 680. Michael Fischer refers to this event as the "Karbala paradigm," and William O. Beeman argues that Khomeini's success is due to his "having been able to use the symbolism of the martyrdom of Hosein and to project it onto the struggle between the throne and the people."[23] As Gustave E. von Grunebaum wrote: "It would be incorrect to say that Husain stands in the center of Shī'a dogma, but it is unquestionably true that contemplation of his personality and fate is the emotional mainspring of the believer's religious experience."[24]

In the Shī'ī tradition, Ḥusayn's death is interpreted as a voluntary sacrifice in the face of treachery and betrayal by Sunnī and other opponents, so that, through his suffering, the Shī'ī faithful could enter paradise. Elizabeth Fernea, who was in Karbala in 1957, describes the event as it then took place.[25] Pilgrims arriving during Muḥarram swelled the population of Karbala, then a town of 30,000 people, to over 1 million, with many of the pilgrims living in black tents erected for them. From the first of the month, when the commemoration began, pilgrims donned mourning clothes; they refrained from bathing and shaving and adopted a simple diet. Pulpits were placed in the street from which the story of Ḥusayn's martyrdom was recited, often with many added details and commentary on current political events. Listeners broke out in tears. Also during this period, at least through the 1950s, groups of men seeking penance, with their bodies stripped to the waist and dyed black or red, roamed the streets, pulling out their hair, inflicting sword wounds upon themselves, and dragging chains behind them. Not infrequently, fights with non-Shī'a developed.

I use the past tense to describe these activities because both the prerevolutionary Iranian government and the Iraqi government formally banned the more extreme of these activities, although many of them continued to be carried out in areas remote from effective state authority. But the pattern of mourning for Ḥusayn's martyrdom is an integral part of the life cycle of most Shī'a, and it provides the Shī'ī community with a sense of self-renewal and victory over death. The ceremonies are replicated on a reduced scale for the deaths of all Shī'a on the third, seventh, and fortieth days after a death and thereafter on the anniversary of the death date. This replication gives the event even more personal significance to individual believers.

On the tenth of Muḥarram, a large procession designed as a funerary parade reenacts the last episodes of Ḥusayn's life and burial. The only props needed in the smaller settings are a coffin (or a bench from a guest house), a few arms, and Ḥusayn's banner. Many versions of these mourning plays exist, often

[23] Fischer, *Iran*, pp. 19–26; William O. Beeman, *Language, Status, and Power in Iran* (Bloomington: Indiana University Press, 1986), p. 71.

[24] Von Grunebaum, *Festivals*, p. 87.

[25] Elizabeth Warnock Fernea, *Guests of the Sheik* (Garden City, NY: Doubleday/Anchor, 1965), pp. 194–208. Since the Iraqi invasion of Iran in 1980, which was followed by a Shī'ī uprising in the Shī'ī-majority south, the Muḥarram celebrations have been significantly curtailed.

FIGURE 10-4. The Iranian cabinet, Tehran, August 1987. A common and highly effective vehicle for communicating government policy is the Friday sermon, often delivered by senior officials who are also clerics. [Photograph courtesy of the Islamic Republic News Agency.]

keyed to local social and political circumstances. The *ta'zīya* for Ḥusayn consists of some 40 to 50 loosely connected episodes. Because the audience knows the "paradigm" of the play, the drama does not rely on suspense but on how the particular scenes are enacted. Anachronisms abound in many presentations. In some versions, European Christian ambassadors rather than Sunnī Muslims have been made to betray Ḥusayn, and Old Testament figures are similarly introduced. The performance is often highly realistic, so that in the nineteenth century condemned criminals sometimes were made to play the part of the slayers of Ḥusayn in case the spectators became so enraged that they attacked the actors. The final scene involves a procession with the martyr's coffin (or in some versions a severed head) to the court of the Sunnī caliph. On the way, Christians, Jews, and Sunnī Muslims are portrayed as bowing before Ḥusayn. The intensity of such public performances, especially when elaborated in the context of other paradigmatic religious events, provides the Shī'ī clergy in Iran with a means of mobilizing public opinion. In the last years of the Shah's rule, political demonstrations were often planned to coincide with the cycle of Shī'ī religious activities. In the Islamic Republic, public events are carefully keyed to religiously significant events and thus motivate people to define contexts and perceive events in similar ways. One analyst refers to Khomeini as a "Great Communicator," as adept at mobilizing support and formulating goals in the Iranian context as Ronald Reagan supposedly was for America.[26]

The tendency of Western and many Sunnī Muslim writers has been to portray Sunnī Islam as "orthodox" in contrast to Shī'ism, a view that distorts the Islamic tradition. A personal report might indicate how I first began to be aware of intersectarian misperceptions within the Muslim community. Shortly before my arrival in Iran for a month's visit in 1968, a Sunnī colleague from a neighboring country warned that I would probably encounter Shī'ī hostility, especially in the smaller towns. For example, I was cautioned that the Shī'a would undoubtedly break any glasses or plates I had used. I encountered no hostility and left Tehran for Baghdad by a bus on which most of my fellow travelers were Shī'ī pilgrims on their way to visit the shrines of southern Iraq. The bus stopped regularly for collective prayers, the pilgrims sang together and shared their food with me. Later I mentioned to an Iranian *mujtāhid* what I had been told about the breaking of dishes and glasses. He laughed and replied that such objects were too expensive to break each time a nonbeliever was offered hospitality. My direct contact with Shī'ī Iran was brief but sufficient to suggest caution toward accepting at face value the often distorted images of "others" generated within the Islamic community among differing sectarian groups or by outside observers.[27]

AN IDEOLOGICAL FRONTIER? THE ALEVI

The ambiguous perceptions by other Muslims of the Alevi of eastern Turkey, Syria, northern Iraq, and Lebanon (where a number of Alevi took refuge in earlier years to avoid repression in their countries of origin) dramatically underscores the difficulty of defining Islam in terms of a supposed orthodoxy without regard to relationships of domination and authority. Thus the "official" recognition of Lebanon's Alevis (*'Alawī*) as part of the Shī'a community has less to do with a change in Alevi beliefs than with changing political relationships.[28] Although a minority, the 'Alawī are politically dominant in Syria. However,

[26] Beeman, *Language*, p. 212. On Khomeini's awareness of how religious discourse could be made to incorporate the political left of the 1960s, including the language of the political left, so that the Quranic notion of the "oppressed of the earth" (*al-mustalẓafūn fī al-'arḍ.*) (Sura 4, verse 97) came to be identified with the Marxist (specifically Franz Fanon's) "wretched of the earth," and the Quranic *al-mustakbarūn* (Sura 16, verses 22–23) with the "oppressors," see Nouchine Yavari-d'Hellencourt, "Le radicalisme Shi'ite de 'Ali Shari'ati" [The Shī'ī Radicalism of 'Ali Shari'ati], in *Radicalismes Islamiques*, vol. 1, ed. Olivier Carré and Paul Dumont (Paris: L'Harmattan, 1985), pp. 83–118, esp. p. 102.

[27] For further discussion of perceptions of intra-Muslim differences, see Robert L. Canfield, "Religious Myth as Ethnic Boundary," in *Ethnic Processes and Intergroup Relations in Contemporary Afghanistan*, ed. Jon W. Anderson and Richard F. Strand, Occasional Paper 15 (New York: Asia Society, 1978), pp. 35–42.

[28] James A. Bill and Carl Leiden, *Politics in the Middle East*, 2nd ed. (Boston and Toronto: Little, Brown, 1984), p. 38.

one leading analyst of Syrian politics cautions against assuming that Syria's 'Alawī are politically unified as a sect and instead suggests that the intertwined alliances developed through family ties, common schooling, and region explain more about patterns of political alliance than religious identity alone.[29] In Chapter 8 we discussed how identity as Alevis and as Kurds is often difficult to distinguish in the Kurdish-speaking regions of eastern Turkey. What is clear is that from the 1920s until very recently, Turkey's secular leadership has sought to limit the role of religion in public life. Nur Yalman, a distinguished Turkish anthropologist, avers that Social Darwinism became the dominant ideology of the Turkish upper classes and a justification for "embracing" Western culture.[30]

In the 1980s, secular-minded Turks began to acknowledge, if not always to welcome, the pervasive and continuing influence of religion in public life.[31] Their caution was due to the role of religious orders in the past, when some orders, such as the Bektāshīya, had enjoyed a privileged status. This order, founded in the thirteenth century, was closely associated with the Janissaries, a professional military body that played an important part in the maintenance of the Ottoman Empire until the early nineteenth century. The order continued to be regarded warily by Ottoman officials and later by those of the Turkish Republic. The influence of this order was such that an estimated 10 to 20 percent of Turkey's adult male population, including not an inconsiderable number of the Alevi, belonged to it in 1925, when religious brotherhoods were outlawed in Turkey. Yet, as orders such as the Bektāshīya declined, others came to the fore, such as Turkey's Nurculuk ("Light") movement, which attracted an especially large following among provincial civil servants, and it has continued to sustain a large following, with supporters even in California.[32] Religious orders (T. *ṭarikat,* Ar. *ṭarīqa*-s) have been driven underground in Turkey but enjoy a continued popularity.

The principal region of Alevi settlement in eastern Turkey forms part of the "shatter zone" of complex religious groupings. Most of the population is Muslim, at least from an external perspective, since the Sunnī, Alevi, Bektashi, and Nuseyri communities of the region do not always acknowledge one another's practices and beliefs as Muslim. To some extent, sectarian divisions

[29] Hanna Batatu, "Some Observations on the Social Roots of Syria's Ruling Military Group and the Causes for its Dominance," *Middle East Journal* 35, no. 3 (Summer 1981), 331–44.

[30] Nur Yalman, "Islamic Reform and the Mystic Tradition in Eastern Turkey," *European Journal of Sociology* 10, no. 1 (May 1969), 41–60. See Niyazi Berkes, *The Development of Secularism in Turkey* (Montreal: McGill University Press, 1964); and Smith, *Islam in Modern History,* pp. 164–208.

[31] For example, a major political scandal occurred in Turkey in early 1987 when the government reluctantly acknowledged that it had accepted funds from a Saudi-backed foundation to pay the salaries of government-employed Muslim clerics who preach to Turkish migrant workers in Western Europe. Many Turks saw such payments as a fundamental challenge to the principles of the Turkish Republic.

[32] John Kingsley Birge, *The Bektashi Order of Dervishes* (London: Luzac & Co., 1937), describes the order's role in consolidating opposition to the government. On the Nurculuk movement, see Şerif Mardin, *Religion and Social Change in Modern Turkey: The Case of Bediüzzaman Said Nursi,* SUNY Series in Near Eastern Studies (Albany: State University of New York Press, 1989).

coincide with linguistic ones: the Nuseyri speak Arabic, many Bektashi speak Turkish, and the Alevi speak both Turkish and Kurdish. But Kurdish-speaking Alevis sometimes claim they are Bektashis, as do Turkish-speaking Turkomen from western Anatolia. Members of both these groups might go to the annual festival at Haci Bektash village held each August. The dividing lines between groups are often ambiguous and shift situationally.[33] But the correlation between sect, language, and community is likewise ambiguous. Ruth Mandel, who has worked extensively with the Alevi, conveys this complexity:

> The majority of the Alevi in the east speak Zaza, and the Sunni speak Kurmanci, but there are Kurmanci-speaking Alevi and Zaza-speaking Sunni. Many people, I think, believe that both Zaza and Kurmanci are Kurdish dialects or languages, and this belief is motivated by social, cultural, or political considerations. From a formal, linguistic perspective, Zaza is an Iranian, not a Kurdish, language. It gets quite complicated, for some of the Zaza-phones claim not to be Kurdish, and say that Kurmanci and Zaza are not mutually intelligible. Others dispute this. To some Zaza Alevis, "Kurd" means Sunni . . . so they don't want to be labeled that. In other contexts the same people might say that they speak Kurdish; still more confusing, they might call the Sunnis "Muslims." Clearly, it depends upon who is the salient "other" in a given context.[34]

I cite Mandel at length because she clearly conveys how assertions of sectarian identity depend on highly nuanced perceptions of Muslim (and, to a lesser extent, non-Muslim) "others," especially when one is member of a nondominant group.

Many Shīʿa (and Sunnī) reject the Alevis as non-Muslims and do not make the distinctions that Alevi do among various groups. Nonetheless, as the name *Alevi* implies, their beliefs and practices have much to do with the role of ʿAlī in Islam. Moreover, because the Alevi are primarily village-based and have been regarded as politically suspect in recent years, they lack a tradition of formal religious scholarship and jurisprudence to produce the sort of "authoritative" discourse possessed by the Sunnī and most Shīʿī groups.

To understand the context of Alevi beliefs and practices in eastern Turkey, Nur Yalman describes a small, bleak peasant village of some 67 houses. He writes that the first thing a visitor notes about the village is the lack of any building showing a minaret and that "there was no call to prayer and no mosque." At the time of his visit, in the 1960s, men had mustaches that covered their upper lip to symbolize the secrecy of their creed, as opposed to the more clipped mustaches of other sectarian groups.[35]

[33] Ruth Mandel (personal communication, 1987) writes: "All Alevis claim to 'love Haci Bektash'—does that make them Bektashis? I'm not sure; it has more to do with [such factors as] the lineage of which their *pir* (spiritual leader) claims to be a part . . . in any case, it is a very fuzzy line, and I certainly wouldn't want to be the one to draw it."

[34] Mandel, personal communication, 1987 (used by permission).

[35] Yalman, "Islamic Reform," p. 50. The Alevi visited by Yalman were clearly confident of their political status since they displayed such a clear marker of sectarian identity.

Alevi ritual practices differ markedly from those of the Sunnī of the region. A brief contrast of ritual and belief from the perspective of the "five pillars" of Islam indicates the singular nature of Alevi beliefs from the dominant Sunnī perspective.[36] In terms of the declaration of faith, Alevis, like the Shī'a, emphasize the role of 'Alī in addition to the oneness of God and the prophecy of Muḥammad. Sunnī Muslims of the prevalent Ḥanafī rite of the region pray five times daily, with a total of forty bowings (*rak'a*-s)—there are eight bowings in each of the five prayers. For the Alevis, two bowings annually in the presence of their spiritual leader (*dede* or *pīr*) suffice. Sunnī-s fast the entire month of Ramaḍān; Alevis consider this a fetish. They fast in the month of Muḥarram for twelve days in memory of the twelve *imām*-s and call this fast *yas*, or "mourning" (for the martyrs of Karbala), not *ṣawm*, as the Ramaḍān fast is known. The Alevis consider the pilgrimage to Mecca "external pretense"; for them, the real pilgrimage takes place in one's heart.

From the dominant Sunnī (or even the Shī'ī) perspective, such Alevi interpretations of the Muslim tradition are unacceptable. Yalman delineates other points of contention: Alevis are reputed by their Sunnī neighbors not to perform ablutions correctly after sexual intercourse, and their secretive religious organization is regarded with suspicion. Most scandalous of all, from a Sunnī perspective, is an annual Alevi feast called *ayin-i cen*, which appears to be as important for the Alevi community as the Feast of Abraham (Ar. *'Īd al-Kabīr*; Turk. *Kurlan Bayrami*) for Sunnī Muslims.[37]

In the village studied by Yalman, this feast occurred when the village's *dede* visited from a neighboring town. Like the Shī'a, the Alevi practice *taqīya* or the dissimulation of their beliefs and practices, and the *ayin-i cen*, at least in Turkey, takes place only when outsiders are not present. This is the time of year when community disputes are resolved, often with the mediation of the *dede* (instead of before the formal services of the state). Members of the community approach the *dede* in pairs, hand in hand, kneeling down and walking on all fours, like lambs, to kiss the hem of his coat. This is when the only obligatory Alevi prayer is performed. *Semah* music, accompanied by a *saz*, a sort of long-necked flute, is performed, and the men and women dance. Some dancers go into trance. Alevi mystical poetry commemorating the martyrs of the Alevi community is recited and, outside of Turkey, the event re-creates or "reimagines" Alevi history in line with contemporary

[36] The following account is based primarily on Yalman, "Islamic Reform," pp. 51–55, with additional materials from Mandel, "Sectarian Splits: Interpretations of Turkish Muslim Identities and History," unpublished paper presented at the American Anthropological Association annual meeting, Philadelphia, December 4, 1986 (used with permission).

[37] For a speaker of Arabic, the word *cem* appears associated with *jam'a* or "gathering," as in *yawm al-jum'a*, literally, "the day of gathering," for Friday, the day of collective prayer. Another connotation, explicit in Iran according to Richard Tapper (personal communication, January 13, 1988), is *jam*, or "wine cup." Mandel, "Sectarian Splits" (p. 6), points out that the etymology of the word is uncertain; some scholars link the term with "*Cemshid*, the Iranian king of epic tradition associated with the creation of society, wine and Bacchanalian attributes." On Kurdish religious doctrines in Iran, see Ziba Mir-Hosseini, "Inner Truth and Outer History: The Two Worlds of the Ahl-i Haqq of Kurdistan," *International Journal of Middle East Studies* 26, no. 2 (May 1994), 267–85.

claims to identity. The climax of the festivity is the "putting out of the candle" (*mum söndürmek*), which some Sunnī claim is associated with "communal sexual intercourse and incest."[38] Contrary to non-Alevi fantasy, this rite culminates with water thrown on 12 burning candles to extinguish them in front of officiating elders. Each candle represents one of the 12 *imām*-s and martyrs. People moan and weep and curse those responsible for the assassination of 'Alī and the other martyrs.

As Mandel reports, Alevi practices have thrived in West Germany because there the Alevi need not be concerned about government interference. In the German "diaspora," in fact, Alevi migrants have been able to establish community-wide networks and elaborate the rituals and the historical sense of self and community through their performance. These wider networks have also facilitated a greater sense of collective political identity. A leading Turkish scholar claims that it was only in the 1970s that the Alevi began consciously to identify themselves as a political group on the basis of shared religious identity.[39] The factionalism that is publicly expressed on occasions such as *ayin-i cen*, especially in the West German context, is a form of "internal discourse" over defining the Alevi community, its "authoritative" discourse, and its sense of limits vis-à-vis the wider Muslim community.

Three main conclusions can be drawn from this brief discussion of Alevi identity. First, it serves as a reminder that orthodoxy and orthopraxy are situationally defined and linked to relationships of dominance and authority. Second, it points to the internal debate within the Muslim community itself and the tendency to maintain distorted perceptions of significant "others." The Alevi, like the Druze of Lebanon and Syria (who, like the Alevi, have a reputation for maintaining a reserve as to the exact nature of their beliefs), may be regarded as particularly extreme examples. Yet similar ranges of perceptions and misperceptions prevail between the Sunnī and Shī'a, between the Ibāḍīyya of Oman and North Africa and their neighbors, and the Aḥmadiyya in Pakistan. Finally, the strength of the Alevi tradition and the capacity of its carriers for self-renewal indicate the persistence of particularistic traditions within the Muslim community. The Alevi community for the most part lacks high scholarship and carriers of "high" formal learning but compensates for this in the strength of its shared local traditions and interpretations of Islamic belief and practice. These "particularistic" interpretations (as seen from a sociological perspective) are not waning in the face of "modernization" but maintain their vitality every bit as much as the Muslim traditions with a wide spectrum of carriers, from highly literate religious intellectuals to peasants and tribesmen.

[38] Yalman, "Islamic Reform," p. 55.

[39] Şerif Mardin, "Centre-Periphery as a Concept for the Study of the Social Transformation of Turkey," in *"Nation" and "State" in Europe: Anthropological Perspectives*, ed. R. D. Grillo (London: Academic Press, 1980), pp. 186–87.

> The impossibility of formulating at any given moment the irreducible elements of Muslim identity was expressed after the 1953 riots against the Aḥmadiyya in Pakistan, when the Pakistani government asked a commission of inquiry to define "Muslim." They reported that the country's religious scholars were unable to agree upon a definition. The commission remarked: "If considerable confusion exists in the minds of our [religious scholars] on such a simple matter, one can easily imagine what the differences on more complicated matters will be." [Punjab Government, *Report on the Court of Inquiry* (Lahore: Government Printing Office, 1954), p. 215.]

THE SUFI TRADITION

Any world religion involves multiple levels of belief and experience, prismatic in their richness and not easily reducible to a set of "basic" principles. One dimension of Islam, which crosscuts both the Sunnī and the Shī'a traditions, emphasizes the formal elaboration of belief and practice, what Marshall Hodgson has termed a *sharī'a*-minded Islam, concerned principally with outward, public credos and behavior (an extreme example of which might be the Saudi religious police, who see that all secular activities cease at the hours of prayer and that all Muslims perform their prayers on time) and the elaborate body of Islamic scholarship and jurisprudence that has been constructed over the years.

Another dimension of the Islamic experience has been glossed as "mysticism" (Ar. *taṣawwuf*), or Sufism, although the notion of mysticism is an elastic one and carries connotations throughout the Islamic world much wider than the intensely personal and often esoteric pursuit of religious truths commonly associated with the term in the West.[40] A mystic—the ambiguities of this term must be kept in mind—is known as a *ṣūfī*. The word *ṣūfī* is sometimes said to originate from the Arabic word for "wool," referring to the coarse wool garments that early Sufis wore to symbolize their lack of concern for the things of this world. Some people also think that *ṣūfī* derives from a word meaning "to be pure." If *sharī'a*-minded Islam was concerned primarily with outward, socially perceived behavior and the well-being of the Islamic body politic, then Sufism in the abstract represents more of a concern with the social and spiritual life of the individual (and, as will be seen, in some cases of specific social groups). Nor are the various manifestations of Sufism best seen as an alternative to *sharī'a*-minded Islam, although at some places and times within the Muslim community, some have argued that certain doctrines and practices are beyond the pale. Rather, it is an intense, personal complement to more formal doctrines, which has resonated in powerful and diverse ways in different contexts and situations.

Sufism encompasses both the highly sophisticated poetry and prose of the elite and practices that, although attracting elite adherents, are also understood

[40] Geertz, *Islam Observed*, p. 24.

and elaborated in more popular forms. Arjomand argues that after the adoption of Shī'ī Islam as the state religion in Iran in 1501, popular Sufism was ruthlessly suppressed for "reasons of state," because it was seen as a potential threat to political and religious authority. Hence in Iran, Sufism continued primarily in its highly cultivated form among the elite.[41]

In Morocco, on the other hand, to provide an example of popular religiosity, the monarchy remains linked with popular, implicit, and locally sustained conceptions of Islam, only some of which are formally articulated by traditionally educated men of learning, reformists, or modernists. The monarch's public image is constantly associated with the nation's religious and material welfare, and his formal statements and actions are scrupulously consistent with Islam, as interpreted by an educated elite. Yet other elaborations of religious practice, particularly the notion of marabouts, or "the pious ones" (*aṣ-ṣāliḥūn;* sing. *aṣ-ṣāliḥ*), are never directly challenged. "The pious ones" are people, living or dead (dead, that is, only from an outside observer's perspective), who, together with their descendants, work as efficacious intermediaries in securing God's blessings (*baraka*) for their clients and supporters.

Belief in the efficacy of the pious ones as saintly intermediaries is usually an implicit ideology expressed more in a set of sustained practices and associated myths than in explicit theology. Pious ones are often thought to be descendants of the Prophet Muḥammad (as is the Moroccan dynasty), 'Umār ibn al-Khaṭṭāb (r. 634–644, the second caliph in Islam), or other religious leaders attributed with *baraka.* Tribes and urban neighborhoods often have special ties with particular pious ones or their descent groups, such as the Sharqāwa of western Morocco. The shrines of the pious ones can be seen throughout North Africa, and the significance of such figures is acknowledged in a variety of ways. In North Africa, it is common for pilgrims to Mecca to first visit the shrines or sanctuaries of local pious ones and to do so again upon their return (see Figure 10-2). Such ritual activities suggest an integrated vision among believers of "local" religious practices linked with more universally accepted rituals such as the pilgrimage to Mecca. Further, there is an array of religious brotherhoods (*ṭarīqa*-s) and lodges (Ar. *zāwiya;* Per. *khānqāh;* Turk. *tekke*) associated with "mystic" practices. As with North African regard for the pious ones, these orders are seen by many Muslims as complementing and enhancing, rather than detracting from, the vitality of the Muslim community, although this view is also subject at times to vigorous internal debate.[42]

[41] Arjomand, *Shadow,* pp. 109, 244.

[42] Two disparate examples indicate the continuing pervasiveness of "mystical" practices. Yann Richard, "L'organisation des Fedâ'iyân-e Eslâm: Mouvement intégriste musulman en Iran (1945–1956)," in *Radicalismes Islamiques,* ed. Carré and Dumont, vol. l, pp. 72–73, describes the Sufi practices, including repeated recitations of the name of God (*dhikr*), of the founder of an important radical sect responsible for a number of political assassinations. Richard argues that such recitations are not just a hagiographic embellishment of a life story but a pervasive element in "radical" practice. Khomeini, he recalls, specialized in teaching philosophy and mysticism in Qum until 1951. Mohammed Tozy and Bruno Etienne, "La Da'wa au Maroc: Prolégomèna théorico-historiques," *ibid.,* vol. 2, pp. 20–21, point to stylistic elements in "fundamentalist" sermons in Morocco and elsewhere that derive from Sufi practices.

> The term "the pious ones" (*aṣ-Ṣāliḥ*) is less familiar to non-Moroccans than "marabout," a term accepted as English usage. "Marabout" has accumulated a baggage of misinterpretation over the years, although it is derived from *murābiṭ* (lit. "the tied one"), a perfectly acceptable Arabic term that, in North Africa, signified pious Muslims who established themselves in tribal territories when the region was not yet thoroughly Islamized. Marabouts constituted the "tie" between Islam and the tribes surrounding them. The term is no longer current and is retained here only when it unambiguously refers to "the pious ones" serving as intermediaries in earlier historical periods. "The pious ones," on the other hand, conveys intact the multivalence of current Moroccan usage. For educated Muslims, a *ṣāliḥ* is revered solely for outstanding piety, and many speak of saint, or maraboutic, "cults" as "pre-Islamic" practices. For many of the nonelite, however, in both towns and in rural areas, recognition of the piety of "the pious ones" is complemented by a belief in their mystical powers. Participants in practices honoring the pious ones or seeking their support are fully aware of the disapproval of some elite but nonetheless regard their vision of Islam as realistic and appropriate. Use of "the pious ones" instead of "marabout" or "saint" evokes the multiplicity of the Moroccan concept and the fact that participation in such a "cult" does not constitute evidence of an alternative, independent interpretation of Islam.

Sufi practices do not appear to have been emphasized in the early development of Islam. From the seventh to the ninth centuries, Sufism seems to have remained largely an individual phenomenon, but gradually it developed a mass appeal.[43] The first Sufi gatherings were reputedly informal meetings for religious discussions, especially among literati. These gatherings were sometimes associated with the repetitions of the names of God, called *dhikr*-s, but these could also properly be recited in mosques. Hence Sufism was not at this stage considered a challenge to the formal practices of *sharī'a*-minded Muslims. A later development was the addition of elaborate rituals, music, and dancing to accompany the *dhikr*, and *these* practices were regarded by some Muslims as a threat to the integrity of Islam.

At first, organized Sufism appears to have gained ground among an intellectual elite constrained by the exigencies of a *sharī'a*-minded Islam. Despite its stated apolitical objectives, Sufism was regarded from the outset as politically suspect (because of its potential for charismatic leadership), with political authorities sometimes using Sufi organizations for their own purposes or regarding them, often with cause, as being so used by others. The Sufi doctrine of the "inner way" or the "spiritual itinerary" toward greater religious experi-

[43] One of the best overall accounts of the development of Sufi thought remains Marshall G. S. Hodgson, *The Venture of Islam: Conscience and History in a World Civilization* (Chicago and London: University of Chicago Press, 1974), vol. 1, pp. 359–409; vol. 2, pp. 201–54.

ence was regarded as especially suspect, as, by its very nature, it claimed a privileged religious insight independent of the community. As a consequence, Sufis began to develop formal disciplines and standard, stylized ways of depicting their experiences. Regular stages in spiritual development were formulated in the classical theories of mystical thought, each called a *ṭarīqa,* or "path." The same term also designates Sufi orders or brotherhoods.

In some versions of "classical" Sufi doctrine, the way consists of seven stages of ascending spiritual insight. Most members of religious orders remain at the lower rungs of these spiritual paths. The upper level is reached when a mystic, in a state of exaltation (*ḥāl*), comprehends the divine attributes. Such people are considered *wālī*-s, or saints, in the classical literature and often were popularly attributed with the ability to perform miracles.

By the eleventh century, particularly in the person of the great scholar and mystic al-Ghazzālī (d. 1111), a synthesis of intellectualized Sufi doctrine and *sharī'a*-minded Islam was reached. At the level of an educated elite, beautiful poetry and literature developed around the notions of mysticism, particularly in the principalities of Muslim Spain and in the Persian-speaking regions of the Islamic world.

In many of the accounts of Sufism written by Muslims and by Western scholars concerned primarily with textual analysis, there is an unfortunate tendency to consider Sufi doctrine as practiced and elaborated by the educated elite as "pure" Sufism and later, popular developments as a corruption of this purer vision. The result is a distorted view of religious development that led an earlier generation of historians to write of the "decline" of the Muslim world rather than to recognize the multiple levels of religious experience in which the "spiritual" aspects of Sufi practice, as interpreted by an elite, were balanced by its functions as a sociopolitical movement intimately tied to other aspects of society.[44] A proliferation of Sufi "paths" developed that were internally differentiated and that appealed to different groups and social classes.

In North Africa, for instance, the Tijānīya order had numerous government officials among its adherents,[45] as did the Bektāshī order in Turkey. Other orders were associated with particular crafts or trades. Some were considered highly respectable; others, such as the Ḥamadsha and the Ḥaddāwa in Morocco, were associated with the use of drugs, trances, and activities considered marginal by the urban bourgeoisie.[46] Until the 1920s, the strength of these orders was such that the majority of adult urban males and many villagers belonged

[44] The assumption of a "decline" of Sufi ideas as they became popularly received unfortunately permeates most of the Orientalist literature on the subject. The irony is that "decline" was coterminous with widespread popularity. See A. J. Arberry, *Sufism: An Account of the Mystics of Islam* (London: Allen & Unwin, 1950); and W. Montgomery Watt, *Muslim Intellectual: A Study of Al-Ghazzali* (Edinburgh: Edinburgh University Press, 1963), esp. pp. 128–33. See also Dale F. Eickelman, *Moroccan Islam: Tradition and Society in a Pilgrimage Center,* Modern Middle East Series 1 (Austin and London: University of Texas Press, 1976), pp. 22–29, on the influential French scholar, Alfred Bel.

[45] Jamil M. Abun-Nasr, *The Tijaniya: A Sufi Order in the Modern World,* Middle Eastern Monographs 7 (London: Royal Institute of International Affairs, 1965).

[46] See, for example, Crapanzano, *The Ḥamadsha.*

to a brotherhood in most parts of the Middle East. A popular saying was: "He who does not have a Sufi master as his guide has Satan to guide him."

The organizational backbone of these orders is important to consider. At its core was the relation of the Sufi master (Ar. *shaykh;* Per. *pīr*) to his disciple (*murīd* in both languages). In formal doctrine, the disciple was supposed to be under the total authority of the shaykh, like a dead body in the hands of its cleanser. Additionally, local religious lodges were organized in a loose hierarchy ordered by the prestige of their shaykhs. But the larger these organizations grew, the more difficulty they had in controlling their members. Subsidiary lodges constantly broke away, with their leaders acting on their own. The dyadic, or two-person, chains of personal authority inherent in the organization of the brotherhoods thus had a built-in weakness. Despite this fact, colonial ethnographers in the nineteenth and early twentieth centuries, especially in North Africa, conceived of the organization of these orders as monolithic "pan-Islamic" conspiracies that could be used by the Ottoman regime and rival colonial powers to weaken colonial rule.[47] In practice, the authority of shaykhs over their followers was usually less than total, as is indicated by the fact that many individuals belonged to more than one order and that only a few orders required that their members join no other. As a whole, however, the hierarchies of dominance established by the religious orders formed a pervasive and popularly understood template for organizing political activities. In many parts of the Muslim world, including among the Turkic peoples of Central Asia, Sufi orders played an important role in spreading Islamic knowledge.[48]

The proliferation and variety of Sufi ways and "pious ones" cannot be sufficiently stressed. Bryan S. Turner has suggested distinctive contrasts between saints in Christianity and in the Muslim world. In early Christianity, sainthood was at first a local and spontaneous phenomenon that gradually became tied to the institutional needs of a bureaucratized church. By the medieval period, saints became officially recognized only after a lengthy process of canonization. There were three implications to this process. First, because of the length of the canonization proceedings, individuals became saints only after they died. Second, because there were stringent tests of piety required by ecclesiastical authorities, most saints were recruited from monasteries and nunneries. Finally, because trained theologians conducted canonization proceedings, theologians had a much better chance than illiterates for canonization.

Becoming a pious one, or marabout, in the Muslim world stands in marked contrast to the Christian tradition. First, with no formal body of orthodoxy accepted throughout the Muslim world, the recognition of sanctity is

[47] See the map in Octave Depont and Xavier Coppolani, *Les confréries religieuses musulmanes* (Algiers: A. Jourdan, 1897 [reprint ed., 1986]), for the most sinister representation of the pervasive, cross-border influence of these orders. The authors were French government specialists on native affairs in Algeria.

[48] Hamid Algar, "Shaykh Zaynullah Rasulev: The Last Great Naqshbandi Shaykh of the Volga-Urals Region," in *Muslims in Central Asia: Expressions of Identity and Change,* ed. Jo-Ann Gross (Durham, NC: Duke University Press, 1992), pp. 112–33; and Alexandre Benningson and S. Enders Wimbush, *Mystics and Commisars: Sufism in the Soviet Union* (Berkeley and Los Angeles: University of California Press, 1985).

local, although some pious ones acquire widespread prominence. Second, whereas Christian saints tend to be orthodox, there is no orthodoxy to which their Muslim counterparts can adhere. Finally, because there are no formal bodies for deciding who are "pious ones," the process of labeling them varies widely. Sometimes a person is considered a pious one on the basis of descent from religious leaders, performing uncanny acts or feats of scholarship, achieving political success, or any combination of these and other attributes.

There is an "essential looseness," to use Turner's phrase, about Islamic religious organization, which means that it is much more responsive to local social contexts than has often been the case in Christianity.[49] Religious orders and lodges accommodated the local beliefs and customs of their adherents, and this led to their sustained popularity in earlier historical periods. In fact, much of the spread of Islam throughout North Africa after the initial Islamic conquests was due to the actions of these orders and lodges. Some of the leaders of these orders and lodges based their legitimacy on genealogies of spiritual authority, which resembled the "teaching licenses" (*ijāza*-s) of men of learning. The source of their teachings could be traced in these chains (*silsila*-s) of authority to the teachings of the Prophet himself. Other lodges claimed genealogical descent from the Prophet Muḥammad. One such leader, the Sudanese Mahdi, Muḥammad Aḥmad (1844–1885), modeled the major activities of his life on those of the Prophet Muḥammad as a means of convincing followers of his legitimacy.[50]

The reasons for the general decline of many of these orders by the early part of this century have been suggested by Michael Gilsenan. In 1964–1966 he studied a twentieth-century Egyptian religious order that continues to thrive, the Ḥāmidīya Shādhilīya.[51] This order was established in the first decades of the

[49] Turner, *Weber and Islam*, pp. 57–62, 66. One of the best assessments of the social origins of pious ones in a Muslim context, based on an analysis of biographical data, is Halima Ferhat and Hamid Triki, "Hagiographie et religion au Maroc médieval," *Hespéris-Tamuda* 24 (1986), 17–51. This study also emphasizes the lack of sharp distinctions between pious ones as intermediaries and as religious scholars and provides insight into the role of female saints (pp. 43–44).

[50] See P. M. Holt, *The Mahdist State in the Sudan, 1881–1898* (Oxford: Clarendon Press, 1958); for discussions of the Sudanese Mahdist movement in the light of later religious developments—descendants of the Mahdi have continued to play important roles in modern Sudanese politics—see John Voll, "Islam: Its Future in the Sudan," *The Muslim World* 63, no. 4 (October 1973), 210–96, and his *Islam: Continuity and Change in the Modern World* (Boulder, CO: Westview Press, 1982). For an account of an Algerian religious figure that is excellent in portraying doctrine, but less so in describing the nature and context of the shaykh's popularity, see Martin Lings, *A Moslem Saint of the Twentieth Century* (London: Allen & Unwin, 1972 [1961]). For an analysis of an order whose political and economic influence actually increased during the colonial and postcolonial eras, see Donald B. Cruise O'Brien, *The Mourides of Senegal* (Oxford: Clarendon Press, 1971), and his *Saints and Politicians: Essays in the Organization of a Senegalese Peasant Society*, African Studies Series 15 (London: Cambridge University Press, 1975).

[51] Gilsenan, *Saint and Sufi*. As in all such sociological arguments, the element of time needs to be emphasized. Kazuo Ohtsuka, a Japanese anthropologist, has studied what he calls "*salafī*," or reformist, Sufism in Cairo from 1986 to 1988. Ohtsuka (personal communication, December 27, 1987) found that many Sufi orders, responding to criticisms from other Muslims arguing for a purification of Islam and a return to "original" (*salafī*) practices, are regaining adherents. Other practices remain closely associated with local politics in Egypt. See Edward B. Reeves, *The Hidden Government: Ritual, Clientelism, and Legitimation in Northern Egypt* (Salt Lake City: University of Utah Press, 1990).

FIGURE 10-5. Members of the Rifā'iya order parading in Cairo on the Prophet's birthday, 1987. [Courtesy Kazuo Ohtsuka.]

twentieth century and was formally recognized by the government in 1926. In the early 1960s, it had between 12,000 and 16,000 members, concentrated for the most part in Cairo and in the larger towns of the Nile Delta.

Gilsenan argues that until the 1920s, religious orders in Egypt provided an "organized associational life" otherwise absent in many Islamic societies. As such, they served as intermediaries between the highborn and the lowborn, rulers and ruled, as well as between people at the same level of society.[52] As a result of basic changes in Egypt's political economy, the heads of the Sufi orders gradually lost their public and political influence. Professional politicians, landowners, lawyers, and journalists took over some of their functions, and mutual aid societies were established to fulfill others. Additionally, the economic position of most of the orders was undermined as a result of government confiscation of some pious endowments (*waqf*-s) and the declining value of others on which they depended. This deprived the leaders of the orders of the resources with which to entertain and aid their followers. Moreover, Sufi teachings and ethics in their conventional form had become less and less responsive to the values of modern society. Many Sufi orders continue to be a major source of emotional gratification for their adherents, but these adherents are mostly peasants and manual laborers. Younger Egyptians no longer seek to join them.

[52] Gilsenan, *Saint and Sufi*, p. 11.

Gilsenan observes that the Ḥāmidīya Shādhilīya order was an exception to this general decline. Its founder, Salāma ibn Ḥasan Salāma (1867–1939), was a minor civil servant, and, as such, he was familiar with the demands of modern bureaucratic organization. He was largely self-taught but popularly respected for his religious learning and his claim to descent from the Prophet. Salāma was a charismatic figure to his followers, and a number of miracle stories circulated during his lifetime. He was claimed capable of confounding the religious scholars opposed to him, known for his understanding of the "secrets" of Islamic mysticism, and charitable and generous to his followers.

Organizationally, the Ḥāmidīya Shādhilīya differs from other orders. Salāma tested his early initiates, so that he had a hard core of knowledgeable and devoted subordinates. He required that his followers join no other brotherhood. Also, the order attracts a white-collar following as well as workers and peasants. Its doctrines and firm organization provide a sense of personal worth and security to middle-class people blocked from occupational advancement (as are many educated Egyptians). Gilsenan characterizes most of the order's adherents as benefiting from, yet not wholly committed to, the new order of Egyptian society. Many individuals who have had their occupational advancement blocked can find alternative satisfaction, he argues, in the order.[53] It offers the fraternal certitude and security that presumably were once provided by the "traditional" social order, yet it is organizationally adapted to the exigencies of modern society.

Gilsenan writes that each role in the Ḥāmidīya Shādhilīya is carefully defined by written charter. Formal reports are periodically required from its branches, and members of the order exhibit discipline and restraint in their public performances, distancing themselves from the ecstatic behavior of some other orders. Because of this bureaucratic structure, the order can keep track of members as they move from town to town and facilitate their adjustment to new locations. Gilsenan suggests that adherence to the primary religious values of the order enables its followers to resolve the frustrations and contradictions they encounter in other aspects of their lives. In Weberian fashion, Gilsenan argues that the order's hierarchical control, lacking in most other orders, enables it to avoid internal schisms, maintain discipline among its members, and emulate the form of valued, "modern" organizations of bureaucracies or industries in which a significant component of its membership participates.

"PIOUS ONES" AND RELIGIOUS ORDERS

Religious orders may, for the moment, be eclipsed by other forms of religiosity, but their political salience in recent historical periods should be kept in mind. One of the first anthropological studies to take them into account was E. E. Evans-Pritchard's study of the Sanūsīya in Libya, which formed the base of the

[53] Ibid., pp. 150–51.

monarchy overthrown by Mu'ammar al-Qadhdhāfi.[54] Evans-Pritchard argues that the Sanūsīya emerged as the most significant religious influence over the tribes of Cyrenaica because the order's leaders adapted its structure to local tribal conditions. He provides a social history of Sanūsī resistance to the Italians, their relations with British military authorities, and how their leadership was transformed into a monarchy. He characterizes the Cyrenaican tribes as segmentarily organized, yet he provides no concrete examples of how these segmentary principles worked or how the Sanūsī lodges were concretely articulated with the tribal structure. Indeed, his narrative is fully comprehensible without recourse to the idea of segmentation. Surprisingly, Evans-Pritchard deals with the transition from the presumed segmentary structure of the tribes to their integration into a "political form . . . on the model of the European state" in a mere two paragraphs.[55] Such a massive transformation of social and political form, if accurately depicted, merits more sustained consideration. Later studies of Islam in a tribal milieu, notably I. M. Lewis's account of the role of saintly lineages in Somalia from precolonial times to independence, are significantly more successful in suggesting how Islam has taken shape in a tribal milieu.[56]

One factor in the proliferation of Sufi brotherhoods is the contrast between the requirements of formal, community-minded religion and the more personalized, often emotionally intense patterns of belief provided by some of the religious orders. Other elements include local conceptions of the social order and the popular understanding of religion, which can be just as creative as elite producers of religious values and practices. The way that North Africans perceive pious ones, or marabouts, suggests the implicit tension between certain Quranic doctrines and local understandings of religion and the social order.

A key Quranic understanding is that all people are equal before God, despite the inequalities found in the social order. Yet the activities of some religious brotherhoods and the often lavish offerings given to pious ones and their descendants in North Africa and to similar figures elsewhere suggest that some Muslims act as if they implicitly accept a hierarchical conception of the relations between people and divinity. In a formal sense, the tenet of the equality of believers before God cannot be reconciled with the notion of access through intermediaries. Yet a reconciliation can be found at the level of practice, in spite

[54] E. E. Evans-Pritchard, *The Sanusiya of Cyrenaica* (Oxford: Clarendon Press, 1949).

[55] Ibid., pp. 104–105. For an account of political development that avoids assuming a sharp dichotomy between tribal and nontribal politics, see Lisa Anderson, *The State and Social Transformation in Tunisia and Libya, 1830–1980* (Princeton, NJ: Princeton University Press, 1980). See also Emrys Peters's analysis of the social structure of the bedouin of Cyrenaica, discussed in Chapter 6; his "From Particularism to Universalism in the Religion of the Cyrenaica Bedouin," *Bulletin of the British Society for Middle Eastern Studies* 3, no. 1 (January 1976), 5–14; and John Davis, *Libyan Politics: Tribe and Revolution*, Society and Culture in the Modern Middle East (London: I. B. Tauris, 1987), pp. 179–211.

[56] I. M. Lewis, *A Pastoral Democracy*, new ed. (New York: Holmes & Meier, 1982 [1961]), esp. pp. 196–241.

FIGURE 10-6. Interior of the Mosque of Ibrāhīm in Hebron, Israel. In the Middle East and North Africa, the significance of many shrines transcends the immediate locality and religious tradition. Many shrines are venerated by Muslims and Jews alike. Similarly, many religious places in the Indian subcontinent are shared by Muslims and Hindus. In this photograph, the *qibila* (prayer niche) facing Mecca, toward which Muslims pray, is seen in the background. The tomb of Rebecca is at the left, and that of Isaac at the right. [Manoug. Courtesy Sonia Alemian. All rights reserved.]

of theological contradictions. The powerful imagery of the role of Morocco's ruling dynasty in this respect has already been raised.

In essence, belief in the efficacy of the pious ones as intermediaries with divinity involves the assumption that whatever might be formally stated about Islam, human relations with the supernatural work in almost the same way as relations among people.[57] In the Moroccan case, the implicit assumption concerning the social order is that people are related in personally contracted dyadic bonds of inferiority and superiority. In a nearly analogous fashion, pious ones are thought to have a "special" relation toward God and with particular people or groups. For Moroccans and other North Africans who implicitly accept such beliefs, the issue is not the existence of marabouts—that is taken for granted—but whether particular pious ones will exercise their powers on one's behalf. They are more likely to do so if a client can claim "closeness"

[57] See Eickelman, *Moroccan Islam*, pp. 155–82, for further discussion of saints, or marabouts, as intermediaries in popular Muslim thought.

FIGURE 10-7. Shrine near Boujad, Morocco. Women often tear strips from their clothing to "remind" pious ones of their requests. [Courtesy of the author.]

(*qarāba*) to a pious one or his descendants. Moroccans who hold this belief are aware that there is no place for it in "official" Islam—"radio Islam," as one Moroccan put it:

> Of course the radio says that everything comes directly from God. But just as the king has his ministers, God has his [pious ones]. If you need a paper from the government office, which is better? Do you go straight to the official and ask for it? You might wait a long time and never receive it. Or do you go to someone who knows you and also knows the official? Of course, you go to the friend, who presents the case to the official. Same thing . . . if you want something from God.

Various offerings and sacrifices are made to marabouts and their descendants. Some, such as the sacrifice of bulls or sheep at the annual festival of a marabout, are annual obligations that ensure that the social groups involved "remain connected" with the marabout and can count on his blessings (*baraka*). Individuals or groups give other gifts in exchange for specific requests. These offerings often are contingent. For instance, it is common for women to go to certain shrines asking for a marabout's help in becoming pregnant. They may tear a strip of cloth from their dress and attach it with henna to the door of a shrine as a "reminder" to the pious one. If the request is granted, then a sheep or other payment is made. At the larger shrines, where descendants of the

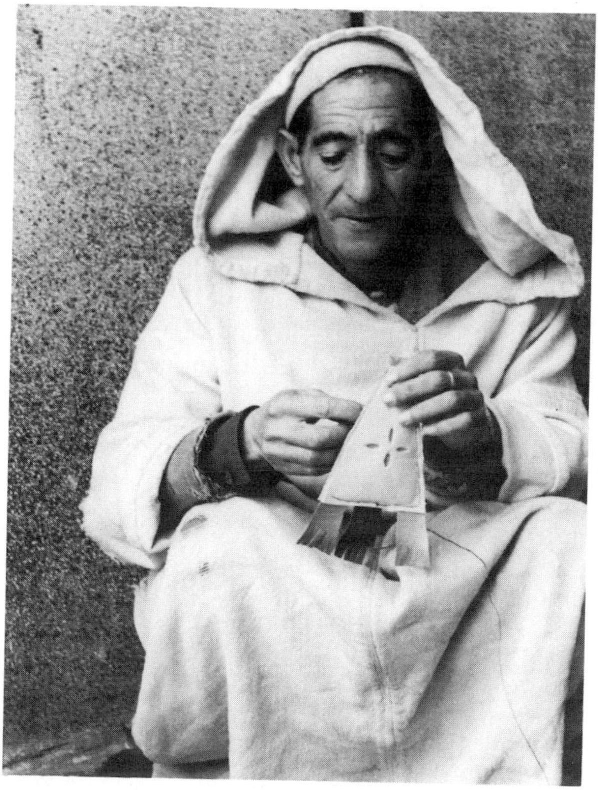

FIGURE 10-8. Preparing amulets for sale at a shrine, Boujad, Morocco. [Courtesy of the author.]

marabout act as custodians, lodging and food may be provided for "visitors" (*zawwār*-s). (The Arabic word for "pilgrim," *ḥājj*, is not used to describe such visits; the pilgrimage to Mecca is considered conceptually separate.) The modest offerings made by women on their own or their placing of "reminders" at larger shrines is discouraged in favor of more substantial offerings in line with the "rank" of the marabout.

Such offerings are thought of in North Africa in terms of the ideology of "obligation" (*ḥaqq*), which informs most other social relationships. As the descendant of one marabout explained: "You must bring a gift to 'open' a matter with God." Offerings and sacrifices create a bond of obligation between the pious one and his client. Just as with other patterns of obligations, those between pious ones and their clients, even if sometimes discussed in terms of the ideology of "blood" relations, are subject to vicissitudes. The reputations of pious ones living and "dead" are as subject to revaluation on the part of the clients as are other concepts of social obligations. Personal and collective ties with pious ones rest on a similar ideological base, but the collective ties merit particular attention because of the emphasis lavished on them by anthropologists. Many tribal collectivities are specifically mentioned in popularly known myths, which serve to legitimate the ties between particular maraboutic descent groups and their clients. Such covenants are represented as being maintained through annual sacrifices, the giving of women to prominent leaders of maraboutic patronymic associations, the claim of a common, distant ancestor between pious ones or their descendants and their clients, and the claim of mere physical propinquity in the distant past.[58]

So pervasive are the basic assumptions concerning the social order upon popular religious conceptions that notions partially parallel to the Muslim pious ones can be found in North African Judaism. Accounts of North African Jewish communities from the 1930s to the 1950s document saints' shrines, local festivals (called *ḥillūla*-s instead of *mūsim*-s, as among Muslims), and sacrifices.[59] Many of these communities continued these practices in modified, and greatly enhanced, form after emigration to Israel. Some North African Jews aver that their *saddiq*-s (Ar. *ṣadīq* or "friend") emigrated with them. The dreams and other events legitimizing these practices appear to parallel their Muslim counterparts.[60] At least one *rebbe* of Moroccan origin has a substantial following both in Israel and in New York.[61]

The understanding of Islam represented by the practices surrounding the pious ones is like other aspects of belief and practice transformed and reinterpreted by changing economic and political conditions. In the past, pious ones and their descent groups served as mediators between tribes and the sultan's court, secured the safe passage of commerce in disturbed areas, and at the same time were often (although not necessarily) respected as religious scholars. Their popular reputations as miracle workers and intermediaries in no way diminished the respect that was accorded their religious learning. Pious ones in tribal areas frequently had extensive contact with religious scholars in principal towns and elsewhere; in some cases they even tutored members of

[58] For an example of such a myth, see ibid., pp. 163–68. An analysis of that particular text in the wider context of the relation between oral narratives and Middle Eastern social forms is provided by Michael E. Meeker, *Literature and Violence in North Arabia*, Cambridge Studies in Cultural Systems 5 (New York: Cambridge University Press, 1979), pp. 214–44. Michael A. Marcus, "'The Saint Has Been Stolen': Sanctity and Social Change in a Tribe of Eastern Morocco," *American Ethnologist* 12, no. 3 (August 1985), 455–67, illustrates how mythic discourse plays a role in contemporary local political activity.

[59] See L. Voinot, *Pèlerinage judéo-musulman du Maroc* (Paris: Éditions Larose, 1948), for a listing of these shrines and a map of their locations.

[60] In addition to the sources on North African Judaism in the Maghrib and in Israel mentioned in Chapters 8 and 9, see Alex Weingrod, "Saints and Shrines, Politics and Culture: A Morocco-Israel Comparison," in *Muslim Travelers*, ed. Eickelman and Piscatori, pp. 217–35. On visitational dreams by *saddiqīm*, see Yoram Bilu and Henry Abramovitch, "In Search of the Saddiq: Visitational Dreams Among Moroccan Jews in Israel," *Psychiatry* 48, no. 1 (February 1985), 83–92. The dreams and their interpretations as reported by the authors strongly resemble their Moroccan Muslim counterparts. See also Eyal Ben-Ari and Yoram Bilu, "Saints' Sanctuaries in Development Towns," in *Israeli Judaism*, ed. Shlomo Deshen, Charles S. Liebman, and Moshe Shokeid, Studies of Israeli Society 7 (New Brunswick, NJ: Transaction, 1995 [1987]), pp. 255–84.

[61] C. T. Bari, *Baba Sali: Our Holy Teacher* (*Rav Yisrael Abuchatzeirah*), trans. Leah Dolinger (New York: Judaica Press, 1986), a hagiography that strongly resembles its Muslim counterparts in style. The Hebrew newspaper *Yedioth Ahronoth* (Brooklyn), November 14, 1986, last page, carried an announcement of a regular meeting of "The American Friends of Yeshivat Baba Sali" at a Central Park South address.

FIGURE 10-9. Women at a grave-shrine, Afghanistan, 1971. Note the miniature cradle on the shrine, lower left. [Courtesy of Nancy Lindisfarne-Tapper.]

the royal family.[62] There frequently was tension between royal and maraboutic authority, but the relationship was often one of complementarity. Earlier social anthropological studies, prepared without the benefit of research based on precolonial historical sources, suggested that saints or marabouts played an interstitial "balancing" role between tribes and royal authority.[63] More recent research, carried out largely by Moroccan scholars more attuned to describing and eliciting the *cultural* understandings of royal and saintly authority, suggests a much closer linkage between maraboutic centers and royal authority than had been recognized by colonial scholarship and sociological accounts. In addition, far from being in opposition to urban-based religious scholars and their supporters, many tribally based marabouts or pious ones were respected by them and shared similar interpretations of Islam, even though popular understanding of the roles of saints or pious ones, both rural and urban, was often at variance with the formal Islamic precepts of the elite. There was no sharp urban/rural dichotomy of belief and ritual practice but rather a contin-

[62] Eickelman, *Moroccan Islam*, pp. 31–64. For southern Morocco in the seventeenth and eighteenth centuries, see Abdellah Hammoudi, "Sainteté, pouvoir et société: Tamgrout aux XVIIe et XVIIIe siècles," *Annales E.S.C.* 35, nos. 3–4 (May–August 1980), 615–41.

[63] The classic statement of this view in English, which has acknowledged antecedents in earlier French scholarship, is Ernest Gellner's *Saints of the Atlas*, The Nature of Human Society Series (Chicago: University of Chicago Press, 1969), discussed in Chapter 5 of this book. Ernest Gellner, "The Roots of Cohesion," *Man* (N.S.) 20, no. 1 (March 1985), 142–55, assesses prior French scholarship.

uum between the two.[64] In spite of the diminished political authority exercised by pious ones during the colonial and postcolonial periods, many tribal collectivities and individuals continue to maintain links with them. The festivals of major saintly figures continue to attract tens of thousands of clients annually.

Belief in the ability of pious ones to serve as intermediaries with divinity is only one of a range of popular religious understandings. In southern Morocco, for instance, resistance to the French as late as 1919 was led by a religious figure from a marginal social group claiming to be a *mahdī,* who continued to organize attacks upon the French even after more established religious figures sought to accommodate the colonial power. After the *mahdī* died, the resistance he initiated continued to oppose the French until it was finally defeated in 1934.[65] The significance of such popular religious leaders has been overlooked, in part because of the reluctance of "establishment" religious scholars—those who define local orthodoxies—to acknowledge the strength of popular religious movements outside their control, the uneasiness of French military intelligence in the early part of this century in comprehending the force of such beliefs, and the fact that many foreign scholars cannot readily assess the documentation on such leaders, most of which is in Arabic. As social anthropology increasingly becomes a "native" enterprise, significant modifications in how popular religious currents are depicted will continue to take place.[66]

THE AUTHORITY OF LEARNING

Some studies of Islam in rural and tribal milieus depict a single, dominant pattern of religious belief and practice. Earlier in this chapter I presented some of the reasons why it is more accurate to regard belief and practice as prismatic, generating and reflecting multiple influences in both urban and rural contexts. This is why it is misleading to speak of firm divisions among various types of religious leaders—including scholars (Ar. *'ulamā',* sing. *'ālim*), Sufis, and *mahdī*-s. In practice these categories overlap. A scholar can become popularly regarded as a pious one for his learning and piety, and an unlearned person similarly can

[64] For incisive rethinking of religious authority in Morocco from the fifteenth through the seventeenth centuries, see Vincent J. Cornell, "The Logic of Analogy and the Role of the Sufi Shaykh in Post-Marinid Morocco," *International Journal of Middle East Studies* 15, no. 1 (February 1983), 67–93. For new work by Moroccan scholars, see Mohamed Kably, *Société, pouvoir et religion au Maroc à la fin du moyen-age,* Islam d'Hier et d'Aujourd'hui (Paris: Maisonneuve et Larose, 1986); Hassan Elboudrari, "Quand les saints font les villes: Lecture anthropologique de la pratique sociale d'un saint marocain du XVIIe siècle," *Annales E.S.C.* 40, no. 3 (May–June 1985), 489–509, and his "Au Maroc: Sharifisme citadin, charisme et historiographie," *Annales E.S.C.* 41 no. 2 (March–April 1986), 433–57.

[65] Abdellah Hammoudi, "Aspects de la mobilisation populaire à la campagne, vus à travers la biographie d'un mahdi mort en 1919," in *Islam et politique au Maghreb,* ed. Ernest Gellner and Jean-Claude Vatin (Paris: Centre National de la Recherche Scientifique, 1981), pp. 47–55.

[66] See, for example, Abdellah Hammoudi, *The Victim and Its Masks: An Essay on Sacrifice and Masquerade in the Maghreb* (Chicago: University of California Press, 1993).

acquire a popular reputation for religious insight. One pervasive element in Islam as a religious tradition is respect for those aspects of belief and ritual that are considered fixed and enduring. Thus, in religious learning in North Africa, there is a valued cognitive style, "a set of basic, deeply interiorized master-patterns of language and thought," that emphasizes the accurate memorization and transmission of knowledge, which is considered fixed. Elsewhere, as in Iran, the cognitive style associated with religious learning places greater emphasis on developing a certain style of argument and questioning.[67] The key exemplar of fixed cognitive style in North Africa is the memorization of the Quran.

Respect for knowledge that is fixed and enduring pervades not only religious knowledge (*'ilm*) but also knowledge of secular subjects and skills (*ma'rifa*). This attitude produces a particular respect for the exact use of the spoken word and of set verses from the Quran, proverbs, and poetry, and influences much of the popular music, rhetoric, art, and oral literature (both religious and secular) throughout the Muslim Middle East. Prior to Western economic and colonial penetration, a major source for the inculcation of this style was the mosque-universities at which advanced students learned the Islamic religious tradition and perpetuated it. Schools such as the Qarawiyīn in Fez, the Yūsufiya in Marrakesh, the Zitūna in Tunis, the Azhar in Cairo, and their equivalents in Mecca and the two Yemens, the Ibāḍī interior of Oman, Najaf in Iraq, and Qum in Iran were all well known throughout the Middle East.

Central Asian equivalents also existed, but from 1928 through 1941, the state carried out a frontal assault on Muslim institutions, closing thousands of mosques and "liquidating" or imprisoning most religious scholars, who were accused of being "spies, saboteurs, counter-revolutionaries and parasites."[68] Only two religious schools existed after the purges of the 1930s. One was opened in Bukhara, Uzbekistan, in 1945, and graduated 10 to 15 students annually. A higher-level school was founded in Tashkent, Uzbekistan, in 1971. As of 1978, it had only 30 students. Graduates secured places within the official administration that the Soviets had set up for Muslim institutions, dividing the regions of significant Muslim populations into four "spiritual directorates": Central Asia and Kazakhstan, Muslims of European Russia and Siberia, the North Caucasus and Daghestan, and the Transcaucasian Muslims.[69]

[67] Part of the discussion in this section was first presented in Dale F. Eickelman, "The Art of Memory: Islamic Education and Its Social Reproduction," *Comparative Studies in Society and History* 20, no. 4 (October 1978), 485–516. The quotation defining cognitive style is from Pierre Bourdieu, "Systems of Education and Systems of Thought," *International Social Science Journal* 19 (1967), 343. See also Eickelman, *Knowledge and Power in Morocco: The Education of a Twentieth Century Notable* (Princeton, NJ: Princeton University Press, 1985). For religious education in Iran, see Fischer, *Iran,* and Mottahedeh, *Mantle;* for the medieval period in Sunnī Islam, see George Makdisi, *The Rise of Colleges: Institutions of Learning in Islam and the West* (Edinburgh: Edinburgh University Press, 1981).

[68] Alexandre Benningsen and S. Enders Wimbush, *Muslims of the Soviet Empire: A Guide* (Bloomington: Indiana University Press, 1986), p. 11.

[69] Ibid., pp. 14–15, 19.

Many observers have commonly assumed that the Soviet repression of 1928–1941 and occasional antireligious campaigns since (for example, in the Khrushchev era) fragmented and ruptured Muslim institutions, practices, and learning. Since Central Asia's sudden independence, though, it is increasingly clear that the official Soviet religious establishment was significantly overshadowed by pervasive and informal "underground" institutions, most of which required official complicity to function. One long-time observer notes the major role of

> the enormous network of unrecognized and frequently untrained 'volunteer' clerics, who established Qur'an schools, preserved shrines, presided at burials, weddings and other rituals and, in the urban Muslim settings at least, monitored the observation of 'traditions'—most of which were Islamic. In Uzbekistan this last function was served through neighbourhood *mahallas* [urban quarters], while in Turkmenistan the watchdogs of traditional Islamic practice were *elats,* or kinship groups of twenty to forty families.[70]

Olcott notes that "Soviet sources generally concealed the information that several religious 'dynasties' flourished in Central Asia, among both the officially-recognized clergy and the unofficial clergy."[71]

Such compromises are not unknown in the Middle East, where, for instance, Egyptian efforts to control religious private voluntary organizations by imposing government bureaucrats on their administrative boards have not prevented religious groups from co-opting them. On paper, the state has achieved its purpose, but in private its efforts at regulation can often be held in check.[72] Such official complicity is clear in the case for Uzbekistan in the 1970s, where clandestine religious schools opened, "missionaries traveled to other cities and rural areas," and books and pamphlets were secretly printed on state-owned (and heavily monitored) presses. For example, Abdujabar Abduvakhitov reports that he saw a book of the writings of the Pakistani religious reformer Abū-l A'lā al-Mawdūdī "bound in the cover of a book entitled *Materials of the XXVth Conference of CPSU*" and distributed for free.[73] In Turkmenistan, President Sapurmurad Niyazov, closely associated with Soviet antireligious campaigns in the pre-1991 era, now sponsors mosques and religious schools, "many of which bear his name," and he has "even erected a large statue of himself making pilgrimage, on the site where [the] main Lenin monument once stood."[74]

[70] Martha Brill Olcott, "Islam and Fundamentalism in Central Asia," in *Muslim Eurasia: Conflicting Legacies*, ed. Yaacov Ro'i, Cummings Center Series (London: Frank Cass, 1995), p. 24.

[71] Ibid.

[72] See Denis J. Sullivan, *Private Voluntary Organizations in Egypt: Islamic Development, Private Initiative, and State Control* (Gainesville: University of Florida Press, 1994), pp. 18, 57–98, 164.

[73] Abdujabar Abduvakhitov, "Islamic Revivalism in Uzbekistan," in *Russia's Muslim Frontiers: New Directions in Cross-Cultural Analysis*, ed. Dale F. Eickelman, Indiana Series in Arab and Islamic Studies (Bloomington: Indiana University Press, 1993), p. 83.

[74] Olcott, "Islam and Fundamentalism," p. 22.

Beginning in the nineteenth century in the Middle East (and during the Soviet era for Central Asia and the Caucasus), the financial base on which many of these institutions depended was increasingly undermined both by "native" regimes such as Muḥammad 'Alī's in Egypt and by colonial regimes such as that of the French in Algeria. Moreover, as European-style schooling, first provided only for specialized military training, rapidly expanded in scope and attracted students from the privileged social strata and more ambitious poorer ones, Islamic schools were left to students of a modest and often rural origin. Some mosque-universities were "reformed," ostensibly to improve their curricula and standards but also to bring them firmly under government control, but these moves only accelerated their decline. Some mosque-universities continued to thrive until fairly recently—those of Morocco until the 1920s and early 1930s, those of the Yemen (*Ṣan'ā'*) and the Sultanate of Oman until the middle of this century. Still, the social networks of influence and patronage formed in part through such mosque-universities have remained remarkably intact in many countries, and the "cognitive style" conveyed by Islamic education retains a popular legitimacy.

The cultural idea of religious knowledge has remained remarkably constant over time throughout the regions of Islamic influence. Writing specifically of medieval Islamic civilization, Marshall Hodgson states that education was "commonly conceived as the teaching of fixed and memorizable statements and formulas which could be learned *without any process of thinking as such.*"[75] This remarkable phrase raises the crucial issue of the meaning of "understanding" associated with such a concept of knowledge. The supposedly fixed and memorizable statements conveyed by education constitute the religious sciences, the totality of knowledge and technique necessary in principle for a Muslim to lead the fullest possible religious life. These memorizable statements also constitute the most valued knowledge. The paradigm of all such knowledge is the Quran; its "mnemonic domination" (*malaka l-ḥifḍ*) is the starting point for the mastery of the religious sciences. To facilitate the task of memorizing other key texts of grammar and law, many are written in rhymed verse.

Two linked propositions can be made concerning the form of Islamic knowledge. The first is that an intellectual tradition that emphasizes fixity and memory, as is characteristic of many other traditions of religious knowledge, can still be capable of flexibility. In practice there is considerable variation over time and place throughout the Islamic world as to the exact bodies of knowledge to be included in the religious sciences. Once this shifting is recognized, the interesting issue is the circumstances under which redefinitions occur, as to what constitutes the proper scope of the religious sciences. The notion of what is meant by "tradition" in Islam, even the "high" tradition of scholarship and learning, may be fixed as to form and style (as the notion of what constitutes "valued" knowledge may be fixed in form and style in any educational system) but not as to content. Former students of mosque-universities have become not

[75] Hodgson, *Venture,* vol. 2, p. 438. (Emphasis added.)

FIGURE 10-10. Discussing a Quranic commentary, Ghazni, Afghanistan, 1971. [Courtesy of Jon Anderson.]

only scholars but also politicians, ministers of state, merchants, and financiers who are quite capable of dealing with contemporary economic and political problems. Hence one must look beyond the mere scope of such learning to understand its significance.

The second proposition is that the cognitive style associated with Islamic education is closely tied to popular understandings of Islam, and it has important analogues in nonreligious spheres of knowledge. This formal congruence has served to enhance the popular legitimacy of religious knowledge and its carriers, but at the same time, it has shaped the ways in which changes are perceived. Earlier in this chapter I indicated how a Moroccan religious judge (*qāḍī*) explained the notion of Islamic law in its jural sense and as a code for personal conduct. Everything within the two parallel lines he drew on a sheet of paper was fixed—the content of Islamic law—everything else constituted innovation. Yet not all innovation is negative; it is tolerated so long as it does not contradict the principles of Islamic law. This formula might not be accepted by all Muslims, but it is one of the several means by which the fixity of tradition can be maintained while accommodating political and economic change. Most Muslims do not possess an exact knowledge of the religious sciences but nonetheless share the assumption that religious knowledge is fixed and knowable and that it is known by men of learning.

To understand the contemporary role of religious learning, it is necessary to have an idea of how many people were traditionally educated and who they were. Contemporary literacy is difficult to measure, let alone the literacy rates of earlier periods, but estimates are necessary to indicate the scope of Islamic education. Thus, for Morocco for the 1920s and 1930s, it appears reasonable to assume that 4 percent of the adult male rural population was literate, allowing for regional variations, and perhaps 10 to 20 percent of the adult male urban population. Similar figures prevail for Oman, a country that had only three "modern" primary schools as late as 1970 and where most education was carried out in mosque-schools.[76]

Two features consistently associated with Islamic education are its rigorous discipline and its lack of explicit explanation of memorized material. Both features are congruent with the concept of knowledge as essentially fixed and, of course, with the notion of reason (*'qāl*) as the ability to discipline one's nature, as explained in Chapter 9. The firm discipline of Quranic education was one of many ways in which the respect for the unchanging word of God could be inculcated in students. In Morocco, many people believe that any part of a student's body struck in the course of memorizing the Quran will never burn in hell; the same notion applies to beatings given by a craftsman to his apprentice.

"Understanding" in the context of such concepts of learning was not measured by any ability to "explain" particular verses. Such explanation (*tafsīr*) was considered a science in itself. Instead, the measure of understanding consisted of the ability to make appropriate use of particular Quranic verses. Originality was shown by working Quranic references into novel but appropriate contexts, just as knowledge and manipulation of secular oral poetry and proverbs were signs of good rhetorical style. This notion of style continues to hold in many parts of the Muslim world.

Mnemonic "possession" of the Quran and related texts is considered a form of cultural capital for those few who achieved its full memorization. Aside from small traditional gifts by the parents of the children to their teachers, Quranic education was free. Yet most students dropped out after a short period to contribute to the support of their families or because they failed to receive parental support for the arduous and imperfectly understood process of learning. In practice, memorization of the Quran was accomplished primarily by the

[76] Sources for the Moroccan estimate are provided in Eickelman, "Art of Memory," p. 492. For Oman, see Dale F. Eickelman, "Religious Knowledge in Inner Oman," *Journal of Oman Studies* 6 (1983), 163–72. Fanny Colonna, *Instituteurs Algériens: 1883–1939* (Paris: Presses de la Fondation Nationale des Sciences Politiques, 1975), p. 30, suggests that around 40 percent of Algeria's male population could read and write just prior to French conquest in the 1830s. After the French conquest in 1830, literacy in Algeria suffered a precipitous decline because the financial basis for religious schools, the system of pious endowments *(awqāf)*, was systematically destroyed.

طرش طريوش انزلوا

انزلوا احضروا اى مذهب

الا ميروجنده الى الاحمر

الا ميروجنوده احضروا

يا خدام هذه الاسماء

و هذا الكاشف فكشفنا عنك

غطاءك فبصرك اليوم

حديد صحيح صح

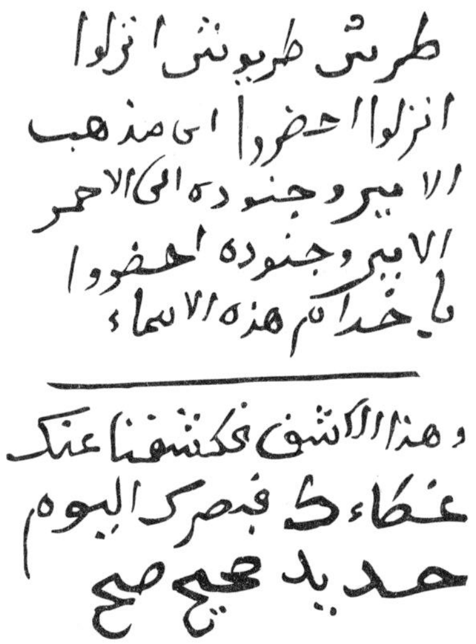

Magic Invocation and Charm.
"Ṭarchun! Ṭaryooshun! Come down!
Come down! Be present! Whither are gone
the prince and his troops? Where are El-Aḥmar
the prince and his troops? Be present
ye servants of these names!"

"And this is the removal. 'And we have removed from thee
thy veil; and thy sight to-day
is piercing.' Correct: correct."

FIGURE 10-11. Invocation for an amulet. Even among illiterates, writing is highly respected. [From Edward William Lane, *An Account of the Manners and Customs of the Modern Egyptians* (London: John Murray, Publishers, Ltd., 1860), p. 269.]

children of relatively prosperous households or those whose fathers or guardians were already literate. Moreover, these children had more opportunities to observe gatherings where the proper use of educated rhetorical style was employed than did poorer students. The biographies of men of learning repeatedly stress the importance of their family milieu in successfully mastering the traditional texts.

The scope of traditional higher education is also significant because of the importance attributed to men of learning in many accounts of the social structure of "traditional" Islamic society. For Morocco in 1931, the year of the first reliable census in the French-controlled part of the country, such students constituted a minuscule 0.02 percent of the population. Mosque-universities in their "traditional" sense (that is, before the al-Azhar reforms of the late nineteenth century and those of Morocco in the 1930s) constituted institutions whose members shared subjectively held ideas and conventions as to how given tasks should be accomplished. They had no sharply defined body of students or faculty, administration, entrance or course examinations, curriculum, or in most cases, unified sources of funds. Teachers (*shaykh*-s) did not form a corporate group as they did in medieval Europe, although older *shaykh*-s served as spokesmen for their colleagues on various occasions. Some also controlled the pious endowment properties (Ar. *waqf; ḥābūs*).[77]

As in any educational system with diffuse, implicit criteria for success, and in which essential skills were not fully embodied in formal learning, the existing elite was favored and certain families often became distinguished for their learning over generations. Despite the great respect in which religious learning and men of learning are held in many parts of the Islamic world, the majority of students at traditional mosque-universities rarely ever used such knowledge in more than an iconic fashion. A student's years at the mosque-university secured ties with people within and without the community of learning, ties that often were of use later in facilitating commercial, political, and entrepreneurial activities. No other preparation, except perhaps association with the sultan's entourage, enabled a person to acquire such a wide range of potential associations, at least so long as there were no major alternatives to Islamic higher education.

In many contexts throughout the Middle East until recent times, Islamic men of learning were at the heart of political affairs. Popular protest often began at the mosque-universities, even though it usually was not initiated by men of learning themselves. Because men of learning tended to be members of the social elite and at the same time appropriated for themselves the symbols of legitimacy provided by religious scholarship, they often represented the will of the population to the government and the intentions of the government to the populace. If the government performed acts that men of learning considered outside the bounds of Islam and if the men of learning were capable of withstanding the ruler's displeasure, the ruler was often compelled to change his course of action. Albert Hourani uses the term "patrician politics" to characterize the nature of their influence.[78] This characterization continues to apply to the officially recognized men of learning of Morocco, Egypt, and the various countries of the Arabian peninsula. Although politically significant, for the most part they take their lead in political matters from state authorities, but at

[77] *Waqf* rentals not only provide revenue to the religious establishment but also create ties of support. Commercial properties are frequently rented to craftsmen and shop owners at less than market value, thus providing an indirect subsidy to them and sustaining yet another form of link between them and the religious establishment. See Clifford Geertz, "Suq: The Bazaar Economy in Sefrou," in Clifford Geertz, Hildred Geertz, and Lawrence Rosen, *Meaning and Order in Moroccan Society* (New York: Cambridge University Press, 1979), pp. 140–50. Gilles Kepel, "Les oulémas, l'intelligentsia et les Islamistes en Égypte" [The 'Ulama, the Intelligentsia, and Islamic Radicals in Egypt], *Revue Française de Science Politique* 35, no. 3 (June 1985), 428–30, notes the loss of authority among traditional men of learning when their sources of independent income from *waqf* properties were undercut, coupled with a drastic 1961 "reform" of al-Azhar University (one of many over the last century) which deprived state-supported men of learning of both independence and prestige.

[78] Albert Hourani, "Ottoman Reform and the Politics of Notables," in *The Beginnings of Modernization in the Middle East: The Nineteenth Century*, ed. William R. Polk and Richard L. Chambers (Chicago and London: University of Chicago Press, 1968), pp. 41–68.

the same time, as in Saudi Arabia, they can on occasion act as a significant constraint on the state.[79]

With the rise of state-supported schooling and the access it provided to employment and government sinecures, the authority of traditional Islamic education was progressively undercut. Nonetheless, the authority of its graduates remains significant, although not unchallenged. Secular state schooling has been available throughout most of the Middle East (and Central Asia) for most of the twentieth century, but it has only been since mid-century that it has become mass education. The timing has varied throughout the region. Mass education began in Egypt shortly after its 1952 revolution, so that large numbers of students reached the university, or tertiary, level only in the late 1960s and early 1970s. In Morocco, which gained its independence in 1956, mass education was implemented somewhat later. Indeed, in the 1960s many teachers had to be imported from Egypt until a sufficient number of Moroccans could be trained. In some parts of the Arabian peninsula, such as Oman, mass schooling began only after 1970.

The result in each case has been to encourage new forms of religious—and political—authority.[80] The shift of religious knowledge from that which is mnemonically possessed to material that can only be consulted in books suggests a major transformation in the nature of knowledge and its carriers. It may still be ideologically maintained that religious knowledge is memorizable and immutable, as is certainly the case for the word of God as recorded in the Quran, but the lack of concrete embodiment of this premise in the carriers of such knowledge indicates a major shift. One consequence is that socially recognized carriers of religious learning are no longer confined to those who have studied authoritative texts in circumstances equivalent to those of the mosque-universities, with their bias toward members of the elite. Those who can interpret what Islam "really" is can now be of more variable social status than was the case when traditional learning was essential to legitimize religious knowledge. A long apprenticeship under an established man of learning is no longer a necessary prerequisite to legitimizing one's own religious knowledge. Carriers of religious knowledge increasingly can be anyone who can claim a strong Islamic commitment, as is the case among many of the educated urban youth. In Uzbekistan's Ferghana Valley, for example, one of the leaders of the Islamic movement in the 1980s and early 1990s was a former garage mechanic.[81] Freed from traditional patterns of learning and scholarship, religious knowledge can be interpreted in a more flexible and directly political fashion by more people. Photocopied tracts and the clandestine dissemination of sermons on cassettes

[79] For Saudi Arabia, see Dale F. Eickelman and James Piscatori, *Muslim Politics,* Princeton Studies in Muslim Politics (Princeton, NJ, and London: Princeton University Press, 1996), pp. 60–63; and for Egypt, see Kepel, "Les oulémas, l'intelligentsia et les Islamistes en Égypte," pp. 426–31.

[80] See Dale F. Eickelman, "Mass Higher Education and the Religious Imagination in Contemporary Arab Societies," *American Ethnologist* 19, no. 4 (November 1992), pp. 1–13.

[81] Abdujabar Abduvakhitov (personal communication, September 28, 1991). See also his "Islamic Revivalism," pp. 79–97.

FIGURE 10-12. Taḥrīr Square, Cairo. With mass education, many persons consider the inexpensive books and pamphlets sold from a sidewalk kiosk just as authoritative as those written by conventionally educated religious scholars. [Courtesy Gregory Starrett. Copyright © 1989.]

now rival the mosque as the center for Islam and challenge those sanctioned by the state.

REFORM AND RADICALISM: SELF-RENEWAL AND INTERNAL DEBATE

The dates in the title of Albert Hourani's *Arabic Thought in the Liberal Age, 1798–1939* suggest that the main impetus for reform in Islamic thought was Western encroachment upon the area.[82] In the preface of the book's reissue, he acknowledges that most studies of Arab intellectual movements, including his own, "did not say enough" about those for whom "the dominant ideas of modern Europe" carried little or no importance, in contrast to ongoing internal

[82] Albert Hourani, *Arabic Thought in the Liberal Age, 1798–1939*, rev. ed. (New York: Oxford University Press, 1970 [1962]), p. viii.

debate within Muslim societies, often phrased in terms of religious debate. Egypt was one center for such reformist activities, Constantinople (Istanbul) another. The influence of nineteenth-century intellectuals on the Islamic body politic was profound, and such activities as the "organization" (*niẓām*)—the word *reform* was scrupulously avoided—of the al-Azhar mosque-university at the instigation of state authorities, ostensibly to "modernize" it, had a profound if delayed impact.

The greatest popular momentum of the reform movement was from the end of the nineteenth century through the 1930s. In Morocco, for example, its growing popularity was linked to the impending threat of European penetration. Reformist thought spread among intellectuals connected with the sultan's court and educated urban merchants informally linked with the milieus of the leading mosque-universities. The movement disseminated the ideas of religious reformers from the Arab "East," such as Jamāl al-Dīn al-Afghānī (1839–1897) and Muḥammad 'Abduh (1849–1905), both of whom attracted disciples throughout the region. Certain religious brotherhoods with modernist tendencies appealed significantly to members of the mercantile and administrative elite.[83]

Muslims in Central Asia and Russia also experienced a vigorous reform movement. Part of this was spearheaded by a talented Tatar journalist and thinker, Ismail Gasprinsky (1851–1914), who resigned as mayor of his Crimean town to devote his life to pan-Islam and pan-Turkism. Writing primarily in Russian, he sought to provide Russia's Muslims with a sense of common identity and, by educating them in their own culture and civilization as well as that of Russia, bring about a *rapproachement* between the two peoples.[84] The movement associated with his name and other early reformers became known as the *jadīdī* ("new") movement, introducing a religious education combined with secular subjects such as history, geography, and arithmetic, in Turkish rather than Persian in regions where Turkic languages predominated. Islam thus would be refocused as a cultural force, and the economic stagnation of Russia's Muslims would end. As in other parts of the Muslim world, newspapers and publishers played a major role in disseminating these ideas among the intelligentsia of small towns, including schoolteachers and minor functionaries. After the 1917 revolution, the Soviet state sought to co-opt the pan-Islam movement but after 1928 decided to destroy it as a political force.[85]

[83] On Afghānī, 'Abduh, and their disciples, see ibid., pp. 103–92. *Islam in Transition: Muslim Perspectives*, ed. John J. Donahue and John L. Esposito (New York: Oxford University Press, 1982), provides translations of and introductions to key reformist and radical writings. See also *Voices of Resurgent Islam*, ed. John L. Esposito (New York: Oxford University Press, 1983), a collection of analytical writings on reformist and radical thought.

[84] Jacob M. Landau, *The Politics of Pan-Islam: Ideology and Organization* (Oxford: Clarendon Press, 1990), pp. 146–47, and his *Pan-Turkism: From Irredentism to Cooperation* (Bloomington: Indiana University Press, 1995), pp. 7–28.

[85] Edward J. Lazzerini, "Beyond Renewal: The Jadīd Response to Pressure for Change in the Modern Age," in *Muslims in Central Asia*, ed. Gross, pp. 151–66; and Abduvakhitov, "Islamic Revivalism," pp. 79–81.

The distinction between reformist and "radical" Muslim thought and movements is more a fine gradation than a sharp boundary and centers on the disposition toward political action. Reformists have placed greatest emphasis on Islamic thought and practice; "radical" Muslim movements are more disposed to participation in the political arena. It would be tempting, but misleading, to see nineteenth-century reform movements as the precursors for subsequent radical thought. The radical vision has co-existed with reformist thought, except that it has become more salient since the early 1970s, and it became most visible in the aftermath of the 1978–1979 Iranian revolution. Yet there are antecedents. Although the Palestinian resistance has been thought of since the 1960s as one of the more secularized political movements in the Arab world, populist Muslim leaders in the 1920s and 1930s were the primary carriers of Palestinian nationalism, displacing an earlier, locality-centered politics of notables. Within Palestine, the major challenge to PLO leadership has been from radical Muslim groups. In this case, as in others, it is not possible to discern a unilineal trajectory of political thought from reformism to radical Islam and secular nationalism.[86]

Ideologically, the reformist movement in the late nineteenth and early twentieth centuries sought to divest Islamic practice of what the reformers considered its particularistic accretions and to return to the essential principles of faith; hence the name of the movement in Arabic, *salafīya,* which suggests a return to the practice of the venerable forebears. In the Muslim world it is common for both modernists and conservatives to justify their ideological position by emphasizing a "return" to original principles, even if the proposed reforms are radically innovative. In western Morocco, I found that the major popular spread of reformist ideas to that region came in the 1930s. The principal carriers were urban merchants, many of whom had been associated with mosque-universities. Reformist Islam gave them an ideological and organizational base to challenge the domination of a maraboutic family in the region that controlled much of the commercial activity. In other regions as well, reformist Islam became, in part, a vehicle for asserting autonomy from the dominant groups of earlier generations and a prototype for the nationalist movement. Organizationally, it was common in the 1930s for merchants and craftsmen caught up in

[86] For the 1920s and 1930s, see Nels Johnson, *Islam and the Politics of Meaning in Palestinian Nationalism* (London and Boston: Kegan Paul International, 1982). One of the best studies of the growth of radical Muslim movements in the occupied Israeli territories is Jean-François Legrain, "Islamistes et lutte nationale Palestinienne dans les territoires occupés par Israel," *Revue Française de Science Politique* 36, no. 2 (April 1986), 227–47, which portrays the internal diversity of radical Muslim thought, its carriers (primarily a younger generation, educated and disillusioned with the ineffectiveness of secular nationalism), and its shifting support, including Israeli military authorities, who at one time viewed religiously based movements as a counter against those expressing sympathy for the PLO (p. 246). For a summary of these developments in both Israel and the occupied territories, see Thomas L. Friedman, "An Islamic Revival Is Quickly Gaining Ground in an Unlikely Place: Israel," *New York Times,* April 30, 1987, p. A6. See also Shaul Mishal and Reuben Aharoni, eds., *Speaking Stones: Communiques from the Intifada Underground* (Syracuse, NY: Syracuse University Press, 1994), which contains translations of leaflets distributed by underground secular and religious groups during the *intifadā* ("uprising" or "shaking off") against the continued Israeli occupation.

the reformist movement to set up loosely knit, often ephemeral committees to negotiate with the local administration on matters such as the construction of schools or road improvements. Reformist Islam had few adherents outside the major cities in this period, but those few were members of influential families.

The popular spread of Algeria's reformist movement is well documented. As Ali Merad has written, before the emergence of the reformist movement, virtually no Algerian Muslim thought that Islam was anything except maraboutism.[87] "Pious ones" were the only religious spokesmen for most Algerians, and the only alternative to them was a French-subsidized "clergy," allowed to conduct Friday prayers in the mosques. An initial impetus for the reform movement was a brief visit by the Egyptian reformer Muḥammad 'Abduh to Algeria in September 1903. 'Abduh's local contacts, although few, were Algerians influential in religious circles.

The popular impact of the reformist movement accelerated after the return of Algerians who had fought with the French in World War I and who were disillusioned about resuming their subservient status. Algerians from all parts of the country began to recognize their common situation despite linguistic and regional differences. (An unintended by-product of French rule was to bring "natives" of different regions into contact with one another.) Distant problems became more familiar as "Young Algerians"—a term that consciously paralleled the earlier "Young Turks" for the Ottoman province of Anatolia—recognized their common status. The small Algerian cadre of French-trained schoolteachers, doctors, journalists, and attorneys formed the movement's vanguard, but their direct influence was limited by their inability to communicate effectively with the vast majority of Algerians. Because marabouts and the "official clergy" had supported the French against the Ottoman Empire (allied with the Germans) during the war, they rapidly lost popular support.

A number of Algerian religious reformers emerged, of whom 'Abd al-Ḥamīd ibn Bādis (ben Badis) (1889–1940), from a leading family of Constantine, was the key leader. A religious scholar, he was influenced by reformist ideas from the Arab East and maintained active ties with Algerians from many walks of life. The elite status of these reformers meant that the French dealt circumspectly with them. Reformists began to visit mosques throughout Algeria, emphasizing in their preachings the unity of Islam, charity, worship, and mutual assistance. While avoiding direct confrontation with the marabouts, who were often strongly embedded in local political networks, they challenged the maraboutic claim of communication with the Prophet, their power of intercession and miraculous healing and magic, and sought to convince Algerians that these were not part of Islamic doctrine. By 1933, the French administration

[87] Ali Merad, *Le réformisme musulman en Algérie de 1925 à 1940,* Recherches Méditerranéenes, Études 7 (Paris and The Hague: Mouton, 1967), discussed at length in Gellner, *Muslim Society,* pp. 149–73. See also Pessah Shinar, "'Ulamā, Marabouts and Government: An Overview of Their Relationships in the French Colonial Maghrib," *Israel Oriental Studies* 10 (1980), 211–29, who makes extensive use of contemporary sources to depict the internal debate within the Muslim community during this period.

placed restrictions on the reformists, especially as some of them had become directly involved in the incipient nationalist movement.

Merad makes two major points. First, maraboutism was the backdrop against which reformist ideologies in Algeria were forged and elaborated. No matter how many educated Muslims deride the implicit assumptions of maraboutism today, the maraboutic interpretation of Islam was a major force in the 1930s, and in many parts of North Africa, it continues to play a significant role. Second, reformism mounted an offensive of educated urban Islam, "intelligible and simple," against a tribal and rural religious orientation. Merad argues that, consciously or not, urban values impregnated the religious conceptions of the reformist movement and paved the way for "rationalist" conceptions of Islam. He goes so far as to say that the carriers of reformist Islam secularized Islam by conveying it as doctrines and practices set apart from other aspects of life.[88]

It can be argued, as Wilfred Cantwell Smith does, that there has been a tendency in the Muslim world, as in the Christian one, for religious traditions that once were "coterminous with human life in all its comprehensiveness" to become transformed so that now "the religious seems to be one facet of a person's life alongside many others."[89] The reformist movement of the late nineteenth and early twentieth centuries was not just a movement of traditionally educated men of learning. It included educated people exposed to other intellectual currents. They changed the terms of discourse as well as the basis for religious authority so that the traditionally educated were no longer the most likely to be the "authoritative" carriers of Islamic thought and practice. Religious discourse could encompass nationalist and anticolonial sympathies and reach wider audiences than its secular counterparts.

The Muslim Brotherhood (*al-Ikhwān al-Muslimūn*), founded in Egypt in 1927 or 1928, grew rapidly because, in place of the religious authority and discourse of traditionally educated men of learning, it offered an alternative that seemed directly related to modern conditions. By the 1930s, it had become a significant religious and political force. By 1948, after the defeat of the Arabs by the new Israeli state, the movement had at least one million active participants, with many more sympathizers, and could be considered the only genuinely popular mass political movement in twentieth-century Egypt.[90] The Brotherhood soon spread to other countries, and similar movements were modeled on it. Its founder, Ḥasan al-Bannā (b. 1906), was assassinated in 1949, perhaps by agents of the Egyptian monarchy, at the height of his career. From the time he entered primary school (and not a religious institution), Ḥasan al-Bannā was

[88] Merad, *Réformisme*, pp. 437–39.

[89] Wilfred Cantwell Smith, *The Meaning and End of Religion* (New York: Macmillan, 1963), p. 124.

[90] The Brotherhood was outlawed in 1948, legalized again in 1951, tolerated after the 1952 revolution (because the Free Officers thought they could successfully co-opt it), but then was ruthlessly repressed from 1954 until the death of Nasser in 1970. See Richard P. Mitchell, *The Society of the Muslim Brothers* (London: Oxford University Press, 1969). For a recent discussion of the variety of political currents within the Muslim Brotherhood, see Sana Abed-Kotob, "The Accommodationists Speak: Goals and Strategies of the Muslim Brotherhood of Egypt," *International Journal of Middle East Studies* 27, no. 3 (August 1995), 321–339.

involved in various religious societies and became strongly influenced by reformist teachings. As with other educated youth of the 1920s, he constantly discussed with his associates the state of Islam and the nation and was concerned with the defection of many of the educated from the Islamic way of life. His followers came to regard him as a charismatic figure. Ikhwān members had to swear complete obedience to the movement, although there were degrees of membership and punishment for negligent members. The Ikhwān's built-in discipline set them apart from most other religious associations (an exception being the order described by Gilsenan, which, however, avoided political activities). Because the Muslim Brotherhood made no distinction between the political and social order and called for the purification of society, successive governments in Egypt and elsewhere saw it as a revolutionary force.[91] The organization was frequently suspected of political violence and experienced a fair share of political violence from a succession of regimes.

Richard P. Mitchell, the leading scholar on the Brotherhood, characterized it "as the first mass-supported and organized, essentially urban-oriented effort to cope with the plight of Islam in the modern world."[92] Mitchell sees a continuity between it and earlier reform movements, including the Wahhābī movement of eighteenth-century Arabia. Members of the movement see themselves as practical successors to the reformist ideas of earlier leaders such as al-Afghānī. The goals of the Muslim Brotherhood have included renewed unity of the Muslim community (Ar. *umma*) and an appeal for personal reform as a prelude to allowing the Muslim community to realize its full potential for development in the modern world. Western influences and institutions are not excluded, provided that they can be harnessed to the service of Islam. At times, such ideological notions have been very much in line with the political goals of conservative Arab and other states. Thus the Saudis supported the Muslim Brotherhood in the 1950s and 1960s, in part as a counterforce to the pan-Arabism of Egypt's Nasser and the secular Ba'th parties of Syria and Iraq, and in later periods, much as they provided support to conservative Turkish preachers among Turkish migrants in West Germany (see earlier in this chapter).[93]

[91] Mitchell, *Muslim Brothers*, p. 312.

[92] Ibid., p. 321.

[93] See Detlev H. Khalid (Khalid Duran), "The Phenomenon of Re-Islamization," *Aussenpolitik* (German Foreign Affairs Review) 29, no. 4 (1978), 433–53. As with other political movements, the Muslim Brotherhood is subject to the vicissitudes of circumstances and external support. In Palestine territories, its strength was among an older generation, especially in Bethlehem and Hebron. In the 1948 war for Israel's independence, Egyptian volunteers with Muslim Brotherhood sympathies were stationed in these two towns. In Jordan, the Muslim Brotherhood was tolerated and at times encouraged because of its opposition to Nasser's pan-Arabism and avoidance of criticism of the Jordanian monarchy. After Brotherhood leadership implicitly criticized the monarchy in late 1985 for seeking a rapprochement with Syria, which strenuously opposes the Brotherhood (at least 30,000 lives may have been lost when Syrian government forces crushed a mini-rebellion led by the Muslim Brotherhood in al-Hama in early 1982), the Brotherhood quickly found that Jordanian tolerance had vanished (Legrain, "Islamistes," pp. 223, 245). By the 1980s it was again tolerated and won 22 seats in Jordan's 1989 parliamentary elections. See Laurie Brand, " 'In the Beginning was the State . . .': The Quest for Civil Society in Jordan," in *Civil Society in the Middle East*, vol. 1, ed. Augustus Richard Norton (Leiden: E. J. Brill, 1995), pp. 163–65.

As Mitchell indicates, it is difficult to ascertain the social origins of quasi-secret movements, especially when they have been declared illegal for significant parts of their existence. Nonetheless, there is a consensus that in spite of its large rural membership, the Muslim Brotherhood is dominated by activists primarily from the urban middle class. Mitchell attended many open meetings of the Brothers between 1953 and 1955 and reports that he saw a fairly regular pattern of attendance: servants, merchants, craftsmen, and a few Azharites, but an "overwhelming majority" of students, civil servants, office workers, and professionals in Western dress—in short, "an emergent and self-conscious Muslim middle class" hostile to imperialism and its "internal" (i.e., indigenous) agents and interested in conservative reform and the implementation of religious life as they conceive it.[94]

Political conditions in Egypt have often been regarded as a bellwether for the Arab Muslim world. The Egyptian revolution in 1952 was thought to exemplify the decline of religious factors and movements in public life, a notion in accord with the assumptions of modernization theory so prevalent in the 1950s and 1960s.[95] Nasser felt sufficiently confident by 1954 that he ordered the arrest of thousands of Muslim Brothers, crushing it as a formal political force in Egypt. After the poorly conceived expedition against the Suez Canal in 1956 by Britain, France, and Israel, and the subsequent precipitate withdrawal of these powers, secular Arab nationalism, with its dream of Arab unity, reached its apogee, which lasted until Israel defeated the Arabs in the June 1967 war.

The vigorous repression of the Muslim Brotherhood movement in the 1950s and the destruction of its leadership, retrospectively seen as moderate, created amenable conditions for fostering more radical religious interpretations and for recruiting a younger generation of radicalized militants unwilling to compromise with existing state authorities. As Gilles Kepel notes, the prisons and prison camps of Nasser's Egypt became vivid metaphors for the moral bankruptcy of existing government and incubators for radical religious thought.[96] *Jahīl* is a Quranic term evoking the state of ignorance, violence, and self-interest that presumably existed prior to the revelation of the Quran and that, for radicals, continues to hamper realization of a full Islamic community. Islamic militants and many other Muslims consider existing state organizations "barbaric" (*jāhilī*) because they do not govern in accordance with Islamic principles.

One of the principal radical ideologues was Sayyid Quṭb (1906–1966). He was born in a village near Assiut, in Upper Egypt, and was educated at a teacher's college. He taught and contributed to various newspapers, went to the United States—his English was good enough so that in 1955 he reviewed the English translation of one of his books—for further training in education,

[94] Mitchell, *Muslim Brothers*, pp. 328–31.

[95] See Leonard Binder, "The Natural History of Development Theory," *Comparative Studies in Society and History* 28, no. 1 (January 1986), 3–33.

[96] Kepel, *Muslim Extremism*. Kepel describes his study as a "grammar and rhetoric" (p. 23) of contemporary radical thought in Egypt.

and joined the Muslim Brotherhood upon his return in 1951. Like al-Bannā, he could not claim the credentials of a traditional man of learning. From 1954 until his execution in 1966, he spent all but eight months (1964–1965) in prison.

His death in prison was precipitated by an alleged assassination attempt against Nasser. While visiting Moscow in August 1965, Nasser announced that the authorities had uncovered a vast plot against the regime. The result was a major roundup of Muslim Brotherhood supporters and, a year later, the hanging of Sayyid Quṭb and others. Whether the regime's strike against the radicals preempted a real plot or was contrived is uncertain, but the authorities, who assumed they had virtually eliminated religiously based opposition, discovered that it had deep roots not only among the peasantry, which the regime had anticipated, but among "lawyers, scientists, doctors, businessmen, university professors, school teachers, and students," for whom Sayyid Quṭb had an almost messianic appeal and therefore constituted a major threat to the regime.[97] In spite of international appeals for clemency, his execution was carried out.

The majority of Sayyid Quṭb's writings were produced in prison. These include a six-volume commentary on the Quran, an abridgment of which, *Signposts* (*Ma'ālim fī al-ṭarīq*) (c. 1965), is one of the most influential radical Muslim texts. Prior to the 1950s, the Muslim Brotherhood never attacked the Egyptian or other Arab Muslim governments as un-Islamic; subsequently, at least the radical elements of the Brotherhood identified the rulers of Egypt and many other Arab states with the Pharaohs of the Quran. A major appeal of Sayyid Quṭb's writings is their ability to offer their readers an explanation in Islamic terms of contemporary political and economic developments and the shortcomings and perceived injustices of existing regimes. When Quṭb's Quranic commentary was published shortly after his execution, in 1966, it was vigorously attacked by several religious spokesmen on behalf of the government. This response, though, only underlined how significant the regime considered his commentary.[98]

The elements of radical discourse have complex origins. Some can be traced back to radical medieval thinkers such as Ibn Taymīya (d. 1328), who argued that it is the duty of rulers to provide the spiritual and material conditions necessary to lead a truly Islamic life. Ironically, Ibn Taymīya's ideas engendered widespread debate and popular support only in the 1970s.[99]

[97] Adeed Dawisha, *The Arab Radicals* (New York: Council on Foreign Relations, 1986), p. 89. For an annotated translation of one of Quṭb's key texts and an account of his career, see William E. Shepard, *Sayyid Qutb and Islamic Activism: A Translation and Critical Analysis of Social Justice in Islam*, Social, Economic, and Political Studies of the Middle East and Asia 54 (Leiden: E. J. Brill, 1996).

[98] Kepel, *Muslim Extremism*, p. 61.

[99] Emanuel Sivan, *Radical Islam: Medieval Theology and Modern Politics* (New Haven, CT, and London: Yale University Press, 1985); and, on both secular and religious contemporary politics, Fouad Ajami, *The Arab Predicament: Arab Political Thought and Practice Since 1967* (New York: Cambridge University Press, 1981). On contemporary Muslim radicalism, see the interesting essay by Henry Munson, Jr., *Islam and Revolution in the Middle East* (New Haven, CT, and London: Yale University Press, 1988).

(Sayyid Quṭb's originality in part lies in concluding that rulers who do not rule by "Islamic" principles are not Muslims at all but illegitimate "Pharaohs.") Another source of Quṭb's writings, and through him a number of radical Muslim thinkers, was the prolific Pakistani neo-fundamentalist intellectual Mawlānā Mawdūdī (1903–1979).[100]

If Sayyid Quṭb emerged in the 1960s as a key ideologue of the radical Islamic movement in Egypt, the organizational muscle of the militants was provided by the developments of the 1970s, especially after the political liberalization that accompanied the latter part of the rule of Anwar al-Sadat (r. 1970–1981). The ideas of most extremist groups are known only through hostile, usually governmental, sources, so it is necessary to exercise caution in evaluating their beliefs and discerning their social origins. Even the names of these groups are subject to distortion. The group headed by Shukrī Muṣṭāfā, who assassinated Sadat in October 1981, called itself the Society of Muslims (*jamā'at al-Muslimīn*) but became known in the press as the Society of Repentance and Emigration (*jamā'at al-takfīr wa-l-hijra*).[101] The group's own name made the government uneasy, although it correctly indicated the group's belief that Muslims who did not adhere to its principles were infidels. Radical beliefs and a dedication to violence kept the numbers of these extremist groups restricted, but their small size and the lack of formal connections among radical groups also kept them outside the effective reach of Egypt's ubiquitous security services.

The appeal of such movements was undoubtedly heightened by a conjuncture of events: Sadat's bold visit to Jerusalem in 1977, a dismal economic situation, and the political unrest in many Muslim states in the aftermath of the Iranian revolution. Such short-term factors are undoubtedly important, although other, long-term ones should be kept in mind. One such factor is the changing face of mass education. Most participants in the radical groups of the 1970s were in their twenties and thirties, the first generation to benefit from the revolution's commitment to mass education. The vast increase in numbers and lowered status of educational credentials meant that diplomas no longer provided the same benefits of prestige and employment that they had earlier. However, one long-term effect of modern mass education was to convey at least the principle (as opposed to pedagogic practice) of individual authority in evaluating written word and doctrine. It facilitated a different notion of religious authority from that conveyed by traditional men of learning.

It is difficult to establish with precision a relationship between belief and social background for those most disposed to support or participate in radical movements. In Egypt, for example, a leading Egyptian sociologist claims that Islamic activists responsible for violent acts against the state tended to be from

[100] For Pakistan and the Indian subcontinent, see Seyyed Vali Reza Nasr, *Mawdudi and the Making of Islamic Revivalism* (New York and Oxford: Oxford University Press, 1996).

[101] Kepel, *Muslim Extremism*, p. 70.

modest backgrounds and were first-generation city dwellers.[102] Kepel stresses the professional middle- and upper-class backgrounds, whereas still another scholar argues that the most successful activist groups contained people of varying social backgrounds and that this mixture across regional and class divides accounted for their success.[103] Similar difficulties face scholars looking at the social origins of participants in fundamentalist movements elsewhere.[104]

The tactics of Sadat's assassins, who justified their act by asserting the *jāhilī* nature of Sadat's rule, profoundly shocked most Egyptians, but denial of the regime's legitimacy on religious grounds had more widespread support. The state's efforts to claim Islamic legitimacy, even at the cost of alienating Egypt's large Coptic minority, suggests the importance attached to it.[105]

The existence of at least 40,000 "independent," privately financed mosques in a poor country such as Egypt in 1981 (when all mosques were at least nominally placed under government supervision), as opposed to only 6000 controlled by the state, suggests the extent to which Islamic thought and practice is considered a vehicle for expression and a potential organizing force for significant elements of the population. An especially sensitive study is provided by Patrick D. Gaffney in *The Prophet's Pulpit*.[106] He studied local preachers, their sermons, and their followings in Minya, Upper (southern) Egypt, between April 1978 and August 1979, a period that "encompasses the first wave of open Muslim militancy." Gaffney contrasts the styles of a range of local preachers, from the traditional to the militants, and follows their sermons over extended periods of time, so that their styles and followings are not merely distilled into "types" but shown as they relate, respond to, and define local, national, and international political events. Much of this discourse is poorly reflected in the Egyptian national press and broadcast media, so Gaffney's

102 Saad Eddin Ibrahim, "Anatomy of Egypt's Militant Islamic Groups: Methodological Note and Preliminary Findings," *International Journal of Middle East Studies* 12, no. 4 (December 1980), 438–39.

103 Kepel, *Muslim Extremism*, Table 5, p. 221; Hamied N. Ansari, "The Islamic Militants in Egyptian Politics," *International Journal of Middle East Studies* 16, no. 1 (March 1984), 123–44.

104 See, for example, Henry Munson, Jr., "The Social Base of Islamic Militancy in Morocco," *Middle East Journal* 40, no. 2 (Spring 1986), 267–84; and the profiles of 125 (out of approximately 160) alleged activists arrested by Omani security authorities in May and June 1994 in Salem Abdullah, *Omani Islamism: An Unexpected Confrontation with the Government*, Occasional Papers Series 8 (Annandale, VA: United Association for Studies and Research, 1995), pp. 25–33. These were convicted by a state security court, meeting in secret session in November 1994. Amnesty International received no responses to various inquiries, but all prisoners were released in November 1995.

105 Hamied N. Ansari, "Sectarian Conflict in Egypt and the Political Expediency of Religion," *Middle East Journal* 38, no. 3 (Summer 1984), 397–418, deals with Sadat's efforts to placate fundamentalist Muslims by adopting policies that exacerbated sectarian conflict between Copts and Muslims.

106 Patrick D. Gaffney, *The Prophet's Pulpit: Islamic Preaching in Contemporary Egypt*, Comparative Studies on Muslim Societies 20 (Berkeley and Los Angeles: University of California Press, 1994). For unusual insight into elite discourse, see Alain Roussillon, "Les 'nouveaux fondamentalistes' en colloque. 'Authenticité et modernité': Les défis de l'identité dans le monde arabe" [The "New Fundamentalists" in Colloquium. Authenticity and Modernity in the Arab World], *Maghreb-Machrek*, no. 107 (January–March 1985), 5–22. Emmanuel Sivan, "The Islamic Republic of Egypt," *Orbis* 31, no. 1 (Spring 1987), 43–53, analyzes an essay, subsequently banned in Egypt, by an Egyptian intellectual who imagines what an Egyptian "Islamic Republic" would be like.

FIGURE 10-13. Advertising in Cairo is adjusting to the "Islamic" look. A billboard near the Muṣṭāfa Maḥmūd private mosque in an upscale district of Cairo reads: "Al-Huda [store] for *muḥajjabat* [proper Islamic attire]. All the requirements for the *muḥajjaba* lady. Elegance and dignity." [Courtesy Gregory Starrett. Copyright © 1989.]

study is useful in showing the contexts in which internal debate occurs and "authoritative" discourse is established.

In Morocco, as in Egypt and elsewhere in the Middle East, some religious interpretations and practices are repressed or held in official disfavor, so an analysis of the strength of Muslim radical activists, let alone those sympathetic to their message, presents a major challenge. Thus estimates of membership in "militant" Islamic associations, even among such definable groups as university students, must remain tentative.[107] In the early 1970s, the Moroccan state tolerated Islamic groups in secondary schools and universities, possibly because political authorities saw them as a counterfoil to leftist political parties. After demonstrations against the presence in Morocco during February and March 1979 of Iran's ex-Shah, such groups were increasingly perceived as a threat by the state. Since then, the Moroccan monarchy has taken firm action to

[107] For a valuable study, similar to Gaffney's on Egypt, which provides a careful reading of the religious discourse and counterdiscourse (and events and actions) as they occurred, see Mohamed Tozy, "Champ et contre champ politico-religieux au Maroc," thesis for the *Doctorat d'État* in political science, presented to the Faculté de Droit et de Science Politique of the Université d'Aix-Marseille, 1984, pp. 241–44. This important study, together with the thinking of key North African Muslim radicals, is discussed in English in Henry Munson, Jr., "Islamic Revivalism in Morocco and Tunisia," *Muslim World* 76, nos. 3–4 (July–October 1986), 203–18. See also Jean-Claude Vatin, "Seduction and Sedition: Islamic Polemical Discourses in the Maghreb," in *Islam,* ed. Roff, pp. 160–79; and my "Religion in Polity and Society," in *The Political Economy of Morocco,* ed. I. William Zartman (New York: Praeger, 1987), pp. 84–97, which formed an earlier version of this discussion on Morocco. On Jordan, see Richard T. Antoun, "Themes and Symbols in the Religious Lesson: A Jordanian Case Study," *International Journal of Middle East Studies* 25, no. 4 (November 1993), 607–24.

contain the minority "Islamic" opposition, in part by co-opting the militants in rhetoric and action. In the 1960s and early 1970s, the monarchy emulated the language of the political left; since the late 1970s, religious slogans have come to the fore.

In the hands of radical Muslim thinkers such as Morocco's ʻAbd as-Salām Yasīn, the militant argument provides an ideology of liberation. Like his predecessors elsewhere, including Egypt's Sayyid Quṭb, Yasīn insists that, except for rule by the Prophet and his first successors, there have been no Islamic governments, only government by Muslims. Yasīn argues that contemporary Muslim societies have been de-Islamicized by imported ideologies and values, the cause of social and moral disorder. Muslim peoples are subjected to injustice and repression by elites whose ideas and conduct derive more from the East and West than from Islam.[108]

Yasīn's argument is necessarily circumspect on how Muslims should liberate themselves from present-day polities, except to argue that the state should allow militant Muslims (*rijāl ad-daʻwa*) the right to speak in exchange for the "official violence" inflicted upon them.[109] He aims to set co-religionists on the "right path" toward a new era, not to directly confront the state. The content of Yasīn's sermons and writings suggests that his principal audience is educated and younger and already familiar with the secular, "imported" ideologies against which he argues. His key terms, derived from Quranic and Arabic phrases, are more evocative for his intended audience than the language and arguments of the secular political parties.

Predictably, a contrasting view of Islam and polity in Morocco is advanced by the monarch. Like Yasīn, the monarch regularly invokes, in a very different way, key religious terms and concepts. Thus, in a 1984 speech opening a new session of parliament and intended in part to counter fundamentalist arguments, Ḥasan II directly linked the monarchy with the lineage of the Prophet, still an important means for claiming popular religious legitimacy in Morocco, and with the Prophet's conduct of state affairs:

> In all modesty, Hassan's school is the school of [my father] Mohammed, . . . and the school of Mohammed V is that of the Prophet. . . . Most of us only know the Prophet as messenger of God, preacher and lawgiver; his political and diplomatic life remain unknown and we await the day when someone firmly attached to his religion and proud of its teachings will write on this subject. . . . You have only to knock on our door and ask for our advice.[110]

The monarch also took measures so that he could claim that key officials in the Ministry of the Interior were well versed in Islamic law, appointed religious officials to advise provincial officials, and in other ways sought to link the gov-

[108] Abdassalam Yassine, *La révolution à l'heure de l'Islam* (Marseille: Presses de l'Université, 1979), p. 11, translated into French by Yasīn himself.

[109] Ibid., p. 19.

[110] Ḥasan II, speech on the opening of parliament, October 15, 1984. French version provided by Maghreb Arabe Presse.

ernmental machinery with religious principles and organization. While many other regimes seek to identify with religious principles to co-opt religious opposition, Morocco is one of the more successful in challenging the militants' claim to authority in interpreting how Islam is supposed to apply to politics and economics.

Less successful, but also indicative of the popular appeal of claims to Islamic legitimacy, are those of Libya's teacher-leader, Mu'ammar al-Qadhdhāfī, who declared that the 1969 coup was an Islamic revolution. Yet, as John Davis points out, Islam did not figure significantly in Qadhdhāfī's speeches until 1975. Before that date, however, alcohol was banned, Libyans were ordered to use the Muslim lunar calendar alongside the Western one, and Qadhdhāfī (in 1970) declared that many religious scholars saw only the "outer coat" of Islam, while he, as an arbiter of doctrine, wanted the "essential part of Islam to be applied."[111] Yet Qadhdhāfī's slim *Green Book,* three pocket-sized tracts of small pages and large type concerning social justice and economy, never uses the word "Islam" in either the English or Arabic versions.[112] The language of the Arabic version makes clear his reliance on many of the key themes of Islamic modernism but not on formal Islamic doctrine or its recognized men of learning. Davis reports that, by 1976, when Qadhdhāfī's claims for Islamic justification of his decrees and statements (such as that Islam condemns private trading) met with resistance from religious leaders, he removed those men from mosques and deprived them of independent incomes from religious endowments. In 1977 he altered the Muslim calendar, as it is used in Libya, so that years were counted not from the time of Muḥammad's emigration (*hijra*) to Medina (A.D. 622) but from the time of the Prophet's death (A.D. 632), making Libyan years about a decade behind the rest of the Muslim world.[113]

As bizarre as many of these activities may appear, and Davis reports that they are erratic to many ordinary Libyans, they are part of an overall pattern of major shifts in styles of religious authority. Qadhdhāfī's efforts to establish his Islamic credentials have been less successful than the efforts of some other Muslim heads of state, but in basing his thoughts on a claim to "direct" interpretation of the message of Islam not filtered through an authoritative scholarly tradition, Qadhdhāfī breaks with earlier forms of religious authority. In this he is not alone; the Ba'th regime in Iraq has used a similar tactic. In 1975, when the regime's relations with Syria deteriorated substantially, government rhetoric invoked many images of the Shī'a in order to shore up its support in southern Iraq. Beginning in 1977, the state even participated in the *'ashūra* ceremonies commemorating the martyrdom of Ḥuṣayn. Similarly, Iraq's public statements became progressively more Islamic as the crisis following its August 1990 invasion of Kuwait deepened. In December 1990, Saḍḍām Ḥusayn

[111] Quoted in Davis, *Libyan Politics,* p. 50.

[112] Muammar al-Qadhafi, *The Green Book,* circa 1975 (for the first two booklets) and 1979 (for the third). Neither the Arabic nor the English version contains date or place of publication. Copies are available from most Libyan People's Bureaus, formerly known as embassies.

[113] Davis, *Libyan Politics,* pp. 44–58.

went so far as to imply that he was a new *mahdī* "whose sacred mission is to purge the Arab and Islamic world, reform Islam and lead the way to a new age."[114]

PARALLELS: CHRISTIANITY AND JUDAISM IN THE MIDDLE EAST

Chapters 8 and 9 have suggested the close, if not always amicable, relationships prevailing among the various communities of the Middle East's three "religions of the book." It is tempting to say that an account of the history and recent political development of non-Muslim sectarian groupings, such as Lebanon's Maronite Christians, with its specifically Christian identifying characteristics removed, would lead many readers unfamiliar with the Middle East to presume that it was a Muslim sect. It displays many of the same "exotic" features—intense, inward-looking ties of loyalty and leadership, opportunistic alliances with other groups, and distorted perceptions of one's sectarian neighbors coexisting with a mix of Western-oriented cosmopolitanism and knowledge of the West and its languages.[115]

Such an interpretation would be highly misleading on several counts. Surely Northern Ireland represents a parallel example of current "Western" sectarian unrest, and it is a salient, but not isolated, example, as ex-Yugoslavia reminds us. For the Middle East as for these "Western" cases, it would be equally misleading to think of sectarian unrest as due to religious factors alone or to discount religious belief as a "dependent variable" ultimately explained by other factors. The factors that figure in understanding the Muslim component of Middle Eastern societies apply equally to other Middle Eastern religious communities and are often remarkably parallel. This does not mean that they are "dominated" by "religious" perceptions to the exclusion of all others, even if some carriers of these religious traditions claim that their particular tradition is a "total" way of life. Economic and political considerations, among others, remain as important in this region as in others.

The subtitle of this section specifies Christianity and Judaism in the Middle East rather than Middle Eastern Judaism or Christianity. In matters of belief and faith—in Judaism and Christianity, as with Islam—such presumably unintended distortions remain common. Perhaps only as Islam begins being perceived as a "Western" religion—now that about 5 percent of France's population, for example, is Muslim—can such unintended exoticism become a matter

[114] Amatzia Baram, "Re-Inventing Nationalism in Ba'thi Iraq, 1968–1994: Supra-Territorial and Territorial Identities and What Lies Below," *Princeton Papers*, no. 5 (Fall–Winter 1996).

[115] For a short introduction to the different Christian sects in Lebanon, see Jonathan Randal, *Going All the Way: Christian Warlords, Israeli Adventurers* (New York: Vintage Books, 1984), pp. 25–60. Matti Moosa, *The Maronites in History* (Syracuse, NY: Syracuse University Press, 1986), does not deal with the modern period, but indicates historical shortcomings in current Maronite claims for the sect's origin.

of the past in Western perceptions.[116] One scholar comments that "until recently, the discipline of Jewish historiography tended to promote a Eurocentric view of Jewish civilization," with Jews under Muslim domination removed to the fringes of research and teaching.[117] Indeed, the term "Middle Eastern" or "Oriental" Judaism unintentionally evokes the perception of a Western-oriented scholarship and creates a tenuous category unrecognized by the people of the region itself (except, perhaps, when "Oriental" Jews in Israel, where the term is current in political circles, act as a coalition against Jews of European origin). Nor will the term "Sefardi" Judaism do. *Sefardi,* as Ross Brann explains, means originating in Spain ("Sefarad"), whereas its counterpart term, *Ashkenazi,* means originating in Germany ("Ashkenaz").

Historically speaking, a Middle Eastern Jew is Sefardi only if claiming descent from a family of Spanish emigrants, as do some of the Jewish communities in Morocco, Tunisia, Turkey, and of course Israel. It does not encompass the Jews of Morocco's High Atlas, the Jews of Yemen, Iraq, or Central Asia (and even China and India). During what Brann calls the "High Middle Ages" (A.D. 900–1200), direct and indirect interaction among Jews of different Middle Eastern countries was strong. One impulse was a localizing one. Thus one of the leading intellects of medieval Judaism, Moses Maimonides (1138–1204), forced to flee Spain, settled in Cairo and was appointed head of the Egyptian Jewish community, but he continued to consider himself a Spaniard.

But the bonds among Jews of different countries was also intense. Across the Muslim-dominated Middle East, "interaction with the new [Islamic] culture in its courtly-scribal, traditionalist, scholastic and folkloristic forms forged a different type of Jew whose outlook and self-expression were to alter the course of Jewish history."[118] Sometimes the parallels were indirect. Thus, as Muslim scholars debated the authenticity of the traditions of the Prophet, the "expressive forms and theological issues" found their parallels among Jewish scholars becoming more intensely concerned "about Jewish tradition and the reliability of its guardians." Arabization (as distinct from Islamization) also played an important role in shaping the style of discourse of religion, commerce, and ideas of the person.[119]

Similar parallels exist of course with the Christian communities in the Middle East. Rarely have the contemporary parallels been more evident than in the apparition in Egypt of the Virgin Mary over a Coptic church in Zītūn, a sub-

[116] The existence of a "French Islam," to use Kepel's term, still comes as a surprise for many French. Publication of his *Suburbs of Islam* was greeted on the cover of the magazine supplement to the Paris newspaper *Le Nouvel Observateur,* October 9–15, 1987, under the title "L'Islam en France: Une enquête-événement de Gilles Kepel" [Islam in France: The Investigative "Happening" of Gilles Kepel]. The book itself was termed a "happening" (*le livre événement*).

[117] Ross Brann, *The Experience of Judaism Under the Orbit of Medieval Islam,* Occasional Papers on the Near East 3 (New York: New York University Center for Near Eastern Studies, 1985), p. 1.

[118] Ibid., p. 2.

[119] Ibid., p. 8. The most comprehensive study of Judaism under Islam is S. D. Goitein's highly readable *A Mediterranean Society,* 5 vols. (Berkeley and Los Angeles: University of California Press, 1967–1988).

urb of Cairo, from April 2, 1968 until several years later. Thousands of pilgrims, both Coptic and Muslim, flocked daily to the site hoping to see the miracle for themselves. As Cynthia Nelson relates, the Virgin commands the respect of both Muslims and Christians in Egypt. Soon after the first apparition, the Coptic Patriarch of Egypt and All Africa announced at a press conference that the Virgin's appearance was genuine. The government subsequently took formal notice of the event. What is significant about the apparition is that it served as a symbol of unity for both Muslims and Christians. Most Egyptians connected the apparition of the Virgin with the Six-Day War of June 1967, "a military defeat that left the country in despair and its people confronting perhaps the severest crisis in their contemporary history."[120] Both Muslims and Copts saw the Virgin as having come to extricate them from their crisis. Copts interpreted her appearance as reaffirming their role in the future of Egypt to the Muslim community. Many of the educated, Christian and Muslim, interpreted the event as a ruse of a foreign intelligence agency (presumably the ubiquitous CIA) or as a warning to unbelievers to restore their faith in the nonvisible and nonrational. Again, the form the transcendent takes is tied to political and social realities, the common elements of which can overshadow differences in the Coptic and Muslim communities.

Two Israeli examples of Jewish movements whose participants are generally not of Middle Eastern origin suggest the need for specificity of time and place in discussing religious doctrines and their carriers. Shlomo Deshen notes that Israel's Orthodox Jews are estimated at less than 5 percent of the nation's Jewish population, yet they have a political significance far beyond their numbers. Although they have not necessarily offered viable solutions to Israel's major political and economic crises, no other version of Judaism has been identified as closely with the symbols of tradition and religious legitimacy central to Israel's national identity.[121]

The development of Israel's ultra-Orthodox (*ḥaredī;* pl. *ḥaredīm*—the Hebrew term connotes "God-fearing") communities since the late 1940s, as studied by Menachem Friedman, is particularly significant.[122] A major part of socialization in Israel is compulsory military service for almost all Jewish youth of both sexes: three years of full-time service upon reaching the age of 18, unless deferred, and at least a month a year thereafter of reserve duty until the

[120] Cynthia Nelson, "Religious Experience, Sacred Symbols, and Social Reality: An Illustration from Egypt," *Humaniora Islamica* 2 (1974), 253–66. For an account of Egypt's Copts 15 years later, and after the June 1981 Coptic-Muslim riots, which left at least 100 dead, see Barbulesco, "Babylone," and Chitham, *Coptic Community.*

[121] Shlomo Deshen, "Israeli Judaism: Introduction to Its Major Patterns," *International Journal of Middle East Studies* 9, no. 2 (May 1978), 141–69; and Don Handelman and Lea Shamgar-Handelman, "Holiday Celebrations in Israeli Kindergartens: Relationships Between Representations of Collectivity and Family in the Nation-State," in *The Frailty of Authority,* ed. Myron J. Aronoff, Political Anthropology 5 (New Brunswick, NJ, and Oxford: Transaction, 1986), pp. 71–103.

[122] Menachem Friedman, "Ḥaredim Confront the Modern City," *Studies in Contemporary Jewry* 2, ed. Peter Y. Medding (Bloomington: Indiana University Press, 1986), pp. 74–96, and discussions with Friedman in Bene Berak, February 20, 1985.

age of 55. The only excluded groups are Israeli Arabs (although Druze and bedouin can join the armed forces) and the ultra-Orthodox. The ultra-Orthodox tradition is Eastern European in origin and was almost wiped out during the Holocaust. When communities of the ultra-Orthodox were reconstituted after World War II, David Ben-Gurion was instrumental in exempting them from military service, one of a number of "special inducements" to encourage young men to undertake years of Orthodox study. The ultra-Orthodox were regarded as "protected" communities by wider Israeli society, to be nurtured and allowed to thrive once more. Yet, because of the new circumstances in which the *ḥaredī* communities were reconstituted in Israel, the nature of their "traditional" learning and their relationship to wider society had significantly altered.

Friedman writes that the traditional Orthodox community in Eastern Europe felt threatened with the erosion of its values through contact with modern society, especially as Jewish youth sought assimilation into "modern" European society in the nineteenth and early twentieth centuries. *Ḥaredī* religiosity emerged in the form of voluntary communities, called "publics" or "circles." These "publics" are voluntary in the sense that they are "not imposed but chosen," and the *ḥaredīm* consider themselves "freed" from religious responsibility to the larger Jewish community, an elite dedicated to Torah study "and to the yeshiva [religious school] from which Jewish existence would draw sustenance."[123]

In Eastern Europe in earlier eras, economic necessity confined specifically religious studies to a select few of the ultra-Orthodox. There were levels of understanding of religious texts, ranging from a rudimentary understanding of ritual forms, legends, and popular stories (*enyakob*) to the study of codified discussions of oral tradition and the study of the Talmud proper. Few students could devote themselves entirely to religious studies. At best, they did so for several years prior to marriage and intermittently thereafter. Only a restricted minority of a community's men could commit themselves completely to religious studies, and the secular world was seen as a threat to their values. However, from the first years in Israel after 1948, the ultra-Orthodox soon found that they could turn relations with the wider Jewish community to their advantage.

One of the major settlements for the ultra-Orthodox in the Tel Aviv area is Bene Berak, where the various *ḥaredī* publics, who share similar lifestyles if not ritual interpretations, live together. Everyone living within the geographic bounds of the community is considered a part of it. An observer entering the community for the first time is struck by the nearly total absence of television antennas. Televisions are discouraged among the ultra-Orthodox as a distraction and for the profane images they carry. One also notes a proliferation of wall posters, in contrast to other Israeli communities. Although some *ḥaredī* news is carried in the national press, most debates are too arcane to concern outsiders, so posters provide community news, announcements of marriages,

[123] Friedman, "Ḥaredim," p. 80.

and, quite often, positions taken in ritual debates. These posters are frequently changed.[124] Friedman, a sociologist engaged in a long-term study of the *ḥaredīm,* visits the community twice a week to photograph these posters and follow the internal debates. Finally, both the men and women of the community have a distinctive dress, in which slight variations suggest the particular "circle" to which a wearer belongs.

Because of outside support, religious studies became more widespread in the 1950s and 1960s than in prior years. Talmudic studies are now the central activity of male youth from the age of five until their late twenties. From the age of five until age thirteen, youth attend first-level yeshiva, supported by the community. Plaques on many of these buildings indicate outside financing, in some cases from institutions in which the *ḥaredīm* cannot participate for religious reasons but from which they can benefit, such as the Israeli National Lottery. In the first years, students return home at night, but by the age of thirteen, they live full time in hostels away from their families. There are no uncontrolled meetings with the opposite sex, and marriages are eventually arranged. Even after marriage, men spend their days in *kollel*-s. Friedman reports that it is a matter of pride for a woman to support a husband engaged in Torah study. In nineteenth-century Europe, these were small-scale institutions for post-yeshiva studies, intended, in the words of one rabbi, for the "spiritually sublime few."[125] After the 1950s, however, the *kollel* became a place where almost anyone who had studied in a *ḥaredī* yeshiva could stay on after marriage, delaying entry into a business or occupation for as long as a decade. As a transitional institution, the *kollel* was ideal. If a student had difficulty in finding an outside job, he could return for part of the day to the *kollel* for continued studies.

Major transformations emerged in both the content of Torah learning and the nature of the *ḥaredīm* community as the time available for studies became longer and more intense. The lower levels of study, such as legends and miracles, disappeared by the mid-1950s. In general, studies engaged in by students at both the lower and higher levels have become more oriented toward the Talmud, which earlier was reserved for a few. And the commentaries now are becoming more involuted and complex than previously. In contrast to the despair of some *ḥaredī* leaders in the late 1940s that the traditions of their fathers were no longer carried on, rabbis by the 1980s commonly expressed the belief that the younger generation was more interested in learning than earlier generations. Some Bene Berak *kollel*-s , such as the "Great Yeshiva" of the Ponavitchers, have up to 450 students at any one time.

There are no entrance examinations to *ḥaredī* yeshivot, but senior rabbis ask students wishing to join what they have read and have them explain a few passages. From such brief interviews, students are placed by level. Once admitted, students determine how to proceed. All students work in pairs. One stu-

[124] Friedman, personal communication, February 20, 1985.

[125] Cited in Friedman, "Ḥaredim," p. 88. Friedman estimated the number of participants in *ḥaredī kollel*-s in Israel at 24,000 in 1986 (personal communication, April 3, 1986).

dent reads from the book to be commented upon, and the other interrupts with challenges or questions of interpretation. Precision in language and expression is highly valued, and less able or serious students, or those who do not attend regularly, find it difficult to work with better students. There are no formal levels or examinations, however. Learning is an end in itself.[126]

Another major development among the *ḥaredīm* is the creation of an educational network for girls (*Beit Yaakov*). The *ḥaredīm* stress that religious laws lay down no limitations to women's education, except that the Talmud be studied. So ultra-Orthodox women train to be teachers, an occupation they can carry out under the supervision of *ḥaredī* institutions and readily adjustable to their household tasks. Women's work outside the home is considered a necessity in current economic conditions, and together with women's desire to learn, it is beginning to transform family roles among the *ḥaredīm*.[127]

Men's education prepares them for few outside jobs. However, unskilled and unspecialized work in Israel is so low in status that it is unacceptable to the *ḥaredīm*. Moreover, because yeshiva training is so specialized, the opportunities for breaking away from the system, which Friedman points out usually means cutting family ties, become increasingly few and make revolt against ultra-Orthodox society unrealistic. Hence today the young are more likely to remain within the "cloister" of the *ḥaredī* community than they were in the past.

The narrow training also limits the economic roles that men can play. Work that demands a high level of skill is generally unrealistic because of the low level of general education. Some men go into commercial niches, where the success of a few (such as in international diamond trading) creates wealth that is often used to support the community's religious leaders. But increasingly, the *ḥaredīm* find their specialized "niche" in providing religious services and accessories (phylacteries, Torah scrolls, wine goblets, and the like) to the wider Jewish community and in salaried state occupations such as army chaplains, judges in the religious courts, supervisors of kosher food preparation, and teachers within state-supported *ḥaredī* schools. Just as a few successful traders keep alive the notion that yeshiva preparation is as good as any other for the "practical" world, so the appointments of a few *ḥaredīm* to posts as judge (*dayan*) in the state rabbinical courts reinforce "the idea that Torah study in haredi yeshivot is eminently practical, in the long run." Wider society, writes Friedman, perceives the *ḥaredīm* "as a kind of living museum of the past, in whose continued existence the nation has an interest," thus facilitating both private donations and Israeli government assistance.

The fact that ultra-Orthodox institutions are expanding and prospering suggests that their scale of funding from outside sources continues to grow. At the same time, crime, drugs, and other problems of the "secular" world are absent from *ḥaredīm* communities. The more they feel alienated from the "secu-

[126] For a sensitive account of a sociologist's participation in *lernen* at more advanced stages in Jerusalem, see Samuel Heilman, *The Gate Behind the Wall: A Pilgrimage to Jerusalem* (New York: Viking/Penguin, 1984).

[127] Friedman, "Ḥaredim," pp. 82–84.

lar" society and its perceived ills, the more their sense of religious superiority increases. Yet the maintenance and development of *ḥaredī* institutions, including the unintended intensification of ultra-orthodox concentration on religious studies, is only made possible by a wider society that supports it but is unable to emulate it (even if it wanted to) without destroying itself.[128]

Another scholar assesses the emergence of "Jewish fundamentalism," which he terms "the single most important force in Israeli politics" since the 1973 Yom Kippur War. Ian Lustick defines Jewish fundamentalism "as a Jewish belief system that requires urgent efforts by its adherents radically to transform Israeli society in conformance with transcendental imperatives," thus excluding such groups as the *ḥaredīm.* Lustick claims that Jewish fundamentalism, advocating maximum territorial demands and the rejection of a negotiated settlement with the Arabs, expresses the beliefs and powerful commitments of 20 percent of Israeli Jews and appeals to an additional 20 to 30 percent of them.[129] He regards this movement as most comprehensively represented by Gush Emunim (the Bloc of the Faithful), a network of more than 10,000 activists who constitute a skilled political cadre and who, like other fundamentalists, believe "that they possess special and direct access to transcendental truth and to the future course of events." Gush Emunim, Lustick writes, is an umbrella organization for several overlapping groups, officially nonpartisan, but represented in the national political arena by "half a dozen cabinet ministers and more than 35 percent of the Knesset, representing five political parties."[130]

In contrast to the original nineteenth-century Zionist ideology, which Lustick argues was intended to transform Jews into a "normal" people occupying their own land and accepted by other peoples on equal terms, the Gush Emunim arose after the June 1967 war and grew even stronger after the 1973 Arab-Israeli conflict. It argues that God ordained a unique and historic purpose for the Jewish people, reflecting "a deep-seated belief that nearly the only distinction worth making among human groups is that between Jews and Gentiles" and that the destiny of Jews can be fulfilled only by liberating the entire land of Israel.[131] Gush Emunim possesses a systematic worldview, although there are disagreements among its members as to leadership and "transcendental" authority (very much like Muslim extremist movements), the territorial extent of Israel, the pace at which territorial gains should be achieved, attitudes toward the Israeli and international opposition (some, Luctick says, openly accept the possibility of a civil war), the role of Arabs in the Jewish state of the future (Meir Kahane, for example, advocated the expulsion of all Arabs from

[128] Ibid., pp. 85–92.

[129] Ian S. Lustick, "Israel's Dangerous Fundamentalists," *Foreign Policy,* no. 68 (Fall 1987), 118–39, esp. 120. For an authoritative, more recent account, see Gideon Aran, "Jewish Zionist Fundamentalism: The Bloc of the Faithful in Israel (Gush Emunim)," in *Fundamentalisms Observed,* ed. Martin E. Marty and R. Scott Appleby, The Fundamentalisms Project 1 (Chicago and London: University of Chicago Press, 1991), pp. 265–344.

[130] Ibid., 119, 127.

[131] Ibid., 122, 125.

Israel and the occupied territories), and the prospects for peace. A few see the possibility of coexistence, but the majority do not.

Handicaps to the movement include cutbacks in subsidies for settlement, a reduction in the flow of new recruits, failure to find meaningful employment for most settlers, and a continued reliance on Arab labor. Most serious of all is the basic problem of a leadership vacuum since the death in 1982 of the movement's first charismatic spokesman, the Rabbi Tzvi Yehuda Kook. The movement became bitterly divided after the arrest in the 1980s of underground Jewish terrorists and the activities of its "vanguardist" elements intent upon destroying Muslim shrines on the Temple Mount in Jerusalem in order to accelerate the Redemption process for the Jewish people and destroy chances for peace negotiations.[132] Political pragmatists in the Gush Emunim movement, intent upon building a consensus among its diverse elements, recognized that any such destruction would turn a significant body of Israeli Jewish opinion against them.

As Lustick stresses, the "worldview" of the Gush Emunim differs radically from that of most Israelis, but the "bloc" is sufficiently committed, organized, and financed (with large donations from private Americans) for it to have influenced Israel's political life far beyond its numbers and contributed to a hardening of positions between Israel's secular Jewish community and its religious extremists. The movement's perceptual and ideological categories serve not only some symbolic purpose but also combine an elaborate exegesis of religious texts with the analysis of contemporary political and historical events in order to guide the continuing struggle toward redemption. For Jewish fundamentalists, "political trends and events contain messages to Jews that provide instructions, reprimands, and rewards."[133]

A similar point can be made about radical Muslim movements. The worldview of both Islamic and Jewish radicals and the nature of their organization bear some similarities. The contemporary radical movements of both religions seek to interpret contemporary events in terms of unique religious categories not necessarily shared even by other religious people in their respective societies. Likewise, they see the need for a radical political transformation of society and are prepared to use force and illegality to achieve their goals. Finally, and perhaps fortunately for the majority of Jews and Muslims who, however disenchanted they are with the conduct of state authorities, fail to be enthused by the agendas of religious radicals, radical groups lacking charismatic leadership are subject to a high level of internal dissension that curbs, to some extent, their ability to unite in the face of opposition or indifference to their programs.

Religion in the civil societies of the Middle East, as elsewhere in the world, is a significant factor in motivating people to perceive events and take actions. The appeal of particular religious interpretations and movements can-

[132] Ibid., 131, 134–36.

[133] Ibid., 127–28.

not be "read" directly from particular conjunctures of politics and economics, although certain settings are more conducive to the spread of certain movements than others. It would be a mistake, however, to try to explain the popularity of specific ideologies and movements on the basis of political and economic factors alone. Much depends on the presence or absence of effective formulators of ideas and organizers and the availability of potential followers. Radical religious interpretations may be more likely to emerge in periods of sustained economic or political crisis. Thus, to many Arabs, the defeat of the Arab states in the war with Israel in 1967 was interpreted as a bankruptcy of secular Arab nationalist movements and of state authorities. An opening was created for radical religious movements with their own vision of the conduct of state affairs. There was no direct chronological parallel with the intensification of radical Judaism in Israel, but after 1973, and especially after Sadat's visit to Jerusalem, a much greater disposition to the ideas and programs of radical Judaism emerged.

Each world religious tradition represented in the Middle East is prismatic, and at no time would it be appropriate to see in each a dominant ideology or organizational form to the exclusion of others. Subordinate forms of discourse and action are present in each of the traditions, and in unexpected ways they can reemerge. With talented innovators and organizers at all levels of society, they can take new forms and achieve positions of dominance.

FURTHER READINGS

On the Zoroastrians, see Shahin Bekhradnia, "The Decline of the Zoroastrian Priesthood and Its Effect on the Iranian Zoroastrian Community in the Twentieth Century," *Journal of the Anthropological Society of Oxford* 23, no. 1 (Hilary 1992), 37–47. The Yazīdīs, now numbering about 150,000, have been characterized as "devil worshippers" by Muslim neighbors, but they share many common beliefs with Christianity and Islam. Their self-representation is that Azaziel, chief of the seven angels, was banished by God (like Satan for Jews and Christians) for disobedience but was subsequently pardoned, so veneration of him is not devil worship. See John S. Guest, *The Yezidis: A Study in Survival* (London: Kegan Paul International, 1987). As indicated in Chapter 7, many small sects, including Nestorian and Chaldaean Christians, coexist in northern Iraq. On the complexities of Lebanon's sectarian groups, see Kamal Salibi, *A House of Many Mansions: The History of Lebanon Reconsidered* (Berkeley and Los Angeles: University of California Press, 1988), esp. pp. 1–37.

Representative but necessarily selective books dealing with understanding Islam include Clifford Geertz, *Islam Observed* (Chicago: University of Chicago Press, 1971 [1968]); for commentaries on Geertz's approach to the study of religion, see, among others, Richard C. Martin, "Clifford Geertz Observed: Understanding Islam as Cultural Symbolism," in *Anthropology and the Study of Religion,* ed. Robert L. Moore and Frank E. Reynolds (Chicago: Center for the Scientific Study of Religion, 1984), pp. 11–30; Henry Munson, Jr., "Geertz on Religion: The Theory and the Practice," *Religion* 16 (1986), 19–32; and Munson's *Religion and Power in Morocco* (New Haven, CT, and London: Yale University Press, 1993). Ernest Gellner, *Muslim Society,* Cambridge Studies in Social Anthropology 32 (Cambridge and New York: Cambridge University Press, 1981), a collection of essays valuable for Gellner's own views—note that "society" in the title is singular, not plural—as for his discussion of other scholars; Michael Gilsenan, *Saint and Sufi in Modern Egypt* (Oxford: Oxford University Press, 1973), and his subsequent *Recognizing Islam: Religion and Society in the Modern Arab World* (New York: Pantheon, 1982); Abdul Hamid M. el-Zein, *The Sacred Meadows: A Structural Analysis of Religious Symbolism in an East African Town* (Evanston, IL: Northwestern University Press, 1974); Dale F. Eickelman, *Moroccan Islam: Tradition and Society in a Pilgrimage Center* (Austin, TX: University of Texas Press, 1976) and *Knowledge and Power in Morocco: The Education of a Twentieth Century Notable* (Princeton, NJ: Princeton University Press, 1985); Clifford Geertz, Hildred Geertz, and Lawrence Rosen, *Meaning and Order in Moroccan Society: Three Essays in Cultural Analysis* (New York: Cambridge University Press, 1979); Michael M. J. Fischer, *Iran: From Religious Dispute to Revolution* (Cambridge: Harvard University Press, 1980); Michael M. J. Fischer and Mehdi Abedi, *Debating Muslims: Cultural Dialogues in Postmodernity and Tradition,* New Directions in Anthropological Writing (Madison: University of Wisconsin Press, 1990); Henry Munson, Jr., *The House of Si Abdallah* (New Haven, CT, and London: Yale University Press, 1984); and Gilles Kepel, *Muslim Extremism in Egypt: The Prophet and Pharaoh,* trans. Jon Rothschild (Berkeley and Los Angeles: University of California Press, 1993 [1984]). For anthropological essays on the study of Muslim societies, see Dale F. Eickelman, "Changing Interpretations of Islamic Movements," in *Islam and the Political Economy of Meaning,* ed. William R. Roff (Berkeley and Los Angeles: University of California Press, 1987), pp. 13–30; and Talal Asad, *The Idea of an Anthropology of Islam,* Occasional Paper Series (Washington, DC: Georgetown University Center for Contemporary Arab Studies, 1986), and his *Genealogies of Religion: Discipline and Reasons of Power in Christianity and Islam* (Baltimore and London: Johns Hopkins University Press, 1993). The idea of an "Islamic anthropology," which is quite different from the anthropology of Islam elaborated by Asad, is further discussed in the last section of Chapter 11, "Writing Middle Eastern Anthropology." For thoughtful discussions of the important issues involved in Islamic studies by Muslim and non-Muslim scholars, see Fazlur Rahman, "Islamic Studies and the Future of Islam," in *Islamic Studies: A Tradition and Its Problems,* ed. Malcolm H. Kerr (Malibu, CA: Undena Publications, 1980), pp. 125–33; and Merryl Wyn Davies, *Knowing One Another: Shaping an Islamic Anthropology* (London and New York: Mansell, 1988).

Perhaps the most seminal scholarly study of the Islamic tradition to date is Marshall G. S. Hodgson's difficult but essential three-volume *Venture of Islam* (Chicago: University of Chicago Press, 1974). Useful complementary readings are Marilyn Robinson Waldman's review of *Venture,* which appeared in *Religious Studies Review* 2, no. 3 (July 1976), 22–35; and Edmund Burke III's introductory and concluding essays in Marshall G. S. Hodgson, *Rethinking World History: Essays on Europe, Islam, and World History,* ed. Edmund Burke III, Studies in Comparative History (Cambridge: Cambridge University Press, 1993). See also Waldman's, "Tradition as a Modality of Change: Islamic Examples," *History of Religions* 25, no. 4 (May 1986), 318–40. See also Charles J. Adams, "Islamic Religious Tradition," in *The Study of the Middle East,* ed. Leonard Binder (New York: Wiley, 1976), pp. 29–95, a bibliographic essay; Bryan S. Turner, *Weber and Islam: A Critical Study* (London and Boston: Routledge & Kegan Paul, 1974); and Richard C. Martin, ed., *Approaches to Islam in Religious Studies* (Tucson: University of Arizona Press, 1985).

The social and economic understanding of events in seventh-century Arabia are currently undergoing major revision as a result of the efforts of both Muslim and non-Muslim scholars. Many of the basic sources are translated into English, and the scholarship based on them is, in most cases, more accessible than was the case even a decade ago. A good place to begin a consideration of this period remains W. Montgomery Watt's *Muhammad at Mecca* (Oxford: Clarendon Press, 1959) and *Muhammad at Medina* (Oxford: Clarendon Press, 1956). Explicitly anthropological analyses of this period include Eric Wolf, "The Social Organization of Mecca and the Origins of Islam," *Southwestern Journal of Anthropology* 7, no. 4 (Winter 1951), 329–56; Barbara C. Aswad, "Social and Ecological

Aspects in the Formation of Islam," reprinted in *Peoples and Cultures of the Middle East*, vol. 1, ed. Louise E. Sweet (Garden City, NY: Natural History Press, 1970 [1963]), pp. 53–73; and Dale F. Eickelman, "Musaylima: An Approach to the Social Anthropology of Seventh Century Arabia," *Journal of the Economic and Social History of the Orient* 10, pt. 1 (July 1967), 17–52. Wolf and Aswad concentrate on the economic background of the rise of Islam; Eickelman is concerned primarily with competing claims to prophetic authority in seventh-century Arabia. Talal Asad, "Ideology, Class and the Origin of the Islamic State," *Economy and Society* 9, no. 4 (November 1980), 451–73, reviews a Marxist analysis in Arabic of the events of the period. A series of articles by R. B. Serjeant on this period is also invaluable. His "Sunnah Jamī'ah: Pacts with the Yathrib Jews and the *Tahrīm* of Yathrib," *Bulletin of the School of Oriental and African Studies* 41, pt. 1 (1978), contains references to his earlier related essays. An anthropologically oriented semantic analysis of the Quran is provided by Toshihiko Izutsu, *God and Man in the Koran: Semantics of the Koranic Weltanschauung*, Studies in the Humanities and Social Relations 5 (Tokyo: Keio Institute of Cultural and Linguistic Studies, 1964), and his *Ethico-Religious Concepts in the Qur'ān*, McGill Islamic Studies 1 (Montreal: McGill University Press, 1966). Izutsu's linguistic approach is paralleled by Muḥammad Shaḥrūr, *al-Kitāb wa-l-Qur'ān: Qirā'a Mu'āṣira* [The Book and the Qur'ān: A Contemporary Reading] (Damascus: Al-Ahālī li-l-Ṭabā'a wa-l-Nashr wa-l-Tawzī'a, 1990). Shaḥrūr's book is banned in many Arabic countries, but this has not kept it from becoming a best-seller throughout the Arab world. See Dale F. Eickelman, "Islamic Liberalism Strikes Back," *Middle East Studies Association Bulletin* 27, no. 2 (December 1993), 163–68. A sweeping reconsideration of the period is Patricia Crone, *Meccan Trade and the Rise of Islam* (Princeton, NJ: Princeton University Press, 1987). Crone argues against Watt's notion of a mercantile revolution at Mecca prompting a "malaise" leading to a reformulation of religious values. As she writes, the evidence for a spiritual "general malaise" in Mecca is inadequate, evidence for a major economic shift correspondingly weak, and a "one-to-one correspondence" between economic factors and the appearance of a prophet tenuous (pp. 231–34). "Ultimately, the Watt thesis boils down to the proposition that a city in a remote corner of Arabia had some social problems to which a preacher responded by founding a world religion. It sounds like an overreaction" (p. 235).

On the interpretation of Islamic law and ideas of justice, see Lawrence Rosen, *The Anthropology of Justice: Law as Culture in Islamic Society* (New York and Cambridge: Cambridge University Press, 1988). Rosen argues that the cultural idea of justice in the Moroccan context is as highly personalized and contextual as is a broad range of relationships in the society. See also Brinkley Messick, *The Calligraphic State: Textual Domination and History in a Muslim Society*, Comparative Studies on Muslim Societies 16 (Berkeley and Los Angeles: University of California Press, 1993), pp. 135–86; Muhammad Khalid Masud, Brinkley Messick, and David S. Powers, eds., *Islamic Legal Interpretation: Muftis and Their Fatwas* (Cambridge, MA, and London: Harvard University Press, 1996); and Frank H. Stewart, "Tribal Law in the Arab World: A Review of the Literature," *International Journal of Middle East Studies* 19, no. 4 (November 1987), 73–90.

On the significance of the pilgrimage and other forms of travel to the religious imagination, see *Muslim Travellers: Pilgrimage, Migration, and the Religious Imagination*, ed. Dale F. Eickelman and James Piscatori (Berkeley and Los Angeles: University of California Press, 1990). For nineteenth-century accounts of the pilgrimage, see C. Snouck Hurgronje, *Mekka in the Latter Part of the Nineteenth Century*, trans. J. H. Monahan (Leiden: E. J. Brill, 1931); and Richard F. Burton, *Personal Narrative of a Pilgrimage to Al-Madinah and Meccah* (New York: Dover, 1964 [1893]). The perils of the journey were increased when European-dominated steamships, often in the hands of unscrupulous, profit-conscious captains, became a common mode of transporting pilgrims. See, for example, Mohammed Amine el Bezzaz, "La chronique scandaleuse du pèlerinage marocain à la Mecque au XIXème siècle," *Hespéris-Tamuda* 20–21 (1982–1983), 319–32.

The best overall introduction to the Shīʿa is Yann Richard, *Shiʿite Islam: Polity, Ideology, and Creed,* Studies in Social Discontinuity (Cambridge, MA: Blackwell, 1995 [1991]). Richard W. Bulliet, *Islam: The View from the Edge,* breaks with older conventions and offers an introduction to Islamic history and politics based on people, including the Iranians, who were never under Ottoman domination. For a brief sketch of divisions among the Shīʿa, see Nikki R. Keddie and Juan R. I. Cole, eds., *Shiʿism and Social Protest* (New Haven, CT: Yale University Press, 1986). For an account of the dissident Babi sect in nineteenth-century Shīʿī Islam in Iran, from which the Baha'i faith emerged, see Peter Smith, *The Babi and Baha'i Religions: From Messianic Shiʿism to a World Religion* (Cambridge: Cambridge University Press, 1987). For Shīʿī practice at the village level in Iran, see Reinhold Loeffler, *Islam in Practice: Religious Beliefs in a Persian Village* (Albany: State University of New York Press, 1988). Yann Richard, "Clercs et intellectuels dans la République islamique d'Iran" [Clerics and Intellectuals in the Islamic Republic of Iran], in *Intellectuels et militants de l'Islam contemporain,* ed. Gilles Kepel and Yann Richard (Paris: Seuil, 1990), pp. 29–70. Roy P. Mottahedeh, *The Mantle of the Prophet: Religion and Politics in Iran* (New York: Simon and Schuster, 1985), through the eyes of contemporary *mullah,* evokes Iran immediately before and after the revolution. On persisting networks of patronage and influence, Judith Lynne Goldstein, "The Paradigm of Protection: Minority 'Big Men' in Iran," *Social Analysis* 9, no. 9 (December 1981), 98–100, notes that the patronage dispensed by key religious figures has its counterpart among Iranian Jews and also mediates intercommunal relations in Iran. For Iraq, see Yitzhak Nakash, *The Shiʿis of Iraq* (Princeton, NJ: Princeton University Press, 1994). On the Shīʿa in Afghanistan, see Robert L. Canfield, "Ethnic, Regional, and Sectarian Alignments in Afghanistan," in *The State, Religion, and Ethnic Politics: Afghanistan, Iran and Pakistan,* ed. Ali Banuazizi and Myron Weiner (Syracuse, NY: Syracuse University Press, 1986), pp. 75–103. On Lebanon's Shīʿī leadership, see Augustus Richard Norton, *Amal and the Shiʿa: Struggle for the Soul of Lebanon,* Modern Middle East Series 13 (Austin and London: University of Texas Press, 1987), pp. 37–58; and Fouad Ajami, *The Vanished Imam: Musa al Sadr and the Shia of Lebanon* (Ithaca, NY, and London: Cornell University Press, 1986). On the Arab Gulf, see James A. Bill, "Resurgent Islam in the Persian Gulf," *Foreign Affairs,* 63, no. 1 (Fall 1984), 108–27. On the galaxy-like connections, as opposed to formal, hierarchical ones, among religiously oriented terrorist groups, see Xavier Raufer, *La nébuleuse: Le terrorisme du Moyen-Orient* (Paris: Fayard, 1987), pp. 153–202.

On the sources of support for the Iranian revolution, a useful point of departure is *The Iranian Revolution and the Islamic Republic,* ed. Nikki R. Keddie and Eric Hooglund, rev. ed. (Boulder, CO: Westview Press, 1985). On the failure to recognize Shīʿī political discontent and the ability to mobilize support for the revolution, see James A. Bill, *The Eagle and the Lion: The Tragedy of American-Iranian Relations* (New Haven, CT, and London: Yale University Press, 1988), pp. 154–260.

On mourning for Ḥusayn, see Peter J. Chelkowski, ed., *Taʿziyeh: Ritual and Drama in Iran* (New York: New York University Press; Tehran: Soroush Press, 1979), especially the essay by William O. Beeman, "Cultural Dimensions of Performance Conventions in Iranian Taʿziyeh," pp. 24–126. Also see Gus Thaiss, "Religious Symbolism and Social Change: The Drama of Husain," in *Scholars, Saints and Sufis,* ed. Nikki Keddie (Berkeley and Los Angeles: University of California Press, 1972), pp. 349–66; and—an account finely tuned to a local social order—Emrys L. Peters, "Aspects of Rank and Status Among Muslims in a Lebanese Village," in *Mediterranean Countrymen,* ed. Julian Pitt-Rivers (Paris and The Hague: Mouton, 1963), pp. 195–200.

On Islam in tribal settings, see *Islam in Tribal Societies: From the Atlas to the Indus,* ed. Akbar S. Ahmed and David M. Hart (London: Routledge & Kegan Paul, 1984). This volume includes a reprint of I. M. Lewis, "Sufism in Somaliland," pp. 127–68 [1955]. For an earlier historical period, Devin De Wesse, *Islamization and Native Religion in the Golden Horde: Baba Tukles and Conversion to Islam in Historical and Epic Tradition* (State College:

Pennsylvania State University Press, 1994), is essential reading. A classic study of religious leadership in a tribal milieu is Fredrik Barth, *Political Leadership Among Swat Pathans,* L.S.E. Monographs on Social Anthropology 19 (London: Athlone Press, 1959), esp. pp. 92–109. Talal Asad, "Market Model, Class Structure and Consent: A Reconsideration of Swat Political Organization," *Man* (N.S.) 7, no. 1 (March 1972), 74–94, offers a critique of Barth, as does Akbar S. Ahmed, *Millennium and Charisma Among Pathans,* International Library in Anthropology (London: Routledge & Kegan Paul, 1976). See also John C. Wilkinson's difficult but detailed *The Imamate Tradition of Oman,* Cambridge Middle East Library (Cambridge: Cambridge University Press, 1987); and Emanuel Marx, "Communal and Individual Pilgrimage: The Religion of Saints' Tombs in South Sinai," in *Regional Cults,* ed. Richard P. Werbner, ASA Monographs 16 (New York and London: Academic Press, 1977), pp. 29–51. An outstanding recent monograph, especially incisive in exploring the "gendered" expression of religious symbolism and practice in a tribal milieu, is Ladislav Holy, *Religion and Custom in a Muslim Society: The Berti of Sudan,* Cambridge Studies in Social and Cultural Anthropology 78 (Cambridge and New York: Cambridge University Press, 1991). Paul Dresch and Bernard Haykel, "Stereotypes and Political Styles: Islamists and Tribesfolk in Yemen," *International Journal of Middle East Studies* 27, no. 4 (November 1995), 405–31, shows the interplay of Muslim politics and tribal identities, avoiding the stereotypes by which both tribes and "Islamist" politics are often represented, including by non-tribal Yemenis.

Religion is also closely linked to many aspects of expressive popular culture. Until the mid-1970s, there were few anthropological studies of expressive language, poetry, music, and other forms of artistic expression in the Middle East, so that Jacques Berque's *Cultural Expression in Arab Society Today,* trans. Robert W. Stookey, Modern Middle East Series 3 (Austin and London: University of Texas Press, 1978), stood almost alone as a comprehensive evocation of the relation of language and artistic expression to society. Even when some modern forms of musical and graphic expression have sought to break away from more traditional art forms, they must do so on the basis of popular understandings, at least if their creators seek a wide audience. A sensitive account of how musicians develop styles in response to their audiences is Philip D. Schuyler, "Berber Professional Musicians in Performance," in *Performance Practice: Ethnomusicological Perspectives,* ed. Gerard Behague, Contributions in Intercultural and Comparative Studies 12 (Westport, CT, and London: Greenwood Press, 1984), pp. 91–148, while Schuyler's "Music Education in Morocco: Three Models," *World of Music* (Berlin) 21 no. 3 (1979), 19–31, explores the parallels between traditional music education and religious education. See also his "The *Rwais* and the *Zawia:* Professional Musicians and the Rural Religious Elite in Southwestern Morocco," *Asian Music* 17, no. 1 (Fall–Winter 1985), 114–31. This particular issue of *Asian Music* is devoted entirely to music in the Muslim world. One can see and hear the music Schuyler discusses in the 1983 film, *Master Musicians of Jahjouka,* available from Mendizza and Associates, Long Beach, CA. Hiromi L. Sakata, *Music in the Mind: The Concepts of Music and Musician in Afghanistan* (Kent, OH: Kent State University Press, 1983), discusses the cultural role of the musician in Afghanistan. For Central Asia, Theodore Levin, *The Hundred Thousand Fools of God: Musical Travels in Central Asia* (Bloomington: Indiana University Press, 1996), explores the changing mix of secular and religious influences and the relationship between performers and their audiences. Finally, Brian Spooner, "Weavers and Dealers: The Authenticity of an Oriental Carpet," in *The Social Life of Things,* ed. Arjun Appadurai (Cambridge: Cambridge University Press, 1986), pp. 195–235, explores how the craft of carpet-weaving and its product are subtly and continuously transformed by the contexts in which they are produced. The transmission of many such crafts—and music is considered a craft, as opposed to an art, in many parts of the Middle East—has important parallels with the form in which religious knowledge was transmitted. For a discussion of dance and religion in the Muslim world, see Anthony Shay, "Dance and Non-Dance: Patterned Movement in Iran and Islam," *Iranian Studies* 28, nos. 1–2 (Winter–Spring 1995), 61–78.

On Islamic learning, in addition to the studies cited in Eickelman, *Knowledge and Power,* see Michael Chamberlain, *Knowledge and Social Practice in Medieval Damascus, 1190–1350,* Cambridge Studies in Islamic Civilization (Cambridge: Cambridge University Press, 1994); and the review essay by Shosham Boaz, "The 'Politics of Notables' in Medieval Islam," *Asian and African Studies* 20, no. 2 (July 1986), 179–215. For medieval Iran, see Richard Bulliet, *The Patricians of Nishapur* (Cambridge, MA: Harvard University Press, 1972). For the nineteenth and twentieth centuries, in addition to studies mentioned earlier, see *Scholars, Saints, and Sufis: Muslim Religious Institutions in the Middle East Since 1500,* ed. Nikki R. Keddie (Berkeley and Los Angeles: University of California Press, 1972).

One of the best-edited volumes assessing Islam and politics throughout the Muslim world is *Islam in the Political Process,* ed. James P. Piscatori (Cambridge and New York: Cambridge University Press, 1983); for Turkey, see Richard Tapper, ed., *Islam in Modern Turkey* (London and New York: I. B. Tauris, 1991). Islamic movements have been less important than ethnonationalism in most of Central Asia, but they are nonetheless politically and socially significant in many regions. See Abduvakhitov, "Islamic Revivalism"; Martha Brill Olcott, "Islam and Fundamentalism in Independent Central Asia," in *Muslim Eurasia: Conflicting Legacies,* ed. Yaacov Ro'i, Cummings Center Series (London: Frank Cass, 1995), pp. 21–39; Nancy Lubin, "Islam and Ethnic Identity in Central Asia: A View from Below," in *Muslim Eurasia,* ed. Ro'i, pp. 53–70; and Muriel Atkin, "Religious, National, and Other Identities in Central Asia," in *Muslims in Central Asia,* ed. Gross, pp. 46–72.

For "Muslim" politics in general, see Eickelman and Piscatori, *Muslim Politics,* which includes annotated references and an extensive bibliography on current developments. See also Gregory Starrett, "The Political Economy of Religious Commodities in Cairo," *American Anthropologist* 97, no. 1 (March 1995), 51–68, and his "The Margins of Print: Children's Religious Literature in Egypt," *Journal of the Royal Anthropological Institute* (N.S.) 2, no. 1 (March 1996), pp. 117–39.

PART V
THE SHAPE OF CHANGE

11

STATE AUTHORITY AND SOCIETY

POPULAR AND ELITE CONCEPTIONS

"Speculation about connections between economics and politics," writes a leading political economist, "becomes much more profitable when one focuses not on the roughest outline, but on the finer features."[1] This applies to understanding politics and political authority in the Middle East and Central Asia, where the "finer features" show up in the language of politics, terms in such common usage that their meaning is taken for granted.

Take the words signifying "people" that have evolved in Iranian political usage, as analyzed by Mohamad Tavakoli-Targhi.[2] Such terms are inherently ambiguous and can be fit into contexts across the political spectrum; they can shift in meaning as relationships of domination change among various classes, parties, and factions, and maintain significance among a wide body of the population throughout these transformations. Tavakoli-Targhi refers to such terms as "floating signifiers" with a "surplus of meaning." The terms for "people" in contemporary Persian usage include *millat* (which, depending upon the words used to modify it, possesses either nationalist or Islamic political connotations), *mardum* (a religiously neutral term used by the

[1] Albert O. Hirschman, *A Bias for Hope: Essays on Development and Latin America* (New Haven, CT, and London: Yale University Press, 1971), p. 9.

[2] Mohamad Tavakoli-Targhi, "'The People' and 'the Popular' in Iranian Political Discourse," paper presented at the Middle East Studies Association annual meeting, Boston, November 1986. (Used with permission.)

Shah beginning in the 1960s), *tudeh* (for members of the Marxist "old left"), and *khalq* (a term associated with the Maoist-inspired left that came into currency in the 1960s).

Tavakoli-Targhi argues that the contextual meanings of these terms, especially *millat*, are linked with patterns of political hegemony and challenges to it. In sixteenth-century Safavi Iran, *millat* signified a distinct Twelver Shīʿī politico-religious identity and hence was not solely confined to subordinate, internally autonomous "peoples of the book," as it was in the Ottoman Empire (the term derives from Arabic and Turkish usage). As Ottoman provinces broke away from the Sublime Porte and became independent in the nineteenth century, *millat* shifted from its religious meaning and began to encompass the idea of a "national" people seeking autonomy.

In nineteenth-century Iran, the term came to signify, not nationhood, but "an ensemble of social forces struggling against foreign intervention and the despotism of the state."[3] However, by the end of the century, especially with popular resistance to the tobacco concession to a British company, *millat* began to be identified with the "Islamic nation" (*millat-i Musalman*). Many Iranians saw the state as having "sold out" to non-Muslim Europeans. To defend the state against the "ideological and organizational" forces mustered against it, Nāṣir al-Dīn Shāh (1848–1896) responded that the weakness of the state and the growing European influence in Iran were due to a weakened *millat*, which, through popular protest, had demonstrated a renewed vitality.[4] Thus the state sought to co-opt the actions and discourse of the opposition. By the time of the 1906 Constitutional Assembly, crowds chanted "Long live *millat-i* Iran," with *millat* now implying a unified people, instead of the earlier usage, which divided them into class, rank, and profession.[5] Later, as factions in the constitutionalist debate developed their positions, *millat* increasingly acquired "secular national, and anti-Islamic connotations."

In the 1950s, the government of nationalist Prime Minister Mohamed Mossadegh was called "the national government" (*hukumat-i milli*), indicating the term's shift to a principally secular nationalist usage. After Mossadegh's overthrow in 1953 and the reinstatement of the Shah (with U.S. and British intelligence support), *millat* again became an oppositional term. Those using it were implicitly anti-Shah, anti-imperialist, and sympathetic to the National Front.[6] When religious leaders mobilized against the Shah in the 1960s, they wrested the term from the secularly oriented nationalists. The crown, in the meantime, used the religiously neutral term of *mardum*, as in such phrases as the "Revolution of the Shah and the People" (*mardum*) and the crown-spon-

[3] Ibid., pp. 5, 8, 10.

[4] Ibid., pp. 12–13.

[5] Ibid., p. 16.

[6] Ibid., pp. 19–23. On U.S. and British involvement in the *coup d'état*, see Mark J. Gasiorowski, "The 1953 *Coup d'Etat* in Iran," *International Journal of Middle East Studies* 19, no. 3 (August 1987), 261–86.

sored political party called *Hizb-i Mardum*.[7] But even *mardum* was taken over by the opposition and provided a point of unity that soon encompassed both the left and the religious opposition.

The final transformation began in 1978, just prior to the overthrow of the Shah, when religious forces reintroduced yet another term, *umat* (Ar. *umma*), a Quranic term for the community of Muslims, using *millat* only in such phrases as *millat-i Musalman* ("the Muslim people") to distinguish it from a more secular usage as "nationalism" (*millatgarā'i*).[8] Thus *millat* came full cycle and was reclaimed as a religious term used in the interests of state authority.

Similar transformations occurred in concepts of political authority throughout the Middle East and Central Asia. Since the nineteenth century, Middle Eastern and Central Asian countries have experienced three major transformations in ideas of political authority and rule: the usages prevailing prior to colonial conquest or domination; the adoption of European-inspired structures of state governance (within the context of colonial rule or as part of autochthonous "reform," usually in response to the threat of European incursion); and the forms that have developed since political independence or in response to demands for greater political participation. These transformations have sometimes been masked by the continued use of an older political vocabulary, such as the Arabic "politics" (*siyāsa*) or "authority" (*sulṭa*) in the Middle East, or by the "revolutionary" language of Soviet Central Asia (or post-1969 Libya, or the former People's Democratic Republic of Yemen, which existed from 1970 to 1990) in which older, forbidden loyalties often remained politically significant. Continued use of the older terms deflected attention from innovation in the concept and practice of state rule. Among Egypt's political elite, for example, "politics" shifted from an earlier usage denoting no more than the practice of governing to one signifying a distinct field of knowledge and practice concerned with "the regulation, management, and supervision of men's affairs." At least for the political elite in the nineteenth century, "politics" signified the discipline, order, control, and well-being of both individuals and the state.[9]

The notion of politics as control (*niẓām*), or ordering by means of discipline and organization, inspired in part by increasing European domination and a desire to emulate or contain the political successes of the dominating powers, was associated with that of renewed national identity under the aegis of Islam in the Middle East and in the Muslim majority regions of Central

[7] The phrase "Revolution of the Shah and the People" was also intended to co-opt the growing strength of the oppositional left in the 1960s. It was evidently borrowed by Morocco's Ḥasan II for his "Revolution of the King with the People" (*thawrat al-mālik ma'a sh-sha'b*). This slogan was replaced in the late 1970s with a more religious one.

[8] Tavakoli-Targhi, "Iranian Political Discourse," pp. 25–27.

[9] Timothy Mitchell, *Colonising Egypt*, Modern Middle East Studies (Cambridge and New York: Cambridge University Press, 1988), pp. 102–104. Mitchell's study traces how the language of authority developed in Egypt. See also Nancy Elizabeth Gallagher, *Medicine and Power in Tunisia, 1780–1900* (Cambridge and New York: Cambridge University Press, 1983), who shows how ideas of health and sanitation can also be linked to authority and domination.

Asia.[10] In earlier epochs, states were considered primarily in the aggregate. Henceforth, despite frequent resistance to expanded state authority, they were, at least in the view of state authorities, individuals to be counted, policed, ordered, taxed, conscripted, and inspected.

By the 1860s, many of the ruling elite advocated a theory of progress in which they constituted the vanguard (*aṭ-ṭalīʿa*). Thus in 1866, Egypt's Foreign Minister explained that his country's Consultative Assembly of Deputies, chosen from families of notables, was a school or "civilizing instrument" more advanced than the people, just as the government was more advanced than the parliament.[11] Such "trickle effect" views, in which change is thought to spread from the elite to the "lower" orders and not the other way around, are often echoed today by technocratic and political cadres infused with Western-style ideas of politics, organization, and "progress" not fully comprehended by the majority of the population. Cadres often presume that the intellectual level and commitment to the public welfare of agents of the state is superior to that of the rest of the population, or that a legislative act or decree suffices to radically reshape sociopolitical organization. Contemporary states of the Middle East and Central Asia frequently claim to represent "the people" (Ar. *ash-shaʿb*) and "the masses" (*al-jamāhīr*), but it is difficult to know how the claims of a self-declared vanguard are understood by citizens presumed to be less "advanced" or even unaware of the new political forms.

In the formerly most advanced Marxist state of the region (it disappeared in 1990 when it joined the Yemen Arab Republic), the People's Democratic Republic of Yemen, there is a significant gap between state rhetoric on the "new" social order and the persistence of "older" tribal and family loyalties and notions of stratification. In the Socialist Popular Libyan Arab Jamāhīriya, which Muʿammar Qadhdhāfī claims has done away with the state to allow people direct participation in governance, the limits of people's participation in the exercise of central political authority remain pervasive and clear, if not publicly discussed.[12]

For Central Asia, the patterns of authority for the Soviet era are only now becoming clear, and they appear at variance with public statements of principle: "Conveyance of élite authority by right of birth, either to family or to clan, is one of the most difficult factors for outsiders to understand about élite politics in Central Asia, even as it is one of the most crucial elements—indeed, perhaps the single most crucial element—which decides an individual's potential

[10] See Rifaʿa al-Tahtawi, "Fatherland and Patriotism," in *Islam in Transition: Muslim Perspectives*, ed. John J. Donahue and John L. Esposito (New York: Oxford University Press, 1982), pp. 11–15; and, for the use of printing technology in Central Asia to spread Muslim reformist thought, see Adeeb Khalid, "Printing, Publishing, and Reform in Tsarist Central Asia," *International Journal of Middle East Studies* 26, no. 2 (May 1994), 187–200.

[11] Mitchell, *Colonising Egypt*, pp. 75–76.

[12] John Davis, *Libyan Politics: Tribe and Revolution*, Society and Culture in the Modern Middle East (London: I. B. Tauris, 1987), pp. 72–80; Norman Cigar, "State and Society in South Yemen," *Problems of Communism* 34, no. 3 (May–June 1985), 41–58.

for authority."[13] Martha Olcott suggests that key Kazakh rivalries relate to descent from rival clans and hordes (*juz*) and that "the majority of Kyrgyzstan President Askar Akaev's most sensitive (and lucrative) appointments have gone to members of his wife's clan; while Niiazov is said to be able to balance rivalries among the five major clans of Turkmenistan (whose seals are represented by the medallions of the state flag) only because he is an orphan, who was raised in a Soviet *internat* (boarding school) and 'clan-neutral.'"[14]

The "transparency" of the last years of the Soviet empire points to the next major transformation of state authority, which came about with the independence and revolutionary movements that developed from the end of World War II through the late 1960s in the West and the 1990s in the Soviet bloc. Egypt's 1952 revolution set a pattern followed by neighboring states, where state authority became more pervasive than in the prerevolutionary period.[15] Educational opportunities, bureaucracy, governmental services, and centralized plans for infrastructure, industrialization, and economic development were vastly expanded over those of the *ancien régime*. Mass mobilization, at least in theory, became the order of the day. In these specific respects, Egypt's experience paralleled not only that of revolutionary regimes elsewhere but also of conservative ones such as Morocco after independence in 1956 and the Sultanate of Oman after its 1970 coup, in which Qaboos ibn Said replaced his father as sultan.

Some observers consider the rise of Mossadegh in Iran in the early 1950s as the point at which Iran would have shifted from a monarchy to another form of regime, except for the successful U.S. and British political intervention, which enabled the Pahlevi monarchy to stay in power until the 1979 Iranian revolution.[16] Others date the transformation from the "White Revolution" of the 1960s, a major effort at land and social reform, later infused with massive funding following the oil price increases of the early 1970s. Yet even independence or the overthrow of old orders, events perceived as the beginning of new social and economic orders, could in retrospect prove deceptive. The overthrow of colonial regimes and foreign-dominated governments did not in itself alter enmeshment in a world economic order that facilitated economic and political dependency. In the 1970s, a Moroccan intellectual wrote of his country's rule

[13] Martha Brill Olcott, "Islam and Fundamentalism in Central Asia," in *Muslim Eurasia: Conflicting Legacies*, ed. Yaacov Ro'i, Cummings Center Series (London: Frank Cass, 1995), 24–25.

[14] Ibid., p. 25.

[15] Ilya Harik, *The Political Mobilization of Peasants* (Bloomington and London: Indiana University Press, 1974); John Waterbury, *The Egypt of Nasser and Sadat: The Political Economy of Two Regimes* (Princeton, NJ, and London: Princeton University Press, 1983), pp. 57–82.

[16] Maridi Nahas, "State-Systems and Revolutionary Challenge: Nasser, Khomeini, and the Middle East," *International Journal of Middle East Studies* 17, no. 4 (November 1985), 507–27, argues that just as the 1815 Congress of Vienna managed for a brief period to hold back the consequences of the French Revolution and irredentism from sweeping the more conservative states (but allowed the flood tides of change to come all the faster afterward), so the Arab Gulf faces a choice between revolutionary Islam and secular republicanism. Given the pattern of external support for the regimes of the area, Nahas's argument, even if not entirely convincing, merits consideration.

since 1956 as "a continuation of the regime of the Protectorate."[17] Or, as Jerrold D. Green suggests for Iran, Max Weber could well have been evoking post-revolutionary Tehran when he wrote:

> As with every apparatus of leadership, so here, one of the necessary conditions of success is to empty the ideas of all content, to concentrate on matters of fact, and to carry through a process of intellectual (i.e., or spiritual) "proletarianisation" in the interests of "discipline." The followers of a warrior of faith, once they have achieved power, tend to degenerate into a thoroughly commonplace class of office-holders.[18]

Religiopolitics, as Green notes, tend to resemble all other political forms, even if the actors seek to "exaggerate the religious content of their actions, while denying the political content."[19]

By the late 1970s, the Middle East entered a third transformation in state authority, marked in part by a growing challenge to the legitimacy of the state and a popular recognition that states had failed to deliver the improvements, participation in decision making, and ideas of social justice and opportunity they had promised. These goals are a stock-in-trade of the rhetoric of both conservative and revolutionary governments, all of which claim to represent the will of the people and their interests. Because of the conjuncture of international market forces, the informal but enduring ties of rural notables, underemployed graduates, restless armed forces, dissident student bodies, and pervasive ethnic and sectarian loyalties, the state is often seen as one actor among many rather than the source of order and change. For many Middle Easterners, the application of Islamic principles to the affairs of state is seen as a promising alternative to nationalism and the interests of those who control the state apparatus.[20]

In the attempt to understand politics in the Middle East, most observers have focused on the formal resources and institutions of state and society. They have usually overlooked the subtle, "informal" forces that provide the basis for civic order. The tendency has been magnified in the face of major social and political upheavals that many Middle Eastern societies have experienced—wars of independence, revolution, coups d'état, invasion, or civil war—in the last half of the twentieth century and, for Central Asia, the sudden collapse of the Soviet empire and the granting of independence.

Understanding the formal structure of "central" institutions, such as the state, is essential, but so is understanding the role of competing and complementary institutions from the political "periphery" of mosque, marketplace,

[17] Abdallah Laroui, *The Crisis of Arab Intellectuals*, trans. Diarmid Cammell (Berkeley and Los Angeles: University of California Press, 1976), p. 53.

[18] Max Weber, cited in Jerrold D. Green, "Islam, Religiopolitics, and Social Change: A Review Article," *Comparative Studies in Society and History* 27, no. 2 (April 1985), 316.

[19] Ibid., p. 317.

[20] See Said Amir Arjomand, "Introduction: Social Movements in the Contemporary Near and Middle East," in *From Nationalism to Revolutionary Islam*, ed. Said Amir Arjomand (London: Macmillan, 1984), pp. 1–27.

and elements of the population previously considered politically inactive or inconsequential. In earlier eras, few people were involved in state-level politics—one observer estimated that no more that 10 percent of Iran's population was politically active when the United States and Great Britain orchestrated the overthrow of Prime Minister Mohamed Mossadegh in 1953.[21] Now large numbers of people follow affairs with interest, even if their voices are muted or unheeded. The rapid rise in recent decades of mass education and mass communication has profoundly influenced ideas of politics, religion, and aspirations of a "just" social order and broadened the spectrum of citizens who feel they should have a political voice.

Moreover, as recent events indicate, the politics of the Middle East and Central Asia are no longer geographically circumscribed. Mass unemployment, migration, and political unrest in North Africa are integral elements in assessing European Community security, and civil war in Algeria has a direct impact on French domestic politics. What Marc Bloch said of ties of dependence in "feudal" Europe applies equally to the emergence of new political forms in the Middle East; successive generations did not consciously create new social forms but gave rise to them "in the process of trying to adapt the old."[22] Terms such as "democracy" and "civil society" may appear incongruous in a Middle Eastern or Central Asian setting, but it is helpful to discern long-term trends and displace conventional wisdom with new questions and conceptual approaches, as has been done in a recent major collaborative study of the Middle East.[23]

It would be misleading to see the emergence of "civil society" in the last few decades as without precedent. The Middle East presents a complex web of social institutions that sustain order when central governments are ineffective or oppressive. If by "civil society" we mean the emergence of institutions autonomous from the state that facilitate orderly economic, social, and political activity, then there are many precedents. They have, for the most part, been overlooked by observers seeking exact correspondence with formal institutions of "Western" civil society. For example, in the Būyid dynasty of tenth- and eleventh-century Iran and Iraq (studied by Roy P. Mottahedeh), recurring crises of royal authority co-existed with relative economic prosperity and an orderly social life made possible by shared understandings of trust, loyalty, and patronage.[24] These understandings and networks of obligations implied a moral order distinct from state or royal authority that extended beyond the bonds of family,

[21] Richard W. Cottam, "United States Middle East Policy in the Cold War Era," in *Russia's Muslim Frontiers: New Directions in Cross-Cultural Analysis*, ed. Dale F. Eickelman, Indiana Series in Arab and Islamic Studies (Bloomington: Indiana University Press, 1993), pp. 21–22.

[22] Marc Bloch, *Feudal Society*, trans. L. A. Manyon (Chicago: University of Chicago Press, 1964), p. 148.

[23] *Civil Society in the Middle East*, ed. Augustus Richard Norton, 2 vols., Social, Economic and Political Studies of the Middle East (Leiden: E. J. Brill, 1995–1996). Parts of the discussion of civil society have been adapted from Dale F. Eickelman's foreword to vol. 2 of this study, pp. ix–xiv.

[24] Roy P. Mottahedeh, *Loyalty and Leadership in an Early Islamic Society* (Princeton, NJ: Princeton University Press, 1980).

tribe, and locality. Similarly, the elaborate commercial and social networks that the Geniza documents reveal for Egypt and the southern Mediterranean from the tenth to the thirteenth centuries suggest pervasive and enduring social and economic ties that frequently transcended boundaries of state and formal political authority for Muslims and non-Muslims alike.[25] Richard Tapper argues that "tribal" regions of the Middle East, instead of being prone to disorder, often offered more opportunities for peace and a just social order than were available through submission to state authorities.[26]

Dynamic civil society can exist without formal political organizations in some contexts because informal organizational structures serve as the framework for effective political, social, and economic action. More than two decades ago, James Bill suggested that an understanding of Iranian politics meant recognizing the significance of the *dawra* (literally, "circle")—an informal group of individuals who meet periodically.[27] These circles could be formed through overlapping professional, religious, political, and economic ties, and networks of interlocking circles disseminated information and views and shaped forms of everyday resistance. Without an effective center or formal leadership for state authorities to co-opt, coerce, or suppress, such networks helped to constrain the arbitrariness of the state and its exercise of authority. Most Iranians assumed that effective access to authority was through informal channels, so recognizing the importance of direct personal ties of trust and obligation, more than ideological preferences or formal institutional structures, is integral to understanding political action.

One scholar has noted with irony that the small-scale monarchies of the Arab Gulf best replicate the attributes of "oligarchic republicanism" that prevailed in the civil society of ancient Athens.[28] Although many residents of such oil-rich states are noncitizens and lack political rights, males with full citizenship participate vigorously in far-reaching debates. In Kuwait, some of these debates take place in the parliament reconstituted after the 1990–1991 Iraqi occupation; others occur in the context of networks of interlocking *diwaniyya*-s (it is tempting to gloss the term as "salon"), which functions much like the Iranian *dawra*. In Kuwait, *diwaniyya*-s can be for men, for women, or, since the late twentieth century, for both men and women. Added to these institutions are the *jama'āt ta'āwuniyya*, neighborhood cooperative societies, which served as significant political arenas when Kuwait was deprived of its parliament, and they

[25] Shlomo D. Goitein, *A Mediterranean Society: The Jewish Communities of the Arab World as Portrayed in the Documents of the Cairo Geniza*, vol. 1, *Economic Foundations* (Berkeley and Los Angeles: University of California Press, 1967).

[26] Richard Tapper, "Anthropologists, Historians, and Tribespeople on Tribe and State Formation in the Middle East," in *Tribes and State Formation in the Middle East*, ed. Philip S. Khoury and Joseph Kostiner (Berkeley and Los Angeles: University of California Press, 1990), pp. 48–73.

[27] James A. Bill, "The Plasticity of Informal Politics: The Case of Iran," *Middle East Journal* 27, no. 2 (Spring 1973), 131–51.

[28] Ghassan Salamé, "Small Is Pluralistic: Democracy as an Instrument of Civil Peace," in *Democracy Without Democrats? The Renewal of Politics in the Muslim World*, ed. Ghassan Salamé (London: I. B. Tauris, 1994), p. 100.

played a significant role in organizing daily life and resistance during the Iraqi occupation.

It might be argued that the Gulf states represent a special case of informal associations, but such ties are also crucial in larger political arenas. In Turkey, for example, the Islamic-oriented Welfare party (RP) won victories in the March 1994 local elections through a strategy that relied on ties of interpersonal trust, taking "full advantage of neighborhood, regional, and other cultural bonds that tie people to one another in mutual assistance as well as its flip side: mutual obligation."[29] In Algeria, the gradual erosion of what Augustus Richard Norton calls the "grand bargain" of the FLN, where citizens gave up political participation in exchange for economic security after Algeria's independence in 1962, became clear only in retrospect. Islamic associations, often existing on the margins of legality through the 1970s, gradually took over where state services had all but collapsed, building mosques, running schools and clinics, and providing services that the state was no longer willing or able to provide.[30] The bonds of reciprocity and obligation created through these activities fostered a sense of moral and spiritual renewal and provided the necessary basis for Islamist organizations to achieve a significant victory in the 1990–1991 Algerian elections.[31]

In some views, civil society has all but collapsed in Algeria and the Sudan, but underlying ties of reciprocity and obligation, concealed from state authorities and from outsiders out of necessity, often exist independent of the state or in defiance of it.[32] These networks make a semblance of collective life possible where the state fails. In Morocco, citizens may be disillusioned with the outcome of the municipal and parliamentary elections that have taken place since 1992, but they do not equate them with prior electoral politics nor do they reject existing political frameworks. Carefully managed, campaigning for the elections has created a sharper sense of what the existing political system promises—even if it fails to deliver.[33]

From Morocco to Turkey, although more tentatively in parts of Central Asia, formal civic institutions have begun to reach a critical mass with associations of migrants, journalists, human rights organizations, doctors, lawyers, women's rights groups, and political parties. They are often built on informal networks of trust and responsibility—the "informal" associations—and the line between formal and informal associations is often exceedingly thin. Even in the Sultanate of Oman, seemingly removed from the vanguard of democratization

[29] Jenny B. White, "Islam and Democracy: The Turkish Experience," *Current History* (January 1995), 11–12, and her "Civic Culture and Islam in Urban Turkey," in *Civil Society: Challenging Western Models*, ed. Chris Hann and E. Dunn (London: Routledge, 1996), pp. 143–54.

[30] Ahmed Rouadjia, *Les frères et la mosquée* (Paris: Karthala, 1990).

[31] Meriem Vergès, "La Casbah d'Alger: Chronique de survie dans un quartier en sursis," in *Exils et royaumes: Les appartenances au monde arabo-musulman aujourd'hui*, ed. Gilles Kepel (Paris: Presses de la Fondation Nationale des Sciences Politiques, 1994), pp. 78–82.

[32] T. Abdou Maliqalim Simone, *In Whose Image? Political Islam and Urban Practices in Sudan* (Chicago: University of Chicago Press, 1994), p. 67.

[33] Dale F. Eickelman, "Re-Imagining Religion and Politics: Moroccan Elections in the 1990s," in *Islam and Secularism in North Africa*, ed. John Reudy (New York: St. Martin's Press, 1994), pp. 269–70.

and the development of civic associations, rising standards of education have created a citizenry that finds ways to breathe life into apparently apolitical or moribund institutions. Discussions about fielding a sports team, improving hygiene in the market, or using a municipal budget to create a library or youth club instead of resurfacing a road or installing street lighting offer citizens opportunities to express their views and learn to get things done. Elsewhere, as in Morocco, the decision by a parents' group to refurbish and pay for a prayer room in a secondary school, to lodge indigent university students, or to offer medical services to the needy may be formally framed as apolitical activities, but they offer citizens opportunities to work together, independent of state initiatives, to achieve common goals.

Although the Middle East has long had distinguished centers of learning, mass education—in particular, mass higher education—has become pervasive only since the 1960s. The result has been a profound change in how Middle Easterners think about person, self, and society. Even if the formal rhetoric of conservative states still stresses a trickle-down theory of development in which all good flows from the top, large numbers of people now have the means to question authority and—thanks to a communications revolution that has caused the efficacy of state censors to wither—the ability to learn about a world unfiltered through state-controlled media.[34]

Seymour Martin Lipset, who defines democracy as "that institutional arrangement for arriving at political decisions in which individuals acquire the power to decide by means of a competitive struggle for the people's vote," views democracy as either present or absent.[35] Yet there are means other than elections to assess the vitality of civil society and movements toward democracy, such as the growing significance of private voluntary associations and changing popular understandings of "just" rule and governance.

An exclusive focus on election results deflects attention from major changes taking place beneath the surface. They suggest that a transition is being made to a less arbitrary, exclusive, and authoritarian rule, notwithstanding the conditions of rapid population growth, stagnating economies, rising unemployment, and a young citizenry who, because of mass education and mass communication, is more articulate than earlier generations and less patient with conventional political arrangements. Even if the "hidden transcript" often remains a better measure of political vitality than the "public" one,[36] disillusion has not led inexorably to revolt or to religious and political radicalism.

[34] Susan Ossman, *Picturing Casablanca: Portraits of Power in a Modern City* (Berkeley and Los Angeles: University of California Press, 1994).

[35] Seymour Martin Lipset, "The Social Requisites of Democracy Revisited," *American Sociological Review* 59, no. 1 (February 1994), 1.

[36] Mounia Bennani-Chraïbi, *Soumis et rebelles: Les jeunes au Maroc* (Paris: CNRS Éditions, 1994), pp. 283–93; and James C. Scott, *Domination and the Arts of Resistance: Hidden Transcripts* (New Haven, CT: Yale University Press, 1990).

To discern these informal patterns, anthropologists, political scientists, and social historians of the Middle East and increasingly of Central Asia have produced valuable studies of local-level politics, administration, and economics. The contribution of anthropology has been to look at the "finer features" of the relationship between political and economic authority and the societies in which it is exercised. The relationship among politics, economics, local concepts of the social order, and programs of "development and progress"—the language used by both revolutionary and conservative regimes to legitimize their rule—is rarely a straightforward one.

Anthropologists have a notion of politics more applicable to many Middle Eastern and Central Asian situations than those who identify the "political" primarily with formal institutions. The basic definition of "institution," it should be recalled, is the accepted and conventional ways of getting specific things done, a notion that clearly goes beyond the limits of formal authority alone. One strength of anthropology is that it is attuned to discerning the political roles and voices of what a Tunisian colleague refers to as "social actors less talkative than the elite,"[37] even if their significance is denied, ignored, or suppressed by the state elite or by political leaders. The views of the nonelite, even if they do not participate in formal political processes, can limit what political leaders propose and accomplish. A riot over price increases in bread, cooking oil, and other basic commodities—in Tehran in 1942, Cairo in 1973, and Casablanca in 1981, among others—can often confirm popular conceptions of political equity and social justice that are less evident from strictly "political" rhetoric.[38] Likewise, the transformation of peasants into an urban proletariat, even under revolutionary regimes, often contains more substantial links with prior values and expectations than revolutionary leaders or modernization theorists have been prepared to assume.[39]

PROBLEMS OF AUTHORITY AND INTERPRETATION

Earlier chapters of this book introduced many of these informal political understandings, but it is useful to indicate here how they relate to past and present political processes in the Middle East and Central Asia and how they shape and constrain state authority.

Talal Asad characterizes the implicit assumptions concerning the ideal type of "oriental" rule made by a prior generation of scholars in the following terms:

[37] Abdelkader Zghal, cited in Nicholas S. Hopkins, *Testour ou la transformation des campagnes maghrébines* (Tunis: Cérès Productions, 1983), p. 48.

[38] See, for example, Stephen L. McFarland, "Anatomy of an Iranian Political Crowd: The Tehran Bread Riot of December 1942," *International Journal of Middle East Studies* 17, no. 1 (February 1985), 51–65.

[39] Pierre Bourdieu, *Algeria 1960*, trans. Richard Nice, Studies in Modern Capitalism (Cambridge: Cambridge University Press, 1979), pp. 1–79.

> An emphasis upon the absolute power of the ruler, and the whimsical, generally illegitimate nature of his demands; on the indifference or involuntary submission on the part of the ruled; on a somewhat irrational form of conflict in which sudden, irresponsible urges to riot are met with violent repression; and, finally, an emphasis on the overall inefficiency and corruption of political life.[40]

In this view of "sultanism," which gets carried over into Western sociology as a classical ideal type, the ruler, to sustain authority, must minimize the independence of his mercenaries, notables, and merchants. A characteristic means of doing this was to make official appointees deliberately insecure so that subordinates could be used as scapegoats for popular discontent, and the ruler could preserve the "fiction that he is benevolent and concerned for the welfare of his subjects."[41] As Bryan S. Turner explains, the paradox of this form of rule is that "the more a ruler has to rely on his mercenaries or slave army, the more dependent he becomes on their power to subjugate the masses." Soon, mercenary armies are able to extract fiefs and regular advantages from the ruler, forcing him to further pauperize the peasantry while continuing to represent himself as the people's benefactor. The result is two forms of protest: periodic outbursts, usually based on religious principles, and "periodic dynastic, political change," which did not result in any change in form of rule but resulted in endemic conflicts over succession.[42]

More recent studies have placed much greater emphasis on economic conditions during the period of Ottoman rule and the effect of those conditions on governance. Roger Owen, for example, relates specific political and social trends to the development of cash crops in Lower (northern) Egypt, Mount Lebanon, and Izmir (Turkey), the rapid spread of maize cultivation during the seventeenth century, and shifting patterns of commerce, factors largely neglected by an earlier generation of scholars.[43] Likewise, many of the "sponta-

[40] Talal Asad, "Two European Images of Non-European Rule," in *Anthropology and the Colonial Encounter*, ed. Talal Asad (London: Ithaca Press; New York: Humanities Press, 1973), p. 107. Edward W. Said, *Orientalism* (New York: Pantheon, 1978), provides a forceful critique of this earlier generation of studies, although his argument is marred by the same sort of ahistorical assumptions that he attributes to Orientalists. For analyses of specific scholars, see Bryan S. Turner, *Weber and Islam: A Critical Study* (London and Boston: Routledge & Kegan Paul, 1974), pp. 122–34; and Roger Owen, "The Middle East in the Eighteenth Century—An 'Islamic' Society in Decline: A Critique of Gibb and Bowen's *Islamic Society and the West*," *Review of Middle East Studies* 1 (1975), 101–12. Owen's study outlines how revised images of the Middle East's past have been forged since the 1960s. Also useful as a counter to the Western image of the "stagnation" of the Ottoman Empire is Albert Hourani, "The Ottoman Background of the Modern Middle East," in his *Emergence of the Modern Middle East* (London: Macmillan, 1981), pp. 1–18.

[41] The notion of the "benevolence" of the ruler, that "if he only knew, then injustice would stop," is not confined to past eras. It was prevalent in Morocco in the late 1960s and Oman through the late 1970s. In both cases, with the spread of mass education and the different attitudes toward authority implicitly spread with it, the "if he only knew" syndrome ceases to explain injustice. An example of this popular attitude toward authority and its erosion in 1940s Iran can be found in Mansur Rafizadeh's autobiographical *Witness: From the Shah to the Secret Arms Deal, An Insider's Account of U.S. Involvement in Iran* (New York: William Morrow, 1987), pp. 7–10. Rafizadeh, a Harvard-educated Iranian, was a senior official in SAVAK, the Shah's secret police.

[42] Turner, *Weber and Islam*, p. 75.

[43] Owen, "The Middle East," p. 110; and Leila Tarazi Fawaz, *An Occasion for War: Civil Conflict in Lebanon and Damascus in 1860* (Berkeley and Los Angeles: University of California Press, 1994), pp. 8–30.

neous" riots in cities and rural regions during Ottoman times are now recognized as popular reactions against accepted notions of political and economic justice. If grain was hoarded by merchants and the price of bread became unconscionable, so-called rioters often became violent only when authorities refused (or were unable) to enforce price levels that were considered just. In some of the Arab Gulf states, merchants and fishermen at the end of the nineteenth century simply moved to another city-state if the ruling family sought to impose what they considered illegitimate exactions. The option of migration provided an informal check on the excesses of rulers.[44] The fact that mosques were often the rallying points for demonstrations suggests that "rioters" considered their demands to be moral and just. The imagined irrationality of the "crowd" has often been nothing more than the inability of earlier scholars to recognize popular assumptions of legitimacy and justice.

Symbolic manifestations of political authority often show significant continuities with the past. Clifford Geertz has described the nineteenth-century "royal progress" in Morocco, a journey by a monarch through his domain that symbolically established or reaffirmed possession of the realm. Geertz argues that an examination of the symbols of power and the nature of power shows that they are often one and the same, a conjunction especially apparent in traditional monarchies but equally prevalent, if more disguised, in recent political systems.[45] In medieval England, the monarch was entertained during the royal progress with public pageants where subjects dressed in costumes depicting the virtues of the realm and the vices that threatened it. In nineteenth-century Morocco, "strength did not have to be represented as other than what it was."

Progresses in Morocco "were not always easy to tell from raids," and society was "a tournament of wills"; hence, so were royal authority and its symbolism. One of Morocco's last precolonial rulers, Sultan Mūlāy Ḥasan I (d. 1894), was usually on the move for half of each year throughout his domains. The mobility of the sultan was a central element in his power and, inseparably, in the concept of royal authority in Morocco. "The realm was unified . . . by a restless searching-out of contact, most of it agonistic, with literally hundreds of lesser centers of power within it."[46]

The durability of the royal progress in expressing political domination is seen in its continued use throughout the colonial era and after Morocco gained its independence in 1956. In the colonial era, royal progresses included officials of the French *résidence* traveling with the sultan (after 1956 the title *sulṭān* was replaced by what Moroccan nationalists considered the more modern-sounding *mālik,* or "king"); French officials appeared alongside the monarch in all formal ceremonials except religious ones. The symbolism of the colonial royal progress also included such features as visits by the sultan to the tomb of the

[44] Peter Lienhardt, "The Authority of Shaykhs in the Gulf: An Essay in Nineteenth-Century History," *Arabian Studies* 2 (1975), 61–75.

[45] Clifford Geertz, "Centers, Kings, and Charisma: Reflections on the Symbolics of Power," in his *Local Knowledge* (New York: Basic Books, 1983), p. 125. This essay was first published in 1977.

[46] Ibid., pp. 134, 136.

unknown soldier in France and other ceremonies visually suggesting the "protected" status of royal authority and the association of the monarchy with the French.

In modified form, the royal progress continues to express Moroccan sovereignty. Ḥasan II's public travels and displays of identity with his kingdom are carefully orchestrated. The "Green March" of King Ḥasan to the Sahara in 1976, along with tens of thousands of Moroccans, can also be seen as a royal progress, one that forced Spain to cede its former Saharan territories to Morocco.[47] In the continued fighting for sovereignty in the Sahara between Morocco and the Polisario movement (the Sahara Democratic Arab Republic, assisted at various times by Algeria and Libya, among others), tribal groups wishing to reaffirm fealty to the Moroccan throne have done so through covenants (*bay'a*-s) in which they offer collective sacrifices of bulls and sheep, very similar to those covenanted to the pious ones at regional shrines.

In a monarchy, the monarch *is* the state, but Middle Eastern monarchies have much in common with their republican counterparts. By naming roads, ports, schools, hospitals, mosques, and stadiums after themselves, rulers inscribe their presence upon the national geography. The ruler's untiring concern for his subjects is affirmed through the repetition of his name, usually bracketed in honorifics, on radio and television, photographs in every place of business and most homes, national days, and commissioned poetry and popular music. These forms of asserting authority may not be as expressive as royal progresses, but they symbolically reaffirm or establish a claim to legitimacy and popular support.

COLONIAL AUTHORITY

Many anthropological studies were conducted during the colonial era in the Middle East, but most of them deal with the colonized or the dominated, and not with the colonizers or with the relations between colonizers and colonized. This is unfortunate from the point of view of understanding authority and domination. As Paul Rabinow suggests, the idea of power "operating primarily through the application of force has been put seriously in question. With fewer than 20,000 soldiers, the French, after all, ran Indochina in the 1920s with a degree of control that the Americans with 500,000 some fifty years later never approached. Power entails more than arms, although it certainly does not exclude them."[48] Just as medicine was considered outside the domain of politi-

[47] The Moroccan newspaper *al-Muḥarrir* (Casablanca), August 16, 1979, described the reception of tribal delegations totaling 300 men and 60 women from the Sahara's Wādī Dhahb region to renew their oath of allegiance to the Moroccan throne. The ceremony involved the sacrifice of sheep and bulls. In the colonial era, similar sacrifices were offered to the French to signify the cessation of hostilities.

[48] Paul Rabinow, "Representations Are Social Facts: Modernity and Post-Modernity in Anthropology," in *Writing Culture: The Poetics and Politics of Ethnography*, ed. James Clifford and George E. Marcus (Berkeley and Los Angeles: University of California Press, 1986), p. 259.

cal authority in nineteenth-century Tunisia, yet intimately related to it, so developmental or "modernization" schemes—for towns, agricultural production, communications, and education—"ordered" territories and populations more effectively than the use of force.[49] It was through the provision of such "benefits," as well as the notion of "security," that colonial regimes sought, often successfully, to justify themselves. Even the forced collectivization of rural Central Asia in the 1920s was achieved in the name of progress and the collective good. A pervasive sign of the collapse of any regime is when it must rely primarily on the use of force to assert its will.

In the re-imagining of the colonial past, nationalists sometimes find it convenient to attribute all cooperation with colonial authorities to compulsion. Yet what is striking in retrospect is how effective most colonial regimes were—at least through the 1940s, but much later in many regions—and often with less force at their disposal than that possessed by later independent regimes.

It is useful here to evoke briefly some of the categories through which colonial authorities "ordered" the societies they came to dominate, because these categories remain highly pervasive, even after the departure of colonial regimes. Many of the contributors to a major book on North Africa in the early 1970s, *Arabs and Berbers*, suggest the continued importance of categories of "ordering" initially created by French colonial sociologists: Arabs and Berbers, town and tribe, lands of submission (to royal authority) and lands of dissidence, and other stereotypic representations.[50] Some of the studies in the volume, notably that of Edmund Burke III, indicate how the ethnographic "authority" of colonial representations of "native" societies was sustained. As late as 1951, when independence movements in the Middle East were gaining momentum, one of the most distinguished French ethnographers (earlier a military intelligence officer) of colonial Morocco brushed aside the delay of 15 years in publication of a book on Moroccan religious brotherhoods by writing that in Islam "evolution is boundlessly slow. For Islam, even more than for other religions, one has to count not in years but in centuries."[51] These sentiments matched precisely the notion of the timeless nature of "oriental" society prevalent in the nineteenth century. Many other studies exist that, like their equivalents elsewhere in the colonial world, ignored almost completely the impact of colonial administration and the "ordering" of colonial society on political life. Local disputes were treated as if they had no wider implications,

[49] Will D. Swearingen, *Moroccan Mirages: Agrarian Dreams and Deceptions, 1912–1986* (Princeton, NJ, and London: Princeton University Press, 1987). One of the few ethnographic studies from the colonial period that recognized the profound effect of the colonial order on notions of work, family, housing, and authority was Charles Le Coeur, *Le rite et l'outil* (Paris: Presses Universitaires de France, 1969 [1939]).

[50] Ernest Gellner and Charles Micaud, eds. *Arabs and Berbers: From Tribe to Nation in North Africa* (London: Duckworth, 1972).

[51] Robert Montagne, in his foreword to Georges Drague [Spillman] *Esquisse d'histoire religieuse du Maroc* (Paris: J. Peyronnet, 1951). Montagne was one of colonial Morocco's outstanding sociologists. See Robert Montagne, *The Berbers: Their Social and Political Organisation*, trans. David Seddon (London: Frank Cass, 1973).

and relations between native officials and foreign administrators were mentioned only in passing.

At one time or another in the past century and a half, most of the Middle East has experienced colonial domination or, in the case of the Arab Gulf states, decisive foreign influence. This fact is significant in two ways. Colonial society can be studied in itself as a unique, and now disappearing, social form, as the discussion of colonial urbanization in Chapter 5 suggests. Second, colonial domination has had a formative influence on the shape of present Middle Eastern polities and societies.

René Maunier, at one time head of the French Academy of Colonial Science, defined colonialism as "occupation with domination and emigration with government."[52] His definition has the advantage of facilitating the comparative study of colonial systems, a field in which Maunier was a leader. His book on the sociology of colonies, a standard text on the subject, discussed the early Phoenician colonies of the Mediterranean, the Roman Empire, and the more recent experience of European colonial expansion and reactions to it.

The notion of "colonial science" is an indication that colonial rule could be rationalized and systematized and was here to stay, an idea perhaps easy to accept (for Europeans at least) in the early 1930s, when congresses were routinely held in Europe and attended by representatives of various colonial administrations. Jacques Berque, a prominent French social historian of colonial rule in North Africa, suggests that 1930 be taken as colonialism's apogee.[53] The year included an International Colonial Exposition in France, which commemorated the centenary of French Algeria.

The 1918 European armistice is a convenient point from which to survey the extent of colonial dominion in the Middle East. All the Levant except Turkey was firmly occupied by colonial powers, and only stiff resistance by the Turks kept Anatolia from succumbing to foreign domination. Syria and Lebanon were under the French, their share of the defeated Ottoman Empire. Iraq was under the British, who also exercised a major influence over the ministates of the Persian/Arab Gulf. British political officers exercised significant control over tribal politics, ordering air strikes when necessary to facilitate "accommodation" to British imperial interests. Saudi Arabia escaped direct European colonial control, primarily because its autonomy suited European colonial powers. Both Jordan and Palestine fell within the British sphere of domination. Egypt had been under English domination since 1882, although,

[52] René Maunier, *The Sociology of Colonies*, trans. E. O. Lorimer (London: Routledge & Kegan Paul, 1949), vol. 1, p. 19. This remains one of the best available accounts of "colonial sociology," and it is all the more valuable for understanding the colonial era because of its unapologetic "insider" perspective.

[53] One of the best accounts of the varieties of colonial experience is Jacques Berque's masterly *French North Africa: The Maghrib Between Two World Wars*, trans. Jean Stewart (New York: Praeger, 1967). Berque's method is to paint vivid word pictures of tribes, towns, people, events, and the attitudes of those who experienced them, often culled from firsthand experience. Berque's father was a key native affairs officer in Algeria, and Berque himself was in colonial service until the mid-1950s, when he began an academic career. See also Abdelkader Zghal, "Nation-Building in the Maghreb," *International Social Science Journal* 23, no. 3 (1971), 435–51.

FIGURE 11-1. Jacques Berque, in uniform, center right, with General Nogues, Résident-Général of Morocco, and notables of Fez, October 1937. In the postcolonial era, Berque became one of France's most distinguished interpreters of Middle Eastern civilizations. [Photo courtesy Jacques Berque.]

like the other countries, significant European control over its finances dated from an earlier period. In the Levant, as in Egypt, there was virtually no European colonial settlement, although Greeks and others worked as artisans in larger cities such as Alexandria, and the British performed many administrative and military functions, effectively blocking training for Middle Easterners. The prevalent thought of such rule, to paraphrase Lord Cromer, one of the British proconsuls in Egypt, was to do what was good for "orientals," not necessarily to do what they thought was good for themselves.

Each North African country from Libya to Morocco experienced colonialism in a different form, but all had a significant population of European settlers. The Ottomans formally ceded Libya to Italy in 1912, a year after the Italians invaded the country. Spain controlled Morocco's northern zone after 1912, as well as its southern fringes, which became known as the Spanish Sahara and the territory of Ifni. The rest of North Africa came under French colonial domination. The earliest French colony in North Africa was Algeria, first occupied by the French in 1830 by means of tactics recognized as brutal even by the advocates of French colonial expansion.[54] Native lands were systematically expropriated, and traditional learning and education were destroyed or eroded. Over time, the presence of a large settler class wrested control of the administration from metropolitan France. Between Algerian French and Algerian Muslims was a marked tradition of violence and mutual incomprehension from the very beginning of colonial rule.

[54] In addition to Berque's *French North Africa* on Algeria, a good point of departure is Pierre Bourdieu's *The Algerians*, trans. Alan C. M. Ross (Boston: Beacon Press, 1962), a book written at the height of the Algerian conflict. Even Algeria, however, indicates how colonial authority took root more through persuasion and "ordering" than through the application of force alone. See Allan Christelow, *Muslim Law Courts and the French Colonial State in Algeria* (Princeton, NJ: Princeton University Press, 1985).

FIGURE 11-2. H. R. P. Dickson, British Resident for Kuwait, and his wife. British political residents in the Arab Gulf states commonly adopted Arab dress as late as the 1930s. [From H. R. P. Dickson, *The Arab of the Desert* (London: George Allen & Unwin, Ltd., 1949), opp. p. 48.]

Morocco, in contrast, was the last North African territory brought under French rule (1912), and it was considered by many French as the jewel of their colonies—an example of "scientific" colonialism at its best. It certainly was the best studied; no Middle Eastern country under English domination has been as thoroughly described ethnographically. The work of colonial ethnographers concerned with Morocco remains valuable today, even if one disagrees with the implicit assumptions of their work and the motivation for it. The corpus is of high quality, and the intensity of the work undertaken makes Morocco "a particularly illuminating place to study the ways in which colonial ethnographers went about their business in the generation or so preceding the First World War."[55]

The French intention to colonize Morocco was clear by the end of the nineteenth century, but opposition by the British and the Germans prevented direct colonization. Domination took place nonetheless. One means was by military expansion in Morocco's southeast, where oases were forced to collaborate with the French or risk destruction of their date palms and herds. Another device (used throughout the Middle East in various guises) was through control of the police of major Moroccan ports, collection of customs revenues, expansion of commercial operations with extraterritorial protection granted to

[55] Edmund Burke III, "Fez, the Setting Sun of Islam: A Study of the Politics of Colonial Ethnography," *Maghreb Review* 2, no. 4 (July–August 1977), 1. For an example of the reevaluation of colonial ethnographic texts, see Abdellah Hammoudi, *The Victim and Its Masks: An Essay on Sacrifice and Masquerade in the Maghreb* (Chicago: University of Chicago Press, 1993).

Moroccans acting in French interests, and, from 1907, creation of the Bank of Morocco to control the country's finances. Ostensibly these measures were to ensure repayment of loans forced upon Morocco by European countries, often on highly disadvantageous terms. By 1907, using as a pretext the struggle over control of the throne between the brothers Mūlāy 'Abd al-'Azīz and Mūlāy Ḥafīḍ, 3000 French and 500 Spanish troops landed at Casablanca and began to occupy the surrounding region to protect the port. The following year the expeditionary force had expanded to 15,000, and beginning in 1910, Morocco was compelled to indemnify the cost of the force.

In November 1911 the French reached an agreement with other major European powers, and the road was clear for the direct occupation of Morocco. Five thousand troops advanced from Algeria to Fez, where Mūlāy Ḥafīḍ was in his palace. The Spaniards occupied points along Morocco's northern coast. Moroccan ability to resist these incursions was virtually nil. In March, the Minister of France at Tangier (where all embassies to Morocco were situated) set out for Fez on horseback. The sultan briefly considered resistance but finally agreed to sign the treaty of the protectorate after six days of being bullied by the French. He abdicated almost immediately afterward in favor of his younger brother, Mūlāy Yūsif. Formal French domination of Morocco had begun.

Louis Hubert Gonzalve Lyautey was appointed first Résident-Général of Morocco (1912–1925). During his administration he set the tone for what was considered an enlightened, "scientific" colonial administration.[56] Lyautey championed "indirect" rule and elaborated an administration that was remarkably economical, requiring only a handful of French to supervise vast expanses of territory. It was almost entirely self-financing. He assiduously cultivated ties with Morocco's urban aristocracy and rural strongmen, often overlooking their excesses in exchange for continued support. Thus, during the pronounced resistance in many regions during the initial takeover of Morocco, Lyautey sent letters by messenger to Moroccan notables—knowing whom to address indicated the sophistication of French intelligence—stating that their interests would be protected if they proved themselves "friends" of France. France, the letters explained, was in Morocco only to defend the interests of the sultan. It is unlikely that many Moroccan notables were convinced by this claim, but they knew the fate of Algeria's elite. Many leaders visited Lyautey directly; others sent emissaries who were reassured of France's intentions. Medical services were made strategically available and used to collect military intelligence, and the French bought grain and animals at high prices to encourage Moroccans to deal with them. When such methods failed, dissident tribes were denied access to markets; transhumant groups were denied vital pastures; and, as a last

[56] See Robin Bidwell's *Morocco Under Colonial Rule: French Administration of Tribal Areas, 1912–1956* (London: Frank Cass, 1973), an account that is especially interesting because Bidwell was previously an administrator in Britain's West Aden Protectorate. For one of the rare interpretive essays concerning who became colonial administrators in various epochs in North Africa, see Vincent Monteil (a former French colonial officer), "Les bureaux arabes au Maghreb (1833–1961)," *Esprit*, no. 29 (November 1961), 575–606.

resort, villages could be burned and crops destroyed. Most military operations were accomplished with relatively few losses; in any case, many soldiers fighting for France were from other French colonies, especially Senegal. Lyautey's tactics worked so well that when many French troops had to be withdrawn at the beginning of World War I and French control was precarious, there was no major rebellion.

Lyautey's patrician image of how Morocco should be ruled prevented the worst excesses of colonial intervention but prevailed most firmly only in those parts of the country *not* coveted by the growing influx of settlers. For many colonizers, the so-called "civilizing mission" of France was a façade for the acquisition of land and resources. Lyautey took the idea of the "civilizing mission" seriously. He insisted on urban planning, the preservation of Morocco's traditional architecture, protection of the interests of Moroccans designated as notables, and training of a colonial elite. He was less successful in limiting the development of a French settler population in Morocco. It grew, along with the flourishing of large commercial enterprises, banks, railroad interests, agribusiness, and mining companies. By the 1920s, the landgrabs of the settler population and large commercial interests had increased, but even in the expropriation of lands held by Moroccans, often by fraud or administrative chicanery, the niceties of colonial rhetoric were preserved. In one case the expropriation of a vast tract of land from a tribe in western Morocco was justified as "educational" for Moroccans, who could see how a European enterprise was run. This dispossession turned tribespeople of many regions into a landless, impoverished proletariat.

French rule in most of Morocco outside the cities froze a local elite into place. Lyautey's policy had been to select local strongmen and maintain them in place if they proved good at the job. If strongmen such as Pasha Ḥājj Thāmi Glāwi of Marrakesh were notorious for their abuses of power, the French rationalized continued support by saying that Moroccans were habituated to ruthless officials. The pasha's ability to grasp the nuances of colonial politics meant that he ran Marrakesh and its many lucrative enterprises to his liking until the last days of French rule.

After the 1920s, there were few changes in local dynasties of privilege and authority until the end of the colonial era. Even then, because of the competitive advantage that such individuals and their families had in the past, a very common pattern was for brothers, uncles, and cousins in a single family to specialize in the complementary fields of agribusiness, administration, and commerce, thus maintaining their privileged position despite major political and economic changes.[57]

[57] On continuity in patterns of the Moroccan elite, see John Waterbury, *The Commander of the Faithful* (New York: Columbia University Press, 1970); and Rémy Leveau, *Le fellah marocain: Defenseur du trône* [The Moroccan Peasant: Defender of the Throne], 2nd ed., Collection "References" 12 (Paris: Presses de la Fondation Nationale des Sciences Politiques, 1985 [1976]). On long-term political change in North Africa, see his *Le sabre et le turban: L'avenir du Maghreb* [The Sword and the Turban: The Future of North Africa] (Paris: François Bourin, 1993), unfortunately unavailable in English.

Morocco was "improved" by the French, but the educational record of the protectorate speaks eloquently about how little emphasis was placed on providing Moroccans with the skills necessary for the "evolution" promised by France's civilizing mission. For French school-aged children in Morocco, education was universal. The education of Jews—for all practical purposes, in the hands of private organizations—was virtually universal in towns and cities. As for Moroccan Muslims, only those recognized as the sons (and, to a much lesser extent, daughters) of notables had relatively easy access to education. Some primary education was provided for other students, but in general it was felt that more than a modicum of education was "unrealistic." Moroccans set up their own system of "free schools," beginning in the 1930s, so that a "modern" education could be obtained. But the standards of these schools were mediocre, and they did not provide the certification necessary for governmental and private employment.

The educational statistics of the protectorate almost speak for themselves; even with a major effort to broaden the educational base after World War II, the results were meager. Of school-aged Muslims in Morocco in 1938, only 1.7 percent were in primary school and 0.1 percent in secondary school; in 1945 the figures were 2.7 percent and 0.2 percent, respectively; in 1950 they were 7.0 percent and 0.6 percent; and in 1955 they were 11.2 percent and 1.2 percent. The dropout rate for primary school alone was 90 percent. As for secondary education, between 1912 and 1956, the years of French rule, only 530 Moroccans passed the French *baccalauréat* examination, a necessary prerequisite to entering the university.[58]

The ironies of protectorate rule were abundant. The formal fiction of a Morocco under French tutelage was preserved, but real political power rested with the French. The sultan could still emerge from his palace on feast days to act as head of the Muslim community and slaughter a sheep on behalf of the Muslims in his domain, but access to him was strictly controlled by the French, and messages to his subordinates had to pass through French hands. Appointments at local administrative levels were chosen from French-approved lists of nominees. In the name of preserving traditional forms, Moroccan ministers were not permitted offices and desks but had to use low-lying benches. Even *qāḍī*-s, or religious judges, could not assume office until they had passed an examination set by a French orientalist who advised the sultan's entourage as to whether the candidate possessed an adequate knowledge of Islamic law.

After World War II, the colonial system elaborated by the French disintegrated. Disparities between Europeans and Moroccans had become too pronounced, with the dislocation of the wartime black market, the Vichy debacle, the expropriation of tribal lands, rising nationalist expectations, and a monarchy that increasingly asserted its autonomy. The French responded with repres-

[58] On education, see John Damis, "Early Moroccan Reactions to the French Protectorate: The Cultural Dimension," *Humaniora Islamica* 1 (1973), 15–31. The cited figures are from Ladislav Cerych, *Européens et marocains, 1930–1956: Sociologie d'une décolonisation* (Bruges: De Tepel, 1964), p. 297; and Waterbury, *Commander*, p. 84.

FIGURE 11-3. Tribunal curateur, Algeria, nineteenth century. Colonial officials sometimes imposed themselves as authoritative arbiters of Muslim jurisprudence. [Photograph from Bibliothèque Nationale, Paris.]

sion and in 1953 made a decisive error in deposing Sultan Muḥammad V in favor of an ineffective relative. The result galvanized Moroccan resistance to French rule. Rural terrorism mounted, and bloody urban demonstrations and strikes became routine. The price of maintaining colonial rule became too high, and by late 1955, the French had negotiated the terms of transition to an independent government.

ECONOMY AND STATE AUTHORITY: TRADITION AND THE PRESENT

Some economists divide the modern Middle East into production and allocation, or rentier, states.[59] A *production state* must secure revenues based on the

[59] Giacomo Luciani, "Allocation vs. Production States: A Theoretical Framework," in *The Rentier State*, ed. Hazem Beblawi and Giacomo Luciani (London: Croom Helm, 1987), pp. 63–82. Davis, *Libyan Politics*, calls allocation states "hydrocarbon societies." Parts of the following analysis were presented in an earlier version in Dale F. Eickelman's "Changing Perceptions of State Authority: Morocco, Egypt, and Oman," in *Foundations of the State in the Arab World*, ed. Chassan Salameh and Marwan Buheiry (London: Croom Helm, 1988), pp. 177–204, and in his "Religion in Polity and Society," in *The Political Economy of Morocco*, ed. I. William Zartman (New York: Praeger, 1987), pp. 84–97.

labor of its citizens, in agriculture, herding, or manufacture. It requires a reasonably effective bureaucracy to collect these charges and is under some pressure to legitimize its exactions. An *allocation state*, a term that fits the major oil-producing countries such as Saudi Arabia, Kuwait, the United Arab Emirates, Qatar, Oman, and Libya, does not derive the majority of its revenues from levies upon its citizens but from revenues received from the rest of the world in payment for its resources.[60] Allocation states require bureaucracies, primarily to deliver services, at least to their citizen populations, and to ensure security, but even these functions can sometimes be performed by foreign personnel. A large proportion of the work force of such states are noncitizens, and in some cases, there are more noncitizens than citizens in the population.

Four Middle Eastern states—Saudi Arabia, Kuwait, Iran, and Iraq—possess 80 percent of the Middle East's proven oil reserves. Other states, notably Algeria and Egypt, possess significant quantities of oil (and natural gas in the case of Algeria), but because of their large populations depend upon remittances from emigrant workers and from nonpetroleum sectors of the economy. All states of the Middle East and Central Asia face similar challenges: rapid population growth, highly unequal distribution of resources (and unequal distribution of resources within the countries themselves), economic distortions caused by the massive influx of oil revenues and, in many cases, the abandonment of less lucrative sectors of the economy, including agriculture, or, as in the case of Uzbekistan, the ravaging of natural resources for short-term gain. Monocrop production of cotton has drained the Aral Sea, which appears to have been quietly written off by the Soviet leadership. Anatoly Khazanov reports that "strong winds lift approximately 200,000 tons of sand intermixed with salt from the dry sea bed every day," depositing it on settlements up to 500 kilometers away. The result is that the "salinization of the area is accompanied by desertification."[61]

Both intraregional labor migration and labor migration to Europe, regarded in the 1960s as a safety valve for overpopulation and stagnant local economies, are now considered to have an equal potential for political and social disruption, especially as such opportunities are rapidly disappearing. Morocco, once vaunted as the granary of Rome, is now a net importer of food, as is Egypt, where agricultural land is being lost to expanded urban settlement.

Although the notion of production and allocation states is particularly useful in delineating some unique features of the smaller, oil-rich states of the Arabian peninsula (and Southeast Asian states such as Brunei), it is misleading to sum up all relevant characteristics of the societies of the region in terms of a single principle. Iran and Iraq, for example, are both oil-rich, but the politics and social dynamics of neither state could readily be categorized as those of an allocation state, even before U.S. sanctions were applied against Iran and international ones against Iraq. Another difficulty with the notion of allocation is

[60] Kazakhstan and Azerbaijan have significant oil deposits, but their economies are still in disarray from the Soviet era, and few economists would call them allocation states.

[61] Anatoly M. Khazanov, *After the USSR: Ethnicity, Nationalism, and Politics in the Commonwealth of Independent States* (Madison: University of Wisconsin Press, 1995), pp. 122–23.

that it deflects attention from historical continuities in leadership, authority, and ideas of justice and equity. Most of the allocation states of the Middle East could be so characterized only since the 1950s, when oil royalties began to accrue in significant amounts. Both types of state are profoundly affected by changing expectations of legitimate rule, in which the leaders of both republics and monarchies assure their citizens that they act on behalf of "the people," one manifestation of which has been vastly expanded educational opportunities in recent decades.

Another common element between production and allocation states is an increasing concern with Islamic radicalism among a younger, educated generation of citizens. The prognosis of some scholars of a growing Islamic political radicalism for the late 1980s and early 1990s can be questioned; nonetheless, the common wisdom of an earlier decade asserting "the growing irrelevance of Islamic standards and criteria in the issues, conflicts, and policy processes of modern Arab politics and the diminishing influence of Islamic authorities in politics" is now very much in question.[62] Each state of the region, both revolutionary and nonrevolutionary, must contend with a citizenry holding varying interpretations of Islam, and many assert that Islam has direct practical application to political and economic affairs. Economic considerations alone are insufficient to explain political and social trends.

Another element that provides continuity in both production and allocation states is long-standing assumptions concerning political and personal loyalties. These provide an organizing framework for associations and networks, both covert and overt, that parallel or limit the authority of the state. A gazetteer of contemporary Middle Eastern polities would reveal multiple instances of tribal, sectarian, ethnic, and factional leaders with followings capable of circumscribing or challenging state authority. Few states possess a complete monopoly on the use of force. For this reason, states are often circumspect about intervention in the affairs of their citizens. In some instances, shared notions of loyalty, trust, and justice allow for a reasonably stable and predictable economic and social life, independent of effective formal government and commercial institutions. Despite the claim of most modern Middle Eastern states that loyalty to the state comes before other obligations, the loyalties of most citizens are significantly more complex. Politics today, as in the past, is wider in scope than state authority alone.

WRITING MIDDLE EASTERN ANTHROPOLOGY

Ethnographic and historical knowledge is politically and socially constructed. The representation of a society in the past or present involves the selection, control, arrangement, organization, and dissemination of knowledge. The prefaces

[62] Michael Hudson, *Arab Politics: The Search for Legitimacy* (New Haven, CT, and London: Yale University Press, 1977), p. 17.

FIGURE 11-4. Campaign poster in Cairo, 1989: "Yes, Islam is the Solution. Religion and State, Justice and Mercy, Freedom and Consultation, Pious Struggle and Outreach. The Islamic Voice in the Consultative Assembly." Because the Muslim Brotherhood is technically illegal, although tolerated, it fields candidates through other political parties, and identifies itself as the sponsor of this poster. [Courtesy Gregory Starrett. Photograph copyright © 1989.]

to most monographs make it clear that anthropologists and historians have long been aware that how they describe and interpret societies and infer the motives of individuals and groups are bound in multiple ways to time, place, context, and audience. Yet only since the 1960s has the discussion of such factors become an integral component of thinking about and "doing" anthropology and history, instead of just a prefatory, marginal, or supplementary activity. In recent decades, scholars have increasingly questioned the "authority" of an earlier generation of scholarly practices and texts. In doing so, they have made more visible the processes by which these texts and their "authority," or ability to persuade an audience of their accuracy and reliability, are maintained.

This heightened concern with *reflexivity* involves explicitly posing the link between power and knowledge not only in terms of the object of anthropological research—the communities and peoples studied—but with the practices of writing and communicating such studies. In anthropology, this concern was initially expressed in terms of how the "colonial encounter" and "Western" political and economic domination framed many classical anthropological and historical texts. Later it encompassed other forms of ethnographic narrative.

There are three main features to the "new wave" in ethnographic writing in which ethnographies developed in Middle Eastern settings have played a decisive role in setting new trends or have served as exemplars of past practice.

First is a heightened awareness of the "multiple voices" constitutive of any society and to representations of them. A second, closely related concern is with the "ethnographic conversation" or, for historians, with the interrogation of historical sources, in order to make visible the means by which the "voices" of the subjects of ethnographic reporting are made part of the ethnographic and historical record or are downplayed or ignored. In "conventional" ethnographic or historical accounts, the author's "monophonic" narrative, with quoted or paraphrased sources, is central to representing or interpreting societies. There have been recent experiments at creating "polyphonic" texts in which "many voices clamor for expression."[63] Yet polyphonic texts are also written and edited texts, even if the author seeks to lend realism to ethnographic reporting by allowing "others" to "speak for themselves" and, in extreme cases, to claim to serve solely as editor, translator, or presenter.

The final concern is writing about writing, the explicit attention to the contexts and practices of ethnographic or historical narrative and presentation. It is important to note that most of the new wave in ethnographic writing—in particular, the concern with understanding "the other" (the term often appears capitalized)—has been created primarily by scholars enmeshed in American and European academic settings and writing in European languages primarily for other academics working in the same intellectual traditions. "Others" who use the term often do so with irony.[64] A comparison with contemporary developments in ethnographic and academic writing in the Middle East by Arabs, Iranians, and Turks working in their own national languages (in addition to European ones, in some cases), and often with very different perceptions of intellectual responsibilities, careers, and audiences, suggests both probable future trends in writing Middle Eastern (and Central Asian) ethnography and implicit built-in limitations to some current trends in writing and interpretation.

Since the late 1960s, most scholars studying Middle Eastern societies have developed an intensified interest in the social construction of knowledge. "Orientalists," to use a term that acquired a pejorative hue only in the late 1960s,[65] developed an interest in understanding how careers, personal background, motivations, conditions of work, and political and economic contexts influenced resulting scholarly texts and their implicit assumptions toward religion and politics in "other" civilizations.[66] Edward Said's *Orientalism* was a late addi-

[63] James Clifford, "Introduction: Partial Truths," in *Writing Culture*, ed. Clifford and Marcus, p. 15.

[64] As does the Sudanese scholar, Abdelwahab El-Affendi, "Studying My Movement: Social Science Without Cynicism," *International Journal of Middle East Studies* 23, no. 1 (February 1991), 83–94.

[65] In Arabian peninsula Arabic, *mustashriq* ("Orientalist," lit., "seeker after the east") can also designate an Arabic-speaking non-Arab businessman or academic and carry no adverse connotation.

[66] See especially Jacques Waardenberg, *L'Islam dans le miroir de l'occident* [Islam in the Mirror of the West], 3rd ed. (Paris and The Hague: Mouton, 1969). For the institutional development of Middle East studies in the United States, see R. Bayly Winder, "Four Decades of Middle Eastern Study," *Middle East Journal* 41, no. 1 (Winter 1987), 40–65.

tion to this body of literature but particularly important because it reached a wide audience.[67]

The earliest "critical" analyses, as studies of the rhetoric of anthropology, history, and related disciplines are often called, for the most part concentrated on such general issues as the relationship between colonial domination or political hegemony and the representation of dominated societies.[68] If the earlier critiques dealt primarily with general issues or with presumably representative, well-known texts, later ones often provided sustained assessments of how training and education, competition for funding and institutional support, professional rivalries, audiences, and shifting economic and political pressures contributed to shaping the intellectual product of "authoritative" historical and ethnographic discourse. Historians, for their part, sought not only to make visible the structure of colonial historiography but also to rewrite it from the perspective of the colonized.[69] Such studies of the past are valuable in themselves, but they also frame issues that can be posed of contemporary scholarship.

An explicit, sustained concern with "doing anthropology" is nonetheless quite recent. A personal note is appropriate here. As a graduate student in the late 1960s at the University of Chicago, I found that the only available course on fieldwork was a noncredit, informal seminar concerned with such "practical" matters as note taking, record keeping, "entry" into field situations, and interviewing and survey techniques. There were no models for exploring systematically how these practices shaped ethnographic "conversations" and the use of archival resources. Independent of the seminar, many of us read with interest a 1968 essay by J. H. Hexter on "doing history," the author's gloss for the more forbidding term, historiography.[70] Hexter argued that historians learn the rhetoric of organizing and presenting their narratives through training and practice, and that this learned rhetoric is an integral part of doing history, not just an optional concern with stylistic flourishes existing independently of "data" and "fact." The implications of Hexter's argument for "doing anthropology" are clear.

The "doing fieldwork" accounts, which appeared with increasing frequency in the 1970s as a complement to, and in some cases virtually as a replacement for, "conventional" ethnographic accounts, brought to the fore the importance of how ethnographic inquiry takes place. Earlier narratives of doing fieldwork were contained in short introductions or were conceived as

[67] Edward Said, *Orientalism* (New York: Pantheon, 1978).

[68] For example, Asad, ed., *Anthropology and the Colonial Encounter*, and the former *Review of Middle East Studies* 1–3 (1975–1978), of which Asad was one of the editors. The *Review*, revived in 1988, appears irregularly.

[69] For example, Germain Ayache, *Les origines de la guerre du Rif* [The Origins of the Riffian War] (Rabat: Société Marocaine des Éditeurs Réunis, 1981).

[70] J. H. Hexter, *Doing History* (Bloomington and London: Indiana University Press, 1971 [1968]). See also Bernard S. Cohn's "Anthropology and History in the 1980s," *Journal of Interdisciplinary History* 12 (1981), 227–52.

adjuncts to more substantive ethnographic inquiries.[71] Later accounts, even if complementary to separate ethnographic studies, dealt directly with the ethnographic apprehension of the "other" and how anthropologists built up their portrayals of "other" societies.[72] Of course, just as "conventional" ethnographies can be shown to be "fictitious" or constructed, so are "doing fieldwork" narratives. Most recently, as in Michael Gilsenan's *Lords of the Lebanese Marches*, there is a complexly interlinked balance among the various perspectives.[73]

As James Clifford comments, the major difference between contemporary ethnographies and those of earlier generations is that "the rhetoric of experienced objectivity" of conventional ethnographic narrative is replaced with "that of the autobiography and the ironic self-portrait." In such accounts, the ethnographer, "a character in a fiction, is at center stage," which is not the case in earlier ethnographic writing.[74] Thus Paul Rabinow's 1977 account is effective in raising some basic issues in anthropological inquiry, but it sets others aside. His text deals mostly with the ethnographer's encounter with Moroccan "others," but it says little about anthropological "others." Members of the "Sefrou project" immediately preceded and were co-present with him for part of the period of field research. Rabinow conferred regularly during field research with Sefrou team members, and they shared informants, notes, and facilities. Surely these conditions of work are as much part of "doing fieldwork" as the encounter with "others," even if the encounters with anthropological "others" are scarcely mentioned in his text. In later writing, Rabinow recognized that "the politics of interpretation" involves not just the conditions in which anthropologists seek to understand "others," but "the conditions of production of anthropological knowledge." The politics of writing anthropology is a subject so close to home that even now anthropologists find difficulty in dealing with the subject with the same rhetorical mixture of familiarity and distance that characterizes most "objective" anthropological and historical writing.[75]

Multiple Voices and Interests

Ethnographers have long been aware of the multiple voices and interests present in any society. "Voice" in this case means how people represent themselves and how analysts attribute material, status, and power "interests" to people. In practice, "voice" and "interest" often merge, as one of the most difficult tasks in

[71] For example, Nadia Abu-Zahra, "Fieldwork Remembered: Tunisia 1955," *Journal of the Anthropological Society of Oxford* 17, no. 5 (Michaelmas 1986), 231–44; and S. al-Sowayan, "The Arabs and Fieldwork" (in Arabic), *al-Ma'thurāt al-Sha'biya* 2, no. 7 (July 1987), 7–20.

[72] An example of this genre is Paul Rabinow, *Reflections on Fieldwork in Morocco* (Berkeley and Los Angeles: University of California Press, 1977).

[73] Michael Gilsenan, *Lords of the Lebanese Marches: Violence and Narrative in an Arab Society* (Berkeley and Los Angeles: University of California Press, 1996).

[74] Clifford, "Introduction," in *Writing Culture*, p. 14.

[75] Paul Rabinow, "Representations Are Social Facts: Modernity and Post-Modernity in Anthropology," in *Writing Culture*, ed. Clifford and Marcus, pp. 253–54.

social science writing is to impute motives to people and groups of people ("Syrians believe that . . ."). Voice and interest can be differentiated by such factors as age, location, language, class, livelihood, gender, sect, and education. Both outsiders to the societies concerned and participants in them have—inadvertently or intentionally—privileged some voices over others. As earlier generations of anthropologists and historians sought to establish coherent, integrated accounts of the "core symbols" of a society, its key social institutions, or "key" semiotic structures to be "read" from representative texts and ritual activities, in the last two decades there has been an increased awareness that many of these accounts achieved coherence and elegance by muting historical transformations or the voices of some key participants.

By the 1970s, competing frameworks emerged for representing the internal economic and political diversity of complex societies such as those of the Middle East; Central Asia remained on the periphery of the ethnographic imagination. Many studies sought to link developments within societies to worldwide economic and political processes. If some studies emphasized European or capitalist "hegemony" at the expense of allowing for creativity among "dominated" peoples, other studies and theoretical approaches sought to redress the balance. Apart from the influential work of Pierre Bourdieu and his colleagues, which by the mid-1970s was translated into English, a range of other creative studies appeared.[76] Talal Asad's *Kababish Arabs* dealt with political leadership in a Sudanese pastoralist tribe.[77] Rather than relying primarily on lineage theory and downplaying the importance of colonial political structures, Asad dealt directly with "external" political and economic influences on the ideas and practice of authority and criticized Weberian notions of power and authority. Other studies were directly or indirectly inspired by Marxist notions of the primacy of economic forces for engendering internal divisions and shaping historical transformations.

An early experiment in representing the divergent voices of a society was a French ethnographer's account of the multiple perspectives of inhabitants of a village in southern Tunisia.[78] Jean Duvignaud, unable to speak Arabic, directed a group of young, mostly middle-class Tunisian sociology students who interviewed the inhabitants. As part of the text offers the "inner" thoughts of an illiterate teen-age girl, presumably not "witnessed" by any member of the ethnographic team, the sense of dramatic event may have overcome more conventional notions of ethnographic reporting. However, the resulting account, which later became a film, represented both the villagers and the consequences of the ethnographic experience for villagers and students. The study was a departure from the "monophonic authority" of con-

[76] See Dale F. Eickelman, "The Political Economy of Meaning," *American Ethnologist* 6, no. 2 (May 1979), 386–93.

[77] Talal Asad, *The Kababish Arabs: Power, Authority and Consent in a Nomadic Tribe* (London: C. Hurst, 1970).

[78] Jean Duvignaud, *Change at Shebeika: Report from a North African Village*, trans. Frances Frenaye (Austin: University of Texas Press, 1977 [1968]).

ventional ethnography, although its alternative rhetorical conventions should not be taken as more authentic because they purport to represent the words and thoughts of the villagers.

An important element of recognizing multiple voices and interests was to relate women's ideologies about gender with those maintained by men, and to link variations in these ideologies with cross-cultural variations in the distribution of power.[79] Other types of studies sought to represent the multiplicity of women's lives and experiences in their own words or in paraphrases, leaving theoretical concerns implicit. The latter strategy has been used particularly by scholars working in Middle Eastern contexts who are interested in reaching wider audiences than would be possible through accounts with explicit theoretical goals.[80] Even if the role of the ethnographer becomes less evident in such accounts, the ethnographer still chooses the voices to represent, translates them (sometimes "inventing" narrative and imputing motives), and edits the narrative.

A particularly interesting collective model for representing the multiple voices of a contemporary Middle Eastern society is *Téhéran au dessous du volcan* [*Tehran Under the Volcano*], a work by French and Iranian scholars.[81] This study uses a combination of narrative, maps, photographs, and the personal testimony of intellectuals, women, students, *mullah*-s, Revolutionary Guards, former prisoners, wealthy businessmen, minorities, the "disinherited" poor, rural immigrants, and others to portray the changes in postrevolutionary Iran. The more analytically oriented contributions deal with such topics as Tehran's stunning demographic growth since the revolution, its division into residential and class areas, and the shifting political and economic importance of various sectors of the city. The mix of first-person narratives (or narratives told as if they were in the first person) and "conventional" ethnographic, geographic, and social historical narrative lends strength to the presentation.

[79] For example, Daisy Hilse Dwyer, *Images and Self-Images: Male and Female in Morocco* (New York: Columbia University Press, 1978).

[80] For example, Erika Friedl, *Women of Deh Koh: Lives in an Iranian Village* (Washington, DC, and London: Smithsonian Institution Press, 1989); Lila Abu-Lughod, *Writing Women's Worlds: Bedouin Stories* (Berkeley and Los Angeles: University of California Press, 1993); Fatima Mernissi, *Doing Daily Battle: Interviews with Moroccan Women*, trans. Mary Jo Lakeland (London: Women's Press, 1988 [1984]); and Deborah Kapchan, *Gender on the Market: Moroccan Women and the Revoicing of Tradition*, New Cultural Studies (Philadelphia: University of Pennsylvania Press, 1996). Paul Pascon and Mekki Bentaher, "Ce que disent 296 jeunes ruraux" [What 296 Rural Youth Say] in *Études sociologiques sur le Maroc*, ed. A. Khatibi (Rabat: Bulletin Économique et Social du Maroc, 1971), pp. 145–287, suggests the limits to "direct" representation. The strength of the Pascon and Bentaher study is to allow the "voices" of rural Moroccan youth to be heard "directly" by an educated and predominantly urban Moroccan audience through verbatim interview extracts, translated into French, loosely organized around such topics as education, sexuality, economic opportunity, and attitudes toward local authorities. However, the study's lack of contextual sociological narrative and analysis limits it to a local audience (or that part of it fluent in French) already familiar, or presuming it is familiar, with rural Morocco.

[81] Bernard Hourcade and Yann Richard, eds., *Téhéran au dessous du volcan, Autrement*, Hors série, 27 (Paris: Autrement Revue, 1987).

The "Ethnographic Conversation"

Heightened awareness of the "ethnographic conversation" is closely related to discerning multiple voices in any society and has served as a bridge to an introspective concern with how ethnographic reporting and narrative are constructed. In this respect, an explicit concern with ethnographic conversation is a logical extension of long-standing ethnographic and sociological interest in the "social construction of reality" and how perceptions are engendered in conversations and formal interviews.[82]

Four American studies on Morocco published within the last decade suggest the range of issues involved. Vincent Crapanzano's *Tuhami*, the earliest of the four accounts to be considered, is an "experimental" life history.[83] The book centers on the "little universe" created by the ethnographer, his interpreter-assistant, and Tuhami, an underemployed Moroccan shantytown dweller whose fantasies, Crapanzano states, are difficult to separate from the existential facts of his life. Crapanzano is self-consciously influenced by a "psychoanalytic orientation" in the questions put to Tuhami, "so embedded is this orientation in contemporary Western thought."[84] Indeed, the last interviews with Tuhami and the interpreter-assistant reflect "the recurrent themes of separation, death, castration, and abandonment."[85] Little attention is given to portraying shantytown existence or to situating Tuhami in a wider social context.

The account is useful for the questions it poses of how relations between ethnographers and informants influence ethnographic perceptions and narratives, and in describing the possibilities of "transference" between ethnographers and informants. Yet in focusing on the relation between the ethnographer and Tuhami, *Tuhami* deals less thoroughly with the interpreter-assistant, to whom the ethnographer says he is "indebted . . . for much of what I have to say about Tuhami." The interpreter-assistant is described in brief introductory and concluding passages as possessing a "faceless presence," providing the "'familiar distance' that was necessary for the frankness of our discourse," and a "frame" for interviews, occupying, "to speak figuratively, the place of God—in Sartre's terms, the place of the unrealized Third."[86] The resulting "little universe" may strike some as turned so intensely upon itself as to preclude other forms of ethnographic representation, but the result is to pose, if not always to

[82] Influential earlier studies include Alfred Schutz, *The Phenomenology of the Social World*, trans. George Walsh and Frederick Lehnert (Evanston, IL: Northwestern University Press, 1967); Erving Goffman, *The Presentation of Self in Everyday Life* (New York: Doubleday, 1959), and Harold Garfinkel, *Studies in Ethnomethodology* (Englewood Cliffs, NJ: Prentice Hall, 1967).

[83] Vincent Crapanzano, *Tuhami: Portrait of a Moroccan* (Chicago: University of Chicago Press, 1980).

[84] Ibid., p. 10.

[85] Ibid., p. 150.

[86] Ibid., pp. 11–13, 146–51. The "unrealized Third" in this case has worked for roughly half a dozen ethnographers of Morocco over a two-decade period. A "The Ethnographers and I" account, perhaps developed in collaboration with a Moroccan anthropologist, might add an important complement to understanding the ethnographic process.

answer, questions useful for generating a self-awareness about ethnographic reporting and texts.

Kevin Dwyer's *Moroccan Dialogues* emphasizes the "structured inequality" of partners in the ethnographic encounter ("Self" and "Other"), with the anthropologist "inextricably linked to his own society's interests."[87] The core of the account is a transcribed, edited, and translated set of interviews with a single informant and an analysis of the implications of the dialogue. As James Clifford notes, "dialogic" encounters between ethnographers and the subjects of their representations are "multisubjective, power-laden, and incongruent."[88] Yet in this respect, ethnographic encounters surely resemble most conversations and show considerable variation. In some encounters, such as those analyzed by Dwyer, the ethnographer cannot leave behind his "dominant" society and is regarded as the dominant partner in the dialogue in a range of subtle ways. The reverse can also hold. As a British colleague who has worked in the Yemen Arab Republic comments, the anthropologist in the Yemen is consistently the subordinate in the "ethnographic" conversation, although the ethnographic conversation is very like any ordinary conversation. Tribesmen were wealthier than the anthropologist, much more skilled in politics, and the dominant figure in any conversation. More often, the ethnographer is involved with a wide range of people in the society studied, with as many variations of influence and control as can be found in other, nonethnographic forms of social encounters.

Dwyer succeeds in rendering visible the encounter of "Self" with "Other,"[89] but it is useful to recall that "Other" can be a highly relative term. "Self" and "Other" can be from the same society, as increasingly is the case in Middle Eastern ethnography, and still face barriers or differences of imputed knowledge, social distance, and authority.[90] To go one step farther, the nuances of "dialogue" described by Dwyer apply to most interviews and social encounters.

Crapanzano's and Dwyer's accounts focus on the encounters of the ethnographer with the subject of his inquiries. The anthropologist is virtually offstage in *The House of Si Abd Allah*, a narrative in which Henry Munson, Jr., represents himself as recorder, translator, and editor of a series of accounts narrated by al-Ḥājj Muḥammad and other members of his family.[91] As in most anthropological field research, recording involved not only edited transcrip-

[87] Kevin Dwyer, *Moroccan Dialogues* (Prospect Heights, IL: Waveland Press, 1987 [1982]), pp. xvii–xviii.

[88] Clifford, "Introduction," in *Writing Culture*, pp. 14–15.

[89] Ibid., p. xxii.

[90] For example, Soraya Altorki, "The Anthropologist in the Field: A Case of 'Indigenous Anthropology' from Saudi Arabia" in *Indigenous Anthropology in Non-Western Countries*, ed. Hussein Faheim (Durham, NC: Carolina Academic Press, 1982), pp. 167–75.

[91] Henry Munson, Jr., *The House of Si Abd Allah: The Oral History of a Moroccan Family*, recorded, translated, and edited by Henry Munson, Jr. (New Haven, CT, and London: Yale University Press, 1984).

tions from tapes, not always contextually practicable or permitted, but the reconstruction of overheard statements and statements attributed to the narrators by third parties (usually members of the family).[92] The result is a persuasive, insightful evocation of the life histories of a Moroccan family of peasant origin, faithfully delivering in translation the rhythm of colloquial Moroccan Arabic and narratives about self. The anthropologist's close personal involvement with the Moroccan narrators and his skillful role in conveying the style of the original narratives are evident, as is his intention to make the narratives the center of his text. There is no prolonged discussion of "Self" and "Other," for to do so would be to displace the center of attention from the narratives that Munson presents.

Dale Eickelman's *Knowledge and Power in Morocco*, the final study considered here, is the biography of a rural Moroccan judge and an account of how the concepts and significance of knowledge and authority communicated in traditional Muslim education shifted from the early years of colonial rule to the present.[93] The study resembles Munson's, in that the relationship between ethnographer and judge is set out in an introductory chapter, where circumstances of the long-term relationship and how the judge and ethnographer worked together are described in detail. As one of the judge's sons later said, his father was much more open than with his own sons about his past, his views on religion and society, and his political and judicial work. Some possible reasons for this, suggested by a psychoanalyst with anthropological training, are mentioned in the text and recognized as important, but, like the account of the relationship between Moroccan and judge, are not the central theme of the book.[94]

Although the judge's voice is present throughout the text, so is the anthropologist's, and the narrative is often deliberately presented in the ethnographer's "voice," which is intended to provide the interpretive tissue and explanations necessary for both a Western audience and for a younger, educated Moroccan one to follow the contours of Islamic education in an earlier era in conveying "authoritative" religious knowledge. Making these ideas of learning, their transmission, and historical transformations intelligible requires a form of narrative different from one focusing on the interpersonal relations of the ethnographer. Were the narrative presented in the judge's words, as opposed to a fictive account in which glosses and reorganization of material were introduced by the anthropologist-editor "as if" the narrative were the judge's alone, it would probably have been unintelligible even to a younger Moroccan audience, let alone a Western one. The judge was not interested in communicating with such an audience, and his narrative required an accompanying interpretation. The narrative of *Knowledge and Power* significantly incorporates the "voice" of the judge and other Moroccans, but it does not mask the role of the ethnographer in organizing the monograph. The judge's statements

[92] Ibid., pp. xii–xiii.

[93] Eickelman, *Knowledge and Power.*

[94] Ibid., pp. 14–36, esp. p. 36.

are treated as interpretations, his efforts to make sense of rapidly shifting political and economic conditions in which he participated.

Another, more situational consideration entered into the choice of narrative form. When dealing with officials and members of the elite in politically volatile situations such as those prevailing in many parts of the Middle East, the ethnographer's "control" over interview contexts is less than is possible with paid informants or assistants. Indeed, if taping is seen in the West as an ultimate guarantor of "authenticity," many Middle Easterners view such devices as a loss of control of discourse. Words, once taped, can be distorted and used for purposes unintended by the speaker or the ethnographer. A tape recorder was regarded as appropriate only for highly formal speech, and I have found the same resistance quite frequently elsewhere in Morocco and consistently with subsequent work in the Arabian peninsula. There was no objection, however, to note taking, as notes were regarded as the ethnographer's record and thus "deniable," although the judge and other individuals, including people in highly sensitive positions, often made every effort to help me get the notes right through subsequent, follow-up interviews.

Unlike the Iranian mullah interviewed by Mottahedeh in the United States,[95] the subject of Eickelman's "social biography" was still an active participant in his own society, a fact that shaped the form the ethnography could take. In sensitive political and social situations, the accurate paraphrase of much unofficial discourse, combined with contextualization and interpretation in the ethnographer's voice, is the only practicable means of representation, and skillfully handled, it can be very effective.[96]

In short, any ethnographer or social historian must strike a balance between the subjectification and objectification of narrative form. An intensive focus on the "ethnographic encounter" can divert attention from the events and experiences through which people have lived, among themselves and in encounters with the West or with Western ethnographers. On the other hand, inattention to the importance of narrative form and its sources of "authority" can lead to an overobjectification of social experience. As one colleague states, "Our interpretive techniques, methods, and ethnographic texts add still more layers to the elementary strata of beliefs which we wish to uncover, yet so do the interpretations of our informants, whose views demonstrably reflect the different interests and positions of competing social groups and, in some cases, of emerging social classes."[97]

[95] Roy P. Mottahedeh, *The Mantle of the Prophet* (New York: Simon and Schuster, 1985).

[96] For example, Davis, *Libyan Politics*, in which the "state theatre" of People's Congresses and similar national public events are represented verbatim but not the "unofficial" voices indicating tribal and lineage loyalties, among others, which nonetheless are persuasively represented in the ethnographer's narrative. For the use of the ethnographer's narrative to contextualize socially sensitive events, see Lila Abu-Lughod, *Veiled Sentiments: Honor and Poetry in a Bedouin Society* (Berkeley and Los Angeles: University of California Press, 1986).

[97] Michael Marcus, "God's Bounty, Men's Deeds: Past and Present in Eastern Morocco" (unpublished manuscript, 1988), who refers to the "oversubjectification" and "undersubjectification" of ethnographic accounts.

"Writing anthropology" has become a separate topic in anthropology in parts of the postmodern West. It involves sustained attention to how ethnographic narratives are constructed, recognition of their intended audiences, and understanding of the institutional conditions and practices that encourage or limit certain forms of presentation, discussion, and analysis. The principal emphasis among "postmodern" anthropologists is with describing Western ethnographies. Yet, for the Middle East, as for many other parts of the non-Western world, a critical density of historians, anthropologists, and sociologists has begun to engage in the study of their own societies and writing for audiences in their own languages. These writings suggest emerging trends in writing Middle Eastern anthropology.

The focus on the "ethnographic encounter" has often diverted attention to how "Westerners" apprehend "other" societies and away from conflicting and contested notions of self and society in non-Western societies themselves. Many of these problems are not just derived from encounters with the West or interpretations of a society intended for "export." This is particularly the case with ideas about history and the past. Defining the past or explaining the social order involves internal debate and competition for control within any society.

An analogy with the varieties of Arabic is useful to indicate challenges common to both Western and Arab ethnographers and historians, and it suggests some of the key issues involved. Contemporary Arabic, in most parts of the Middle East, can be thought of as possessing a continuum of levels, each possessing its own morphology, lexicon, and syntax. In Egypt, for instance, most "Egyptian speakers are competent in more than one level, but equally most speakers are incompetent in one or several of Egypt's native foreign languages (to coin an oxymoron)."[98] Classical Arabic is used for prayers and formal rhetoric. Modern standard Arabic, the lingua franca of educated people, is used for radio and television, newspapers, and academic writing. The spoken language of the highly educated, often mixed with words and syntax from European languages, and that of the illiterate constitute other levels. To add to the intricacies, Arabs from one region of the Middle East are often unable to comprehend the equivalent level of Arabic in another. A Moroccan publisher told me of a meeting in Casablanca with an Iraqi business associate where the common language had to be English. The Iraqi, educated outside the Arab world, was proficient only in spoken Baghdad Arabic, which was unintelligible to the Moroccan.

There are analogous levels of history and conceptions of self and past. Paul Dresch, in *Tribes, Government, and History in Yemen*, an account based equally on ethnographic research and Yemeni classical and contemporary historical writing in Arabic, points out that even present-day Yemeni historians and sociologists pass over almost in silence the role of tribes in Yemeni society.[99]

[98] Robert Irwin, "Native Foreign Languages," *Times Literary Supplement* (London), January 15–21, 1988, p. 67.

[99] Paul Dresch, *Tribes, Government and History in Yemen* (Oxford: Oxford University Press, 1989).

They are fully aware of the significance of tribal organization and authority on contemporary politics, but until recently they lacked appropriate rhetorical and ideological forms to incorporate them into discussions of central authority and Muslim society. Many modern Arab intellectuals deal with tribes as a "vestige" of earlier civilizational stages; medieval Muslim historiography, with a few rare exceptions, likewise discusses tribal organization as antithetical to Islam, even though the country's religious leadership depended on tribal support. Allowing Yemeni sources to "speak for themselves," without ethnographic analysis and the presentation of subordinate voices would not adequately represent the important theme of tribal identity. In Morocco, Michael Marcus represents the regional and local conceptions of history contained in poems, myths, and popular narratives that often diverge significantly from "authoritative" and "official" versions of the past.[100] The importance of eliciting multiple histories, including those of nondominant groups, is increasingly recognized by a new generation of historians in the Middle East.[101]

The combined expansion of facilities for higher education and the shift to the use of national languages for graduate education, both very recent developments, has had a significant impact on the nature of anthropological and historical writing in the Middle East. It has created new, locally based scholarly communities, the institutional and critical apparatus necessary to maintain peer review (at least in some instances), and, with the shift to national languages, new audiences interested in ethnography and local history.

Studies based on Morocco, demographically the Arab world's second largest country after Egypt, suggest the scale and significance of these developments. By the late 1960s, Morocco's scholarly community in the human sciences took off in terms of numbers and quality, and American, British, and French scholars were concurrently conducting field studies there. Broadly similar trajectories of writing can be traced for other countries of the Arab world and for Iran and Turkey, but the sustained intensity over the last two decades of publications on Morocco by both Moroccans and non-Moroccans makes it an appropriate point of departure for indicating current trends.

In the late 1960s, there was only one university in Morocco, and entry to it was highly restricted. Now there are eight, and the university system continues to expand.[102] French was the primary language of instruction for history and

[100] Michael A. Marcus, "'The Saint Has Been Stolen': Sanctity and Social Change in a Tribe of Eastern Morocco," *American Ethnologist* 12, no. 3 (August 1985), 455–67.

[101] For example, Jocelyne Dakhlia, "Le sens des origines: Comment on raconte l'histoire dans une société maghrébine" [The Sense of Origins: How History Is Narrated in a North African Society] *Revue Historique* 278, no. 2 (1987), 401–27; see also her *L'Oubli de la cité*, Textes à l'appui (Paris: Éditions la Découverte, 1990); and Abdelahad Sebti, "Au Maroc: Sharifisme citadin, charisme et historiographie" [Morocco: Urban Descent from the Prophet, Charisma, and Historiography] *Annales E.S.C.* 41, no. 2 (March–April 1986), 433–57.

[102] For statistics indicating this rapid growth and its impact on the development of sociology in Morocco, see Sa'īd bin Sa'īd, "Development and the Creation of a Framework for Teaching Sociology in Moroccan Educational Institutions" (in Arabic), *Majalla al-'Ulum al-Ijtima'iya* (Rabat) 14, no. 4 (Winter 1982), 83–113.

sociology until the late 1960s, and it was a major factor in restricting growth in these fields. By the early 1970s, Arabization had begun in earnest for higher education. The change occurred over several years and was not an easy one for either students or staff. In Morocco, as in Tunisia and other countries, intellectuals who had been trained in French (and in a few cases, English), could speak colloquial Arabic, but they were unable to lecture in modern standard Arabic.

As both Moroccan and Tunisian colleagues explain, even if one's native language is Arabic, the challenge of lecturing in one's own language, let alone writing in it after having been educated almost exclusively in French or English, is a daunting task. In addition, books and teaching resources, which often take years to develop, were nonexistent or unobtainable.

The intellectual implications of Arabization appeared gradually. One of the most significant was a renewed interest in studying one's own society by historians, anthropologists, and sociologists, who had often been more concerned with generalized theories of "development" than with the specifics of their own societies. Thus it was with a sense of excitement that I attended the doctoral defense of a young Moroccan historian in Rabat in July 1976, one of the first to be presented in Arabic in Morocco. As in France, dissertation defenses are public events, and this one was attended by over 1000 students and faculty, as well as the national press. The dissertation, subsequently published, dealt with the nineteenth-century economic, social, and political history of a region of the High Atlas Mountains not far from where Ernest Gellner conducted field research in the early 1950s.[103] It was based primarily on family and tribal documents, firmly placing the region's past within the compass of known history, as opposed to the largely speculative assertions about the past by an earlier generation of anthropologists. The study demonstrated a command of Western social and historical thought but was not limited by it. Of equal interest was the dissertation's jury, composed of several distinguished Moroccan historians and a senior French scholar, Germain Ayache, who, as part of a personal commitment to "decolonizing" history and participating in the formation of a new, Arabized generation of Moroccan scholars, had learned to lecture in modern standard Arabic a decade earlier.

A corollary of the shift to Arabic as the primary language for scholarship in Morocco and the rapid expansion of higher education has been an impressive growth in local publishing, including scholarly books and periodicals. Several hundred titles are now published annually in Morocco, and in recent years the number and quality of scholarly journals have also increased. These periodicals serve as vehicles for lively debate and timely critical review.[104] Unlike

[103] Aḥmad Tawfīq, *Moroccan Society in the Nineteenth Century: Inūltān, 1850–1912* (in Arabic), 2nd ed. (Casablanca: al-Najāḥ Press, 1984 [1978]).

[104] Particularly important is *al-Kitāb al-Maghribī* [The Moroccan Book] (1983–), which provides comprehensive reviews of books and scholarly articles either concerning Morocco or published in Morocco. Another important periodical is *Abḥāth* (1982–), which specializes in the social sciences. For a comprehensive discussion of the Moroccan publishing industry, see Michael W. Albin, "Moroccan-American Bibliography," in *The Atlantic Connection: 200 Years of Moroccan-American Relations, 1786–1986*, ed. Jerome B. Bookin-Weiner and Mohamed El Mansour (Rabat: Edino Press, 1990), pp. 5–18.

imported books in French and English, which are often prohibitively expensive, the price of locally published books and journals is kept low—with an average price of just over U.S. $4.00 per copy for books—so they are widely circulated and read.

The shift to the use of the region's languages does not, however, lead to scholarly or intellectual self-sufficiency. Colleagues writing and teaching in various Middle Eastern languages—Arabic, Persian, Turkish, and Hebrew—recognize that they require at least a reading knowledge of major European languages to keep abreast of current developments in their discipline and to conduct basic research on their own countries. The need to strike a delicate balance between the use of materials in local and foreign languages is especially apparent in university teaching, where students, unlike many instructors, are often still uncomfortable with the use of foreign languages and have not yet had—and for a new generation, may never have—an opportunity to receive advanced training outside their country or region of origin.

An appreciation of what goes on in university classrooms is as important as understanding more advanced scholarly contributions. For this reason, whenever I visit foreign (and domestic) academic institutions, I try to visit classes to understand the conditions under which colleagues work and think. Let me provide two examples here, one from the occupied West Bank and the other from Kuwait. In both cases, the availability of appropriate books and the use of foreign languages were critical issues.

In the occupied West Bank in February 1985—dates are important when situations are in rapid flux—I was invited to sit in on the first meeting of a course on the "Sociology of the Family," taught by a young Palestinian then completing a doctoral dissertation in anthropology at a foreign university. There were about 25 students, both men and women, most of whom were preparing for careers in the health sciences, for which the course was required.

Discussion was entirely in Arabic, although all students had at least a working command of written English. Many also had a command of spoken Hebrew. The instructor explained the syllabus, which included units on the study of the family in general, but she drew on examples specific to the Middle East: the Israeli kibbutz, the family in the Arab world, and the family in refugee camps, the instructor's particular research concern. The principal reading for the course was an Egyptian textbook, although the instructor said that its approach to the subject was "rather limited."[105] However, the instructor continued, it was the only available book in Arabic. To supplement this book, she stated that there would be additional reading materials in English. A student immediately raised his hand to say that many students find English difficult. Others nodded assent. The instructor replied that she would go through the materials carefully with the students but made clear that they were essential for understanding the subject matter.

[105] The English citations for the book stopped with the early 1950s, and there were few citations of Arabic literature published outside of Egypt.

Two sensitive issues were at play. One was the lack of adequate teaching materials in Arabic. Reliable translations into Arabic, even of classical studies in social thought, are still uncommon, let alone more contemporary ones. Conveying this to students without being perceived as valuing "foreign" scholarship over Arab scholarship is a difficult task. Second is the problem of censorship. Scholarly books are subject in varying degrees to censorship throughout the Arab world, but West Bank universities at the time had to submit assigned books to Israeli military authorities for approval, a procedure described by many administrators as cumbersome and capricious.[106]

In Kuwait, sociology and anthropology are taught almost entirely in Arabic. Most undergraduate students have only a basic knowledge of English, but the instructors, even when trained entirely in the Arab world, are all bilingual, even if many choose to write primarily in Arabic. Course readings are primarily in Arabic, although a small amount of supplementary work in English is often assigned. Required readings include textbooks and collections of readings, often translated, of necessity, from English by the instructors because of the paucity of appropriate materials.[107]

I participated in several undergraduate classes at Kuwait University in December 1987. In contrast to Egypt and Morocco, where financial constraints mean that classes of 300 to more than 1000 students are unexceptional, most classes at Kuwait University have between 15 and 40 students. Most students are Kuwaiti nationals, although there is a sprinkling of students from the other Arab Gulf states. Women sit on one side of the classroom and men on the other. For women, there is a variety of dress styles, often reflecting religious sect and personal commitment to Islam. Men's dress is more uniform, although the presence or absence of a beard and the style of beard can communicate attitudes toward religion.

In one of the anthropology classes I attended, the day's discussion concerned American ethnicity and concepts of class. The instructor wrote several key terms and foreign names on the blackboard in English and Arabic. After a short lecture, the instructor shifted to a question-and-answer format, enabling him to gauge what the students knew and how well they could discuss the assigned readings. "Can American ethnicity be compared to the differences we

[106] For the conditions of West Bank universities in the 1980s, see Penny Johnson, "The Routine of Repression," *Merip Middle East Report* 18, no. 1 (January–February 1988), 6–7. Censorship of academic books in the Arab world would make a particularly interesting sociological study. Unlike publications in Turkey and Iran, which basically pass through only one censoring authority, Arab world publications intended for regional distribution—almost a necessity, given the small domestic markets in many Arab countries—must pass through several censors. Some countries have arrangements with major publishers so that prior approval of texts can be obtained; others simply seize offending material once it is published or distributed. The net result is to damage the infrastructure necessary to support academic publication and research and to impede the circulation of ideas in Arabic. The only solace for authors is the recognition that some state authorities take the printed word more seriously than do liberal regimes. Ironically, the response of many scholars is to publish in European languages, as materials in these languages, perhaps because limited in local circulation, are often subject to less rigorous scrutiny.

[107] Kuwait University, Student Bookstore, "Books Remaining After 1987–1988" (in Arabic) (mimeo).

have here in Kuwait between Sunnī and Shī'a?" he asked. "What about tribal differences here in the Gulf? Can we call these 'ethnic'?" Through discussing questions such as these during the class session, the students seemed to improve their practical understanding of the abstract social science concepts presented and to apply them to both their own and different cultural contexts.

The textbooks used in anthropology and sociology courses in Kuwait (and elsewhere in the Arab world) show no dramatic differences from their European and American counterparts. One newly introduced text was jointly written by a Kuwaiti cultural anthropologist and a Palestinian physical anthropologist teaching at Kuwait University.[108] The section on physical anthropology looks much like its American counterpart in terms of coverage, and (quite appropriately) places no particular emphasis on the Arab world as such. The section on cultural anthropology describes the history of the discipline, linguistics, the notion of fieldwork, and key concepts used at various periods in the development of anthropology and provides short descriptions of various world cultures. There is an effort to explain some notions through the analysis of current trends in the Western world, such as the tendency in English to replace gender-weighted terms, such as "chairman" with "chairperson."[109]

Occasionally, the text uses the English terms only, without translation, implying a basic bilingualism in university students that could not be taken for granted, for example, in an American context. Many examples, however, come from the Arab world, and the bibliography is equally divided between foreign sources, primarily derived from American anthropology, and Arab ones.

In practice, at least in university circles, the boundary between "Western" and "Muslim" knowledge is becoming increasingly blurred. A Syrian colleague with a distinguished international reputation based on writing in Arabic and several European languages reflected on his teaching career over the past quarter-century.

> At the beginning, I taught only the elite. They knew the names of the European philosophers and writers and often had read them. Imagine my challenge at the

[108] Muḥammad Sulaymān al-Ḥaddād and Muḥammad Yūsif al-Najjār, *Anthropology: An Introduction to the Science of Man* (in Arabic) (Kuwait: International Press, 1987). See also Seteney Shami, "Socio-cultural Anthropology in Arab Universities," *Current Anthropology* 30, no. 5 (December 1989), 649–54. A Turkish equivalent is Bozkurt Güvenç, *Man and Culture* (in Turkish) (Istanbul: Remzi Kitzbevi, 3rd printing, 1979). Its section headings include "The Birth of Anthropology," "Boundaries of Understanding Race," "The Social Sciences and Anthropology," "The Development of Anthropology," "Man as a Bio-Cultural and Historical Being," "Relations of Production, Consumption, and Exchange," "Class Formation," and "Kinship, Descent, and Marriage." There is little specific reference in the book to Turkey. Readers are often used throughout the region to provide students with an introduction to selected texts. A Turkish example is Oğuz Ari, ed., *Reader in Village Sociology* (in Turkish) (Istanbul: Bogazici University Publications, 1977), which contains articles on how to study such topics as class, domestic budgets, basic resources, and income patterns in village settings. In contrast to its American counterparts, there is much more interest in gathering quantifiable data than in analyses of values or opinions. Values are treated primarily in the context of opinion surveys and formal questionnaires. I am grateful to Richard Tapper for discussions of the content of Persian and Turkish textbooks and ethnographies.

[109] Ibid., p. 416.

University of Damascus as my students increasingly became the sons of peasants. I don't begin at the same point with them, but after two or three years, they begin to understand Kant's notion of enlightenment, existentialism, and other issues. They know that these are ideas and philosophies that originated in the West, but the origins of these ideas don't have to make a major difference. Their minds are open, and they develop these ideas in an Arab context.[110]

In this respect, my colleague's approach reflected that of the Zairian-born anthropologist and literary critic V. Y. Mudimbe, commenting on the efforts to assert an "African" anthropology without Western antecedents (just as some aspire to an "Islamic" anthropology). Mudimbe writes: "It seems impossible to imagine any anthropology without a Western epistemological link." For Mudimbe, Western traditions of science, including anthropology, are "part of Africa's present-day heritage." Rather than cut African anthropology from its epistemological roots, Mudimbe argues that "one might also conceive the intellectual signs of otherness not as a project for the foundation of a new science, but rather as a mode of reexamining the journeys of human knowledge in a world of competing propositions and choices."[111]

Advanced work intended for colleagues and scholars in the Middle East shows subtle but significant differences from the "standard" output of American and European scholarly communities. Scholars in countries such as Turkey, Morocco, or Kuwait are under implicit pressure to communicate across disciplinary boundaries, rather than just to fellow practitioners of their specific discipline, and to the wider community outside academe. Many scholars possess more politically activist notions of the role of knowledge, derived in part from the shared notion that intellectuals in societies where access to higher education has been severely limited until recent decades have special responsibilities to society at large. Moreover, scholars in the social sciences are much more likely to engage in the study of their own society and region. Part of the reason for this is practical, such as the lack of library facilities and the resources and incentives necessary to engage in the comparative study of other countries. Another reason is that students and other readers are primarily interested in understanding their own societies and not distant "other" societies.

For the most part, ethnographies written in Arabic, Persian, and Turkish are aimed primarily at local audiences. For example, one issue addressed by Bozkurt Güvenç, a prominent Turkish anthropologist, is the question of contemporary Turkish national identity. Since at least the eighteenth century, the elite of the Ottoman Empire, with its capital in Constantinople (present-day Istanbul), had begun to strengthen its bonds with Europe. With the proclamation of the secular Republic of Turkey in 1923, modern Turkey's founder, Mustapha Kemal Atatürk, sought to "insulate" Turks from their Ottoman and Muslim past in order to forge a new cultural identity. Güvenç observes that Atatürk succeeded in creating a distinct Turkish national identity, "but only for

[110] Interview, Damascus, March 20, 1996.

[111] V. Y. Mudimbe, *The Invention of Africa: Gnosis, Philosophy, and the Order of Knowledge* (Bloomington: Indiana University Press, 1988), pp. 18, 79.

the post-World War I generation of Turks. The challenge now is to give the vast majority of Turks who were untouched by the Turkish Revolution a sense of what it means to be a Turk. It is a task of turning peasants, who still make up the bulk of our population, into Turkish nationals." Likewise, when Güvenç writes in Turkish on Japanese society, he does so for an audience of co-nationals eager to explore possible comparisons between their own society and Japanese society, which they perceive as having undergone a successful "modernization" without sacrificing their national identity.[112] The issue is a critical one for many contemporary Turkish intellectuals.

As scholarly traditions in new or newly expanded universities of the Middle East have begun to assume more permanent shape, incremental shifts have taken place in the sociological, social anthropological, and historical issues discussed and how they are treated. For countries where colonial domination came to an end in the 1950s and 1960s, the first historical studies by younger scholars from those countries often focused on the nationalist movement or on decolonizing some aspect of the "basic" historical narratives of their countries. In anthropology and sociology there was a corresponding emphasis on studies of "development" or "modernization." Such studies had the advantage of suggesting the practical uses of these disciplines to governments hard pressed for cash. An historian writing of comparable trends elsewhere has referred to this wave of scholars studying their own countries as a concern with the historical and anthropological "topsoil," a sort of intellectual strip mining.[113]

Recent studies show considerably more variation, largely within the range of their Western counterparts. Kuwait again serves as an indicator. One journal article assesses the strengths and weaknesses of various studies on the Middle East through the 1970s; another argues that the nineteenth-century scholar W. Robertson Smith, influential in developing E. E. Evans-Pritchard's ideas of segmentary lineage theory, directly cited and developed the ideas of Ibn Khaldūn (d. 1406), showing a larger indirect Arab input to contemporary anthropology than has been commonly recognized.[114] A recent collective study deals with the bedouin influence upon Kuwait society, with essays on such topics as intergenerational social change, popular crafts, bedouin "social traits" in Kuwaiti society, linguistic change in bedouin poetry, and the effects of sedentarization, and it provides a comprehensive bibliography, citing relevant sources in Western languages.[115]

[112] Bozkurt Güvenç, "Turning Peasants into Turks," *Wilson Center Reports* (Washington, D.C., June 1986), 3–4, and his *Japon Kültürü* [Japanese Culture], 2nd ed. (Ankara: Iş Bank of Turkey Cultural Publications, 1983 [1980]), based on field research in Japan (interview, Ankara, June 8, 1988).

[113] Roff, "Malaysia," p. 238.

[114] Sulaymān Khalaf, "A Critical Reading of Structuralism and Its Uses in the Anthropology of Middle Eastern Societies" (in Arabic), *Journal of the Social Sciences* (Kuwait) 13, no. 4 (Winter 1985), 369–99; al-Sayyid Aḥmad Ḥāmid, "Ibn Khaldun's Influence in Social Anthropology: An Anthropological Reading of His *Muqaddimah*" (in Arabic), *Journal of the Social Sciences* (Kuwait) 15, no. 3 (Autumn 1987), 171–87.

[115] Muḥammad al-Ḥaddād, Fāṭima al-Khalīfa, Badr al-Dīn al-Khuṣūṣī et al., *The Bedouin Heritage: An Introduction to the Study of Bedouin Society in Kuwait* (in Arabic) (Kuwait: Kuwait Institute for Scientific Research, 1987).

An example of a study with wider scope and a more explicit theoretical orientation is *Toward an Arab Sociology*, a symposium of 19 sociologists and anthropologists from throughout the Arab world published by the Center for Arab Unity Studies.[116] The papers suggest that many of the basic intellectual problems are not unlike those faced by sociologists and social anthropologists in the West, and that the much-heralded crises of Western sociology are largely paralleled by equivalent discussions outside of Western circles and are based on a similar range of theoretical issues modified, often substantially, to apply to the Arab world. With only a few exceptions, most contributions show a familiarity with relevant writings in English and French sociology and historiography, and many of the contributions deal with substantive issues rather than programmatic themes. Another recent study concerns long-term changes in ideas of hierarchy and social class in the Arabian peninsula and the influence of the oil economy on state structures and authority; another courageously explores the issue of sectarian and minority identities in the Arab world.[117] Unlike those of many of their Western counterparts, the text and notes of these studies incorporate references to sources in both Arabic and relevant European languages.

There have been significant shifts in attitudes toward Western scholarship on the Middle East in the past two decades. Generalized, stereotyped criticisms of Western scholarship are much less common than in earlier periods.[118] In their place have come circumstantial, critical assessments of particular studies or intellectual approaches. Representative of this new wave is the work of Bahraini anthropologist Abdallāh A. Yateem, who is engaged in a long-term project of translating key anthropological writings into Arabic. His audience is

[116] Center for Arab Unity Studies (Beirut), *Toward an Arab Sociology* (in Arabic) (Beirut: Center for Arab Unity Studies, 1986). This center, which also publishes the monthly *al-Mustaqbal al-'Arabī* [The Arab Future], has become one of the major regional centers for promoting quality research in the human sciences in the Arab world.

[117] Khaldūn Ḥasan al-Naqīb, *Society and State in the Gulf and the Arabian Peninsula* (in Arabic) (Beirut: Center for Arab Unity Studies, 1987).

[118] There are, of course, exceptions to this overall trend. Consider, for example, a book by a British-trained social anthropologist and Pakistani Ministry of the Interior official, Akbar Ahmed's *Toward Islamic Anthropology: Definitions, Dogma, and Directions* (Ann Arbor, MI: New Era Publications, 1986), which purports to be a review of "Western anthropology" and a statement of what an Islamic anthropology ought to be. Roughly 37 of the book's 55 pages demonstrating the discipline's "general theoretical stagnation" consist of direct but unmarked quotations from a 1964 book by John Beattie (which is incorrectly attributed to his son!), with only a general note in the acknowledgments that Ahmed has "borrowed extensively" in order to "faithfully" reflect Western anthropology (p. 5). Clearly, a book of two decades ago cannot be considered a reliable guide to developments since then. Islamic anthropology is defined "loosely as the study of Muslim groups by scholars committed to the universalistic principles of Islam," a definition that "does not preclude non-Muslims" (p. 56), presumably so long as they conform to Islam's "universalistic principles," as understood by Ahmed or other arbiters entrusted with defining them. Ahmed's "Islamic anthropology" thus appears to be a step backward in linking anthropology to a fixed doctrine, the very thing that Ahmed and others rightly decry in earlier studies of the "Orient." For further discussion of Ahmed's argument, see Richard Tapper's review in *Man* (N.S.) 23, no. 3 (September 1988). For a more considered vision of an anthropology of Islam, see Talal Asad, *The Idea of an Anthropology of Islam*, Occasional Papers Series (Washington, DC: Georgetown University Center for Contemporary Arab Studies, 1986).

FIGURE 11-5. Abdullah A. Yateem, anthropologist and editor in chief of *al-Bahrain al-Thaqafiya* [Cultural Bahrain]. Translations from European languages into Arabic and from Arabic into other languages play an important role in expanding disciplinary understandings. [Photograph courtesy Abdullah A. Yateem.]

not just fellow specialists but a wider, educated audience in the Arabic-speaking world. In this respect, the audience for his writings (published in the Arab Gulf and, for wider circulation throughout the Arab world, Beirut) resembles an audience in France more than that of the United States, where the reading public is more fragmented.

Although part of his project involves the explanation of key anthropological writings, Yateem has focused primarily on published interviews with key anthropologists—Ernest Gellner, Claude Lévi-Strauss, Raymond Firth, and Clifford Geertz—about their work and professional goals. At the same time, his more specialized writing outlines his professional goals. Take, for example, a recent article on the relevance of Lévi-Strauss's notion of the structural study of kinship.[119] He writes that although Lévi-Strauss's work on kinship, structuralism, and philosophy has been influential since the late 1940s, he remains relatively unknown among Arab anthropologists and the Arab public in general, in contrast to theories in literary criticism. Arab anthropologists, he argues, still use the earlier theories of structural functionalism (see the last section of Chapter 2) to explain kinship, and that applying Lévi-Strauss's notions to ideas of

[119] ʿAbdallāh A. Yatīm, "Claude Lévi Strauss' Theory of Kinship [*qarāba*]: A Reading in Contemporary Anthropology," *Majallat al-ʿulūm al-ijtimāʿiya* 24, no. 2 (Summer 1996), 87–128.

family and relationships in the Arab world can offer significant insight into the nature of Arab kinship systems. As with Mudimbe, Yateem focuses on the ideas, regardless of their provenance, and one can point to many conferences throughout the Middle East that approach studies with a similar attitude.

The French-Arabic monthly *Prologues/Muqaddimāt* (Casablanca) takes much the same approach and specializes in presenting arguments that address current issues and that, for reason of language, are often inaccessible to an Arab audience. The Fall 1995 issue, for example, had an interview with Mohamed Arkoun, an Algerian Muslim intellectual living in France, on the theme of Islam and democracy; articles on Marshall Hodgson's idea of Islam in world history; the linguistic situation in Morocco (where French, English, formal Arabic, colloquial Arabic, Spanish, and the Berber languages intermingle in many of the larger towns); and an interview with Aḥmad Tawfīq (now director of Morocco's National Library) on recent studies of Sufism in Morocco.[120]

There is a renewed interest in understanding Western scholarship on its own terms, even in unlikely settings. In the aftermath of the 1978–1979 revolution in Iran, there was a flood of translations of virtually all works dealing with Iran, including many that had been banned under the prerevolutionary regime. These were often prepared by university faculty paid salaries but unable to teach because classes had not yet resumed, and the new censorship apparatus was not yet in place. Book prices were low, so books were widely circulated. More recently, with censorship better organized, obstacles similar to the old ones have surfaced, although many works continue to be approved.[121]

When studies in European languages are made available for the first time in Middle Eastern languages, different questions are often asked of them, and they appear in a fresh light. For example, for Eickelman's *Moroccan Islam*, the Arabic translator's introduction and annotation of the text suggests what is needed to interpret a "foreigner's" ethnography of aspects of Moroccan religion and society that most Moroccans take for granted.[122] The translator specifies that the text can be read as an indication of how Westerners seek to understand Muslim societies, explains a "sociological" approach to the study of religion and why a Western audience not interested in Morocco for its own sake (as Moroccans necessarily are) might find the form of argument in the book of theoretical interest.

If, for Western audiences, there is a comfortable assumption among some practitioners of the social sciences that their theoretical language and abstract terms are universal in application, the glosses provided by the translator on basic sociological terms, theoretical developments, historical references, and the like unequivocally indicate how much of the theoretical work of "Western" social science is bound to specific audiences. For an English-speaking audience,

[120] *Prologues: Revue Maghrébine du Livre* (Casablanca), no. 4 (Fall 1995).

[121] See Azadeh Entechami, "La survie culturelle" [Cultural Survival], in *Téhéran*, ed. Hourcade and Richard, pp. 109–13.

[122] Dale F. Eickelman, *Religion and Society: A Study in the Social History of Western Morocco* (in Arabic), trans. Mohammed Aafif (Casablanca: Dār Tubkāl, 1989).

Moroccan Islam incorporated contextual glosses on Muslim concepts and Moroccan historical events that are unnecessary for a Moroccan audience. To be accessible for an educated Arab audience, the text required glosses instead on "standard" references of the social sciences. The net result is to present the book in an accessible manner to a new audience interested in seeing how a foreign scholar interprets their religious tradition. In part, the study joins internal debate within Morocco itself, where a primary goal of the human sciences is to facilitate the understanding of Moroccan society. Reciprocally, the translation and the translator's preface make the implicit assumptions of the original text more visible.

In recent years, there has been a recognition of the strengths and limitations of different perspectives toward scholarship in the humanities and social sciences, rather than the presumption, sometimes advocated in earlier years, that scholars of particular nationalities or religious backgrounds had particular advantages over the study of particular topics. As a leading Moroccan historian explains, the native scholar is not automatically advantaged over the foreign one. The foreign scholar often is less suspect of participating in local conflicts and rivalries and can speak to a wider range of persons. The outsider is obliged to ask basic questions about the nature of the social world that natives are supposed to know and therefore do not or ordinarily cannot discuss with one another.

Any assessment of trends must necessarily be tentative, but there is a turn away from the simplistic rejection of "Western" social sciences and toward assessments of specific studies and intellectual approaches. At the same time, there is a greater awareness of how the institutional and intellectual contexts within which academic work is carried out shape the intellectual product. There are, of course, "Western" works that continue to disregard appropriate scholarship generated within the Middle East, but these works are just as likely to be criticized by scholars enmeshed in Western academic contexts as those enmeshed in non-Western ones. Thus Edward Said, who earlier excepted Clifford Geertz's *Islam Observed* (1968) from his general critique of Western scholarship on Islam and the Middle East, notes in a later interview that Geertz's 1979 essay on Moroccan markets "has literally not a single Moroccan source cited for the study of Moroccan marketplace ritual! That couldn't happen in Latin American anthropology."[123] Scholars in the Middle East hold one another to equivalent standards in the use of sources in relevant languages, both for access to "basic" data and for the development and exchange of theoretical perspectives. Indeed, despite often inadequate libraries, the awareness and use of sources in

[123] Edward Said, "Orientalism Revisited," *Merip Middle East Reports* 18, no. 1 (January–February 1988), 34. The essay to which Said refers is Clifford Geertz, "Suq: The Bazaar Economy in Sefrou," in Clifford Geertz, Hildred Geertz, and Lawrence Rosen, *Meaning and Order in Moroccan Society* (Cambridge and New York: Cambridge University Press, 1979), pp. 123–313. What Said has in mind by "marketplace ritual" is unclear, since Geertz cites studies on other aspects of markets by Moroccans.

Western languages is more pervasive in the Middle East than is the Western use of scholarship in Middle Eastern languages.

The intellectual shifts engendered by the growing use of Middle Eastern languages for scholarship in the region and the growth of a university-educated audience for their intellectual product have been incremental rather than revolutionary, even in revolutionary settings. Indeed, the major constraints are often internal. Said comments, presumably with hyperbole, on intellectual "production" in the Middle East: "Everything is politicized in the most reductive and mindless way. Nothing is free from being saturated with immediate political reference, which means that it's virtually impossible to portray things on a more nuanced palette."[124] There are institutional limits to scholars of different intellectual and cultural orientations, and an awareness of these among scholars, regardless of their religious or national identities or the institutional and political contexts, can only improve an understanding of the region. In Middle Eastern and Central Asian contexts in general, there is less concern with reading societies as "texts" or with understanding texts for their own sake than in some scholarly circles. Instead, ethnographic and historical texts are intended to facilitate understanding of political, economic, and historical events and struggles.

As an ironic reminder that words and figures of speech still bear a direct relation with the "real" world, books are banned and their authors imprisoned, even when the intended audiences are academic and removed from the front lines of political struggle. Such experiences suggest limits to the postmodernist concern with texts displacing what people do with texts, and the issues of which texts are intended to facilitate understanding. They also suggest an enhanced understanding of ethnographic and historical narrative and the political and economic influences, direct and indirect, by which ethnographies and histories are shaped and constrained.

FURTHER READINGS

On the subtleties of changing political vocabulary in Arabic, see Ami Ayalon, *Language and Change in the Middle East: The Evolution of Modern Arabic Political Discourse* (New York and Oxford: Oxford University Press, 1987).

For a discussion of how patterns of medieval Middle Eastern authority have figured in Western sociological thought, see Bryan S. Turner, *Weber and Islam: A Critical Study* (London and Boston: Routledge & Kegan Paul, 1974), pp. 75–92. See also his *Marx and the End of Orientalism*, Controversies in Sociology, 7 (London: Allen & Unwin, 1978), as well as Maxime Rodinson, *Marxism and the Muslim World*, trans. Jean Matthews (New York and London: Monthly Review Press, 1981). Other assessments of "classical" Muslim political society include Fred M. Donner, *The Early Islamic Conquests* (Princeton, NJ: Princeton University Press, 1981); Patricia Crone, *Slaves on Horses* (Cambridge: Cambridge University Press, 1980); and Roy P. Mottahedeh, *Loyalty and Leadership in an Early Islamic Society* (Princeton, NJ: Princeton University Press, 1980).

[124] Said, "Orientalism Revisited," p. 34.

On colonial North Africa, in addition to sources cited in the notes, see See Dale F. Eickelman, *Moroccan Islam: Tradition and Society in a Pilgrimage Center*, Modern Middle East Series 1 (Austin and London: University of Texas Press, 1976), pp. 218–30; Dale F. Eickelman, *Knowledge and Power in Morocco: The Education of a Twentieth Century Notable* (Princeton, NJ: Princeton University Press, 1985), pp. 107–80 (for an account of the rural notables who sustained French rule); David Seddon, *Moroccan Peasants: A Century of Change in the Eastern Rif, 1870–1970* (Folkstone, Kent: Dawson Press, 1981); and Paul Pascon, *Capitalism and Agriculture in the Haouz of Marrakesh*, trans. C. Edwin Vaughan and Veronique Ingman (New York: Methuen, 1986 [1977]). For urban Morocco, especially from the perspective of its larger cities, see Janet L. Abu-Lughod, *Rabat: Urban Apartheid in Morocco* (Princeton, NJ: Princeton University Press, 1980). A useful long-term study of the relation between political forms and economic conditions elsewhere in North Africa is Lucette Valensi, *Tunisian Peasants in the Eighteenth and Nineteenth Centuries*, trans. Beth Archer, Studies in Modern Capitalism (Cambridge: Cambridge University Press; Paris: Éditions de la Maison des Science de l'Homme, 1985 [1977]).

For the contemporary political situation, see the bibliographic essay and references in Dale F. Eickelman and James Piscatori, *Muslim Politics* (Princeton, NJ, and London: Princeton University Press, 1996).

On writing Middle Eastern and Central Asian anthropologies and histories, see, for example, Edmund Burke III, "The Sociology of Islam: The French Tradition," in *Islamic Studies: A Tradition and Its Problems*, ed. Malcolm H. Kerr (Malibu, CA: Undena Publications, 1980), pp. 75–88; Ernest Gellner, "The Roots of Cohesion," *Man* (N.S.) 20, no. 1 (March 1985), 142–55; and, for recent scholarship with important parallels for the Middle East, William R. Roff, "Malaysia, Sdn. Bhd." [Malaysia, Incorporated], in *Historia: Essays in Commemoration of the 25th Anniversary of the Dept. of History, University of Malaya*, ed. M. Abu Bakr et al. (Kuala Lumpur: Malaysia Historical Society, 1984), pp. 236–40. His subject is the historical writing that immediately followed independence. For a Moroccan's view of colonial historiography, see Abdallah Laroui, *The History of the Maghreb: An Interpretive Essay*, trans. Ralph Mannheim (Princeton, NJ: Princeton University Press, 1977 [1970]). For Muslim Central Asia (and Russian views of the "Muslim East"), Victor A. Shnirelman, *Who Gets the Past? Competition for Ancestors Among Non-Russian Intellectuals in Russia* (Washington, DC: Woodrow Wilson Center Press, 1996), offers an excellent introduction to the ethnopolitical nationalism that dominates post-independence writing about the area, together with Philip L. Kohl and Gocha R. Tsetskhladze, "Nationalism, Politics, and the Practice of Archaeology in the Caucasus," in *Nationalism, Politics, and the Practice of Archaeology*, ed. Philip L. Kohl and Clare Fawcett (Cambridge: Cambridge University Press, 1995), pp. 149–74. See also Garay Menicucci, "Glasnost, the Coup, and Soviet Arabist Historians," *International Journal of Middle East Studies* 24, no. 4 (November 1992), 559–77.

On the writing of anthropology in the Middle East, Richard Tapper (personal communication, March 5, 1988) suggests that there is not a distinctive Turkish anthropology as such, but a variety of anthropologies by Turkish scholars that apply Western approaches to the study of Turkish situations. As in European settings, there is a tendency of academic departments to reproduce the same form of work as their founders—village and local studies. One influential study is Ali Reza Balaman, *Marriage and Kinship: Social Anthropological Approaches* (in Turkish) (Izmir: Ileri Kitap, 1982). The book is a study of the author's own village, but it is intended to serve as a model for conducting similar studies elsewhere. A study heavily influenced by Oscar Lewis's influential work in the 1960s of life among Mexican slum dwellers is Orhan Türkdoğan, *The Culture of Poverty* (in Turkish) (Istanbul: Dede Korkut, 1974). Other studies deal with the role of women in Turkish society, ritual kinship (*kirvelik*), and migration and squatter settlements. An excellent sense of the scope of contemporary Turkish anthropology is offered by the volume published to commemorate Professor Güvenç on his retirement: *Humana: Bozkurt Güvenç'e Armağan*, ed. N. Serpil Altuntek, Suavi Aydın, and İsmail H. Demirdöven, Başvuru Eserleri Dizisi 24 (Ankara: T. C. Küktür Bakanliği, 1994). In brief, it reaffirms Tapper's characterization of Turkish anthropology (and sociology) as wide-ranging and diverse.

In Persian, the influential novelist Jalal Al-e Ahmad (1923–1969), the author of *Gharbzadegi* [Weststruckness], trans. John Green and Ahmad Alizadeh (Lexington, MA: Mazda Publishers, 1982 [1962]), also wrote ethnographic studies based on life in his own village, using the sort of "village and I" approach that is returning to favor in anthropological circles. These studies include *Owrāzān: Topography, Customs, Folklore, Dialect* (Tehran: Danesh, 1954), and the frequently reprinted *Peasants of Boluke-e zahra* (Tehran: Amir Kebir, 1958). Iranians rapidly translate foreign publications concerning Iran, and many Iranians now resident in Iran and elsewhere conduct field studies of Iran, cited elsewhere in this volume, which are addressed both to Iranians and to a wider anthropological community.

There are recent appraisals of Western anthropological writings on the Middle East. Michael Gilsenan, "Very Like a Camel: The Appearance of an Anthropologist's Middle East," in *Localizing Strategies: Regional Traditions of Ethnographic Writing*, ed. Richard Fardon (Washington, DC: Smithsonian Institution Press; Edinburgh: Scottish Academic Press, 1990), pp. 222–39, nicely captures for a wide audience the changing assumptions and styles of training of anthropologists from the 1960s to the late 1980s. See also, in the same volume, Brian V. Street, "Orientalist Discourses in the Anthropology of Iran, Afghanistan, and Pakistan," pp. 240–59, and Charles Lindholm, "The New Middle Eastern Ethnography," *Journal of the Royal Anthropological Institute* (N.S.) 1, no. 4 (December 1995), 805–20, the latter of which focuses on trends in the English-speaking world.

GLOSSARY

Terms are defined according to local usage. Many terms, especially religious ones, appear in slightly different forms in each of the major languages of the Middle East and Central Asia; not all variants are given here. Spellings consequently often reflect local usage and not the conventions of the major literary languages. Page numbers indicate where the terms are explained in context.

P = Persian; A = Arabic; T = Turkish; H = Hebrew

afrāngī (A, Egypt): urban (lit. "French"); the opposite of **baladī**, 112

Āl (A): family, clan, people.

ᶜAlāwī (A), **Alevi** (T): Shīᶜī religious sect found in Turkey, Iraq, Syria, and Lebanon, 265, 266, 269

ᶜālim, pl. **ᶜulamā'** (A): religious scholar, 288–297

amīr, pl. **umarā'** (A): prince or tribal chief, 79, 80, 86, 87, 258

ᶜār (Mor. A): conditional curse or compulsion, 234, 238

ᶜaṣabīya (A): "group feeling" or solidarity (Ibn Khaldūn), 28, 153

ᶜashīra (Syr. A): tribe, 85

ᶜāshūrā (A): the tenth day of the lunar month of Muḥarram and a day of voluntary fast. For the Shīᶜa, the day also commemorates the martyrdom of Ḥusayn at Karbala, 309

aṣl (A): descent, 243

āyātullāh (A and P): principal Shiᶜī religious leader, 266

badawī; pl. **badū** (A): camel-herding pastoralists or their descendants (Arabian Peninsula), 54, 121, 144. Also **badāwa**, the state of being bedouin.

baladī (A, esp. Egypt): countrified; of country origin, 112

bālah (Yemeni A): men's poetic competitions, 175

baraka (A): supernatural blessing; abundance, 275, 284

baten (P); **bāṭin** (A): hidden; concealed, 229

bayᶜa (A): oath of fealty; homage, 338

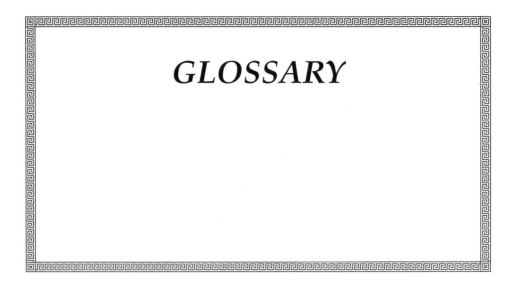

bayt (A): house; household.

bāzār (P): marketplace, 102

bin ᶜamm (A): father's brother's son (for a list of kinship terms, see Chapter 7).

bint ᶜamm (A): father's brother's daughter, 158, 169, 170

bishᶜa (A, Egypt): ordeal in customary bedouin law in which judicial truth is determined by an accused person licking a hot iron. An unburned tongue signifies truth, 246

blād al-makhzan (Mor. A): "lands of government" (lit. "storehouse"), 55

blād as-sība (Mor. A): "lands of dissidence," 55

çarşi (T): market, 102

dam (A): blood, also metaphorically, to imply kinship, 243

dār (A): house; tribal territory, 135

darb (Mor. A): quarter; neighborhood, 158

dawra (A), **dowreh** (P): circle; discussion group, 231

dawwār (Mor. A): rural local community, 135, 137

dede (Kurdish): religious leader, 272. See also **pīr**.

dhikr (A): Sufi term for repetition of certain words or phrases in praise of God, 257m, 276

dīwāniyya (A, Arab Gulf): regular private gathering of friends and associates for conversation and discussion, 332

diya (A): blood money; recompense for bodily injury, 131

dughrī (A and H): "straight" or "direct" speech. For the different connotations in the two languages, see 230n

dürüstlük (T): trustworthiness, 118

fakhdh, pl. **fukhūdh** (A): subdivision of a tribe; lit. "thigh," 84, 85

falaj, pl. **aflāj** (A): irrigation canal, partially underground (Oman), 11

fallāḥ, pl. **fallāḥūn** (A): peasant; farmer cultivator, 54

fqīh (classical **faqīh),** pl. **fuqahā'** (A): person who knows Islamic law; Quranic teacher, 155

gecekondu (T): shantytown, 108

ghaṭṭāra (A): irrigation canal, partially underground (Morocco), 11

ghinnāwa (A, Egyptian bedouin): short, lyric poem, 242

guyandeh (P): female religious leader, 184

ḥābūs, pl. **aḥbās** (North African A): religious bequest; same as **waqf**, 295

ḥaḍāra (A): settlement; civilization, 53, 54, 73, 121, 154

ḥaḍarī (A): urban, "civilized."

ḥajj (A): pilgrimage to Mecca, 260–64

ḥājjī (A): pilgrim, also the title assumed by one who has made the pilgrimage, 264

ḥāl (A): Sufi term for mystic exaltation, 277

ḥamūla (A): kinship group (esp. Arabs in Israel and Palestine), 151–52, 153

ḥaqq (A): obligation; share or right; truth, 234, 237, 285

ḥaram (A): religious sanctuary; that which is sacred or forbidden, 262, 263

ḥaredī, pl. **ḥaredīm** (H): lit. "the God-fearing"; ultra-Orthodox Jews, 312–316

ḥasab (A): honor acquired through one's deeds, 153

ḥasham (A): restrained, modest, possessing **ḥshūmiyya**, 243

ḥayyān (Omani A): family cluster, 153, 159, 199

hijra (A): emigration, flight, 309

ḥillūla (Mor. A, H): festival for a Jewish saint, 286

ḥshūmīya (A): propriety; deference, 234, 238

ḥurma (A): honor, 196

Ibāḍīya (A): subdivision of the Muslim community; found principally in Oman, East Africa, Algeria, and Libya.

ᶜId al-Kabīr (A): the Great Feast, or Feast of Abraham, 179, 263, 272

iḥrām (A): white seamless garment worn by pilgrims to Mecca, 262, 263

ijāza (A): teaching license, 279

ijmāᶜa (A): consensus, 256

ᶜilm, pl. **ᶜulūm** (A): religious knowledge; religious scholarship, 289

imām (A): spiritual leader; prayer leader, 67, 258, 264, 267, 272, 273

ᶜirḍ (A): honor, 83

jāhilī (A): an "ignorant" person, also one unaware of Islam or not heeding its call, 303, 306

jāhilīya (A): the pre-Islamic time of ignorance.

jamāᶜa (A): gnroup or council, 136, 272n

jamāhīr (A): the "masses," 328

jihād (A): religious struggle or endeavor.

juz (Mongol): clan, horde, 123

Kaᶜba (A): sacred enclosure at Mecca, 35, 43, 261, 263, 264

khalīfa (A): deputy, caliph, 265

khān (P): tribal leader, 29, 123

khanīth (A): male transsexual prostitute.

khānqah (P): religious lodge, 275

khaṭba (A): engagement, 167

khayma (A): tent, household (pastoralists), 135

khuṭba (A): Friday sermon, 167

khūwa (A): brotherhood; tax paid for protection to a more powerful tribal group, 70

kibbutz, pl. **kibbutzīm** (H): collective settlement, 362

kollel (H): place of residence and study in which ultra-Orthodox male youth pursue religious learning, 314

kubbār (plural, A): persons of high social standing (North Africa), "big people," 154

kunya, pl. **kunan** (A): surname, 179, 181

laqab, pl. **alqāb** (A): nickname, 178

madīna; pl. **mudun** (A): town; traditional urban quarters (North Africa), 101–10

maḥalla (A), **mehelle** (T and Uzbek): urban quarter, 105. Also, in Morocco, a "royal progress," 337–338

mahdī (A): rightly guided one; religious leader, 265, 279, 288, 310

makrūh (A): reprehensible, 185

maktūb (A): written, foreordained, 235

malaka l-ḥifḍ (A): mnemonic domination; the faculty of memory, 291

mālik; pl. **mulūk** (A): king, sovereign, 337

mallāḥ (A): Jewish quarter, 102, 213

marabout (A. **murābiṭ**). See **ṣāliḥ**, 137, 284–85

mardum (P): people, 325

maᶜrifa (A): secular knowledge, 289

maᶜrūf (A): known; used with reference to distinguished or noble families.

mawlid (A); **mevlûd** (T): celebration of the Prophet's birthday or the anniversary of a death; panegyric poem praising Muḥammad, 198

milla (A, P, and T): religious community or "people," 325

mimūna (A, Moroccan Jews): visit to saint's shrine after Passover, 218

moshav, pl. **moshavīm** (H): agricultural colony, 240

muḍīf (Iraqi A): guest house, 217

mujtāhid (A and P): Shīᶜī religious leader, 266, 269

mulk (A): royal authority; sovereignty.

mullah (P): village preacher, 119, 266, 321

murīd (A): Sufi term for student or disciple, 278

mushā' (A): collective landownership, 152

mūsim (Mor. A): an annual festival in honor of a saint or "pious one," 137, 138

muṭᶜa (A and P): temporary marriage (Shīᶜa), 190, 191, 198

muwaḥḥidūn, al- (A): "the Unitarians," followers of the Saudi religious leader Ibn ᶜAbd al-Wahhāb (1703/4–1792), 36

nafs (A): self; passions, 197

nasab (A): honor from descent, descent, 153

nazdīk (P): nearness or closeness, 232

nīf (Algerian A): honor, 196

nisba, pl. **nisab** (A): name derived from occupation or origin, 179

nīya (A): faith; intent, 262

niẓām (A): order; organization, 298, 327

nuqqāṣ (Yemeni A): lit. "deficient," a "lower" social category, 67–68

oğlu (Uzbek): son of, 178

pīr (P): Sufi master, 271, 272, 278

qabīla (Mor. A), **gabīla** (Saudi A), pl. **qabā'il**: tribe, 67–68, 85

qāḍī, pl. **quḍā'** (A): religious judge, 67, 256, 257, 292

ᶜqāl (A): reason, 166, 197, 234, 236, 243, 284

qanāt (A and P): irrigation canal, partially underground, 11

qarāba (A): nearness or closeness, 104, 136, 151–52, 154, 243, 284

qarīb (A): "close," related.

qaṣba (A): citadel or fortress; **qasaba** (P) and **kasaba** (T): small town, 102

qāt (Yemeni A): mild narcotic plant, the leaves of which are chewed in the Yemens, Somalia, Djibouti, and coastal Kenya, 66–69

qawm (A and P): people or nation; kinship term in parts of Afghanistan, 82, 151, 153, 201

qudrat Allāh (A): God's will, 234

rakᶜa (A): a bending of the torso from an upright position, followed by prostrations, in Islamic prayer, 272

Ramaḍān (A): Muslim lunar month of fasting, 117, 236, 259, 272

rasūl (A): messenger; envoy, 259

rebbe (H, Yiddish): teacher, 286

rukn, pl. **arkān** (A): pillar, principle, 255

sabra (H): native-born Israeli Jews of European descent, 230n

saddiq (H), **ṣadīq** (A): lit. "friend"; used by North African Jews to designate saints, 286

ṣafāyi bāṭin (P): integrity; inner purity, 229

salafīya (A): Islamic reform movement, 299

ṣalāt, pl. **salawāt** (A): ritual Islamic prayers, 259

ṣāliḥ (A): "pious one," or saint; a person, living or dead, thought to have a special relation toward God that enables him or her to ask for God's grace on behalf of clients and to communicate it to them (North Africa), 275, 276

ṣawm (A): fast, 259, 272

sayyid, pl. **sāda** (A): descendants of the Prophet (esp. Iraq and the Yemens), 60, 64, 67–68

ṣdāq (A): bridewealth, 166

shaᶜb (A): people, 328

shahāda (A): declaration of faith, 259

shahr (P); **şehir** (T): town or city, 102, 180n

sharaf (A): honor, 83, 129

sharīᶜa (A): the revealed, or canonical, law of Islam, 256, 257, 258, 274, 276, 277

shārif, pl. **shurafā'** (A): descendant of the Prophet through his daughter, Fāṭima, and his son-in-law, ᶜAlī, 60–64

shaykh, pl. **shuyūkh** (A): tribal or religious leader, 60, 64, 75–76, 79, 81, 85, 87, 278, 279n, 295

Shīᶜa (A): sect; major subdivision of the Muslim community, 265 (See also index).

shūra (A): consultation; **istishāra** (A): to ask for advice.

silsila (A): chain; patrilineal genealogy, 279

siyāsa (A, P): politics, policy, 327

ṣūfī (A): Muslim mystic, 274

sulṭa (A): political authority, 327

sulṭān (A): ruler, sovereign, 327

Sunnī (A): major subdivision of the Muslim community. Some 90 percent of the world's Muslims are Sunnī. See index.

sūq; pl. **aswāq** (A): market, 102, 103

ta[c]**āruf** (A and P): etiquette, 229, 230, 232

tafsīr (A): science of interpreting the Quran, 293

taḥrīk (Mor. A): competitive display of horsemanship, 137

ṭalī[c]**a** (A): vanguard, 328

taqīya (A): concealment, 265, 272

ṭarīqa, pl. **ṭuruq** (A): religious order, 270, 275, 277

taṣawwuf (A): mysticism; Sufism, 274

ṭāṭā (Berber): contractual ritual alliance, 138

ṭawāf (A): act of circumambulating the Ka[c]ba, 263

ta[c]**zīya** (A and P): mourning, 62, 267, 268

tekke (T): religious lodge, 275

thiqa (A): confidence.

umma (A): Muslim community, 257, 302

vilayet-i faqīh (P and A): Shī[c]ī doctrine of the sovereignty of the jurist.

Wahhābī (A): followers of Ibn [c]Abd al-Wahhāb, more properly known as al-Muwaḥḥidūn, or "the Unitarians." Located primarily in Saudi Arabia, 35, 302

wālī, pl. **awliyā'** (A): saint (North Africa); provincial governor (Oman) (pl. **wulā'**), 277

waqf, pl. **awqāf** (A): pious endowment, 280, 293n, 295

zaher (P), **ẓāhir** (A): manifest, external, unconcealed, apparent, 229

za[c]**im,** pl. **zu**[c]**amā'** (A): leader or strongman (esp. Lebanon).

zakāt (A): alms tax, 259

zāwiya, pl. **zāwāya** (A): religious lodge, 275

zawwār (A): lit. "visitor." Refers in Morocco to a descendant or worker for a shrine who collects donations on behalf of the "pious one," 285

zerangī (P): cleverness; insincerity, 229

ziyāra (A): visit (to a saint's shrine), 264

INDEX

AUTHOR INDEX

SUBJECT INDEX